International Economics

International Economics

SECOND EDITION

Dominick Salvatore Chairman and Professor
Department of Economics, Fordham University

Macmillan Publishing Company
New York
Collier Macmillan Publishers
London

Macmillan Publishing Company
866 Third Avenue, New York, New York 10022

Collier Macmillan Canada, Inc.

Library of Congress Cataloging in Publication Data

Salvatore, Dominick.
  International economics.

  Includes bibliographies and indexes.
  1. International economic relations.   I. Title.
HF1411.S239   1987   337'.09'048   86-8633
ISBN 0-02-405360-0

Printing: 1 2 3 4 5 6 7 8   Year: 7 8 9 0 1 2 3 4 5

ISBN 0-02-405360-0

To Lucille

Preface

This is the second edition of a text that has enjoyed a very gratifying market success, having been used in over 150 colleges and universities throughout the United States, Canada, and other English speaking countries. All of the features that made the first edition one of the leading texts in the United States have been retained in the second edition, but the content has been thoroughly updated and expanded to include many new significant topics. The following are among the new topics included in the second edition: the specific-factors model, growth with factor immobility, trade in differentiated products, the rise of trade protectionism, the international debt, exchange rate dynamics, exchange rate futures and options, efficiency of the foreign exchange markets, the Eurobond and Euronote markets, and the portfolio balance approach.

The second edition also clearly examines the many significant changes and trends that have occurred in the international economy since the first edition of this text was published four years ago. While inflation and the price of petroleum have declined significantly, unemployment has remained high throughout the world and protectionism has risen to dangerous levels. Exchange rates have shown excessive volatility, and this has led to increased demands for reforms of the present monetary system. The huge international debt of developing countries is threatening not only economic development in poor lands but the very stability of the entire world banking system as well. The internationalization of capital markets has accelerated, and new international financial instruments and practices have become widespread; these developments have further eroded governments' control over internal monetary matters. In this rapidly changing world, the United States has often been caught in a turn of events that has significantly affected its well-being but which has to a large extent been beyond its control.

The main objective of the second edition of this text is to present a comprehensive, up-to-date and clear exposition of the theory and principles of international economics that are essential for understanding and evaluating the international economic problems and issues of the late 1980s.

Audience and Level

This text attempts to overcome the shortcomings of other international economics texts in which the level of analysis is either too complicated or too simplistic. The text presents all of the principles and theories essential for a thorough understanding of international economics. It does so on an intuitive level in the text itself, while presenting more rigorous analysis in the appendices at the end of most chapters. Thus, the book is designed for flexibility.

In the typical one-semester undergraduate course in international economics, instructors would probably want to cover the ten core chapters (2–3, 5, 8, 13–17, 20) and exclude the appendices. The many examples and real world cases discussed also makes the text very suitable for international economics courses in business programs. In first-year graduate courses in international economics and business, instructors may want to cover the appendices also and assign readings from the extensive bibliography at the end of each chapter.

Organization of the Book

The book is organized into four parts. Part I (Chapters 2–7) deals with the pure theory of international trade (i.e., the basis and the gains from trade). Part II (Chapters 8–12) deals with commercial policies (i.e., obstructions to the flow of trade). Part III (Chapters 13 and 14) deals with foreign exchange markets and the measurement of a nation's balance of payments. Part IV (Chapters 15–20) examines the various mechanisms to adjust balance of payments disequilibria and the workings of the present international monetary system. As pointed out earlier, there are ten core chapters: 2–3, 5, 8, 13–17, 20.

Teaching Aids

A unique feature of this book is that the same example is utilized in all the chapters dealing with the same basic concept. For example, the same graphical and numerical model is referred to in Chapters 2 through 10 (the chapters that deal with the pure theory of trade and commercial policies). This greatly reduces the real burden on the student, who does not have to start afresh with a new example each time. Furthermore, actual numbers are used in the examples and the graphs are presented on scales. Theories and concepts are always related to the real world with meaningful and up-to-date examples. All of these features make the various concepts and theories more concrete, accessible, and pertinent to the student.

Each chapter contains a number of teaching aids to make the text easier to use in the classroom. The sections of each chapter are numbered for easy reference. Longer sections are broken into two or more numbered subsections. All of the graphs and diagrams are carefully explained in the text and then summarized briefly in the captions.

Each chapter ends with the following teaching aids:

Summary—A paragraph reviews each section of the text.

A Look ahead—Describes what follows in the subsequent chapter.

Chapter Glossary—Gives the definition of important terms introduced in bold-face in the chapter. A separate index of glossary terms in alphabetical order is provided at the end of the book for easy cross-reference.

Questions for Review—At least one question for each section in the chapter.

Problems—These ask the student to calculate a specific measure or explain a particular theory or issue graphically. Brief answers to selected problems are provided at the end of the book for feedback. These are indicated by an asterisk (*).

Appendices—(except for Chapters 1 and 11)—As discussed earlier, these develop in a more rigorous, but careful and clear fashion, material that is presented on an intuitive level in the chapter.

Selected Bibliography—The most important references are included along with specific notes indicating the topic they deal with. A separate author index is included at the end of the book.

An *Instructor's Manual* prepared by the author is available which includes chapter objectives and lecture suggestions, answers to the end-of-chapter problems, and a set of 12 multiple-choice questions, with answers, for each chapter.

Acknowledgements

This text grew out of the undergraduate and graduate courses in international economics that I have been teaching at Fordham University over the past 15 years. I was very fortunate to have had many excellent students, who with their questions and comments contributed much to the clarity of exposition of this text.

I owe a great intellectual debt to my brilliant former teachers of international economics, Professor Arthur I. Bloomfield and Professor Michael Michaely. I have received much useful advice by Professors Bela Balassa (Johns Hopkins University and the World Bank), Robert Baldwin (University of Wis-

consin), Jagdish Bhagwati (Columbia University), John Bilson (University of
Chicago), William Branson (Princeton University), Richard Cooper (Harvard
University), W.M. Corden (Australian National University), Robert Feenstra
(Columbia University), Gerald Helleiner (University of Toronto), Lawrence Klein
(University of Pennsylvania), Ronald McKinnon (Stanford University), Mi-
chael Mussa (University of Chicago and Council of Economic Advisors), and
Robert Stern (University of Michigan).

I have also received assistance in preparing the second edition of this text
by various people in a number of well-known international Organizations:
Charles Gardner, Jeorge Ordenes and George Tavlas of the International Mon-
etary Fund; Gershon Feder and Michael Michaely of the World Bank; Antonio
Costa of OECD; Michael Mussa of the President's Council of Economic Advi-
sors; Victor Fuchs and Robert E. Lipsey of the National Bureau of Economics
Research; and Shuaib Yolah, Goran Ohlin, V.K. Sastry, Gamal Elish, Fred
Campano, D. Choi, Massimo D'Angelo, Julio Gomez, Augusto Silvany, Karl
Souvant, and Douglas Walker of the United Nations.

John Piderit, Edward Dowling, William Hogan, Clive Daniels, Edward
Sheehey, Darryl McLeod, and Siamack Shojai, my colleagues in the Economics Department, have also provided much useful advice. John Piderit, in particular, read through the entire manuscript and made many valuable suggestions that greatly improved the text. My graduate assistants: Anita Longobardi,
Cristina Cadac, Cristina Gaspar, Luis Mejia-Maya, and Cecilia Winters have
provided much help with many aspects of the project.

The following Professors read through the entire manuscript and made many
valuable suggestions: Professor Dennis R. Appleyard of the University of North
Carolina, Taeho Bark of Georgetown University, Joseph C. Breda of the Ari-
zona State University, Professor Liam P. Ebril of Cornell University, Roy J.
Hensley of the University of Miami, Professor W.E. Khun of the University of
Nebraska-Lincoln, Professor Stanley Lawson of St. John's University, and Professor Patrick O'Sullivan of the State University of New York.

Other Professors who provided valuable comments are: Andrew Blair of the
University of Pittsburgh, Roger Even Bove of West Chester University, Francis
Colella of Simpson College, Evangelos Djinopolos of Fairleigh Dickinson Uni-
versity, Ali Ebrahimi of Pace University, Holger Engberg of New York University, George Georgiou of the Towson State University, Reza Gorashi of Stock-
ton College, Nick Gianaris of Fordham University, Fred Glahe and William
Kaempfer of the University of Colorado, Henry Golstein of the University of
Oregon, Sara Gordon of St. John's University, Syed Hussain of the University
of Wisconsin, Demetrius Karantelis of Assumption College, Joseph Kiernan of
Fairleigh Dickinson University, Richard Kjetsaa of Manhattanville College, Ki-
shore Kulkarni of the University of Central Kansas, J.S. LaCascia of Marshall
University, Richard Levich of New York University, Cho Kin Leung of Wil-
liam Patterson College, Jerry McElroy of Saint Mary's College, Farhad Mir-
hady of San Francisco State University, George Mungia of the University of
Santo Domingo, Kee-Jim Ngiam of Carleton University, Shreekant Palekar of

the University of Mexico, Anthony Pavlick of the University of Wisconsin, Vedat Sayar of Brooklyn College, Lezcek Stachow of St. Anselm College, Michael Szenberg of Pace University, Richard Torrisi of the University of Hartford, Stanislaw Wasowski of Georgetown University, Behzad Yaghmaian of Rutgers University, Darrel Young of the University of Texas, Helen Youngelson of Portland State University, Eden Yu of the University of Oklahoma, as well as Dr. Glenn DeSouza, Senior Consultant of Arthur D. Little; Dr. Leroy Laney of the Federal Reserve Bank of Dallas; Dr. Vincent Malanga, Vice-President of Shilling & Company; Dr. John McAuley, Vice-President for Global Portfolio Management at Chemical Bank; and Dr. Morris Morkre and David Tarr of the Federal Trade Commission.

Finally, I would like to express my gratitude to the entire staff at Macmillan, especially Chip Price, Jack Repcheck, John Travis, Jackie Kennen, David Claughen, Harold Stancil, Nick Sklitsis, for their kind and skillful assistance, and to Angela Bates and Marie Sundberg, the department secretaries, for their efficiency and cheerful disposition.

D. S.

Summary Table of Contents

CHAPTER 1   *Introduction*   *1*

PART I   *The Pure Theory of International Trade*   *11*

CHAPTER 2   *The Law of Comparative Advantage*   *13*

CHAPTER 3   *The Modern Theory of International Trade*   *39*

CHAPTER 4   *Offer Curves and the Terms of Trade*   *66*

CHAPTER 5   *Factor Endowments and Heckscher-Ohlin Theory*   *91*

CHAPTER 6   *Empirical Tests and Complementary Trade Theories*   *123*

CHAPTER 7   *Economic Growth and International Trade*   *151*

PART II   *Commercial Policies*   *181*

CHAPTER 8   *Trade Restrictions: Tariffs*   *183*

CHAPTER 9   *Other Trade Restrictions and United States Commercial Policy*   *217*

CHAPTER 10   *Economic Integration: Customs Unions*   *247*

CHAPTER 11   *International Trade and Economic Development*   *266*

CHAPTER 12   *International Resource Movements and*
             Multinational Corporations   *296*

PART III   *Foreign Exchange Markets and the*
           Balance of Payments   *321*
  CHAPTER 13   *The Foreign Exchange Markets*   *323*
  CHAPTER 14   *The Balance of Payments*   *362*

PART IV   *Adjustment in the Balance of Payments*
          and Domestic Stability   *393*
  CHAPTER 15   *Price Adjustment Mechanism*   *395*
  CHAPTER 16   *The Income Adjustment Mechanism and*
               Synthesis of Automatic Adjustments   *429*
  CHAPTER 17   *Adjustment Policies*   *459*
  CHAPTER 18   *The Monetary and Portfolio Balance*
               Approaches   *494*
  CHAPTER 19   *Flexible Versus Fixed Exchange Rates*   *522*
  CHAPTER 20   *The International Monetary System:*
               Past and Present   *546*

  Glossary Index   *593*
  Name Index   *597*
  Subject Index   *600*

Contents

CHAPTER 1 *Introduction*   *1*

   1.1 The Importance of International Economics   1
   1.2 International Trade and the Nation's Standard of Living   2
   1.3 The Subject Matter of International Economics   4
   1.4 The Purpose of International Economic Theories and Policies   5
   1.5 Organization of the Book   6
   1.6 Methodology of the Book   7

   Summary 7 • **A Look Ahead** 8 • **Glossary** 8 • **Questions for Review** 8 • **Problems** 9 • **Selected Bibliography** 10

PART I: *The Pure Theory of International Trade*   *11*

   CHAPTER 2 *The Law of Comparative Advantage*   *13*

   2.1 Introduction   13
   2.2 The Mercantilists' Views on Trade   14
   2.3 Trade Based on Absolute Advantage: Adam Smith   15
      2.3a Absolute Advantage   15
      2.3b Illustration of Absolute Advantage   16
   2.4 Trade Based on Comparative Advantage   17
      2.4a The Law of Comparative Advantage   18
      2.4b The Gains from Trade   19
      2.4c Exception to the Law of Comparative Advantage   20
      2.4d Comparative Advantage with Money   21
   2.5 Comparative Advantage and Opportunity Costs   23
      2.5a Comparative Advantage and the Labor Theory of Value   23

       2.5b   The Opportunity Cost Theory   24

       2.5c   The Production Possibility Frontier under Constant Costs   24

       2.5d   Opportunity Costs and Relative Commodity Prices   26

  2.6   The Basis and the Gains from Trade Under Constant Costs   27

       2.6a   Illustration of the Gains from Trade   27

       2.6b   Alternative Illustration of the Gains from Trade   28

       2.6c   The Small Country Case   30

Summary 32 • A Look Ahead 33 • Glossary 33 • Questions for Review 34 • Problems 34

Appendix: A2.1   Comparative Advantage with more than Two Commodities   36

            A2.2   Comparative Advantage with more than Two Nations   37

Selected Bibliography   38

CHAPTER 3   *The Modern Theory of International Trade*   39

  3.1   Introduction   39

  3.2   The Production Frontier with Increasing Costs   40

       3.2a   Illustration of Increasing Costs   40

       3.2b   The Marginal Rate of Transformation   41

       3.2c   Reasons for Increasing Opportunity Costs and Different Production Frontiers   41

  3.3   Community Indifference Curves   42

       3.3a   Illustration of Community Indifference Curves   43

       3.3b   The Marginal Rate of Substitution   44

       3.3c   Some Difficulties with Community Indifference Curves   44

  3.4   Equilibrium in Isolation   45

       3.4a   Illustration of Equilibrium in Isolation   45

       3.4b   Equilibrium Relative Commodity Prices and Comparative Advantage   46

  3.5   The Basis and the Gains from Trade with Increasing Costs   47

       3.5a   Illustration of the Basis for and the Gains from Trade with Increasing Costs   47

       3.5b   Equilibrium Relative Commodity Prices with Trade   49

       3.5c   Incomplete Specialization   50

       3.5d   Small Country Case with Increasing Costs   50

       3.5e   The Gains from Exchange and from Specialization   51

  3.6   Trade Based on Differences in Tastes   52

       3.6a   Illustration of Trade Based on Differences in Tastes   52

Summary 54 • A Look Ahead 55 • Glossary 55 • Questions for Review 55 • Problems 56

Appendix: A3.1 Productions Functions, Isoquants, Isocosts and
                     Equilibrium   57
           A3.2 Production Theory with Two Nations, Two
                     Commodities and Two Factors   59
           A3.3 Derivation of the Edgeworth Box Diagram and
                     Production Frontiers   60
           A3.4 Some Important Conclusions   64
Selected Bibliography   65

CHAPTER **4** *Offer Curves and the Terms of Trade*   **66**

4.1 Introduction   66
4.2 The Offer Curve of a Nation   66
     4.2a Origin and Definition of Offer Curves   67
     4.2b Derivation of the Offer Curve of Nation 1   67
     4.2c The Shape of the Offer Curve of Nation 1   67
4.3 The Offer Curve of the Other Nation   68
     4.3a Derivation of the Offer Curve of Nation 2   68
     4.3b Shape of the Offer Curve of Nation 2   70
4.4 The Equilibrium Relative Commodity Price with Trade   70
     4.4a Illustration of Equilibrium   70
     4.4b The Small Country Case   71
4.5 The Terms of Trade   72
     4.5a Definition and Measurement of the Terms of Trade   73
     4.5b Illustration of the Terms of Trade   73
4.6 Extension and Evaluation of our Trade Model   74
     4.6a Usefulness of the Model   74
     4.6b Extension of the Model   75
     4.6c Some Apparent Shortcomings of the Model   77

Summary 78 • **A Look Ahead** 79 • **Glossary** 79 • **Questions for
Review** 79 • **Problems** 79
Appendix: A4.1 Derivation of a Trade Indifference Curve for
                     Nation 1   80
           A4.2 Derivation of Nation 1's Trade Indifference Map   82
           A4.3 Formal Derivation of Nation 1's Offer Curve   83
           A4.4 Outline of the Formal Derivation of Nation 2's Offer
                     Curve   85
           A4.5 General Equilibrium of Production, Consumption and
                     Trade   87
           A4.6 Multiple and Unstable Equilibria   88
Selected Bibliography   90

CHAPTER 5 *Factor Endowments and Heckscher-Ohlin Theory* **91**

5.1 Introduction   91

5.2 Assumptions of the Theory   92

    5.2a The Assumptions   92

    5.2b Meaning of the Assumptions   93

5.3 Factor Intensity, Factor Abundance and the Shape of the Production Frontier   94

    5.3a Factor Intensity   94

    5.3b Factor Abundance   96

    5.3c Factor Abundance and the Shape of the Production Frontier   98

5.4 Factor Endowments and the Heckscher-Ohlin Theory   99

    5.4a The Heckscher-Ohlin Theorem   99

    5.4b General Equilibrium Framework of the Heckscher-Ohlin Theory   100

    5.4c Illustration of the Heckscher-Ohlin Theory   102

5.5 Factor-Price Equalization and Income Distribution   104

    5.5a The Factor-Price Equalization Theorem   104

    5.5b Relative and Absolute Factor-Price Equilization   105

    5.5c Effect of Trade on the Distribution of Income   107

    5.5d Empirical Relevance   108

5.6 The Heckscher-Ohlin Model—A General Equilibrium Model   109

Summary   110   •   **A Look Ahead**   111   •   **Glossary**   111   •   **Questions for Review**   112   •   **Problems**   113

Appendix: A5.1   The Edgeworth Box Diagram of Nation 1 and Nation 2   114

    A5.2   Relative Factor-Price Equalization   115

    A5.3   Absolute Factor-Price Equalization   118

    A5.4   Effect of Trade on the Short-Run Distribution of Income: The Specific-Factors Model   119

    A5.5   Comparative Static Analysis for a Change in Tastes   121

Selected Bibliography   121

CHAPTER 6 *Empirical Tests and Complementary Trade Theories* **123**

6.1 Introduction   123

6.2 Empirical Tests of the Ricardian Model   124

6.3 Empirical Tests of the Heckscher-Ohlin Model   126

    6.3a Empirical Results—The Leontief Paradox   126

    6.3b Explanations of the Leontief Paradox   128

    6.3c Factor-Intensity Reversal   129

6.4 Complementary Trade Theories   131
    6.4a   *Trade Based on Economies of Sale*   131
    6.4b   *Trade Based on Differentiated Products*   134
    6.4c   *Trade Based on Technological Gaps and Product Cycles*   135
6.5 Transportation Costs and Nontraded Commodities   137
6.6 Some General Conclusions on the Heckscher-Ohlin Model and
      Complementary Trade Theories   139

Summary   141   •   **A Look Ahead**   142   •   **Glossary**   142   •   **Questions
for Review**   143   •   **Problems**   143
Appendix: A6.1   Illustration of Factor-Intensity Reversal   144
          A6.2   The Elasticity of Substitution and Factor-Intensity
                Reversal   146
          A6.3   Empirical Tests of Factor-Intensity Reversal   147
Selected Bibliography   148

CHAPTER **7**   *Economic Growth and International Trade*   *151*

7.1 Introduction   151
7.2 Growth of Factors of Production   152
    7.2a   *Labor Growth and Capital Accumulation Over Time*   152
    7.2b   *The Rybczynski Theorem*   154
7.3 Technical Progress   155
    7.3a   *Neutral, Labor-Saving and Capital-Saving Technical Progress*   156
    7.3b   *Technical Progress and the Nation's Production Frontier*   156
7.4 Growth and Trade: The Small Country Case   158
    7.4a   *The Effect of Growth on Trade*   158
    7.4b   *Illustration of Factor Growth, Trade and Welfare*   159
    7.4c   *Technical Progress, Trade and Welfare*   161
7.5 Growth and Trade: The Large Country Case   162
    7.5a   *Growth and the Nation's Terms of Trade and Welfare*   162
    7.5b   *Immiserizing Growth*   163
    7.5c   *Illustration of Beneficial Growth and Trade*   166
7.6 Growth, Change in Tastes and Trade in Both Nations   166
    7.6a   *Growth and Trade in Both Nations*   166
    7.6b   *Change in Tastes and Trade in Both Nations*   169

Summary   170   •   **A Look Ahead**   171   •   **Glossary**   171   •   **Questions
for Review**   172   •   **Problems**   172
Appendix: A7.1   Formal Proof of the Rybczynski Theorem   173
          A7.2   Growth with Factor Immobility   176
          A7.3   Graphical Analysis of Hicksian Technical
                Progress   77
Selected Bibliography   179

PART II: *Commercial Policies*   *181*

CHAPTER 8   *Trade Restrictions: Tariffs*   *183*

8.1   Introduction   183
8.2   General Equilibrium Analysis of a Tariff in a Small Country   184
    8.2a   General Equilibrium Effects of a Tariff in a Small Country   *184*
    8.2b   Illustration of the Effects of a Tariff in a Small Country   *185*
    8.2c   The Stolper-Samuelson Theorem   *188*
8.3   General Equilibrium Analysis of a Tariff in a Large Country   188
    8.3a   General Equilibrium Effects of a Tariff in a Large Country   *189*
    8.3b   Illustration of the Effects of a Tariff in a Large Country   *189*
8.4   The Optimum Tariff   191
    8.4a   The Meaning of the Concept of Optimum Tariff and
        Retaliation   *191*
    8.4b   Illustration of the Optimum Tariff and Retaliation   *192*
8.5   Partial Equilibrium Effects of a Tariff   193
    8.5a   Partial Equilibrium Effects of a Tariff   *193*
    8.5b   Illustration of the Partial Equilibrium Effects of a Tariff   *194*
8.6   The Theory of Tariff Structure   196
    8.6a   The Rate of Effective Protection   *196*
    8.6b   Generalizations and Evaluation of the Theory of Effective
        Protection   *198*

**Summary   200   •   A Look Ahead   200   •   Glossary   201   •   Questions
for Review   201   •   Problems   202**
Appendix: A8.1   The Stolper-Samuelson Theorem Graphically   203
         **A8.2   Exception to the Stolper-Samuelson Theorem—The
              Metzler Case   205**
         A8.3   Short-run Effect of a Tariff on Factors' Income   207
         A8.4   Measurement of the Optimum Tariff   208
         **A8.5   Partial Equilibrium Effects of a Tariff in a Large
              Nation   210**
         **A8.6   Derivation of the Formula for the Rate of Effective
              Protection   213**
Selected Bibliography   215

CHAPTER 9   *Other Trade Restrictions and United States
               Commercial Policy*   *217*

9.1   Introduction   217
9.2   Quotas   218
    9.2a   The Effects of an Import Quota   *218*
    9.2b   Comparison of an Import Quota to an Import Tariff   *219*
9.3   Other Nontariff Barriers   220
    9.3a   Voluntary Export Restraints   *220*

9.3b *Technical, Administrative and Other Regulations*   *221*
9.3c *International Cartels*   *222*
9.3d *Dumping*   *223*

9.4 **Arguments for Protection**   **224**
9.4a *Fallacious and Questionable Arguments for Protection*   *224*
9.4b *The Infant-Industry Argument for Protection*   *225*
9.4c *Other Qualified Arguments for Protection*   *226*

9.5 **History of United States Commercial Policy**   **226**
9.5a *The Trade Agreements Act of 1934*   *227*
9.5b *The General Agreement on Tariffs and Trade (GATT)*   *228*
9.5c *The 1962 Trade Expansion Act and the Kennedy Round*   *229*
9.5d *The Trade Reform Act of 1974 and the Tokyo Round*   *230*

9.6 **Current Trade Problems**   **230**
9.6a *The New Protectionism and Trade Negotiations*   *231*
9.6b *Other Trade Problems*   *233*

Summary **234** • **A Look Ahead** **235** • **Glossary** **236** • **Questions for Review** **237** • **Problems** **238**
Appendix: **A9.1** **Centralized Cartels**   **239**
A9.2 **International Price Discrimination**   **240**
A9.3 **Taxes and Subsidies to Correct Domestic Distortions**   **241**
A9.4 **State Trading**   **242**
Selected Bibliography   **244**

CHAPTER 10 *Economic Integration: Customs Unions*   **247**

10.1 Introduction   **247**
10.2 Trade-Creating Customs Unions   **248**
10.2a *Trade Creation*   *248*
10.2b *Illustration of a Trade-Creating Customs Union*   *249*
10.3 Trade-Diverting Customs Unions   **250**
10.3a *Trade Diversion*   *250*
10.3b *Illustration of a Trade-Diverting Customs Union*   *251*
10.4 The Theory of the Second Best and Other Static Welfare Effects of Customs Unions   **253**
10.4a *The Theory of the Second Best*   *253*
10.4b *Conditions More Likely to Lead to Increased Welfare*   *253*
10.4c *Other Static Welfare Effects of Customs Unions*   *254*
10.5 Dynamic Benefits from Customs Unions   **255**
10.6 History of Attempts at Economic Integration   **256**
10.6a *The European Economic Community*   *256*
10.6b *The European Free Trade Association*   *257*
10.6c *Attempts at Economic Integration Among Developing Nations*   *258*

Summary 259 • **A Look Ahead** 260 • **Glossary** 260 • **Questions for Review** 261 • **Problems** 261
Appendix: General Equilibrium Analysis of the Static Effects of a Trade-Diverting Customs Union 262
Selected Bibliography 264

CHAPTER 11 *International Trade and Economic Development*   *266*

11.1   Introduction   266
11.2   The Importance of Trade to Development   267
    11.2a   Trade Theory and Economic Development   267
    11.2b   Trade as an Engine of Growth   268
    11.2c   The Contributions of Trade to Development   270
11.3   The Terms of Trade and Economic Development   271
    11.3a   The Various Terms of Trade   271
    11.3b   Alleged Reasons for Deterioration in the Commodity Terms of Trade   273
    11.3c   Historical Movement in the Commodity Terms of Trade   274
11.4   Export Instability and Economic Development   276
    11.4a   Causes and Effects of Export Instability   276
    11.4b   Measurements of Export Instability and Its Effect on Development   278
    11.4c   International Commodity Agreements   279
11.5   Import Substitution Versus Export Orientation   281
    11.5a   Development Through Import Substitution versus Exports   281
    11.5b   The Experience with Import Substitution   282
11.6   Current Problems and Demands of Developing Countries   284
    11.6a   Poverty in Developing Countries   284
    11.6b   International Debt Problem of Developing Countries   285
    11.6c   Trade Problems of Developing Countries   286
    11.6d   Demands for a New International Economic Order   287

Summary 289 • **A Look Ahead** 290 • **Glossary** 290 • **Questions for Review** 291 • **Problems** 292
Selected Bibliography 293

CHAPTER 12 *International Resource Movements and Multinational Corporations*   *296*

12.1   Introduction   296
12.2   Some Data on International Capital Flows   297
12.3   Motives for International Capital Flows   300
    12.3a   Motives for International Portfolio Investments   300
    12.3b   Motives for Direct Foreign Investments   301

12.4 Welfare Effects of International Capital Flows   **303**
    12.4a *Effects on the Investing and Host Countries*   *303*
    12.4b *Other Effects on the Investing and Host Countries*   *304*
12.5 Multinational Corporations   **306**
    12.5a *Reasons for the Existence of Multinational Corporations*   *306*
    12.5b *Problems Created by Multinational Corporations in the Home Country*   *309*
    12.5c *Problems Created by Multinational Corporations in the Host Country*   *310*
12.6 Motives and Welfare Effects of International Labor Migration   **311**
    12.6a *Motives for International Labor Migration*   *311*
    12.6b *Welfare Effects of International Labor Migration*   *312*
    12.6c *Other Welfare Effects of International Labor Migration*   *313*

Summary **315** • **A Look Ahead** **316** • **Glossary** **316** • **Questions for Review** **317** • **Problems** **317**
Appendix: The Transfer Problem   **318**
Selected Bibliography   **319**

PART III: *Foreign Exchange Markets and the Balance of Payments*   *321*

CHAPTER 13 *The Foreign Exchange Markets*   *323*

13.1 Introduction   *323*
13.2 Functions of the Foreign Exchange Markets   *324*
13.3 The Foreign Exchange Rates   *326*
    13.3a *The Equilibrium Foreign Exchange Rates*   *326*
    13.3b *Arbitrage*   *329*
    13.3c *Spot and Forward Rates*   *330*
    13.3d *Foreign Exchange Futures and Options*   *333*
13.4 Foreign Exchange Risks, Hedging, and Speculation   *334*
    13.4a *Foreign Exchange Risks*   *334*
    13.4b *Hedging*   *337*
    13.4c *Speculation*   *339*
13.5 Interest Arbitrage and the Efficiency of Foreign Exchange Markets   *341*
    13.5a *Uncovered Interest Arbitrage*   *341*
    13.5b *Covered Interest Arbitrage*   *342*
    13.5c *The Efficiency of Foreign Exchange Markets*   *344*
13.6 Eurocurrency, Eurobond, and Euronote Markets   *345*
    13.6a *Description of the Eurocurrency Markets*   *345*
    13.6b *Operation and Effects of Eurocurrency Markets*   *346*
    13.6c *The Eurobond and Euronote Markets*   *348*

Summary 349 • **A Look Ahead** 350 • **Glossary** 350 • **Questions for Review** 351 • **Problems** 352

Appendix: A13.1 Derivation of the Demand and Supply Curves for Foreign Exchange 353

A13.2 Covered Interest Arbitrage and Interest Parity Theory 356

A13.3 Derivation of the Formula for the Covered Interest Arbitrage Margin 358

Selected Bibliography 361

CHAPTER **14** *The Balance of Payments* 362

14.1 Introduction 363
14.2 Balance-of-Payments Accounting Principles 363
    14.2a Debits and Credits 364
    14.2b Double-Entry Bookkeeping 365
14.3 The International Transactions of the United States in 1984 367
14.4 Accounting Balances and Disequilibrium in International Transactions 370
    14.4a Accounting Balances 371
    14.4b Disequilibrium in International Transactions 372
14.5 Brief Postwar International Monetary History of the United States 375
14.6 The International Investment Position of the United States 378

Summary 380 • **A Look Ahead** 381 • **Glossary** 381 • **Questions for Review** 382 • **Problems** 383

Appendix: A14.1 The International Transactions of the United States: 1960–1984 384

A14.2 The Basic Balance and the Net Liquidity Balance 384

A14.3 The IMF Method of Reporting International Transactions 389

Selected Bibliography 391

PART **IV:** *Adjustment in the Balance of Payments and Domestic Stability* 393

CHAPTER **15** *Price Adjustment Mechanism* 395

15.1 Introduction 395
15.2 Adjustment with Flexible Exchange Rates 397
    15.2a Balance-of-Payments Adjustments with Exchange Rate Changes 397

15.2b   *Derivation of the Demand Curve for Foreign Exchange*   398
15.2c   *Derivation of the Supply Curve for Foreign Exchange*   400
15.2d   *Effect of Exchange Rate Changes on Domestic Prices and the Terms
          of Trade*   402
15.3   **Stability of Foreign Exchange Markets**   403
15.3a   *Stable and Unstable Foreign Exchange Markets*   403
15.3b   *The Marshall-Lerner Condition*   405
15.4   **Elasticities in the Real World**   406
15.4a   *Elasticity Estimates*   406
15.4b   *Evaluation of Elasticity Measurements*   407
15.5   **Purchasing-Power Parity**   409
15.5a   *Absolute Purchasing-Power Parity Theory*   409
15.5b   *Relative Purchasing-Power Parity Theory*   410
15.6   **Adjustment Under the Gold Standard**   413
15.6a   *The Gold Standard*   413
15.6b   *The Price-Specie-Flow Mechanism*   414

Summary   416 • **A Look Ahead**   417 • **Glossary**   417 • **Questions
for Review**   418 • **Problems**   418
Appendix: **A15.1**   **The Effect of Exchange Rate Changes On Domestic
                             Prices**   419
              A15.2   **Derivation of the Marshall-Lerner Condition**   421
              A15.3   **Stability of Foreign Exchange Markets Once
                             Again**   424
              A15.4   **Derivation of the Gold Points and Gold Flows Under
                             the Gold Standard**   425
Selected Bibliography   427

CHAPTER 16   *The Income Adjustment Mechanism and
                  Synthesis of Automatic Adjustments*   **429**
16.1   Introduction   429
16.2   Income Determination in a Closed Economy   430
16.2a   *Determination of the Equilibrium National Income in a Closed
          Economy*   430
16.2b   *The Multiplier in a Closed Economy*   433
16.3   Income Determination in a Small Open Economy   434
16.3a   *The Import Function*   435
16.3b   *Determination of the Equilibrium National Income in a Small Open
          Economy*   436
16.3c   *Graphical Determination of the Equilibrium National
          Income*   437
16.3d   *The Foreign Trade Multiplier*   439
16.4   Foreign Repercussions   441
16.5   The Absorption Approach   443

16.6 Monetary Adjustments and Synthesis of the Automatic
Adjustments 445

16.6a *Monetary Adjustments* 445

16.6b *Synthesis of Automatic Adjustments* 446

16.6c *Automatic Adjustments in the Real World* 447

16.6d *Disadvantages of Automatic Adjustments* 448

Summary 449 • **A Look Ahead** 450 • **Glossary** 450 • **Questions
for Review** 451 • **Problems** 452

Appendix: A16.1 Derivation of Foreign Trade Multipliers with Foreign
Repercussions 453

A16.2 The Transfer Problem Once Again 455

Selected Bibliography 457

CHAPTER 17 *Adjustment Policies* *459*

17.1 Introduction 459

17.2 Internal and External Balance with Expenditure-Changing
and Expenditure-Switching Policies 461

17.3 Equilibrium in the Goods Market, in the Money Market, and
in the Balance of Payments 464

17.4 Fiscal and Monetary Policies for Internal and External
Balance with Fixed Exchange Rates 467

17.4a *Fiscal and Monetary Policies from External Balance and
Unemployment* 467

17.4b *Fiscal and Monetary Policies from External Deficit and
Unemployment* 469

17.4c *Fiscal and Monetary Policies with Elastic Capital Flows* 471

17.5 The Policy Mix and Price Changes 472

17.5a *The Policy Mix and Internal and External Balance* 473

17.5b *Evaluation of the Policy Mix and Price Changes* 475

17.5c *Policy Mix in the Real World* 477

17.6 Direct Controls 478

17.6a *Commercial Controls* 478

17.6b *Exchange Controls* 478

17.6c *Other Direct Controls and International Cooperation* 480

Summary 480 • **A Look Ahead** 481 • **Glossary** 482 • **Questions
for Review** 482 • **Problems** 483

Appendix: A17.1 Derivation of the *IS* Curve 484

A17.2 Derivation of the *LM* Curve 486

A17.3 Derivation of the *FE* Curve 488

A17.4 The *IS-LM-FE* Model with Exchange Rate
Changes 490

A17.5 Mathematical Summary 491

Selected Bibliography 492

CHAPTER 18   *The Monetary and Portfolio Balance Approaches*   *494*

18.1   Introduction   494
18.2   The Monetary Approach Under Fixed Exchange Rates   495
    18.2a   Causes and Adjustment of External Imbalances   *496*
    18.2b   Further Aspects of the Adjustment Process   *498*
    18.2c   Control Over the Nation's Money Supply   *500*
18.3   Policy Implications of the Monetary Approach Under Fixed Exchange Rates and Inflation in the World Economy   501
    18.3a   Policy Implications of the Monetary Approach Under Fixed Exchange Rates   *501*
    18.3b   The Monetary Approach and Inflation in the World Economy Under Fixed Exchange Rates   *503*
18.4   The Monetary Approach Under Flexible Exchange Rates   504
18.5   The Portfolio Balance Approach and Exchange Rate Dynamics   506
    18.5a   The Portfolio Balance Approach   *506*
    18.5b   Exchange Rate Dynamics   *507*
18.6   Evaluation and Empirical Tests of the Monetary and Portfolio Balance Approaches   509

Summary   511   •   **A Look Ahead**   512   •   **Glossary**   512   •   **Questions for Review**   512   •   **Problems**   513
Appendix: A18.1   A Mathematical Model of the Monetary Approach   514
    A18.2   The Exchange Rate Under the Monetary Approach   516
    A18.3   A Mathematical Model of the Portfolio Balance Approach   518
Selected Bibliography   519

CHAPTER 19   *Flexible Versus Fixed Exchange Rates*   *522*

19.1   Introduction   522
19.2   The Case for Flexible Exchange Rates   523
    19.2a   Market Efficiency   *523*
    19.2b   Policy Advantages   *524*
19.3   The Case for Fixed Exchange Rates   526
    19.3a   Less Uncertainty   *526*
    19.3b   Stabilizing Speculation   *528*
    19.3c   Price Discipline   *530*
19.4   Optimum Currency Areas   532
19.5   Exchange Rate Bands, Adjustable Pegs, and Crawling Pegs   534
    19.5a   Exchange Rate Bands   *534*

    19.5b   Adjustable Peg Systems   536
    19.5c   Crawling Pegs   537
19.6   Managed Floating   537

Summary **540** • **A Look Ahead** **541** • **Glossary** **541** • **Questions for Review** **541** • **Problems** **542**
Appendix: Exchange Rate Arrangements   542
Selected Bibliography   544

CHAPTER 20   *The International Monetary System: Past and Present*   *546*

20.1   Introduction   546
20.2   The Gold Standard and the Interwar Experience   548
    20.2a   The Gold Standard Period (1880–1914)   548
    20.2b   The Interwar Experience   550
20.3   The Bretton Woods System   551
    20.3a   The Gold-Exchange Standard (1947–1971)   551
    20.3b   Borrowing from the International Monetary Fund   553
20.4   Operation and Evolution of the Bretton Woods System   554
    20.4a   The Operation of the Bretton Woods System   554
    20.4b   Evolution of the Bretton Woods System   556
20.5   United States Balance-of-Payments Deficits and Collapse of the Bretton Woods System   557
    20.5a   The United States Balance-of-Payments Deficits   558
    20.5b   The Collapse of the Bretton Woods System   560
20.6   The Present International Monetary System   562
    20.6a   The Operation of the Present System   562
    20.6b   The European Monetary System   565
    20.6c   Problems with Present Exchange Rate Arrangements   568
    20.6d   Other Current International Economic Problems   570

Summary **573** • **Glossary** **574** • **Questions for Review** **576** • **Problems** **577**
Appendix: International Reserves: 1950–1985   577
Selected Bibliography   579

Answers to Selected Problems   *582*

Glossary Index   *593*

Name Index   *597*

Subject Index   *600*

CHAPTER 1

Introduction

1.1 The Importance of International Economics

When an American purchases a Toyota car or a Sony television, a Mercedes automobile or a bottle of Beck's beer, a Michelin tire or a bottle of Courvoisier cognac, an Olivetti typewriter or a Gucci handbag, J & B scotch or a Burburrys' raincoat, a Longines or an Omega watch, he or she is obviously buying a foreign product. These are but a few examples of the numerous products available to American consumers that are obviously made in and imported from other nations. Often we are not aware that the products we use, or parts of them, were in fact produced abroad. For example, imported cloth is used in American-made suits; many American brand-name shoes are actually manufactured abroad; the mineral tungsten in our light bulbs is imported, and so is all the coffee we drink, the bananas we eat, and so on.

As tourists, we need to exchange American dollars for British pounds, French francs, Italian liras, and so on to pay for hotel rooms, meals, sightseeing trips and souvenirs. Our news programs and the pages of our daily newspapers are filled with reports on the high value of the dollar in relation to other currencies, the huge U.S. balance of trade deficit, demands for protection of our textile and steel industries against imports, the dangers of trade wars, complaints that Japan does not allow American products to be sold there as freely as Japanese products are sold in the United States, the danger of developing countries defaulting on their huge international debt (a great deal of which is

1

held by American commercial banks), the spread of inflationary and recessionary pressures internationally, and so on.

Similarly, concern is often expressed about such topics as the opportunities and problems created by legal and illegal immigration and by international capital movements and international corporations, the demands of developing nations for a "new economic order" and the redistribution of wealth from rich nations to poorer ones, leakages of high technology secrets, and exports of arms and nuclear plants.

All of these topics and many more are either directly or indirectly the subject matter of international economics. Some knowledge of international economics is thus necessary to understand what goes on in the world of today and to be informed consumers, citizens, and voters. On a more practical level, the study of international economics is required for numerous jobs in multinational corporations, international banking, government agencies such as the Department of Commerce, and international organizations such as the United Nations, the World Bank, and the International Monetary Fund.

1.2   International Trade and the Nation's Standard of Living

The United States, stretching across a continent and rich in a variety of human and natural resources, can produce, relatively efficiently, most of the products it needs. Contrast this with small industrial nations such as Switzerland and Austria that have a few very specialized resources and produce a much smaller range of products which they export in exchange for the many items they must import. Even large industrial nations such as Japan, West Germany, France, England, and Italy rely crucially on international trade. For developing nations, exports provide employment opportunities and earnings to pay for many foreign products that cannot presently be produced domestically and the advanced technology not available at home.

A rough measure of the economic relationship among nations, or their **interdependence,** is given by the percentage of their merchandise imports to their gross national product (GNP). This ranges from a low of about 9 percent for the United States to a high of 31 percent for Switzerland among industrial nations, and from a low of 7 percent for India to a high of 40 percent for Malaysia and Costa Rica among developing nations. Table 1-1 gives these figures for a group of industrial and developing nations arranged from largest to smallest in population. Note the close *inverse* relationship between a nation's size and the percentage of its merchandise imports to GNP.

Even though the United States relies to a relatively small extent on international trade, a great deal of its high standard of living depends on it. First of all, there are many commodities—coffee, bananas, cocoa, tea, scotch, cognac—which the country does not produce at all. In addition, the United States

TABLE 1-1. *Economic Interdependence as Measured by the Percentage of Merchandise Imports to GNP, 1984*

Industrial Nation	Population (millions)	Percentage of Imports to GNP	Developing Nation	Population (millions)	Percentage of Imports to GNP
United States	235	9	India	733	7
Japan	120	11	Brazil	133	8
Germany	61	25	Pakistan	90	18
Italy	57	24	Philippines	53	20
United Kingdom	56	25	Egypt	46	31
France	55	21	Korea	40	38
Canada	25	24	Malaysia	15	40
Sweden	8	29	Tunisia	7	38
Switzerland	6	31	Costa Rica	2	40

Source: IMF, *International Financial Statistics Yearbook* (Washington, D.C.: International Monetary Fund, 1985).

has no deposits of such minerals as tin, tungsten, and chromium, which are important to certain industrial processes, and it has only dwindling reserves of petroleum, copper and many other minerals. Much more important *quantitatively* for the nation's standard of living are the many products that could be produced domestically but only much less efficiently than abroad. These account for most of the *benefits or gains from trade.*

Nevertheless, the United States could probably withdraw from world trade and still survive without too drastic a decline in its standard of living. The same cannot be said of such nations as Japan, West Germany, England, or Italy—not to speak of Switzerland or Austria. Even the Soviet Union and the People's Republic of China, which for political and military reasons value self-sufficiency very highly, have come to acknowledge their need to import high technology products, foreign capital, and even grains, soybeans, and other agricultural commodities. In general, the economic interdependence among nations has been on the increase over the years, particularly since World War II, as measured by the more rapid growth of world trade than output.

But there are many other crucial ways in which nations are interdependent, so that economic events and policies in one nation significantly affect other nations (and vice versa). For example, if the United States stimulates its economy, part of the increased demand for goods and services by its citizens spills into imports, which stimulate the economy of other nations that export those commodities. On the other hand, if the United States reduces the growth in its money supply to combat inflation, this will raise interest rates in the United States and attract funds (capital) from abroad. As we will see in Part IV of the text, this inflow of funds to the United States increases the international value of the dollar, which in turn stimulates U.S. imports and discourages U.S. exports. This then leads to a trade deficit, which dampens economic activity in the U.S. and stimulates economic activity abroad.

Finally, trade negotiations that reduce trade barriers across nations may lead to an increase in the exports of high technology goods (such as computers) and thus to an increase in employment and wages in those industries in the United States, but it may also increase imports of shoes and textiles, therefore reducing employment and wages in those industries in the United States. Thus, we see how closely linked or interdependent nations are in today's world and how government policies directed toward purely domestic problems can have significant international repercussions.

1.3   The Subject Matter of International Economics

International economics deals with the economic interdependence among nations. It analyzes the flow of goods, services, and payments between a nation and the rest of the world, the policies directed at regulating this flow, and their effect on the nation's welfare. This economic interdependence among nations is affected by, and in turn influences, the political, social, cultural, and military relations among nations.

Specifically, international economics deals with the pure theory of trade, the theory of commercial policy, foreign exchange markets and the balance of payments, and adjustment in the balance of payments. The **pure theory of trade** analyzes the basis for and the gains from trade. The **theory of commercial policy** examines the reasons for and the effects of trade restrictions. **Foreign exchange markets** are the framework for the exchange of one national currency for another, while the **balance of payments** measures a nation's total receipts from and the total payments to the rest of the world. Finally, **adjustment in the balance of payments** is concerned with the mechanisms for correcting balance-of-payments disequilibria (i.e., deficits and surpluses) under different international monetary systems and their effect on a nation's welfare.

The pure theory of trade and the theory of commercial policies are the **microeconomic** aspects of international economics because they deal with *individual* nations treated as single units and with the (relative) price of *individual* commodities. On the other hand, since the balance of payments deals with *total* receipts and payments while adjustment policies affect the level of *national* income and the *general* price index, they represent the **macroeconomic** aspects of international economics. These are often referred to as **international finance.**

International economic relations differ from inter-regional economic relations (i.e., the economic relations among different parts of the same nation), thus requiring somewhat different tools of analysis and justifying international economics as a distinct branch of economics. That is, nations usually impose some restrictions on the flow of goods, services, and factors across their borders while generally imposing no such restrictions internally. In addition, international flows are to some extent hampered by differences in language, customs, and laws. Further, international flows of goods, services, and resources give rise to payments and receipts in foreign currencies, which change in value over time.

International economics has enjoyed a long, continuous, and rich development over the past two centuries with contributions from some of the world's most distinguished economists, including *Adam Smith, David Ricardo, John Stuart Mill, Alfred Marshall, John Maynard Keynes,* and *Paul Samuelson.* We will be examining the contribution made by each of these and by other great economists in the following chapters. Other special branches of economics are of more recent vintage, and none can claim such a distinguished list of contributors and background.

1.4 The Purpose of International Economic Theories and Policies

The purpose of economic theory in general is to predict and explain. That is, economic theory abstracts from the details surrounding an economic event in order to isolate the few variables and relationships deemed most important in predicting and explaining the event. Along these lines, international economic theory usually assumes a two-nation, two-commodity, two-factor world. It further assumes no trade restrictions to begin with, perfect mobility of factors within the nations but no international mobility, perfect competition in all commodity and factor markets, and no transportation costs.

These assumptions may seem unduly restrictive. However, most of the conclusions reached on the basis of these simplifying assumptions hold even when they are relaxed so as to deal with a world of more than two nations, commodities and factors, a world where there is some international mobility of factors, imperfect competition, transportation costs, and trade restrictions.

Starting with the simplifying assumptions mentioned above, international economic theory examines the basis for and the gains from trade, the reasons for and the effects of trade restrictions, policies directed at regulating the flows of international payments and receipts, and the effects of these policies on a nation's welfare.

While most of international economics represents the application of general microeconomic and macroeconomic principles to the international context, many theoretical advances were made in the field of international economics itself and only subsequently found their way into the body of general economic theory. One example is the so-called "theory of the second best" (discussed in section 10.4a). Production and general equilibrium theory, welfare economics and growth theory, and many other theories have also benefited from work in the international sphere. These contributions attest to the vitality and importance of international economics as a special branch of economics.

1.5 Organization of the Book

This book is organized into four parts. Part I (Chapters 2–7) deals with the pure theory of international trade. It starts with the explanation of the important theory of comparative advantage in Chapter 2, examines the basis for and the gains from trade in Chapter 3, and defines the tool of analysis called "offer curve" in Chapter 4. The Heckscher-Ohlin, or modern, theory of international trade is presented in Chapter 5, and tested empirically and extended in Chapter 6. Chapter 7 deals with growth.

Part II (Chapters 8–12) deals with commercial policies. Chapter 8 examines tariffs, the most important of the trade restrictions, while Chapter 9 extends the discussion to other trade restrictions, evaluates the justifications usually given for trade restrictions, and summarizes their history. Chapter 10 deals with economic integration, Chapter 11 with the effects of international trade on economic development, and Chapter 12 with international resource movements and multinational corporations.

Part III (Chapters 13 and 14) deals with foreign exchange markets and the measurement of a nation's balance of payments. A clear grasp of these two chapters is crucial for understanding Part IV, on the adjustment to balance of payments disequilibria. Besides presenting the theory, Chapter 13 also examines the actual operation of foreign exchange markets and therefore is of great practical relevance to students of international economics, particularly business majors.

Part IV (Chapters 15–20) deals with the various mechanisms for adjusting balance-of-payments disequilibria. Chapter 15 covers the adjustment mechanism that operates by changing the relationship between domestic and foreign prices, while Chapter 16 examines the income adjustment mechanism and presents a synthesis of the automatic adjustment mechanisms. Chapter 17 deals with adjustment policies; Chapter 18 presents the "monetary approach" to the balance of payments; Chapter 19 compares fixed versus flexible exchange rates; and Chapter 20 examines the operation of the international monetary system over time, especially its present functioning and current international economic problems.

This book starts on an abstract and theoretical level and then becomes more applied in nature and policy oriented. The reason is that one must understand the nature of the problem before seeking appropriate policies for its solution. In the last part of the book (Part IV) some integration of the microeconomic and macroeconomic tools of analysis is achieved. Each part starts with simple concepts and gradually and systematically proceeds to the more complex and difficult.

1.6 Methodology of the Book

This text presents all of the principles and theories for a thorough understanding of international economics. But it does so on an intuitive level in the text itself, while presenting more rigorous proofs requiring intermediate microeconomics in the appendices at the end of most chapters. Thus, the book is designed for flexibility depending on a student's academic background. To make the concepts and theories presented more accessible and concrete, the same example is followed through in all chapters dealing with the same basic concept and actual numbers are used in examples.

Each chapter contains six sections plus a summary, a look ahead, a glossary of important terms, questions for review, problems, one or more appendices (except for this chapter and Chapters 11 and 19), and a selected bibliography. Sections of each chapter are numbered for easy reference (as in this chapter). Long sections are broken down into two or more numbered subsections.

Each section of the chapter is summarized in one paragraph in the **summary.** Following the summary a paragraph under the title of **a look ahead** tells what follows in the subsequent chapter. The purpose of this is to integrate the material more closely and show the relationship between the various chapters. Important terms are printed in boldface when they are first introduced and explained (as in this chapter), and are then collected with their definitions in the **glossary** at the end of the chapter.

There is one question (made up of several parts) reviewing the most important concepts or theories presented in each section of the chapter. These appear in the **questions for review** at the end of the chapter. This is followed by a section of **problems.** There is one problem (usually made up of several parts) for each section of the chapter. These problems differ from the questions for review in that they ask the student to get pencil and paper and draw a graph illustrating a particular theory or actually calculate a specific measure. These graphs and calculations are challenging but not tricky or time consuming. They are intended to show whether or not the student understands the material covered in the chapter to the point where he or she can use it to analyze similar problems. The student is urged to work through these problems because only with his or her active participation will international economics truly come alive.

The **selected bibliography** gives the most important references, clearly indicating the particular concept or theory to which they refer.

Summary

1. Some knowledge of international economics is necessary to understand what goes on in the world of today and to be informed consumers, citizens, and voters. On a more practical level, the study of international economics is required for numerous jobs in international corporations, international banking, various government agencies, and international organizations.

2. The United States relies on international trade to obtain many products that it does not produce

and some minerals (either because there are no deposits in this country or because domestic reserves are dwindling). More important *quantitatively* for the nation's standard of living are many products that could be produced domestically but only much less efficiently than abroad. International trade is even more crucial to the well-being of other industrial nations and developing nations.

3. International economics deals with the pure theory of trade, the theory of commercial policy, foreign exchange markets and balance of payments, and adjustment in the balance of payments. The first two topics are the microeconomic aspects of international economics; the latter two are the macroeconomic aspects, also known as international finance.

4. Starting with many simplifying assumptions, international economic theories examine the basis for and the gains from trade, the reasons for and the effects of trade restrictions, the politics directed at regulating the flow of international payments and receipts, and the effects of these policies on a nation's welfare.

5. The book is organized into four parts. Part I (Chapters 2–7) deals with the pure theory of trade. Part II (Chapters 8–12) examines commercial policies. Part III (Chapters 13–14) covers foreign exchange markets and the balance of payments. Part IV (Chapters 15–20) examines the various mechanisms to adjust balance-of-payments disequilibria.

6. The text is designed for maximum flexibility to be used in classes of international economics populated by students with different academic backgrounds and levels of preparation. Each chapter is divided into numbered sections and subsections and includes a summary, a look ahead, a glossary of important terms, questions for review, problems, one or more appendices (except for this chapter and Chapters 11 and 19), and a selected bibliography.

A Look Ahead

In Chapter 2, we begin our presentation of the pure theory of international trade and present the law of comparative advantage. This is one of the most important and still unchallenged laws of economics, with many interesting and practical applications. The law of comparative advantage is the cornerstone of the pure theory of international trade and it is crucial to master it completely before going on to other chapters.

Glossary

Interdependence The (economic) relationships among nations.

Pure theory of trade Analyzes the basis for and gains from trade.

Theory of commercial policy Examines the reasons for and the effects of trade restrictions.

Foreign exchange markets The framework for the exchange of one national currency for another.

Balance of payments The measure of a nation's total receipts from and total payments to the rest of the world.

Adjustment in the balance of payments The operation and effects of the mechanisms for correcting balance-of-payments disequilibria.

Microeconomic The study of individual units, such as a particular nation and the relative price of a single commodity.

Macroeconomic The study of the whole or the aggregate, such as the total receipts and payments of a nation and the general price index.

International finance The study of foreign exchange markets, the balance of payments, and adjustment to balance-of-payments disequilibria.

Questions for Review

1. Why is it important to study international economics? What are some of the most important current events that are part of the general subject matter of international economics? Why are they important? How do they affect the political and military relations between the United States and Japan? The United States and the Soviet Union?

2. How is international trade related to the standard of living of the United States? Of other large industrial nations? Of small industrial nations? Of developing nations? For which of these groups of nations is international trade most crucial? How can we get a rough measure of the interdependence of each nation with the rest of the world?

3. What does the pure theory of trade deal with? The theory of commercial policy? Why are they known as the microeconomic aspects of international economics? What are foreign exchange markets and what is the balance of payments? What is meant by adjustment in the balance of payments? Why are these topics known as the macroeconomic aspects of international economics? What is meant by international finance?

4. What is the purpose of economic theory in general? Of international economic theories and policies in particular? What simplifying assumptions do we make in studying international economics? Why are these assumptions usually justified?

5. Why does the study of international economics usually begin with the presentation of the pure theory of trade? Why must we discuss theories before examining policies? Which aspects of international economics are more abstract? Which are more applied in nature?

6. From your previous course(s) in economics, do you recall the concepts of demand, supply, and equilibrium? Do you recall the meaning of the elasticity of demand? Perfect competition? Factor markets? The production frontier? The law of diminishing returns? The marginal productivity theory? (If you do not remember some of these concepts, quickly review them from your principles text or class notes.)

Problems

*1. Go through your daily newspaper and identify:
   (a) 5 news items of an international economic character;

* = answer provided at the end of the book.

(b) the importance or effect of each of these news items on the United States economy;
(c) the importance of each of these news items to you personally.

2. This question will involve you in measuring the economic interdependence of some nations.
   (a) Identify any five industrial and any five developing nations not shown in Table 1-1.
   (b) Go to your school library and find the latest edition of *International Financial Statistics*, published by the International Monetary Fund. This book is usually in the reference section of a library, but look it up in the card catalogue and/or ask the librarian for help if you cannot locate it. If your library does not have this book, skip the rest of this problem and go on to the next.
   (c) Utilizing the data in *International Financial Statistics*, find the degree of economic interdependence for the ten nations you have chosen and construct a table analogous to Table 1-1. Is the economic interdependence of the smaller nations in each group greater than that of the larger nations?

3. Take your principles of economics text (even if you have already had intermediate theory) and from the table of contents:
   (a) identify the topics presented in the microeconomics parts of the text;
   (b) identify the topics presented in the macroeconomics parts of the text;
   (c) compare the contents of the microeconomic parts of your principles text with the content of Parts I and II of this text;
   (d) compare the contents of the macroeconomic parts of your principles text with the content of Parts III and IV of this text.

4. (a) What does consumer demand theory predict will happen to the quantity demanded of a commodity if its price rises (for example, as a result of a tax) while everything else is held constant?
   (b) What do you predict would happen to the quantity of imports of a commodity if its

price to domestic consumers rose (for example, as a result of a tax on imports)?

5. (a) How can a government eliminate or reduce a budget deficit?

  (b) How can a nation eliminate or reduce a balance-of-payments deficit?

*6. How does the organization of the text compare with the natural breakdown of the subject matter of international economics?

Selected Bibliography

A very popular paperback in the Schaum's Outline Series in Economics that gives a problem-solving approach to international economics and can be used with this and any other text is:
- D. Salvatore, *Theory and Problems of International Economics*, 2nd ed. (New York: McGraw-Hill, 1984).

An excellent discussion of the concept and measurement of interdependence is found in:
- R. N. Cooper, *Economic Policy in an Interdependent World* (Cambridge, Mass.: M.I.T. Press, 1985).
- M. Michaely, *Trade, Income Levels, and Dependence* (Amsterdam: North-Holland, 1985).

Two books of readings on current events in international economics, specifically for undergraduates, are:
- J. Adams, *The Contemporary International Economy: A Reader* (New York: St. Martin's Press, 1985).
- R. E. Baldwin and J. D. Richardson, *International Trade and Finance* (Boston: Little, Brown, 1986).

* = answer provided at the end of the book.

Books that reprint many classic articles from economic journals and are useful for advanced undergraduates and graduate students are:
- J. N. Bhagwati, *International Trade* (Baltimore: Penguin, 1969).
- J. N. Bhagwati, *International Trade: Selected Readings* (Cambridge, Mass.: M.I.T. Press, 1981).
- R. N. Cooper, *International Finance* (Baltimore: Penguin, 1969).
- R. E. Caves and H. G. Johnson, *Readings in International Economics* (Homewood, Ill.: Irwin, 1968).
- H. S. Ellis and L. A. Metzler, *Readings in the Theory of International Trade* (Homewood, Ill.: Irwin, 1950).

Some excellent surveys in trade theory for more advanced students are:
- J. N. Bhagwati, "The Pure Theory of International Trade," *Economic Journal,* March 1964.
- J. Chipman, "A Survey of the Theory of International Trade, Parts I–III," *Econometrica,* July 1965, October 1965, October 1966.
- J. N. Bhagwati and T. N. Srinivasan, *Lectures on International Trade* (Cambridge, Mass.: M.I.T. Press, 1983).
- R. W. Jones and P. B. Kenen, *Handbook of International Economics*, Vol. 1 (Amsterdam: North-Holland, 1984).

The classic surveys in international finance for the more advanced students are:
- J. E. Meade, *The Balance of Payments* (London: Oxford University Press, 1951).
- R. M. Stern, *The Balance of Payments: Theory and Economic Policy* (Chicago: Aldine, 1973).
- R. W. Jones and P. B. Kenen, *Handbook of International Economics*, Vol. 2 (Amsterdam: North-Holland, 1985).

PART I

The Pure Theory of International Trade

Part 1 (Chapters 2–7) deals with the pure theory of international trade. It starts with the presentation and explanation of the very important theory of comparative advantage in Chapter 2, examines the basis for and the gains from trade in Chapter 3, and defines the tool of analysis called "offer curve" in Chapter 4. Chapter 5 presents the Heckscher-Ohlin, or modern, theory of international trade. Chapter 6 examines empirical tests and complementary trade theories. Chapter 7 deals with growth and its effects on international trade.

CHAPTER 2

The Law of Comparative Advantage

2.1 Introduction

In this chapter, we examine the development of trade theory from the seventeenth century through the first part of the twentieth century. This historical approach is useful not because we are interested in the "history of economic thought" as such but because it is a convenient way of introducing the concepts and theories of international trade from the simple to the more complex and realistic.

The basic questions that we seek to answer in this chapter are:

1. What is the **basis for trade** and what are the **gains from trade?** Presumably (and as in the case of an individual) a nation will voluntarily engage in trade only if it benefits from trade. But how are gains from trade generated? How large are the gains and how are they divided among the trading nations?

2. What is the **pattern of trade?** That is, what commodities are traded and which commodities are exported and imported by each nation?

We begin with a brief discussion of the economic doctrines known as mercantilism that prevailed during the seventeenth and eighteenth centuries. We then go on to discuss the theory of absolute advantage developed by Adam Smith. It remained, however, for David Ricardo, writing some forty years after Smith, to truly explain the pattern of and the gains from trade with his law of comparative advantage. The law of comparative advantage is one of the most important laws of economics, with applicability to nations as well as to individuals and useful for exposing many serious fallacies in apparently logical reasoning.

One difficulty remained. Ricardo had based his explanation of the law of comparative advantage on the labor theory of value, which was subsequently rejected. In the first part of this century, Haberler came to the "rescue" of Ricardo by explaining the law of comparative advantage in terms of the opportunity cost theory, as reflected in production possibility frontiers, or transformation curves.

For simplicity, our discussion will initially refer to only two nations and two commodities. In the appendix to this chapter, the conclusions will be generalized to trade in more than two commodities and among more than two nations.

2.2   The Mercantilists' Views on Trade

Economics as an organized science can be said to have originated with the publication in 1776 of *The Wealth of Nations* by *Adam Smith.* However, writings on international trade preceded this date in such countries as England, Spain, France, Portugal, and the Netherlands as they developed into modern national states. Specifically, during the seventeenth and eighteenth centuries a group of men (merchants, bankers, government officials, and even philosophers) wrote essays and pamphlets on international trade that advocated an economic philosophy known as **mercantilism.** Briefly, the mercantilists maintained that the way for a nation to become rich and powerful was to export more than it imported. The resulting export surplus would then be settled by an inflow of bullion, or precious metals, primarily gold and silver. The more gold and silver a nation had, the richer and more powerful it was. Thus, the government had to do all in its power to stimulate the nation's exports and discourage and restrict imports (particularly the import of luxury consumption goods). However, since all nations could not simultaneously have an export surplus and the amount of gold and silver was fixed at any particular point in time, one nation could gain only at the expense of other nations. The mercantilists thus preached economic nationalism, believing as they did that national interests were basically in conflict.

Note that the mercantilists measured the wealth of a nation by the stock of precious metals it possessed. In contrast, today we measure the wealth of a nation by its stock of human, man-made, and natural resources available for producing goods and services. The greater is this stock of useful resources, the greater is the *flow* of goods and services to satisfy human wants, and the higher the standard of living in the nation.

At a more sophisticated level of analysis, there were more rational reasons for the mercantilists' desire for the accumulation of precious metals. This can be understood if it is remembered that the mercantilists were writing primarily for rulers and to enhance national power. With more gold, rulers could maintain larger and better armies and consolidate their power at home; improved armies and navies also made it possible for them to acquire more colonies. In addition, more gold meant more money (i.e., more gold coins) in circulation and greater business activity. Further, by encouraging exports and restricting imports, the government would stimulate national output and employment.

In any event, mercantilists advocated strict government control of all economic activity and preached economic nationalism because they believed that a nation could gain in trade only at the expense of other nations. These views are important for two reasons. First, the ideas of Adam Smith, David Ricardo and other classical economists can best be understood if they are regarded as reactions to the mercantilists' views on trade and the role of the government. Second, today there seems to be a resurgence of neo-mercantilism as nations plagued by high levels of unemployment seek to restrict imports in an effort to stimulate domestic production and employment.

2.3   Trade Based on Absolute Advantage: Adam Smith

Smith started with the simple truth that for two nations to trade with each other *voluntarily,* both nations must gain. If one nation gained nothing or lost, it would simply refuse to trade. But how does this *mutually beneficial* trade take place and from where do these gains from trade come?

2.3a   Absolute Advantage

According to Adam Smith, trade between two nations is based on **absolute advantage.** When one nation is more efficient than (or has an absolute advantage over) another in the production of one commodity but is less efficient than (or has an absolute disadvantage with respect to) the other nation in producing a second commodity, then both nations can gain by each *specializing* in the production of the commodity of its absolute advantage and exchanging part of its output with the other nation for the commodity of its absolute disadvantage. By this process, resources are utilized in the most efficient way and the output of *both* commodities will rise. This increase in the output of both commodities measures the gains from specialization in production available to be divided between the two nations through trade.

For example, because of climatic conditions, Canada is efficient in growing wheat but inefficient in growing bananas (hot houses would have to be used). On the other hand, Nicaragua is efficient in growing bananas but inefficient in growing wheat. Thus, Canada has an absolute advantage over Nicaragua in the cultivation of wheat but an absolute disadvantage in the cultivation of bananas. The opposite is true for Nicaragua.

Under these circumstances, both nations would benefit if each specialized in the production of the commodity of its absolute advantage and then traded with the other nation. Canada would specialize in the production of wheat (i.e., produce more than needed domestically) and exchange some of it for (surplus) bananas grown in Nicaragua. As a result, both more wheat and more bananas would be grown and consumed, and both Canada and Nicaragua would gain.

In this respect, a nation behaves no differently from an individual who does not attempt to produce all the commodities he needs. Rather, he produces only that commodity which he can produce most efficiently and then exchanges part of his output for the other commodities he needs or wants. This way, total output and the welfare of all individuals is maximized.

Thus, while the mercantilists believed that one nation could gain only at the expense of another nation and advocated strict government control of all economic activity and trade, Adam Smith (and the other classical economists who followed him) believed that all nations would gain from free trade and strongly advocated a policy of **laissez-faire** (i.e., as little as possible government interference with the economic system). Free trade would cause world resources to be utilized most efficiently and would maximize world welfare. There were to be only a few exceptions to this policy of laissez-faire and free trade. One of these was the protection of industries important for national defense.

In view of this, it seems paradoxical that today most nations impose many restrictions on the free flow of international trade. Trade restrictions are invariably rationalized in terms of national welfare. In reality, trade restrictions are advocated by the few industries and their workers who are hurt by imports. As such, trade restrictions benefit the few at the expense of the many (who will have to pay higher prices for competing domestic goods). These issues will be examined in detail in Part II.

Also to be noted is that Smith's theory served the interest of factory owners (who were able to pay lower wages because of cheaper food imports) and harmed land owners in England (because food became less scarce due to cheaper imports), and it shows the link between social pressures and the development of new economic theories to support them.

2.3b   Illustration of Absolute Advantage

We will now look at a *numerical* example of absolute advantage that will serve to establish a frame of reference for presentation of the more challenging theory of comparative advantage in the next section.

Table 2-1 shows that one hour of labor time produces six bushels of wheat in the United States but only one in the United Kingdom. On the other hand, one hour of labor time produces five yards of cloth in the United Kingdom but only four in the United States. Thus, the United States is more efficient than, or has an absolute advantage over, the United Kingdom in the production of wheat, while the United Kingdom is more efficient than, or has an

TABLE 2-1.   Absolute Advantage

	U.S.	U.K.
Wheat (bushels/man-hour)	6	1
Cloth (yards/man-hour)	4	5

absolute advantage over, the United States in the production of cloth. With trade, the United States would specialize in the production of wheat and exchange part of it for British cloth. The opposite is true for the United Kingdom.

If the United States exchanges six bushels of wheat (6W) for six yards of British cloth (6C), the United States gains 2C or saves ½ man-hour or 30 minutes of labor time (since the U.S. can only exchange 6W for 4C domestically). Similarly, the 6W that the United Kingdom receives from the United States is equivalent to or would require six man-hours of labor time to produce in the United Kingdom. These same six man-hours can produce 30C in the United Kingdom (6 hours times 5 yards of cloth per man-hour). By being able to exchange 6C (requiring a little over one hour to produce to the United Kingdom) for 6W with the United States, the United Kingdom gains 24C or saves almost five man-hours.

The fact that the United Kingdom gains much more than the United States is not important at this time. What is important is that *both* nations can gain from specialization in production and trade. (We will see in Chapter 4 how the rate at which commodities are exchanged for one another is determined, and also examine the closely related question of how the gains from trade are divided among the trading nations.)

Absolute advantage, however, can explain only a very small part of world trade today, such as the trade between developed and developing countries. Most of world trade, especially trade among developed countries, could not be explained by absolute advantage. It remained for David Ricardo, with the law of comparative advantage, to truly explain the basis for and the gains from trade. Indeed, absolute advantage will be seen to be only a special case of the more general theory of comparative advantage.

2.4   Trade Based on Comparative Advantage

In 1817 *Ricardo* published his *Principles of Political Economy and Taxation*, in which he presented the law of comparative advantage. This is one of the most important and still unchallenged laws of economics, with many practical applications. In this section, we will first define the law of comparative advantage. Then we will restate it with a simple numerical example, and finally prove it by demonstrating that both nations can indeed gain by each specializing in the production and exporting the commodity of its comparative advantage. In section 2.6, we will prove the law *graphically*.

2.4a   The Law of Comparative Advantage

According to the **law of comparative advantage,** even if one nation is less efficient than (has an absolute disadvantage with respect to) the other nation in the production of *both* commodities, there is still a basis for mutually beneficial trade. The first nation should specialize in the production of and export the commodity in which its absolute disadvantage is smaller (this is the commodity of its *comparative advantage*) and import the commodity in which its absolute disadvantage is greater (this is the commodity of its *comparative disadvantage*).

The statement of the law can be clarified by looking at Table 2-2. The only difference between Table 2-2 and 2-1 is that the United Kingdom now produces only two yards of cloth per man-hour instead of five. Thus, the United Kingdom now has an absolute disadvantage in the production of *both* wheat and cloth with respect to the United States.

TABLE 2-2.   Comparative Advantage

	U.S.	U.K.
Wheat (bushels/man-hour)	6	1
Cloth (yards/man-hour)	4	2

However, since United Kingdom labor is half as productive in cloth but six times less productive in wheat with respect to the United States, *the United Kingdom has a comparative advantage in cloth.* On the other hand, the United States has an absolute advantage in both wheat and cloth with respect to the United Kingdom, but since its absolute advantage is greater in wheat (6:1) than in cloth (4:2), *the United States has a comparative advantage in wheat.* To summarize, the United States' absolute advantage is greater in wheat and so the United States has a comparative advantage in wheat. The United Kingdom's absolute disadvantage is smaller in cloth so that its comparative advantage lies in cloth. According to the law of comparative advantage, both nations can gain if the United States specializes in the production of wheat and exports some of it in exchange for British cloth. (At the same time, the United Kingdom is specializing in the production of and exporting cloth.)

Note that in a two-nation, two-commodities world, once it is determined that one nation has a comparative advantage in one commodity, then the other nation *must* necessarily have a comparative advantage in the other commodity.

2.4b The Gains from Trade

So far, we have stated the law of comparative advantage in words, then restated it with a simple numerical example. However, we have not yet proved the law. To do so, we must be able to show that the United States and the United Kingdom can both gain by each specializing in the production of and exporting the commodity of its comparative advantage.

To start with, we know that the United States would be indifferent to trade if it received only 4C from the United Kingdom in exchange for 6W, since the United States can produce exactly 4C domestically by utilizing the resources released in giving up 6W (see Table 2-2). And the United States would certainly not trade if it received less than 4C for 6W. Similarly, the United Kingdom would be indifferent to trade if it had to give up 2C for each 1W it received from the United States, and it certainly would not trade if it had to give up more than 2C for 1W.

To show that both nations can gain, suppose the United States could exchange 6W for 6C with the United Kingdom. The United States would then gain 2C (or save ½ hour of labor time) since the United States could only exchange 6W for 4C domestically. To see that the United Kingdom would also gain, note that the 6W that the United Kingdom receives from the United States would require six man-hours to produce in the United Kingdom. The United Kingdom could instead use these six man-hours to produce 12C and give up only 6C for 6W from the United States. Thus, the United Kingdom would gain 6C or save three hours of labor time. Once again, the fact that the United Kingdom gains more from trade than the United States is not important at this point. What is important is that both nations can gain from trade even if one of them (in this case the United Kingdom) is less efficient than the other in the production of both commodities.

We can convince ourselves of this by looking at a simple example from everyday life. Suppose a lawyer can type twice as fast as his secretary. The lawyer then has an absolute advantage over his secretary in both the practice of law and typing. However, since the secretary cannot even practice law without a law degree, the lawyer has a greater absolute advantage or a comparative advantage in law, and the secretary has a comparative advantage in typing. According to the law of comparative advantage, the lawyer should spend all of his time practicing law and let his secretary do the typing. For example, if the lawyer earns $100 per hour practicing law and must pay his secretary $10 per hour to do the typing, he would actually lose $80 for each hour that he typed. The reason for this is that he would save $20 (since he can type twice as fast as his secretary) but forgo earning $100 in the practice of law.

Returning to the United States and the United Kingdom, we saw that both nations would gain by exchanging 6W for 6C. However, this is not the only rate of exchange at which mutually beneficial trade can take place. Since the United States could exchange 6W for 4C domestically (in the sense that both require 1 man-hour to produce), the United States would gain if it could exchange 6W for more than 4C from the United Kingdom. On the other hand, in the United Kingdom 6W = 12C (in the sense that both require 6 man-hours to produce). Anything less than 12C that the United Kingdom must give up to obtain 6W from the United States represents a gain from trade for the United Kingdom. To summarize, the United States gains to the extent that it can exchange 6W for more than 4C from the United Kingdom. The United Kingdom gains to the extent that it can give up less than 12C for 6W from the United States. Thus the range for mutually advantageous trade is:

$$4C < 6W < 12C$$

The spread between 12C and 4C (i.e., 8C) represents the total gains from trade available to be shared by the two nations by trading 6W. For example, we have seen that when 6W are exchanged for 6C, the United States gains 2C and the United Kingdom 6C, making a total of 8C. The closer the rate of exchange is to 4C = 6W (the *domestic*, or *internal*, rate in the United States—see Table 2-2), the smaller is the share of the gain going to the United States and the larger the share of the gain going to the United Kingdom. On the other hand, the closer the rate of exchange is to 6W = 12C (the domestic, or internal, rate in the United Kingdom), the greater is the gain of the United States relative to that of the United Kingdom.

For example, if the United States exchanged 6W for 8C with the United Kingdom, both nations would gain 4C, for a total gain of 8C. If the United States could exchange 6W for 10C, it would gain 6C and the United Kingdom only 2C. (Of course, the gains from trade are proportionately greater when more than 6W are traded.) In Chapter 4, we will see how this rate of exchange is actually determined in the real world by demand as well as supply considerations. The rate of exchange will also determine how the total gains from trade are actually shared by the trading nations. Up to this point, all we have wanted to do was to prove that mutually beneficial trade can take place even if one nation is less efficient than the other in the production of both commodities.

So far, the gains from specialization in production and trade have been measured in terms of cloth. However, the gains from trade could also be measured exclusively in terms of wheat or, more realistically, in terms of both wheat and cloth. This will be done in the graphical presentation of the law of comparative advantage in section 2.6.

2.4c Exception to the Law of Comparative Advantage

There is one (not very common) **exception to the law of comparative advantage.** This occurs when the absolute disadvantage that one nation has with respect to another nation is the *same* in both commodities. For example, if one man-hour produced 3W instead of 1W in the United Kingdom (see Table

2-2), the United Kingdom would be exactly half as productive as the United States in both wheat and cloth. The United Kingdom (and the United States) would then have a comparative advantage in neither commodity, and no mutually beneficial trade could take place.

The reason for this is that (as earlier) the United States will trade only if it can exchange 6W for more than 4C. However, now the United Kingdom is not willing to give up more than 4C to obtain 6W from the United States because the United Kingdom can produce either 6W or 4C with two man-hours domestically. Under these circumstances, no mutually beneficial trade can take place.

This requires a slight modification in the statement of the law of comparative advantage to read as follows: Even if one nation has an absolute disadvantage with respect to the other nation in the production of both commodities, there is still a basis for mutually beneficial trade, *unless the absolute disadvantage (that one nation has with respect to the other nation) is exactly the same or in the same proportion for the two commodities.* While it is important to note this exception in theory, its occurrence is rare and a matter of coincidence so that the applicability of the law of comparative advantage is not much affected.

2.4d Comparative Advantage with Money

According to the law of comparative advantage (and disregarding the exception noted above), even if one nation (the United Kingdom in this case) has an absolute disadvantage in the production of both commodities with respect to the other nation (the United States), there is still a basis for mutually beneficial trade. But how, you may ask, can the United Kingdom export anything to the United States if it is less efficient than the United States in the production of both commodities? The answer is that wages in the United Kingdom will be sufficiently lower than wages in the United States so as to make the price of cloth (the commodity in which the United Kingdom has a comparative advantage) lower in the United Kingdom, and the price of wheat lower in the United States *when both commodities are expressed in terms of the currency of either nation.* Let us see how this works.

Suppose that the wage rate in the United States is $6 per hour. Since one man-hour produces 6W in the United States (see Table 2-2), the price of a bushel of wheat is $P_W = \$1$. On the other hand, since one man-hour produces 4C, $P_C = \$1.50$ (from $6/4C$). Suppose that at the same time the wage rate in England is £1 per hour (the symbol "£" stands for pound, the United Kingdom currency). Since one man-hour produces 1W in the United Kingdom (see Table 2-2), $P_W = £1$ in the United Kingdom. Similarly, since one man-hour produces 2C, $P_C = £0.5$. If the exchange rate between the pound and the dollar is £1 = $2, then $P_W = £1 = \$2$ and $P_C = £0.5 = \$1$ in the United Kingdom. Table 2-3 shows the dollar price of wheat and cloth in the United States and the United Kingdom at the exchange rate of £1 = $2.

TABLE 2-3. *Dollar Price of Wheat and Cloth in the United States and United Kingdom at £1 = $2*

	U.S.	U.K.
Price of one bushel of wheat	$1.00	$2.00
Price of one yard of cloth	1.50	1.00

From Table 2-3 we can see that the dollar price of wheat (the commodity in which the United States has a comparative advantage) is lower in the United States than in the United Kingdom. On the other hand, the dollar price of cloth (the commodity in which the United Kingdom has a comparative advantage) is lower in the United Kingdom. (The result would be the same if the price of both commodities had been expressed in pounds.)

With the dollar price of wheat lower in the United States, businessmen would buy wheat there and sell it in the United Kingdom, where they would buy cloth to sell in the United States. Even though United Kingdom labor is half as productive as United States labor in cloth production (see Table 2-2), United Kingdom labor receives only one-third of the United States wage rate (£1 = $2 as opposed to $6 in the United States), so that the dollar price of cloth is lower in the United Kingdom. To put it differently, the inefficiency of United Kingdom labor relative to United States labor in cloth production is more than compensated by the lower wages in the United Kingdom. As a result, the dollar price of cloth is less in the United Kingdom, so that the United Kingdom can export cloth to the United States. This is always the case as long as the United Kingdom wage rate is between ⅙ and ½ of the United States wage rate (the same as the productivity difference between the United Kingdom and the United States in the production of wheat and cloth).

If the exchange rate between the dollar and the pound was instead £1 = $1 (so that the United Kingdom wage rate was exactly ⅙ the United States wage rate), then the dollar price of wheat in the United Kingdom would be $P_W = £1 = \$1$. Since this is the same price as in the United States (see Table 2-3), the United States could not export wheat to the United Kingdom at this exchange rate. At the same time, $P_C = £0.5 = \$0.50$ in the United Kingdom, and the United Kingdom would export even more cloth than before to the United States. Trade would be unbalanced in favor of the United Kingdom and the exchange rate between the dollar and the pound (i.e., the dollar price of the pound) would have to rise.

On the other hand, if the exchange rate was £1 = $3 (so that the United Kingdom wage rate was exactly ½ the United States wage rate), the price of cloth in the United Kingdom would be $P_C = £0.5 = \$1.50$ (the same as in the United States—see Table 2-3). As a result, the United Kingdom could not export cloth to the United States. Trade would be unbalanced in favor of the

United States and the exchange rate would have to fall. The rate of exchange between the dollar and the pound will eventually settle at the level that will result in balanced trade (in the absence of any other international transaction). We will return to this point in the appendix to this chapter and in much greater detail in Parts III and IV, which deal with international finance.

Thus, the argument that could be advanced in the United States that it needs to protect the high wages and standard of living of its workers against cheap British labor is generally false. Similarly faulty is the opposing argument that could be advanced in the United Kingdom that its labor needs protection against more efficient United States labor. These arguments are certainly inconsistent, and both are basically incorrect.

2.5 Comparative Advantage and Opportunity Costs

Ricardo based his law of comparative advantage on a number of simplifying assumptions: (1) only two nations and two commodities, (2) free trade, (3) perfect mobility of labor within each nation but immobility between the two nations, (4) constant costs of production, (5) no transportation costs, (6) no technical change, and (7) the labor theory of value. While assumptions one through six can easily be relaxed, assumption seven (i.e., that the labor theory of value holds) is basically wrong and should not be used in *explaining* comparative advantage.

2.5a Comparative Advantage and the Labor Theory of Value

Under the **labor of value,** the value or price of a commodity depends exclusively on the amount of labor going into the production of the commodity. This implies that (1) either labor is the only factor of production or that labor is used in the *same* fixed proportion in the production of all commodities and (2) that labor is homogeneous (i.e., of only one type). Since neither of these assumptions is true, the labor theory of value must be rejected.

Specifically, labor is neither the only factor of production nor is it homogeneous, and labor is not used in the same fixed proportion in the production of all commodities. For example, much more capital equipment per worker is required to produce some products (such as steel) than to produce other products (such as textiles). In addition, there is usually some possibility of substitution between labor, capital and other factors in the production of most commodities. Furthermore, labor is obviously not homogeneous but varies greatly in training, productivity, and wages.

By rejecting the labor theory of value we must also reject Ricardo's *explanation* of comparative advantage, but not the law of comparative advantage itself. The law of comparative advantage can be explained on the basis of the opportunity cost theory (which is acceptable).

2.5b   The Opportunity Cost Theory

In 1936 *Haberler* "rescued" the law of comparative advantage by basing it on the **opportunity cost theory** rather than on the (unacceptable) labor theory of value. In this form, the law of comparative advantage is sometimes referred to as the *law of comparative cost.*

According to the opportunity cost theory, the cost of a commodity is the amount of a second commodity that must be given up to release just enough resources to produce one additional unit of the first commodity. No assumption is here made that labor is the only factor of production or that labor is homogeneous. Nor is it assumed that the cost or price of a commodity depends on or can be inferred exclusively from its labor content. Consequently, the nation with the lower opportunity cost in the production of a commodity has a comparative advantage in that commodity (and a comparative disadvantage in the second commodity).

For example, if in the absence of trade the United States must give up two-thirds of a unit of cloth to release just enough resources to produce one additional unit of wheat domestically, then *the opportunity cost of wheat is two-thirds of a unit of cloth* (i.e., 1W = 2/3C in the United States). If 1W = 2C in the United Kingdom, then the opportunity cost of wheat (in terms of the amount of cloth that must be given up) is lower in the United States than in the United Kingdom, and the United States would have a comparative (cost) advantage over the United Kingdom in wheat. In a two-nation, two-commodity world, the United Kingdom would then have a comparative advantage in cloth.

According to the law of comparative advantage, the United States should specialize in producing wheat and export some of it in exchange for British cloth. This is exactly what we concluded earlier with the law of comparative advantage based on the labor theory of value, but now our explanation is based on the opportunity cost theory.

2.5c   The Production Possibility Frontier under Constant Costs

Opportunity costs can be illustrated with the production possibility frontier, or transformation curve. The **production possibility frontier** is a curve that shows the *alternative* combinations of the two commodities that a nation can produce by fully utilizing all of its resources with the best technology available to it.

Table 2-4 gives the (hypothetical) production possibility schedules of wheat (in million bushels/year) and cloth (in million yards/year) for the United States and the United Kingdom. We see that the United States can produce 180W and 0C, 150W and 20C, or 120W and 40C, down to 0W and 120C. For each 30W that the United States gives up, just enough resources are released to produce an additional 20C. That is, 30W = 20C (in the sense that both require the same amount of resources). Thus, the opportunity cost of one unit of wheat in the United States is 1W = ⅔C (the same as in Table 2-2) and remains con-

TABLE 2-4. ***Production Possibility Schedules for Wheat and Cloth in the United States and the United Kingdom***

United States		United Kingdom	
Wheat	*Cloth*	*Wheat*	*Cloth*
180	0	60	0
150	20	50	20
120	40	40	40
90	60	30	60
60	80	20	80
30	100	10	100
0	120	0	120

stant. On the other hand, the United Kingdom can produce 60W and 0C, 50W and 20C, or 40W and 40C, down to 0W and 120C. It can increase its output by 20C for each 10W it gives up. Thus, the opportunity cost of wheat in the United Kingdom is 1W = 2C and remains constant.

The United States and United Kingdom production possibility schedules given in Table 2-4 are graphed as production possibility frontiers in Figure 2-1. Each point on a frontier represented one combination of wheat and cloth that the nation can produce. For example, at point *A*, the United States produces 90W and 60C. At point *A'*, the United Kingdom produces 40W and 40C.

Points inside, or below, the production possibility frontier are also possible but are inefficient, in the sense that the nation either has some idle resources and/or is not using the best technology available to it. On the other hand, points above the production frontier cannot be achieved with the resources and technology currently available to the nation.

The downward, or negative, slope of the production possibility frontiers in Figure 2-1 indicates that if the United States and the United Kingdom want to produce more wheat, they must give up some of their cloth production. The fact that the production possibility frontiers of both nations are straight lines reflects the fact that their opportunity costs are constant. That is, for each additional 1W to be produced, the United States must give up ⅔C and the United Kingdom must give up 2C *no matter from which point on its production possibility frontier the nation starts.*

Constant opportunity costs arise when (1) resources or factors of production are either perfect substitutes for each other or are used in fixed proportion in the production of both commodities, and (2) all units of the same factor are homogeneous or of exactly the same quality. Then, as each nation transfers resources from the production of cloth to the production of wheat, it will not have to use resources that are less and less suited to wheat production, no matter how much wheat it is already producing. The same is true for the production of more cloth. Thus, we have constant costs in the sense that the same amount of one commodity must be given up to produce each additional unit of the second commodity.

While opportunity costs are constant in each nation, they differ among nations, providing the basis for trade. Constant costs are not realistic, however. They are discussed only because they serve as a convenient introduction to the more realistic case of increasing costs discussed in the next chapter.

2.5d Opportunity Costs and Relative Commodity Prices

We have seen that the opportunity cost of wheat is equal to the amount of cloth that the nation must give up to release just enough resources to produce one additional unit of wheat. This is given by the (absolute) slope of the production possibility frontier, or transformation curve, and is sometimes referred to as the *marginal rate of transformation.*

Figure 2-1 shows that the (absolute) slope of the United States transformation curve is $120/180 = 2/3 =$ opportunity cost of wheat in the United States and remains constant. The slope of the United Kingdom transformation curve is $120/60 = 2 =$ opportunity cost of wheat in the United Kingdom and remains constant. On the assumptions that prices equal costs of production and that

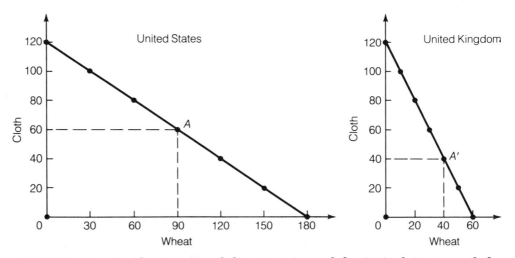

FIGURE 2-1.   Production Possibility Frontiers of the United States and the United Kingdom.

The U.S. and U.K. production frontiers are obtained by plotting the values in Table 2-4. The frontiers are downward, or negatively, sloped, indicating that as each nation produces more wheat, it must give up some cloth. Straight line production possibility frontiers reflect constant opportunity costs.

the nation does produce both some wheat and some cloth, the opportunity cost of wheat is equal to the price of wheat relative to the price of cloth (P_W/P_C).

Thus, $P_W/P_C = 2/3$ in the United States, and inversely $P_C/P_W = 3/2 = 1.5$. In the United Kingdom, $P_W/P_C = 2$, and $P_C/P_W = 1/2$. The lower P_W/P_C in the United States (2/3 as opposed to 2) is a reflection of the United States comparative advantage in wheat. Similarly, the lower P_C/P_W in the United Kingdom (1/2 as opposed to 3/2) reflects its comparative advantage in cloth. Note that under constant costs, P_W/P_C is determined exclusively by production, or supply, considerations in each nation. Demand considerations do not enter at all in the determination of **relative commodity prices.**

To conclude, we can say that the difference in relative commodity prices between the two nations (given by the difference in the slope of their transformation curves) is a reflection of their comparative advantage and provides the basis for mutually beneficial trade.

2.6 The Basis for and the Gains from Trade Under Constant Costs

In the absence of trade, a nation can only consume the commodities that it produces. As a result, the nation's production possibility frontier also represents its *consumption frontier*. Which combination of commodities the nation actually chooses to produce and consume depends on the people's tastes, or demand considerations.

2.6a Illustration of the Gains from Trade

In the absence of trade, the United States might choose to produce and consume combination A (90W and 60C) on its production possibility frontier (see Figure 2-2), and the United Kingdom might choose combination A' (40W and 40C).

With trade possible, the United States would specialize in the production of wheat (the commodity of its comparative advantage) and produce at point B (180W and 0C) on its production possibility frontier. Similarly, the United Kingdom would specialize in the production of cloth and produce at B' (0W and 120C). If the United States then exchanges 70W for 70C with the United Kingdom, it ends up consuming at point E (110W and 70C), and the United Kingdom ends up consuming at E' (70W and 50C). Thus, the United States gains 20W and 10C from trade (compare point E with point A in Figure 2-2), and the United Kingdom gains 30W and 10C (compare point A' with point E').

The increased consumption of both wheat and cloth in both nations was made possible by the increased output that resulted as each nation specialized in the production of the commodity of its comparative advantage. That is, in

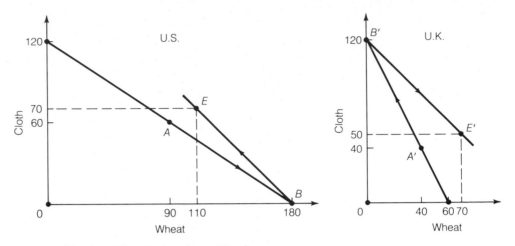

FIGURE 2-2. The Gains from Trade

In the absence of trade, the U.S. produces and consumes at *A,* and the U.K. at *A'*. With trade, the U.S. specializes in the production of wheat and produces at *B,* while the U.K. specializes in the production of cloth and produces at *B'*. By exchanging 70W for 70C with the U.K., the U.S. ends up consuming at *E* (and gains 20W and 10C), while the U.K. ends up consuming at *E'* and gains 30W and 10C).

the absence of trade, the United States produced 90W and the United Kingdom 40W, for a total of 130W. With specialization in production and trade, 180W are produced (all in the United States). Similarly, in the absence of trade, the United States produced 60C and the United Kingdom 40C, for a total of 100C. With specialization in production and trade, 120C are produced (all in the United Kingdom).

It is this increase in output of 50W and 20C resulting from specialization in production that is shared by the United States and the United Kingdom and represents their gains from trade. Recall that in the absence of trade, the United States would not specialize in the production of wheat because it also wanted to consume some cloth. Similarly, the United Kingdom would not specialize in the production of cloth in the absence of trade because it also wanted to consume some wheat.

2.6b   Alternative Illustration of the Gains from Trade

An alternative graphical illustration of the gains from trade under constant costs is shown in Figure 2-3. This is obtained by rotating by 180 degrees the United Kingdom production possibility frontier of Figure 2-2 and superimposing it on the United States production possibility frontier in such a way that points *B* and *B'* coincide.

In Figure 2-3 (as in Figure 2-2), the United States produces and consumes at *A* in the absence of trade, and the United Kingdom at *A'*. With trade, the

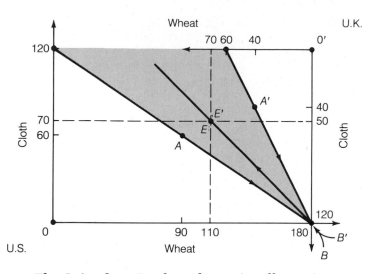

FIGURE 2-3. The Gains from Trade—Alternative Illustration

The figure is obtained by rotating by 180 degrees the U.K. production possibility frontier of Figure 2-2 and superimposing it on the U.S. production possibility frontier in such a way that points B and B' coincide. The shaded wedge-shaped area between the two frontiers shows the total gains from trade. Line BE (the same as $B'E'$) divides the total gains from trade between the two nations.

United States specializes in the production of wheat and produces at B, while the United Kingdom specializes in the production of cloth and produces at B'. *By exchanging 70W for 70C with the United Kingdom, the United States ends up consuming at E, and the United Kingdom at E'* (which now coincides with E). The gains from trade are shown by $E>A$ in the United States, and by $E'>A'$ in the United Kingdom (when measured from origin $0'$).

With the United States specializing in the production of wheat and the United Kingdom specializing in cloth, the total output of wheat increased by 50W (the horizontal distance between points A and A' in Figure 2-3), and the total output of cloth increased by 20C (the vertical distance between A and A'). Points E and E' indicate how these gains in production are divided between the two nations. The greater is the difference in the absolute slope of the production possibility frontiers of the two nations, the greater is the shaded wedge-shaped area representing the total gains from specialization and trade available for them to share. Line BE (the same as $B'E'$) then divides these total gains between the two nations.

Figure 2-3 can also be used to show the basis for and the gains from trade in terms of relative commodity prices. With P_W/P_C larger than 2/3 and lower than 2, both nations gain from trade. Since in our example 70W are exchanged for 70C, $P_W/P_C=1$ (the slope of line BE) with trade. The United States then gains because by giving up 1W it gets 1C through trade as opposed to 2/3C domestically (i.e., in the absence of trade). The United Kingdom also gains because it can get each unit of wheat that it wants to consume by giving up only 1C through trade rather than 2C in the absence of trade.

The closer P_W/P_C with trade settles to 2/3 (the United States domestic, or internal, rate of exchange), the greater is the share of the gains from trade going to the United Kingdom. On the other hand, the closer P_W/P_C with trade comes to 2 (the United Kingdom domestic, or internal, rate of exchange), the greater is the share of the gains from trade accruing to the United States.

In Chapter 4, we will see that the greater is the strength or intensity of the United States' demand for British cloth, the closer P_W/P_C will settle to the value of 2/3 with trade, and the smaller will be the share of the gains from trade going to the United States. On the other hand, the greater is the United Kingdom's demand for American wheat, the closer P_W/P_C will settle to the value of 2 with trade, and the smaller will be the United Kingdom's share of the gains from trade. Thus, we can say that while comparative costs, or supply considerations, determine the range within which mutually advantageous trade can take place, demand conditions determine precisely what the actual rate of exchange will be within those limits.

In our example, $P_W/P_C=1$ with trade. This is the **equilibrium commodity terms of trade** in the sense that at $P_W/P_C=1$ the quantity of wheat imports *demanded* by the United Kingdom (70W) exactly equals the quantity of wheat exports *supplied* by the United States, and the quantity of cloth imports *demanded* by the United States (70C) exactly equals the quantity of cloth exports *supplied* by the United Kingdom. At $P_W/P_C>1$, the quantity of wheat exports supplied by the United States would *exceed* the quantity of wheat imports demanded by the United Kingdom and P_W/P_C would fall toward the equilibrium value of 1. At $P_W/P_C<1$, the quantity of wheat imports demanded by the United Kingdom would *exceed* the quantity of wheat exports supplied by the United States and P_W/P_C would rise toward the equilibrium level of 1. (The same conclusion would be reached in terms of the demand and supply of imports and exports of cloth.)

Figure 2-3 can also be used to illustrate the exception to the law of comparative advantage discussed earlier. That is, if the United States' absolute advantage over the United Kingdom was the same or in the same proportion in both wheat and cloth, then the production possibility frontiers of the United States and the United Kingdom would have exactly the same absolute slope, indicating equal P_W/P_C in the two nations in the absence of trade. As a result, there would be no shaded wedge-shaped area and no possibility for mutually beneficial trade.

2.6c   The Small Country Case

So far we have assumed that with trade each nation specializes completely in production of the commodity of its comparative advantage. For example, the United States uses all of its resources in the production of wheat and produces no cloth when trade is possible, while the United Kingdom uses all of its resources in the production of cloth and produces no wheat (see points B and B' in Figures 2-2 and 2-3).

Complete specialization in production is usually the case under constant (opportunity) costs, when trade is possible. The reason for this is that *if* it pays for the United States to exchange 1W for 1C with the United Kingdom, then it will *also* pay for the United States to obtain all of its cloth from the United Kingdom in exchange for wheat, *since the opportunity cost of wheat remains constant in terms of cloth in the United States.*

There is only one exception to complete specialization in both nations under constant costs. This arises when one nation is too small to satisfy all of the demand of its trade partner for a commodity. For example, if the United Kingdom was too small to satisfy the entire United States demand for 70C, the United Kingdom would specialize completely in the production of cloth (the commodity of its comparative advantage), but the United States would continue to produce some cloth even with trade. However, trade between the two would now take place at the United States pre-trade $P_W/P_C = 2/3$, so that all of the gains from trade would now accrue to the United Kingdom. This is the **small country case** shown in Figure 2-4.

In Figure 2-4, we assume that the United Kingdom is now only half as large as before (so that its production possibility frontier crosses the commodity

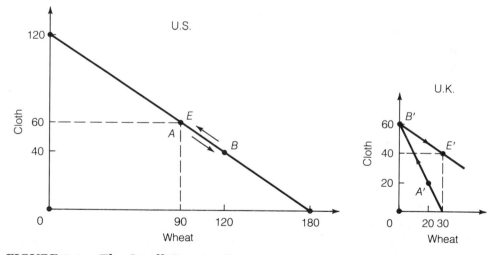

FIGURE 2-4. The Small Country Case

The United Kingdom is now assumed to be half its former size and unable to satisfy all of the U.S. demand for cloth. With trade, the United Kingdom specializes completely in the production of cloth (point B'), while the United States continues to produce some cloth (point B). Trade takes place at the U.S. pretrade P_W/P_C, and all of the gains from trade accrue to the United Kingdom (compare E' with A' in the U.K. and E with A in the U.S.).

axes at 30W and 60C), and produces and consumes at A' (20W and 20C) in the absence of trade, while the United States is at A (the same as before). Since $P_W/P_C = 2$ in the United Kingdom (as earlier), it has the same comparative advantage over the United States as before and specializes completely in the production of cloth (point B'). By then exchanging 20C for 30W from the United States, the United Kingdom gets to E' and gains 10W and 20C in consumption. On the other hand, the United States produces at B with trade, and by exchanging 30W for 20C with the United Kingdom ends up consuming at E (which now coincides with A). Thus, the United States now gains nothing from trading with the United Kingdom.

The obvious question is then, why would the United States trade with the United Kingdom if it gains nothing? We can answer only by looking at a slightly more realistic case in which there is at least one other "large" trading nation with a comparative advantage in cloth. The rate at which the United States exchanges wheat for cloth would then be determined by supply and demand considerations in the United States and in the other large nation, so that both nations gain from trade. The United Kingdom (the assumed small nation) would then "join in" and trade at the prevailing exchange rate of wheat for cloth on the world market and, without affecting that rate, would gain all the benefits *from its own trade*. This is sometimes referred to "as the importance of being unimportant."

This benefit, however, is not without cost, since the small nation faces the risk of a possible future reduction in demand for the only commodity it produces. This could create serious difficulties for the small nation. Furthermore, the small nation also relies for its survival on the willingness of the large nation to continue trading.

Summary

1. This chapter examined the development of trade theory from the mercantilists to Smith, Ricardo and Haberler. We sought to answer two basic questions: (a) What is the basis for and what are the gains from trade? (b) What is the pattern of trade?

2. The mercantilists believed that a nation could gain in international trade only at the expense of other nations. As a result, they advocated restrictions on imports, incentives for exports, and strict government regulation of all economic activities.

3. According to Adam Smith, trade is based on absolute advantage and benefits both nations (the discussion assumes a two-nation, two-commodity world). That is, when each nation specializes in the production of the commodity of its absolute advantage and exchanges part of its output for the commodity of its absolute disadvantage, both nations end up consuming more of both commodities. Absolute advantage, however, explains only a small portion of international trade today.

4. David Ricardo introduced the law of comparative advantage. This postulates that even if one nation is less efficient than the other nation in the production of both commodities, there is still a basis for mutually beneficial trade (as long as the absolute disadvantage that the first nation has with respect to the second is not the same in both commodities). The less efficient nation should specialize in the production and export the commodity in which its absolute disadvantage is less (this is the commodity of its comparative advantage). Ricardo, however, explained his law of comparative advantage in terms of the labor theory of value, which is unacceptable.

5. Gottfried Haberler came to the "rescue" by explaining the law of comparative advantage in terms of the opportunity cost theory. This states that the cost of a commodity is the amount of a second commodity that must be given up to release just enough resources to produce one additional unit of the first commodity. The opportunity cost of a commodity is equal to the relative price of that commodity and is given by the (absolute) slope of the production possibility frontier. A straight line production possibility frontier reflects constant opportunity costs.

6. In the absence of trade, a nation's production possibility frontier is also its consumption frontier. With trade, each nation can specialize in production of the commodity of its comparative advantage and exchange part of its output with the other nation for the commodity of its comparative disadvantage. By so doing, both nations end up consuming more of both commodities than without trade.

A Look Ahead

In Chapter 3, we will examine the basis for the gains from trade, as well as the pattern of trade in the more realistic case of increasing costs. Our model will then be completed in Chapter 4, where we will see how the rate at which commodities are exchanged in international trade is actually determined. This will also determine how the gains from trade are in fact divided between the two trading nations.

Glossary

Basis for trade The forces that give rise to trade between two nations. This was absolute advantage according to Adam Smith and comparative advantage according to David Ricardo.

Gains from trade The increase in consumption in each nation resulting from specialization in production and trading.

Pattern of trade The commodities exported and imported by each nation.

Mercantilism The body of writings prevailing during the seventeenth and eighteenth centuries which postulated that the way for a nation to become richer was to restrict imports and stimulate exports. Thus, one nation could gain only at the expense of other nations.

Absolute advantage The greater efficiency that one nation may have over another in the production of a commodity. This was the basis for trade for Adam Smith.

Laissez-faire The policy of minimum government interference in or regulation of economic activity, advocated by Adam Smith and other classical economists.

Law of comparative advantage Explains how mutually beneficial trade can take place even when one nation is less efficient than, or has an absolute disadvantage with respect to, another nation in the production of all commodities. The less efficient nation should specialize in and export the commodity in which its absolute disadvantage is smaller (the commodity of its comparative advantage), and should import the other commodity.

Exception to the law of comparative advantage The case where the absolute advantage that one nation has over another in production is the same or in the same proportion in both commodities.

Labor theory of value The theory that the cost or price of a commodity is determined by or can be inferred exclusively from its labor content.

Opportunity cost theory The theory that the cost of a commodity is the amount of a second commodity that must be given up to release just enough resources to produce one more unit of the first commodity.

Production possibility frontier A curve showing the various alternative combinations of two commodities that a nation can produce by fully utilizing all of its resources with the best technology available to it.

Constant opportunity costs Equal costs to produce each additional unit of a commodity in terms of the amount of a second commodity that must be given up. Under constant costs, a nation's production possibility frontier is a straight line.

Relative commodity prices The price of one commodity divided by the price of another commodity. This equals the opportunity cost of the first commodity and is given by the absolute slope of the production possibility frontier.

Equilibrium commodity terms of trade The relative commodity price at which commodities exchange for one another.

Complete specialization The utilization of all of a nation's resources in the production of only one commodity with trade. This usually occurs under constant costs.

Small country case The situation where trade takes place at the pretrade relative commodity prices in the large nation, so that the small nation receives all of the benefits from trade.

Questions for Review

1. What are the basic questions that we seek to answer in this chapter? In what way is the model presented in this chapter an abstraction or a simplification of the real world? Can the model be generalized?
2. What were the mercantilists' views on trade? How does their concept of national wealth differ from today's view? Why is it important to study the mercantilists' views on trade? How were their views different from those of Adam Smith? What is the relevance of all this today?
3. What was the basis for and the pattern of trade according to Adam Smith? How were gains from trade generated? What policies did Smith advocate on international trade? What did he think was the proper function of government in the economic life of the nation?
4. In what way was Ricardo's law of comparative advantage superior to Smith's theory of absolute advantage? How do gains from trade arise with comparative advantage? How can a nation which is less efficient than another nation in the production of all commodities export anything to the second nation? What is the exception to the law of comparative advantage? How important is it?
5. Why is Ricardo's explanation of the law of comparative advantage unacceptable? What acceptable theory can be used to explain the law? What is the relationship between opportunity costs and the production possibility frontier of a nation? How does the production possibility frontier look under constant opportunity costs? What is the relationship between the opportunity cost of a commodity and the relative price of that commodity? How can they be visualized graphically?
6. Why is a nation's production possibility frontier the same as its consumption frontier in the absence of trade? How does the nation decide how much of each commodity to consume in the absence of trade? What is meant by complete specialization in production with trade? When do we have incomplete specialization with trade? How are the gains from trade shared by the trading nations?

Problems

*1. The table below shows bushels of wheat and the yards of cloth that the United States and the United Kingdom can produce with one

* = answer provided at the end of the book.

	Case A		Case B		Case C		Case D	
	U.S.	U.K.	U.S.	U.K.	U.S.	U.K.	U.S.	U.K.
Wheat (bushels/man-hour)	4	1	4	1	4	1	4	2
Cloth (yards/man-hour)	1	2	3	2	2	2	2	1

hour of labor time under four different hypothetical situations. *In each case* identify the commodity in which the United States and the United Kingdom have:

(a) an absolute advantage or disadvantage;

(b) a comparative advantage or disadvantage.

(c) Indicate whether or not trade is possible in each case and the basis for trade.

*2. Suppose that in case B of problem 1 the United States exchanges 4W for 4C with the United Kingdom.

(a) How much does the United States gain?

(b) How much does the United Kingdom gain?

(c) What is the range for mutually beneficial trade?

(d) How much would each nation gain if they exchanged 4W for 6C instead?

3. Use the information in case B for problem 1 and assume that labor is the only factor of production and is homogeneous (i.e., all of one type).

(a) What is the cost *in terms of labor content* of producing wheat and cloth in the United States and the United Kingdom?

(b) What is the dollar price of wheat and cloth in the United States if the wage rate is $6?

(c) What is the pound price of wheat and cloth in the United Kingdom if the wage rate is £1?

4. Answer the following questions with reference to problem 3.

(a) What is the dollar price of wheat and cloth in the United Kingdom if the exchange rate between the pound and the dollar is £1 = $2? Would the United States be able to export wheat to the United Kingdom at this exchange rate? Would the United

Kingdom be able to export cloth to the United States at this exchange rate?

(b) What if the exchange rate between the dollar and the pound were £1 = $4?

(c) What if the exchange rate were £1 = $1?

(d) What is the *range* of exchange rates that will allow the United States to export wheat to the United Kingdom and the United Kingdom to export cloth to the United States?

5. Assume that the data in case B in problem 1 refers to millions of bushels of wheat and millions of yards of cloth.

(a) Plot on graph paper the production frontiers of the United States and the United Kingdom.

(b) What is the relative price of wheat (i.e., P_W/P_C) in the United States and in the United Kingdom?

(c) What is the relative price of cloth (i.e., P_C/P_W) in the United States and in the United Kingdom?

6. Using the United States and United Kingdom production frontiers from problem 5, assume that the no trade or autarky point is 3W and ¾C (in million units) in the United States and ½W and 1C in the United Kingdom. Also assume that with the opening of trade the United States exchanges 1W for 1C with the United Kingdom.

(a) Show graphically for the United States and the United Kingdom, the autarky point of production and consumption, the point of production and consumption with trade, and the gains from trade.

(b) Repeat (a) assuming that the United States and the United Kingdom exchange 1W for ¾C. How much would each nation gain from trade in this case? Why?

APPENDIX——————————

We now extend the theory of comparative advantage first to the case of more than two commodities and then to the case of more than two nations. In each case, we will see that the theory of comparative advantage is easily generalized.

A2.1 Comparative Advantage with More than Two Commodities

Table 2–5 shows the dollar and the pound cost, or price, of five commodities in the United States and the United Kingdom. (In economics, "cost" includes the return of all factors including "normal profits"; thus "cost" and "price" are used interchangeably here.)

TABLE 2-5. Commodity Prices in the United States and United Kingdom

Commodity	Price in the U.S.	Price in the U.K.
A	$ 2	£6
B	4	4
C	6	3
D	8	2
E	10	1

To determine which commodities will be exported and imported by the United States and the United Kingdom, we must first express all commodity prices in terms of the same currency and then compare prices in the two nations. For example, if the exchange rate between the dollar and the pound is £1 = $2, the *dollar* prices of the commodities in the United Kingdom are:

Commodity	A	B	C	D	E
Dollar price in the U.K.	12	8	6	4	2

At this exchange rate, the dollar prices of commodities A and B are lower in the United States than in the United Kingdom; commodity C is equally priced in the two nations; and the dollar prices of commodities D and E are lower in the United Kingdom. As a result, the United States will export commodities A and B to the United Kingdom and import commodities D and E from the United Kingdom. Commodity C will not be traded.

Now assume that the exchange rate between the dollar and the pound is £1 = $3. The dollar prices of the commodities in the United Kingdom would be:

Commodity	A	B	C	D	E
Dollar price in the U.K.	18	12	9	6	3

At this higher exchange rate, the dollar prices of commodities A, B and C are lower in the United States, while the dollar prices of commodities D and E are lower in the United Kingdom. Thus, the United States would export commodities A, B and C to the United Kingdom and import commodities D and E from the United Kingdom. Note that commodity C, which was not traded at the exchange rate of £1 = $2, is now exported by the United States at the exchange rate of £1 = $3.

Finally, if the exchange rate was £1 = $1, the dollar prices of the commodities in the United Kingdom would be:

Commodity	A	B	C	D	E
Dollar price in the U.K.	6	4	3	2	1

In this case, the United States would export only commodity A to the United Kingdom and import all other commodities with the exception of commodity B (which would not be traded because it is now equally priced in the two nations).

The actual exchange rate between the dollar and the pound will settle at the level at which the *value of United States exports to the United Kingdom exactly equals the value of the United States imports from the United Kingdom* (in the absence of other international transactions). Once this equilibrium exchange rate is established, we will be able to determine exactly which commodities are exported by the United States and which are exported by the United Kingdom. Each nation will then have a comparative advantage in the commodities that it exports at the particular equilibrium exchange rate established.

What we can say on the basis of Table 2-5 is that the United States comparative advantage is greatest in commodity A, and the United States must export at least this commodity. For this to be possible, the exchange rate between the dollar and the pound must be £1>$0.33. The United Kingdom comparative advantage is highest in commodity E, so that the United Kingdom must export at least commodity E. For this to be possible, the exchange rate between the dollar and the pound must be £1<$10. This discussion can be generalized to cover many more commodities.

A2.2 Comparative Advantage with More than Two Nations

Suppose that instead of two nations and five commodities we have two commodities (wheat and cloth) and five nations (A, B, C, D and E). Table 2-6 ranks these nations from lowest to highest in terms of their internal P_W/P_C values. With trade, the equilibrium P_W/P_C will settle somewhere between 1 and 5. That is, $1<P_w/P_c<5$.

If the equilibrium $P_W/P_C=3$ with trade, Nations A and B will export wheat to nations D and E in exchange for cloth. Nation C will not engage in inter-

TABLE 2-6. *Ranking of Nations in Terms of Internal Pw/Pc*

Nation	A	B	C	D	E
Pw/Pc	1	2	3	4	5

national trade in this case because its pretrade P_W/P_C equals the equilibrium P_W/P_C with trade. Given a trade equilibrium $P_W/P_C = 4$, Nations A, B and C will export wheat to Nation E in exchange for cloth, and Nation D will not engage in international trade. If the equilibrium $P_W/P_C = 2$ with trade, Nation A will export wheat to all the other nations, with the exception of Nation B, in exchange for cloth.

This discussion can easily be extended to any number of countries. However, generalizing our analysis to many commodities *and* many nations at the same time becomes cumbersome and is unnecessary. What is important at this point is that the conclusions reached on the basis of our simple model with only two nations and two commodities *can* be generalized and are indeed applicable to the case of many nations and many commodities.

Problem   Set up an example of trade with three commodities and three nations in such a way that each of the three nations exports one of the commodities to, and imports one of the commodities from, each of the other two nations.

Selected Bibliography

For a problem-solving approach to the material covered in this chapter, with many examples and solved problems, see:
- D. Salvatore, *Theory and Problems of International Economics*, 2nd ed. (New York: McGraw-Hill, 1984), chs. 1, 2 (sects. 2.1 to 2.3).

A preclassical mercantilistic view on international trade can be found in:
- P. C. Newman, A. D. Gayer, and M. H. Spencer, *Source Readings in Economic Thought* (New York: Norton, 1954), pp. 24–53.

For Smith's and Ricardo's views on international trade, see:
- A. Smith, *The Wealth of Nations* (New York: The Modern Library, 1937), Book I, ch. 3; Book IV, chs. 1–3, 6–8.

- David Ricardo, *The Principles of Political Economy and Taxation* (Homewood, Ill.: Irwin, 1963), ch. 7.

An excellent exposition of the classical theory of comparative advantage can be found in:
- G. Haberler, *The Theory of International Trade* (London: W. Hodge and Co., 1936), chs. 9–10.
- J. Viner, *Studies in the Theory of International Trade* (New York: Harper and Brothers, 1937), ch. 7.

For a more advanced and definitive exposition of the theory of comparative advantage, see:
- J. N. Bhagwati, "The Pure Theory of International Trade: A Survey," *Economic Journal*, March 1964.
- J. S. Chipman, "A Survey of the Theory of International Trade," *Econometrica*, July 1965.

CHAPTER 3

The Modern Theory of International Trade

3.1 Introduction

This chapter extends our simple trade model to the more realistic case of increasing opportunity costs. Demand conditions are also introduced with community indifference curves. We then see how these forces of demand and supply determine the equilibrium relative commodity price in each nation in the absence of trade. This will also indicate the commodity of comparative advantage for each nation.

Subsequently, we examine how, with trade, each nation gains by specializing in the production of the commodity of its comparative advantage and exporting some of its output in exchange for the commodity of its comparative disadvantage. The last section of the chapter shows how mutually beneficial trade is possible even when two nations are exactly alike except for tastes.

In this and in the following chapters, it will be convenient to generalize the presentation and deal with Nation 1 and Nation 2 (instead of the United States and United Kingdom) and commodity X and commodity Y (instead of cloth and wheat).

The appendix to this chapter is a review of those aspects of production theory which are essential for understanding the material presented in the *appendices* of the chapters that follow. This and the subsequent appendices can be omitted without loss of continuity in the text.

3.2   The Production Frontier with Increasing Costs

It is more realistic for a nation to face increasing rather than constant opportunity costs. **Increasing opportunity costs** mean that the nation must give up more and more of one commodity to release just enough resources to produce each additional unit of another commodity. Increasing opportunity costs result in a production frontier that is concave from the origin (rather than a straight line).

3.2a   Illustration of Increasing Costs

Figure 3-1 shows the hypothetical production frontier of commodities X and Y for Nation 1 and Nation 2. Both production frontiers are concave from the origin, reflecting the fact that each nation incurs increasing opportunity costs in the production of *both* commodities.

Suppose that Nation 1 wants to produce more of commodity X, starting from point A on its production frontier. Since at point A the nation is already utilizing all of its resources with the best technology available, the nation can only produce more of X by reducing the output of commodity Y. (In Chapter

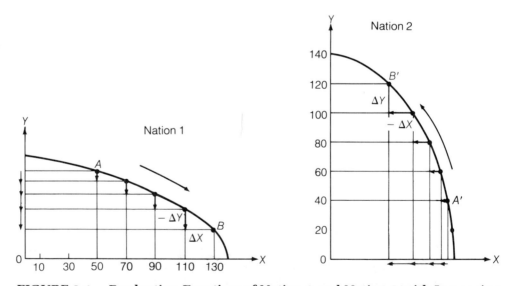

FIGURE 3-1.   Production Frontiers of Nation 1 and Nation 2 with Increasing Costs

Concave production frontiers reflect increasing opportunity costs in each nation in the production of *both* commodities. Thus Nation 1 must give up more and more of Y for each additional batch of 20X that it produces. This is illustrated by downward arrows of increasing length. Similarly, Nation 2 incurs increasing opportunity costs in terms of forgone X (illustrated by the increasing length of the leftward arrows) for each additional batch of 20Y it produces.

2, we saw that this is the reason production frontiers are negatively sloped.)

Figure 3-1 shows that for each additional batch of 20X that Nation 1 produces, it must give up more and more Y. The increasing opportunity costs in terms of Y that Nation 1 faces are reflected in the longer and longer downward arrows in the figure, and result in a production frontier that is concave from the origin.

Nation 1 also faces increasing opportunity costs in the production of Y. This could be demonstrated graphically by showing that Nation 1 has to give up increasing amounts of X for each additional batch of 20Y that it produces. However, instead of showing this for Nation 1, we demonstrate increasing opportunity costs in the production of Y with the production frontier of Nation 2 in Figure 3-1.

Moving upward from point *A'* along the production frontier of Nation 2, we observe leftward arrows of increasing length, reflecting the increasing amounts of X that Nation 2 must give up to produce each additional batch of 20Y. Thus, concave production frontiers for Nation 1 and Nation 2 reflect increasing opportunity costs in each nation in the production of *both* commodities.

3.2b   The Marginal Rate of Transformation

The **marginal rate of transformation (MRT)** of X for Y refers to the amount of Y that a nation must give up to produce each additional unit of X. Thus, MRT is another name for the opportunity cost of X (the commodity measured along the horizontal axis) and is given by the (absolute) *slope* of the production frontier at the point of production.

If in Figure 3-1 the slope of the production frontier (MRT) of Nation 1 at point *A* is ¼, this means that Nation 1 must give up ¼ of a unit of Y to release just enough resources to produce one additional unit of X at this point. Similarly, if the slope, or MRT, equals 1 at point *B*, this means that Nation 1 must give up one unit of Y to produce one additional unit of X at this point.

Thus, a movement from point *A* down to point *B* along the production frontier of Nation 1 involves an increase in the slope (MRT) from ¼ (at point *A*) to 1 (at point *B*) and reflects the increasing opportunity costs in producing more X. This is in contrast to the case of a straight line production frontier (as in Chapter 2), where the opportunity cost of X is constant regardless of the level of output and is given by the constant value of the slope (MRT) of the production frontier.

3.2c   Reasons for Increasing Opportunity Costs and Different Production Frontiers

We have examined the meaning of increasing opportunity costs as reflected in concave production frontiers. But how do increasing opportunity costs arise? And why are they more realistic than constant opportunity costs?

Increasing opportunity costs arise because resources or factors of production (1) are not homogeneous (i.e., all units of the same factor are not identical or of the same quality) and (2) are not used in the *same* fixed proportion or intensity in the production of all commodities. This means that as the nation produces more of a commodity, it must utilize resources that become progressively less efficient or less suited for the production of that commodity. As a result, the nation must give up more and more of the second commodity to release just enough resources to produce each additional unit of the first commodity.

For example, suppose some of a nation's land is flat and suited for growing wheat, and some is hilly and better suited for grazing and milk production. The nation originally specialized in wheat but now wants to concentrate on producing milk. By transferring its hilly areas from wheat growing to grazing, the nation gives up very little wheat and obtains a great deal of milk. Thus the opportunity cost of milk in terms of the amount of wheat given up is initially small. But if this transfer process continues, eventually flat land which is better suited for wheat growing will have to be used for grazing. As a result, the opportunity cost of milk will rise and the production frontier will be concave from the origin.

The difference in the production frontiers of Nation 1 and Nation 2 in Figure 3-1 is due to the fact that the two nations have different factor endowments or resources at this disposal and/or use different technologies in production. In the real world, the production frontiers of different nations will usually differ since practically no two nations have identical factor endowments (even if they could have access to the same technology).

As the supply or availability of factors and/or technology changes over time, a nation's production frontier shifts. The type and extent of these shifts depend on the type and extent of the changes that take place. These are examined in detail in Chapter 7, which deals with economic growth and its effect on international trade.

3.3   Community Indifference Curves

So far, we have discussed production, or supply, considerations in a nation, as reflected in its production frontier. We now introduce the tastes, or demand preferences, in a nation. These are given by community (or social) indifference curves.

A **community indifference curve** shows the various combinations of two commodities which yield equal satisfaction to the community or nation. Higher curves refer to greater satisfaction, lower curves to less satisfaction. Community indifference curves are negatively sloped and convex from the origin. And to be useful, they must not cross. (Readers familiar with an individual's

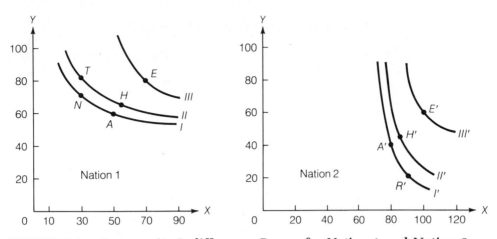

FIGURE 3-2. Community Indifference Curves for Nation 1 and Nation 2

A community indifference curve shows the various combinations of X and Y that yield equal satisfaction to the community or nation. A higher curve refers to a higher level of satisfaction. Community indifference curves are downward, or negatively, sloped and convex from the origin; to be useful, they must not cross. The declining slope of the curve reflects the diminishing marginal rate of substitution (MRS) of X for Y in consumption.

indifference curves will note that community indifference curves are almost completely analogous.)

3.3a   Illustration of Community Indifference Curves

Figure 3-2 shows three hypothetical indifference curves for Nation 1 and Nation 2. They differ on the assumption that tastes, or demand preferences, are different in the two nations.

Points N and A give equal satisfaction to Nation 1 since they are both on indifference curves I. Points T and H refer to a higher level of satisfaction since they are on a higher indifference curve (II). Even though T involves more Y but less of X than A, satisfaction is greater at T because it is in on indifference curve II. Point E refers to still greater satisfaction since it is on indifference curve III. For Nation 2, $A' = R' < H' < E'$.

Note that the community indifference curves in Figure 3-2 are negatively sloped. This is always the case because as a nation consumes more of X, it must consume less of Y. Thus, as Nation 1 moves from N to A on indifference curve I, it consumes more of X but less of Y. Similarly, as Nation 2 moves from A' to R' on indifference curve I', it consumes more of X but less of Y. If a nation continued to consume the same amount of Y as it increased its consumption of X, the nation would necessarily move to a higher indifference curve.

3.3b   The Marginal Rate of Substitution

The **marginal rate of substitution (MRS)** of X for Y in consumption refers to the amount of Y that a nation could give up for one extra unit of X *and still remain on the same indifference curve*. This is given by the (absolute) slope of the community indifference curve at the point of consumption and declines as the nation moves down the curve. For example, the slope, or MRS, of indifference curve I is greater at point *N* than at point *A* (see Figure 3-2). Similarly, the slope, or MRS, of indifference curve I' is greater at point *A'* than at *R'*.

The MRS falls because of diminishing marginal utility in consuming more and more units of any commodity. That is, the more of X a nation is consuming, the less the satisfaction it receives from each additional unit of X. As a result, the nation is willing to give up less and less of Y to obtain each additional unit of X. Another way of stating this is that the less of Y the nation is left with, the more valuable it considers each remaining unit of Y. Thus, once again, we come to the conclusion that the nation is willing to give up less and less of Y to obtain each additional unit of X.

Declining MRS causes community indifference curves to be convex from the origin. Thus, while *increasing* opportunity costs result in *concave* production frontiers, *diminishing* marginal rates of substitution in consumption result in *convex* community indifference curves. In section 3.4, we will see that this convexity property of community indifference curves is necessary to reach a unique (i.e., a single) equilibrium point.

3.3c   Some Difficulties with Community Indifference Curves

As we said earlier, to be useful, community indifference curves must not intersect (cross). A point of intersection would refer to equal satisfaction on two different community indifference curves, which is inconsistent with their definition. Thus, the indifference curves of Nation 1 and Nation 2 in Figure 3-2 are drawn as nonintersecting.

However, a particular set, or map, of community indifference curves refers to a particular *income distribution* within the nation. A different income distribution would result in a completely new set of indifference curves, which might intersect previous indifference curves.

This is precisely what may happen as a nation opens trade or expands its level of trade. Exporters will benefit while domestic producers competing with imports will suffer. There is also a differential impact upon consumers depending upon whether an individual's consumption pattern is oriented more toward the X or the Y good. Thus, trade will change the distribution of real income in the nation and *may* cause indifference curves to intersect. In that case, we would not use community indifference curves to determine whether the opening or the expansion of trade increased the nation's welfare.

One way out of this impasse is through the so-called *compensation prin-*

ciple. According to this principle, the nation benefits from trade if the gainers would be better off (i.e., retain some of their gain) even after fully compensating the losers. This is true regardless of whether compensation actually occurs. (One way that compensation would occur is for the government to tax enough of the gain to fully compensate the losers with subsidies or tax relief.) Alternatively, we could make a number of restrictive assumptions about tastes, incomes, and patterns of consumption that would preclude intersecting community indifference curves.

Although the compensation principle or restrictive assumptions do not completely eliminate all the conceptual difficulties inherent in using community indifference curves, they do allow us to draw them as nonintersecting (so that we can continue to make use of them, even if a bit cautiously).

3.4   Equilibrium in Isolation

In section 3.2, we discussed production frontiers, which illustrate the production, or supply, conditions in a nation. In section 3.3, we examined community indifference curves, which reflect the tastes, or demand preferences, in a nation. We will now see how the interaction of these forces of demand and supply determines the equilibrium point, or point of maximum social welfare, in a nation in isolation (i.e., in the absence of trade).

In the absence of trade, a nation is in equilibrium when it reaches the highest indifference curve possible given its production frontier. This occurs at the point where a community indifference curve is tangent to the nation's production frontier. The common slope of the two curves at the tangency point gives the internal equilibrium relative commodity price in the nation and reflects the nation's comparative advantage. Let us see what all this means.

3.4a   Illustration of Equilibrium in Isolation

Figure 3-3 brings together the production frontiers of Figure 3-1 and the community indifference curves of Figure 3-2. We see in Figure 3-3, that indifference curve I is the highest indifference curve that Nation 1 can reach with its production frontier. Thus, Nation 1 is in equilibrium, or maximizes its welfare, when it produces and consumes at point A in the absence of trade, or **autarky.** Similarly, Nation 2 is in equilibrium at point A', where its production frontier is tangent to indifference curve I'.

Note that since community indifference curves are convex from the origin and drawn as nonintersecting, there is only one such point of tangency, or equilibrium. Furthermore, we can be certain that one such equilibrium point exists because there are an infinite number of indifference curves (i.e., the indifference map is dense). Points on lower indifference curves are possible but would not maximize the nation's welfare. On the other hand, the nation

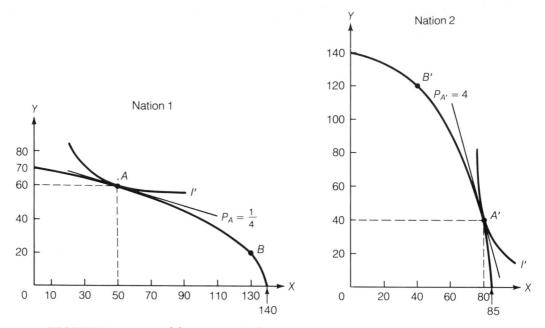

FIGURE 3-3.   Equilibrium in Isolation

Nation 1 is in equilibrium, or maximizes its welfare, in isolation by producing and consuming at point *A*, where its production frontier reaches (is tangent to) indifference curve I (the highest possible). Similarly, Nation 2 is in equilibrium at point *A'*, where its production frontier is tangent to indifference curve I'. The equilibrium relative price of X in Nation 1 is given by the slope of the common tangent to its production frontier and indifference curve I at point *A*. This is $P_A = \frac{1}{4}$. For Nation 2, $P_{A'} = 4$. Since the relative price of X is lower in Nation 1 than in Nation 2, Nation 1 has a comparative advantage in commodity X and Nation 2 in commodity Y.

cannot reach higher indifference curves with the resources and technology presently available.

3.4b   Equilibrium Relative Commodity Prices and Comparative Advantage

The **equilibrium relative commodity price in isolation** is given by the slope of the common tangent to the nation's production frontier and indifference curve at the autarky point of production and consumption. Thus, the equilibrium relative price of X is $P_A = P_X/P_Y = \frac{1}{4}$ in Nation 1 and $P_{A'} = P_X/P_Y = 4$ in Nation 2 in isolation (see Figure 3-3). Relative prices are different in the two nations because their production frontiers and indifference curves differ in shape and location.

Since in isolation $P_A < P_{A'}$, Nation 1 has a comparative advantage in commodity X and Nation 2 in commodity Y. It follows that both nations can gain if Nation 1 specializes in the production of and exports X in exchange for Y from Nation 2. How this takes place will be seen in the next section.

Figure 3-3 illustrates that the forces of supply (as given by the nation's production frontier) and the forces of demand (as summarized by the nation's indifference map) *together* determine the equilibrium relative commodity prices in each nation in autarky. For example, if indifference curve I had been of a different shape, it would have been tangent to the production frontier at a different point, and determined a different relative price of X in Nation 1. The same would be true for Nation 2. This is in contrast to the fixed costs case, where the equilibrium P_X/P_Y is constant in each nation regardless of the level of output and conditions of demand, and is given by the constant slope of the nation's production frontier.

3.5   The Basis For and the Gains From Trade with Increasing Costs

A difference in relative commodity prices between two nations is a reflection of their comparative advantage and forms the basis for mutually beneficial trade. The nation with the lower relative price for a commodity has a comparative advantage in that commodity and a comparative disadvantage in the other commodity, with respect to the second nation. Each nation should then specialize in production of the commodity of its comparative advantage (i.e., produce more of the commodity than it wants to consume domestically) and exchange part of its output with the other nation for the commodity of its comparative disadvantage.

However, as each nation specializes in production of the commodity of its comparative advantage, it incurs increasing opportunity costs. Specialization will continue until relative commodity prices in the two nations become equal at the level at which trade is in equilibrium. By then trading with each other, both nations end up consuming more than in the absence of trade.

3.5a   Illustration of the Basis for and the Gains from Trade with Increasing Costs

We have seen (Figure 3-3) that in the absence of trade the equilibrium relative price of X is $P_A = ¼$ in Nation 1 and $P_{A'} = 4$ in Nation 2. Thus, Nation 1 has a comparative advantage in commodity X and Nation 2 in commodity Y.

Suppose that trade between the two nations becomes possible (e.g., through the elimination of government obstacles to trade or a drastic reduction in transportation costs). Nation 1 should now specialize in the production and export of commodity X in exchange for commodity Y from Nation 2. How this takes place is illustrated by Figure 3-4.

Starting from point *A* (the equilibrium point in isolation), as Nation 1 spe-

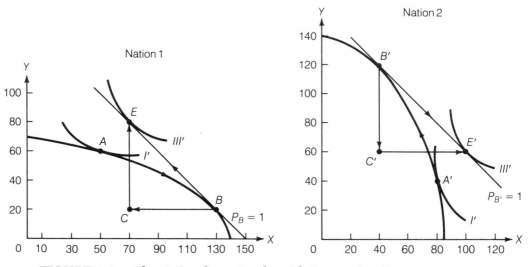

FIGURE 3-4.   The Gains from Trade with Increasing Costs

With trade, Nation 1 moves from point *A* to point *B* in production. By then exchanging 60X for 60Y with Nation 2 (see trade triangle *BCE*), Nation 1 ends up consuming at point *E* (on indifference curve III). Thus, Nation 1 gains 20X and 20Y from trade (compare autarky point *A* with point *E*). Similarly, Nation 2 moves from *A'* to *B'* in production. By then exchanging 60Y for 60X with Nation 1 (see trade triangle *B'C'E'*), Nation 2 ends up consuming at point *E'* and also gains 20X and 20Y. $P_B = P_{B'} = 1$ is the equilibrium relative price—the price at which trade is balanced.

cializes in the production of X and moves *down* its production frontier, it incurs increasing opportunity costs in the production of X. This is reflected in the *increasing slope* of its production frontier. Starting from point *A'*, as Nation 2 specializes in the production of Y and moves *upward* along its production frontier, it experiences increasing opportunity costs in the production of Y. This is reflected in the *decline in the slope* of its production frontier (a reduction in the opportunity cost of X, which means a rise in the opportunity cost of Y).

This process of specialization in production continues until relative commodity prices (the slope of the production frontiers) become equal in the two nations. The common relative price (slope) with trade will be somewhere between the pretrade relative prices of ¼ and 4, at the level at which trade is balanced. In Figure 3-4, this is $P_B = P_{B'} = 1$.

With trade, Nation 1 moves from point *A* down to point *B* in production. By then exchanging 60X for 60Y with Nation 2 (see trade triangle *BCE*), Nation 1 ends up consuming at Point *E* (70X and 80Y) on its indifference curve III. This is the highest level of satisfaction that Nation 1 can reach with trade at $P_X/P_Y = 1$. Thus, Nation 1 gains 20X and 20Y from its no-trade equilibrium point (compare point *E* on indifference curve III with point *A* on indifference curve I).

Similarly, Nation 2 moves from point A' up to point B' in production and, by exchanging 60Y for 60X with Nation 1 (see trade triangle $B'C'E'$), it ends up consuming at point E' (100X and 60Y) on its indifference curve III'. Thus, Nation 2 also gains 20X and 20Y from specialization in production and trade.

Note that with specialization in productions and trade, each nation can consume outside its production frontier (which also represents its no-trade consumption frontier).

3.5b   Equilibrium Relative Commodity Prices with Trade

The **equilibrium relative commodity price with trade** is the common relative price in both nations at which trade is balanced. In Figure 3-4, this is $P_B = P_{B'} = 1$. At this relative price, the amount of X that Nation 1 wants to export (60X) equals the amount of X that Nation 2 wants to import (60X). Similarly, the amount of Y that Nation 2 wants to export (60Y) exactly matches the amount of Y that Nation 1 wants to import at this price (60Y).

Any other relative price could not persist because trade would be unbalanced. For example, at $P_X/P_Y = 2$, Nation 1 would want to export more of X than Nation 2 would be willing to import at this high price. As a result, the relative price of X would fall toward the equilibrium level of 1. Similarly, at a relative price of X lower than 1, Nation 2 would want to import more of X than Nation 1 would be willing to export at this low price, and the relative price of X would rise. Thus, the relative price of X would gravitate toward the equilibrium price of 1. (The same conclusion would be reached in terms of Y.)

The equilibrium relative price in Figure 3-4 was determined by trial and error; that is, various relative prices were tried until the one that balanced trade was found. There is a more rigorous theoretical way to determine the equilibrium relative price with trade. This makes use of so-called offer curves and is discussed in the next chapter.

All we need to say at this point is that the greater is Nation 1's desire for Y (the commodity exported by Nation 2) and the weaker is Nation 2's desire for X (the commodity exported by Nation 1), the closer the equilibrium price with trade will be to ¼ (the pretrade equilibrium price in Nation 1) and the smaller will be Nation 1's share of the gain. Once the equilibrium relative price with trade is determined, we will know exactly how the gains from trade are divided between the two nations, and our trade model will be complete. In Figure 3-4, the equilibrium relative price of X with trade ($P_B = P_{B'} = 1$) results in equal gains (20X and 20Y) for Nation 1 and Nation 2, but this need not be the case.

Of course, if the *pretrade* relative price had been the same in both nations (an unlikely occurrence), there would be no comparative advantage or disadvantage to speak of in either nation, and no specialization in production or mutually beneficial trade would take place.

3.5c   Incomplete Specialization

There is one basic difference between our trade model under increasing costs and the constant opportunity costs case. Under constant costs, both nations specialize completely in production of the commodity of their comparative advantage (i.e., produce only that commodity). For example, in Figure 2-2 and 2-3, the United States specialized completely in wheat production, and the United Kingdom specialized completely in cloth production. Since it paid for the United States to exchange some wheat for British cloth, it paid for the United States to obtain all of its cloth from the United Kingdom in exchange for wheat, because the opportunity cost of wheat remained constant in the United States. The same was true for the United Kingdom in terms of cloth production.

In contrast, under increasing opportunity costs, there is **incomplete specialization** in production in both nations. For example, while Nation 1 produces more of X (the commodity of its comparative advantage) with trade, it continues to produce some Y (see point *B* in Figure 3-4). Similarly, Nation 2 continues to produce some X with trade (see point *B'* in Figure 3-4).

The reason for this is that as Nation 1 specializes in the production of X, it incurs increasing opportunity costs in producing X. Similarly, as Nation 2 produces more Y, it incurs increasing opportunity costs in Y (which means declining opportunity costs of X). Thus, as each nation specializes in production of the commodity of its comparative advantage, relative commodity prices move toward each other (i.e., become less unequal) until they are identical in both nations.

At that point, it does not pay for either nation to continue to expand production of the commodity of its comparative advantage. This occurs before either nation has completely specialized in production. In Figure 3-4, $P_B = P_{B'} = 1$ before Nation 1 or Nation 2 has completely specialized in production.

3.5d   Small Country Case with Increasing Costs

Recall that under fixed costs, the only exception to complete specialization in production that occurred in the small country case. There, only the small nation specialized completely in production of the commodity of its comparative advantage. The large nation continued to produce both commodities even with trade (see Figure 2-4) because the small nation could not satisfy all of the demand for imports of the large nation. In the increasing costs case, however, we find incomplete specialization even in the small nation.

We can use Figure 3-4 to illustrate the small country case with increasing costs. Let us assume that Nation 1 is now a very small country, which is in equilibrium at point *A* (the same as before) in the absence of trade, and that Nation 2 is a very large country or even the rest of the world. (The diagram for Nation 2 in Figure 3-4 is to be completely disregarded in this case.)

Suppose that the equilibrium relative price of X on the world market is 1

$(P_W=1)$, and it is not affected by trade with small Nation 1. Since in the absence of trade, the relative price of X in Nation 1 $(P_A=\frac{1}{4})$ is lower than the world market price, Nation 1 has a comparative advantage in X. With the opening of trade, Nation 1 specializes in the production of X until it reaches point B on its production frontier, where $P_B=1=P_W$. Even though Nation 1 is now considered to be a small country, it still does not specialize completely in the production of X (as would be the case under constant costs).

By exchanging 60X for 60Y, Nation 1 reaches point E on indifference curve III and gains 20X and 20Y (compared with its autarky point A on indifference curve I). Note that this is exactly what occurred when Nation 1 was *not* considered to be small. The only difference is that now Nation 1 does not affect relative prices in Nation 2 (or the rest of the world), and Nation 1 captures all the benefits from trade (which now amount to only 20X and 20Y).

3.5e   The Gains from Exchange and from Specialization

A nation's gains from trade can be broken into two components: the gains from exchange and the gains from specialization. Figure 3-5 illustrates this breakdown for *small* Nation 1. (For simplicity, the autarky price line, $P_A=\frac{1}{4}$, and indifference curve I, are omitted from the figure.)

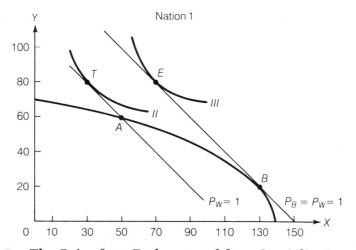

FIGURE 3-5.   The Gains from Exchange and from Specialization

If Nation 1 could not specialize in the production of X with the opening of trade but continued to produce at point A, Nation 1 could export 20X in exchange for 20Y at the prevailing world price of $P_W=1$, and end up consuming at point T on indifference curve II. The increase in consumption from point A (in autarky) to point T represents the gains from exchange alone. If Nation 1 subsequently did specialize in the production of X and produced at point B, it would then consume at point E on indifference curve III. The increase in consumption from T to E would represent the gains from specialization in production.

Suppose that, for whatever reason, Nation 1 could *not* specialize in the production of X with the opening of trade but continued to produce at point A. Starting from point A, Nation 1 could export 20X in exchange for 20Y at the prevailing world relative price of $P_W = 1$, and end up consuming at point T on indifference curve II. Even though Nation 1 consumes less of X and more of Y at point T in relation to point A, it is better off than it was in autarky because T is on higher indifference curve II. The movement from point A to point T in consumption measures the **gains from exchange.**

If subsequently Nation 1 also specialized in the production of X and produced at point B, it could then exchange 60X for 60Y with the rest of the world and consume at point E on indifference curve III (thereby gaining even more). The movement from T to E in consumption measures the **gains from specialization** in production.

In sum, the movement from A (on indifference curve I) to T (on indifference curve II) is made possible by exchange alone. This takes place even if Nation 1 remains at point A (the autarky point) in production. The movement from point T to point E (on indifference curve III) represents the gains resulting from specialization in production.

Note that Nation 1 is not in equilibrium in production at point A with trade because $P_A < P_W$. To be in equilibrium in production, Nation 1 should expand its production of X until it reaches point B, where $P_B = P_W = 1$. Nation 2's gains from trade can similarly be broken down into gains from exchange and gains from specialization.

3.6   Trade Based on Differences in Tastes

The difference in *pretrade* relative commodity prices between Nation 1 and Nation 2 in Figures 3-3 and 3-4 was based on the difference in the production frontier and indifference curves in the two nations. This determined the comparative advantage of each nation and set the stage for specialization in production and mutually beneficial trade.

With increasing costs, even if two nations have identical production possibility frontiers (which is unlikely), there will still be a basis for mutually beneficial trade if tastes, or demand preferences, in the two nations differ. The nation with the relatively smaller demand or preference for a commodity will have a lower autarky relative price for, and a comparative advantage in, that commodity. The process of specialization in production and trade would then follow, exactly as described in the previous section.

3.6a   Illustration of Trade Based on Differences in Tastes

Trade based solely on differences in tastes is illustrated with Figure 3-6. Since the production frontiers of the two nations are now assumed to be identical, they are represented by a single curve. With indifference curve I tangent to

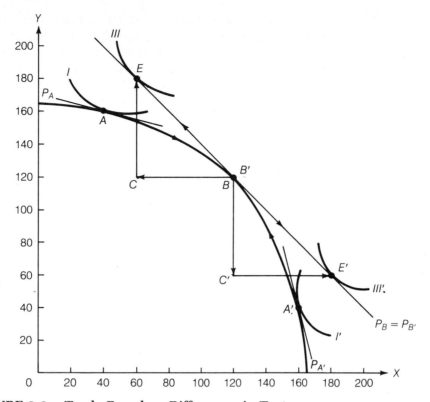

FIGURE 3-6. Trade Based on Differences in Tastes

Nations 1 and 2 have identical production frontiers (shown by a single curve) but different tastes (indifference curves). In isolation, Nation 1 produces and consumes at point A and Nation 2 at point A'. Since $P_A < P_{A'}$, Nation 1 has a comparative advantage in X and Nation 2 in Y. With trade, Nation 1 specializes in the production of X and produces at B, while Nation 2 specializes in Y and produces at B' (which coincides with B). By exchanging 60X for 60Y with each other (see trade triangles BCE and $B'C'E'$), Nation 1 ends up consuming at E (thereby gaining 20X and 20Y), while Nation 2 consumes at E' (and also gains 20X and 20Y).

the production frontier at point A for Nation 1 and indifference curve I' tangent at point A' for Nation 2, the pretrade relative price of X is lower in Nation 1. Thus, Nation 1 has a comparative advantage in commodity X and Nation 2 in commodity Y.

   With the opening of trade, Nation 1 specializes in the production of X (and moves down its production frontier), while Nation 2 specializes in Y (and moves up its own production frontier). Specialization continues until P_W/P_Y is the same in both nations and trade is balanced. This occurs at point B (which coincides with point B'), where $P_B = P_{B'} = 1$. Nation 1 then exchanges 60X for 60Y with Nation 2 (see trade triangle BCE) and ends up consuming at point E on its indifference curve III. Nation 1 thus gains 20X and 20Y as compared with point *A*. Similarly, Nation 2 exchanges 60Y for 60X with Nation 1 (see trade triangle *B'C'E'*) and ends up consuming at point *E'* on its indifference curve III' (also gaining 20X and 20Y from point *A'*). Note that when trade is based solely on taste differences, the patterns of production become more similar as both nations depart from autarky.

Thus, mutually beneficial trade can be based exclusively on a difference in tastes between two nations. In Chapter 5, we will examine the opposite case, where trade between the two nations is based exclusively on a difference in factor endowments and production frontiers. (This will be referred to as the Heckscher-Ohlin model.) Only if the production frontier and the indifference curves are identical in both nations (or the difference in production frontiers is exactly neutralized, or offset, by the difference in the indifference curves) will the pretrade relative commodity prices be equal in both nations, ruling out the possibility of mutually beneficial trade.

Summary

1. This chapter extended our simple trade model to the more realistic case of increasing opportunity costs. It also introduced demand conditions in the form of community indifference curves. We then went on to examine how the interaction of these forces of demand and supply determines each nation's comparative advantage and set the stage for specialization in production and mutually beneficial trade.

2. Increasing opportunity costs mean that the nation must give up more and more of one commodity to release just enough resources to produce each additional unit of another commodity. This is reflected in a production frontier that is concave from the origin. The slope of the production frontier gives the marginal rate of transformation (MRT). Increasing opportunity costs arise because resources are not homogeneous, and they are not used in the same fixed proportion in the production of all commodities. Production frontiers differ because of different factor endowments and/or technology in different nations.

3. A community indifference curve shows the various combinations of two commodities which yield equal satisfaction to the community or nation. Higher curves refer to a greater level of satisfaction. Community indifference curves are negatively sloped and convex from the origin.

And to be useful, they must not cross. The slope of an indifference curve gives the marginal rate of substitution in consumption (MRS), or the amount of commodity Y that a nation could give up for each extra unit of commodity X and still remain on the same indifference curve. Trade affects the income distribution within a nation and can result in intersecting indifference curves. This difficulty can be overcome by the compensation principle, which states that the nation gains from trade if the gainers would retain some of their gain even after fully compensating losers. Alternatively, some restrictive assumptions could be made.

4. In the absence of trade, a nation is in equilibrium when it reaches the highest indifference curve possible with its production frontier. This occurs at the point where a community indifference curve is tangent to the nation's production frontier. The common slope of the two curves at the tangency point gives the internal equilibrium relative commodity price in the nation and reflects the nation's comparative advantage.

5. With trade, each nation specializes in production of the commodity of its comparative advantage and faces increasing opportunity costs. Specialization in production proceeds until relative commodity prices in the two nations are equalized at the level at which trade is in equilibrium. By then trading, each nation ends up consuming on a higher indifference curve than in the absence of trade. With increasing costs, specialization in production is incomplete, even in a small nation. The gains from trade can be broken down into gains from exchange and gains from specialization in production.

6. With increasing costs, even if two nations have identical production frontiers, there is still a basis for mutually beneficial trade if tastes, or demand preferences, differ in the two nations. The nation with the relatively smaller demand or preference for a commodity will have a lower autarky relative price for, and a comparative advantage in, that commodity. This will set the stage of specialization in production and mutually beneficial trade, as described above.

A Look Ahead

In Chapter 4, we will introduce the concept of offer curves and examine how the intersection of the offer curves of two nations defines the equilibrium relative commodity price with trade and the terms of trade of each nation. The intersection of offer curves also determines each nation's share of the gains from trade. With this addition, our simple trade model will be complete. In Chapter 5, we will see how this simple trade model was extended by Heckscher and Ohlin.

Glossary

Increasing opportunity costs The increasing amounts of one commodity that a nation must give up to release just enough resources to produce each additional unit of another commodity. This is reflected in a production frontier that is concave from the origin.

Marginal rate of transformation (MRT) The amount of one commodity that a nation must give up to produce each additional unit of another commodity. This is another name for the opportunity cost of a commodity and is given by the slope of the production frontier at the point of production.

Community indifference curve The curve that shows the various combinations of two commodities which yield equal satisfaction to the community or nation. Community indifference curves are negatively sloped, convex from the origin, and should not cross.

Marginal rate of substitution (MRS) The amount of one commodity that a nation could give up in exchange for one extra unit of a second commodity and still remain on the same indifference curve. It is given by the slope of the community indifference curve at the point of consumption and declines as the nation consumes more of the second commodity.

Autarky The absence of trade, or isolation.

Equilibrium relative commodity price in isolation The relative commodity price at which a nation is maximizing its welfare in isolation. It is given by the slope of the common tangent to the nation's production frontier and indifference curve at the autarky point of production and consumption.

Equilibrium relative commodity price with trade The common relative commodity price in two nations at which trade is balanced.

Incomplete specialization The continued production of both commodities in both nations with increasing costs, even with trade and even in a small nation.

Gains from exchange The increase in consumption resulting from exchange alone and with the nation continuing to produce at the autarky point.

Gains from specialization The increase in consumption resulting from specialization in production.

Questions for Review

1. In what way is the material in this chapter more realistic than that of Chapter 2? How are the tastes, or demand preferences, of a nation introduced in this chapter? Why are they needed?

2. Why does a production frontier that is concave from the origin indicate increasing opportunity costs in both commodities? What does the slope of the production frontier measure? How does that slope change as the nation produces more of the commodity measured along the horizontal axis? More of the commodity measured along the vertical axis? What is the reason for increasing opportunity costs? Why do the production frontiers of different nations have different shapes?

3. What does a community indifference curve measure? What are its characteristics? What does the slope of an indifference curve measure? Why does it decline as the nation consumes more of the commodity measured along the horizontal axis? What are some difficulties with community indifference curves? How can they be overcome?

4. What is meant by the equilibrium relative commodity price in isolation? How is this price determined in each nation? How does it define the nation's comparative advantage?

5. Why does specialization in production with trade proceed only up to the point where relative commodity prices in the two nations are equalized? How is the equilibrium relative commodity price with trade determined? Why is there incomplete specialization in production (even in a smaller nation) with increasing opportunity costs? How are the results under increasing costs different from the fixed costs case? What is meant by gains from exchange? By gains from specialization?

6. Can specialization in production and mutually beneficial trade be based solely on a difference in tastes between two nations? How is this different from the more general case? Can specialization in production and mutually beneficial trade be based exclusively on a difference in factor endowments and/or technology between two nations?

Problems

1. On one set of axes, sketch a fairly large production frontier concave from the origin. Starting near the midpoint on the production frontier, use arrows to show that the nation

incurs increasing opportunity costs in producing:
   (a) more of X (the commodity measured along the horizontal axis) and more of Y.
   (b) How does the slope of the production frontier change as the nation produces more of X? More of Y? What do these changes reflect?

2. On another set of axes, sketch three community indifference curves, making the top two curves cross each other.
   (a) Why have you drawn community indifference curves downward, or negatively, sloped?
   (b) What does the slope of the curves measure? Why is the slope of each curve smaller for lower points?
   (c) Which of the two intersecting indifference curves shows a greater level of satisfaction to the right of the point of intersection? To the left? Why is this inconsistent with the definition of indifference curves? What conclusion can you reach?

*3. On one set of axes, sketch a community indifference curve tangent to the fairly flat section of a concave production frontier. On a second set of axes, sketch another (different) community indifference curve tangent to the fairly steep portion of another (different) concave production frontier.
   (a) Draw in the line showing the equilibrium relative commodity price in isolation in each nation.
   (b) Which is the commodity of comparative advantage for each nation?
   (c) Under what (unusual) condition would there be no such a thing as comparative advantage or disadvantage between the two nations?

*4. On the graphs of problem 3, show for each nation with trade:
   (a) the direction (by an arrow on the production frontier) of specialization in production and the equilibrium point of production and consumption.
   (b) How much does each nation gain in consumption compared with its autarky

point? Which of the two nations gains more from trade? Why?

5. On one set of axes, sketch a community indifference curve tangent to the fairly flat section of a concave production frontier and show the nation's autarky equilibrium relative commodity price, labeling it P_A. Assume that this graph refers to a very small nation whose trade does not affect relative prices on the world market, given by P_W.

   (a) Show on the graph the process of specialization in production, the amount traded, and the gains from trade.

   (b) Why doesn't this small nation specialize completely in production of the commodity of its comparative advantage? How does this differ from the constant costs case?

6. On two sets of axes, draw identical concave production frontiers with different community indifference curves tangent to them.

   (a) Indicate the autarky equilibrium relative commodity price in each nation.

   (b) Show the process of specialization in production and mutually beneficial trade.

   (c) What would have happened if the two community indifference curves had also been identical? Sketch a graph of this situation.

   (d) What would have happened if the production frontiers were identical and the community indifference curves different, but we had constant opportunity costs? Can you draw a graph of this?

APPENDIX

In this appendix, we review those aspects of production theory which are essential for understanding the material presented in subsequent appendices. We begin with a review of production functions, isoquants, isocosts, and equilibrium. We then illustrate these concepts for two nations, two commodities, and two factors. Next, we derive the Edgeworth box diagram and, from it, the production frontier of each nation. Finally, we use the Edgeworth box diagram to show the change in the ratio of resource use as each nation specializes in production with trade.

A3.1 Production Functions, Isoquants, Isocosts, and Equilibrium

A **production function** gives the *maximum* quantities of a commodity that a firm can produce with various amounts of factor inputs. This purely technological relationship is supplied by engineers and is represented by isoquants.

An **isoquant** is a curve that shows the various combinations of two factors, say, capital (K) and labor (L), that a firm can use to produce a specific level of output. Higher isoquants refer to larger outputs and lower ones to smaller outputs. Isoquants have the same general characteristics of indifference curves. They are negatively sloped, convex from the origin, and do not cross. (However, isoquants give a cardinal measure of output while indifference curves give only an ordinal measure of utility.)

Isoquants are negative sloped because a firm using less K must use more L to remain on the same isoquant. The (absolute) slope of the isoquant is called the **marginal rate of technical substitution of labor for capital in production (MRTS)** and measures how much K the firm can give up by increasing L by one unit and still remain on the same isoquant. As a firm moves down an isoquant and uses more L and less K, it finds it more and more difficult to replace K with L. That is, the marginal rate of technical substitution of L for K (or slope of the isoquant) diminishes. This makes the isoquant convex from the origin. Finally, isoquants do not cross because an intersection would imply the same level of output on two isoquants, which is inconsistent with their definition.

In Figure 3-7, the curve labeled 1X is the isoquant for one arbitrarily defined unit of commodity X, and curve 2X is the isoquant for two units of X. Note that the isoquants are negatively sloped and convex from the origin and that they do not cross.

An **isocost** is a line that shows the various combinations of K and L that a firm can hire for a given expenditure, or total outlay (TO), at given factor prices. For example, suppose that the total outlay of the firm in Figure 3-7 is $TO = \$30$, that the price of a unit of capital is $P_K = \$10$, and that the wage rate is $P_L = \$5$. Under these conditions, the firm can hire either 3K (the vertical intercept) or 6L (the horizontal intercept) or any combination of L and K shown on the straight line (isocost). The (absolute) slope of the isocost of $\frac{3}{6} = \frac{1}{2}$ gives the relative price of L (the factor plotted along the horizontal axis). That is, $P_L/P_K = \$5/\$10 = \frac{1}{2}$. A $TO = \$60$ and unchanged factor prices give a new isocost parallel to the first one and twice as far from the origin (see Figure 3-7).

A **producer** is in **equilibrium** when he maximizes output for a given cost outlay (i.e., when he reaches the highest isoquant possible with a given isocost). This occurs where an isoquant is tangent to an isocost (i.e., MRTS $= P_L/P_K$). In Figure 3-7, the producer is in equilibrium at point A_1, producing 1X with the lower isocost, and at point A_2, producing 2X with the higher isocost. Note that isoquant 2X involves twice as much output as isoquant 1X, is twice as far from the origin, and requires twice as much outlay as K and L to be reached. The straight line from the origin connecting equilibrium points A_1 and A_2 is called the **expansion path** and shows the constant $K/L = \frac{1}{4}$ in producing 1X and 2X.

All the characteristics we have mentioned imply a production function that is **homogeneous of degree one,** or shows **constant returns to scale.** We will make much use of this production function in international economics because of its useful properties. Since the K/L ratio remains the same with this production function (as long as factor prices do not change), the productivity of K and L also remains the same, regardless of the level of output. Furthermore, with this type of production function, all the isoquants that refer to the

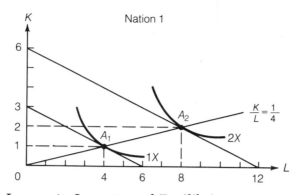

FIGURE 3-7.   Isoquants, Isocosts, and Equilibrium

Isoquants 1X and 2X give the various combinations of K and L that the firm can use to produce one and two units of X, respectively. Isoquants are negatively sloped, convex, and do not cross. An *isocost* shows the various amounts of K and L that a firm can hire with a given total outlay (*TO*). The lines from $3K$ to $6L$ and from $6K$ to $12L$ are isocosts. The (absolute) slope of the isocost measures P_L/P_K. *Equilibrium* is at points A_1 and A_2, where the firm reaches the highest isoquant possible for a given *TO*. At A_2 the firm produces twice as much output and uses twice as much K and L as at A_1. The straight line through the origin joining A_1 and A_2 is the *expansion path* and gives the constant K/L ratio in producing 1X and 2X.

production of various quantities of a particular commodity look exactly alike or have identical shape (see Figure 3-7).

A3.2   Production Theory with Two Nations, Two Commodities, and Two Factors

Figure 3-8 extends Figure 3-7 to deal with the case of two nations, two commodities, and two factors. Figure 3-8 shows isoquants for commodity X and commodity Y for Nation 1 and Nation 2. Note that commodity Y is produced with a higher K/L ratio in both nations. Thus, we say that Y is K-intensive and X is the L-intensive commodity. Note also that the K/L ratio is lower in Nation 1 than in Nation 2 for both X and Y. The reason for this is that the relative price of labor (i.e., P_L/P_K, or slope of the isocosts) is lower in Nation 1 than in Nation 2.

If, for whatever reason, the relative price of labor (i.e., P_L/P_K) rose in both nations, each nation would substitute K for L in the production of both commodities to minimize costs. As a result, the K/L ratio would rise in both nations in the production of both commodities.

Even though both X and Y are more K-intensive in Nation 2 than in Nation 1, X is always the L-intensive commodity in both nations. This important fact is reflected in the isoquants of X and Y intersecting only once (see Figure

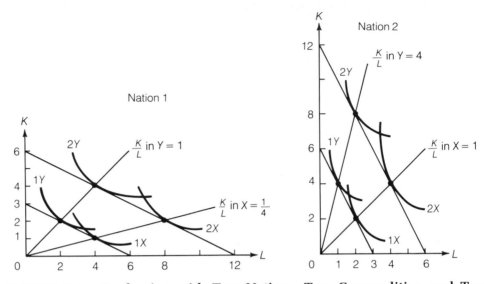

FIGURE 3-8. Production with Two Nations, Two Commodities, and Two Factors

Y is the *K*-intensive commodity in both nations. The *K/L* ratio is lower in Nation 1 than in Nation 2 in both X and Y because P_L/P_K is lower in Nation 1. Since Y is always the *L*-intensive and X is always the *K*-intensive commodity in both nations, the X and Y isoquants intersect only once in each nation.

3-8), and it will be of great use in the appendix to Chapter 6, which deals with factor-intensity reversal.

A3.3 Derivation of the Edgeworth Box Diagram and Production Frontiers

We will now use the knowledge gained from Figure 3-8 to derive the Edgeworth box diagram and, from it, the production frontier of each nation. This is illustrated in Figure 3-9 for Nation 1 and in Figure 3-10 for Nation 2.

Our discussion will first concentrate on the top panel of Figure 3-9. The dimensions of the box in the top panel reflect the total amount of L (measured by the length of the box) and K (the height of the box) available in Nation 1 at a given time.

The lower left-hand corner of the box (O_X) represents the zero origin for commodity X, and X-isoquants farther from O_X refer to greater outputs of X. On the other hand, the top right-hand corner (O_Y) represents the zero origin for commodity Y, and Y-isoquants farther from O_Y refer to greater outputs of Y.

Any point within the box indicates how much of the *total* amount of labor

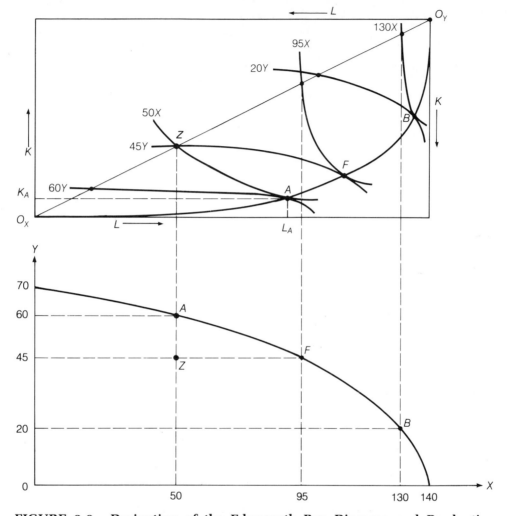

FIGURE 3-9. Derivation of the Edgeworth Box Diagram and Production Frontier for Nation 1

The size of the box in the top panel gives the total amount of L and K available to Nation 1. The bottom left-hand corner is the origin for X, so that higher X outputs are given by X-isoquants farther away from this origin. The top right-hand corner is the origin for Y, and higher Y outputs are given by Y-isoquants farther from this origin. Any point in the box gives how much K and L are used in the production of X and Y, respectively. The line joining points of tangency of X and Y isoquants is called the *contract curve*. Any point not on the contract curve is not efficient because the nation could produce more of one commodity without reducing the output of the other. The contract curve is not a straight line because factor prices change to keep K and L fully employed. By mapping the contract curve from input to output space, we derive the production frontier of Nation 1 in the bottom panel.

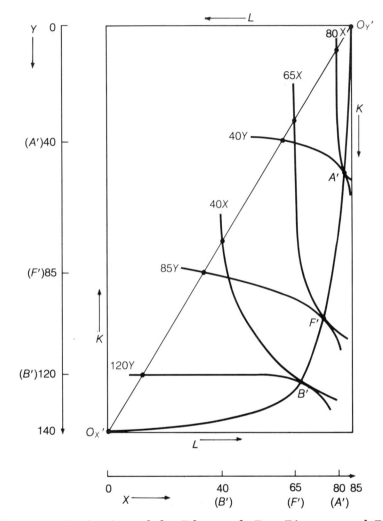

FIGURE 3-10.   Derivation of the Edgeworth Box Diagram and Production Frontier for Nation 2

The dimensions of its Edgeworth box indicate that Nation 2 has a relative abundance of K compared with Nation 1. Efficiency considerations require that Nation 2 produce on its contract curve shown by the line joining $O_{X'}$ to $O_{Y'}$ through points A', F', and B'. The amount of commodity X produced at points A', F', and B' is given by the points where the X-isoquant through each crosses the diagonal. This output is then projected down to the X-axis at the bottom of the figure. Similarly, the amount of commodity Y produced at points A', F', and B' is given by the points where the Y-isoquant through each (and tangent to an X-isoquant) crosses the diagonal. This output is then projected to the Y-axis at the left of the figure.

available ($\bar{L}$) and how much of the total amount of capital available ($\bar{K}$) are used in the production of X and Y. For example, at point A, L_A and K_A are used to produce 50X, and the remaining quantities, or $\bar{L} - L_A$ and $\bar{K} - K_A$, are used in the production of 60Y (see Figure 3-9).

By joining all points in the box where an X-isoquant is tangent to a Y-isoquant, we get the nation's **production contract curve.** Thus, the contract curve of Nation 1 is given by the line joining O_X to O_Y through points A, F, and B. At any point not on the contract curve, production is not efficient because the nation could increase its output of one commodity without reducing its output of the other.

For example, from point Z in the figure, Nation 1 could move to point F and produce more of X (i.e., 95X instead of 50X) and the same amount of Y (both Z and F are on the isoquant for 45Y). Or Nation 1 could move from point Z to point A and produce more Y (i.e., 60Y instead of 45Y) and the same amount of X (both Z and A are on the isoquant for 50X). Or Nation 1 could produce a little more of both X and Y and end up on the contract curve somewhere between A and F (the isoquants for this are not shown in the figure). Once on its contract curve, Nation 1 could only expand the output of one commodity by reducing the output of the other. The fact that the contract curve bulges toward the lower right-hand corner indicates that commodity X is the L-intensive commodity in Nation 1.

By transposing the contract curve from the input space in the top panel to the output space in the bottom panel, we derive Nation 1's production frontier shown in the bottom panel. For example, from point Z where the isoquant for 50X crosses the straight-line diagonal $O_X O_Y$ in the top panel, we get point A (i.e., 50X) in the bottom panel. Note that point A in the bottom panel is directly below point Z in the top panel, rather than directly below point A in the top panel because output is *measured* at constant K/L (i.e., along the straight-line diagonal). The measurement along the diagonal reflects the fact that imputs are being used to measure outputs (with constant returns to scale).

Even though outputs are measured along the diagonal, efficiency considerations (discussed earlier) require that Nation 1 produce 50X at point A in the top panel where the X-isoquant for 50X is *tangent* to the Y-isoquant for 60Y. This gives point A in the bottom panel, referring to the output of 50X and 60Y. If Nation 1 produced at point Z instead of point A in the top panel, Nation 1 would produce 50X but only 45Y, giving point Z *inside* the production frontier in the bottom panel.

Similarly, directly below the point in the top panel where the X-isoquant showing 95X crosses the diagonal, we get point F, referring to 95X and 45Y, on the production frontier in the bottom panel. Finally, point B on the isoquants for 130X and 20Y in the top panel is projected down to point B, referring to 130X and 20Y, on the production frontier in the bottom panel. Thus, there is a one-to-one correspondence between the contract curve and the production frontier, with each point on the contract curve uniquely defining one point on the production frontier.

Note that the output of commodity X is proportional to the distance from origin O_X along the diagonal because of our assumption of constant returns to scale. Similarly, the output of commodity Y is proportional to the distance from origin O_Y along the diagonal. (This is the reason for measuring outputs along the diagonal.) Also note that the X-intercept and the Y-intercept of the production frontier correspond to the length and height of the Edgeworth box.

Figure 3-10 shows the Edgeworth box for Nation 2. The dimensions of the box indicate that Nation 2 has a relative abundance of K compared with Nation 1. As with Nation 1, the amount of commodity X produced at points A', F', and B' is given by the points where the X-isoquant through each point crosses the diagonal. This output is then projected down to the X-axis at the bottom of the figure. Similarly, the amount of commodity Y produced at points A', F', and B's given by the points where the Y-isoquant through each point (and tangent to an X-isoquant) crosses the diagonal. This output is then projected to the Y-axis at the left of the figure. For example, the X-isoquant through B' crosses the diagonal at an output of 40X (see the X-axis at the bottom of the figure). Similarly, the Y-isoquant through point B' crosses the diagonal at the output of 120Y (see the Y-axis at the left of the figure). These give the coordinates of point B' of 40X and 120Y on Nation 2's production frontier (not shown). The other points on Nation 2's production frontier are similarly derived. Note that the production frontiers for Nation 1 and Nation 2 that we have just derived are the ones that we used earlier in this chapter. However, we have now derived rather than assumed them.

Problem   Derive from Figure 3-10 Nation 2's production frontier. Which commodity is *L*-intensive in Nation 2? Why?

A3.4   Some Important Conclusions

The movement from point *A* to point *B* on Nation 1's *contract curve* (see Figure 3-9) refers to an increase in the production of X (the commodity of its comparative advantage) and results in a rise in the K/L ratio. This rise in the K/L ratio is measured by the increase in the slope of a straight line (not drawn) from origin O_X to point *B* as opposed to point *A*. The same movement from point *A* to point *B* also raises the K/L ratio in the production of Y. This is measured by the increase in the slope of a line from origin O_Y to point *B* as opposed to point *A*.

The rise in the K/L ratio in the production of both commodities in Nation 1 can be explained as follows. Since Y is K-intensive, as Nation 1 reduces its output of Y, capital and labor are released in a ratio that exceeds the K/L ratio used in expanding the production of X. There would then be a tendency for some of the nation's capital to be unemployed, causing the relative price of K to fall (i.e., P_L/P_K to rise).

As a result, Nation 1 will substitute K for L in the production of both commodities until all available K is once again fully utilized. Thus, the K/L ratio in Nation 1 rises in the production of both commodities. This also explains why the production contract curve is not a straight line but becomes steeper as Nation 1 produces more X (i.e., it moves farther from origin O_X). *The contract curve would be a straight line only if relative factor prices remained unchanged, and here factor prices change.* The rise in P_L/P_K in Nation 1 can be visualized in the top panel of Figure 3-9 by the greater slope of the common tangent to the isoquants at point B as opposed to point A (to keep the figure simple, such tangents are not actually drawn). We will review and expand these results in the appendix to Chapter 5, where we prove the factor-price equalization theorem of the Heckscher-Ohlin trade model.

Problem   Explain why, as Nation 2 moves from point A' to point B' on its contract curve (i.e., specializes in the production of Y, the commodity of its comparative advantage), its K/L ratio *falls* in the production of both X and Y. (If you cannot, reread section A3.4).

Selected Bibliography

For a problem-solving approach to the material covered in this chapter, with many examples and solved problems, see:
- D. Salvatore, *Theory and Problems of International Economics*, 2nd ed. (New York: McGraw-Hill, 1984), ch. 2 (sects. 2.4 and 2.5) and ch. 3 (sects. 3.1 and 3.2).

For a diagrammatic presentation of cost conditions in international trade, see:
- G. Haberler, *The Theory of International Trade* (London: W. Hodge and Co., 1936), ch. 12.
- A. P. Lerner, "The Diagrammatic Representation of Cost Conditions in International Trade," *Economica*, 1932. Reprinted in A. P. Lerner, *Essays in Economic Analysis* (London: Macmillan, 1953).

Two excellent articles on the use of community indifference curves in international trade are:
- W. W. Leontief, "The Use of Indifference Curves in International Trade," *Quarterly Journal of Economics*, 1933. Reprinted in H. S. Ellis and L. M. Metzler, *Readings in the Theory of International Trade* (Homewood, Ill.: Irwin, 1950).
- P. A. Samuelson, "Social Indifference Curves," *Quarterly Journal of Economics*, 1956.

For an exposition of the gains from trade, see:
- P. A. Samuelson, "The Gains from International Trade," *Canadian Journal of Economics and Political Science*, 1939. Reprinted in H. S. Ellis and L. M. Metzler, *Readings in the Theory of International Trade* (Homewood, Ill.: Irwin, 1950). Also reprinted in J. Bhagwati, *International Trade: Selected Readings* (Cambridge, Mass.: M.I.T. Press, 1981).
- P. Kenen, "Distribution Demand and Equilibrium in International Trade: A Diagrammatic Analysis," *Kyklos*, December 1959. Reprinted in R. E. Caves and H. G. Johnson, *Readings in International Economics* (Homewood, Ill.: Irwin, 1968).
- P. A. Samuelson, "The Gains from International Trade Once Again," *Economic Journal*, 1962.

For a review of, or introduction to, production theory, as well as for the derivation of the Edgeworth box diagram and production frontiers, see:
- D. Salvatore, *Microeconomics: Theory and Applications* (New York: Macmillan, 1986), chs. 7, 17 (sects. 17.3 and 17.4).
- D. Salvatore, *Microeconomic Theory*, 2nd ed. (New York: McGraw-Hill, 1983), chs. 7, 14 (sects. 14.3 and 14.7).

CHAPTER 4

Offer Curves and the Terms of Trade

4.1 Introduction

We saw in Chapter 3 that a difference in relative commodity prices between two nations in isolation is a reflection of their comparative advantage and forms the basis for mutually beneficial trade. The equilibrium relative commodity price at which trade takes place was then found by trial and error at the level at which trade was balanced. In this chapter, we present a more rigorous theoretical way of determining the equilibrium relative commodity price with trade. This method makes use of offer curves.

The offer curve of Nation 1 is derived in section 4.2, and the offer curve of Nation 2 in section 4.3. In section 4.4, we examine how the interaction of the offer curves of the two nations defines the equilibrium relative commodity price with trade. Section 4.5 considers the meaning, measurement, and importance of the terms of trade. Section 4.6 extends and evaluates our trade model. The appendix to this chapter presents the *formal* derivation of offer curves, utilizing more complex analytical techniques. It also examines the case of multiple and unstable equilibria.

4.2 The Offer Curve of a Nation

In this section, we define offer curves and note their origin. We then derive the offer curve of a nation and examine the reasons for its shape.

4.2a   Origin and Definition of Offer Curves

Offer curves (sometimes referred to as **reciprocal demand curves**) were devised and introduced into international economies by *Marshall* and *Edgeworth*, two British economists of the turn of the century. Since then, offer curves have been used extensively in international economics, especially for pedagogical purposes.

The offer curve of a nation shows how much of its import commodity the nation demands to be willing to supply various amounts of its export commodity. As the definition indicates, offer curves incorporate elements of both demand and supply. Alternatively, we can say that the offer curve of a nation shows the willingness of the nation to import and export at various relative commodity prices.

The offer curve of a nation can be derived rather easily and somewhat informally from the nation's production frontier, its indifference map, and the various hypothetical relative commodity prices at which trade could take place. The formal derivation of offer curves presented in the appendix is based on the work of *Meade*, another British economist and Nobel Prize winner.

4.2b   Derivation of the Offer Curve of Nation 1

In the left panel panel of Figure 4-1, Nation 1 starts at the no-trade (or autarky) point A, as in Figure 3-3. If trade takes place at $P_B = P_X/P_Y = 1$, Nation 1 moves to point B in production, trades 60X for 60Y with Nation 2, and reaches point E on its indifference curve III. (So far this is exactly the same as in Figure 3-4.) This gives point E in the right panel of Figure 4-1.

At $P_F = P_X/P_Y = \frac{1}{2}$ (see the left panel of Figure 4-1), Nation 1 would move instead from point A to point F in production, exchange 40X for 20Y with Nation 2, and reach point H on its indifference curve II. This gives point H in the right panel. Joining the origin with points H and E and other points similarly obtained, we generate Nation 1's offer curve in the right panel. The offer curve of Nation 1 shows how much imports of commodity Y Nation 1 requires to be willing to export various quantities of commodity X.

To keep the left panel simple, we omitted the autarky price line $P_A = \frac{1}{4}$ and indifference curve I tangent to the production frontier and P_A at point A. Note that P_A, P_F, and P_B in the right panel refer to the same P_X/P_Y as P_A, P_F, and P_B in the left panel because they refer to the same *absolute* slope.

4.2c   Shape of the Offer Curve of Nation 1

The offer curve of Nation 1 in the right panel of Figure 4-1 lies above the autarky price line $P_A = \frac{1}{4}$ and bulges toward the X-axis, measuring the commodity of its comparative advantage and export. Note, however, that for a sufficiently small volume of trade, Nation 1 would trade at P_A (i.e., over a

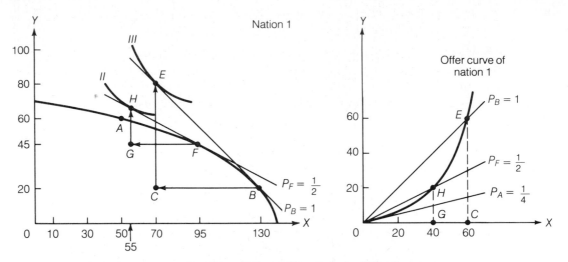

FIGURE 4-1.   Derivation of the Offer Curve of Nation 1

In the left panel, Nation 1 starts at pretrade equilibrium point *A*. If trade takes place at $P_B = 1$, Nation 1 moves to point *B* in production, exchanges 60X for 60Y with Nation 2, and reaches point *E*. This gives point *E* in the right panel. At $P_F = \frac{1}{2}$ in the left panel, Nation 1 would move instead from point *A* to point *F* in production, exchange 40X for 20Y with Nation 2, and reach point *H*. This gives point *H* in the right panel. Joining the origin with points *H* and *E* in the right panel, we generate Nation 1's offer curve. This shows how much imports of commodity Y Nation 1 requires to be willing to export various quantities of commodity X.

short range near the origin, its offer curve coincides with its autarky price line P_A).

To induce Nation 1 to export more of commodity X, P_X/P_Y must rise. Thus, at $P_F = \frac{1}{2}$, Nation 1 would export 40X, and at $P_B = 1$, it would export 60X. There are two reasons for this: (1) Nation 1 incurs increasing opportunity costs in producing more of commodity X (for export), and (2) the more of commodity Y Nation 1 consumes, the lower the extra, or marginal, satisfaction it receives from each additional unit of commodity Y imported.

4.3   The Offer Curve of the Other Nation

The offer curve of the trade partner is derived in a completely analogous way, that is, from its production frontier, its indifference map, and the various relative commodity prices at which trade could take place.

4.3a   Derivation of the Offer Curve of Nation 2

In the left panel of Figure 4-2, Nation 2 starts at the autarky equilibrium point A', as in Figure 3-3. If trade takes place at $P_B = P_X/P_Y = 1$, Nation 2 moves to point B' in production, exchanges 60Y for 60X with Nation 1, and reaches

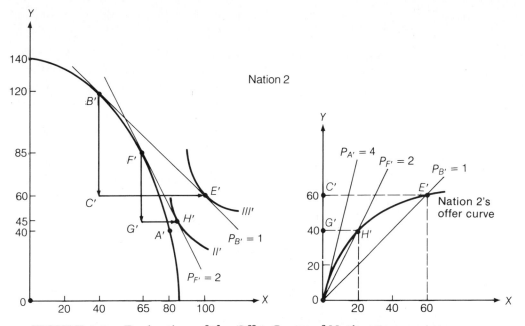

FIGURE 4-2.   Derivation of the Offer Curve of Nation 2

In the left panel, Nation 2 starts at pretrade equilibrium point A'. If trade takes place at $P_{B'} = 1$, Nation 2 moves to point B' in production, exchanges 60Y for 60X with Nation 1, and reaches point E'. This gives point E' in the right panel. At $P_{F'} = 2$ in the left panel, Nation 2 would move instead from A' to F' in production, exchange 40Y for 20X with Nation 1, and reach H'. This gives point H' in the right panel. Joining the origin with points H' and E' in the right panel, we generate Nation 2's offer curve. This shows how much imports of commodity X Nation 2 demands to be willing to supply various amounts of commodity Y for export.

point E' on its indifference curve III'. (So far this is exactly the same as in Figure 3-4.) Trade triangle $B'C'E'$ in the left panel of Figure 4-2 corresponds to trade triangle $O'C'E'$ in the right panel, and we get point E' on Nation 2's offer curve.

At $P_{F'} = P_X/P_Y = 2$ in the left panel, Nation 2 would move instead to point F' in production, exchange 40Y for 20X with Nation 1, and reach point H' on its indifference curve II'. Trade triangle $F'G'H'$ in the left panel corresponds to trade triangle $O'G'H'$ in the right panel, and we get point H' on Nation 2's offer curve.

Joining the origin with points H' and E' and other points similarly obtained, we generate Nation 2's offer curve in the right panel. The offer curve of Nation 2 shows how much imports of commodity X Nation 2 demands to be willing to export various quantities of commodity Y.

Once again, we omitted the autarky price line $P_{A'} = 4$ and indifference curve I' tangent to the production frontier and $P_{A'}$ at point A'. Note that $P_{A'}$, $P_{F'}$, and $P_{B'}$ in the right panel refer to the same P_X/P_Y as $P_{A'}$, $P_{F'}$, and $P_{B'}$ in the left panel because they refer to the same *absolute* slope.

4.3b   Shape of the Offer Curve of Nation 2

The offer curve of Nation 2 in the right panel of Figure 4-2 lies *below* its autarky price line $P_{A'} = 4$ and bulges toward the Y-axis, measuring the commodity of its comparative advantage and export. Note, however, that for a sufficiently small volume of trade, Nation 2 would trade at $P_{A'} = 4$ (i.e., over a short range near the origin, its offer curve coincides with its autarky price line $P_{A'}$).

To induce Nation 2 to export more of commodity Y, the relative price of Y must rise. This means that its reciprocal (i.e., P_X/P_Y) must fall. Thus, at $P_{F'} = 2$, Nation 2 would export 40Y and at $P_{B'} = 1$, it would export 60Y.

Once again, Nation 2 requires a higher relative price of Y to be induced to export more of Y because: (1) Nation 2 incurs increasing opportunity costs in producing more of commodity Y (for export), and (2) the more of commodity X Nation 2 consumes, the lower the extra, or marginal, satisfaction it receives from each additional unit of commodity X imported.

4.4   The Equilibrium Relative Commodity Price with Trade

The intersection of the offer curves of the two nations defines the equilibrium relative commodity price at which trade takes place between them. Only at this equilibrium price will trade be balanced between the two nations. At any other relative commodity price, the *desired* quantities of imports and exports of the two commodities would not be equal. This would put pressure on the relative commodity price to move toward its equilibrium level.

4.4a   Illustration of Equilibrium

The offer curves of Nation 1 and Nation 2 in Figure 4-3 are those derived in Figures 4-1 and 4-2. These two offer curves intersect at point E, defining equilibrium $P_X/P_Y = P_B = P_{B'} = 1$. At P_B, Nation 1 offers 60X for 60Y (point E on Nation 1's offer curve) and Nation 2 offers exactly 60Y for 60X (point E' on Nation 2's offer curve). Thus trade is in equilibrium at P_B.

At any other P_X/P_Y, trade would not be in equilibrium. For example, at $P_F = \frac{1}{2}$, the 40X that Nation 1 would export (see point H in Figure 4-3) would fall short of the imports of commodity X demanded by Nation 2 at this relatively low price of X. (This is given by a point, not shown in Figure 4-3, where the extended price line P_F crosses the extended offer curve of Nation 2.)

The excess import demand for commodity X at $P_F = \frac{1}{2}$ by Nation 2 tends to drive P_X/P_Y up. As this occurs, Nation 1 will supply more of commodity X for export (i.e., Nation 1 will move up its offer curve), while Nation 2 will reduce

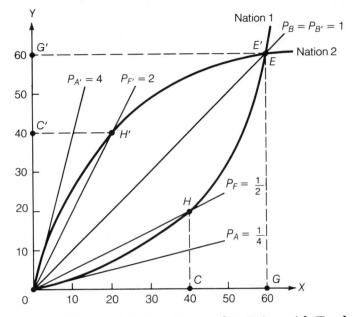

FIGURE 4-3.   Equilibrium Relative Commodity Price with Trade

The offer curves of Nation 1 and Nation 2 are those of Figures 4-1 and 4-2. The offer curves intersect at point E, defining the equilibrium relative commodity price $P_B = 1$. At P_B, trade is in equilibrium because Nation 1 offers to exchange 60X for 60Y and Nation 2 offers exactly 60Y for 60X. At any $P_X/P_Y < 1$, the quantity of exports of commodity X supplied by Nation 1 would fall short of the quantity of imports of commodity X demanded by Nation 2. This would drive the relative commodity price up to the equilibrium level. The opposite would be true at $P_X/P_Y > 1$.

its import demand for commodity X (i.e., Nation 2 will move down its offer curve). This will continue until supply and demand become equal at P_B. The pressure for P_F to move toward P_B could also be explained in terms of commodity Y and arises at any other P_X/P_Y, such as $P_F \neq P_B$.

Note that the equilibrium relative commodity price of $P_B = 1$ with trade (determined in Figure 4-3 by the intersection of the offer curves of Nation 1 and Nation 2) is identical to that found by trial and error in Figure 3-4. At $P_B = 1$, both nations happen to gain equally from trade (refer to Figure 3-4).

4.4b The Small Country Case

If one of the two trading nations is very small, it is possible that the offer curve of the small nation will intersect the straight-line segment of the large nation's offer curve near the origin. In that case, the small nation will trade at the pretrade relative commodity price prevailing in the large nation (i.e., the small nation is a price taker, just like a perfectly competitive firm), and the small nation will capture all of the benefits from trade.

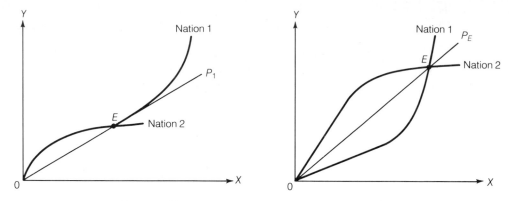

FIGURE 4-4. The Small Country and the Constant Costs Case

In the left panel, Nation 2 is the small nation. Its offer curve intersects at point E the straight-line segment of Nation 1's offer curve near the origin. Trade takes place at P_1, the pretrade relative commodity price in Nation 1, and Nation 2 captures all of the benefits from trade. In the right panel, both nations face constant costs, and their offer curves are straight lines until they both become completely specialized in production. Then, the offer curves assume their regular shape and determine at their intersection at point E, the equilibrium relative commodity price of P_E.

In the left panel of Figure 4-4, Nation 2 is the small nation and we *magnified* the portion of the offer curve of nation 1 (the large nation) near the origin (where nation 1's offer curve coincides with P_1, the pretrade relative commodity price in Nation 1). The equilibrium volume of trade is given by point E and trade takes place at P_1. Thus, Nation 2 is a price taker and captures all of the benefits from trade. The same would be true even if Nation 2 were not a small nation, as long as Nation 1 faced constant opportunity costs and did not specialize completely in the production of commodity X with trade. However, as pointed out in section 3.2, constant opportunity costs are not very realistic.

In the unlikely event that both nations faced constant costs, the offer curves of both would be straight lines until both nations became completely specialized in production. Afterwards, offer curves would assume their normal shape and determine the equilibrium relative commodity price where they crossed. This is shown in the right panel of Figure 4-4, where the equilibrium relative commodity price is P_E and is determined by the intersection of the two nations' offer curves at point E.

4.5 The Terms of Trade

In this section, we define the terms of trade of each nation and illustrate their measurement. We also discuss the meaning of a change in a nation's terms of trade.

4.5a   Definition and Measurement of the Terms of Trade

The **terms of trade** of a nation are defined as the ratio of the price of its export commodity to the price of its import commodity. Since in a two-nation world, the exports of a nation are the imports of its trade partner, the terms of trade of the latter are equal to the inverse, or reciprocal, of the terms of trade of the former.

In a world of many (rather than just two) traded commodities, the terms of trade of a nation are given by the ratio of the price *index* of its exports to the price *index* of its imports. This ratio is usually multiplied by 100 in order to express the terms of trade in percentages. These terms of trade are often referred to as the **commodity or net barter terms of trade** to distinguish them from other measures of the terms of trade presented in Chapter 11 in connection with trade and development.

As supply and demand considerations change over time, offer curves will shift, changing the volume and the terms of trade. An improvement in a nation's terms of trade is usually regarded as beneficial to the nation *in the sense* that the prices that the nation receives for its exports rise relative to the prices that it pays for imports.

4.5b   Illustration of the Terms of Trade

Since Nation 1 exports commodity X and imports commodity Y, the terms of trade of Nation 1 are given by P_X/P_Y. From Figure 4-3, these are $P_X/P_Y = P_B = 1$ or 100 (in percentages). If Nation 1 exported and imported many commodities, P_X would be the *index* of its export prices and P_Y would be the *index* of its import prices.

Since Nation 2 exports commodity Y and imports commodity X, the terms of trade of Nation 2 are given by P_Y/P_X. Note that this is the inverse, or reciprocal, of Nation 1's terms of trade and also equals 1 or 100 (in percentages) in this case.

If through time, the terms of trade of Nation 1 rise, say, from 100 to 120, this means that Nation 1's export prices rose 20 percent in relation to its import prices. This would also mean that the terms of trade of Nation 2 have deteriorated from 100 to (100/120)100 = 83. Note that we can always set a nation's terms of trade equal to 100 in the base period, so that changes in its terms of trade over time can be measured in percentages.

Even if Nation 1's terms of trade improve over time, we cannot conclude that Nation 1 is *necessarily* better off because of this, or that Nation 2 is necessarily worse off because of the deterioration in its terms of trade. Changes in a nation's terms of trade are the result of many forces at work both in that nation and in the rest of the world, and we cannot determine their net effect on the nation's welfare by simply looking at the change in its terms of trade. To answer this question, we need more information and analysis, but we will postpone this until Chapter 11.

4.6 Extension and Evaluation of Our Trade Model

We now examine what our model has accomplished, how the model can be extended, and some remaining apparent shortcomings.

4.6a Usefulness of the Model

The trade model presented thus far summarizes clearly and concisely a remarkable amount of useful information and analysis. It shows the conditions of production, or supply, in the two nations, the tastes, or demand prefer-

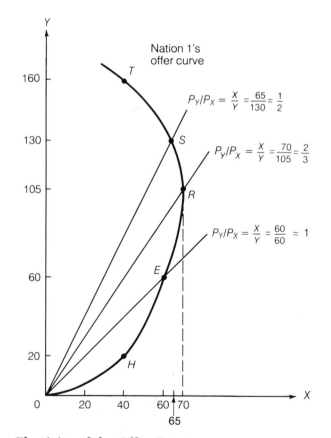

FIGURE 4-5. Elasticity of the Offer Curve

Nation 1's offer curve is elastic up to point R because as P_Y/P_X falls to $\frac{2}{3}$, Nation 1's expenditures on imports of commodity Y increase in terms of the quantity of its exports of commodity X. Nation 1's offer curve is inelastic past point R because as P_Y/P_X falls below $\frac{2}{3}$, Nation 1's expenditures on imports of commodity Y decline in terms of its exports of commodity X. Nation 1's offer curve is unitary elastic at point R (i.e., where the offer curve is vertical) because at $P_Y/P_X = \frac{2}{3}$, Nation 1's expenditures on imports of commodity Y are maximum in terms of its exports of commodity X.

ences, the autarky point of production and consumption, the equilibrium relative commodity price in the absence of trade, and the comparative advantage of each nation (refer to Figure 3-3). It also shows the degree of specialization in production with trade, the volume of trade, the terms of trade, the gains from trade, and the share of these gains going to each nation (see Figures 3-4 and 4-3).

The shape of the nation's offer curve also tells us whether it is elastic or not at various points. This is illustrated with Figure 4-5, which shows Nation 1's offer curve as backward bending past point R. (This offer curve is simply an extension of the offer curve of Nation 1 in Figures 4-1 and 4-3, and it will actually be derived in section A4.3 in the appendix.)

Up to point R, Nation 1's offer curve is elastic because, as P_Y/P_X falls to ⅔, Nation 1's expenditures on imports of commodity Y increase *in terms of its exports of commodity X*. Nation 1's offer curve is inelastic past point R because, as P_Y/P_X falls below ⅔, Nation 1's expenditures on imports of commodity Y decline in terms of its exports of commodity X. Nation 1's offer curve is unitary elastic at point R (i.e., where the offer curve is vertical) because at $P_Y/P_X = ⅔$, Nation 1's expenditures on imports of commodity Y are maximum in terms of its exports of commodity X. (Review the relationship between price, elasticity, and total expenditures from your principles text.)

Thus, Nation 1's offer curve is elastic over its positively inclined portion, inelastic over its backward bending portion, and unitary elastic at the point where it is vertical. Similarly, Nation 2's offer curve (not shown in the figure) is elastic over its positively inclined portion, becomes unitary elastic at its highest point (i.e., where it has zero slope or is horizontal), and then becomes inelastic when it bends downward (i.e., when it becomes negatively inclined).

4.6b Extension of the Model

Our trade model can easily be extended to analyze changes in tastes, technology, and factor endowments over time. While these topics are examined in detail in Chapter 7, dealing with economic growth and international trade, it is useful at this point briefly to anticipate that discussion to gain greater familiarity with offer curves as tools of analysis and to highlight the effect of changes in the economic forces represented by offer curves.

If a nation's tastes change and desire for its import commodity increases, the nation's offer curve will rotate closer to the axis measuring the commodity of its comparative advantage. The reason for this is that the nation is now willing to give up more of its export commodity in exchange for any given amount of the imported commodity because of its increased desire for the imported commodity. This results in an expanded volume of trade but in a deterioration in the nation's terms of trade. This is illustrated with Figure 4-6.

In Figure 4-6, Nation 1's terms of trade deteriorate from $P_X/P_Y = 1$ at point E_1 to $P_X/P_Y = ½$ at point E_2 and the volume of trade increases after Nation 1's

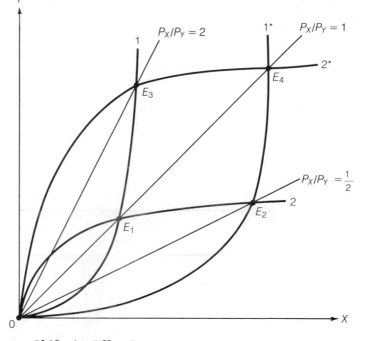

FIGURE 4-6. Shifts in Offer Curves

An increase in Nation 1's desire for its import commodity Y (or an improvement in its technology or availability of resources) that rotates its offer curve from 1 to 1* will cause Nation 1's terms of trade to deteriorate from $P_X/P_Y=1$ to $P_X/P_Y=\frac{1}{2}$ and the volume of trade to increase. Similarly, an increase in Nation 2's desire for its import commodity X that rotates its offer curve from 2 to 2* will cause Nation 2's terms of trade to deteriorate from $P_Y/P_X=1$ to $P_Y/P_X=\frac{1}{2}$ (the inverse of $P_X/P_Y=2$) and the volume of trade to increase. With offer curves 1 and 2 rotating to 1* and 2*, respectively, the terms of trade of each nation remain unchanged at $P_X/P_Y=P_Y/P_X=1$, and the volume of trade will greatly expand.

offer curve shifts (rotates) from 1 to 1* as a result of its increased desire for its imported commodity Y. The same could be true if an improvement in technology or an increase in resources shifted Nation 1's offer curve to 1*.

Similarly, an increase in Nation 2's desire for imports of commodity X, an improvement in its technology, or increased availability of resources over time will rotate Nation 2's offer curve upward (counter-clockwise). This will result in a deterioration in Nation 2's terms of trade and an expansion of trade. For example, if Nation 2's offer curve rotates from 2 to 2* while assuming no change in Nation 1, then Nation 2's terms of trade deteriorate from $P_Y/P_X=1$ at point E_1 to $P_Y/P_X=\frac{1}{2}$ (the inverse, or reciprocal, of $P_X/P_Y=2$) at point E_3 and the volume of trade expands.

If the offer curves of Nation 1 and Nation 2 rotate to 1* and 2*, respectively, the terms of trade of the two nations remain unchanged at $P_X/P_Y = P_Y/P_X = 1$ at point E_4, and the volume of trade will greatly expand (see Figure 4-6). Of course, with shifts of different sizes in the two nations' offer curves, the terms of trade of the two nations will be different.

A reduction in a nation's desire for its import commodity or in its resources over time will rotate the nation's offer curve in the opposite direction from that indicated above and result in opposite changes in the volume and the terms of trade (see problem 6, with answer provided at the end of the text).

4.6c   Some Apparent Shortcomings of the Model

Our trade model is a complete **general equilibrium model** except for the fact that it deals with only two nations (Nation 1 and Nation 2), two commodities (X and Y), and two factors (labor and capital). The real world is much more complex than that, including as it does over 150 nations, thousands of commodities, and hundreds of different resources or factors of production.

However, the purpose of theory is to simplify and generalize. A good theory abstracts from numerous details and isolates the few most important determinants or explanations of an economic event, with a view to predicting and eventually controlling economic phenomena. Thus, our simple trade model seems to do admirably well (pending its further theoretical extension and empirical verification, undertaken in Chapters 5 and 6).

A somewhat more valid shortcoming of our trade model is the fact that offer curves cannot be easily derived *in the real world*. They can be derived in the real world only by analyzing the interaction of all the intricate production and consumption relationships within and among nations. To a large extent, offer curves thus represent the *final result of a very complex set of forces which are extremely difficult to analyze and evaluate*. It is often (and justifiably) said that guessing the shape of offer curves and reading off the results means jumping to the final conclusion of a very complicated process without analyzing it.

While this shortcoming of offer curves is certainly valid, it must be remembered that they are not absolutely essential to our trade model. Indeed, we were able to find the equilibrium volume of trade and the terms of trade in Chapter 3 (Figure 3-4) by trial and error and without the use of offer curves. Furthermore, the fact that offer curves cannot be derived easily, or cannot be derived at all, in the real world does not eliminate their pedagogical value in defining the equilibrium volume of trade and terms of trade. We will find offer curves useful in the analysis of growth in Chapter 7, and for the analysis of the welfare effects of tariffs in Chapter 8. Finally, the appendix will examine some of the relationships between offer curves and the usual demand and supply curves for imports and exports (from which offer curves would have to be derived).

Our trade model (at least as developed up to now) has two other apparent shortcomings: it does not explicitly isolate the basis for comparative advantage, nor does it indicate the effect of trade on the returns, or earnings, of the various resources or factors of production. That is, comparative advantage simply resulted from and was reflected in the difference in the autarky relative commodity prices in the two nations, without anything being said explicitly as to which of the numerous production or demand considerations was primarily responsible for it. Similarly, practically nothing was or could be said about the effect of specialization in production and trade on the absolute and relative earnings of the various factors of production in each nation.

Fortunately, these disadvantages can and will be overcome by further extending our trade model, following the work of Heckscher and Ohlin. This is done in the next chapter.

Summary

1. In this chapter, we derived the offer curves of two nations and used them to determine the equilibrium volume of trade and the equilibrium relative commodity price at which trade takes place between them. The results obtained here confirm those reached in Chapter 3 by a process of trial and error.

2. The offer curve of a nation shows how much of its import commodity the nation demands to be willing to supply various amounts of its export commodity. The offer curve of a nation can be derived from its production frontier, its indifference map, and the various relative commodity prices at which trade could take place. A more formal derivation of offer curves is presented in the appendix.

3. The offer curve of each nation bends toward the axis measuring the commodity of its comparative advantage. The offer curves of two nations will lie between their pretrade, or autarky, relative commodity prices. To induce a nation to export more of a commodity, the relative price of the commodity must rise. The reason for this is that the nation incurs increasing opportunity costs in producing more of its export commodity, while it receives diminishing satisfaction from each additional unit of the commodity it imports.

4. The intersection of the offer curves of two nations defines the equilibrium relative commodity price at which trade takes place between them. Only at this equilibrium price will trade be balanced. At any other relative commodity price, the desired quantities of imports and exports of the two commodities would not be equal. This would put pressure on the relative commodity price to move toward its equilibrium level. However, if one nation is very small, or its trade partner faces constant costs, trade will take place at the autarky relative commodity price of the trade partner, and the small or the other nation will capture all of the gains from trade.

5. The terms of trade of a nation are defined as the ratio of the price of its export commodity to the price of its import commodity. The terms of trade of the trade partner are then equal to the inverse, or reciprocal, of the terms of trade of the other nation. With more than two commodities traded, we use the index of export to import prices and multiply by 100 to express the terms of trade in percentages. Through time, offer curves shift and the terms of trade change. However, changes in a nation's welfare cannot be inferred by simply examining the change in its terms of trade.

6. From its shape, we can determine whether a nation's offer curve is elastic, inelastic, or unitary elastic at various points. Change in a nation's tastes, technology, or factor endowments over time can be analyzed in terms of shifts in the nation's offer curve. Such shifts will affect the volume and the terms of trade. Our trade model is a general equilibrium model except for the fact that it deals with only two nations, two commodities, and two factors. Offer curves are very difficult to derive in the real world, but they are not absolutely essential to our model.

A Look Ahead

In Chapter 5, we will extend our trade model in order to identify the single most important determinant of the difference in the pretrade relative commodity prices and comparative advantage among nations. This will also allow us to examine the effect that international trade has on the relative price and income of the various factors of production. Our trade model so extended is referred to as the Heckscher-Ohlin model. In Chapter 6, the Heckscher-Ohlin model will be empirically verified and extended.

Glossary

Offer curve   A curve that shows how much of its import commodity a nation demands to be willing to supply various amounts of its export commodity, or the willingness of the nation to import and export at various relative commodity prices.

Reciprocal demand curve   Another name for the offer curve.

Terms of trade   The ratio of the price of a nation's export commodity to the price of its import commodity. With more than two commodities traded, we use the index of export to import prices. The terms of trade are usually given in percentages.

Commodity or net barter terms of trade   A more precise name for the (commodity) terms of trade.

General equilibrium model   An economic model that studies the behavior of all producers, consumers, and traders simultaneously.

Questions for Review

1. What is the usefulness of offer curves? How are they related to the trade model of Figure 3-4?
2. What do offer curves show? How are they derived? What is their shape? What explains their shape?
3. How do offer curves define the equilibrium relative commodity price at which trade takes place? Why couldn't any other relative commodity price persist? What are the forces that would push any non-equilibrium relative commodity price toward the equilibrium level?
4. What do the terms of trade measure? What is the relationship between the terms of trade in a world of two trading nations? How are the terms of trade measured in a world of more than two traded commodities? What does an improvement in a nation's terms of trade mean? What effect does this have on the nation's welfare?
5. Under what conditions will trade take place at the pretrade relative commodity price in one of the nations? How does the shape of a nation's offer curve determine whether it is elastic, inelastic, or unitary elastic at various points? How does a change in tastes, technology, or the availability of resources affect the nation's offer curve?
6. In what way does our trade model represent a general equilibrium model? In what way it does not? What is a shortcoming of offer curves? In what ways does our trade model require further extension?

Problems

1. Try to work this problem without looking at the text.
   (a) Derive a nation's offer curve from its production frontier, its indifference map, and two relative commodity prices at which trade could take place (i.e., sketch a figure similar to Figure 4-1).
   (b) Do the same for the trade partner (i.e., sketch a figure similar to Figure 4-2).
   (c) Bring together on another graph the offer curves that you derived in parts a and b, and determine the equilibrium relative commodity price at which trade would take place.
2. In what way is a nation's offer curve similar to:
   (a) a demand curve;
   (b) a supply curve?
   (c) In what way is the offer curve *different*

from the usual demand and supply curves? (Hint: remember what was measured along the vertical axis of the usual demand and supply curve diagrams and consider how this differs in drawing an offer curve. If you still cannot answer, see the sixth paragraph of section A4.3).

*3. Sketch a figure similar to Figure 4-3.
   (a) Extend the P_F price line and the offer curve of Nation 1 until they cross. (Let the offer curve of Nation 1 bend backward in extending it.)
   (b) Using the figure you sketched, explain the forces that push P_F toward P_B in terms of commodity Y.
   (c) What does the backward bending (negatively sloped) segment of Nation 1's offer curve indicate?

4. To show how nations can share unequally in the benefits from trade:
   (a) Sketch a figure showing the offer curve of a nation having a much greater curvature than the offer curve of its trade partner.
   (b) Which nation gains most from trade, the nation with the offer curve of greater or lesser curvature?
   (c) Can you explain why?

5. Suppose that the terms of trade of a nation improved from 100 to 110 over a given period of time.
   (a) By how much did the terms of trade of its trade partner deteriorate?
   (b) In what sense can this be said to be unfavorable to the trade partner? Does this mean that the welfare of the trade partner has definitely declined?

*6. Starting from the curves of Nation 1 and Nation 2 in Figure 4-3, show the effect of the following on the terms of trade of each nation and on the volume of trade:
   (a) a decrease in Nation 1's desire for imports of commodity Y;
   (b) a decrease in Nation 2's desire for imports of commodity X;
   (c) a decrease in each nation's desire for its import commodity in such a way as to leave the terms of trade of each nation unchanged.

APPENDIX————————————————

This appendix presents the formal derivation of offer curves, using a technique perfected by James Meade. In section A4.1, we derive a trade indifference curve for Nation 1, and in section A4.2, its trade indifference map. In section A4.3, Nation 1's offer curve is derived from its trade indifference map and various relative commodity prices at which trade could take place. Section A4.4 outlines the derivation of Nation 2's offer curve in relation to the Nation 1's offer curve. In section A4.5, we present the complete general equilibrium model showing production, consumption, and trade in both nations simultaneously. Finally, in section A4.6, we examine multiple and unstable equilibria.

A4.1   Derivation of a Trade Indifference Curve for Nation 1

The second (upper-left) quadrant of Figure 4-7 shows the familiar production frontier and community indifference curve I for Nation 1. The only difference between this and Figure 3-3 is that now the production frontier and commu-

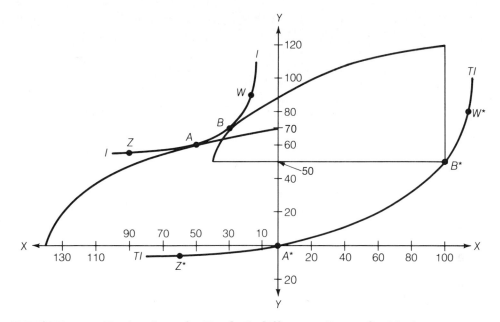

FIGURE 4-7.   Derivation of a Trade Indifference Curve for Nation 1

Trade indifference curve TI is derived by sliding Nation 1's production frontier, or block, along its indifference curve I so that the production block remains tangent to indifference curve I and the commodity axes are kept parallel at all times. As we do this, the *origin* of the production block will trace out TI. This shows the various *trade* situations that would keep Nation 1 at the same level of welfare as in the initial no-trade situation (given by point A on indifference curve I).

nity indifference curve I are in the second rather than the first quadrant, and quantities are measured from right to left instead of from left to right (the reason for this will become evident in a moment). As in Figure 3-3, Nation 1 is in equilibrium at point A in the absence of trade by producing and consuming 50X and 60Y.

Now let us slide Nation 1's production block, or frontier, along indifference curve I so that the production block remains tangent to indifference curve I and the commodity axes are kept parallel at all times. As we do this, the *origin* of the production block will trace out curve TI (see Figure 4-7). Point A* is derived from the tangency at A, point B* from the tangency at B, point W* from the tangency at W (not shown to keep the figure simple) and point Z* from the tangency at Z.

Curve TI is Nation 1's trade indifference curve corresponding to its indifference curve I. TI shows the various *trade* situations that would keep Nation 1 at the same level of welfare as in the initial no-trade situation. For example, Nation 1 is as well off at point A as at point B since both points A and B are on the same community indifference curve I. However, at point A, Nation 1 produces and consumes 50X and 60Y without trade. At point B, Nation 1 would produce 130X and 20Y (with reference to the origin at B^*) and consume 30X and 70Y (with reference to the origin at O or A^*) by exporting 100X in exchange for 50Y (see the figure).

Thus a **trade indifference curve** shows the various trade situations that provide a nation equal welfare. The level of welfare shown by a trade indifference curve is given by the community indifference curve from which the trade indifference curve is derived. Also note the slope of the trade indifference curve at any point is equal to the slope at the corresponding point on the commodity indifference curve from which the trade indifference curve is derived.

A4.2   Derivation of Nation 1's Trade Indifference Map

There is one trade indifference curve for each community indifference curve. Higher community indifference curves (reflecting greater national welfare) will give higher trade indifference curves. Thus a nation's *trade* indifference map can be derived from its indifference curve map.

Figure 4-8 shows the derivation of trade indifference curve TI from community indifference curve I (as in Figure 4-7), and the derivation of trade indifference curve TIII from community indifference curve III for Nation 1.

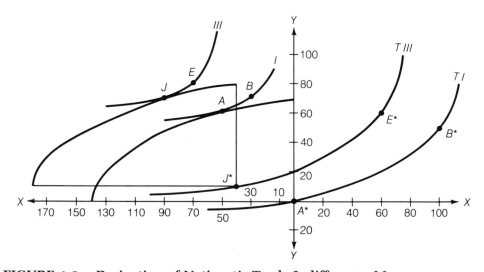

FIGURE 4-8.   Derivation of Nation 1's Trade Indifference Map

Trade indifference curve TI is derived from Nation 1's indifference curve I, as shown in Figure 4-7. Trade indifference curve TIII is similarly derived by sliding Nation 1's production block along its indifference curve III while keeping the axes always parallel. Higher community indifference curve III gives higher trade indifference curve TIII. For each indifference curve, we could derive the corresponding trade indifference curve and obtain the entire trade indifference map of Nation 1.

Note that community indifference curve III is the one shown in Figure 3-2. To reach community indifference curve III in Figure 4-8, the production block must be shifted up parallel to the axes until it is tangent to that community indifference curve. Thus, the tangency point *J* gives *J** on TIII. Tangency point *E* would give *E** on TIII, and so on.

Figure 4-8 shows only the derivation of TI and TIII (to keep the figure simple). However, for each indifference curve for Nation 1, we could derive the corresponding trade indifference curve and obtain the entire trade indifference map of Nation 1.

A4.3   Formal Derivation of Nation 1's Offer Curve

A nation's offer curve is the locus of tangencies of the relative commodity price lines at which trade could take place with the nation's trade indifference curves. The formal derivation of Nation 1's offer curve is shown in Figure 4-9.

In Figure 4-9, TI to TVI are Nation 1's trade indifference curves derived from its production block and community indifference curves, as illustrated in Figure 4-8. Lines P_A, P_F, P_B, $P_{F'}$, and $P_{A'}$ from the origin refer to relative prices of commodity X at which trade could take place (as in Figure 4-3).

Joining the origin with tangency points H, E, R, S, and T gives Nation 1's offer curve. This is the same offer curve that we derived with a simpler technique in Figure 4-1. The only difference is that now we have derived the top and backward bending portion of Nation 1's offer curve as well. As defined earlier, Nation 1's offer curve shows the amount of imports of commodity Y that Nation 1 demands to be willing to supply various amounts of commodity X for export. Note that the greater Nation 1's terms of trade are, the higher is the trade indifference curve reached and the greater Nation 1's welfare.

From Figure 4-9, we can see that as its terms of trade rise from $P_A = \frac{1}{4}$ to $P_M = 1\frac{1}{2}$, Nation 1 offers more and more exports of commodity X in exchange for more and more imports of commodity Y. At point R, Nation 1 offers the maximum amount of 70X for export. Past point R, Nation 1 will only export less and less of commodity X in exchange for more and more imports of commodity Y. The reason for the backward bend in Nation 1's offer curve past point R is generally the same as the reason (discussed in section 4.2b) that gives the offer curve its shape and curvature before the bend. Past point R, the opportunity cost of X has risen so much and the marginal utility or satisfaction from each additional unit of imported Y has fallen so much that Nation 1 is only willing to offer less and less of X for more and more of Y.

The shape of Nation 1's offer curve can also be explained in terms of the substitution and income effects on Nation 1's *home demand* for commodity X. As P_X/P_Y rises, Nation 1 tends to produce more of commodity X and demand less of it. As a result, Nation 1 has more of commodity X available for export. At the same time, as P_X/P_Y rises, the income of Nation 1 tends to rise

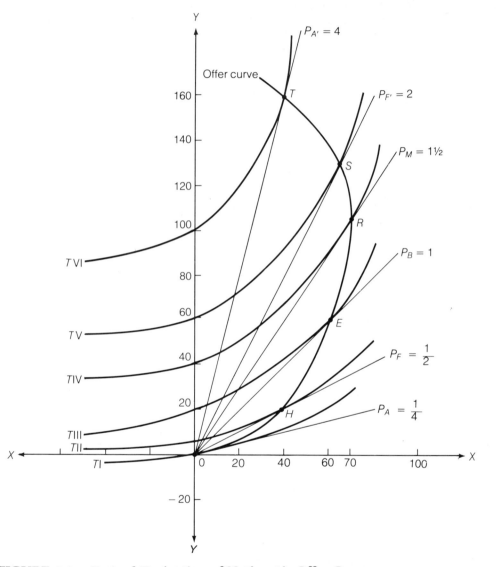

FIGURE 4-9.   Formal Derivation of Nation 1's Offer Curve

Curves TI to TVI are Nation 1's trade indifference curves derived from its production block and community indifference curves, as illustrated in Figure 4-8. Lines P_A, P_F, P_B, P_M, $P_{F'}$, and $P_{A'}$ from the origin refer to relative prices of commodity X at which trade could take place. Joining the origin with tangency points of price lines with trade indifference curves gives Nation 1's offer curve. This is elastic up to point R, unitary elastic at point R, and inelastic over its backward bending portion.

(because it exports commodity X), and when income rises, more of every normal good is demanded in Nation 1, including commodity X. Thus, by itself, the income effect tends to reduce the amount of commodity X available to Nation 1 for export, while the substitution effect tends to increase it. These effects operate simultaneously. Up to $P_X/P_Y = 1\frac{1}{2}$ (i.e., up to point R), the substitution effect overwhelms the opposite income effect, and Nation 1 supplies more of commodity X for export. At $P_X/P_Y > 1\frac{1}{2}$, the income effect overwhelms the opposite substitution effect, and Nation 1 supplies less of commodity X for export (i.e., Nation 1's offer curve bends backward).

Note that Nation 1's offer curve also represents its demand for imports of commodity Y, *not in terms of the price of imports (as along a usual demand curve), but in terms of total expenditures in terms of the nation's exports of commodity X*. As Nation 1's terms of trade rise (and P_Y/P_X falls) so that it demands more imported Y, its expenditures in terms of commodity X rise up to point R, reach the maximum at point R, and fall past R. Thus, the nation's offer curve is elastic up to point R, unitary elastic at point R, and inelastic past point R.

We can now understand (at least intuitively) why the nation with the weaker or less intense demand for the other nation's export commodity has an offer curve with a greater curvature (i.e., less elasticity) and gains more from trade than the nation with the stronger or more intense demand (refer to problem 4). This is sometimes referred to as the **law of reciprocal demand,** first expounded numerically by *Mill* (another British classical economist) and subsequently generalized and visualized with offer curves, or reciprocal demand curves.

Problem   Starting with Nation 1's offer curve, the more advanced student should attempt to sketch (a) Nation 1's demand curve for imports of commodity Y (with P_Y/P_X along the vertical axis), and (b) Nation 1's supply curve for exports of commodity X (with P_X/P_Y along the vertical axis).

A4.4   Outline of the Formal Derivation of Nation 2's Offer Curve

Nation 2's offer curve can be formally derived in a completely analogous way from its trade indifference map and the various relative commodity prices at which trade could take place. This is outlined in Figure 4-10 without repeating the entire process.

Quadrant 2 of Figure 4-10 shows Nation 1's production frontier, or block, and indifference curves I and III, while quadrant 4 shows the same things for Nation 2. Nation 2's production frontier and indifference curves are placed in quadrant 4 so that its offer curve will be derived in the proper relationship to Nation 1's offer curve in quadrant 1.

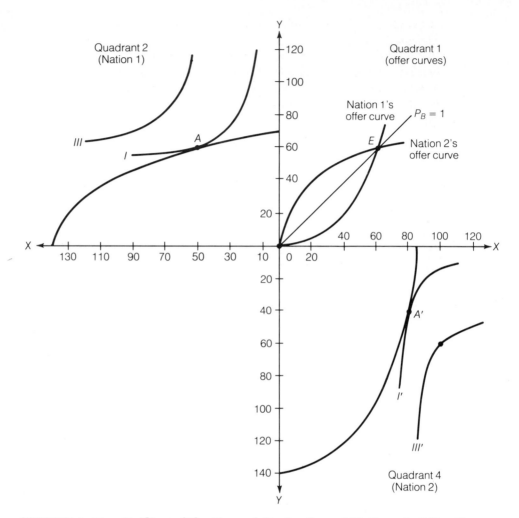

FIGURE 4-10.   Outline of the Formal Derivation of Nation 2's Offer Curve

Nation 2's offer curve can be formally derived from its trade indifference map and the various relative commodity prices at which trade could take place, as was done for Nation 1. This is simply outlined here without repeating the entire process. Thus, Nation 1's offer curve in quadrant 1 is derived from its production block and indifference curves in quadrant 2 and bends in the same direction as its indifference curves. Nation 2's offer curve in quadrant 1 could similarly be derived from its production block and indifference curves in quadrant 4 and bends in the same direction as its indifference curves.

Nation 1's offer curve in quadrant 1 of Figure 4-10 was derived from its trade indifference map in Figure 4-9. Note that Nation 1's offer curve bends in the same direction as its community indifference curves. In a completely analogous way, Nation 2's offer curve in quadrant 1 of Figure 4-10 can be derived from its trade indifference map and bends in the same direction as its community indifference curves in quadrant 4.

The offer curves of Nation 1 and Nation 2 in quadrant 1 of Figure 4-10 are the offer curves of Figure 4-3 and define the equilibrium relative commodity price of $P_B = 1$ at their intersection. As will be seen in the next section, only at point E does general equilibrium exist.

Problem Draw a figure showing Nation 2's trade indifference curves that would give its offer curve, including its backward bending portion.

A4.5 General Equilibrium of Production, Consumption, and Trade

Figure 4-11 brings together in one diagram all the information about production, consumption, and trade for the two nations in equilibrium. The production blocks of Nation 1 and Nation 2 are joined at point E^* (the same as point E in Figure 4-10), where the offer curves of the two nations cross.

With trade, Nation 1 produces 130X and 20Y (point E with reference to point E^*) and consumes 70X and 80Y (the same point E but with reference to the origin, O) by exchanging 60X for 60Y with Nation 2. On the other hand, Nation 2 produces 40X and 120Y (point E' with reference to point to E^*) and consumes 100X and 60Y (the same point E' but with reference to the origin) by exchanging 60Y for 60X with Nation 1.

International trade is in equilibrium with 60X exchanged for 60Y at $P_B = 1$. This is shown by the intersection of offer curves 1 and 2 at point E^*. $P_B = 1$ is also the relative commodity price of X prevailing *domestically* in Nations 1 and 2 (see the relative price line tangent to each nation's production blocks at points E and E', respectively). Thus, producers, consumers, and traders in both nations all respond to the same set of equilibrium relative commodity prices.

Note that point E on Nation 1's indifference curve III measures consumption in relation to the origin, O, while the same point E on Nation 1's production block measures production from point E^*. Finding Nation 1's indifference curve III tangent to its production block at point E seems different but is in fact entirely consistent and confirms the results of Figure 3-4 for Nation 1. The same is true for Nation 2.

Figure 4-11 summarizes and confirms all of our previous results and the conclusions of our trade model (compare, for example, Figure 4-11 with Figure 3-4). Thus, Figure 4-11 is a complete general equilibrium model (except for the fact that it deals with only two nations and two commodities). The figure is admittedly complicated. But this is because it summarizes in a single graph a tremendous amount of very useful information. Figure 4-11 is the pinnacle of the neoclassical trade model. The rewards of mastering it are great indeed in terms of future deeper understanding.

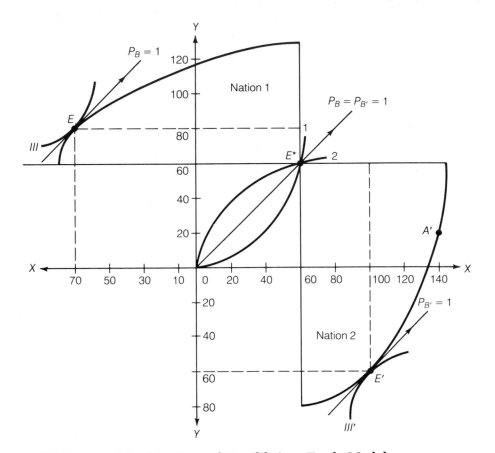

FIGURE 4-11.   Meade's General Equilibrium Trade Model

The production blocks of Nations 1 and 2 are joined at point E^* (the same as point E in Figure 4-10), where the offer curves of the two nations cross. With trade, Nation 1 produces 130X and 20Y (point E with reference to point E^*) and consumes 70X and 80Y (the same point E but with reference to the origin) by exchanging 60X for 60Y with Nation 2. On the other hand, Nation 2 produces 40X and 120Y and consumes 100X and 60Y by exchanging 60Y for 60X with Nation 1. International trade is in equilibrium at point E^*. $P_B=1$ is the equilibrium relative commodity price prevailing in international trade and domestically in each nation.

A4.6   Multiple and Unstable Equilibria

In Figure 4-12, offer curve 1 and offer curve 2 intersect at three points (A, B, and C) where at least one of the offer curves is inelastic. Equilibrium points B and C are stable, while equilibrium point A is unstable. The reason is that a small displacement from point A will give rise to economic forces that will

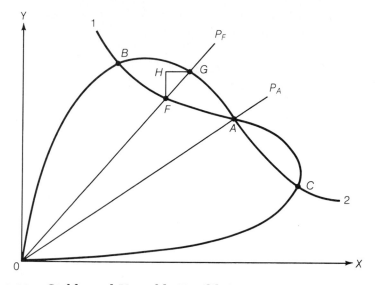

FIGURE 4-12. Stable and Unstable Equilibria

Equilibrium point *A* is unstable because any displacement from it will give rise to economic forces that will automatically move the nations even farther away from it and toward either point *B* or point *C*. For example, at P_F, Nation 2 demands *GH* more of commodity X than Nation 1 is willing to export at that price. At the same time, Nation 1 demands *FH* less of commodity Y than Nation 2 wants to export at P_F. For both reasons, P_X/P_Y will rise until point *B* is reached. Any small displacement away from point *B* will push the nations back to point *B*. On the other hand, if P_X/P_Y falls below P_A, the nations will be pushed toward stable equilibrium point *C*.

automatically shift the equilibrium point farther away from *A* and toward either *B* or *C*.

For example, at P_F, Nation 2 will demand *GH* more of commodity X than Nation 1 is willing to export at that price. At the same time, Nation 1 will demand *FH* less of commodity Y than Nation 2 wants to export at P_F. For both reasons, P_X/P_Y will rise until point *B* is reached. Past point *B*, Nation 1 will demand more of commodity Y than Nation 2 is willing to offer, and Nation 2 will demand less of commodity X than Nation 1 wants to export, so that P_X/P_Y will fall until the nations have moved back to point *B*. Thus, point *B* is a point of stable equilibrium.

On the other hand, if for whatever reason P_X/P_Y falls below P_A (see Figure 4-12), automatic forces will come into play that will push the nations to equilibrium point *C*, which is also a point of stable equilibrium.

Problem   Draw two relative commodity price lines on Figure 4-12, one between point *A* and point *C* and one intersecting both offer curves to the right of point *C*. Starting from each of the two price lines that you have drawn, explain the forces that will automatically push the nations toward equilibrium point C.

Selected Bibliography

For a problem-solving approach to the material covered in this chapter, see:
- D. Salvatore, *Theory and Problems of International Economics,* 2nd ed. (New York: McGraw-Hill, 1984), ch. 3 (sects. 3.3 to 3.6).

An excellent discussion of offer curves is found in:
- G. Haberler, *The Theory of International Trade* (London: W. Hodge and Co., 1936), ch. 11.
- J. Viner, *Studies in the Theory of International Trade* (New York: Harper and Brothers, 1937), ch. 9.
- A. P. Lerner, "The Diagrammatic Representation of Demand Conditions in International Trade," *Economica,* 1934. Reprinted in A. P. Lerner, *Essays in Economic Analysis* (London: Macmillan, 1953).

For the formal derivation of offer curves perfected by Meade and presented in the appendix to this chapter, see:
- J. E. Meade, *A Geometry of International Trade* (London: George Allen and Unwin, 1952), chs. 1–4.

CHAPTER 5

Factor Endowments and Heckscher-Ohlin Theory

5.1 Introduction

In this chapter, we extend our trade model in two important directions. First, we explain the basis of (i.e., what determines) comparative advantage. That is, we have seen in previous chapters that the difference in relative commodity prices between two nations is evidence of their comparative advantage and the basis for mutually beneficial trade. We now go one step further and explain the reason, or cause, for the difference in relative commodity prices and comparative advantage between the two nations. The second way we extend our trade model is to analyze the effect that international trade has on the earnings of factors of production in the two trading nations. That is, we want to examine the effect of international trade on the earnings of labor as well as on international differences in earnings.

These two important questions were left largely unanswered by Smith, Ricardo, and Mill. According to classical economists, comparative advantage was based on the difference in the *productivity of labor* (the only factor of production they explicitly considered) among nations, but they provided no explanation for such a difference in productivity, except for possible differences in climate. The Heckscher-Ohlin theory goes much beyond that by extending the trade model of the previous two chapters to examine the basis for comparative advantage and the effect that trade has on factor earnings in the two nations.

Section 5.2 deals with the assumptions of the theory. Section 5.3 clarifies the meaning of factor intensity and factor abundance, and explains how the latter is related to factor prices and the shape of the production frontier in each nation. Section 5.4 presents the Heckscher-Ohlin model proper and illustrates it graphically. Section 5.5 examines the effect of international trade on factor earnings and income distribution in the two nations. Section 5.6 concludes the chapter by briefly examining the general equilibrium nature of the complete trade model. The appendix to the chapter presents the formal derivation of the factor-price equalization theorem.

5.2   Assumptions of the Theory

The Heckscher-Ohlin theory is based on a number of simplifying assumptions (some made only implicitly by Heckscher and Ohlin). Rather than note these assumptions along the way as they are needed in the analysis, it is both logical and convenient to present them together and explain their meaning at this point. This will not only allow us to view the theory to be presented in a better perspective but will also make the presentation smoother and more direct. To make the theory more realistic, we will relax these assumptions in the next chapter and examine the effect that such relaxation has on the conclusions reached in this chapter.

5.2a   The Assumptions

The Heckscher-Ohlin theory is based on the following assumptions:

1. There are two nations (Nation 1 and Nation 2), two commodities (commodity X and commodity Y), and two factors of production (labor and capital).
2. Both nations use the same technology in production.
3. Commodity X is labor intensive and commodity Y is capital intensive in both nations.
4. Constant returns to scale in the production of both commodities in both nations.
5. Incomplete specialization in production in both nations.
6. Equal tastes in both nations.
7. Perfect competition in both commodities and factor markets in both nations.
8. Perfect factor mobility within each nation but no international factor mobility.
9. No transportation costs, tariffs, or other obstructions to the free flow of international trade.

5.2b Meaning of the Assumptions

The meaning of assumption 1 (two nations, two commodities, and two factors) is clear, and it is made in order to be able to illustrate the theory with a two-dimensional figure. This assumption is made with the knowledge (discussed in the next chapter) that its relaxation (so as to deal with the more realistic case of more than two nations, more than two commodities, and more than two factors) will leave the conclusions of the theory basically unchanged.

Assumption 2 (that both nations use the **same technology**) means that both nations have access to and use the same general production techniques. That is, if factor prices were the same in both nations, producers in both nations would use exactly the same amount of labor and capital in the production of each commodity. Since factor prices usually differ, producers in each nation will use more of the relatively cheaper factor in the nation to minimize their costs of production.

Assumption 3 (that commodity X is **labor intensive** and commodity Y is **capital intensive**) means that commodity X requires relatively more labor to produce than commodity Y in both nations. In a more technical and precise way, this means that the **labor-capital ratio** (L/K) is higher for commodity X than for commodity Y in both nations at the same relative factor prices. This is equivalent to saying that the **capital-labor ratio** (K/L) is *lower for X than for Y*. But it does not mean that the K/L ratio for X is the same in Nation 1 and Nation 2, only that K/L is lower for X than for Y in both nations. This point is so important that we will use section 5.3a to clarify it.

Assumption 4 (**constant returns to scale** in the production of both commodities in both nations) means that increasing the amount of labor and capital used in the production of any commodity will increase output of that commodity in the same proportion. For example, if Nation 1 increases by 10 percent both the amount of labor and the amount of capital that it uses in the production of commodity X, its output of commodity X will also increase by 10 percent. If it doubles the amount of both labor and capital used, its output of X will also double. The same is true for commodity Y and in Nation 2.

Assumption 5 (incomplete specialization in production in both nations) means that even with free trade both nations continue to produce both commodities. This implies that neither of the two nations is "very small."

Assumption 6 (equal tastes in both nations) means that demand preferences, as reflected in the shape and location of indifference curves, are identical in both nations. Thus, when relative commodity prices are equal in the two nations (as, for example, with free trade), both nations will consume X and Y in the same proportion. This will be illustrated in section 5.3c.

Assumption 7 (**perfect competition** in both commodities and factor markets) means that producers, consumers, and traders of commodity X and commodity Y in both nations are each too small to affect the price of these commodities. The same is true for each user and supplier of labor time and capital. Perfect competition also means that, in the long run, commodity prices equal their costs of production, leaving no (economic) profit after all costs (including implicit costs) are taken into account. Finally, perfect competition means that all producers, consumers, and owners of factors of production have perfect knowledge of commodity prices and factor earnings in all parts of the nation and in all industries.

Assumption 8 (perfect **internal factor mobility** but no international factor mobility) means that labor and capital are free to move, and indeed do move quickly, from areas and industries of lower earnings to areas and industries of higher earnings until earnings for the same type of labor and capital are the same in all areas, uses, and industries of the nation. On the other hand, there is zero **international factor mobility** (i.e., no mobility of factors among nations), so that international differences in factor earnings would persist indefinitely in the absence of international trade.

Assumption 9 (no transportation costs, tariffs, or other obstructions to the free flow of international trade) means that specialization in production proceeds until relative (and absolute) commodity prices are the same in both nations with trade. If we allowed for transportation costs and tariffs, specialization would proceed only until relative (and absolute) commodity prices differed by no more than the costs of transportation and the tariff on each unit of the commodity traded.

5.3   Factor Intensity, Factor Abundance, and the Shape of the Production Frontier

Since the Heckscher-Ohlin theory to be presented in section 5.4 is expressed in terms of factor intensity and factor abundance, it is crucial that the meaning of these terms be very clear and precise. Hence, the meaning of factor intensity is explained and illustrated in section 5.3a. In section 5.3b, we examine the meaning of factor abundance and its relationship to factor prices. Finally, in section 5.3c, we examine the relationship between factor abundance and the shape of the production frontier of each nation.

5.3a   Factor Intensity

In a world of two commodities (X and Y) and two factors (labor and capital), we say that commodity Y is *capital intensive* if the capital-labor ratio (K/L) used in the production of Y is greater than K/L used in the production of X.

For example, if two units of capital ($2K$) and two units of labor ($2L$) are required to produce one unit of commodity Y, the capital-labor ratio is one. That is, $K/L = 2/2 = 1$ in the production of Y. If at the same time $1K$ and $4L$ are required to produce one unit of X, $K/L = 1/4$ for commodity X. Since $K/L = 1$ for Y and $K/L = 1/4$ for X, we say that Y is K intensive and X is L intensive.

Note that it is not the *absolute* amount of capital and labor used in the production of commodities X and Y that is important in measuring the capital and labor intensity of the two commodities, but the amount of capital *per unit of labor* (i.e., K/L). For example, suppose that 3K and 12L (instead of 1K and 4L) are required to produce 1X, while to produce 1Y requires 2K and 2L (as indicated earlier). Even though to produce 1X requires 3K while to produce 1Y requires only 2K, commodity Y would still be the K-intensive commodity because K/L is higher for Y than for X. That is, K/L = 2/2 = 1 for Y, but K/L = 3/12 = 1/4 for X.

If we plotted capital (K) along the vertical axis of a graph and labor (L) along the horizontal axis, and production took place along a straight-line ray from the origin, the slope of the line would measure the capital-labor ratio (K/L) in the production of the commodity. This is shown in Figure 5-1.

Figure 5-1 shows that Nation 1 can produce 1Y with 2K and 2L. With 4K and 4L, Nation 1 can produce 2Y because of constant returns to scale (assumption 4). Thus, K/L = 2/2 = 4/4 = 1 for Y. This is given by the slope of 1 for the ray from the origin for commodity Y in Nation 1 (see the figure). On the other hand, 1K and 4L are required to produce 1X, and 2K and 8L to produce

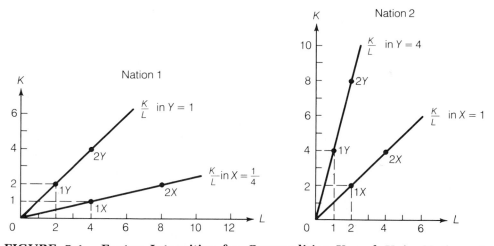

FIGURE 5-1.   Factor Intensities for Commodities X and Y in Nations 1 and 2

In Nation 1, the capital-labor ratio (K/L) equals 1 for commodity Y and K/L = 1/4 for commodity X. These are given by the slope of the ray from the origin for each commodity in Nation 1. Thus, commodity Y is the K-intensive commodity in Nation 1. In Nation 2, K/L = 4 for Y and K/L = 1 for X. Thus, commodity Y is the K-intensive and commodity X is the L-intensive commodity in both nations. Nation 2 uses a higher K/L than Nation 1 in the production of both commodities because the relative price of capital (r/w) is lower in Nation 2. If r/w declined, producers would substitute K for L in the production of both commodities to minimize their costs of production. As a result, K/L would rise for both commodities.

2X, in Nation 1. Thus $K/L = 1/4$ for X in Nation 1. This is given by the slope of 1/4 for the ray from the origin for commodity X in Nation 1. Since K/L, or the slope of the ray from the origin, is higher for commodity Y than for commodity X, we say that commodity Y is K intensive and commodity X is L intensive in Nation 1.

In Nation 2, K/L (or the slope of the ray) is 4 for Y and 1 for X (see Figure 5-1). Therefore, Y is the K-intensive commodity and X is the L-intensive commodity in Nation 2 also. This is illustrated by the fact that the ray from the origin for commodity Y is steeper (i.e., has a greater slope) than the ray for commodity X in both nations.

Even though commodity Y is K intensive in relation to commodity X in both nations, *Nation 2 uses a higher K/L in producing both Y and X than Nation 1.* For Y, $K/L = 4$ in Nation 2 but $K/L = 1$ in Nation 1. For X, $K/L = 1$ in Nation 2 but $K/L = 1/4$ in Nation 1. The obvious question is why does Nation 2 use more K-intensive production techniques in both commodities than Nation 1? The answer is that capital must be relatively cheaper in Nation 2 than in Nation 1, so that producers in Nation 2 use relatively more capital in the production of both commodities to minimize their costs of production. But why is capital relatively cheaper in Nation 2? To answer this question, we must define factor abundance and examine its relationship to factor prices.

Before doing this, however, we must settle one other related point of crucial importance. This refers to what happens if, for whatever reason, the relative price of capital falls. Producers would substitute capital for labor in the production of both commodities to minimize their costs of production. As a result, both commodities would become more K intensive. However, only if K/L in the production of commodity Y exceeds K/L in the production of commodity X *at all possible relative factor prices* can we say *unequivocally* that commodity Y is the K-intensive commodity. This is basically an empirical question and will be explored in the next chapter. For now, we will assume that this is true (i.e., that commodity Y remains the K-intensive commodity at all possible relative factor prices.

To summarize, we say that commodity Y is unequivocally the K-intensive commodity if K/L is higher for commodity Y than for commodity X at all possible relative factor prices. Nation 2 uses a higher K/L in the production of both commodities because the relative price of capital is lower in Nation 2 than in Nation 1. If the relative price of capital declines, producers will substitute K for L in the production of both commodities to minimize their costs of production. Thus, K/L will rise for both commodities, but Y continues to be the K-intensive commodity.

5.3b   Factor Abundance

There are two ways to define **factor abundance.** One way is in terms of *physical units* (i.e., in terms of the overall amount of capital and labor available to each nation). Another way to define factor abundance is in terms of **relative**

factor prices (i.e., in terms of the rental price of capital and the price of labor time in each nation).

According to the definition in terms of physical units, Nation 2 is capital abundant if the ratio of the total amount of capital to the total amount of labor (TK/TL) available in Nation 2 is *greater* than that in Nation 1 (i.e., if TK/TL for Nation 2 exceeds TK/TL for Nation 1). Note that it is not the absolute amount of capital and labor available in each nation that is important but the *ratio* of the total amount of capital to the total amount of labor. Thus, Nation 2 can have less capital than Nation 1 and still be the capital-abundant nation if TK/TL in Nation 2 exceeds TK/TL in Nation 1.

According to the definition in terms of factor prices, Nation 2 is capital abundant if the ratio of the rental price of capital to the price of labor time (P_K/P_L) is *lower* in Nation 2 than in Nation 1 (i.e., if P_K/P_L in Nation 2 is smaller than P_K/P_L in Nation 1). Since the rental price of capital is usually taken to be the interest rate (r) while the price of labor time is the wage rate (w), $P_K/P_L = r/w$. Once again, it is not the absolute level of r that determines whether or not a nation is the K-abundant nation but r/w. For example, r may be higher in Nation 2 than in Nation 1, but Nation 2 will still be the K-abundant nation if r/w is lower there than in Nation 1.

The relationship between the two definitions of factor abundance is clear. The definition of factor abundance in terms of physical units considers only the supply of factors. The definition in terms of relative factor prices considers both demand and supply (since we know from principles of economics that the price of a commodity or factor is determined by both demand and supply considerations under perfect competition). Also from principles of economics, we know that the demand for a factor of production is a **derived demand**—derived from the demand for the final commodity that requires the factor in its production.

Since we have assumed that tastes, or demand preferences, are the same in both nations, the two definitions of factor abundance give the same conclusions in our case. That is, with TK/TL larger in Nation 2 than in Nation 1 in the face of equal demand conditions (and technology), P_K/P_L will be smaller in Nation 2. Thus, Nation 2 is the K-abundant nation in terms of both definitions.

This is not always the case. For example, it is conceivable that the demand for commodity Y (the K-intensive commodity) and therefore the demand for capital could be so much higher in Nation 2 than in Nation 1 (despite the relatively greater supply of capital in Nation 2). In that case, Nation 2 would be considered K abundant according to the definition in physical terms and L abundant according to the definition in terms of relative factor prices.

In such situations, it is the definition in terms of relative factor prices that should be used. That is, a nation is K abundant if the relative price of capital is lower in it than in the other nation. In our case, there is no such contradiction between the two definitions. Nation 2 is K abundant and Nation 1 is L abundant in terms of both definitions. We will assume this to be the case throughout the rest of the chapter, unless otherwise explicitly indicated.

5.3c   Factor Abundance and the Shape of the Production Frontier

Since Nation 2 is the *K*-abundant nation and commodity Y is the *K*-intensive commodity, Nation 2 can produce *relatively* more of commodity Y than Nation 1. On the other hand, since Nation 1 is the *L*-abundant nation and commodity X is the *L*-intensive commodity, Nation 1 can produce relatively more of commodity X than Nation 2. This gives a production frontier for Nation 1 that is relatively flatter and wider than the production frontier of Nation 2 (if we measure X along the horizontal axis).

In Figure 5-2, we plotted on the same set of axes the production frontiers of Nation 1 and Nation 2. (These are the same production frontiers introduced with Figure 3-1 and used throughout Chapters 3 and 4). Since Nation 1 is the *L*-abundant nation and commodity X is the *L*-intensive commodity, Nation 1's

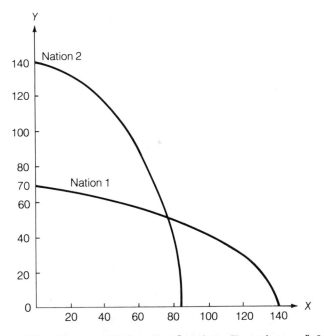

FIGURE 5-2.   The Shape of the Production Frontiers of Nation 1 and Nation 2

The production frontier of Nation 1 is flatter and wider than the production frontier of Nation 2, indicating that Nation 1 can produce relatively more of commodity X than Nation 2. The reason for this is that Nation 1 is the *L*-abundant nation and commodity X is the *L*-intensive commodity.

production frontier is skewed toward the horizontal axis measuring commodity X. On the other hand, since Nation 2 is the K-abundant nation and commodity Y is the K-intensive commodity, Nation 2's production frontier is skewed toward the vertical axis measuring commodity Y. The production frontiers are plotted on the same set of axes so that the difference in their shape is more clearly evident and because this will facilitate the illustration of the Heckscher-Ohlin model in section 5.4c.

Having clarified the meaning of factor intensity and factor abundance, we are now ready to present the Heckscher-Ohlin theory.

5.4 Factor Endowments and the Heckscher-Ohlin Theory

In 1919 *Eli Heckscher*, a Swedish economist, published an article entitled "The Effect of Foreign Trade on the Distribution of Income," in which he presented the outline of what was to become the "modern theory of international trade." The article went largely unnoticed for over ten years until *Bertil Ohlin*, another Swedish economist and former student of Heckscher, picked it up, built on it, clarified it, and in 1933 published his famous book *Interregional and International Trade*.

We will only discuss Ohlin's work since it incorporates all that Heckscher had said in his article and much more. However, since the essence of the model was first introduced by Heckscher, due credit is given to him by calling the theory the Heckscher-Ohlin theory. Ohlin, on his part, shared (with James Meade) the 1977 Nobel Prize in economics for his work in international trade.

The **Heckscher-Ohlin (H-O) theory** can be presented in a nutshell in the form of two theorems: the so-called *H-O theorem* (which deals with and predicts the pattern of trade) and the *factor-price equalization theorem* (which deals with the effect of international trade on factor prices). The factor-price equalization theorem will be discussed in section 5.5. In this section, we present and discuss the H-O theorem. We begin with the statement of the theorem and briefly explain its meaning. Then we examine the general equilibrium nature of the H-O theory, and finally we give a geometrical interpretation of the model.

5.4a The Heckscher-Ohlin Theorem

Starting with the assumptions presented in section 5.2, we can state the **Heckscher-Ohlin theorem** as follows: *A nation will export the commodity whose production requires the intensive use of the nation's relatively abundant and cheap factor and import the commodity whose production requires the intensive use of the nation's relatively scarce and expensive factor.* In short, the relatively labor-rich nation exports the relatively labor-intensive commodity and imports the relatively capital-intensive commodity.

In terms of our previous discussion, this means that Nation 1 exports commodity X because commodity X is the *L*-intensive commodity and *L* is the relatively abundant and cheap factor in Nation 1. On the other hand, Nation 2 exports commodity Y because commodity Y is the *K*-intensive commodity and *K* is the relatively abundant and cheap factor in Nation 2 (i.e., *r/w* is lower in Nation 2 than in Nation 1).

Of all the possible reasons for differences in relative commodity prices and comparative advantage among nations, the H-O theorem isolates the difference in relative factor abundance, or *factor endowments*, among nations as the basic cause or determinant of comparative advantage and international trade. For this reason, the H-O model is often referred to as the **factor-proportions** or **factor-endowment theory.** That is, each nation specializes in the production of and exports the commodity intensive in its relatively abundant and cheap factor and imports the commodity intensive in its relatively scarce and expensive factor.

Thus, the H-O theorem *explains* comparative advantage rather than assuming it (as was the case for classical economists). That is, the H-O theorem postulates that the difference in relative factor abundance and prices is the *cause* of the pretrade difference in relative commodity prices between two nations. This difference in *relative* factor and *relative* commodity prices is then translated into a difference in *absolute* factor and commodity prices between the two nations (as outlined in section 2.4d). It is this difference in absolute commodity prices between the two nations that is the *immediate* cause of trade.

5.4b   General Equilibrium Framework of the Heckscher-Ohlin Theory

The general equilibrium nature of the H-O theory can be visualized and summarized with the use of Figure 5-3. Starting at the lower right-hand corner of the diagram, we see that tastes and the distribution in the ownership of factors of production (i.e., the distribution of income) together determine the demand for commodities. The demand for commodities determines the derived demand for the factors required to produce them. The demand for factors of production together with the supply of the factors determines the price of factors of production under perfect competition. The price of factors of production, together with technology, determines the price of final commodities. The difference in relative commodity prices between nations determines comparative advantage and the pattern of trade (i.e., which nation exports which commodity).

Figure 5-3 shows clearly how all economic forces jointly determine the price of final commodities. This is what is meant when we say that the H-O model is a general equilibrium model.

However, out of all these forces working together, the H-O theorem isolates the difference in the *physical* availability or supply of factors of production among nations (in the face of equal tastes and technology) to explain the dif-

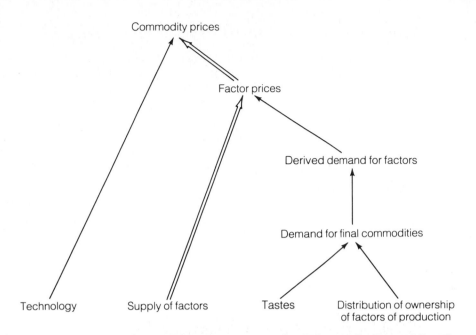

FIGURE 5-3.   General Equilibrium Framework of the Heckscher-Ohlin Theory

Beginning at the lower right-hand corner of the diagram, we see that the distribution of ownership of factors of production or income and tastes determine the demand for commodities. The demand for factors of production is then derived from the demand for final commodities. The demand for and supply of factors determine the price of factors. The price of factors and technology determine the price of final commodities. The difference in relative commodity prices among nations then determines comparative advantage and the pattern of trade.

ference in relative commodity prices and trade among nations. Specifically, Ohlin assumed equal tastes (and income distribution) among nations. This gave rise to similar demands for final commodities and factors of production in different nations. Thus, it is the difference in the supply of the various factors of production in different nations that is the cause of different relative factor prices in different nations. Finally, the same technology but different factor prices leads to different relative commodity prices and trade among nations. Thus, the difference in the relative supply of factors leading to the difference in relative factor prices and commodity prices is shown by the double lines in Figure 5-3.

To be noted is that the H-O model does not require that tastes, distribution of income, and technology be exactly the same in the two nations. It only requires that they be broadly the same for these results to follow. The assumptions of equal tastes, distribution of income, and technology do simplify the exposition and graphical illustration of the theory. They will be relaxed in the next chapter.

5.4c   Illustration of the Heckscher-Ohlin Theory

The H-O theory is illustrated in Figure 5-4. The left panel of the figure shows the production frontiers of Nation 1 and Nation 2, as in Figure 5-2. As indicated in section 5.3c, Nation 1's production frontier is skewed along the X axis because commodity X is the *L*-intensive commodity, Nation 1 is the *L*-abundant nation, and both nations use the same technology. Furthermore, since the two nations have equal tastes, they face the same indifference map. Indifference curve I (which is common for both nations) is tangent to Nation 1's production frontier at Point *A* and to Nation 2's production frontier at *A'*. Indifference curve I is the highest indifference curve that Nation 1 and Nation 2 can reach in isolation, and points *A* and *A'* represent their equilibrium points of production and consumption in the absence of trade.

The tangency of indifference curve I at points *A* and *A'* defines the no-trade, or autarky, equilibrium relative commodity prices of P_A in Nation 1 and $P_{A'}$ in Nation 2 (see the figure). Since $P_A < P_{A'}$, Nation 1 has a comparative

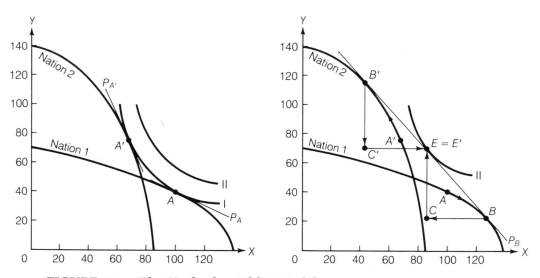

FIGURE 5-4.   The Heckscher-Ohlin Model

Indifference curve I is common to both nations because of the assumption of equal tastes. Indifference curve I is tangent to the production frontier of Nation 1 at point *A* and tangent to the production frontier of Nation 2 at *A'*. This defines the no-trade equilibrium relative commodity price of P_A in Nation 1 and $P_{A'}$ in Nation 2 (see the left panel). Since $P_A < P_{A'}$, Nation 1 has a comparative advantage in commodity X and Nation 2 in commodity Y. With trade (see the right panel) Nation 1 produces at point *B* by exchanging X for Y reaches point *E* in consumption (see trade triangle *BCE*). Nation 2 produces at *B'* and by exchanging Y for X reaches point *E'* (which coincides with *E*). Both nations gain from trade because they consume on higher indifference curve II.

advantage in commodity X, and Nation 2 has a comparative advantage in commodity Y.

The right panel shows that with trade Nation 1 specializes in the production of commodity X, and Nation 2 specializes in the production of commodity Y (see the direction of the arrows on the production frontiers of the two nations). Specialization in production proceeds until Nation 1 has reached point B and Nation 2 has reached point B' where the transformation curves of the two nations are tangent to the common relative price line P_B. Nation 1 will then export commodity X in exchange for commodity Y and consume at point E on indifference curve II (see trade triangle BCE). On the other hand, Nation 2 will export Y for X and consume at point E', which coincides with point E (see trade triangle B'C'E').

Note that Nation 1's exports of commodity X equal Nation 2's imports of commodity X (i.e., $BC = C'E'$). Similarly, Nation 2's exports of commodity Y equal Nation 1's imports of commodity Y (i.e., $B'C' = CE$). At $P_X/P_Y > P_B$, Nation 1 wants to export more of commodity X than Nation 2 wants to import at this high relative price of X, and P_X/P_Y falls toward P_B. On the other hand, at $P_X/P_Y < P_B$, Nation 1 wants to export less of commodity X than Nation 2 wants to import at this low relative price of X, and P_X/P_Y rises toward P_B. This tendency of P_X/P_Y could also be explained in terms of commodity Y.

Also to be noted is that point E involves more of Y but less of X than point A. Nevertheless, Nation 1 gains from trade because point E is on higher indifference curve II. Similarly, even though point E' involves more X but less Y than point A', Nation 2 is also better off because point E' is on higher indifference curve II. This pattern of specialization in production and trade and consumption will remain the same until there is a change in the underlying demand or supply conditions in commodity and factor markets in either or both nations.

It is now instructive briefly to compare Figure 5-4 with Figure 3-4. In Figure 3-4, the difference in the production frontiers of the two nations is reinforced by their difference in tastes, thus making the autarky relative commodity prices in the two nations differ even more than in Figure 5-4. On the other hand, the tastes of the two nations could be different in such a way as to make mutually beneficial trade impossible. This would occur if the different indifference curves in the two nations were tangent to their respective and different production frontiers in such a way as to result in equal autarky relative commodity prices in the two nations. This is assigned as an end-of-chapter problem and discussed in detail in the next chapter.

Finally, if Nation 1, say, was much smaller than Nation 2, it is conceivable that Nation 1's production frontier would lie entirely inside Nation 2's production frontier when plotted on the same set of axes. This would make no difference to the analysis as long as the production frontiers differed in the same general way (i.e., Nation 1's production frontier is flat and wide, while Nation 2's production frontier is tall and slim) and as long as specialization remained incomplete even in the small nation with trade. In this case, however, the two nations would consume commodities X and Y in the same proportion rather than in the same amount (as in Figure 5-4). See problem 5, with answer at the end of the text.

5.5 Factor-Price Equalization and Income Distribution

In this section, we examine the *factor-price equalization theorem*, which is really a corollary since it follows directly from the H-O theorem and holds only if the H-O theorem holds. It was *Paul Samuelson* (1976 Nobel Prize in economics) who rigorously proved this factor-price equalization theorem (corollary). For this reason, it is sometimes referred to as the Heckscher-Ohlin-Samuelson theorem (H-O-S theorem, for short).

In section 5.5a, we state the theorem and explain its meaning. Section 5.5b presents an intuitive proof of the factor-price equalization theorem. In section 5.5c, we examine the related question of the effect of international trade on the distribution of income within each trading nation. Finally, in section 5.5d, we briefly consider the empirical relevance of this theorem. The rigorous proof of the factor-price equalization theorem is presented in the appendix to this chapter. The proof requires the tools of analysis of intermediate microeconomic theory presented in the appendix to Chapter 3.

5.5a The Factor-Price Equalization Theorem

Starting with the assumptions given in section 5.2a, we can state the **factor-price equalization (H-O-S) theorem** as follows: *International trade will bring about equalization in the relative and absolute returns to homogeneous factors across nations.* As such, international trade is a substitute for the international mobility of factors.

What this means is that international trade will cause the wages of homogeneous labor (i.e., labor with the same level of training, skills, and productivity) to be the same in all trading nations (if all of the assumptions of section 5.2a hold). Similarly, international trade will cause the return to homogeneous capital (i.e., capital of the same productivity and risk) to be the same in all trading nations. That is, international trade will make w the same in Nation 1 and Nation 2; similarly, it will cause r to be the same in both nations. Both relative and absolute factor prices will be equalized.

From section 5.4, we know that in the absence of trade the relative price of commodity X is lower in Nation 1 than in Nation 2 because the relative price of labor, or the wage rate, is lower in Nation 1. As Nation 1 specializes in the production of commodity X (the *L*-intensive commodity) and reduces its production of commodity Y (the *K*-intensive commodity), the relative demand for labor rises, causing wages (w) to rise, while the relative demand for capital falls, causing the interest rate (r) to fall. The exact opposite occurs in Nation

2. That is, as Nation 2 specializes in the production of Y and reduces its production of X with trade, its demand for L falls, causing w to fall, while its demand for K rises, causing r to rise.

To summarize, international trade causes w to rise in Nation 1 (the low-wage nation) and to fall in Nation 2 (the high-wage nation). Thus international trade reduces the pretrade difference in w between the two nations. Similarly, international trade causes r to fall in Nation 1 (the K-expensive nation) and to rise in Nation 2 (the K-cheap nation), thus reducing the pretrade difference in r between the two nations. This proves that international trade *tends to reduce* the pretrade difference in w and r between the two nations.

We can go further and demonstrate that international trade not only tends to reduce the international difference in the returns to homogeneous factors, but would in fact bring about complete equalization in relative factor prices when all of the assumptions made hold. This is so because as long as relative factor prices differ, relative commodity prices differ and trade continues to expand. But the expansion of trade reduces the difference in factor prices between nations. Thus, international trade keeps expanding until relative commodity prices are completely equalized, which means that relative factor prices have also become equal in the two nations.

5.5b Relative and Absolute Factor-Price Equalization

We can show graphically that relative factor prices are equalized by trade in the two nations (if all the assumptions of section 5.2a hold). In Figure 5-5, the relative price of labor (w/r) is measured along the horizontal axis and the relative price of commodity X (P_X/P_Y) is measured along the vertical axis. Before trade, Nation 1 is at point A, with $w/r = (w/r)_1$ and $P_X/P_Y = P_A$ while Nation 2 is at point A', with $w/r = (w/r)_2$ and $P_X/P_Y = P_{A'}$. Since w/r is lower in Nation 1 than in Nation 2 in the absence of trade, P_A is lower than $P_{A'}$ so that Nation 1 has a comparative advantage in commodity X.

As Nation 1 (the relatively L-abundant nation) specializes in the production of commodity X (the L-intensive commodity) and reduces the production of commodity Y, the demand for labor increases relative to the demand for capital and w/r rises in Nation 1. On the other hand, as Nation 2 (the K-abundant nation) specializes in the production of commodity Y (the K-intensive commodity), its relative demand for capital increases and r/w rises (i.e., w/r falls). This will continue until point $B = B'$, at which $P_B = P_{B'}$ and $w/r = (w/r)^*$ in both nations (see Figure 5-5). Note that $P_B = P_{B'}$ only if w/r is identical in the two nations, since both nations use the same technology (by assumption). Note also that $P_B = P_{B'}$ lies between P_A and $P_{A'}$, and $(w/r)^*$ lies between $(w/r)_1$ and $(w/r)_2$. To summarize, P_X/P_Y will become equal as a result of trade and this will cause w/r to also become equal in the two nations (as long as both nations continue to produce both commodities). A more rigorous and difficult proof of the relative factor-price equalization theorem is given in the appendix.

The above proves complete equalization of *relative* factor prices, not abso-

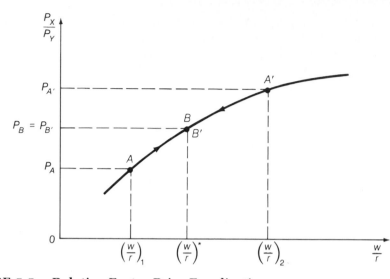

FIGURE 5-5.   Relative Factor Price Equalization

The horizontal axis measures w/r and the vertical axis P_X/P_Y. Before trade, Nation 1 is at point A, with $w/r = (w/r)_1$ and $P_X/P_Y = P_A$ while Nation 2 is at point A', with $w/r = (w/r)_2$ and $P_X/P_Y = P_{A'}$. Since w/r is lower in Nation 1 than in Nation 2, P_A is lower than $P_{A'}$ so that Nation 1 has a comparative advantage in commodity X. As Nation 1 specializes in the production of commodity X with trade and increases the demand for labor relative to capital, w/r rises. As Nation 2 specializes in the production of commodity Y and increases its relative demand for capital, r/w rises (i.e., w/r falls). This will continue until point $B = B'$, at which $P_B = P_{B'}$ and $w/r = (w/r)^*$ in both nations.

lute factor prices. Equalization of *absolute* factor prices means that free international trade also equalizes the real wages for the same type of labor in the two nations and the real rate of interest for the same type of capital in the two nations. However, given that trade equalizes relative factor prices, that perfect competition exists in all commodity and factor markets, and given the additional assumptions that both nations use the same technology and face constant returns to scale in the production of both commodities, it follows that trade also equalizes the absolute returns to homogeneous factors. A rigorous and difficult proof of absolute factor-price equalization is presented in the appendix to this chapter following the proof of relative factor-price equalization.

Note that trade acts as a substitute for the international mobility of factors of production in its effect on factor prices. With perfect mobility (i.e., with complete information and no legal restrictions or transportation costs), labor would migrate from the low-wage nation to the high-wage nation until wages in the two nations became equal. Similarly, capital would move from the low-interest to the high-interest nation until the rate of interest was equalized in the two nations. While trade operates on the demand for factors, factor mobility operates on the supply of factors. However, the result is complete equalization in the absolute returns of homogeneous factors in either case. With some (rather than perfect) international mobility of factors, a smaller volume of trade would be required to bring about equality in factor returns between the two nations.

5.5c   Effect of Trade on the Distribution of Income

While in the previous section we examined the effect of international trade on the difference in factor prices *between nations,* in this section we analyze the effect of international trade on relative factor prices and income *within each nation.* These two questions are certainly related, but they are not the same.

Specifically, we have seen in section 5.5a that international trade tends to equalize w in the two nations and also to equalize r in the two nations. We now want to examine how international trade affects real wages and the real income of labor in relation to real interest rates and the real income of owners of capital *within* each nation. Does the real wage and income of labor rise or fall in relation to the real interest rate and earnings of owners of capital in the same nation as a result of international trade?

From our discussion in section 5.5a, we know that trade increases the price of the nation's abundant and cheap factor and reduces the price of its scarce and expensive factor. In terms of our example, w rises and r falls in Nation 1, while w falls and r rises in Nation 2. Since labor and capital are assumed to remain fully employed before and after trade, the real income of labor and the real income of owners of capital move in the same direction as the movement in factor prices. Thus, trade causes the real income of labor to rise and the real income of owners of capital to fall in Nation 1 (the nation with cheap labor and expensive capital). On the other hand, international trade causes the real income of labor to fall and the real income of owners of capital to rise in Nation 2 (the nation with expensive labor and cheap capital).

Since in developed nations (e.g., the United States, West Germany, Japan, France, Britain, Italy, etc.) capital is the relatively abundant factor (as in our Nation 2), international trade tends to reduce the real income of labor and increase the real income of owners of capital. This is why labor unions in developed nations generally favor trade restrictions. On the other hand, in less developed nations (e.g., India, Egypt, Brazil, Argentina, Greece, etc.) labor is the relatively abundant factor, and international trade will increase the real income of labor and reduce the real income of owners of capital. These results, however, are based on the assumption that factors are perfectly mobile among the nation's industries. While this is likely to be the case in the long run, it may not be true in the short run, when some factors, say capital, may be *immobile.* In that case, the above conclusions need to be modified and can be analyzed with the **specific-factors model** presented in the appendix.

Since according to the Heckscher-Ohlin theory international trade causes real wages and the real income of labor to fall in a capital-abundant and labor-scarce nation such as the United States, shouldn't the U.S. government restrict trade? The answer is almost invariably no. The reason is that the loss that trade causes to labor is less than the gain received by owners of capital. With an appropriate redistribution policy of taxes on owners of capital and subsidies to labor, both broad classes of factors of production can benefit from international trade. Such a redistribution policy can take not only the form of retraining labor displaced by imports but may also take the form of tax relief for labor and provision of some social services. We will return to this important question in our discussion of trade restrictions in Chapters 8 and 9.

5.5d Empirical Relevance

Has international trade equalized the returns to homogeneous factors in different nations in the real world? Even casual observation clearly indicates that it has not. Thus, wages are much higher for doctors, engineers, technicians, mechanics, secretaries, and laborers in the United States and West Germany than in Korea and Mexico.

The reason for this is that many of the simplifying assumptions on which the H-O-S theory rests do not hold in the real world. For example, nations do not use exactly the same technology, and transportation costs and trade barriers prevent the equalization of relative commodity prices in different nations. Furthermore, many industries operate under conditions of imperfect competition and non-constant returns to scale. It should not, therefore, be surprising that international trade has not equalized wages and interest rates for homogeneous factors in different nations.

Under these circumstances, it is more realistic to ask whether international trade has *reduced,* rather than completely eliminated, the international difference in the returns to homogeneous factors. While international trade seems to have reduced international differences in *relative* factor prices, it is more difficult to give a clear-cut answer as to its effect on *absolute* differences.

The reason for this is that, even if international trade has operated to reduce absolute differences in factor returns among nations, many other forces were operating at the same time, preventing any such relationship from becoming clearly evident. For example, while international trade may have tended to reduce the difference in real wages and incomes for the same type of labor between the United States and Argentina, technological advances occurred more rapidly in the United States than in Argentina, so that the difference in earnings has in fact increased. This seems indeed to have been the case between developed nations as a group and developing nations since World War II.

Once again, this does not disprove the factor-price equalization theorem, since in the absence of trade these international differences might have been much greater than they are now. In any event, the factor-price equalization theorem is useful because it identifies crucial variables affecting factor prices and provides important insights into the general equilibrium nature of our trade model and economics in general.

One thing the factor-price equalization theorem *does not say* is that international trade will eliminate or reduce international differences in *per capita incomes.* It only predicts that international trade will eliminate or reduce international differences in the returns to *homogeneous factors.* Even if real wages were to be equalized among nations, their per capital incomes could still remain widely different. Per capita income depends on many other forces not directly related to the factor-price equalization theorem. These other forces include the ratio of skilled to unskilled labor, the participation rate in the labor force, the dependency rate, the type of effort made by workers, and so on. For example, Japan has a higher ratio of skilled to unskilled labor than India, a higher participation rate and lower dependency rate, and Japanese workers seem to thrive on work and precision. Thus, even if wages for the same type of labor were exactly the same in Japan and India, Japan would end up with a much higher per capita income than India.

5.6 The Heckscher-Ohlin Model—A General Equilibrium Model

The Heckscher-Ohlin model can be used to trace the effect of a change in any economic force throughout the economy of the nation and in international trade. For example, suppose that tastes change in Nation 1 (the L-abundant and L-cheap nation) so that consumers demand more of commodity X (the L-intensive commodity) and less of commodity Y (the K-intensive commodity). Suppose that Nation 1 is India, commodity X is textiles, and commodity Y is food. (For the opposite change in tastes, see problem 6 with answer at the end of the text.)

Starting from the no-trade equilibrium position, this change in tastes increases the relative price of textiles in India. This can be visualized by the fact that India's indifference map shifts toward the X (textiles) axis so that an indifference curve is tangent to the steeper segment of India's production frontier (because of increasing opportunity costs) after the increase in demand for textiles.

As the relative price of textiles rises, domestic producers in India will shift labor and capital from the production of food to the production of textiles. Since textiles are L intensive in relation to food, the demand for labor and therefore the wage rate will rise in India. At the same time, as the demand for food falls, the demand for and thus the price of capital will fall. With labor becoming relatively more expensive, producers in India will substitute capital for labor in the production of both textiles and food. Thus, K/L will rise in the production of both textiles and food in India.

Even with this rise in relative wages and in the relative price of textiles, India still remains the *L*-abundant and low-wage nation with respect to a nation such as the United States. However, the pretrade difference in the relative price of textiles between India and the United States is now somewhat smaller than before the change in tastes in India. As a result, the volume of trade required to equalize relative commodity prices and hence factor prices is smaller than before. That is, India need now export a smaller quantity of textiles and import less food than before for the relative price of textiles in India and the United States to be equalized. Similarly, the gap in real wages between India and the United States is now smaller and can be more quickly and easily closed (i.e., with a smaller volume of trade).

Since many of the assumptions required for complete equalization of relative commodity and factor prices do not hold in the real world, great differences can be expected and in fact do remain between real wages in India and the United States. Nevertheless, trade would tend to reduce these differences, and the model does identify the forces that must be considered to analyze the effect of trade on the differences in relative and absolute commodity and factor prices between India and the United States.

The change in tastes introduced above is perhaps the simplest change in economic conditions that could occur. Over time, other changes can and certainly do occur. Technology usually improves. Some factors of production, such as a nation's labor force, increase with population growth. New mineral deposits may be discovered and uses found for previously unusable resources. On the other hand, some resources, such as mineral deposits and forests, can become depleted by excessive use. It may be very difficult to analyze such changes in terms of their effect on factor prices and incomes within the nation and on the nation's comparative advantage. While our trade model developed so far (except briefly in section 4.6b) is entirely static (i.e., can be regarded as a snapshot picture at a given point in time), it can incorporate many of these changes over time. This is done in Chapter 7, where we discuss the effect of growth on comparative advantage and on factor prices and incomes.

Summary

1. The Heckscher-Ohlin theory presented in this chapter extends our trade model of previous chapters to explain the basis of (what determines) comparative advantage and to examine the effect of international trade on the earnings of factors of production. These two important questions were left largely unanswered by classical economists.

2. The Heckscher-Ohlin theory is based on a number of simplifying assumptions (some made only implicitly by Heckscher and Ohlin). These are: (1) two nations, two commodities, and two factors of productions; (2) both nations use the same technology; (3) the same commodity is labor intensive in both nations; (4) constant returns to scale; (5) incomplete specialization in production; (6) equal tastes in both nations; (7) perfect competition in both commodities and factor markets; (8) perfect internal but no international mobility of factors; (9) no transportation costs, tariffs or other obstruction to the free flow of international trade. These assumptions will be relaxed in Chapter 6.

3. In a world of two nations (Nation 1 and Nation 2), two commodities (X and Y), and two factors (labor and capital), we say that commodity Y is capital intensive if the capital-labor ratio (K/L) used in the production of Y is *greater* than K/L for X in both nations. We also say that Nation 2 is the K-abundant nation if the relative price of capital (r/w) is *lower* there than in Nation 1. Thus, Nation 2's production frontier is skewed toward the Y axis and Nation 1's is skewed toward the X axis.

4. Since the relative price of capital is lower in Nation 2, producers there will use more K-intensive techniques in the production of both commodities in relation to Nation 1. Producers would also substitute K for L (causing K/L to rise) in the production of both commodities if the relative price of capital *declined*. Commodity Y is *unequivocally* the K-intensive commodity if K/L remains higher for Y than for X in both nations at all relative factor prices.

5. The Heckscher-Ohlin, or factor-endowment, theory can be expressed in terms of two theorems. According to the Heckscher-Ohlin (H-O) theorem, a nation will export the commodity intensive in its relatively abundant and cheap factor and import the commodity intensive in its relatively scarce and expensive factor. According to the factor-price equalization (H-O-S) theorem, international trade will bring about equalization of relative and absolute returns to homogeneous factors across nations.

6. Out of all the possible forces that could cause a difference in pretrade relative commodity prices between nations, Heckscher and Ohlin isolate the difference in factor endowments (in the face of equal technology and tastes) as the basic determinant or cause of comparative advantage. International trade can also be a substitute for the international mobility of factors in equalizing relative and absolute returns to homogeneous factors across nations. The general equilibrium nature of the H-O theory arises from the fact that all commodity and factor markets are components of an overall unified system so that a change in any part affects every other part.

A Look Ahead

Chapter 6 will present results of empirical tests of the Heckscher-Ohlin theory to see whether its predictions correspond to what actually takes place in the real world. We will be particularly interested in examining whether factor endowments do indeed determine comparative advantage and the pattern of trade. We will then extend the Heckscher-Ohlin theory by relaxing the assumptions on which it rests and evaluate alternative trade theories.

Glossary

Same technology Equal production techniques; it results in equal K/L in the production of each commodity in both nations if relative factor prices are the same in both nations.

Labor-intensive commodity The commodity with the higher labor-capital ratio (L/K) at all relative factor prices.

Capital-intensive commodity The commodity with the higher capital-labor ratio (K/L) at all relative factor prices.

Labor-capital ratio (L/K) Measures the amount of labor per unit of capital used in the production of a commodity; it is the inverse, or reciprocal, of K/L.

Capital-labor ratio (K/L) Measures the amount of capital per unit of labor used in the production of a commodity; it is the inverse, or reciprocal, of L/K.

Constant returns to scale The production condition whereby increasing by a given percentage the amount of all factors used in the production of a commodity will increase output of the commodity by the same percentage.

Perfect competition The market condition where (1) there are many buyers and sellers of a given commodity or factor, each too small to affect the price of the commodity or factor; (2) all units of the same commodity or factor are homogeneous, or of the same quality; (3) there is perfect knowledge and information on all markets; and (4) there is perfect internal mobility of factors of production.

Internal factor mobility   The movement within a nation of factors of production from areas and industries of lower earnings to areas and industries of higher earnings.

International factor mobility   The movement of factors of production across national boundaries, usually from nations of lower earnings to nations of higher earnings.

Factor abundance   Refers to the factor of production available in greater proportion and at a lower relative price in a nation than in another nation.

Relative factor prices   The ratio of the price of one factor of production to the price of the other factor. With labor and capital as the factors of production, the relative price of labor is w/r and the relative price of capital is the inverse, or r/w.

Derived demand   The demand for factors of production that arises from the demand for final commodities that are produced using the particular factors.

Heckscher-Ohlin (H-O) theory   The broadly verified hypothesis that a nation exports those commodities whose production requires intensive use of the nation's relatively abundant and cheap factor; it also predicts that international trade will bring about equalization in relative and absolute returns to homogeneous factors across nations (when all the assumptions of the theory hold).

Heckscher-Ohlin (H-O) theorem   The part of the Heckscher-Ohlin theory that postulates that a nation will export the commodity intensive in its relatively abundant and cheap factor and import the commodity intensive in its relatively scarce and expensive factor.

Factor endowments   See factor abundance.

Factor-proportions or **factor-endowment theory**   See Heckscher-Ohlin theory.

Factor-price equalization (H-O-S) theorem   The part of the H-O theory that predicts, under highly restrictive assumptions, that international trade will bring about equalization in relative and absolute returns to homogeneous factors across nations.

Specific-factors model   The model to analyze the effect of a change in commodity price on the returns of factors in a nation when at least one factor is not mobile between industries.

Questions for Review

1. In what ways does the Heckscher-Ohlin theory represent an extension of the trade model presented in the previous chapters? What did classical economists say on these matters?
2. State the assumptions of the Heckscher-Ohlin theory. What is the meaning and importance of each of these assumptions?
3. What is meant by labor-intensive commodity? Capital-intensive commodity? Capital-labor ratio? What is meant by capital-abundant nation? What determines the shape of the production frontier of each nation?
4. What determines the capital-labor ratio in the production of each commodity in both nations? Which of the two nations uses a higher capital-labor ratio in the production of both commodities? Why? Under what circumstance would the capital-labor ratio be the same in the production of each commodity in both nations? If labor and capital can be substituted for each other in the production of both commodities, when can we say that one commodity is capital intensive and the other labor intensive?
5. What does the Heckscher-Ohlin theory say? Which force do Heckscher and Ohlin identify as the basic determinant of comparative advantage and trade? What does the factor-price equalization theorem say? What is its relationship to the international mobility of factors of production?
6. Explain why the Heckscher-Ohlin theory is a general equilibrium model. How does a change in tastes in favor of the commodity of the nation's comparative advantage affect the pretrade relative price of that commodity in the nation? What effect will this have on the comparative advantage of the nation and on the volume of trade? What is the effect of these changes on the trade partner?

Problems

1. Draw two set of axes, one for Nation 1 and the other for Nation 2, measuring labor along the horizontal axis and capital along the vertical axis.
   (a) Show by straight lines through the origin that K/L is higher for commodity Y than for commodity X in both nations in the absence of trade and that K/L is higher in Nation 2 than in Nation 1 for both commodities.
   (b) What happens to the slope of the lines measuring K/L of each commodity in Nation 2 if r/w rises in Nation 2 as a result of international trade?
   (c) What happens to the slope of the lines measuring K/L in Nation 1 if r/w falls in Nation 1 as a result of international trade?
   (d) Given the results of parts b and c, does international trade increase or reduce the difference in the K/L in the production of each commodity in the two nations as compared with the pretrade situation?

2. Without looking at the text:
   (a) sketch a figure similar to Figure 5-4 showing the autarky equilibrium point in each nation and the point of production and consumption in each nation with trade.
   (b) With reference to your figure in part a, explain what determines the comparative advantage of each nation.
   (c) Why do the two nations consume different amounts of the two commodities in the absence of trade but the same amount with trade?

3. Starting with the production frontiers for Nation 1 and Nation 2 shown in Figure 5-4, do the following:
   (a) Show graphically that even with a small difference in tastes in the two nations, Nation 1 would continue to have a comparative advantage in commodity X.
   (b) Show graphically that sufficiently different tastes in the two nations could conceivably neutralize the difference in their factor endowments and lead to equal rel-

ative commodity prices in the two nations in the absence of trade.
   (c) Show that with an even greater difference in tastes in the two nations, Nation 1 could end up exporting the capital-intensive commodity.

4. A difference in factor endowments will cause the production frontiers of two nations to be shaped differently.
   (a) What else could cause their production frontiers to have different shapes? What assumption made by Heckscher and Ohlin prevented this in the Heckscher-Ohlin model?
   (b) What are other possible causes of a difference in relative commodity prices between the two nations in the absence of trade?

*5. Assume that Nation 1 is much smaller than Nation 2.
   (a) Sketch the production frontier of Nation 1 entirely inside the production frontier of Nation 2 but with Nation 1's production frontier retaining its general shape (i.e., its bias in favor of commodity X, plotted on the horizontal axis). Show the relative price of commodity X in both nations in the absence of trade if both nations have the same tastes so that they consume commodities X and Y in the same *proportion* (i.e., along the same straight line through the origin cutting the production frontiers of the two nations). In which commodity does Nation 1 have a comparative advantage?
   (b) Using the above figure, show the process of specialization in production and trade. Note that it may be easier at this point to redraw the production frontier of each nation on a separate set of axes (as in Figure 3-4).

*6. Starting from the pretrade equilibrium point in Figure 5-4, assume that tastes in Nation 1 change favor of the commodity of its comparative *disadvantage* (i.e., in favor of commodity Y).
   (a) What is the effect of this change in tastes on P_X/P_Y in Nation 1? How did you reach such a conclusion?

(b) What is the effect of this change in tastes on *r/w* in Nation 1?

(c) What is the effect of this on the volume of trade and on the trade partner?

APPENDIX————————————————————

This appendix presents the formal proof of the factor-price equalization theorem. Section A5.1 repeats (with some modifications to fit our present aim) the Edgeworth box diagrams of Nation 1 and Nation 2 from Figures 3-9 and 3-10. Section A5.2 then examines how international trade brings about equality in *relative* factor prices in the two nations. Section A5.3 shows that *absolute* factor prices are also equalized across nations as a result of international trade. Section A5.4 examines the effect of trade on the short-run distribution of income with the specific-factors model. Section A5.5 utilizes the tools developed in this appendix to retrace in a more formal manner the analysis of the change in tastes in Nation 1 presented in section 5.6.

A5.1   The Edgeworth Box Diagram for Nation 1 and Nation 2

Figure 5-6 shows the Edgeworth box diagram of Nation 2 superimposed on the box diagram of Nation 1 in such a way that their origins for commodity X coincide. The origins for commodity Y differ because Nation 1 has a relative abundance of labor whereas Nation 2 has a relative abundance of capital. The box diagrams are superimposed on each other to facilitate the analysis to follow.

Because both nations use the *same technology*, the isoquants for commodity X in the two nations are identical (and are measured from the common origin O_X). Similarly, the isoquants for commodity Y in the two nations are also identical (but are measured from origin O_Y for Nation 1 and from origin $O_{Y'}$ for Nation 2). X-isoquants farther from O_X refer to progressively higher outputs of X, while Y-isoquants farther from O_Y or $O_{Y'}$ refer to greater outputs of Y.

By joining all points where an X-isoquant is tangent to a Y-isoquant in each nation, we obtain the nation's production contract curve. Points *A, F,* and *B* on Nation 1's production contract curve in Figure 5-6 refer to corresponding points on Nation 1's production frontier (see Figure 3-9). Similarly, points *A',* *F',* and *B'* on Nation 2's production contract curve refer to corresponding points on Nation 2's production frontier. Note that the contract curves of both nations bulge toward the lower right-hand corner because commodity X is the *L*-intensive commodity in both nations.

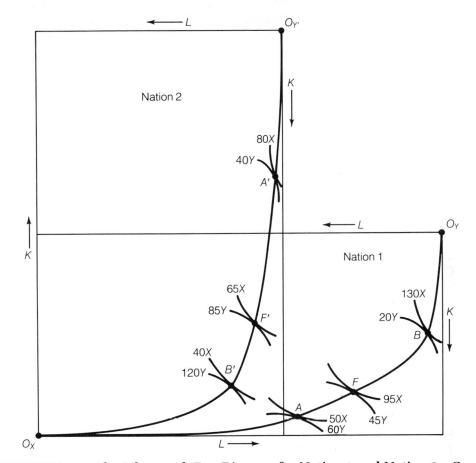

FIGURE 5-6.   The Edgeworth Box Diagram for Nation 1 and Nation 2—Once Again

The Edgeworth box diagram of nation 2 from Figure 3-10 is superimposed on the box diagram for Nation 1 from Figure 3-9 in such a way that their origins for commodity X coincide. Because both nations use the same technology, the isoquants of commodity X are identical in the two nations. The same is true for the Y-isoquants. The points on each nation's production contract curve refer to corresponding points on the nation's production frontier. The contract curves of both nations bulge toward the lower right-hand corner because commodity X is the L-intensive commodity in both nations.

A5.2   Relative Factor-Price Equalization

Figure 5-7 repeats Figure 5-6 but omits (to keep the figure simple) all iso-quants as well as points F and F' (which are not needed in the subsequent analysis). The no-trade equilibrium point is A in Nation 1 and A' in Nation 2 (as in Figures 3-3 and 3-4). The K/L ratio in the production of commodity X

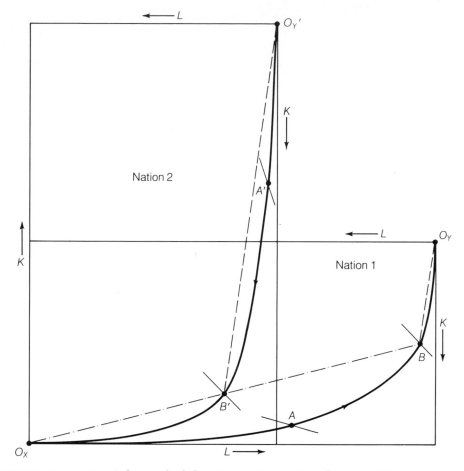

FIGURE 5-7.   Formal Proof of the Factor-Price Equalization Theorem

At the no-trade equilibrium point *A* in Nation 1 and *A'* in Nation 2, *K/L* is lower in the production of both commodities in Nation 1 than in Nation 2. These are given by the lower slopes of straight lines (not shown) from O_X and O_Y or $O_{Y'}$ to points *A* and *A'*. Since *w/r* (the absolute slope of the solid line through point *A*) is lower in Nation 1 and commodity X is *L*-intensive, Nation 1 specializes in the production of commodity X until it reaches point *B*. Nation 2 specializes in Y until it reaches point *B'*. At *B* and *B'*, *K/L* and therefore *w/r* are the same in both nations.

is smaller in Nation 1 than in Nation 2. This is given by the lesser slope of the line (not shown) from origin O_X to point *A* as opposed to point *A'*. Similarly, the *K/L* ratio in the production of commodity Y is also smaller in Nation 1 than in Nation 2. This is given by the smaller slope of the line (not shown) from O_Y to point *A* as opposed to the slope of the line (also not shown) from $O_{Y'}$ to point *A'*.

Since Nation 1 uses a smaller amount of capital per unit of labor (*K/L*) in the production of both commodities with respect to Nation 2, the productivity of labor and therefore the wage rate (w) is lower, while the productivity of capital and therefore the rate of interest (r) is higher, in Nation 1 than in Nation 2. This is always the case when both nations use a production function that is homogeneous of degree one, showing constant returns to scale (as assumed throughout).

With a lower w and a higher r, w/r is lower in Nation 1 than in Nation 2. This is consistent with the relative physical abundance of labor in Nation 1 and capital in Nation 2. The lower w/r in Nation 1 at autarky point A is reflected in the smaller (absolute) slope of the (short and solid) straight line through point A as opposed to the corresponding line at point A'. (The straight lines are the common tangents to the X- and Y-isoquants—not shown in Figure 5-7—at point A and point A'.)

To summarize, we can say that at the no-trade equilibrium point A, Nation 1 uses a smaller K/L ratio in the production of both commodities with respect to Nation 2. This results in lower productivity of labor and higher productivity of capital in Nation 1 than in Nation 2. As a result, w/r is lower in Nation 1 (the L-abundant nation) than in Nation 2.

Since Nation 1 is the L-abundant nation and commodity X is the L-intensive commodity, with the opening of trade Nation 1 will specialize in the production of commodity X (i.e., will move from point A toward O_Y along its production contract curve). Similarly, Nation 2 will specialize in the production of commodity Y and move from point A' toward O_X. Specialization in production continues until Nation 1 reaches point B and Nation 2 reaches point B', where K/L is the same in each commodity in both nations. This is given by the slope of the dashed line from O_X through points B' and B for commodity X, and by the parallel dashed lines from O_Y and $O_{Y'}$ to points B and B' for commodity Y, for Nation 1 and Nation 2, respectively.

Note that as Nation 1 moves from point A to point B, K/L rises in the production of both commodities. This is reflected by the steeper slope of the dashed lines from O_X and O_Y to point B as opposed to point A. As a result of this increase in K/L, the productivity and therefore the wage of labor rises in Nation 1 (the low-wage nation). On the other hand, as Nation 2 moves from point A' to B', K/L falls in the production of both commodities. This is reflected by the smaller slope of the dashed lines from $O_{Y'}$ and O_X to point B' as opposed to point A'. As a result of this decline in K/L, the productivity and therefore the wage of labor falls in Nation 2 (the high-wage nation). The exact opposite is true for capital.

In the absence of trade, w/r was lower in Nation 1 than in Nation 2 (see the absolute slopes of the solid straight lines through points A and A'). As Nation 1 (the low-wage nation) specializes in the production of commodity X, K/L and w/r rise in the production of both commodities in Nation 1. As Nation 2 (the high-wage nation) specializes in the production of commodity Y, K/L and w/r fall in the production of both commodities. Specialization in production continues until K/L and w/r have become equal in the two nations. This occurs when Nation 1 produces at point B and Nation 2 produces at point B′ with trade. This concludes our formal proof that international trade equalizes relative factor prices in the two nations when all the assumptions listed in section 5.2a hold.

Problem Show graphically that with sufficiently less capital available Nation 1 would have become completely specialized in the production of commodity X before relative factor prices became equal in the two nations.

A5.3 Absolute Factor-Price Equalization

This proof of absolute factor-price equalization is more difficult than the proof of relative factor-price equalization and is seldom if ever covered in undergraduate courses, even when all students in the course have had intermediate microeconomics and macroeconomics. The proof is included here only for the sake of completeness and for more advanced undergraduate students and first-year graduate students.

The proof makes use of **Euler's theorem.** According to Euler's theorem, if constant returns to scale prevail in production and if each factor is rewarded (paid) according to its productivity, the output produced is exhausted and just exhausted. Specifically, the marginal physical product of labor (*MPL*) times the amount of labor used in production (*L*) plus the marginal physical product of capital (*MPK*) times the amount of capital used in production (*K*) exactly equals the output produced. The same is true for commodity Y. In equation form, Euler's theorem in the production of commodity X can be expressed as:

$$(MPL)(L) + (MPK)(K) = X \qquad\qquad (5\text{A-}1)$$

Dividing both sides by *L* and rearranging:

$$X/L = MPL + (MPK)(K)/L \qquad\qquad (5\text{A-}2)$$

Factoring out *MPL*:

$$X/L = MPL[1 + (K/L)(MPK/MPL)] \qquad\qquad (5\text{A-}3)$$

With trade, Nation 1 produces at point B and Nation 2 produces at point B′. Since at points B and B′, *w/r* is the same in both nations, *MPK/MPL* is also the same in both nations. We also know that at points B and B′, *K/L* in the production of commodity X is the same in both nations. Finally, *X/L* is the average product of labor in the production of commodity X—and this is also the same in the two nations because of the assumptions of constant returns to scale and the same technology. As a result, the last remaining component (*MPL*) in equation 5A-3 must also be the same in the production of commodity X *in both nations* if equation 5A-3 is to hold.

Since the real wage is equal to MPL, the equality of MPL in the two nations means that real wages are the same in the two nations in the production of commodity X. With perfect competition and perfect internal factor mobility, real wages in the production of commodity Y are equal to real wages in the production of commodity X in each nation as well. In a completely analogous way, we can prove that the rate of interest is the same in the two nations in the production of both commodities. This concludes our proof that international trade equalizes absolute factor prices in the production of both commodities in both nations (under highly restrictive assumptions). That is, we have proved that real wages (w) are the same in both nations in the production of both commodities. Similarly, the real rate of interest (r) is also the same in both nations in the production of both commodities.

A5.4   Effect of Trade on the Short-Run Distribution of Income: The Specific-Factors Model

Suppose that in Nation 1 (the L-abundant nation) labor is mobile between industries but capital is not. Since labor is mobile, the wage of labor will be the same in the production of commodities X and Y in Nation 1. The equilibrium wage and the amount of labor employed in the production of X and Y in Nation 1 are given by the intersection of the value of the marginal product of labor curve in the production of X and Y. From microeconomic theory, we know that the value of the marginal product of labor in the production of X is equal to the price of commodity X times the marginal physical product of labor in the production of X. That is, $VMPL_X = (P_X)(MPL_X)$. Similarly, $VMPL_Y = (P_Y)(MPL_Y)$. We also know that if a firm employs more labor with a given amount of capital, VMPL declines because of the law of diminishing returns. Finally, to maximize profits, firms will employ labor until the wage they must pay equals the value of the marginal product of labor (i.e., until $w = VMPL$).

We can show the no-trade equilibrium wage and employment of labor in the production of commodities X and Y in Nation 1 with the aid of Figure 5-8. In the figure, the horizontal axis measures the total supply of labor available to Nation 1 and the vertical axis measures the wage rate. To begin with, concentrate on the $VMPL_X$ curve (which is read from right to left, as usual) and on the $VMPL_Y$ curve (which is read from right to left). The equilibrium wage rate is ED and is determined at the intersection of the $VMPL_X$ and $VMPL_Y$ curves. The wage rate is identical in the production of X and Y because of perfect labor mobility in the nation between the two industries. The amount of OD of labor is used in the production of X and the remainder, or DO', is used in the production of Y.

Since Nation 1 (the L-abundant nation) has a comparative advantage in commodity X (the L-intensive commodity), the opening of trade increases P_X/P_Y. Since $VMPL_X = (P_X)(MPL_X)$, the increase in P_X shifts the $VMPL_X$ curve upward

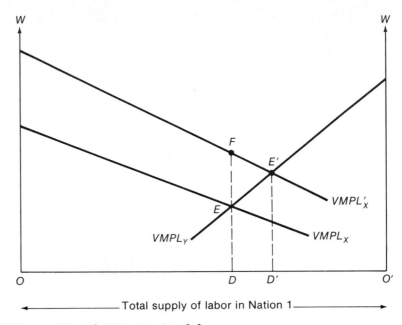

Total supply of labor in Nation 1

FIGURE 5-8. Specific-Factors Model

Labor is mobile between industries but capital is not. The horizontal axis measures the total supply of L available to Nation 1 and the vertical axis the wage rate (w). Before trade, the intersection of the $VMPL_X$ and $VMPL_Y$ curves determines $w = ED$ in the two industries. OD of L is used in the production of X and DO' in Y. With trade, P_X/P_Y increases and shifts $VMPL_X$ up to $VMPL'_X$. w rises from ED to $E'D'$, and DD' of L shifts from Y to X. Since w rises less than P_X, w falls in terms of X but rises in terms of Y (since P_Y is unchanged). With more L used with fixed K in the production of X, $VMPK_X$ and r increase in terms of both X and Y. With less L used with fixed K in Y, $VMPK_Y$ and r fall in terms of both commodities.

proportionately, by EF, to $VMPL'_X$. The wage rate increases less than proportionately, from ED to $E'D'$, and DD' units of labor shifts from the production of Y to the production of X. Since w increases by less than the increase in P_X, w falls in terms of X but rises in terms of Y (since P_Y is unchanged). Thus, the effect of the increase in P_X of the real income of labor is ambiguous and depends on spending patterns. Workers who consume mainly commodity X will be worse off, while those who consume mainly commodity Y will be better off.

The rewards (r) to the specific factor (capital) change unambiguously, however. Since the specific capital in the production of commodity X has more labor to work with, $VMPK_X$ and r increase in terms of both commodities X and Y. On the other hand, since less labor is used with the fixed capital in the production of commodity Y, $VMPK_Y$ and r fall in terms of commodity X, and therefore in terms of commodity Y as well.

Thus, with the opening of trade, the real income of the immobile capital (the nation's scarce factor) rises in the production of X and falls in the production of Y, while real wages (which are equal in the production of both commodities) fall in terms of commodity X and rise in terms of commodity Y. This is the result we obtain in the short run with the specific-factors model when capital is immobile between the two industries of the nation. In the long run, however, when both capital and labor are fully mobile between the two industries in the nation, the Heckscher-Ohlin model postulates that the opening of trade leads to a reduction in the real income of owners of capital (Nation 1's scarce factor) and an increase in the real income of labor (Nation 1's abundant factor).

Problem   What effect will the opening of trade have on the real income of labor and capital in Nation 2 (the K-abundant nation) if L is mobile between the two industries in Nation 2 but K is not?

A5.5   Comparative Static Analysis of a Change in Tastes

We can now see how to use Figure 5-7 to retrace the analysis of a change in tastes presented in section 5.7. There, it was assumed that, starting from its no-trade equilibrium point, Nation 1 (the L-abundant and L-cheap nation) increased its demand for commodity X (the L-intensive commodity) because of a change in tastes. In terms of Figure 5-7, this means that the no-trade equilibrium point A on Nation 1's production contract curve is farther away from O_X and closer to O_Y in the absence of trade.

This change in tastes would cause K/L and w/r to be higher than before in the production of both commodities in Nation 1 (see Figure 5-7). As a result, the distance that Nation 1 needs to travel along its production contract curve (i.e., the degree of specialization in the production of commodity X) with trade in order to reach point B is less than before the change in tastes. That is, with a smaller pretrade difference in relative commodity and factor prices between the two nations after the change in tastes, a smaller degree of specialization in production and trade is required to equalize relative commodity and factor prices between the two nations (see the figure). This confirms the conclusions reached in section 5.7 and also shows how to use Figure 5-7 for analyses of this type.

Problem   Use Figure 5-7 to analyze the effect of an increase in Nation 1's demand for commodity Y (the K-intensive commodity) because of a change in tastes, starting from its no-trade equilibrium point.

Selected Bibliography

For a problem-solving approach to the material covered in this chapter, see:

• D. Salvatore, *Theory and Problems of Inter-* *national Economics*, 2nd ed. (New York, McGraw-Hill, 1984), ch. 4 (sect. 4.1).

The original sources for the Heckscher-Ohlin theory are:

- E. F. Heckscher, "The Effect of Foreign Trade on the Distribution of Income," *Ekonomisk Tidskrift,* 1919. Reprinted in H. S. Ellis and L. M. Metzler, *Readings in the Theory of International Trade* (Homewood Ill.: Irwin, 1950).
- B. Ohlin, *Interregional and International Trade* (Cambridge, Mass.: Harvard University Press, 1933).

The original proof of the factor-price equalization theorem is found in:

- P. A. Samuelson, "International Trade and the Equalization of Factor Prices," *Economic Journal,* June, 1948.
- P. A. Samuelson, "International Factor-Price Equalization Once Again," *Economic Journal,* June 1949. Reprinted in J. N. Bhagwati, *International Trade: Selected Readings* (Cambridge, Mass.: M.I.T. Press, 1981).

For the effect of international trade on the distribution of income, see:

- W. F. Stolper and P. A. Samuelson, "Protection and Real Wages," *Review of Economic Studies,* November 1941. Reprinted in H. S. Ellis and L. M. Metzler, *Readings in the Theory of International Trade* (Homewood, Ill.: Irwin, 1950).

Excellent syntheses of the Heckscher-Ohlin theory are found in:

- R. W. Jones, "Factor Proportions and the Heckscher-Ohlin Theorem," *Review of Economic Studies,* January 1956.
- H. G. Johnson, "Factor Endowments, International Trade and Factor Prices," *Manchester School of Economics and Social Studies,* September 1957. Reprinted in R. E. Caves and H. G. Johnson, *Readings in International Economics* (Homewood, Ill.: Irwin, 1968).
- K. Lancaster, "The Heckscher-Ohlin Trade Model: A Geometric Treatment," *Economica,* February 1957. Reprinted in J. N. Bhagwati, *International Trade: Selected Readings* (Baltimore: Penguin, 1969).

For excellent surveys of the Heckscher-Ohlin theory, see:

- J. N. Bhagwati, "The Pure Theory of International Trade: A Survey," *Economic Journal,* 1964.
- J. S. Chipman, "A Survey of the Theory of International Trade," *Econometrica,* 1965.

For the specific-factors model, see:

- R. W. Jones, "A Three-Factor Model in Theory, Trade, and History," in J. N. Bhagwati et al., eds. *Trade, Balance of Payments, and Growth: Essays in Honor of Charles P. Kindleberger* (Amsterdam: North-Holland, 1971).
- M. Mussa, "Tariffs and the Distribution of Income: The Importance of Factor Specificity, Substitutability, and Intensity in the Short and Long Run," *Journal of Political Economy,* November 1974.

CHAPTER 6

Empirical Tests and Complementary Trade Theories

6.1 Introduction

In previous chapters, we have seen that comparative advantage is reflected in a difference in relative commodity prices across nations. For *Ricardo* (Chapter 2), such a difference in relative commodity prices was based on the difference in the productivity of labor (the only factor of production that he explicitly considered) in the two nations. For *Haberler* (Chapter 3), comparative advantage was based on the difference in factor endowments and/or technology (as reflected in different production frontiers) in the two nations, reinforced (or at least not completely neutralized) by differences in tastes. Finally, *Heckscher and Ohlin* (Chapter 5) based comparative advantage on the difference in factor endowments in the two nations on the assumption of equal technology and tastes.

We now would like to examine the results of empirical tests of Ricardo's and Heckscher and Ohlin's trade models. A model must be successfully tested empirically before it is accepted as a theory. The greater the number of successful empirical tests is, the greater the confidence we have in the model. On the other hand, a model that is contradicted by empirical evidence must be rejected and an alternative model drawn up.

In section 6.2, we examine briefly some empirical tests that seem to verify Ricardo's trade model. Section 6.3 presents many important but somewhat inconclusive empirical tests of the Heckscher-Ohlin trade model. In section

6.4, we examine trade theories that are complementary to the basic Heckscher-Ohlin model so as to be able to explain an important portion of international trade not explained by the basic H-O model. In section 6.5, we examine transportation costs and nontraded commodities. Finally, in section 6.6, we present some general conclusions on the status of trade theory, in general, and the Heckscher-Ohlin model, in particular, as the assumptions of the latter are relaxed and made more realistic.

In the appendix to this chapter, we analyze the theoretical condition known as factor-intensity reversal, utilizing somewhat more advanced tools of analysis. We also summarize some important and advanced empirical tests on the prevalence of this phenomenon in the real world.

6.2   Empirical Tests of the Ricardian Model

The first empirical test of the Ricardian trade model was conducted by *MacDougall* in 1951 and 1952 using labor productivity and export data for 25 industries in the United States and the United Kingdom for the year 1937.

Since wages were twice as high in the United States as in the United Kingdom, MacDougall argued that costs of production would be lower in the United States in those industries where American labor was more than twice as productive as British labor. These would be the industries in which the United States had a comparative advantage with respect to the United Kingdom and in which it would undersell the United Kingdom in third markets (i.e., in the rest of the world). On the other hand, the United Kingdom would have a comparative advantage and undersell the United States in those industries where the productivity of British labor was more than one-half the productivity of American labor.

In his test MacDougall excluded trade between the United States and the United Kingdom because tariffs varied widely from industry to industry, tending to offset the differences in labor productivity between the two nations. At the same time, both nations faced generally equal tariffs in third markets. The exclusion of trade between the United States and the United Kingdom did not bias the test because their exports to each other constituted less than 5 percent of their total exports.

Figure 6-1 summarizes MacDougall's results. The vertical axis measures the ratio of output per United States worker to output per United Kingdom worker. The higher this ratio, the greater the relative productivity of United States labor. The horizontal axis measures the ratio of United States exports to United Kingdom exports to third markets. The higher this ratio, the larger are United States exports in relation to United Kingdom exports to the rest of the world. Note that the scales are logarithmic (so that equal distances refer to equal *percentage* changes) rather than arithmetic (where equal distances would measure equal *absolute* changes).

The points in the figure show a clear *positive* relationship between labor

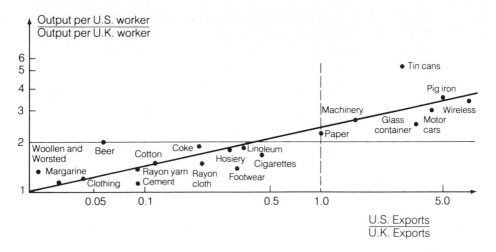

FIGURE 6-1.   Labor Productivity and Comparative Advantage—United States and United Kingdom

The figure shows a positive relationship between labor productivity and export shares for 20 industries in the United States and the United Kingdom, thus confirming the Ricardian trade model. *Source:* Adapted from G. D. A. MacDougall, "British and American Exports: A Study suggested by the Theory of Comparative Costs," *Economic Journal,* December 1951, p. 703.

productivity and exports. That is, those industries where the productivity of labor is relatively higher in the United States than in the United Kingdom are the industries with the higher ratios of United States to United Kingdom exports. This was true for the 20 industries shown in the figure out of the total of 25 industries studied by MacDougall. This positive relationship between labor productivity and exports in the United States and the United Kingdom was confirmed by subsequent studies by *Balassa* using 1950 data and *Stern* using 1950 and 1959 data.

These empirical studies all seem to support the Ricardian theory of comparative advantage. That is, the actual pattern of trade seems to be based on the different labor productivities in different industries in the two nations. Production costs other than labor costs, demand considerations, political ties, and various obstructions to the flow of international trade did not break the link between relative labor productivity and export shares.

One possible question remained. Why did the United States not capture the entire export market from the United Kingdom (rather than only a rising share of exports) in those industries where it enjoyed a cost advantage (i.e., where the ratio of the productivity of United States labor to United Kingdom labor was greater than 2)? MacDougall answered that this was mainly due to product differentiation. That is, the output of the same industry in the United States and the United Kingdom is not homogeneous. An American car is not identical to a British car. Even if the American car is cheaper, some consumers in the rest of the world may still prefer the British car. Thus the United Kingdom continues to export some cars even at a higher price. However, as the price difference grows, the United Kingdom's share of car exports can be expected to decline. The same is true for most other products. Similarly, the United States continues to export to third markets some commodities in which it has a cost disadvantage with respect to the United Kingdom. We will return to this important point in section 6.4b.

Even though the simple Ricardian trade model has to a large extent been empirically verified, it has a serious shortcoming in that it assumes rather than explains comparative advantage. As pointed out in section 5.1, Ricardo and classical economists in general provided no explanation for the difference in labor productivity and comparative advantage between nations, and they could not say much as to the effect of international trade on the earnings of factors of production. By providing answers to both of these important questions, the Heckscher-Ohlin model is certainly superior on theoretical grounds to the Ricardian, or classical, trade model.

6.3   Empirical Tests of the Heckscher-Ohlin Model

This section presents and evaluates the results of empirical tests of the Heckscher-Ohlin model. These results and their interpretation are not as straightforward and clear-cut as those for the Ricardian model.

In section 6.3a, we present the results of the original empirical test of the Heckscher-Ohlin model, conducted by Leontief. Since these results seemed to conflict with the model, many attempts were made to reconcile them with the model, and in the process numerous other empirical tests were undertaken. These are discussed in section 6.3b. In section 6.3c, we discuss the situation called factor-intensity reversal, which, if very prevalent, would lead to rejection of the H-O model. Empirical tests, however, indicate that this is not a very frequent occurrence in the real world.

6.3a   Empirical Results—The Leontief Paradox

The first empirical test of the Heckscher-Ohlin model was conducted by *Wassily Leontief* in 1951 using United States data for the year 1947. Since the United States was the most K-abundant nation in the world, Leontief expected to find that it exported K-intensive commodities and imported L-intensive commodities.

For this test, Leontief utilized the input-output table of the U.S. economy to calculate the amount of labor and capital in a "representative bundle" of $1 million worth of United States exports and import substitutes for the year 1947. (The **input-output table** is a table showing the origin and destination of each product in the economy. Leontief himself had contributed importantly to the development of this new technique of analysis and received the Nobel Prize in 1973 for his contributions.)

To be noted is that Leontief estimated K/L of United States import substitutes rather than imports. **Import substitutes** are commodities, such as automobiles, that the United States produces at home but also imports from abroad (because of incomplete specialization in production). Leontief was forced to use United States data on import substitutes because *foreign* production data on actual United States imports were not available. However, Leontief correctly reasoned that even though United States import substitutes would be more K intensive than actual imports (because K was relatively cheaper in the United States than abroad), they should still be less K intensive than United States exports if the H-O model held true. Of course, the use of United States data on import substitutes, instead of foreign data on actual United States imports, also eliminated from the calculations commodities, such as coffee and bananas, not produced at all in the United States.

The results of Leontief's test were startling. United States import substitutes were about 30 percent more K-intensive than United States exports. That is, the United States seemed to export L-intensive commodities and import K-intensive commodities. This was the opposite of what the H-O model predicted and became known as the **Leontief paradox.**

In the same study, Leontief tried to rationalize his results rather than reject the H-O model. He argued that what we had here was an optical illusion: since in 1947 United States labor was about three times as productive as foreign labor, the United States was really an L-abundant nation if we multiplied the United States labor force by three and compared this figure to the availability of capital in the nation. Therefore, it was only appropriate that United States exports should be L-intensive in relation to United States import substitutes. This explanation is not acceptable, and Leontief himself subsequently withdrew it. The reason is that while United States labor was definitely more productive than foreign labor (though the multiple of three used by Leontief was largely arbitrary), so was United States capital. Therefore, both United States labor *and* United States capital should be multiplied by about the same multiple, leaving the relative abundance of capital in the United States more or less unaffected.

Similarly invalid is another explanation that postulated that United States tastes were biased so strongly in favor of K-intensive commodities as to result in higher relative prices for these commodities in the United States. Therefore, the United States would export relatively L-intensive commodities. The reason this explanation is not acceptable is that tastes are known to be similar across nations. A study by *Houthakker* in 1957 on household consumption patterns in many countries found that the income elasticity of demand for food, clothing, housing, and other classes of goods was remarkably similar across nations. As a result, this explanation of the Leontief paradox based on a difference in tastes is also unacceptable.

6.3b   Explanations of the Leontief Paradox

One possible explanation of the paradox is that the year 1947, which Leontief used for the test, was too close to World War II to be representative. Leontief himself answered this criticism by repeating his study in 1956 using the 1947 input-output table of the United States economy but 1951 trade data. (The year 1951 is usually taken to mark the completion of post-war reconstruction.) This analysis showed that United States exports were only 6 percent more *L*-intensive than United States import substitutes. Leontief had reduced the paradox but had not eliminated it.

A more general source of bias is that Leontief used a two-factor model (*L* and *K*), thus abstracting from other factors such as natural resources (soil, climate, mineral deposits, forests, etc.). However, a commodity might be intensive in natural resources so that classifying it as either *K*- or *L*-intensive (with a two-factor model) would clearly be inappropriate. Furthermore, many production processes using natural resources such as coal mining, steel production, and farming also require large amounts of physical capital. The U.S. dependence on imports of many natural resources, therefore, might help explain the large capital intensity of U.S. import-competing industries.

United States tariff policy was another source of bias in the Leontief study. A tariff is nothing else than a tax on imports. As such, it reduces imports and stimulates the domestic production of import substitutes. In a 1954 study, *Kravis* found that the most heavily protected industries in the United States were the *L*-intensive industries. This biased the pattern of trade and reduced the labor intensity of United States import substitutes, thus contributing to the existence of the Leontief paradox.

Perhaps the most important source of bias was the fact that Leontief included in his measure of capital only physical capital (such as machinery, other equipment, buildings, and so on) and completely ignored human capital. **Human capital** refers to the education, job training, and health embodied in workers, which increase their productivity. The implication is that since United States labor embodies more human capital than foreign labor, adding the human capital component to physical capital would make United States exports more *K* intensive relative to United States import substitutes. (In fairness to Leontief it must be said that the analysis of human capital became fully developed and fashionable only following the work of Schultz in 1961 and Becker in 1964.)

Somewhat related to human capital is the influence of research and development (R&D) on U.S. exports. The "knowledge" capital resulting from R&D leads to an increase in the value of output derived from a given stock of material and human resources. Even casual observation shows that most U.S. exports are R&D and skill-intensive. Thus, human and knowledge capital are important considerations in determining the pattern of U.S. trade. These were not considered by Leontief in his study.

The most important of the numerous empirical studies following a human capital approach were undertaken by Kravis, Keesing, Kenen, and Baldwin. In two studies published in 1956, *Kravis* found that wages in United States exports industries in both 1947 and 1951 were about 15 percent higher than wages in United States import-competing industries. Kravis correctly argued that the higher wages in United States exports industries were a reflection of the greater productivity and human capital embodied in United States exports than in United States import substitutes.

In a 1966 study, *Keesing* found that United States exports were more skill-intensive than the exports of nine other industrial nations for the year 1957. This reflected the fact that the United States had the most highly trained labor force, embodying more human capital than other nations.

It remained for *Kenen*, in a 1965 study, to actually estimate the human capital embodied in United States exports and import-competing goods, add these estimates to the physical capital requirements, and then recompute K/L for United States exports and United States import substitutes. Using 1947 data and without excluding products with an important natural resource content (as in the original Leontief study), Kenen succeeded in eliminating the Leontief paradox.

In a 1971 study, *Baldwin* updated Leontief's study by using the United States input-output table of 1958 and United States trade data for 1962. Baldwin found that including human capital was not sufficient to eliminate the paradox unless goods using natural resources intensively were excluded. However, a great deal of United States trade is based on agricultural and petroleum products. Furthermore, the paradox remained for developing nations as a group and for Canada. Similar paradoxical results arose in using other countries' data. A 1977 study by *Branson* and *Monoyios* also raised some questions on the appropriateness of combining human and physical capital into a single measure for the purpose of testing the H-O trade model.

An important step in resolving the paradox was provided by *Leamer* in 1980. Since the U.S. was a net exporter of capital and labor services, Leamer argued that we should compare the K/L ratio in production versus consumption, rather than in exports versus imports. Taking this approach to Leontief 1947 data, Leamer found that the K/L ratio embodied in U.S. production was indeed greater than that embodied in U.S. consumption, so that the paradox disappears. This was confirmed in a 1981 study by *Stern* and *Maskus* using 1972 data. Additional empirical tests may be required, however, to fully confirm the H-O theory. In the meantime, the model is retained while awaiting further empirical testing.

6.3c Factor-Intensity Reversal

Factor-intensity reversal refers to the situation where a given commodity is the *L*-intensive commodity in the *L*-abundant nation and the *K*-intensive commodity in the *K*-abundant nation. For example, factor-intensity reversal is present if commodity X is the *L*-intensive commodity in Nation 1 (the low-wage nation) and the *K*-intensive comodity in Nation 2 (the high-wage nation).

To determine when and why factor-intensity reversal occurs, we use the concept of the elasticity of substitution of factors in production. The **elasticity of substitution** measures the degree or ease with which one factor can be substituted for another in production as the relative price of the factor declines. For example, suppose that the elasticity of substitution of *L* for *K* is much greater in the production of commodity X than in the production of commodity Y. This means that it is much easier to substitute *L* for *K* (or vice versa) in the production of comodity X than in the production of commodity Y.

Factor-intensity reversal is more likely to occur when the *difference* in the elasticity of substitution of *L* for *K* in the production of the two commodities is greater. With a large elasticity of substitution of *L* for *K* in the production of commodity X, Nation 1 will produce commodity X with *L*-intensive techniques because its wages are low. On the other hand, Nation 2 will produce commodity X with *K*-intensive techniques because its wages are high. If at the same time the elasticity of substitution of *L* for *K* is very low in the production of commodity Y, the two nations will be forced to use similar techniques in producing commodity Y even though their relative factor prices may differ greatly. As a result, comodity X will be the *L*-intensive commodity in Nation 1 and the *K*-intensive comodity in Nation 2, and we have a case of factor-intensity reversal.

When factor-intensity reversal is present, both the H-O theorem and the factor-price equalization theorem do not hold. The H-O model fails because it would predict that Nation 1 (the *L*-abundant nation) would export commodity X (its *L*-intensive commodity) and that Nation 2 (the *K*-abundant nation) would also export commodity X (its *K*-intensive commodity). Since the two nations cannot possibly export the same *homogeneous* commodity to each other, the H-O model no longer predicts the pattern of trade.

With factor-intensity reversal, the factor-price equalization theorem also fails to hold. The reason for this is that as Nation 1 specializes in the production of commodity X and demands more *L*, the relative and the absolute wage rate will rise in Nation 1 (the low-wage nation). On the other hand, since Nation 2 cannot export commodity X to Nation 1, it will have to specialize in the production of and export commodity Y. Since commodity Y is the *L*-intensive commodity in Nation 2, the demand for *L* and thus wages will also rise in Nation 2. What happens to the *difference* in relative and absolute wages between Nation 1 and Nation 2 depends on how fast wages rise in each nation. The difference in relative and absolute wages between the two nations could decline, increase, or remain unchanged as a result of international trade, so that the factor-price equalization theorem no longer holds.

That factor-intensity reversal does occur in the real world is beyond doubt. The question is how prevalent it is. If factor reversal is very prevalent, the entire H-O theory must be rejected. If it occurs but rarely, we can retain the

H-O model and treat factor reversal as an exception. The frequency of factor reversal in the real world is an empirical question.

The first empirical research on this topic was a study conducted by *Minhas* in 1962, in which he found factor reversal to be fairly prevalent, occurring in about one-third of the cases that he studied. However, by correcting an important source of bias in the Minhas study, Leontief showed in 1964 that factor reversal occurred in only about 8 percent of the cases studied, and that if two industries with an important natural resource content were excluded, factor reversal occurred in only 1 percent of the cases.

A study by *Ball* published in 1966 and testing another aspect of Minhas' results confirmed Leontief's conclusion that factor-intensity reversal seems to be a rather rare occurrence in the real world. As a result, the assumption that one commodity is *L*-intensive and the other commodity is *K*-intensive (assumption 3 in section 5.2) at all *relevant* relative factor prices generally holds, so that the H-O model can be retained.

6.4   Complementary Trade Theories

While the H-O model is retained, there is a significant portion of international trade not explained by the basic H-O model. In this section, we examine other important trade theories in an attempt to fill the gap.

In section 6.4a, we examine trade based on increasing returns to scale. In section 6.4b, we discuss trade based on differentiated products. Finally, in section 6.4c, we analyze trade based on technological gaps and product cycles. Some economists view these as *alternative* trade theories. However, since these trade models are not comprehensive and explain only the portion of international trade that the H-O model cannot explain, we regard them as complementary to the H-O model rather than as alternative or substitute trade models. We will return to this topic in section 6.6, where we summarize the status of the H-O model and international trade theory in general.

6.4a   Trade Based on Economies of Scale

One of the assumptions of the H-O model was that both commodities were produced under conditions of constant returns to scale in the two nations (assumption 4 in section 5.2). With increasing returns to scale, mutually beneficial trade can take place even when the two nations are identical in every respect. This is a type of trade that the H-O model does not explain.

Increasing returns to scale refers to the production situation where output grows proportionately more than the increase in inputs or factors of production. That is, if all inputs are doubled, output is more than doubled. If all inputs are tripled, output is more than tripled. Increasing returns to scale *may* occur because at a larger scale of operation a greater division of labor and specialization becomes possible. That is, each worker can specialize in performing a simple repetitive task with a resulting increase in productivity. Furthermore, a larger scale of operation may permit the introduction of more specialized and productive machinery than would be feasible at a smaller scale of operation.

Figure 6-2 shows how mutually beneficial trade can be based on increasing returns to scale. If the two nations are assumed to be identical in every respect, we can use a single production frontier and a single indifference map to refer to both nations. Increasing returns to scale result in production frontiers that are *convex* from the origin, or inward-bending. With identical production frontiers and indifference maps, the no-trade equilibrium relative commodity prices in the two nations are also identical. In Figure 6-2, this is $P_X/P_Y = P_A$ in both nations and is given by the slope of the common tangent to the production frontier and indifference curve I at point A.

With trade, Nation 1 could specialize completely in the production of commodity X and produce at point B. Nation 2 would then specialize completely in the production of commodity Y and produce at point B'. By then exchang-

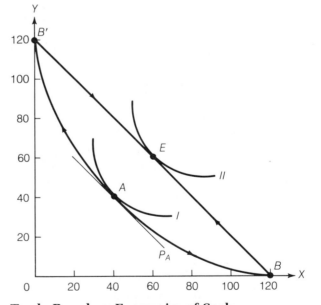

FIGURE 6-2. Trade Based on Economies of Scale

With identical and convex to the origin (because of economies of scale) production frontiers and indifference maps, the no-trade equilibrium relative commodity price in the two nations is identical and given by P_A. With trade, Nation 1 could specialize completely in the production of commodity X and produce at point B. Nation 2 would then specialize completely in the production of commodity Y and produce at point B'. By then exchanging 60X for 60Y with each other, each nation would end up consuming at point E on indifference curve II, thus gaining 20X and 20Y.

ing 60X for 60Y with each other, each nation would end up consuming at point E on indifference curve II, thus gaining 20X and 20Y. These gains from trade arise from economies of scale in the production of only one comodity in each nation. In the absence of trade, the two nations would not specialize in the production of only one commodity because each nation wants to consume both commodities.

Note that the no-trade equilibrium point A is unable in the sense that if, for whatever reason, Nation 1 moves to the right of point A along its production frontier, the relative price of X (the slope of the production frontier) will fall and will continue to fall until Nation 1 becomes completely specialized in the production of commodity X. Similarly, if Nation 2 moves to the left of point A along its production frontier, P_X/P_Y will rise (so that its inverse, or P_Y/P_X, falls) until Nation 2 becomes completely specialized in the production of commodity Y.

Several additional aspects of the above analysis and Figure 6-2 must be clarified. First of all, it is a matter of complete indifference which of the two nations specializes in the production of commodity X or commodity Y. Second, it should be clear, at least intuitively, that the two nations need not be identical in every respect for mutually beneficial trade to result from increasing returns to scale. Third, if economies of scale persist over a sufficiently long range of outputs, one or a few firms will capture the entire market for a given product, leading to **monopoly** (a single producer of a commodity for which there is no close substitute) or **oligopoly** (a few producers of a homogeneous or differentiated product).

Furthermore, it has recently become evident that economies of scale in industrialized nations result primarily from having each firm or plant produce only one or at most a few varieties and styles of the same product rather than many different varieties and styles. This is crucial in keeping unit costs low. With few varieties and styles, more specialized and faster machinery can be developed for a continuous operation and a longer production run.

For example, even before the formation of the European Economic Community, or Common Market, plant size in most industries was about the same in Europe and the United States. However, unit costs were much higher in Europe, primarily because European plants produced many more varieties and styles of a product than their American counterparts. As tariffs were reduced and finally eliminated and trade expanded within the European Community, each European plant could specialize in the production of only a few varieties and styles of a product, and unit costs fell sharply.

Somewhat related to economies of scale is the hypothesis advanced by *Linder* in 1961 that a nation exports those manufactured products for which a large domestic market exists. These are products that appeal to the majority of the population. In the process of satisfying such a market, the nation acquires the necessary experience and efficiency to be able subsequently to export these commodities to other nations with similar tastes and income levels. The nation will import those products that appeal to the low- and high-income minorities. While confirmed for his native Sweden, Linder's hypothesis has not been confirmed for other nations. It also cannot explain, for example, why such non-Christian nations as Japan and Korea export artificial Christmas trees and Christmas cards in the absence of a domestic market for these products.

6.4b   Trade Based on Differentiated Products

A large portion of the output of modern economies involves differentiated rather than homogeneous products. Thus, a Chevrolet is not identical to a Toyota, a Volkswagen, a Fiat, or a Renault. As a result, a great deal of international trade can and does involve the exchange of *differentiated products* of the same industry or broad product group. That is, a great deal of international trade is **intra-industry trade** in differentiated products as opposed to inter-industry trade in completely different products.

This became apparent when all tariffs and other obstructions to the flow of trade among members of the European Economic Community, or Common Market, were removed. *Balassa* found in 1967 that the volume of trade surged but most of the increase involved the exchange of differentiated products *within* each broad and industrial classification. That is, German cars were exchanged for French and Italian cars, French washing machines were exchanged for German washing machines, and Italian typewriters for German and French typewriters, and so on.

Grubel and *Lloyd* have estimated that almost 50 percent of the trade among industrialized countries involves the exchange of differentiated products of the same industry in the various nations. As might be expected, this figure is smaller for developing countries and in agricultural products, where product differentiation is less prevalent.

These large two-way flows of differentiated products within the same general product class among industrialized nations result from the fact that producers in each nation tend to cater to "majority" tastes within their nation. This leaves pockets of "minority" tastes, which are more effectively and efficiently satisfied by imports. For example, most Germans prefer Volkswagens to Renaults because Volkswagens more nearly reflect tastes and driving conditions in Germany. However, some Germans do buy Renaults. This type of international trade not only increases the range of choices available to consumers within each nation but also increases the level of competition among producers of the same class of products in various nations. These are important benefits not explicitly considered by the basic H-O trade model.

Several other interesting considerations must be pointed out with respect to the intra-industry trade models developed by *Krugman, Lancaster, Helpman*, and others since 1979. First, while trade in the H-O model is based on different factor endowments (labor, capital, natural resources, and technology), intra-industry trade is likely to be larger among economies of similar size and factor proportions.

Secondly, product differentiation and economies of scale are closely related. As pointed out in the previous subsection, international competition forces firms in each industrial nation to produce only a few varieties and styles of a product in order to take advantage of economies of scale and lower per-unit production costs. The nation then imports other varieties and styles of the commodity from other nations. Thus, inter-industry trade can be explained by the standard H-O model (i.e., by comparative advantage), while intra-industry trade can be explained by product differentiation and economies of scale.

Thirdly, with differentiated products produced under economies of scale, pre-trade relative commodity prices may no longer accurately predict the pattern of trade. Specifically, a large country may produce a commodity at lower cost than a smaller country in the absence of trade (because of larger national economies of scale). With trade, however, all countries can take advantage of economies of scale to the same extent, and the smaller country could conceivably undersell the larger nation in the same commodity.

Finally, as contrasted to the H-O model, which predicts that trade will lower the return of the nation's scarce factor, with intra-industry trade based on economies of scale it is possible for all factors to gain. This may explain why the formation of the European Common Market and the great postwar trade liberalization in manufactured goods met little resistance by interest groups.

Related to intra-industry trade is the sharp increase in international trade in parts or components of a product. International corporations often produce various parts of a product in different nations to minimize their costs of production. For example, the motors of some Ford Fiestas are produced in the United Kingdom, the transmissions in France, the clutches in Spain, and the parts assembled in West Germany. Similarly, German and Japanese cameras are often assembled in Singapore to take advantage of the much cheaper labor there. The utilization of each nation's comparative advantage to minimize total production costs can be regarded as an extension of the basic H-O model to modern production conditions. This pattern also provides greatly needed employment opportunities in some developing nations. We will return to this topic in Chapter 12, which deals with international resource movements and multinational corporations.

6.4c Trade Based on Technological Gaps and Product Cycles

Apart from the relative availability of labor, capital, and natural resources, and the existence of product differentiation and economies of scale, technology can also be a separate determinant of international trade. Two models that explain international trade on the basis of technological change are the technological gap model and the product cycle model. As time is involved in a fundamental way in both of these models, they can be said to be dynamic in nature as opposed to the mostly static H-O model.

According to the **technological gap model** sketched by *Posner* in 1961, a great deal of the trade among industrialized countries is based on the introduction of new products and new production processes. These give the innovating firm and nation a *temporary* monopoly in the world market. Such a temporary monopoly is often based on patents and copyrights granted to stimulate the flow of inventions.

As the most technologically advanced nation, the United States exports a large number of new high-technology products. However, as foreign producers acquire the new technology, they eventually are able to conquer markets abroad, and even the United States market for the product, because of their lower labor costs. In the meantime, United States producers may have introduced still newer products and production processes and be able to export these products based on the new technological gap established. However, this model does not explain the size of technological gaps and does not probe the reason that technological gaps arise or exactly how they are eliminated over time.

A generalization and extension of the technological gap model is the **product cycle model,** which was fully developed by *Vernon* in 1966. According to this model, when a new product is introduced, it usually requires highly skilled labor to produce. As the product matures and acquires mass acceptance, it becomes standardized; it can then be produced by mass production techniques and less skilled labor. Therefore, comparative advantage in the product shifts from the advanced nation that originally introduced it to less advanced nations where labor is relatively cheaper. This may be accompanied by foreign direct investments from the innovating nation to nations with cheaper labor.

Vernon also pointed out that high-income and labor-saving products are most likely to be introduced by producers in the U.S. and in other rich nations because there the opportunities for doing so are greatest and because the development of these new products requires proximity to markets so as to benefit from consumer feedback in modifying the product, and to provide service.

A classic example of the product cycle model is provided by the experience of United States and Japanese radio manufacturers since World War II. Immediately after the war, United States firms dominated the international market for radios, based on vacuum tubes developed in the United States. However, within a few years, Japan was able to capture a large share of the market by copying United States technology and utilizing cheaper labor. The United States recaptured technological leadership with the development of transistors. But, once again, in a few short years, Japan imitated the technology and was able to undersell the United States. Subsequently, the United States reacquired its ability to compete successfully with Japan by introducing printed circuits. It remains to be seen whether this latest technology will finally result in radios being labor or capital intensive and whether the United States will be able to stay in the market—or whether both the United States and Japan will eventually be displaced by still cheaper producers in such nations as Korea and Taiwan.

In a 1967 study, *Grubber*, *Mehta*, and *Vernon* found a strong correlation between expenditures on research and development (R&D) and export performance. The authors took expenditures on research and development as a proxy for the *temporary* comparative advantage that firms and nations have in new products and new production processes. As such, these results tend to support both the technological gap model and the closely related product cycle model. In a 1983 study, Bowen found that the technological lead of the U.S. based on R&D has narrowed with respect to Europe and Japan.

Note that trade in these models is originally based on new technology developed by the relatively abundant factors in industrialized nations (such as highly skilled labor and expenditures on research and development). Subsequently, through imitation and product standardization, less developed nations gain a comparative advantage based on their relatively cheaper labor. As such, trade may be said to be based on relative factor abundance. Therefore, the technological gap and product cycle models can be regarded as extensions of the basic H-O model into a technologically·dynamic world, rather than as alternative trade models. In short, the product cycle model tries to explain *dynamic* comparative advantage for new products and new production processes as opposed to the *basic* H-O model, which explains *static* comparative advantage. We return to this source of growth, and change in comparative advantage over time in the next chapter.

6.5 Transportation Costs and Nontraded Commodities

So far, we have assumed that transportation costs are zero (assumption 9 in section 5.2). In this section, we relax this assumption and analyze the effect on the basic H-O model.

Transportation costs include freight charges, costs of loading and unloading, insurance premiums, and interest charges while goods are in transit. Thus, we are here using the term "transportation costs" to include all the costs of transferring goods from one location (nation) to another. A homogeneous good will be traded internationally only if the pretrade price difference in the two nations exceeds the cost of transporting the good from one nation to the other. Consideration of transportation costs explains why many goods and services are not traded at all internationally. These are referred to as **nontraded goods and services.** They are the goods and services for which transportation costs exceed price differences across nations. Thus, cement is not traded internationally except in border areas. Similarly, a person does not travel from London to New York simply to get a haircut.

There are two ways of analyzing transportation costs. One is by **general equilibrium analysis,** which utilizes the nations' production frontiers or offer curves and expresses transportation costs in terms of relative commodity prices. A more straightforward method is to analyze the absolute, or money, cost of transportation with **partial equilibrium analysis.** This holds constant the rate of exchange between the two currencies, the level of income, and everything else in the two nations, except the amount produced, consumed, and traded of the commodity under consideration. This is shown in Figure 6-3.

In Figure 6-3, the common vertical axis measures the dollar price of commodity X in Nation 1 and in Nation 2. Increasing quantities of commodity X are measured by a movement to the right from the common origin (as usual) for Nation 2. Increasing quantities of commodity X for Nation 1 are instead measured by a movement to the left from the common origin. Note that Nation 1's demand curve for commodity X (D_X) is negatively inclined (slopes downward), while its supply curve of commodity X (S_X) is positively inclined, *as we move from right to left* as we should for Nation 1.

In the absence of trade, Nation 1 produces and consumes 50X at the equilibrium price of $P_X = \$5$ (given by the intersection of D_X and S_X in Nation 1). Nation 2 produces and consumes 50X at $P_X = \$11$. With the opening of trade, Nation 1 will export commodity X to Nation 2. As it does, P_X rises in Nation 1 and falls in Nation 2. With a transportation cost of $2 per unit, P_X in Nation

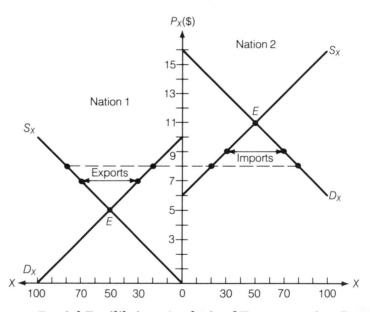

FIGURE 6-3. Partial Equilibrium Analysis of Transportation Costs

The common vertical axis measures the dollar price of commodity X in the two nations. A movement to the left from the common origin measures increasing quantities of commodity X for Nation 1. In the absence of trade, Nation 1 will produce and consume 50X at $P_X = \$5$. Nation 2 will produce and consume 50X at $P_X = \$11$. With transportation costs of $2 per unit, $P_X = \$7$ in Nation 1 and $P_X = \$9$ in Nation 2. At $P_X = \$7$, Nation 1 will produce 70X, consume 30X, and export 40X. At $P_X = \$9$, Nation 2 will produce 30X, import 40X, and consume 70X.

2 will exceed P_X in Nation 1 by \$2. This cost will be shared by the two nations so as to balance trade. This occurs when $P_X = \$7$ in Nation 1 and $P_X = \$9$ in Nation 2. At $P_X = \$7$, Nation 1 will produce 70X, consume domestically 30X, and export 40X to Nation 2. At $P_X = \$9$, Nation 2 will produce 30X, import 40X, and consume 70X.

Note that in the absence of transportation costs, $P_X = \$8$ in both nations and 60X are traded. Thus, transportation costs reduce the level of specialization in production and also the volume and gains from trade. Furthermore, since the absolute (and relative) price of commodity X differs in the two nations with transportation costs, their factor prices will not be completely equalized even if all the other assumptions of the H-O model hold.

Finally, because of the way Figure 6-3 was drawn, the cost of transportation is shared equally by the two nations. In general, the more steeply inclined D_X and S_X are in Nation 1 relative to Nation 2, the greater is the share of transportation costs paid by Nation 1. (The proof of this proposition and the general equilibrium analysis of transportation costs is assigned as an end-of-chapter problem.)

6.6   Some General Conclusions on the Heckscher-Ohlin Model and Complementary Trade Theories

We now present some general conclusions as to the status of international trade theory in general, and the H-O model in particular, in light of the empirical testing and the development of the complementary trade theories discussed above. It is useful to organize the presentation in terms of the assumptions of the H-O model discussed in section 5.2. That is, what effect will making the assumptions of the model more realistic have on the basic H-O model?

Relaxing the first assumption (two nations, two commodities, and two factors) to include more than two nations, more than two commodities, and more than two factors, while certainly complicating the analysis, leaves the H-O model basically valid, as long as the number of commodities is equal to or larger than the number of factors. One complication that arises in dealing with more than two factors is that we can no longer classify a commodity as simply L or K intensive but will require the construction of a factor-intensity *index* to predict the pattern of trade. This can be complex, but should still be possible.

The assumption of the same technology in the two nations is not generally valid. Trade can be based on a difference in technology, as in the technological gap and product cycle models. However, as pointed out in section 6.4c, these models could be regarded as dynamic extensions of the basic H-O model.

The assumption that commodity X is L intensive and commodity Y is K

intensive in both nations implies the absence of factor-intensity reversal. As pointed out in section 6.3c, factor-intensity reversal would lead to the rejection of the H-O model. However, empirical studies indicate that factor-intensity reversal is fairly rare in the real world. It seems that the Leontief paradox could be eliminated by the inclusion of human capital, the exclusion of commodities intensive in natural resources, and comparing the K/L ratio in production versus consumption, rather than in exports versus imports.

While the H-O model assumed constant returns to scale, international trade can also be based on increasing returns to scale. Thus, increasing returns to scale can be regarded as *complementary* to the H-O model in that they try to explain a portion of international trade not covered by the basic H-O model.

The fifth assumption of the H-O model was incomplete specialization in both nations. If trade brings about complete specialization in production in one of the nations, relative commodity prices will be equalized but factor prices will not. For example, if in Figure 5-7, the amount of capital available to Nation 1 was so much less than point B (at which factor prices would be equalized in the two nations) is outside the Edgeworth box for Nation 1 (and, therefore, unattainable), factor prices would not be equalized in the two nations, even though relative commodity prices are.

The assumption of equal tastes has been more or less verified empirically. Tastes are certainly not sufficiently different across nations to overcome differences in the relative *physical* availability of factors of production, in explaining different relative commodity prices and trade among nations.

The assumption of perfect competition is more troublesome. It seems that about one-half of the trade in manufactured goods among industrialized nations is based on product differentiation and economies of scale, which are not easily reconciled with the H-O factor-endowment model. To explain intraindustry trade, we need new models which are complementary to the basic H-O model.

As pointed out in section 5.5a, international factor mobility can be a substitute for international trade in bringing about equality of relative commodity and factor prices among nations. With some, but less than perfect, international factor mobility, the volume of trade required to bring about relative commodity and factor price equalization would be less. This only modifies the basic H-O model and it does not take away its validity.

Similarly, transportation costs and other nonprohibitive obstructions to the flow of international trade reduce the volume and the benefits of international trade, but they only modify (rather than to lead to rejection of) the H-O theorem and the factor-equalization theorem.

The general conclusions that emerge from all of this are:

1. Empirical tests to date have been somewhat inconclusive, and the H-O model has been neither proved nor disproved.
2. Relaxing most of the assumptions on which the model rests only modifies the model and does not lead to its rejection.

3. The H-O model seems to offer a reasonable explanation for international trade in nonindustrial goods, especially for trade based on the natural resource endowments of the nation, but it leaves a substantial portion of international trade unexplained. This is particularly true for the trade in differentiated manufactured products among industrial countries.

4. Complementary or alternative explanations (based on economies of scale, differentiated products, and dynamic changes in technology) are required to account for the portion of international trade not covered by the basic H-O model. The hope is that in the future some of these other explanations of international trade can be merged into a single and more general theory. However, international trade may be too complex a phenomenon to be explained by a single comprehensive theory.

Summary

1. The first empirical test of the Ricardian trade model was conducted by MacDougall in 1951 and 1952 using 1937 data. The results indicated that those industries where labor productivity was relatively higher in the United States than in the United Kingdom were the industries with the higher ratios of United States to United Kingdom exports to third markets. These results were confirmed by Balassa using 1950 data and Stern using 1950 and 1959 data. Thus, it can be seen that comparative advantage seems to be based on a difference in labor productivity, as postulated by Ricardo. However, the Ricardian model explains neither the reason for the difference in labor productivity across nations nor the effect of international trade on the earnings of factors.

2. The first empirical test of the H-O model was conducted by Leontief using 1947 United States data. Leontief found that United States import substitutes were about 30 percent more K intensive than United States exports. Since the United States is the most K-abundant nation, this result was the opposite of what the H-O model predicted and became known as the Leontief paradox. This paradox could be explained by (1) 1947 being a nonrepresentative year, (2) the use of a two-factor (L and K) model, (3) the fact that United States tariffs gave more protection to L-intensive industries, (4) the exclusion of human capital from the calculations. Kravis, Keesing, Kenen, and Baldwin demonstrated that United States exports embody more human capital than United States imports, and this could indeed contribute to explaining part of the paradox. The paradox was eliminated by Leamer, and Stern and Maskus by comparing the K/L ratio in U.S. production vs. U.S. consumption, rather than in exports vs. imports.

3. Factor-intensity reversal refers to the situation where a commodity is L intensive in the L-abundant nation and K intensive in the K-abundant nation. This may occur when the elasticity of substitution of factors in production varies greatly for the two commodities. With factor reversal, both the H-O theorem and the factor-price equalization theorem fail. Minhas conducted a test in 1962 that showed that factor reversal was fairly prevalent. Leontief and Ball demonstrated, however, that Minhas' results were biased and that factor reversal was a rather rare occurrence. Therefore, the H-O model could be retained.

4. There is an important portion of international trade not explained by the basic H-O model. A great deal of trade in manufactured products among industrial nations now involves differentiated products and economies of scale, with each nation producing only some varieties of a given product and importing other varieties from other nations. To explain this trade, new trade theories are required. Some trade is also the result of technological gaps and product cycles. Vernon postulated that a new product is usually introduced by an industrial nation and pro-

duced with skilled labor. As the product matures and is standardized, it will be produced with less skilled labor in other nations.

5. With transportation costs, only those commodities whose pretrade price difference exceeds the cost of transporting them from one nation to another will be traded. When trade is in equilibrium, the relative price of traded commodities in the two nations will differ by the cost of transportation. This will also prevent complete factor-price equalization.

6. The status of the H-O model and international trade theory in general can be summarized as follows: (1) empirical tests have neither proved nor disproved the H-O model; (2) relaxing most of the assumptions of the H-O model merely modifies the model and does not lead to its rejection; (3) the H-O model seems to offer a good explanation of trade in nonindustrial goods but leaves unexplained an important portion of international trade, particularly the trade in industrial goods; (4) complementary or alternative explanations are required to account for the portion of international trade not covered by the basic H-O model. These are based on economies of scale, differentiated products, and dynamic changes in technology.

A Look Ahead

The international trade theory discussed so far is, with few exceptions (such as the product cycle model), completely static in nature. That is, given the resource endowments, technology, and tastes of two nations, we proceeded to determine the comparative advantage of each nation and examine the resulting gains from trade. In the next chapter, we will analyze in detail the effect of changes in factor endowments, technology, and tastes on the comparative advantage of each nation, the volume of trade, the terms of trade, and the welfare of each nation. Though this does not make our trade theory exactly dynamic, it does show that it can be extended to incorporate the effect of changes in underlying conditions through time.

Glossary

Input-output table A matrix or table showing the origin and destination of each product in the economy.

Import substitutes Commodities (such as automobiles in the United States) that a nation products at home but also imports from other nations (because of incomplete specialization in production).

Leontief paradox The empirical finding that United States import substitutes were more K intensive than United States exports. This is contrary to the H-O trade model, which predicts that, as the most K-abundant nation, the United States should import L-intensive products and export K-intensive products.

Human capital The education, job training, and health embodied in workers, which increase their productivity.

Factor-intensity reversal The situation where a commodity is L intensive when the relative price of labor is low and K intensive when the relative price of capital is low. If prevalent, this would lead to rejection of the H-O trade model.

Elasticity of substitution The degree or ease with which one factor can be substituted for another in production when the price of the factor declines.

Differentiated products The somewhat different products (such as automobiles, cigarettes, and soaps) produced by different manufacturers in the same industry or general product group.

Intra-industry trade International trade in the differentiated products of the same industry or broad product group.

Increasing returns to scale The production situation where output grows proportionately more than the increase in inputs or factors of production. For example, doubling all inputs more than doubles output.

Monopoly The form of market organization where there is a single producer of a commodity for which there is no close substitute.

Oligopoly The form of market organization

where there are only a few producers of a homogeneous or differentiated product.

Technological gap model   The hypothesis that a portion of international trade is based on the introduction of new products or processes.

Product cycle model   The hypothesis, advanced by Vernon, that new products introduced by industrial nations and produced with skilled labor eventually become standardized and can be produced in other nations with less skilled labor.

Transportation costs   Freight charges, costs of loading and unloading, insurance premiums, and interest charges while goods are in transit.

Nontraded goods and services   Those goods and services which are not traded internationally because the cost of transporting them exceeds the international price difference.

Partial equilibrium analysis   The study of individual decision-making units (such as persons or firms) and individual markets in isolation (i.e., abstracting from all the interconnections that exist between the individual, firm, or market and the rest of the economy).

Questions for Review

1. What results did MacDougall get when he tested the Ricardian trade model empirically? Were these results confirmed or rejected by the empirical tests of Balassa and Stern? What theoretical shortcomings of the Ricardian model make it necessary to look for better trade models?

2. What is meant by the Leontief paradox? What are some possible explanations of the paradox? How can human capital contribute to the explanation of the paradox? What were the results of empirical tests on the relationship between human capital and international trade? How was the paradox seemingly resolved recently?

3. What is meant by factor-intensity reversal? How is this related to the elasticity of substitution of factors in production? Why would

the prevalence of factor reversal lead to rejection of the H-O theorem and the factor-price equalization theorem? What were the results of empirical tests on the prevalence of factor reversal in the real world?

4. Why are theories complementary to the H-O model required? How can trade be based on economies of scale? What was the principal cause of the economies of scale that resulted from the formation of the European Economic Community? How can trade be based on product differentiation? How does the technological gap model explain international trade? How does this differ from the product cycle model? Can you give an example of the product cycle explanation of international trade?

5. What is the relationship between transportation costs and nontraded goods and services? How do transportation costs affect the H-O theorem? How do they affect the factor-price equalization theorem?

6. What overall conclusion emerges from the empirical tests to date on the H-O model? What effect does relaxation of the assumptions have on the H-O model? What part of international trade does the H-O model seem best suited to explain? What part of international trade is the H-O model unable to explain? What should be the aim of future theoretical and empirical work in international trade theory?

Problems

*1. Comment on the following quotation: "The assumptions necessary to bring about complete equality in the returns to homogeneous factors among nations are so restrictive and unrepresentative of actual reality that the theory can be said to prove the opposite of what it seems to say—namely, that there is no chance whatsoever that factor prices will ever be equalized by free commodity trade."

2. (a) Discuss the meaning and importance of the Leontief paradox.

(b) Summarize the empirical results of Kravis, Keesing, Kenen, and Baldwin on the importance of human capital in helping to resolve the paradox.

(c) How was the paradox seemingly resolved by Leamer, and Stern and Maskus?

*3. (a) Draw a figure similar to Figure 5-4 showing factor-intensity reversal.

(b) With reference to your figure, explain how factor reversal could take place.

(c) Summarize the empirical results of Minhas, Leontief, and Ball on the prevalence of factor reversal in the real world.

4. Explain why, with factor-intensity reversal, international differences in the price of capital can decrease, increase, or remain unchanged.

5. Draw a separate figure, similar to Figure 6-2, for each of two nations showing how mu-

tually beneficial trade can take place between them based on economies of scale, if the two nations:

(a) have identical production frontiers but different tastes;

(b) have equal tastes but different production frontiers;

(c) have different production frontiers and tastes.

6. Show how transportation costs:

(a) can be analyzed with production frontiers (hint: relative commodity prices with trade will differ by the cost of transportation);

(b) can be analyzed with offer curves;

(c) fall more heavily on the nation with the steeper demand and supply curves for the traded commodity, using a figure similar to Figure 6-3.

APPENDIX

We now examine factor-intensity reversal utilizing the more advanced analytical tools reviewed in the appendix to Chapter 3. Section A6.1 gives a diagrammatic presentation of factor-intensity reversal. Section A6.2 presents the formula to measure the elasticity of substitution of L for K in production and examines its relationship to factor-intensity reversal. Section A6.3 then discusses the method used to conduct empirical tests to determine the prevalence of factor-intensity reversal in the real world.

A6.1   Illustration of Factor-Intensity Reversal

Figure 6-4 shows a single isoquant for commodity X and a single isoquant for commodity Y. From section A3.1, we know that with a homogeneous production function of degree one, a single isoquant completely describes the entire production function of each commodity. Furthermore, since both nations are assumed to use the same technology, we can use the single X- and Y-isoquants to refer to both nations.

Figure 6-4 shows that at $w/r = 1/2$, commodity X is produced at Point A, where the X-isoquant is tangent to the isocost line with slope (w/r) equal to $1/2$ and $K/L = 6/18 = 1/3$. Commodity Y is produced at point B, where the Y-isoquant is tangent to the same isocost line with slope (w/r) equal to $1/2$ and $K/L = 9/12 = 3/4$. Thus, at $w/r = 1/2$, K/L is higher for commodity Y, so that commodity X is the relatively *L*-intensive commodity.

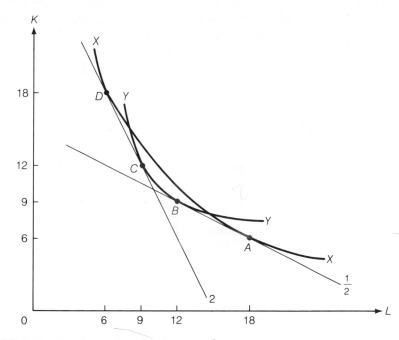

FIGURE 6-4. Factor-Intensity Reversal

At $w/r=\frac{1}{2}$, commodity X is produced at point A with $K/L=6/18=\frac{1}{3}$, while commodity Y is produced at point B with $K/L=9/12=\frac{3}{4}$. Thus, commodity X is the L-intensive commodity. On the other hand, at $w/r=2$, commodity Y is produced at point C with $K/L=12/9=\frac{4}{3}$, while commodity X is produced at point D with $K/L=18/6=3$. Thus, commodity X is L intensive at $w/r=\frac{1}{2}$ and K intensive at $w/r=2$ in relation to commodity Y, and factor-intensity reversal is present.

On the other hand, at $w/r=2$, commodity Y is produced at point C, where the Y-isoquant is tangent to the isocost line with slope (w/r) equal to 2 and $K/L=12/9=4/3$. Commodity X is produced at point D, where the X-isoquant is tangent to the same isocost line with slope (w/r) equal to 2 and $K/L=18/6=3$. Thus, at $w/r=2$, commodity X is the relatively K-intensive commodity.

As a result, commodity X is L intensive at $w/r=1/2$ and K intensive at $w/r=2$ with respect to commodity Y, and we say that factor-intensity reversal is present.

With factor-intensity reversal, both the H-O theorem and the factor-price equalization theorem must be rejected. To see this, suppose that Nation 1 is the relatively L-abundant nation with $w/r=1/2$, while Nation 2 is the relatively K-abundant nation with $w/r=2$. With $w/r=1/2$, Nation 1 should specialize in the production of and export commodity X because Nation 1 is the L-abundant nation and commodity X is the L-intensive commodity there. With $w/r=2$, Nation 2 should specialize in the production of and export commodity X because Nation 2 is the K-abundant nation and commodity X is the K-intensive commodity there. Since both nations cannot export to each other the same *homogeneous* commodity (i.e., commodity X), the H-O theorem no longer predicts the pattern of trade.

When the H-O model does not hold, the factor-price equalization theorem also fails. To see this, note that as Nation 1 (the low-wage nation) specializes in the production of commodity X (the L-intensive commodity), the demand for labor rises, and w/r and w rise in Nation 1. With Nation 1 specializing in and exporting commodity X to Nation 2, Nation 2 must specialize in and export *commodity* Y to Nation 1 (since the two nations could not possibly export the same homogeneous commodity to each other). However, since commodity Y is the L-intensive commodity in Nation 2, the demand for labor rises, and w/r and w rise in Nation 2 (the high-wage nation) also. Thus wages rise both in Nation 1 (the low-wage nation) and in Nation 2 (the high-wage nation).

If wages rise faster in Nation 1 than in Nation 2, the difference in wages between the two nations declines, as predicted by the factor-price equalization theorem. If wages rise more slowly in Nation 1 than in Nation 2, the wage difference increases. If wages rise by the same amount in both nations, the wage difference remains unchanged. Since there is no *a priori* way to determine the effect of international trade on the difference in factor prices in each case, we must reject the factor-price equalization theorem.

From Figure 6-4, we can see that factor-intensity reversal arises because the X-isoquant has a much smaller curvature than the Y-isoquant and the X- and Y-isoquants *cross twice within the two relative factor price lines*. When the two isoquants have similar curvature, they will only cross once and there is no factor-intensity reversal.

Problem   Draw a figure similar to Figure 6-4 with the X-isoquant and the Y-isoquant crossing only once within the relative factor price lines of the two nations and show that in that case there is no factor-intensity reversal.

A6.2   The Elasticity of Substitution and Factor-Intensity Reversal

We said above that for factor-intensity reversal to occur, the X-isoquant and the Y-isoquant must have a sufficiently *different* curvature to cross twice within the relative factor price lines prevailing in the two nations. The curvature of an isoquant measures the ease with which L can be substituted for K in production as the relative price of labor (i.e., w/r) declines. When w/r falls, producers will want to substitute L for K in the production of both commodities to minimize their costs of production.

The flatter (i.e., the smaller the curvature of) an isoquant, the easier it is to substitute L for K (and vice versa) in production. A measure of the curvature of an isoquant and the ease with which one factor can be substituted for another in production is given by the elasticity of substitution. The **elasticity of substitution** of L for K in production *(e)* is measured by the following formula:

$$e = \frac{\Delta(K/L)/(K/L)}{\Delta(\text{slope})/(\text{slope})}$$

For example, the elasticity of substitution of *L* for *K* for commodity X between point *D* and point *A* is calculated as follows. $K/L = 3$ at point *D* and $K/L = \frac{1}{3}$ at point *A* in Figure 6-4. Therefore, the change in K/L for a movement from point *D* to point *A* along the X-isoquant is $3 - \frac{1}{3} = 2\frac{2}{3} = 8/3$. Thus, $\Delta(K/L)/(K/L) = (8/3)/3 = 8/9$. The absolute slope of the X-isoquant is 2 at point *D* and $\frac{1}{2}$ at point *A*. Therefore, $\Delta(\text{slope}) = 2 - \frac{1}{2} = 1\frac{1}{2} = 3/2$. Thus, $\Delta(\text{slope})/(\text{slope}) = (3/2)/2 = 3/4$. Substituting these values into the formula, we get:

$$e = \frac{\Delta(K/L)/(K/L)}{\Delta(\text{slope})/(\text{slope})} = \frac{8/9}{3/4} = 32/27 = 1.19$$

Similarly, the elasticity of substitution of *L* and *K* between point *C* and point *B* along the Y-isoquant is:

$$e = \frac{\Delta(K/L)/(K/L)}{\Delta(\text{slope})/(\text{slope})} = \frac{[(4/3)-(3/4)]/(4/3)}{(2-\frac{1}{2})/(2)} = \frac{(7/12)/(4/3)}{(1\frac{1}{2})/2} = \frac{21/48}{3/4} = 84/144 = 0.58$$

Thus, the X-isoquant has a much smaller curvature and a much greater elasticity of substitution than the Y-isoquant. It is this difference in curvature and elasticity of substitution between the X-isoquant and the Y-isoquant that results in their crossing twice within the relative factor price lines, giving factor-intensity reversal. Note that a difference in the curvature of the isoquants and in the elasticity of substitution is a necessary but not sufficient condition for factor-intensity reversal. For factor reversal to occur, the elasticity of substitution must be sufficiently different so that the isoquants of the two commodities cross *within* the relative factor price lines of the two nations.

Problem Calculate the elasticity of substitution of *L* and *K* for your X-isoquant and Y-isoquant of the previous problem (where there is no factor-intensity reversal), and verify that the elasticity of substitution for the two isoquants does not differ much because of their similar curvature. Assume that the coordinates are: A (4,2), B (3,3), C (3,2.5), D (2,4), and that the absolute slope of the isoquants is 1 at points A and C and 2 at B and D.

A6.3 Empirical Tests of Factor-Intensity Reversal

Until 1961, economists used almost exclusively the **Cobb-Douglas production function** in their work. This implied that the elasticity of substitution of *L* for *K* was equal to 1 in the production of all commodities. As a result, this production function was not at all useful to measure the prevalence of factor-intensity reversal in the real world.

Partially in response to the need to measure factor-intensity reversal in international trade, a new production function was developed in 1961 by *Arrow, Chenery, Minhas,* and *Solow* called the **constant elasticity of substitution (CES) production function.** As its name implies, the CES production function kept the elasticity of substitution of L for K constant for each industry but allowed the elasticity of substitution to vary from industry to industry.

It was this CES production function that Minhas used to measure factor-intensity reversal. That is, Minhas found that the elasticity of substitution of *L* for *K* differed widely in the six industries that he studied and that factor-intensity reversal occurred in one-third of the cases. This rate of occurrence is too frequent for factor reversal to be treated as an exception and, if true, it would have seriously damaged the H-O model.

However, *Leontief* calculated the elasticity of substitution of all 21 industries used to derive the CES production function (rather than just the six selected by Minhas) and found that factor reversal occurred in only 8 percent of the cases. Furthermore, when he removed two industries intensive in natural resources, factor reversal fell to about 1 percent of the cases. Thus, Leontief concluded that factor-intensity reversal is a rather rare occurrence and that the H-O model should not be rejected on account of this.

Minhas also conducted another test in his study. He calculated *K/L* for the same 20 industries in the United States and Japan, ranked these industries according to the *K/L* in each nation, and then found the coefficient of rank correlation between the industry rankings in the two nations. Since the United States was the relatively *K*-abundant nation, all industries could be expected to be more *K*-intensive in the United States than in Japan. However, the *K*-intensity *ranking* of the industries would have to be very similar in the United States and Japan in order for factor-intensity reversal to be rare. That is, the most *K*-intensive industries in the United States should also be the most *K*-intensive industries in Japan. Minhas found that the rank correlation was only 0.34 and concluded that factor reversal was fairly common.

However, *Ball* found that when agriculture and two industries intensive in natural resources were removed from the list, the rank correlation rose to 0.77, so that, once again, the conclusion could be reached that factor-intensity reversal is not a common occurrence.

Selected Bibliography

For a problem-solving approach to the topics covered in this chapter, see:
• D. Salvatore, *Theory and Problems of International Economics,* 2nd ed. (New York, McGraw-Hill, 1984), ch. 4 (sects. 4.2 to 4.6).

An excellent and advanced survey of developments in the pure theory of international trade over the past twenty years is found in:
• R. W. Jones and P. B. Kenen, *Handbook of International Economics,* Vol. 1 (Amsterdam: North-Holland, 1984). Reviewed by D. Salvatore in *Kyklos,* March (No. 2) 1986.

Empirical tests of the Ricardian trade theory are found in:
- G. D. A. MacDougal, "British and American Exports: A Study Suggested by the Theory of Comparative Costs," *Economic Journal*, December 1951 and September 1952. Reprinted in R. E. Caves and H. G. Johnson, *Readings in International Economics* (Homewood Ill.: Irwin, 1968).
- B. Balassa, "An Empirical Demonstration of Classical Comparative Cost Theory," *Review of Economics and Statistics*, August 1963.
- R. M. Stern, "British and American Productivity and Comparative Costs in International Trade," *Oxford Economic Papers*, October 1962.

For an excellent theoretical presentation of factor-intensity reversal, see:
- M. Michaely, "Factor Proportions in International Trade: Comment on the State of the Theory," *Kyklos*, June 1964.

The first empirical test of the H-O model, which gave rise to the so-called Leontief paradox, is:
- W. Leontief, "Domestic Production and Foreign Trade: The American Capital Position Reexamined," *Economia Internazionale*, February 1954. Reprinted in R. E. Caves and H. G. Johnson, *Readings in International Economics* (Homewood, Ill.: Irwin, 1968), and in J. N. Bhagwati, *International Trade: Selected Readings* (Baltimore: Penguin, 1969).

For the study on the similarity of consumers' tastes in many nations, see:
- H. Houthakker, "An International Comparison of Household Expenditure Patterns," *Econometrica*, October 1957.

Attempts to explain the Leontief paradox are found in:
- W. Leontief, "Factor Proportions and the Structure of American Trade: Further Theoretical and Empirical Analysis," *Review of Economics and Statistics,* November 1956.
- I. B. Kravis, "Wages and Foreign Trade," *Review of Economics and Statistics*, February 1956.
- I. B. Kravis, "Availability and Other Influences on the Commodity Composition of Trade," *Journal of Political Economy*, April 1956.
- D. B. Keesing, "Labor Skills and Comparative Advantage," *American Economic Review*, May 1966.
- P. Kenen, "Nature, Capital and Trade," *Journal of Political Economy*, October 1965.
- R. E. Baldwin, "Determinants of the Commodity Structure of U.S. Trade," *American Economic Review*, March 1971.
- E. E. Leamer, "The Leontief Paradox Reconsidered," *Journal of Political Economy*, June 1980.
- R. M. Stern and K. E. Maskus, "Determinants of the Structure of U.S. Foreign Trade," *Journal of International Economics,* May 1981.
- E. E. Leamer, *Sources of International Comparative Advantage* (Cambridge, Mass.: M.I.T. Press, 1984).

The article criticizing the procedure of combining human and physical capital in the attempts to explain the Leontief paradox is:
- W. H. Branson and N. Monoyios, "Factor Inputs in U.S. Trade," *Journal of International Economics*, May 1977.

Sources for the empirical studies on factor-intensity reversal discussed in the text are:
- B. S. Minhas, "The Homohypallagic Production Function, Factor Intensity Reversals and the Heckscher-Ohlin Theorem," *Journal of Political Economy*, April 1962. Reprinted in J. N. Bhagwati, *International Trade: Selected Readings* (Baltimore: Penguin, 1969).
- W. Leontief, "An International Comparison of Factor Costs and Factor Use:
A Review Article," *American Economic Review*, June 1964.
- D. P. S. Ball, "Factor Intensity Reversals: An International Comparison of Factor Costs and Factor Use," *Journal of Political Economy*, February 1966.

The Linder hypothesis is presented in:
- S. B. Linder, *An Essay on Trade and Transformation* (New York: Wiley, 1961).

For intra-industry trade, see:
- B. Balassa, "Trade Creation and Trade Diver-

sion in the European Common Market," *Economic Journal*, March 1967.

- H. G. Grubel and P. J. Lloyd, *Intra-Industry Trade: The Theory and Measurement of International Trade in Differentiated Products* (London: Macmillan, and New York: Halsted, 1975).
- P. R. Krugman, "Scale Economies, Product Differentiation, and the Pattern of Trade," *American Economic Review*, December 1980.
- K. Lancaster, "Intra-industry Trade under Perfect Monopolistic Competition," *Journal of International Economics*, 1980.
- E. Helpman, "International Trade in the Presence of Product Differentiation, Economies of Scale and Monopolistic Competition: A Chamberlin-Heckscher-Ohlin Approach," *Journal of International Economics*, August 1981.
- H. Helpman and P. R. Krugman, *Market Structure and Foreign Trade* (Cambridge, Mass.: M.I.T. Press, 1985.

The original presentation of the monopolistically competitive model based on differentiated products, from which the models on intra-industry trade originate, is found in:

- E. H. Chamberlin, *The Theory of Monopolistic Competition* (Cambridge, Mass.: Harvard University Press, 1933).

For the technological gap and product cycle models, see:

- M. V. Posner, "International Trade and Technical Change," *Oxford Economic Papers*, 1961.
- R. Vernon, "International Investment and International Trade in the Product Cycle," *Quarterly Journal of Economics*, May 1966.

Reprinted in R. E. Baldwin and J. D. Richardson, *International Trade and Finance Readings* (Boston: Little, Brown, 1981).

- W. Gruber, D. Mehta, and R. Vernon, "The R&D Factor in International Trade and Investment of United States Industries," *Journal of Political Economy*, February 1967.
- H. P. Bowen, "Changes in the International Distribution of Resources and their Impact on U.S. Comparative Advantage," *Review of Economics and Statistics*, August 1983.

The source of the constant elasticity of substitution (CES) production function used to test for factor-intensity reversal discussed in section A6.3 is:

- K. Arrow, H. B. Chenery, B. Minhas, and R. M. Solow, "Capital-Labor Substitution and Economic Efficiency," *Review of Economics and Statistics*, August 1961.

For a more extensive discussion and applications of the elasticity of substitution, see:

- D. Salvatore, *Microeconomics: Theory and Applications* (New York: Macmillan, 1986), ch. 9 (sect. 9.2).
- D. Salvatore, *Microeconomic Theory*, 2nd ed. (New York: MacGraw-Hill, 1983), ch. 7 (sect. 7.5).

The most important sources of international trade data are:

- United States, *Statistical Yearbook* (New York: United Nations, Yearly).
- International Monetary Fund, *International Financial Statistics* (Washington, D.C.: International Monetary Fund, Monthly and Summarized Yearly).

CHAPTER 7

Economic Growth and International Trade

7.1 Introduction

The trade theory discussed thus far is completely static in nature. That is, given the nation's factor endowments, technology, and tastes, we proceeded to determine the nation's comparative advantage and the gains from trade. However, factor endowments change through time; technology usually improves; and tastes may also change. As a result, the nation's comparative advantage also changes over time.

In this chapter, we extend our trade model to incorporate these changes. We show how a change in factor endowments and/or an improvement in technology affects the nation's production frontier. These changes, together with possible changes in tastes, affect the nation's offer curve, the volume and the terms of trade, and the gains from trade.

In section 7.2, we illustrate the effect of a change in factor endowments on the nation's production frontier and examine the Rybczynski theorem. In section 7.3, we define the different types of technical progress and illustrate their effect on the nation's production frontier. Section 7.4 deals with and illustrates the effect of growth on trade and welfare in a nation that is too small to affect the terms of trade. Section 7.5 extends the analysis to the more complex case of the large nation. Finally, section 7.6 examines the effect of growth and changes in tastes in both nations on the volume and terms of trade. The appendix presents the formal proof of the Rybczynski theorem, examines growth

151

when one factor is not mobile within the nation, and gives a graphical presentation of Hicksian technical progress.

Throughout this chapter and in the appendix, we will have the opportunity to utilize most of the tools of analysis developed in previous chapters and truly see trade theory at work. The type of analysis that we will be performing is known as comparative statics (as opposed to dynamic analysis). *Comparative statics* analyzes the effect on the equilibrium position resulting from a change in underlying economic conditions and without regard to the transitional period and process of adjustment. *Dynamic analysis,* on the other hand, deals with the time path and the process of adjustment itself. Dynamic trade theory is still in its infancy. However, our comparative statics analysis can carry us a long way in analyzing the effect on international trade resulting from changes in factor endowments, technology, and tastes over time.

7.2   Growth of Factors of Production

Through time, a nation's population usually grows and, with it, the size of its labor force. Similarly, by utilizing part of its resources to produce capital equipment, the nation increases its stock of capital. Capital refers to all the man-made means of production, such as machinery, factories, office buildings, transportation, and communications, and also to the education and training of the labor force, all of which greatly enhance the nation's ability to produce goods and services.

Though there are many different types of labor and capital, we will assume for simplicity that all units of labor and capital are homogeneous (i.e., identical), as we have done in previous chapters. This will leave us with two factors—labor (L) and capital (K)—so that we can conveniently continue to use plane geometry for our analysis. In the real world, of course, there are also natural resources, and these can be depleted (such as minerals) or new ones found through discoveries or new applications.

We will also continue to assume that the nation experiencing growth is producing two commodities (commodity X, which is L intensive, and commodity Y, which is K intensive) under constant returns to scale.

7.2a   Labor Growth and Capital Accumulation Over Time

An increase in the endowment of labor and capital over time causes the nation's production frontier to shift outward. The type and degree of the shift depend on the rate at which L and K grow. If L and K grow at the same rate, the nation's production frontier will shift out evenly in all directions at the rate of factor growth. As a result, the slope of the old and new production frontiers (before and after factor growth) will be the same at any point where they are cut by a ray from the origin. This is the case of **balanced growth.**

If only the endowment of L grows, the output of both commodities grows because L is used in the production of both commodities and L can be substituted for K to some extent in the production of both commodities. However, the output of commodity X (the L-intensive commodity) grows faster than the output of commodity Y (the K-intensive commodity). The opposite is true if only the endowment of K grows. If L and K grow at different rates, the outward shift in the nation's production frontier can similarly be determined.

Figure 7-1 shows various types of hypothetical factor growth in Nation 1. The growth of factor endowments are exaggerated to make the illustrations clearer.) The presentation is completely analogous for Nation 2 and will be left as end-of-chapter problems.

The left panel of Figure 7-1 shows the case of balanced growth under the assumption that the amounts of L and K available to Nation 1 double. With constant returns to scale, the maximum amount that Nation 1 can produce of each commodity also doubles, from 140X to 280X or from 70Y to 140Y. Note that the shape of the expanded production frontier is identical to the shape of the production frontier before growth, so that the slope of the two production frontiers, or P_X/P_Y, is the same at points such as B and B′ where they are cut by a ray from the origin.

The right panel repeats Nation 1's production frontier before growth (with intercepts of 140X and 70Y) and shows two additional production frontiers—one with only L doubling (solid line) and the other with only K doubling (dashed line). When only L doubles, the production frontier shifts more along the X axis measuring the L-intensive commodity. If only K doubles, the production frontier shifts more along the Y axis measuring the K-intensive commodity. Note that when only L doubles, the maximum output of commodity X does not double (i.e., it only rises from 140X to 275X). For X to double,

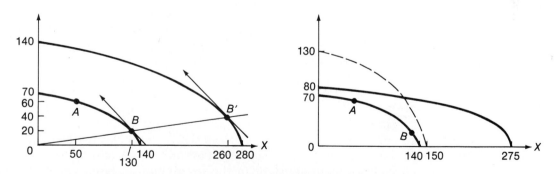

FIGURE 7-1.　Growth of Labor and Capital over Time

The left panel shows the case of balanced growth with L and K doubling under constant returns to scale. The two production frontiers have identical shapes and the same slope, or P_X/P_Y, along any ray from the origin. The right panel shows the case when only L or only K doubles. When only L doubles, the output of commodity X (the L-intensive commodity) grows proportionately more than the output of Y (but less than doubles). Similarly, when only K doubles, the output of Y grows proportionately more than that of X but less than doubles (see the dashed production frontier).

both L and K must double. Similarly, when only K doubles, the maximum output of commodity Y less than doubles (from 70Y to 135Y).

When both L and K grow at the same rate and we have constant returns to scale in the production of both commodities, the productivity and therefore the returns of L and K remain the same after growth as they were before growth took place. If the dependency rate (i.e., the ratio of dependents to the total population) also remains unchanged, real per capita income and the welfare of the nation tend to remain unchanged. If only L grows (or L grows proportionately more than K), K/L will fall and so will the productivity of L, the returns to L, and real per capita income. If, on the other hand, only the endowment of K grows (or K grows proportionately more than L), K/L will rise and so will the productivity of L, the returns to L, and real per capita income.

7.2b   The Rybczynski Theorem

The **Rybczynski theorem** postulates that at constant commodity prices, an increase in the endowment of one factor will increase by a greater proportion the output of the commodity intensive in that factor and will reduce the output of the other commodity. For example, if only L grows in Nation 1, then the output of commodity X (the L-intensive commodity) expands more than proportionately while the output of commodity Y (the K-intensive commodity) declines at constant P_X and P_Y.

Figure 7-2 shows the production frontier of Nation 1 before and after only L doubles (as in the right panel of Figure 7-1). With trade but before growth, Nation 1 produces at point B (i.e., 130X and 20Y) at $P_X/P_Y = P_B = 1$, as in previous chapters. After only L doubles and with P_X/P_Y remaining at $P_B = 1$, Nation 1 would produce at point M on its new and expanded production frontier. At point M, Nation 1 produces 270X but only 10Y. Thus, the output of commodity X more than doubled while the output of commodity Y declined (as predicted by Rybczynski theorem). Doubling L *and* transferring some L and K from the production of commodity Y more than doubles the output of commodity X.

The formal graphical proof of the Rybczynski theorem will be presented in the appendix. We will here give an intuitive but still adequate proof of the theorem. The proof is as follows. For *commodity* prices to remain constant with the growth of one factor, *factor* prices (i.e., w and r) must also remain constant. But factor prices can remain constant only if K/L and the productivity of L and K also remain constant in the production of both commodities. The only way to fully employ all of the increase in L and still leave K/L unchanged in the production of both commodities is for the output of commodity Y (the K-intensive commodity) to fall in order to release enough K (and a little L) to absorb all of the increase in L in the production of commodity X (the L-intensive commodity). Thus, the output of commodity X rises while the output of commodity Y declines at constant commodity prices. In fact, the increase in the output of commodity X expands a greater proportion than the

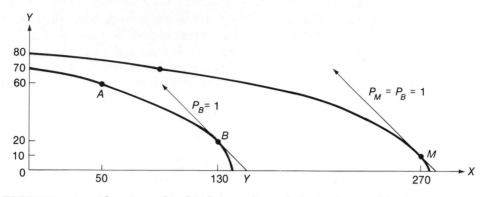

FIGURE 7-2.   The Growth of Labor Only and the Rybczynski Theorem

With trade but before growth, Nation 1 produces at point B (130X and 20Y) at $P_X/P_Y = P_B = 1$, as in previous chapters. After only L doubles and with P_X/P_Y remaining at $P_B = 1$, Nation 1 produces at point M (270X and 10Y) on its new and expanded production frontier. Thus, the output of X (the L-intensive commodity) expanded and the output of Y (the K-intensive commodity) declined, as postulated by the Rybczynski theorem.

expansion in the amount of labor because some labor and capital are also transferred from the production of commodity Y to the production of commodity X. This is called the *magnification effect* and is formally proved in section A7.1 of the appendix.

To summarize, we can say that for P_X and P_Y (and therefore P_X/P_Y) to remain the same, w and r must be constant. But w and r can remain the same only if K/L remains constant in the production of both commodities. The only way for this to occur and also absorb all of the increase in L is to reduce the output of Y so as to release K/L in the greater proportion used in Y, and combine the released K with the additional L at the lower K/L used in the production of X. Thus, the output of X rises and that of Y falls. In fact, the output of X increases by a greater proportion than the increase in L. Similarly, when only K increases, the output of Y rises more than proportionately and that of X falls.

If one of the factors of production is not mobile within the nation, the results differ and depend on whether it is the growing or the nongrowing factor that is immobile. This is examined in section A7.2 of the appendix using the specific-factors model introduced in the appendix to chapter 5 (section A5.4).

7.3 Technical Progress

Several empirical studies have indicated that most of the increase in real per capita income in industrial nations is due to technical progress and much less to capital accumulation. However, the analysis of technical progress is much more complex than the analysis of factor growth because there are several definitions and types of technical progress and they can take place at different rates in the production of either or both commodities.

The most appropriate definitions of technical progress for our purposes are those advanced by *John Hicks*, the British economist who shared the 1972 Nobel Prize in economics. In section 7.3a, we define the different types of Hicksian technical progress. In section 7.3b, we then examine the effect that the different types of Hicksian technical progress have on the nation's production frontier. Throughout our discussion, we will assume that constant returns to scale prevail before and after technical progress takes place and that technical progress occurs in a once-and-for-all fashion.

7.3a   Neutral, Labor-Saving, and Capital-Saving Technical Progress

Technical progress is usually classified into neutral, labor saving, or capital saving. All technical progress (regardless of its type) reduces the amount of both labor and capital required to produce any given level of output. The different types of Hicksian technical progress specify how this takes place.

Neutral technical progress increases the productivity of L and K in the same proportion so that K/L remains the same after the neutral technical progress as it was before *at unchanged relative factor prices* (w/r). That is, with unchanged w/r, there is no substitution of L for K (or vice versa) in production so that K/L remains unchanged. All that happens is that a given output can now be produced with less L and less K.

Labor-saving technical progress increases the productivity of K proportionately more than the productivity of L. As a result, K is substituted for L in production and K/L rises at unchanged w/r. Since more K is used per unit of L, this type of technical progress is called labor saving. Note that a given output can now be produced with fewer units of L and K but with a higher K/L.

Capital-saving technical progress increases the productivity of L proportionately more than the productivity of K. As a result, L is substituted for K in production and L/K rises (K/L falls) at unchanged w/r. Since more L is used per unit of K, this type of technical progress is called capital saving. Note that a given output can now be produced with fewer units of L and K but with a higher L/K (a lower K/L).

The appendix to this chapter gives a rigorous graphical interpretation of the Hicksian definitions of technical progress, utilizing somewhat more advanced tools of analysis.

7.3b   Technical Progress and the Nation's Production Frontier

As in the case of factor growth, all types of technical progress cause the nation's production frontier to shift outward. The type and degree of the shift depend on the type and rate of technical progress in either or both commodities. We will here deal only with neutral technical progress. Non-neutral technical progress is extremely complex and can only be handled mathematically in the most advanced graduate texts.

With the same rate of neutral technical progress in the production of both commodities, the nation's production frontier will shift out evenly in all directions at the same rate at which technical progress takes place. This has the same effect on the nation's production frontier as balanced factor growth. Thus, the slope of the nation's old and new production frontiers (before and after this type of technical progress) will be the same at any point where they are cut by a ray from the origin.

For example, suppose that the productivity of L and K doubles in the production of commodity X and commodity Y in Nation 1 and constant returns to scale prevail in the production of both commodities. The graph for this type of technical progress is identical to the left panel of Figure 7-1, where the supply of both L and K doubled, and so the graph is not repeated here.

Figure 7-3 shows Nation 1's production frontier before technical progress and after the productivity of L and K doubled in the production of commodity X only, or in the production of commodity Y only (the dashed production frontier).

When the productivity of L and K doubles in the production of commodity X only, the output of X doubles for each output level of commodity Y. For

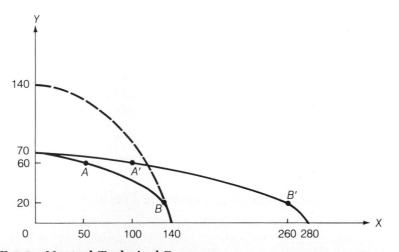

FIGURE 7-3   Neutral Technical Progress

The figure shows Nation 1's production frontier before technical progress and after the productivity of L and K doubled in the production of commodity X only, or in the production of commodity Y only (the dashed frontier). Note that if Nation 1 uses all of its resources in the production of the commodity in which the productivity of L and K doubled, the output of the commodity also doubles. On the other hand, if Nation 1 uses all of its resources in the production of the commodity in which no technical progress occurred, the output of that commodity remains unchanged.

example, at the unchanged output of 60Y, the output of commodity X rises from 50X before technical progress to 100X afterward (points A and A', respectively, in the figure). Similarly, at the unchanged output of 20Y, the output of commodity X increases from 130X to 260X (points B and B'). When all of Nation 1's resources are used in the production of commodity X, the output of X also doubles (from 140X to 280X). Note that the output of commodity Y remains unchanged at 70Y if all of the nation's resources are used in the production of commodity Y and technical progress took place in the production of commodity X only.

The reasoning is analogous to explain the shift in the production frontier when the productivity of L and K doubles only in the production of commodity Y (the dashed production frontier in Figure 7-3). The student should carefully examine the difference between Figure 7-3 and the right panel of Figure 7-1.

Finally, it must be pointed out that, in the absence of trade, all types of technical progress tend to increase the nation's welfare. The reason is that with a higher production frontier and the same L and population, each citizen could be made better off after growth than before by an appropriate redistribution policy. The question of the effect of growth on trade and welfare will be explored in the remainder of this chapter.

7.4   Growth and Trade: The Small Country Case

We will now build on the discussion of the previous two sections and analyze the effect of growth on production, consumption, trade, and welfare when the nation is too small to affect the relative commodity prices at which it trades (so that the nation's terms of trade remain constant). In section 7.4a, we discuss growth in general and define protrade, antitrade, and neutral production and consumption. Using these definitions, we illustrate the effect of one type of factor growth in section 7.4b and analyze the effect of technical progress in section 7.4c. Section 7.5 then examines the more realistic case where the nation *does* affect relative commodity prices by its trading.

7.4a   The Effect of Growth on Trade

We have seen so far that factor growth and technical progress result in an outward shift in the nation's production frontier. What happens to the volume of trade depends on the rates at which the output of the nation's exportable and importable commodities grow and on the consumption pattern of the nation as its national income expands through growth and trade.

If the output of the nation's exportable commodity grows proportionately more than the output of its importable commodity at constant relative commodity prices, then growth tends to lead to a greater than proportionate expansion of trade and is said to be **protrade**. Otherwise it is **antitrade** or **neu-**

tral. The expansion of output has a neutral trade effect if it leads to the same rate of expansion of trade. On the other hand, if the nation's consumption of its importable commodity increases proportionately more than the nation's consumption of its exportable commodity at constant prices, then the consumption effect tends to lead to a greater than proportionate expansion of trade and is said to be protrade. Otherwise, the expansion in consumption is antitrade or neutral.

Thus, production and consumption can be protrade (if they lead to a greater than proportionate increase in trade at constant relative commodity prices) or antitrade or neutral. *Production is protrade if the output of the nation's exportable commodity increases proportionately more* than the output of its importable commodity. *Consumption is protrade if the nation's consumption of its importable commodity increases proportionately more* than consumption of its exportable commodity.

What in fact happens to the volume of trade in the process of growth depends on the net result of these production and consumption effects. If both production and consumption are protrade, the volume of trade expands proportionately faster than output. If production and consumption are both antitrade, the volume of trade expands proportionately less than output and may even decline absolutely. If production is protrade and consumption antitrade or vice versa, what happens to the volume of trade depends on the net effect of these two opposing forces. In the unlikely event that both production and consumption are neutral, trade expands at the same rate as output.

Since growth can result from different types and rates of factor growth and technical progress, and production and consumption can be protrade, antitrade, or neutral, the effect of growth on trade and welfare will vary from case to case. Thus, the approach must necessarily be taxonomic (i.e., in the form of "if this is the case, then this is the outcome"). As a result, all we can do is give some examples and indicate the forces that must be analyzed to determine what is likely to happen in any particular situation.

7.4b   Illustration of Factor Growth, Trade, and Welfare

The top panel of Figure 7-4 reproduces Figure 7-2, which shows that L doubles in Nation 1 and that Nation 1's terms of trade do not change with growth and trade. That is, before growth, Nation 1 produced at point B, traded 60X for 60Y at $P_B = 1$, and reached indifference curve III (as in previous chapters). When L doubles in Nation 1, its production frontier shifts outward as explained in section 7.2a. If Nation 1 is too small to affect relative commodity prices, it will produce at point M, where the new expanded production frontier is tangent to $P_M = P_B = 1$. At point M, Nation 1 produces more than twice of commodity X than at point B but less of commodity Y, as postulated by the Rybczynski theorem. At $P_M = P_B = 1$, Nation 1 exchanges 150X for 150Y and consumes at point Z on its community indifference curve VII.

Since the output of commodity X (Nation 1's exportable commodity) in-

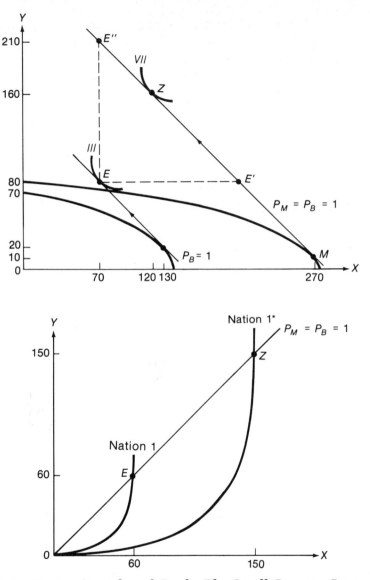

FIGURE 7-4. Factor Growth and Trade: The Small Country Case

The top panel shows that after L doubles, Nation 1 exchanges 150X for 150Y at $P_M = P_B = 1$ and reaches indifference curve VII. Since the consumption of both X and Y rises with growth, both commodities are normal goods. Since L doubled but consumption less than doubled (compare point Z to point E), the social welfare of Nation 1 declined. The bottom panel shows that with free trade before growth, Nation 1 exchanged 60X for 60Y at $P_X/P_Y = P_B = 1$. With free trade after growth, Nation 1 exchanges 150X for 150Y at $P_X/P_Y = P_M = P_B = 1$.

creased while the output of commodity Y declined, the growth of output is protrade. Similarly, since the consumption of commodity Y (Nation 1's importable commodity) increased proportionately more than the consumption of commodity X (i.e., point Z is to the left of a ray from the origin though point E), the growth of consumption is also protrade. With both production and consumption protrade, the volume of trade expanded proportionately more than the output of commodity X.

Note that with growth and trade, Nation 1's *consumption* frontier is given by straight line P_M tangent to the new expanded production frontier at point M. The fact that consumption of both commodities increased with growth and trade means that both commodities are **normal goods.** Only if commodity Y had been an **inferior good,** would Nation 1 have consumed a smaller absolute amount of Y (i.e., to the right and below point E' on line P_M). Similarly, Nation 1 would have consumed a smaller absolute amount of commodity X (i.e., to the left and above point E'') only if commodity X had been an inferior good.

The bottom panel of Figure 7-4 utilizes offer curves to show the same growth of trade for Nation 1 at constant terms of trade. That is, with free trade before growth, Nation 1 exchanged 60X for 60Y at $P_X/P_Y = P_B = 1$. With free trade after growth, Nation 1 exchanges 150X for 150Y at $P_X/P_Y = P_M = P_B = 1$. The straight line showing the constant terms of trade also represents the straight-line segment of Nation 2's (or the rest of the world's) offer curve (see section 4.4b). It is because Nation 1 is very small that its offer curve before and after growth intersects the straight-line segment of Nation 2's (the large nation's) offer curve and the terms of trade remain constant.

Note that Nation 1 is worse off after growth because its labor force (and population) doubled while its total consumption less than doubled (compare point Z with 120X and 160Y after growth to point E with 70X and 80Y before growth). Thus, the consumption and welfare of Nation 1's "representative" citizen decline as a result of this type of growth. A representative citizen is one with the identical tastes and consumption pattern of the nation as a whole but with quantities scaled down by the total number of citizens in the nation.

7.4c Technical Progress, Trade, and Welfare

We have seen in section 7.3b that *neutral technical progress at the same rate in the production of both commodities* leads to a proportionate expansion in the output of both commodities at constant relative commodity prices. If consumption of each commodity also increases proportionately in the nation, the volume of trade will also increase at the same rate at constant terms of trade. That is, the neutral expansion of production and consumption leads to the same rate of expansion of trade. With neutral production and protrade consumption, the volume of trade would expand proportionately more than production. With neutral production and antitrade consumption, the volume of trade would expand proportionately less than production. However, regardless of what happens to the volume of trade, the welfare of the representative citizen will increase with constant L and population and constant terms of trade.

Neutral technical progress in the production of the exportable commodity only is protrade. For example, if neutral technical progress takes place only in the production of commodity X in Nation 1, then Nation 1's production frontier expands only along the X axis, as indicated in Figure 7-3. At constant terms of trade, Nation 1's output of commodity X will increase even more than in Figure 7-4 while the output of commodity Y declines (as in Figure 7-4). Nation 1 will reach an indifference curve higher than VII, and the volume of trade will expand even more than in Figure 7-4. What is even more important is that with a constant population and labor force, the welfare of the representative citizen now rises (as opposed to the case where only L grows in Figure 7-4).

On the other hand, *neutral technical progress only in the production of commodity Y* (the importable commodity) *is antitrade,* and Nation 1's production frontier will expand only along the Y axis (the dashed production frontier in Figure 7-3). If the terms of trade, tastes, and population also remain unchanged, the volume of trade tends to decline but national welfare increases. This is similar to the growth of K only in Nation 1 and will be examined in section 7.5c. The case where neutral technical change occurs at different rates in the two commodities may lead to a rise or fall in the volume of trade but always increases welfare. The same is generally true for nonneutral technical progress. Thus, technical progress, depending on the type, may increase or decrease trade, but it will always increase social welfare in a small nation.

7.5   Growth and Trade: The Large Country Case

We will now build on our presentation of section 7.4 to analyze the effect of growth on production, consumption, trade, and welfare when the nation is sufficiently large to affect the relative commodity prices at which it trades (so that the nation's terms of trade change). In section 7.5a, we examine the effect of growth on the nation's terms of trade and welfare. In section 7.5b, we deal with the case where growth, by itself, might improve the nation's welfare but its terms of trade deteriorate so much as to make the nation worse off after growth than before. Finally, in section 7.5c, we examine the case where growth leads to improvement in the country's terms of trade and welfare.

7.5a   Growth and the Nation's Terms of Trade and Welfare

If growth, regardless of its source or type, expands the nation's volume of trade at constant prices, then the nation's terms of trade tend to deteriorate. On the other hand, if growth reduces the nation's volume of trade at constant prices, the nation's terms of trade tend to improve. This is referred to as the **terms-of-trade effect** of growth.

The effect of growth on the nation's welfare depends on the net result of the terms-of-trade effect and a wealth effect. The *wealth effect* refers to the change in the output per worker or per person as a result of growth. A positive wealth effect, by itself, tends to increase the nation's welfare. Otherwise, the nation's welfare tends to decline or remain unchanged. If the wealth effect is positive and the nation's terms of trade improve as a result of growth and trade, the nation's welfare will definitely increase. If they are both unfavorable, the nation's welfare will definitely decline. If the wealth effect and the terms-of-trade effect move in opposite directions, the nation's welfare may deteriorate, improve, or remain unchanged depending on the relative strength of these two opposing forces.

For example, if only L doubles in Nation 1, the wealth effect, by itself, tends to reduce Nation 1's welfare. This was the case shown in Figure 7-4. Furthermore, since this type of growth tends to expand the volume of trade of Nation 1 at $P_M = P_B = 1$, Nation 1's terms of trade also tend to decline. Thus, the welfare of Nation 1 will decline for both reasons. This case is illustrated in Figure 7-5.

Figure 7-5 is identical to Figure 7-4 except that now Nation 1 is assumed to be large enough to affect relative commodity prices. With the terms of trade deteriorating from $P_M = P_B = 1$ to $P_N = \frac{1}{2}$ with growth and trade, Nation 1 produces at point N, exchanges 140X for 70Y with Nation 2, and consumes at point T on indifference curve IV (see the top panel). Since the welfare of Nation 1 declined (i.e., the wealth effect was negative) even when it was too small to affect its terms of trade, and now its terms of trade have also deteriorated, the welfare of Nation 1 declines even more. This is reflected in indifference curve IV being lower than indifference curve VII.

The bottom panel of Figure 7-5 shows with offer curves the effect of this type of growth on the volume and the terms of trade when Nation 1 does not affect its terms of trade (as in the bottom panel of Figure 7-4) and when it does.

7.5b Immiserizing Growth

Even if the wealth effect, by itself, tends to increase the nation's welfare, the terms of trade may deteriorate so much as to lead to a net decline in the nation's welfare. This case was termed **immiserizing growth** by *Jagdish Bhagwati* and is illustrated in Figure 7-6.

Figure 7-6 reproduces from Figure 7-3 the production frontier of Nation 1 before and after neutral technical progress doubled the productivity of L and K in the production of commodity X only. The wealth effect, by itself, would increase Nation 1's welfare at constant prices because Nation 1's output increases while its labor force *(L)* and population remain constant. However,

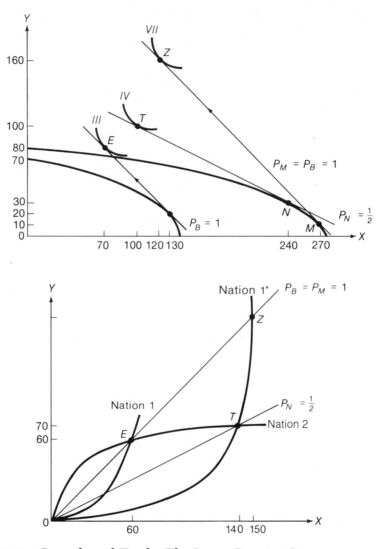

FIGURE 7-5. Growth and Trade: The Large Country Case

Figure 7-5 is identical to Figure 7-4 except that now Nation 1 is assumed to be large enough to affect the terms of trade. With the terms of trade deteriorating from $P_M = P_B = 1$ to $P_N = \frac{1}{2}$ with growth and trade, Nation 1 produces at point N, exchanges 140X for 70Y with Nation 2, and consumes at point T on indifference curve IV (see the top panel). Since indifference curve IV is lower than VII, the nation's welfare will decline even more now. The bottom panel shows with offer curves the effect of this type of growth on the volume and the terms of trade when Nation 1 does and does not affect its terms of trade.

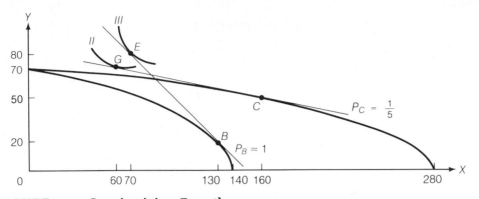

FIGURE 7-6.   Immiserizing Growth

This figure reproduces from Figure 7-3 the production frontier of Nation 1 before and after neutral technical progress increased the productivity of L and K in the production of commodity X only. With this type of technical progress, the wealth effect, by itself, would increase the welfare of Nation 1. However, Nation 1's terms of trade deteriorate drastically from $P_B = 1$ to $P_C = \frac{1}{5}$, so that Nation 1 produces at point C, exports 100X for only 20Y, and consumes at point G on indifference curve II (which is lower than indifference curve III, which Nation 1 reached with free trade *before* growth).

since this type of technical progress tends to increase the volume of trade, Nation 1's terms of trade tend to deteriorate. With a drastic deterioration in its terms of trade, for example, from $P_B = 1$ to $P_C = \frac{1}{5}$, Nation 1 would produce at point C, export 100X for only 20Y, and consume at point G on indifference curve II (which is lower than indifference curve III, which Nation 1 reached with free trade *before* growth).

Immiserizing growth is more likely to occur in Nation 1 when (a) growth tends to increase substantially Nation 1's exports at constant terms of trade; (b) Nation 1 is large so that the attempt to expand its exports substantially will cause a deterioration in its terms of trade; (c) the income elasticity of Nation 2's (or the rest of the world's) demand for Nation 1's exports is very low so that Nation 1's terms of trade will deteriorate substantially; and (d) Nation 1 is so heavily dependent on trade that a substantial deterioration in its terms of trade will lead to a reduction in national welfare.

Immiserizing growth does not seem very prevalent in the real world. When it does take place, it is more likely to occur in developing than in developed nations. Even though the terms of trade of developing nations seem to have deteriorated somewhat over time, increases in production have more than made up for this, and their real per capita incomes and welfare have generally increased. Real per capita incomes would have increased much faster if the population of developing nations had not grown so rapidly in recent decades. These questions and many others will be fully analyzed in Chapter 11, which deals with international trade and economic development.

7.5c   Illustration of Beneficial Growth and Trade

We now examine the case where only K (Nation 1's scarce factor) doubles in Nation 1 so that the wealth effect, by itself, tends to increase the nation's welfare. The results would be very similar with neutral technical progress in the production of only commodity Y (the K-intensive commodity) in Nation 1. Since this type of growth tends to reduce the volume of trade at constant prices, Nation 1's terms of trade tend to improve. With both the wealth and terms-of-trade effects favorable, Nation 1's welfare definitely improves. This is illustrated in Figure 7-7.

The top panel of the figure shows Nation 1's production frontier before growth and after only K doubles (the dashed production frontier from the right panel of Figure 7-1). At the constant relative commodity price of $P_B = 1$, Nation 1 would produce 110X and 105Y (point R in the top panel), exchange 15X for 15Y with Nation 2, and consume at point U on indifference curve V. With L and population unchanged, this type of growth would increase Nation 1's welfare.

Furthermore, since Nation 1's trade volume declines at constant prices (from the free trade but pregrowth situation at point E), Nation 1's terms of trade also improve, from $P_R = P_B = 1$ to $P_S = 2$. At $P_S = 2$, Nation 1 produces 120X and 90Y at point S, exchanges 20X for 40Y, and consumes at point W on indifference curve VI. Thus, Nation 1's welfare increases because of both wealth and terms-of-trade effects.

The bottom panel of Figure 7-7 shows with offer curves the effect of this type of growth on the volume and the terms of trade when Nation 1 does not and when it does affect its terms of trade. The reader should carefully compare Figure 7-7, where both wealth and terms-of-trade effects are favorable (so that Nation 1's welfare increases for both reasons), with Figure 7-5, where both effects are unfavorable and Nation 1's welfare declines for both reasons.

7.6   Growth, Change in Tastes, and Trade in Both Nations

Up to now we have assumed that growth took place only in Nation 1. As a result, only Nation 1's production frontier and offer curve shifted. We now extend our analysis to incorporate growth in both nations. When this occurs, the production frontiers and offer curves of both nations shift. We will now use offer curves to analyze the effect of growth and change in tastes in both nations.

7.6a   Growth and Trade in Both Nations

Figure 7-8 shows the effect on the volume and terms of trade of various types of growth in either or both nations. We assume that both nations are large. The offer curves labeled "1" and "2" are the original (pregrowth) offer curves

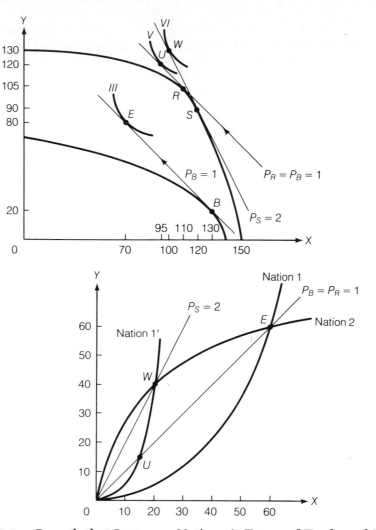

FIGURE 7-7.   Growth that Improves Nation 1's Terms of Trade and Welfare

If K (Nation 1's scarce factor) doubles in Nation 1, production would take place at point R at the unchanged terms of trade of $P_R = P_B = 1$ (see the top panel). Nation 1 would exchange 15X for 15Y with Nation 2 and consume at point U on indifference curve V. However, if Nation 1 is large, its terms of trade will improve because it is willing to export less of X at $P_R = P_B = 1$. At $P_S = 2$, Nation 1 produces at point S, exchanges 20X for 40Y with Nation 2, and consumes at point W on indifference curve VI. Nation 1's welfare increases because of both a favorable wealth and terms-of-trade effect. The bottom panel shows with offer curves the effect of this type of growth on the volume and the terms of trade when Nation 1 does not and when it does affect its terms of trade. Compare this to Figure 7-5.

of Nation 1 and Nation 2, respectively. Offer curves "1*" and "2*" and offer curves "1'" and "2'" are the offer curves of Nation 1 and Nation 2, respectively, with various types of growth. A relative commodity price line is not drawn through each equilibrium point in order not to clutter the figure. However, Nation 1's terms of trade (i.e., P_X/P_Y) at each equilibrium point is obtained by dividing the *quantity of commodity Y by the quantity of commodity X* traded at that point. Nation 2's terms of trade at the same equilibrium point is then simply the inverse, or reciprocal, of Nation 1's terms of trade.

With the original pregrowth offer curves 1 and 2, Nation 1 exchanges 60X for 60Y with Nation 2 at $P_B = 1$ (see equilibrium point E_1). If L doubles in Nation 1 (as in Figure 7-5), its offer curve rotates clockwise from 1 to 1* and Nation 1 exports 140X for 70Y (point E_2). In this case, Nation 1's terms of trade deteriorate to $P_X/P_Y = 70Y/140X = ½$ and Nation 2's terms of trade improve to $P_Y/P_X = 2$.

If growth occurs only in Nation 2 and its offer curve rotates counterclock-

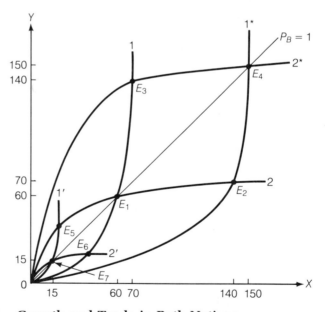

FIGURE 7-8.   Growth and Trade in Both Nations

If L (Nation 1's abundant factor) doubles in Nation 1, its offer curve rotates from 1 to 1*, giving equilibrium E_2 with a larger volume but lower terms of trade for Nation 1. If K (Nation 2's abundant factor) increases in Nation 2 and its offer curve rotates from 2 to 2*, equilibrium occurs at E_3 with a larger volume but lower terms of trade for Nation 2. If instead K doubles in Nation 1, its offer curve rotates to 1' with a reduction in volume but an increase in Nation 1's terms of trade. If L increases in Nation 2 and its offer curve rotates to 2', equilibrium occurs at E_6 with a reduction in volume but an improvement in Nation 2's terms of trade. If both offer curves shift to 1' and 2', the volume of trade declines even more (see E_7), and the terms of trade of both nations remain unchanged.

wise from 2 to 2*, we get equilibrium point E_3. This might result, for example, from a doubling of K (the abundant factor) in Nation 2. At E_3, Nation 2 exchanges 140Y for 70X with Nation 1; thus Nation 2's terms of trade deteriorate to $P_Y/P_X = \frac{1}{2}$ and Nation 1's terms of trade improve to $P_X/P_Y = 2$. With growth in both nations and offer curves 1* and 2*, we get equilibrium point E_4. The volume of trade expands to 140X for 140Y, but the terms of trade remain at 1 in both nations.

On the other hand, if K doubles in Nation 1 (as in Figure 7-7), its offer curve would rotate counterclockwise from 1 to 1′ and give equilibrium point E_5. Nation 1 would then exchange 20X for 40Y with Nation 2 so that Nation 1's terms of trade would improve to 2 and Nation 2's terms of trade would deteriorate to $\frac{1}{2}$. If instead Nation 2's labor only grows in such a manner that its offer curve rotates clockwise to 2′, we get equilibrium point E_6. This might result, for example, from a doubling of L (the scarce factor) in Nation 2. Nation 2 would then exchange 20Y for 40X with Nation 1, and Nation 2's terms of trade would increase to 2 while Nation 1's terms of trade would decline to $\frac{1}{2}$. If growth occurred in both nations in such a way that offer curve 1 rotated to 1′ and offer curve 2 rotated to 2′, then the volume of trade would be only 15X for 15Y, and both nations' terms of trade would remain unchanged at the level of 1 (see equilibrium point E_7).

With balanced growth or neutral technical progress in the production of both commodities in both nations, both nations' offer curves will shift outward and move closer to the axis measuring the nation's exportable commodity. In that case, the volume of trade will expand and the terms of trade can remain unchanged or improve for one nation and deteriorate for the other, depending on the shape (i.e., the curvature) of each nation's offer curve and on the degree by which each offer curve rotates.

7.6b   Change in Tastes and Trade in Both Nations

Through time not only do economies grow but national tastes are also likely to change. As we have seen, growth affects a nation's offer curve through the effect that growth has on the nation's production frontier. Similarly, a change in tastes affects a nation's offer curve through the effect that the change in tastes has on the nation's indifference map.

If Nation 1's desire for commodity Y (Nation 2's exportable commodity) increases, Nation 1 will be willing to offer more of commodity X (its exportable commodity) for each unit of commodity Y imported. Another way of stating this is that Nation 1 will be willing to accept less of commodity Y for a given amount of commodity X that it exports. This will cause Nation 1's offer curve to rotate clockwise, say from 1 to 1* in Figure 7-8, causing an increase in the volume of trade but a decline in Nation 1's terms of trade.

On the other hand, if Nation 2's tastes for commodity X increase, its offer curve will rotate counterclockwise, say from 2 or 2*, increasing the volume of trade but reducing Nation 2's terms of trade. If tastes change in the opposite direction, the offer curves will rotate in the opposite direction. If tastes change in both nations, both offer curves will rotate. What happens to the volume of trade and the terms of trade then depends on the type and degree of the change in tastes taking place in each nation, just as in the case of growth.

Summarizing, we can say that with growth and/or a change in tastes in both nations, both nations' offer curves will shift, changing the volume and/or the terms of trade. Regardless of its source, a shift in a nation's offer curve toward the axis measuring its exportable commodity tends to expand trade at constant prices and reduce the nation's terms of trade. Opposite shifts in the nation's offer curve tend to reduce the volume of trade at constant prices and improve the nation's terms of trade. For a given shift in its offer curve, the nation's terms of trade will change more the greater the curvature is of its trade partner's offer curve.

Summary

1. The trade theory discussed in previous chapters was completely static in nature. That is, given the nation's factor endowments, technology, and tastes, we proceeded to determine its comparative advantage and the gains from trade. However, factor endowments change through time; technology usually improves; and tastes may also change. In this chapter, we examined the effect of these changes on the equilibrium position. This is known as comparative static analysis.

2. With constant returns to scale and constant prices, if L and K grow at the same rate (balanced growth), the nation's production frontier will shift out evenly in all directions at the rate of factor growth and output per worker will remain constant. If L grows faster than K, the nation's production frontier will shift proportionately more in the direction of the L-intensive commodity and output per worker will decline. The opposite is true if K grows faster than L. The **Rybczynski theorem** postulates that at constant commodity prices, an increase in the endowment of one factor will increase by a greater proportion the output of the commodity intensive in that factor and will reduce the output of the other commodity.

3. All technical progress reduces the amount of L and K required to produce any given output, shifts the production frontier outward, and tends to increase the nation's welfare. Hicksian neutral technical progress increases the productiv-
ity of L and K in the same proportion and has the same effect on the nation's production frontier as balanced factor growth. As a result, K/L remains unchanged at constant relative factor prices (w/r). L-saving technical progress increases the productivity of K proportionately more than the productivity of L. As a result, K is substituted for L in production so that K/L rises at unchanged w/r. K-saving technical progress is the opposite of L-saving technical progress.

4. Production and consumption can be protrade (if they lead to a greater than proportionate increase in trade at constant prices), antitrade, or neutral. Production is protrade if the output of the nation's exportable commodity increases proportionately more than the output of its importable commodity. Consumption is protrade if the nation's consumption of its importable commodity increases proportionately more than consumption of its exportable commodity. What happens to the volume of trade in the process of growth depends on the net result of the production and consumption effects.

5. If growth, regardless of its source and type, increases the nation's volume of trade at constant prices, the nation's terms of trade tend to deteriorate. Otherwise, the nation's terms of trade tend to remain unchanged or improve. The effect of growth on the nation's welfare depends on a wealth effect also. This refers to the change in output per worker or per person as a result of growth. If both the terms-of-trade and wealth effects of growth are favorable, the nation's welfare will definitely improve. Otherwise, it will remain the same or decline, depending on the net result of these two effects. The case where an unfavorable terms-of-trade effect overwhelms even a favorable wealth effect and leads to a decline in the nation's welfare is known as "immiserizing growth."

6. With growth and/or a change in tastes in both nations, both nations' offer curves will shift, changing the volume and/or the terms of trade. Regardless of its source, a shift in a nation's offer curve toward the axis measuring its exportable commodity tends to expand trade at constant prices and reduce the nation's terms of trade. Opposite shifts in the nation's offer curve tend to reduce the volume of trade at constant prices and improve the nation's terms of trade. For a given shift in its offer curve, the nation's terms of trade will change more the greater the curvature is of its trade partner's offer curve.

A Look Ahead

This chapter concludes our presentation of the pure theory of international trade. We now go on to Part II, dealing with commercial policies. We begin with a discussion of tariffs in Chapter 8. We will be primarily concerned with the welfare effects of tariffs on the nation imposing a tariff and on the rest of the world. The welfare effects of tariffs will be analyzed from a general equilibrium and from a partial equilibrium point of view, utilizing the tools of analysis and figures developed in Part I.

Glossary

Comparative statics   Studies and compares two or more equilibrium positions (resulting from changes in underlying economic conditions) without regard to the transitional period and process of adjustment.

Dynamic analysis   Deals with the time path and process of adjustment from one equilibrium position to another.

Balanced growth   Equal rates of factor growth and technological progress in the production of both commodities.

Rybczynski theorem   Postulates that at constant commodity prices, an increase in the endowment of one factor will increase by a greater proportion the output of the commodity intensive in that factor and will reduce the output of the other commodity.

Labor-saving technical progress   Technical progress that increases the productivity of capital proportionately more than the productivity of labor and results in an increase in K/L at constant relative factor prices.

Capital-saving technical progress   Technical progress that increases the productivity of labor proportionately more than the productivity of capital and results in an increase in L/K at constant relative factor prices.

Protrade production and consumption   Increases in production and consumption that lead to greater than proportionate increases in the volume of trade.

Antitrade production and consumption   Increases in production and consumption that lead to a smaller than proportionate increase (or even an absolute decline) in the volume of trade.

Neutral production and consumption   Increases in production and consumption that lead to proportionate increases in the volume of trade.

Normal goods   Those goods for which consumption changes in the same direction as a change in income (so that the income elasticity of demand is positive).

Inferior goods   Those goods for which consumption declines absolutely if income rises and increases absolutely if income falls (so that the income elasticity of demand is negative).

Terms-of-trade effect   The change in the relative commodity prices at which a nation trades resulting from the tendency of the volume of trade to change as a result of growth in the nation.

Wealth effect   The change in the output per worker or per person as a result of growth in the nation.

Immiserizing growth The situation where a nation's terms of trade deteriorate so much as a result of growth that the nation is worse off after growth than before, even if growth without trade tends to improve the nation's welfare.

Questions for Review

1. What is meant when we say that the trade theory discussed in previous chapters is static in nature? What is meant by comparative statics? How can our trade theory of previous chapters be extended to incorporate changes in the nation's factor endowments, technology, and tastes? Is the resulting trade theory a dynamic theory of international trade? Why?

2. What effect do the various types of factor growth have on the growing nation's production frontier? What is meant by balanced growth? What does the Rybczynski theorem postulate?

3. Explain neutral, labor-saving, and capital-saving technical progress. How does neutral technical progress in the production of either or both commodities affect the nation's production frontier? Which type of technical progress corresponds to balanced factor growth as far as its effect on the growing nation's production frontier?

4. What is meant by production and/or consumption being protrade, antitrade, or neutral? Which sources of growth are most likely to be protrade? Which sources of growth are most likely to be antitrade? Which types of commodities are most likely to result in protrade consumption? Antitrade consumption?

5. What is the terms-of-trade effect of growth? What is the wealth effect of growth? How can we measure the change in the welfare of the nation as a result of growth and trade when the nation is too small to affect relative commodity prices? When the nation is large enough to affect relative commodity prices? Which type of growth will most likely lead to a decline in the nation's welfare? What is meant by immiserizing growth? Which type

of growth will most likely lead to an increase in the nation's welfare?

6. What is the effect on the volume and terms of trade if a nation's offer curve shifts or rotates toward the axis measuring its exportable commodity? What type of growth and/or change in tastes in the nation will cause its offer curve to shift or rotate this way? How does the shape of the trade partner's offer curve affect the change in the terms of trade resulting from a given shift in a nation's offer curve?

Problems

*1. Starting with Nation 2's pregrowth production frontier of previous chapters, draw a new production frontier for Nation 2 showing:
   (a) that the amount of both capital and labor available to Nation 2 doubled;
   (b) that only the amount of capital doubled;
   (c) that only the amount of labor doubled;
   (d) the Rybczynski theorem for the doubling of the amount of capital only.

2. Starting with Nation 2's pregrowth production frontier, draw a production frontier for Nation 2 showing neutral technical progress that doubles the productivity of labor and capital in the production of:
   (a) both commodity X and commodity Y;
   (b) commodity Y only;
   (c) commodity X only;
   (d) Compare the graphs in this problem with those of problem 1.

3. Draw for Nation 2 a figure analogous to Figure 7-4 (both panels) under the following assumptions:
   (1) Only the amount of capital doubles in Nation 2.
   (2) The free trade equilibrium relative commodity price is $P_X/P_Y = 1$.
   (3) Nation 2 is too small to affect the relative commodity prices at which it trades before and after growth.
   (4) Nation 2 exports 150Y after growth.
       (Hint: the bottom panel of the figure that you are asked to draw is already part of Figure 7-8.)

4. Draw for Nation 2 a figure (built on your figure in problem 3) analogous to Figure 7-5 (both panels) under the following assumptions:
   (1) Nation 2 is now large enough to affect the relative commodity prices at which it trades.
   (2) The terms of trade of Nation 2 deteriorate from $P_Y/P_X = 1$ with free trade before growth to $P_Y/P_X = \frac{1}{2}$ with growth and free trade.
   (3) Nation 2 exports 140Y with growth and free trade.
       (Hint: the bottom panel of the figure that you are asked to draw is already part of Figure 7-8).
*5. Draw a figure analogous to Figure 7-6 showing immiserizing growth for Nation 2 when the productivity of capital and labor doubled only in the production of commodity Y in Nation 2.

6. Draw for Nation 2 a figure analogous to Figure 7-7 (both panels) under the following assumptions:
   (1) Only the amount of labor doubles in Nation 2.
   (2) The terms of trade of Nation 2 improve from $P_Y/P_X = 1$ with free trade before growth to $P_Y/P_X = 2$ with growth and free trade.
   (3) Nation 2 exports 20Y with growth and free trade.
       (Hint: the bottom panel of the figure that you are asked to draw is already part of Figure 7-8).

Appendix——————————

This appendix presents the formal proof of the Rybczynski theorem in section A7.1, it examines growth when one factor is not mobile within the nation in section A7.2, and it gives a graphical interpretation of Hicksian neutral, labor-saving, and capital-saving technical progress in section A7.3.

A7.1 Formal Proof of the Rybczynski Theorem

As discussed in section 7.2b, the Rybczynski theorem postulates that at constant commodity prices, an increase in the endowment of one factor will increase by a greater proportion the output of the commodity intensive in that factor and will reduce the output of the other commodity.

The formal proof of the Rybczynski theorem presented here closely follows the analysis for the derivation of a nation's offer curve from its Edgeworth box diagram presented in section A3.3. Starting from Figure 3-9, we formally prove the Rybczynski theorem for the case where only the amount of labor doubles in Nation 1.

The theorem could be proved either by starting from the free trade production point B (as in Figure 7-2) or by starting from the autarky, or no-trade, production and consumption equilibrium point A (from previous chapters). The starting point is immaterial as long as the new production point after growth is compared with the particular initial point chosen and commodity prices are kept at the same level as at the initial equilibrium point. We will start from point A because that will also allow us to examine the implications of the Rybczynski theorem for relative commodity prices in the absence of trade.

Figure 7-9 shows the proof. Point A on Nation 1's production frontier (in the bottom part of Figure 7-9) is derived from point A in Nation 1's Edgeworth box diagram (in the top of the figure) before the amount of labor doubles. This is exactly as in Figure 3-9. After the amount of labor doubles, Nation 1's Edgeworth box doubles in length but remains the same height (because the amount of capital is kept constant).

For commodity prices to remain constant, factor prices must remain constant. But relative factor prices can remain constant only if K/L and the productivity of L and K remain constant in the production of both commodities. The only way for K/L to remain constant and all of L and K to remain fully employed after L doubles, is for production in Nation 1 to move from point A

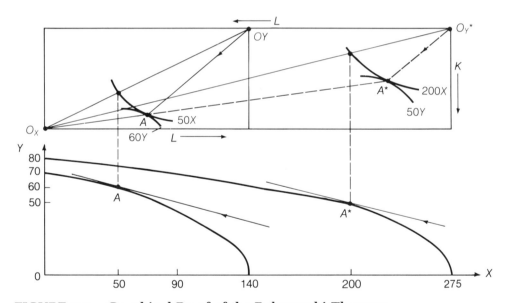

FIGURE 7-9.   Graphical Proof of the Rybczynski Theorem

Point A on Nation 1's production frontier (in the bottom part of the figure) is derived from point A in Nation 1's Edgeworth box (in the top part of the figure). This is exactly as in Figure 3-9. Doubling L doubles the size of the box. For P_X and P_Y to remain the same, w and r must remain constant. But w and r can remain constant only if K/L remains constant in the production of both commodities. Point A^* in the top and bottom parts of the figure is the only point where this is possible and all of the increase in L is fully absorbed. At point A^*, K/L in the production of both commodities is the same as at point A. At A^*, the output of commodity X (the L-intensive commodity) more than doubles while the output of commodity Y declines, as postulated by the Rybczynski theorem.

to point A^* in the Edgeworth box in the top part of the figure. At points A and A^*, K/L in the production of commodity X is the same because point A^* lies on the same ray from origin O_X as point A. Similarly, K/L in the production of commodity Y at point A^* is the same as at point A because the dashed ray from origin O_Y^* to point A^* has the same slope as the ray from origin O_Y to point A. Point A^* is the only point in the Edgeworth box consistent with full employment of all resources after L has doubled and with K/L constant in the production of both commodities. Note that isoquants have the same slope at point A and A^* indicating that w/r is the same at both points.

Since point A^* is much farther from origin O_X than point A in the Edgeworth box, Nation 1's output of commodity X has increased. On the other hand, since point A^* is closer to origin O_Y^* than point A is to origin O_Y, Nation 1's output of commodity Y has declined. These are reflected in the movement from point A on Nation 1's production frontier before L doubled to point A^* on its production frontier after L doubled. That is, at point A on its production frontier before growth, Nation 1 produced 50X and 60Y, whereas at point A^* on its production frontier after growth, Nation 1 produces 200X but only 50Y at $P_A = P_A^* = \frac{1}{4}$. Doubling L more than doubles (in this case, it quadruples) the output of commodity X. That is, the growth of L has a magnified effect on the growth of the output of commodity X (the L-intensive commodity). This completes our proof of the Rybczynski theorem.

After proving that the output of commodity Y falls at constant P_X/P_Y, we must immediately add that P_X/P_Y cannot remain constant unless commodity Y is an inferior good. Only then would the consumption of commodity Y decline absolutely in Nation 1 with the growth of its real *national* income and no trade. Barring inferior goods, P_X/P_Y must fall (P_Y/P_X rises) so that absolutely more of commodity Y is also produced and consumed after growth and with no trade. Thus, keeping relative commodity prices constant is only a way of analyzing what would happen to the output of each commodity *if relative commodity prices remained constant.*

However, relative commodity prices cannot remain constant unless commodity Y is inferior or if there is free trade and Nation 1 is assumed to be too small to affect the relative commodity prices at which it trades. In that case, Nation 1 can consume more of both commodities after growth even with constant relative commodity prices and without commodity Y having to be an inferior good. This is exactly what Figure 7-4 shows.

Problem (a) Starting from pretrade, or autarky, equilibrium point A^* in Nation 2, prove graphically the Rybczynski theorem for a doubling in the amount of K in Nation 2. (b) What restrictive assumption is required for production and consumption actually to occur at the new equilibrium point after the doubling of K in Nation 2? (c) How are relative commodity prices likely to change as a result of growth only? As the result of both growth and free trade?

A7.2   Growth with Factor Immobility

We know from the Rybczynski theorem that at constant commodity prices, an increase in the endowment of one factor will increase by a greater proportion the output of the commodity intensive in that factor and will reduce the output of the other commodity. We also know that factor prices are constant at constant commodity prices.

We now want to analyze the effect of factor growth when one of the factors is not mobile between the nation's industries and commodity prices are constant. We can analyze this case by using the specific-factors model developed in section A5.4 of the appendix to Chapter 5. We will see that the results differ from those predicted by the Rybczynski theorem and depend on whether it is the growing or the nongrowing factor that is immobile within the nation.

The left panel of Figure 7-10 refers to an increase in the supply of labor (the relatively abundant and mobile factor in Nation 1) and the right panel refers to an increase in the supply of capital (the scarce and the immobile factor in Nation 1). In *both panels,* we begin (as in Figure 5-8) with a total supply of labor in the nation equal to OO'. The equilibrium wage in both industries is ED and is determined by the intersection of the $VMPL_X$ and $VMPL_Y$ curves. OD of labor is used in the production of commodity X and DO' in the production of commodity Y.

Let us now concentrate on the *left panel* of Figure 7-10, where the supply of labor increases and labor is mobile while capital is not. If the supply of labor increases by $O'O^* = EF = DG$, from OO' to OO^*, the new equilibrium

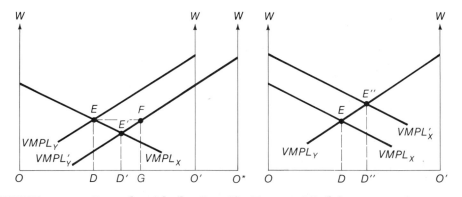

FIGURE 7-10. Growth with the Specific-Factors Model

Before growth and with L mobile and K immobile in the nation, $w = ED$, and OD of L is used to produce X and DO' to produce Y in both panels. In the left panel, an increase in L of $O'O^* = EF = DG$ results in a fall in wages to $E'D'$, and DD' more L used in the production of X and $D'G$ in Y. The output of X and Y increases, and r rises in both industries. In the right panel, K increases in the production of X only. This causes the $VMPL_X$ curve to shift up to $VMPL'_X$. The wage rate rises to $w = E''D''$ and DD'' of L is transferred from X to Y. The output of X rises and that of Y falls, and r falls in both industries with unchanged commodity prices.

wage in both industries is $E'D'$ and is determined at the intersection of the $VMPL_X$ and $VMPL'_Y$ curves. Of the DG increase in the supply of labor, DD' is employed in the production of commodity X and $D'G$ in the production of commodity Y. Since the amount of capital used in each industry does not change but the amount of labor increases, the output of both commodities increases. However, the output of commodity X increases by more than the output of commodity Y because commodity X is L intensive and more of the increase in labor is employed in the production of commodity X. Furthermore, since more labor is used in each industry with unchanged amounts of capital, the $VMPK$ and the return on capital (r) rise in both industries.

Thus, when the supply of labor increases and labor is mobile but capital is not, the output of both commodities increases, and w falls and r rises in both industries, at constant commodity prices. In the long run (when both labor and capital are mobile within the nation), an increase in the supply of labor increases the output of commodity X by a greater proportion, reduces the output of commodity Y, and leaves w and r unchanged at constant commodity prices (the Rybczynski theorem).

Let us turn to the *right panel* of Figure 7-10, where the supply of capital (Nation 1's scarce and immobile factor) increases in the production of commodity X only. Since each unit of labor in the production of commodity X will have more capital to work with, the $VMPL_X$ curve shifts up to $VMPL'_X$. The intersection of the $VMPL'_X$ and $VMPL_Y$ curves now determines the new and higher equilibrium wage of $E''D''$ in both industries, and DD'' of labor is transferred from the production of commodity Y to the production of commodity X. Since w rises in both industries, r must fall in both in order for commodity prices to remain constant (as assumed). Furthermore, since both more capital and more labor are used in the production of commodity X, the output of commodity X rises. On the other hand, since the same amount of capital but less labor is used in the production of commodity Y, the output of commodity Y declines. Thus, in this case, the change in outputs are similar to those postulated by the Rybczynski theorem.

All of the above results, however, are based on the assumption that commodity prices do not change. Since the output of commodity X increases while that of Y falls (or increases by less than the increase in the output of X), P_X/P_Y is likely to fall, and this lowers the terms of trade of the nation (unless Nation 1 is small) and modifies the effects of growth on factor prices derived above (on the basis of unchanged commodity prices).

Problem   What happens if the supply of capital increases in Nation 1 in the production of commodity Y only?

A7.3   Graphical Analysis of Hicksian Technical Progress

In this section we give a graphical interpretation of the Hicksian classification of neutral, L-saving, and K-saving technical progress using isoquants (reviewed in sections A3.1 and A3.2). We also examine the effect of the various types of technical progress on relative factor prices.

All innovations, regardless of their type, can be represented by a shift toward the origin of the isoquant referring to any given level of output. This indicates that fewer inputs or factors are required to produce any level of output after technical progress has occurred. The distinction between various types of technical progress is based on the effect that each has on K/L at constant relative factor prices (w/r).

Hicksian technical progress is *neutral* if it leaves K/L unchanged. Technical progress is *labor saving* if it tends to increase K/L and *capital saving* if it tends to reduce K/L. These are shown in Figure 7-11.

In all three panels of the figure, we begin at point A_1, where 100X is produced with 4L and 4K before technical progress occurs. After neutral technical progress, the same 100X can be produced with 2L and 2K (point A_2 in the left panel), leaving $K/L = 1$ at unchanged $w/r = 1$ (the absolute slope of the isocosts). With L-saving technical progress, the same 100X can be produced with 3K and 1L (point A_3 in the middle panel) and $K/L = 3$ at unchanged $w/r = 1$. Finally, with K-saving technical progress, the same 100X can be produced with 1K and 3L (point A_3 in the right panel) and $K/L = \frac{1}{3}$ at unchanged $w/r = 1$.

At point A_2 in the middle panel, the ratio of the marginal productivity of K to the interest rate (i.e., MPK/r) exceeds MPL/w, and so K is substituted for L in the production of commodity X. As K is substituted for L, r/w will tend

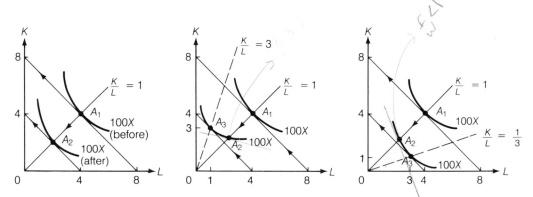

FIGURE 7-11. Hicksian Neutral, *L*-Saving, and *K*-Saving Technical Progess

In all three panels of the figure, we begin at point A_1, where 100X is produced with 4L and 4K before technical progress occurs. After neutral technical progress, the same 100X can be produced with 2L and 2K (point A_2 in the left panel), leaving $K/L = 1$ at unchanged $w/r = 1$ (the absolute slope of the isocosts). With L-saving technical progress, the same 100X can be produced with 3K and 1L (point A_3 in the middle panel) and $K/L = 3$ at unchanged $w/r = 1$. Finally, with K-saving technical progress, the same 100X can be produced with 1K and 3L (point A_3 in the right panel) and $K/L = \frac{1}{3}$ at unchanged $w/r = 1$.

to rise, thus moderating the tendency of K/L to rise. In any event, r is likely to rise in relation to w as a result of the L-saving innovation.

On the other hand, at point A_2 in the right panel, MPL/w exceeds MPK/r, and so L is substituted for K in the production of commodity X. As L is substituted for K, w/r will tend to rise, this moderating the tendency of K/L to fall (i.e., L/K to rise). In any event, w is likely to rise in relation to r as a result of the K-saving innovation.

Thus, a greater proportionate increase in the amount of L and/or an K-saving innovation tends to reduce K/L and w/r. This tendency will be greater if the L-saving innovation takes place in the production of the K-intensive commodity. On the other hand, a greater proportionate increase in the amount of K and/or an L-saving innovation tends to increase K/L and w/r. This tendency will be greater if the K-saving innovation takes place in the production of the L-intensive commodity. This is the case because then the demand for labor grows the most. To these effects on w/r resulting purely from internal growth would have to be added the effects resulting from international trade in order to determine the net effect on w/r resulting from both growth and trade. These were discussed in the chapter itself.

Problem   Using the tools of analysis developed in this chapter, comment in detail on the following statement: Capital investments tend to increase real wages while technical progress, depending on its type, may increase or reduce real wages.

Selected Bibliography

For a problem-solving approach to the material covered in this chapter, see:

- D. Salvatore, *Theory and Problems of International Economics*, 2nd ed. (New York, McGraw-Hill, 1984), ch. 5.

For an overall theoretical discussion and empirical test of the relationship between international trade and economic development, see:

- D. Salvatore, "A Simultaneous Equations Model of Trade and Development with Dynamic Policy Simulations," *Kyklos*, March (No. 1) 1983.

Important papers on the topics of growth, trade, and welfare are:

- T. M. Rybczynski, "Factor Endowments and Relative Commodity Prices," *Economica*, November 1955. Reprinted in R. E. Caves and

H. G. Johnson, *Readings in International Economics* (Homewood Ill.: Irwin, 1968).

- R. Findlay and H. Grubert, "Factor Intensities, Technological Progress, and International Trade," *Oxford Economic Papers*, February 1959. Reprinted in J. N. Bhagwati, *International Economics: Selected Readings* (Baltimore: Penguin, 1969).

- J. N. Bhagwati, "Immiserizing Growth," *Review of Economic Studies*, June 1958. Reprinted in R. E. Caves and H. G. Johnson, *Readings in International Economics* (Homewood Ill.: Irwin, 1968), and in R. C. Feenstra, *The Theory of Commercial Policy* (Cambridge, Mass.: M.I.T. Press, 1983).

- W. M. Corden, "The Effects of Trade on the Rate of Growth," in J. N. Bhagwati *et al.*, *Trade, Balance of Payments and Growth* (Amsterdam: North-Holland, 1971).

- H. G. Johnson, "Trade and Growth: A Geo-

metrical Exposition," *Journal of International Economics*, February 1971.
- A. Smith, "Capital Theory and Trade Theory," in R. W. Jones and P. B. Kenen, eds., *Handbook of International Economics*, Vol. 1 (Amsterdam: North-Holland, 1984).
- M. C. Kemp and N. V. Long, "Natural Resources in Trade Models," in R. W. Jones and P. B. Kenen, eds., *Handbook of International Economics*, Vol. 1 (Amsterdam: North-Holland, 1984).

The original Hicksian classification of technological progress is found in:
- J. R. Hicks, *The Theory of Wages* (London: Macmillan, 1932), ch. 6.

PART II

Commercial Policies

Part II (Chapters 8-12) deals with commercial policies. Chapter 8 examines tariffs, the most important of the trade restrictions; Chapter 9 extends the discussion to other trade restrictions, evaluates the justification usually given for trade restrictions, and summarizes their history. Chapter 10 deals with economic integration, Chapter 11 with the effect of international trade on economic development, and Chapter 12 with international resource movements and multinational corporations.

CHAPTER 8

Trade Restrictions: Tariffs

8.1 Introduction

We have seen in Part I that free trade maximizes world output and benefits all nations. However, practically all nations impose some restrictions on the free flow of international trade. Since these restrictions and regulations deal with the nation's trade or commerce, they are generally known as **commercial policies.** While trade restrictions are invariably rationalized in terms of national welfare, in reality they are usually advocated by those special groups in the nation that stand to benefit from such restrictions.

The most important type of trade restriction is the tariff. A tariff is a tax or duty levied on the traded commodity as it crosses a national boundary. In this chapter we deal with tariffs and discuss other trade restrictions in the next chapter. An **import tariff** is a duty on the imported commodity, while an **export tariff** is a duty on the exported commodity. Import tariffs are more important than export tariffs, and most of our discussion will deal with import tariffs. Export tariffs are prohibited by the U.S. Constitution but are often applied by developing countries on their traditional exports (such as Ghana on its cocoa and Brazil on its coffee) to get better prices and raise revenues. Developing nations rely heavily on export tariffs to raise revenues because of their ease of collection. On the other hand, industrial countries invariably impose tariffs or other trade restrictions to protect some (usually L-intensive) industry, while using mostly income taxes to raise revenues.

Tariffs can be ad valorem, specific, or compound. The **ad valorem tariff** is expressed as a fixed *percentage* of the value of the traded commodity. The **specific tariff** is expressed as a fixed *sum* per physical unit of the traded commodity. Finally, a **compound tariff** is a combination of an ad valorem and a specific tariff. For example, a 10 percent ad valorem tariff on bicycles would result in the payment to customs officials of the sum of $10 on each $100 imported bicycle and the sum of $20 on each $200 imported bicycle. On the other hand, a specific tariff of $10 on imported bicycles means that customs officials collect the fixed sum of $10 on each imported bicycle regardless of its price. Finally, a compound duty of 5 percent ad valorem and a specific duty of $10 on imported bicycles would result in the collection by customs officials of the sum of $15 on each $100 bicycle and $20 on each $200 imported bicycle. The United States uses the ad valorem and the specific tariff with about equal frequency, whereas European countries rely mainly on the ad valorem tariff. Most of our presentation in this chapter will be in terms of ad valorem import tariffs.

Tariffs have generally declined in industrial nations since World War II and now average less than 10 percent on manufactured goods. However, trade in agricultural commodities is still subject to many direct quantitative and other nontariff trade barriers. These will be discussed in section 8.6 and in the next chapter.

In this chapter, we analyze the effects of a tariff on production, consumption, trade, and welfare in the nation imposing the tariff and on its trade partner(s). In section 8.2, we analyze the general equilibrium effects of a tariff in a country that is too small to affect world prices by its trading. We relax this assumption and deal with a large country in section 8.3. In section 8.4, we examine the concept of the optimum tariff. In sections 8.5 and 8.6, we deal with the partial equilibrium effects of a tariff and the theory of tariff structure, respectively.

The general equilibrium effects of a tariff are analyzed before the partial equilibrium effects because (contrary to the usual case) the former are somewhat easier to deal with than the latter and also follow more directly from the material covered in previous chapters. The appendix then analyzes graphically the Stolper-Samuelson theorem and its exception, examines the short-run effect of a tariff on factors income, shows the measurement of the optimum tariff and the partial equilibrium effects of a tariff in a large nation, and derives the formula for the rate of effective protection.

8.2 General Equilibrium Analysis of a Tariff in a Small Country

In this section, we use general equilibrium analysis to study the effects of a tariff on production, consumption, trade, and welfare when the nation is too small to affect world prices by its trading. In the next section, we will relax this assumption and deal with the more realistic and complex case where the nation is large enough to affect world prices by its trading.

8.2a General Equilibrium Effects of a Tariff in a Small Country

When a very small nation imposes a tariff, it will not affect prices on the world market. However, the domestic price of the importable commodity will rise by the full amount of the tariff for individual producers and consumers in the small nation. As a result, domestic production of the importable commodity will expand while domestic consumption and imports will fall. Domestic production of the importable commodity will expand as long as and until domestic producers can match the world price of the imported commodity plus the tariff. On the other hand, consumers in the small nation will reduce their consumption of the importable commodity because of the rise in its domestic price. With larger domestic production and smaller domestic consumption of the importable commodity, the small nation's imports of the commodity will decline.

Although the price of the importable commodity rises by the full amount of the tariff for *individual* producers and consumers in the small nation, its price remains constant for the *small nation as a whole* since the nation itself collects the tariff. For example, if the international price of importable commodity X is $1 per unit and the nation imposes a 100 percent ad valorem tariff on imports of commodity X, domestic producers can compete with imports as long as they can produce and sell commodity X at a price no higher than $2. Consumers will have to pay $2 per unit of commodity X, whether imported or domestically produced (we assume throughout that the imported commodity and the domestically produced commodity are identical). However, since the nation itself collects the $1 tariff on each unit of commodity X imported, the price of commodity X remains $1 as far as the nation as a whole is concerned.

The divergency between the price of the importable commodity for individual producers and consumers (which includes the tariff) and the price for the nation as a whole (which excludes the tariff and remains the same as the world price) is crucial for the graphical analysis in section 8.2b. We further assume that the government of the small tariff-imposing nation uses the tariff revenue to subsidize public consumption (such as schools, police, etc.) and/or for general income tax relief. That is, the government of the small nation will need to collect less taxes internally to provide basic services by using the tariff revenue.

8.2b Illustration of the Effects of a Tariff in a Small Country

We will illustrate the general equilibrium effects of a tariff by continuing to utilize our familiar Nation 1 and Nation 2 from previous chapters. We start by using Nation 2's production frontier because it is somewhat more convenient for the type of analysis that we need to perform now. The same analysis for Nation 1 is left as end-of-chapter problems. The only conclusion that we need to remember from previous chapters is that Nation 2 is the capital-abundant nation specializing in the production of commodity Y (the capital-intensive commodity), which it exports in exchange for imports of commodity X.

From Figure 8-1, we see that if $P_X/P_Y = 1$ on the world market and Nation 2 is too small to affect world prices, it produces at point B, exchanges 60Y for

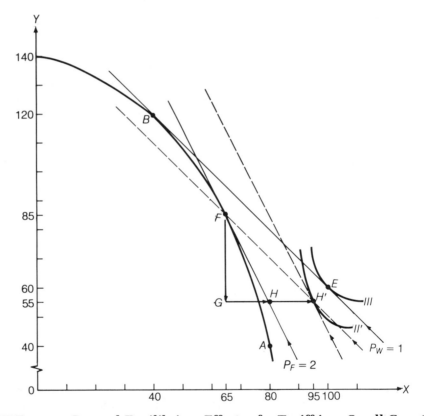

FIGURE 8–1.   General Equilibrium Effects of a Tariff in a Small Country

At $P_X/P_Y = 1$ on the world market, the small nation produces at point B and consumes at point E (as in the right panel of Figure 3–4). With a 100 percent ad valorem tariff on imports of commodity X, $P_X/P_Y = 2$ for individuals in the nation, production takes place at point F, and the nation exports 30Y (FG) for 30X, of which 15X (HH') is collected by the government as a tariff. Since we assume that the government redistributes the tariff revenue in full to its citizens, consumption with the tariff takes place on indifference curve ll' at point H', where the two dashed lines cross. Thus, free trade consumption and welfare (point E) are superior to consumption and welfare with the tariff (point H').

60X with the rest of the world, and consumes at point E on its indifference curve III with free trade. (For convenience, we now omit the prime that we attached to all letters on the graphs for Nation 2 in previous chapters.)

If the nation now imposes a 100 percent ad valorem tariff on imports of commodity X, the relative price of X rises to $P_X/P_Y = 2$ for domestic producers and consumers but remains at $P_X/P_Y = 1$ on the world market and for the nation as a whole (since the nation itself collects the tariff). Facing $P_X/P_Y = 2$, domestic producers will produce at point F, where price line $P_F = 2$ is tangent to the nation's production frontier. Thus, the nation produces more of importable commodity X and less of exportable commodity Y after imposition of the tariff than under free trade (compare point F to point B). The figure also shows that for exports of FG, or 30Y, the nation demands imports of GH', or 30X, of which GH, or 15X, goes directly to the nation's consumers and HH' (i.e., the remaining 15X) is collected in kind by the government in the form of the 100 percent import tariff on commodity X.

Note that indifference curve II' is tangent to the dashed line parallel to P_F = 2 because individual consumers in the nation face the tariff-inclusive price of $P_X/P_Y = 2$. However, since the government collects and *redistributes* the tariff in the form of public consumption and/or tax relief, indifference curve II' must also be on the dashed line parallel to $P_W = 1$ (since the nation as a whole still faces the world price of $P_X/P_Y = 1$). Thus, the new consumption point H' is defined by the intersection of the two dashed lines (and therefore is on both). The angle between the two dashed lines (which is equal to the angle between price lines $P_W = 1$ and $P_F = 2$) is equal to the tariff *rate* of 100 percent. With production at point F and consumption at point H', the nation exports 30Y for 30X after imposition of the tariff (as opposed to 60Y for 60X before imposition of the tariff).

To summarize, the nation produces at point B with free trade and exports 60Y for 60X at $P_W = 1$. With the 100 percent import tariff on commodity X, $P_X/P_Y = 2$ for individual producers and consumers in the nation but remains at $P_W = 1$ on the world market and for the nation as a whole. Production then takes place at point F; thus more of importable commodity X is produced in the nation with the tariff than under free trade. 30Y is exchanged for 30X, of which 15X is collected in kind by the government of the nation in the form of a 100 percent import tariff on commodity X. Consumption takes place at point H' on indifference curve II' after imposition of the tariff. This is below the free trade consumption point E on indifference curve III because, with the tariff, specialization in production is less and so are the gains from trade.

With a 300 percent import tariff on commodity X, $P_X/P_Y = 4$ for domestic producers and consumers, and the nation would return to its autarky point A in production and consumption (see the figure). Such an import tariff is called a **prohibitive tariff.** The 300 percent import tariff on commodity X is the *minimum ad valorem rate* that would make the tariff prohibitive in this case. Higher tariffs remain prohibitive, and the nation would continue to produce and consume at point A.

8.2c   The Stolper-Samuelson Theorem

According to the **Stolper-Samuelson theorem,** the real return to the nation's scarce factor of production will rise with the imposition of a tariff. For example, when Nation 2 (the K-abundant nation) imposes an import tariff on commodity X (its L-intensive commodity), P_X/P_Y rises for domestic producers and consumers and so will the real wage of labor (Nation 2's scarce factor).

The reason for this is that as P_X/P_Y rises as a result of the import tariff on commodity X, Nation 2 will produce more of commodity X and less of commodity Y (compare point F with point B in Figure 8-1). The expansion in the production of commodity X (the L-intensive commodity) requires L/K in a higher proportion than is released by reducing the output of commodity Y (the K-intensive commodity). As a result, w/r rises and K is substituted for L so that K/L rises in the production of both commodities (this is shown graphically in section A8.1 in the appendix). As each unit of L is now combined with more K, the productivity of L rises and therefore w rises. Thus, imposition of an import tariff on commodity X by Nation 2 increases P_X/P_Y in the nation and increases the earnings of L (the nation's scarce factor of production).

Since the productivity of labor increases in the production of both commodities, not only the money wage but also the real wage rises in Nation 2. With labor fully employed before and after imposition of the tariff, this also means that the total earnings of labor and its share of the national income are now greater. Since national income is reduced by the tariff (compare point H' to point E in Figure 8-1), and the share of total income going to L is higher, the interest rate and the total earnings of K fall in Nation 2. Thus, while the small nation as a whole is harmed by the tariff, its scarce factor benefits at the expense of its abundant factor (refer to section 5.5c).

For example, when a small industrial and K-abundant nation, such as Switzerland, imposes a tariff on the imports of an L-intensive commodity, w rises. That is why labor unions in industrial nations generally favor import tariffs. However, the reduction in the earnings of the owners of capital exceed the gains of labor so that the nation as a whole loses. The Stolper-Samuelson theorem is always true for small nations and is usually true for large nations as well. However, for large nations, the analysis is further complicated by the fact that they affect world prices by their trading.

8.3   General Equilibrium Analysis of a Tariff in a Large Country

In this section, we extend our general equilibrium analysis of the production, consumption, trade, and welfare effects of a tariff to the case of a nation large enough to affect international prices by its trading.

8.3a General Equilibrium Effects of a Tariff in a Large Country

To analyze the general equilibrium effects of a tariff in a large nation, it is more convenient to utilize offer curves. When a nation imposes a tariff, its offer curve shifts or rotates toward the axis measuring its importable commodity by the amount of the import tariff. The reason is that for any amount of the export commodity, importers now want sufficiently more of the import commodity to also cover (i.e., pay for) the tariff. The fact that the nation is large is reflected in the trade partner's (or rest of the world's) offer curve having some curvature rather than being a straight line.

Under these circumstances, imposition of a tariff by a large nation reduces the volume of trade but improves the nation's terms of trade. The reduction in the volume of trade, by itself, tends to reduce the nation's welfare, while the improvement in its terms of trade tends to increase the nation's welfare. Whether the nation's welfare actually rises or falls depends on the net effect of these two opposing forces. This is to be contrasted to the case of a small country imposing a tariff, where the volume of trade declines but the terms of trade remain unchanged so that the small nation's welfare always declines.

8.3b Illustration of the Effects of a Tariff in a Large Country

The imposition by Nation 2 of a 100 percent ad valorem tariff on its imports of commodity X is reflected in Nation 2's offer curve rotating to offer curve 2' in Figure 8–2. Note that tariff-distorted offer curve 2' is at every point 100 percent or twice as distant from the Y axis as offer curve 2 (compare, for example, point H' to point H and point E' to point D in the figure).

Before imposition of the tariff, the intersection of offer curve 2 and offer curve 1 defined equilibrium point E, at which Nation 2 exchanged 60Y for 60X at $P_X/P_Y = P_W = 1$. After imposition of the tariff, the intersection of offer curve 2' and offer curve 1 defines the new equilibrium point E', at which Nation 2 exchanges 40Y for 50X at the new world price of $P_X/P_Y = P_{W'} = 0.8$. Thus, the terms of trade of *Nation 1* (the rest of the world) deteriorated from $P_X/P_Y = P_W = 1$ to $P_X/P_Y = P_{W'} = 0.8$. On the other hand, Nation 2's terms of trade improved from $P_Y/P_X = 1/P_W = 1$ to $P_Y/P_X = 1/P_{W'} = 1/0.8 = 1.25$. Note that for any tariff *rate*, the steeper or less elastic Nation 1's (or the rest of the world's) offer curve is, the more its terms of trade deteriorate and Nation 2's improve.

Thus, when large Nation 2 imposes a tariff, the volume of trade declines but its terms of trade improve. Depending on the net effect of these two opposing forces, Nation 2's welfare can increase, decrease, or remain unchanged. This is to be contrasted to the previous case where Nation 2 was assumed to be a small nation and did not affect world prices by its trading. In that case, Nation 1's (or the rest of the world's) offer curve is represented by straight line $P_W = 1$ in Figure 8–2. Nation 2's imposition of the 100 percent import tariff on commodity X then reduces the volume of trade from 60Y for 60X

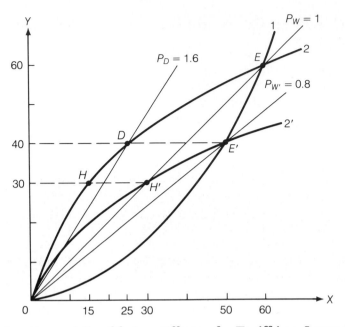

FIGURE 8–2. General Equilibrium Effects of a Tariff in a Large Country

Free trade offer curves 1 and 2 define equilibrium point E and $P_X/P_Y = 1$ in both nations. A 100 percent ad valorem import tariff on commodity X by Nation 2 rotates its offer curve to 2′, defining the new equilibrium point E'. At point E' the volume of trade is less than under free trade and $P_X/P_Y = 0.8$. This means that Nation 2's terms of trade improved to $P_Y/P_X = 1.25$. The change in Nation 2's welfare depends on the net effect from the higher terms of trade but lower volume of trade. However, since the government collects half of the imports of commodity X as tariff, P_X/P_Y for individuals in Nation 2 rise from $P_X/P_Y = 1$ under free trade to $P_X/P_Y = P_D = 1.6$ with the tariff.

under free trade to 30Y for 30X with the tariff, at unchanged $P_W = 1$ (compare point E to point H' in Figure 8–2 and Figure 8–1). As a result, the welfare of (small) Nation 2 always declines with a tariff.

Returning to our present case where Nation 2 is assumed to be large, we have seen in Figure 8–2 that with tariff-distorted offer curve 2′, Nation 2 is in equilibrium at point E' by exchanging 40Y for 50X so that $P_X/P_Y = P_W' = 0.8$ on the world market and for Nation 2 as a whole. However, of the 50X imported by Nation 2 at equilibrium point E', 25X is collected in kind by the government of Nation 2 as the 100 percent import tariff on commodity X and only the remaining 25X goes directly to individual consumers. As a result, for individual consumers and producers in Nation 2, $P_X/P_Y = P_D = 1.6$, or twice as much as the price on the world market and for the nation as a whole (see the figure).

Since the relative price of importable commodity X rises for individual consumers and producers in Nation 2, the Stolper-Samuelson theorem also holds (and w rises) when we assume that Nation 2 is large. Only in the unusual case where P_X/P_Y falls for individual consumers and producers after the nation imposes a tariff will the theorem not hold and w falls in nation 2. This is known as the **Metzler case** and is discussed in section A8.2 in the appendix.

Also to be pointed out is that the Stolper-Samuelson theorem refers to the long run when all factors are mobile between the nation's industries. If one of the two factors (say, capital) is immobile (so that we are in the short run), the effect of a tariff on factors' income will differ from that postulated by the Stolper-Samuelson theorem and is examined in section A8.3 of the appendix with the specific-factors model.

8.4 The Optimum Tariff

In this section, we examine how a *large* nation can increase its welfare over the free trade position by imposing a so-called optimum tariff. However, since the gains of the nation come at the expense of other nations, the latter are likely to retaliate, and in the end all nations usually lose.

8.4a The Meaning of the Concept of Optimum Tariff and Retaliation

As we saw in section 8.3b and Figure 8–2, when a large nation imposes a tariff, the volume of trade declines but the nation's terms of trade improve. The decline in the volume of trade, by itself, tends to reduce the nation's welfare. On the other hand, the improvement in its terms of trade, by itself, tends to increase the nation's welfare.

The **optimum tariff** is that rate of tariff that maximizes the net benefit resulting from improvement in the nation's terms of trade against the negative effect resulting from reduction in the volume of trade. That is, starting from the free trade position, as the nation increases its tariff rate, its welfare increases up to a maximum (the optimum tariff) and then declines as the tariff rate is raised past the optimum. Eventually the nation is pushed back toward the autarky point with a prohibitive tariff.

However, as the terms of trade of the nation imposing the tariff improve, those of the trade partner deteriorate, since they are the inverse, or reciprocal, of the terms of trade of the tariff-imposing nation. Facing both a lower volume of trade and deteriorating terms of trade, the trade partner's welfare definitely declines. As a result, the trade partner is likely to retaliate and impose an optimum tariff on its own. While recapturing most of its losses with the improvement in its terms of trade, retaliation by the trade partner will definitely reduce the volume of trade still further. The first nation may then itself retaliate. If the process continues, all nations usually end up losing all or most of the gains from trade.

Note that even when the trade partner does not retaliate when one nation imposes the optimum tariff, the gains of the tariff-imposing nation are less than the losses of the trade partner, so that the world as a whole is worse off than under free trade. It is in this sense that free trade maximizes world welfare.

8.4b Illustration of the Optimum Tariff and Retaliation

Figure 8–3 repeats free trade offer curves 1 and 2 from Figure 8–2 defining equilibrium point E at $P_W = 1$. Suppose that with the optimum tariff, Nation 2's offer curve rotates to 2*. (Why the tariff associated with offer curve 2* is an optimum tariff will be explained in section A8.4 in the appendix.) If Nation 1 does not retaliate, the intersection of offer curve 2* and offer curve 1 defines the new equilibrium point E^*, at which Nation 2 exchanges 25Y for 40X so that $P_X/P_Y = P_W^* = 0.625$ on the world market and for Nation 2 as a

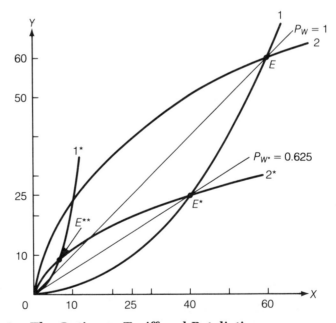

FIGURE 8–3. The Optimum Tariff and Retaliation

Offer curves 1 and 2 define free trade equilibrium point E and $P_X/P_Y = 1$, as in Figure 8–2. If the optimum tariff for Nation 2 rotates its offer curve to 2*, Nation 2's terms of trade improve to $P_Y/P_X = 1/P_W^* = 1/0.625 = 1.6$. At equilibrium point E^*, Nation 2 is at its highest possible welfare and is better off than at the free trade equilibrium point E. However, since Nation 1's welfare is reduced, it is likely to retaliate with an optimum tariff of its own, shown by offer curve 1* and equilibrium at point E^{**}. Nation 2 may then itself retaliate so that in the end both nations are likely to lose all or most of the benefits from trade.

whole. As a result, Nation 1's (the rest of the world's) terms of trade deteriorate from $P_X/P_Y = P_W = 1$ to $P_X/P_Y = P_{W*} = 0.625$, and Nation 2's terms of trade improve to $P_Y/P_X = 1/P_W^* = 1/0.625 = 1.6$.

With the tariff associated with offer curve 2*, not only does the improvement in Nation 2's welfare resulting from its improved terms of trade exceed the reduction in welfare due to the decline in volume of trade, but it represents the highest welfare that Nation 2 can achieve with a tariff (and exceeds its free trade welfare). (Again, the reason why the tariff associated with offer curve 2* is the optimum tariff will be explained in section A8.4 in the appendix by utilizing the trade indifference curves derived in section A4.1 in the appendix to Chapter 4. Here we simply examine the effect of the optimum tariff on the nation imposing it and on its trade partner.)

However, with deteriorated terms of trade and a smaller volume of trade, Nation 1 is definitely worse off than under free trade. As a result, Nation 1 is likely to retaliate and impose an optimum tariff of its own, shown by offer curve 1*. With offer curves 1* and 2*, equilibrium moves to point E^{**}. Now Nation 1's terms of trade are higher and Nation 2's are lower than under free trade, but the volume of trade is much smaller. At this point, Nation 2 is itself likely to retaliate, and in the end both nations may end up at the origin of Figure 8–3, representing the autarky position for both nations. By so doing, all of the gains from trade are lost.

Note that we have been implicitly discussing the optimum *import* tariff. More advanced treaties show, however, that an optimum import tariff is equivalent to an optimum *export* tariff. Finally, note that the optimum tariff for a small country is zero since a tariff will not affect its terms of trade and will only cause the volume of trade to decline (see points E and H' in Figure 8–2). Thus, no tariff can increase the small nation's welfare over its free trade position even if the trade partner does not retaliate.

8.5 Partial Equilibrium Analysis of a Tariff

Some effects of a tariff are best studied with partial equilibrium analysis. This type of analysis is most appropriate when a small nation imposes a tariff on imports competing with the output of a small domestic industry. Then the tariff will affect neither world prices (because the nation is small) nor the rest of the economy perceptibly (because the industry is small).

8.5a Partial Equilibrium Effects of a Tariff

When a small nation imposes a tariff on imports competing with the output of a small domestic industry, the price of the importable commodity rises by the full amount of the tariff for individuals in the nation. As a result, domestic production of the importable commodity rises, and domestic consumption and imports of the commodity fall. Revenues are also collected by the government. In addition, the tariff redistributes income from domestic consumers (who pay a higher price for the commodity) to domestic producers of the commodity (who receive the higher price) and from the nation's abundant factor (producing exportables) to the nation's scarce factor (producing importables). This leads to inefficiencies referred to as the protection cost or deadweight loss of the tariff. (A tariff will also have a balance-of-payments effect, but this is discussed in section 17.6, after we have examined the concept and measurement of the balance of payments.)

8.5b   Illustration of the Partial Equilibrium Effects of a Tariff

The partial equilibrium effects of a tariff can be analyzed with Figure 8–4, in which D_X is the demand curve and S_X is the supply curve of commodity X in Nation 2. Nation 2 is now assumed to be small and so is industry X. In the absence of trade, the intersection of D_X and S_X defines equilibrium point E, at which 30X is demanded and supplied at $P_X=\$3$ in Nation 2. With free trade at the world price of $P_X=\$1$, Nation 1 will consume 70X (AB), of which 10X (AC) is produced domestically and the remainder of 60X (CB) is imported (as

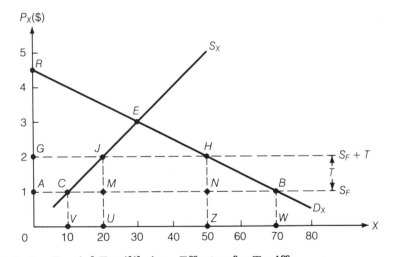

FIGURE 8–4.   Partial Equilibrium Effects of a Tariff

D_X and S_X represent Nation 2's demand and supply curves of commodity X. At the free trade price of $P_X=\$1$, Nation 2 consumes 70X (AB), of which 10X (AC) is produced domestically and 60X (CB) is imported. With a 100 percent import tariff on commodity X, P_X rises to $2 for individuals in Nation 2. At $P_X=\$2$, Nation 2 consumes 50X (GH), of which 20X (GJ) is produced domestically and 30X (JH) is imported. Thus, the consumption effect of the tariff is (−)20X (BN); the production effect is 10X (CM); the trade effect equals (−)30X (BN+CM); the revenue effect is $30 (MJHN); the increase in rent or producers' surplus is $15 (AGJC); and the protection cost, or deadweight loss, of the tariff is $15 (CJM+BHN).

in Figure 8–1). The horizontal dashed line S_F represents the infinitely elastic free trade foreign supply curve of commodity X to Nation 2.

If Nation 2 now imposes a 100 percent ad valorem tariff on the imports of commodity X, P_X for individual producers and consumers in Nation 2 will rise to $2. At $P_X = \$2$, Nation 2 will consume 50X *(GH)*, of which 20X *(GJ)* is produced domestically and the remainder of 30X *(JH)* is imported. The horizontal dashed line $S_F + T$ represents the new tariff-inclusive foreign supply curve of commodity X to Nation 2. Thus, the **consumption effect of the tariff** (i.e., the reduction in domestic consumption) equals 20X *(BN)*; the **production effect** (i.e., the expansion of domestic production resulting from the tariff) equals 10X *(CM)*; the **trade effect** (i.e., the decline in imports) equals 30X *(BN + CM)*; and the **revenue effect** (i.e., the revenue collected by the government) equals $30 ($1 on each of the 30X imported, or *MJHN*).

Note that for the same $1 increase in P_X in Nation 2 as a result of the tariff, the more elastic and flatter D_X is, the greater is the consumption effect (see the figure). Similarly, the more elastic S_X is, the greater is the production effect. Thus, the more elastic D_X and S_X are in Nation 2, the greater is the trade effect of the tariff (i.e., the greater is the reduction in Nation 2's imports of commodity X) and the smaller is the revenue effect of the tariff.

At the free trade $P_X/P_Y = \$1$, consumers are willing to pay the total of 0RBW for 70X. Since they only need to pay 0ABW, ARB represents consumers' surplus. The **consumers' surplus** (measured by the area under the demand curve and above the going price) is $122.50 (the area of triangle ARB) under free trade and $62.50 (the area of triangle RHG) with the tariff. Of the $60 reduction in consumers' surplus ($122.50 − $62.50 = area of AGHB), $30 *(MJHN)* is collected by the government as tariff revenue; $15 *(AGJC)* is redistributed to domestic producers in the form of increased rent; and the remaining $15 *(CJM + BHN)* represents the protection cost, or deadweight loss, to the economy (as explained shortly).

The increased rent of $15 *(AGJC)* redistributed to producers with the tariff can be explained as follows. At free trade $P_X = \$1$, domestic producers produce 10X and receive revenues of $10. With the tariff and $P_X = \$2$, they produce 20X and receive $40. Of the $30 increase in the revenue of producers, $15 (area *CJUV* under S_X between C and J) represents the increase in their costs of production, while the remainder of $15 *(AGJC)* represents an increase in **rent** or **producers' surplus** (defined as a payment that need not be made in the long run in order to induce domestic producers to supply the additional 10X with the tariff). The increase in producers' surplus is sometimes referred to as the subsidy effect of the tariff.

The production component *(CJM)* of the **protection cost, or deadweight loss,** arises because, with the tariff, some domestic resources are transferred from the more efficient production of exportable commodity Y to the less efficient production of importable commodity X in Nation 2. The consumption component *(BHN)* of the protection cost, or deadweight loss, arises because the tariff artificially increases P_X in relation to P_Y and distorts the pattern of consumption in Nation 2. These represent real costs or losses for Nation 2.

To summarize, the 100 percent tariff on commodity X results in a consumption effect of $(-)20X$ *(BN)*; a production effect of 10X *(CM)*; a trade effect of $(-)30X$ *(BN + CM)*; a revenue effect of $30 *(MJHN)*; an increase in rent, or producers' surplus, of $15 *(AGJC)*; and a protection cost, or deadweight loss, of $15 *(CJM + BHN)*.

The above are the partial equilibrium effects of a tariff in a small nation (i.e., in a nation that does not affect commodity pricing by its trading). The partial equilibrium effects of a tariff imposed by a large nation are more complex to analyze and are presented for the more advanced student in section A8.5 of the appendix.

8.6   The Theory of Tariff Structure

So far, we have discussed the **nominal tariff** on imports of a final commodity. We now extend the partial equilibrium analysis of the previous section to define, measure, and examine the importance of the rate of effective protection. This is a relatively new concept developed only since the 1960s but widely used today.

8.6a   The Rate of Effective Protection

When a domestic import-competing industry utilizes some imported inputs, the nominal tariff rate on imports of the final commodity is usually not a good measure of the degree of protection actually provided to domestic producers of the commodity. This is instead given by the **rate of effective protection,** which measures the percentage increase in domestic value added in the production of a commodity as a result of tariffs. **Domestic value added** equals the price of the final commodity minus the cost of the imported inputs going into the production of the commodity.

For example, if $80 of imported cotton goes into the production of a $100 suit, the free trade value added by domestic labor and capital *(V)* equals $20 ($100 − $80). A nominal tariff of 10 percent on imported suits but no duty on cotton imports increases the price of a suit to domestic consumers to $110 so that domestic value added *(V')* becomes $30 ($110 − $80). The rate of effective protection (g) measuring the increase in domestic value added is thus:

$$g = \frac{V' - V}{V} = \frac{\$30 - \$20}{\$20} = \frac{\$10}{\$20} = 0.5 \text{ or } 50\% \qquad (8\text{-}1)$$

If the nation also imposes a 5 percent tariff on cotton imports, the cost of the imported cotton going into a suit rises from $80 to $84 and V' falls to $26 ($110 − $84). The rate of effective protection in this case would be:

$$g = \frac{V' - V}{V} = \frac{\$26 - \$20}{\$20} = \frac{\$6}{\$20} = 0.3 \text{ or } 30\% \qquad (8\text{-}2)$$

Note that in both cases the rate of effective protection differs from (exceeds) the nominal tariff rate. It is this rate of effective protection that measures the degree of protection *actually* provided to domestic producers. The higher the rate is of effective protection given an industry, the greater is the incentive for domestic producers in the industry to expand output—regardless of the nominal tariff rate. Thus, while the nominal tariff rate is calculated on the price of the final commodity and, by affecting that price, is important to consumers in their consumption decisions, the rate of effective protection is important to domestic producers in their production decisions.

The rate of effective protection is usually calculated by the following formula (derived in the appendix from the definition given above):

$$g = \frac{t - a_i t_i}{1 - a_i} \qquad (8\text{-}3)$$

where g = the rate of effective protection to producers of the final commodity

t = the nominal tariff rate on consumers of the final commodity

a_i = the ratio of the cost of the imported input to the price of the final commodity in the absence of tariffs

t_i = the nominal tariff rate on the imported input

In the above example, $t = 10$ percent or 0.1, $a_i = \$80/\$100 = 0.8$, and t_i is first assumed to be zero and then 5 percent. When $t_i = 0$,

$$g = \frac{0.1 - (0.8)(0)}{1.0 - 0.8} = \frac{0.1 - 0}{0.2} = \frac{0.1}{0.2} = 0.5 \text{ or } 50\% \text{ (as found earlier)}$$

On the other hand, when $t_i = 5$ percent,

$$g = \frac{0.1 - (0.8)(0.05)}{1.0 - 0.8} = \frac{0.1 - 0.04}{0.2} = \frac{0.06}{0.2} = 0.3 \text{ or } 30\%$$

If $t_i = 10$ percent instead,

$$g = \frac{0.1 - (0.8)(0.1)}{1.0 - 0.8} = \frac{0.1 - 0.08}{0.2} = \frac{0.02}{0.2} = 0.1 \text{ or } 10\% \text{ (and equals } t)$$

With $t_i = 20$ percent,

$$g = \frac{0.1 - (0.8)(0.2)}{1.0 - 0.8} = \frac{0.1 - 0.16}{0.2} = \frac{-0.06}{0.2} = -0.3 \text{ or } -30\%$$

8.6b   Generalization and Evaluation of the Theory of Effective Protection

From examining formula 8–3 and the results obtained with it, we can reach the following important conclusions on the relationship between the rate of effective protection (g) and the nominal tariff (t) rate on the final commodity:

1. If $a_i = 0$, $g = t$.
2. For given values of a_i and t_i, g is larger the greater is the value of t.
3. For given values of t and t_i, g is larger the greater is the value of a_i.
4. The value of g exceeds, is equal to, or is smaller than t, as t_i is smaller than, equal to, or larger than t (see the first three examples above).
5. When $a_i t_i$ exceeds t, the rate of effective protection is negative (see the last example above).

Note that a tariff on imported inputs is a tax on domestic producers that increases their costs of production, reduces the rate of effective protection provided by a given nominal tariff on the final commodity, and therefore discourages domestic production. In some cases (see conclusion 5 above), even with a positive nominal tariff on the final commodity, less of the commodity is produced domestically than would be under free trade.

Clearly, the nominal tariff rate could be very deceptive and gives not even a rough idea of the degree of protection actually provided to domestic producers of the import-competing product. This is illustrated in Table 8–1, which gives the nominal and effective tariff rates for a number of products, as well as the median nominal and effective tariff rates for all products, in the United States, the European Economic Community (EEC), and Japan. Note that the median rate of effective protection on all products is everywhere more than

TABLE 8-1.   Nominal (t) and Effective (g) Tariff Rates

	U.S.		EEC		Japan	
	t	g	t	g	t	g
Meat and meat products	5.9	10.3	19.5	36.6	17.9	69.1
Preserved fruits and vegetables	14.8	36.8	20.5	44.9	18.5	49.3
Milk, cheese, and butter	10.8	36.9	22.0	59.9	37.3	248.8
Cocoa products and chocolates	4.2	16.2	12.8	34.6	22.8	80.7
Leather and leather products	7.0	12.8	7.8	14.6	14.8	22.6
Soaps and detergents	7.9	19.3	7.5	14.4	16.6	44.4
Cigars and cigarettes	68.0	113.2	87.1	147.3	339.5	405.6
Overall median tarriff rate	8.6	18.0	12.2	33.1	16.5	45.4

Source: Adapted from A. J. Yeats, "Effective Tariff Protection in the United States, the European Economic Community, and Japan," *The Quarterly Review of Economics and Business,* Summer 1974.

TABLE 8-2. *Nominal (t) and Effective (g) Tariff Rates*

	U.S.		EEC		Japan	
	t	g	t	g	t	g
Raw cotton	6.1	—	0.0	—	0.0	—
Cotton yarn	8.3	12.0	7.0	22.8	8.1	25.8
Cotton fabrics	15.6	30.7	13.6	29.7	7.2	34.9
Groundnuts, green	18.2	—	0.0	—	0.0	—
Groundnut oil, crude and cake	18.4	24.6	7.5	92.9	7.6	93.7
Groundnut oil, refined	22.0	64.9	15.0	186.4	10.1	324.8

Source: Adapted from A. J. Yeats, "Effective Tariff Protection in the United States, the European Economic Community, and Japan," *The Quarterly Review of Economics and Business,* Summer 1974.

twice the median nominal tariff rate, and both tariff rates are lowest in the United States and highest in Japan.

Furthermore, most industrial nations have a "cascading" tariff structure with very low or zero nominal tariffs on raw materials and higher and higher rates the greater is the degree of processing. This makes the rate of effective protection on a final commodity with imported inputs much greater than the nominal tariff rate would indicate. The highest rates of effective protection in industrial nations are often found on simple labor-intensive commodities, such as textiles, in which developing nations have or can soon acquire a comparative advantage and, as such, are of crucial importance to their development (these questions will be analyzed in detail in Chapter 11). Table 8–2 gives an idea of the cascading effect of tariffs from raw cotton to cotton fabrics and from green groundnuts to refined groundnut oil in the United States, the European Economic Community, and Japan.

However, even the rate of effective protection must be used cautiously because of its partial equilibrium nature. Specifically, the theory assumes that the international prices of the commodity and of imported inputs are not affected by tariffs, and that inputs are used in fixed proportions in production. Both assumptions are of doubtful validity. For example, when the price of an imported input rises for domestic producers as a result of an import tariff, they are likely to substitute cheaper domestic or imported inputs in production. Despite these shortcomings, the rate of effective protection is definitely superior to the nominal tariff rate in estimating the degree of protection actually afforded domestic producers of the import-competing product. Recently, more and more attention is being paid to rates of effective protection in international tariff negotiations (these are discussed in the next chapter).

Formula 8-3 can easily be extended to the case of more than one imported input subject to different nominal tariffs. This is done by using the sum of $a_i t_i$ for each imported input in the numerator and the sum of a_i for each imported input in the denominator of the formula. (It is this more general formula that is actually derived in the appendix; the case of a single imported input discussed above is a simpler special case.)

Summary

1. While free trade maximizes world welfare, most nations impose some trade restrictions that benefit special groups in the nation. The most important type of trade restriction is the tariff. This is a tax or duty on imports or exports. The *ad valorem tariff* is expressed as a percentage of the value of the traded commodity, whereas the specific tariff is a fixed sum per unit. The two are sometimes combined into a compound tariff. The most common is the ad valorem import tariff. These have generally declined over the past 40 years and today average less than 10 percent on manufactured goods in industrial nations.

2. When a small nation imposes an import tariff, the domestic price of the importable commodity rises by the full amount of the tariff for individuals in the nation. As a result, domestic production of the importable commodity expands while domestic consumption and imports fall. However, the nation as a whole faces the unchanged world price since the nation itself collects the tariff. These general equilibrium effects of a tariff can be analyzed with the trade models developed in Part I and by assuming that the nation redistributes the tariff revenue fully to its citizens in the form of subsidized public consumption and/or general income tax relief.

3. According to the Stolper-Samuelson theorem, an increase in the relative price of a commodity (for example, as a result of a tariff) raises the return or earnings of the factor used intensively in its production. For example, if a capital-abundant nation imposes an import tariff on the labor-intensive commodity, wages in the nation will rise.

4. When a large nation imposes an import tariff, its offer curve rotates toward the axis measuring its importable commodity by the amount of the tariff, reducing the volume of trade but improving the nation's terms of trade. The optimum tariff is one that maximizes the net benefit resulting from improvement in the nation's terms of trade against the negative effect resulting from reduction in the volume of trade. However, since the nation's benefit comes at the expense of other nations, the latter are likely to retaliate, so that in the end all nations usually lose.

5. Partial equilibrium analysis of a tariff utilizes the nation's demand and supply curves of the importable commodity and assumes that the domestic price of the importable commodity rises by the full amount of the tariff. It measures the reduction in domestic consumption, increase in domestic production, reduction in imports, revenue collected, and redistribution of income from domestic consumers (who pay a higher price for the commodity) to domestic producers (who receive a higher price) as a result of the tariff. A tariff leads to inefficiencies referred to as protection cost or deadweight loss.

6. The appropriate measure of the degree of protection actually provided to domestic producers is given by the rate of effective protection. This measures the percentage increase in domestic value added as a result of the tariff structure. The rate of effective protection (g) usually differs widely from the nominal tariff rate on the commodity (t), and g can even be negative for a positive value of t. The two rates are equal only when the nominal rate on imported inputs equals the nominal rate on the final commodity or if there are no imported inputs. Rates of effective protection in industrial nations are generally more than twice the corresponding nominal rates and are higher the more processed the product. However, these calculations must be used cautiously because of their partial equilibrium nature.

A Look Ahead

Chapter 9 extends our discussion to nontariff trade restrictions, such as quotas, and examines the similarities and differences between tariffs and other forms of trade restriction. It then goes on to analyze the various arguments for tariffs and other trade restrictions and finds that very few of these arguments are justified on close economic scrutiny. The chapter concludes with an overview of the historical experience with attempts at international trade liberalization, particularly since the end of World War II.

Glossary

Commercial policies The regulations governing a nation's commerce or international trade.

Import tariff A tax or duty on imports.

Export tariff A tax or duty on exports.

Ad valorem tariff A tariff expressed as a fixed *percentage* of the value of a traded commodity.

Specific tariff A tariff expressed as a fixed *sum* per unit of a traded commodity.

Compound tariff A combination of an ad valorem and a specific tariff.

Prohibitive tariff A tariff sufficiently high to stop all international trade so that the nation returns to autarky.

Stolper-Samuelson theorem Postulates that an increase in the price of a commodity (for example, as a result of a tariff) raises the return or earnings of the scarce factor used intensively in the production of the commodity.

Metzler case The exception to the Stolper-Samuelson theorem.

Optimum tariff The rate of tariff that maximizes the benefit resulting from improvement in the nation's terms of trade against the negative effect resulting from reduction in the volume of trade.

Consumption effect of a tariff The reduction in domestic consumption of a commodity resulting from the increase in its price due to a tariff.

Production effect of a tariff The increase in domestic production of a commodity resulting from the increase in its price due to a tariff.

Trade effect of a tariff The reduction in the volume of trade in the commodity affected by a tariff.

Revenue effect of a tariff The revenue collected by the government from the tariff.

Consumers' surplus The difference between what consumers are willing to pay for a specific amount of a commodity and what they actually pay for it.

Rent or **producers' surplus** A payment that need not be made in the long run in order to induce producers to supply a specific amount of a commodity or factor services.

Protection cost or **deadweight loss of a tariff** The real losses in a nation's welfare because of inefficiencies in production and distortions in consumption resulting from a tariff.

Nominal tariff A tariff (such as an ad valorem one) calculated on the price of a final commodity.

Rate of effective protection The percentage increase in domestic value added in the production of a commodity as a result of tariffs.

Domestic value added Equals the price of a final commodity minus the cost of the imported inputs going into the production of the commodity.

Questions for Review

1. What is meant by an ad valorem, a specific, and a compound tariff? Are import or export tariffs more common in industrial nations? In developing nations? What is the primary function of tariffs in industrial nations? In developing nations? What is a prohibitive tariff?

2. Using general equilibrium analysis, indicate the effect of an import tariff imposed by a small nation on the relative commodity price of the importable commodity for individuals in the nation and for the nation as whole. What is the effect of the tariff on the degree of specialization in production in the nation? The volume of trade? The welfare of the nation? The distribution of income between the nation's relatively abundant and scarce factors?

3. Using general equilibrium analysis and assuming that a nation is large, indicate the ef-

fect of an import tariff on the nation's offer curve, the nation's terms of trade, the volume of trade, the nation's welfare, and the distribution of income between the nation's relatively abundant and scarce factors.

4. What is meant by the optimum tariff? What is its relationship to changes in the nation's terms of trade and volume of trade? Why are other nations likely to retaliate when a nation imposes an optimum tariff (or for that matter, any import tariff)? What is likely to be the final outcome resulting from the process of retaliation?

5. When is partial equilibrium analysis of a tariff justified? How is this performed? What is meant by the consumption, production, trade, revenue, and redistribution effects of a tariff? What is meant by the protection cost, or deadweight loss, of a tariff? How is this measured?

6. What is the difference between a nominal tariff and an effective tariff? What is the usefulness of the concept of effective protection? How is the rate of effective protection measured? What is the tariff structure of industrial nations? Why is this of special concern to developing nations? What is the most serious shortcoming of the concept and measure of effective protection?

Problems

*1. Starting with the trade model of Figure 3–4 for Nation 1 and assuming that Nation 1 is small, draw a figure analogous to Figure 8–1 showing the general equilibrium effects resulting when Nation 1 imposes a 100 percent ad valorem import tariff on commodity Y, starting from its free trade position. (Hint: see Figure 4–1 but assume that, with the tariff, individuals exchange 30X for 15Y, instead of the 40X for 20Y in Figure 4–1.)

*2. (a) Using the Stolper-Samuelson theorem, indicate the effect on the distribution of income between labor and capital in Nation 1 (assumed to be a small nation) when it imposes an import tariff on commodity Y.

(b) Explain the forces at work that lead to this redistribution of income in a way analogous to the explanation given in section 8.2c for the redistribution of income in Nation 2 when that nation imposed an import tariff on commodity X.

(c) How would the result be affected if Nation 1 were instead assumed to be a large nation?

3. Starting with the free trade offer curve of Nation 1 and Nation 2 in Figure 8–2 and building on your figure in problem 1, draw a figure analogous to Figure 8–2 showing the general equilibrium effects of the 100 percent ad valorem import tariff on commodity Y imposed by Nation 1, now assumed to be a large nation.

4. (a) Draw a figure analogous to Figure 8–3 for Nation 1 showing that with the optimum tariff Nation 1 will trade 25X for 40Y and also showing the effect of Nation 2 retaliating with an optimum tariff of its own.

(b) What happens if the two nations retaliate against each other's optimum tariff several times?

5. Draw a figure similar to Figure 8–4 for Nation 1 but with the quantity of commodity Y on the horizontal axis and the dollar price of Y on the vertical axis. Draw S_Y for Nation 1, identical to S_X for Nation 2 in Figure 8–4, but draw D_Y for Nation 1 crossing the vertical axis at $P_Y = \$8$ and the horizontal axis at 80Y. Finally, assume that $P_Y = \$1$ under free trade and that Nation 1 then imposes a 100 percent ad valorem import tariff on commodity Y. With regard to your figure, indicate the following for Nation 1:

(a) the level of consumption, production, and imports of commodity Y at the free trade price of $P_Y = \$1$;

(b) the level of consumption, production, and imports of commodity Y after Nation 1 imposes the 100 percent ad valorem tariff on commodity Y.

(c) What are the consumption, production, trade, and revenue effects of the tariff?

(d) What is the dollar value of the consumers' surplus before the imposition of the tariff? After the imposition of the tariff?

(e) Of the increase in the revenue of producers with the tariff (as compared with their revenues under free trade), how much represents increased production costs? Increased rent, or producers' surplus?

(f) What is the dollar value of the protection cost, or deadweight loss, of the tariff?

6. (a) Calculate the rate of effective protection when t (the nominal tariff on the final commodity) is 40 percent, a_i (the ratio of the cost of the imported input to the price of the final commodity in the absence of tariffs) is 0.5, and t_i (the nominal tariff on the imported input) is 40 percent. Recalculate g with the following changes:

(b) $t_i = 20$ percent;

(c) $t_i = 0$;

(d) $t_i = 80$ percent;

(e) $t_i = 100$ percent;

(f) $t_i = 20$ percent and $a_i = 0.6$

(g) What general conclusions can you reach from the above results about the relationship between g and t?

APPENDIX

This appendix analyzes graphically the Stolper-Samuelson theorem and its exception, examines the short-run effect of a tariff on factors' income, shows the measurement of the optimum tariff and the partial equilibrium effects of a tariff in a large nation, and derives the formula for the rate of effective protection.

A8.1 The Stolper-Samuelson Theorem Graphically

According to the Stolper-Samuelson theorem (see section 8.2c), the real return to the nation's scarce factor of production will rise with the imposition of a tariff. For example, when Nation 2 (the K-abundant nation) imposes an import tariff on commodity X (its L-intensive commodity), P_X/P_Y rises for domestic producers and consumers and so will the real wage of labor (Nation 2's scarce factor).

The rise in P_X/P_Y and the resulting expansion of the output of commodity X and contraction of the output of commodity Y when Nation 2 imposes an import tariff on commodity X are clearly shown in Figure 8–1. Here we want to show that the tariff also results in an increase in K/L in the production of both commodities and thus increases the wage of labor (the nation's scarce factor), as postulated by the Stolper-Samuelson theorem.

To do this, we utilize the Edgeworth box diagram for Nation 2 in Figure 8–5 (from Figures 3–10 and 5–6, but omitting the prime on the letters). In Figure 8–5, point A is the autarky production point, point B is the free trade production point, and point F is the production point with 100 percent import tariff on commodity X. Note that point F is farther away from origin O_X and closer to origin O_Y than point B, indicating that with the rise in P_X/P_Y as a result of the import tariff on commodity X, Nation 2 produces more of commodity X and less of commodity Y.

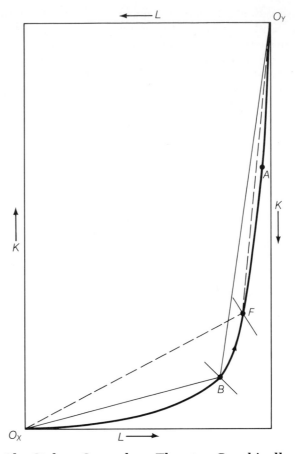

FIGURE 8–5.   The Stolper-Samuelson Theorem Graphically

When Nation 2 imposes an import tariff on commodity X, P_X/P_Y rises and the nation moves from free trade point B to point F on its production contract curve and produces more of commodity X but less of commodity Y. Since both *dashed* lines from the origins to point F are steeper than both *solid* lines from the origins to point B, K/L is higher in the production of both commodities with the tariff than under free trade. As more capital is used per unit of labor, the productivity of labor rises and therefore the income of labor is higher after the tariff is levied, as postulated by the theorem.

The slope of the *solid* line from origin O_X to point B measures K/L in the production of commodity X, and the slope of the *solid* line from origin O_Y to point B measures K/L in the production of commodity Y *under free trade*. With production at point F (after the import tariff on commodity X), K/L in the production of commodity X and commodity Y is measured by the slope of the *dashed* lines from origins O_X and O_Y, respectively, to point F. Since the dashed line from each origin is steeper than the solid line (see the figure), K/L

is higher in the production of both commodities after the imposition of the import tariff on commodity X than under free trade.

As each unit of labor is combined with more capital in the production of both commodities after the tariff on commodity X, the productivity of labor increases and therefore the wage rate rises in the production of both commodities. This is reflected in the fact that the absolute slope of the short solid line through point *F* (measuring *w*/*r*) is greater than the absolute slope of the short solid line through point *B*. With the assumption of perfect competition in factor markets, wages will be equalized in the production of both commodities.

Problem Utilizing the Edgeworth box diagram for *Nation 1* in the top panel of Figure 3–9 and in Figure 5–6, show that a 100 percent import tariff on commodity Y alters production from point *B* to point *F*, reduces *K/L* in the production of both commodities, and thus increases the productivity and income of capital in Nation 1.

A8.2 Exception to the Stolper-Samuelson Theorem: The Metzler Case

In the unusual case where a tariff lowers rather than raises the relative price of the importable commodity to individuals in the nation, the income of the nation's scarce factor also falls, and the Stolper-Samuelson theorem no longer holds. To examine this case (discovered by Metzler), we first look at the left panel of Figure 8–6, where the theorem *does* hold. This is identical to Figure 8–2 except that now we deal with an *export* rather than an import tariff because this makes the graphical analysis more straightforward.

The left panel of Figure 8–6 shows that *individual* exporters in Nation 2 must export 55Y, of which 15Y *(D′E′)* is collected in kind by their government in the form of an *export* tariff and the remaining 40Y goes to foreigners in exchange for 50X. As a result, $P_X/P_Y = P_D' = 1.1$ for individuals in Nation 2 with the tariff, as opposed to $P_X/P_Y = P_W = 1$ under free trade.

Note that the rise in P_X/P_Y for individuals in Nation 2 would be greater if the shift from offer curve 2 to 2′ was due to an import rather than an export tariff (see $P_D = 1.6$ in Figure 8–2), but what is important for the Stolper-Samuelson theorem to hold is only that P_X/P_Y rises for individuals in Nation 2. The reason for this is that when P_X/P_Y rises, *whether from an import or export tariff*, L and K are transferred from the production of commodity Y to the production of commodity X, *K/L* rises in the production of both commodities and so will the productivity and the income of labor (exactly as described in section A8.1).

Only in the unusual case where Nation 1's (or the rest of the world's) offer curve bends backward and becomes negatively inclined or inelastic after a

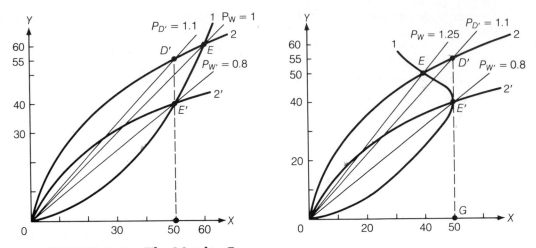

FIGURE 8–6.   The Metzler Case

The left panel shows that when Nation 2 imposes an export tariff, the relative price of commodity X falls to $P_X/P_Y = 0.8$ for the nation as a whole but rises to $P_X/P_Y = 1.1$ for individuals (because of the tariff) as compared with free trade $P_X/P_Y = 1$. Since P_X/P_Y rises for individuals in Nation 2, Nation 2 produces more of commodity X (the L-intensive commodity) and the income of labor rises, so that the Stolper-Samuelson theorem holds. In the right panel, free trade $P_X/P_Y = 1.25$ (at point E,) and the same export tariff by Nation 2 results in $P_X/P_Y = 1.1$ for individuals in Nation 2. Since P_X/P_Y falls for individuals when Nation 2 imposes a tariff, the income of labor falls. Thus, the Stolper-Samuelson theorem no longer holds, and we have the Metzler case. This results because Nation 1's offer curve bends backward or is inelastic past point E' in the right panel.

point (as in the right panel in Figure 8–6), P_X/P_Y may fall rather than rise for individuals in Nation 2 (compared with the free trade equilibrium price). In that case, the Stolper-Samuelson theorem would no longer hold. Specifically, the right panel of Figure 8–6 shows that at the free trade equilibrium point E (given by the intersection of offer curves 1 and 2), $P_W = 1.25$. The imposition of the export tariff by Nation 2 rotates offer curve 2 to 2′, giving equilibrium point E' with $P_{W}' = 0.8$ for Nation 2 as a whole and the rest of the world. However, individuals in Nation 2 will have to pay the export tariff of 15Y ($D'E'$) so that $P_X/P_Y = P_{D'} = 1.1$ for individuals in Nation 2.

Since the imposition of the export tariff reduces P_X/P_Y for individuals in Nation 2 (from $P_X/P_Y = 1.25$ under free trade to $P_X/P_Y = 1.1$ with the export tariff), the Stolper-Samuelson theorem no longer holds. That is, the fall in P_X/P_Y as Nation 2 imposes a tariff causes Nation 2 to produce less of commodity X and more of commodity Y. Since commodity Y is the K-intensive commodity, K/L falls in the production of both commodities and so will the productivity and income of labor (Nation 2's scarce factor). This is the opposite of what the Stolper-Samuelson theorem postulates and is known as the Metzler case.

The Metzler case, however, is unusual. A necessary and sufficient condition for its occurrence is that the other nation's (or the rest of the world's) offer curve bends backward or is inelastic over the range of the tariff and that all of the export tariff collected by the government is spent on consumption of the importable commodity.

Problem   Draw a figure analogous to Figure 8–6 showing in the left panel that the Stolper-Samuelson theorem holds *when Nation 1 imposes an export tariff* and showing the Metzler case in the right panel.

A8.3   Short-Run Effect of a Tariff on Factors Income

The Stolper-Samuelson theorem refers to the long run when all factors are mobile between the nation's industries. Suppose, however, that labor is mobile but some capital is specific to the production of commodity X and some capital is specific to the production of commodity Y, so that we are in the short run. The short-run effect of a tariff on factors income differs from that postulated by the Stolper-Samuelson theorem for the long run and can be analyzed with the use of the specific-factors model developed in section A5.4.

Suppose we examine the case of Nation 2 (the K-abundant nation) which exports commodity Y (the K-intensive commodity) and imports commodity X. In Figure 8–7, distance OO' refers to the total supply of labor available to Nation 2 and the vertical axis measures the wage rate. Under free trade, the

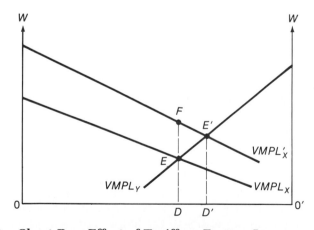

FIGURE 8–7.   Short-Run Effect of Tariff on Factors Income

An import tariff imposed by Nation 2 (K-abundant) usually increases P_X and shifts the $VMPL_X$ curve upward to $VMPL'_X$. The wage rate increases less than proportionately, and DD' of labor (the nation's mobile factor) is transferred from the production of Y to the production of X. The real wage falls in terms of X but rises in terms of Y. The real return of capital (the nation's immobile factor) rises in terms of X but falls in terms of Y.

equilibrium wage rate is ED in both industries of Nation 2 and is determined by the intersection of the $VMPL_X$ and $VMPL_Y$ curves. OD of labor is used in the production of commodity X and DO' in the production of Y.

If Nation 2 now imposes a tariff on the importation of commodity X so that P_X rises in Nation 2, the $VMPL_X$ curve shifts upward proportionately, say, to $VMPL'_X$. This increases the wage rate from ED to $E'D'$, and DD' units of labor is transferred from the production of commodity Y to the production of commodity X. Since w increases by less than the increase in P_X, w falls in terms of X but rises in terms of Y (since P_Y is unchanged).

Since the specific capital in the production of commodity X has more labor to work with, the real $VMPK_X$ and r increase in terms of both commodities X and Y. On the other hand, since less labor is used with the fixed capital in the production of commodity Y, $VMPK_Y$ and r fall in terms of commodity X, and therefore in terms of commodity Y as well.

Thus, the imposition of an import tariff on commodity X by Nation 2 (the K-abundant nation) leads to the real income of labor (the mobile factor) falling in terms of X and rising in terms of Y in both industries of Nation 2, and to the real income and return to capital (the immobile factor) rising in the production of X and falling in the production of Y. These results are to be contrasted to those obtained by the Stolper-Samuelson theorem when both labor and capital are mobile, which postulates that an import tariff increases real w and reduces real r in the K-abundant nation (our Nation 2).

Problem   What effect on real w and r will the imposition of an import tariff on commodity Y (the K-intensive commodity) have in Nation 1 (the L-abundant nation) if labor is mobile but capital is not?

A8.4   Measurement of the Optimum Tariff

In section 8.4a, we defined the optimum tariff as that rate of tariff that maximizes the net benefit resulting from the improvement in the nation's terms of trade against the negative effect resulting from the reduction in the volume of trade. The reason offer curve 2* in Figure 8–3 is associated with the optimum tariff for Nation 2 is that point E^* is on the *highest trade indifference curve* that Nation 2 can achieve with any tariff. This is shown by TI in Figure 8–8, which is otherwise identical to Figure 8–3.

Trade indifference curves were derived for Nation 1 in section A4.1. Other trade indifference curves for Nation 2 have the same general shape as TI in Figure 8.8 but are either to the left of TI (and, therefore, refer to a lower welfare for Nation 2) or to the right of TI (and, as such, are superior to TI but cannot be reached by Nation 2).

Thus, the optimum tariff is the tariff rate that makes the nation reach its highest trade indifference curve possible. This is the trade indifference curve that is tangent to the trade partner's offer curve. Thus, TI is tangent to Nation

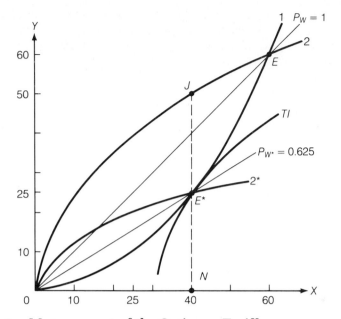

FIGURE 8–8.   Measurement of the Optimum Tariff

Offer curve 2* is associated with the optimum tariff rate for Nation 2 because equilibrium point E* is on the highest trade indifference curve Nation 2 can reach. This is given by Tl, which is tangent to Nation 1's offer curve. Nation 2 can get to equilibrium point E* on Tl by imposing a 100 percent ad valorem export tariff (since $JE^* = E^*N$). Nation 2 cannot reach a trade indifference curve higher than Tl. On the other hand, any tariff other than the optimum rate of 100 percent will put the nation on a trade indifference curve lower than Tl.

1's (or the rest of the world's) offer curve. To reach TI and point E^*, Nation 2 must impose that import or export tariff which rotates its offer curve from 2 to 2*.

Nation 2 can cause its offer curve to rotate from 2 to 2* by imposing a 100 percent ad valorem export tariff on commodity Y. Specifically, at equilibrium point E^*, Nation 2's exporters will export 50Y (*JN*), of which 25Y (*JE**) is collected by the government of Nation 2 as an export tax on commodity Y, and the remainder of 25Y (*E*N*) goes to foreigners in exchange for 40X. Note that Nation 2 could also get its offer curve to rotate from 2 to 2* with a seemingly much larger import tariff on commodity X. In reality, the optimum export tariff *rate* is equal to the optimum import tariff rate (even though this does not seem so in Figure 8–7). This can be proved adequately only with mathematics in more advanced graduate texts.

However, since it is more likely for a nation to have some monopoly power over its exports (for example, Brazil over coffee exports and petroleum-exporting countries over petroleum exports through OPEC) than it is for a nation to have some monopsony power over its imports, our discussion of the optimum tariff is perhaps more relevant in terms of exports than imports.

The optimum export or import tariff rate (t^*) can also be calculated with the following formula:

$$t^* = \frac{1}{e-1} \tag{8A-1}$$

where e is the (absolute value of the) elasticity of the trade partner's offer curve (as defined in section 4.6a). Thus, when e is infinite (i.e., when the trade partner's offer curve is a straight line, which also means that Nation 2 is a small nation), then the optimum tariff for Nation 2 is zero (see the formula). On the other hand, when Nation 1's (or the rest of the world's) offer curve has some curvature (so that e is less than infinite), t^* has a positive value. The lower is the value of e (i.e., the greater is the curvature of the trade partner's offer curve), the greater is the value of t^*. However, formula 8A–1 is not very operational because in order to use it to calculate the optimum tariff, we must first identify point E^* (see the figure).

As pointed out in section 8.4b, the gain to a nation from the optimum tariff comes at the expense of the trade partner, who is likely to retaliate. The process of retaliation may continue until in the end both nations lose all or most of the gains from trade. The volume of trade may shrink to zero unless, by coincidence, both nations happen to be imposing their optimum tariff *simultaneously*, given the trade partner's tariff.

Problem   (a) Draw a figure analogous to Figure 8–8 showing the optimum export tariff on commodity X *for Nation 1*. (Hint: for the general shape of Nation 1's trade indifference curves, see Figure 4–7.) Can you show on the same figure the optimum tariff for Nation 2 after Nation 1 has already imposed its optimum tariff? (Hint: see Figure 8–3.) (b) What are the approximate terms of trade of Nation 1 and Nation 2 after Nation 1 has imposed an optimum tariff and Nation 2 has retaliated with an optimum tariff of its own? (c) How has the welfare of each nation changed from the free trade position?

A8.5   Partial Equilibrium Effects of a Tariff in a Large Nation

In section 8.5, we examined the partial equilibrium effects of a tariff in a small nation (i.e., one that does not affect commodity prices by its trading). We now extend the analysis to examine the partial equilibrium effects of a tariff imposed by a large nation. These results extend the general equilibrium analysis of a tariff in a large nation presented in section 8.3.

The partial equilibrium effects of a tariff in a large nation can be examined by using Figure 8–9, which is similar but more complex than Figure 8–4. In the right side of Figure 8–9, D_H is the *domestic* demand curve and S_H is the *domestic* supply curve for commodity X in the *large* nation. In the absence of trade, $P_X = \$3.33$ and 167X are produced and consumed in the nation.

If P_X is lower on the world market than in the nation, the opening of trade will lead the nation to import commodity X until the domestic and foreign price of commodity X are equal (on the assumption of free trade and no transportation costs). To see how this takes place, we must introduce the world supply curve of exports of commodity X to our nation. This is given by S_F on the left side of the figure. S_F is positively sloped (when moving from right to left) because our nation is now assumed to be large enough to affect world prices. For example, to induce the rest of the world to increase the quantity

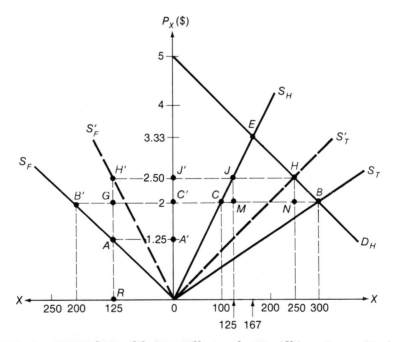

FIGURE 8–9. Partial Equilibrium Effects of a Tariff in a Large Nation

D_H is the domestic demand curve and S_H is the domestic supply curve. S_F on the left side is the foreign supply curve of exports to the nation. $S_T = S_H + S_F$. With free trade, D_H and D_T determine $P_X = \$2$ and $Q_X = J'H = 300X$ ($C'C = 100X$ produced at home and $CB = 200X$ imported). With a 100 percent tariff, S_F shifts up to S'_F and S_T to S'_T. D_H and S'_T determine $P_X = \$2.50$ but foreign producers receive only \$125 *(RA = OA')*. Of $Q_X = 250$, $J'J = 125X$ are produced at home and $JH = 125X$ are imported. The consumption effect in the nation is BN, the production effect is CM, the trade effect is $BN + CM$, the revenue effect is $AH'J'A'$ (of which $MJHN = C'J'H'G'$ is collected from domestic consumers and $A'C'GA$ from foreign producers). The protection cost is $CJM + BHN$. The nation has a net welfare gain that is smaller than the welfare loss of foreign producers.

exported to our nation from 125X (point A on the S_F curve) to 200X (point B' on S_F), the price of commodity X must rise from $P_X = \$1.25$ to $P_X = \$2$.

With free trade and no transportation costs, the total supply curve of commodity X to the nation is S_T and is obtained by adding *laterally* the S_H and the S_F curves. For example, at $P_X = \$2$, $C'C = 100X$ will be supplied by domestic producers and $CB = C'B' = 200X$ by foreign producers, for a total of $C'B = 300X$. The intersection of the D_H and D_T curves now gives equilibrium point B, at which $P_X = \$2$ and $Q_X = C'B = 300X$ (of which $C'C = 100X$ are supplied by domestic producers and $CB = C'B' = 200X$ by foreign suppliers). This compares with $P_X = \$3.33$ at which 167X are produced and consumed domestically in the nation in the absence of trade (point E).

If now the nation imposes a 100 percent ad valorem tariff on the importation of commodity X, S_F on the left side of the figure will shift up or rotate upward to S'_F, which is twice as steep as S_F. That is, foreign producers must now be offered twice as high a price as before the nation imposed the import tariff to supply the same quantity of exports of commodity X. For example, at $P_X = \$1.25$, foreign producers were willing to export 125X to the nation (point A on the S_F curve) before the nation imposed the tariff, but required a $P_X = \$2.50$ with the 100 percent tariff (point H' on the S'_F curve). This gives S'_F as the new supply curve of exports by foreigners to the nation.

In order to determine the equilibrium point when the nation imposes the tariff, we must now add laterally the domestic supply curve of commodity X in the nation (S_H on the right side of the figure) to the foreign supply curve of exports with the tariff (S'_F on the left side of the figure). This gives S'_T as the new total supply curve of commodity X to the nation on the right side of the figure. For example, at $P_X = \$2.50$, $J'J = 125X$ will be supplied by domestic producers and $JH = J'H' = 125X$ by foreign producers. Thus, with D_H and S'_T, $P_X = \$2.50$ and 250X will be consumed in the nation (125X produced at home and 125X imported). The price of commodity X to domestic consumers rises from $P_X = \$2.00$ under free trade to $\$2.50$ with the tariff. Foreign producers, however, receive only $P_X = RA = \$1.25$, or half of the $P_X = \$2.50$ paid by domestic consumers in the nation for each of the 125X they export to the nation. The other half ($AH' = A'J' = \$1.25$) is collected as a tariff by the nation on each unit of commodity X imported.

The partial equilibrium effect on the nation resulting from its imposition of a 100 percent ad valorem tariff on commodity X can now be measured. The tariff will result in a consumption effect of $(-)50X$ *(BN)*; a production effect of $(+)25X$ *(CM)*; a trade effect of $(+)75X$ *(BN + CM)*; a revenue effect of $\$156.25$ ($AH' = A'J'$ times $JH = J'H'$, which is equal to area $AH'J'A'$); of this revenue effect, $MJHN = C'J'H'G = \$62.50$ comes from domestic consumers and the remainder of $A'C'GA = \$93.75$ ($\$156.25 - \$62.50$) comes from foreign producers. The protection cost or deadweight loss is $\$18.75$ *(CJM + BHN)*. Therefore, the nation obtains a welfare *gain* equal to the $\$93.75$ of *net* tariff revenue extracted from foreigners *minus* the protection cost or deadweight loss of $\$18.75$. This gives an overall net welfare gain of $\$75$.

Foreign producers, on the other hand, lose $A'C'B'A = \$121.88$ of producers' surplus due to the reduction in the price they receive for commodity X from $P_X = \$2$ under free trade to $P_X = \$1.25$ when the nation imposes the tariff. This is made up of two parts: $A'C'GA = \$93.75$ (the amount extracted from foreign producers by the reduction in P_X they receive with the tariff) plus $AGB' = \$28.13$ (the terms of trade effect on the foreign supply).

Thus, the nation imposing the tariff receives an overall gain of $75, while foreign producers face an overall loss of $121.88. Since losses exceed gains, the world as a whole suffers a net welfare loss of $46.88 ($121.88 − $75). This is exactly equal to the protection cost or deadweight loss in the nation of $18.75 plus the terms of trade loss of foreign suppliers of $28.13 (i.e., $CJM + BHN + AGB'$). Of course, with a different size of tariff and different shapes of demand and supply curves, the results would differ.

Problem What is the relationship between the price elasticity of S_H and S_F and the price of the commodity under free trade and with the tariff?

A8.6 Derivation of the Formula for the Rate of Effective Protection

In section 8.6a, we defined the rate of effective protection as the percentage increase in domestic value added as a result of tariffs. This was given by equation 8−1, repeated below as equation 8A−2:

$$g = \frac{V' - V}{V} \tag{8A-2}$$

where g is the rate of effective protection, V is the domestic value added under free trade, and V′ equals the domestic value added with a tariff on imports of the final commodity and/or on imported inputs used in the domestic production of the commodity.

We now want to derive equation 8−3 in section 8.6a from equation 8A−2. This is accomplished by defining V and V′ in terms of the international price of the final commodity under free trade and with tariffs, substituting these values into equation 8A−2, and simplifying to get equation 8−3.

Suppose that the fixed international free trade price of a commodity (for example, a suit) is p. (Thus, we are dealing with a small nation, so that we start the analysis from section 8.5 in the text rather than from section A8.5.) Suppose also that a number of imported inputs (such as cotton, buttons, etc.), also fixed in price on the world market, go into the domestic production of suits. The sum of the costs of these imported inputs going into the domestic production of a suit under free trade is:

$$a_1 p + a_2 p + \ldots + a_n p = \Sigma a_i p \tag{8A-3}$$

where i refers to any of the n imported inputs and $a_i p$ is the cost of imported input i going into the domestic production of a suit.

Thus, the domestic value added in a suit produced in the nation under free trade equals the international fixed price of the suit under free trade minus the cost of all imported inputs at their fixed international free trade price. That is,

$$V = p - p\Sigma a_i = p(1 - \Sigma a_i) \tag{8A-4}$$

With a tariff on suit imports and on imported inputs going into the domestic production of suits, the domestic value added (V') is:

$$V' = p(1 + t) - p\Sigma a_i(1 + t_i) \tag{8A-5}$$

where t is the nominal ad valorem tariff rate on suit imports, and t_i is the nominal ad valorem tariff rate on the imported input i going into the domestic production of suits. Note that t_i may differ for different imported inputs.

Substituting the values from equation 8A–4 and equation 8A–5 into equation 8A–2, we get:

$$g = \frac{V' - V}{V} = \frac{p(1 + t) - p\Sigma a_i(1 + t_i) - p(1 - \Sigma a_i)}{p(1 - \Sigma a_i)}$$

Since there is a p in each term in the numerator and denominator, we can cancel them out, and by also removing the parentheses, we get:

$$g = \frac{1 + t - \Sigma a_i - \Sigma a_i t_i - 1 + \Sigma a_i}{1 - \Sigma a_i}$$

Cancelling out equal terms in the numerator, we get equation 8A–6:

$$g = \frac{t - \Sigma a_i t_i}{1 - \Sigma a_i} \tag{8A-6}$$

If there is only one imported input going into the production of the commodity, the Σ sign is removed from the numerator and the denominator of equation 8A–6 and we end up with equation 8–3 given in section 8.6.

A shortcoming of the theory of effective protection is that it assumes technologically fixed coefficients of production (i.e., no factor substitution is possible) and that the international prices of the imported commodity and imported inputs are not affected by tariffs (i.e., the nation is a small nation).

Problem   (a) What effect will the imposition of a tariff on imported inputs going into the domestic production of a commodity have on the size of the consumption, production, trade, revenue, and redistribution effect of the tariff on the final commodity? (b) What effect will it have on the size of the protection cost, or deadweight loss, of the tariff? (Hint: determine which curve shifts and in which direction in Figure 8–4 as a result of the tariff on imported inputs.)

Selected Bibliography

For a problem-solving approach to the theory of tariffs, see:
- D. Salvatore, *Theory and Problems of International Economics*, 2nd ed. (New York: McGraw-Hill, 1984), ch. 6.

An excellent discussion of interdependence is found in:
- R. N. Cooper, *Economic Policy in an Interdependent World* (Cambridge, Mass.: M.I.T. Press, 1985).
- M. Michaely, *Trade, Income Levels, and Dependence* (Amsterdam: North-Holland, 1984).

Comprehensive surveys of commercial policy, in general, and the theory of tariffs, in particular, are:
- W. M. Corden, *The Theory of Protection* (London: Oxford University Press, 1971).
- W. M. Corden, *Trade Policy and Economic Welfare* (London: Oxford University press, 1974).
- H. G. Johnson, *Aspects of the Theory of Tariffs* (London: Allen & Unwin, 1974).
- M. Michaely, *Theory of Commercial Policy* (Chicago: University of Chicago Press, 1977).
- J. N. Bhagwati and T. N. Srinivisan, *Lectures on International Trade* (Cambridge, Mass.: M.I.T. Press, 1983).
- W. M. Corden, "The Normative Theory of International Trade," in R. W. Jones and P. B. Kenen, *Handbook of International Economics* (Amsterdam: North-Holland, 1984).
- J. N. Bhagwati, in R. C. Feenstra, ed., *The Theory of Commercial Policy* (Cambridge, Mass.: M.I.T. Press, 1983).

The Stolper-Samuelson theorem, the Metzler case, and the conditions for the occurrence of the Metzler case, respectively, are found in:
- W. F. Stolper and P. A. Samuelson, "Protection and Real Wages," *Review of Economic Studies*, November 1941. Reprinted in H. S. Ellis and L. M. Metzler, *Readings in the Theory of International Trade* (Homewood, Ill.: Irwin, 1950).
- L. A. Metzler, "Tariffs, the Terms of Trade and the Distribution of National Income," *Journal of Political Economy*, February 1949. Reprinted in R. E. Caves and H. G. Johnson, *Readings in International Economics* (Homewood, Ill.: Irwin, 1968).
- B. Sodersten and K. Vind, "Tariffs and Trade in General Equilibrium," *American Economic Review*, June 1968.

The classics on the optimum tariff and an excellent later work are:
- A. P. Lerner, "The Symmetry between Import and Export Taxes," *Economica*, August 1936. Reprinted in R. E. Caves and H. G. Johnson, *Readings in International Economics* (Homewood, Ill.: Irwin, 1968).
- T. Scitovsky, "A Reconsideration of the Theory of Tariffs," *Review of Economic Studies*, no. 2, 1942. Reprinted in H. S. Ellis and L. M. Metzler, *Readings in the Theory of International Trade* (Homewood, Ill.: Irwin, 1950).
- V. J. de Graff, "On Optimum Tariff Structures," *Review of Economic Studies*, no 1, 1949.

The standard works on the theory of tariff structure and the rate of effective protection are:
- W. M. Corden, *The Theory of Protection* (London: Oxford University Press, 1971).
- H. G. Johnson, "The Theory of Tariff Structure with Special Reference to World Trade and Development," in H. G. Johnson and P. B. Kenen, *Trade and Development* (Geneva: United Nations, 1965).
- H. G. Grubel and H. G. Johnson, *Effective Tariff Protection* (Geneva: United Nations, 1971).

For some measurements of rates of effective protection, see:
- B. Balassa, "Tariff Protection in Industrial Countries: An Evaluation," *Journal of Politi-*

cal Economy, December 1965. Reprinted in R. E. Caves and H. G. Johnson, *Readings in International Economics* (Homewood, Ill.: Irwin, 1968).

• B. Balassa *et al.*, *The Structure of Protection in Developing Countries* (Baltimore: Johns Hopkins University Press, 1971).

• A. J. Yeats, "Effective Tariff Protection in the United States, the European Economic Community, and Japan," *Quarterly Review of Economics and Business*, Summer 1974.

• M. Szenberg, J. Lombardi, and E. Lee, *Welfare Effects of Trade Restrictions*, (New York: Academic Press, 1977).

CHAPTER 9

Other Trade Restrictions and United States Commercial Policy

9.1 Introduction

Although tariffs are the most important form of trade restriction, there are other types of trade barriers, such as quotas, voluntary export restraints, and technical, administrative and other regulations. Trade restrictions result also from the existence of international cartels and "dumping." As tariff levels are negotiated down, the *relative* importance of these other trade barriers is increasing.

In this chapter, we analyze the effect of nontariff trade barriers, evaluate the various arguments for protection, and present the highlights of United States commercial policy. Specifically, section 9.2 examines the effects of an import quota and compares them to the effects of an import tariff. Section 9.3 deals with other nontariff trade barriers and includes a discussion of international cartels and dumping. In section 9.4, the various arguments for protection are presented and evaluated, from the clearly fallacious ones to those that seem to make some economic sense. Section 9.5 briefly surveys the history of United States commercial policy from 1934 to the present. Finally, section 9.6 examines remaining problems and the future of trade liberalization. The appendix analyzes graphically the operation of centralized cartels, international price discrimination, and the use of taxes and subsidies instead of tariffs to correct domestic distortions. It also analyzes state trading.

217

9.2 Quotas

A **quota** is the most important nontariff trade barrier. It is a *direct* quantitative restriction on the amount of a commodity allowed to be imported or exported. Import quotas are far more common and important than export quotas, and so we deal exclusively with import quotas in this section. We first analyze the effects of an import quota with the same type of partial equilibrium analysis used in section 8.5b to analyze the effects of an import tariff. Subsequently, we note the similarities and differences between an import quota and an equivalent import tariff.

9.2a The Effects of an Import Quota

Import quotas can be used to protect a domestic industry, to protect domestic agriculture, and/or for balance-of-payments reasons. Import quotas were very common in Western Europe immediately after World War II. Today they are used by practically all industrial nations to protect their agriculture, and by developing nations to stimulate import substitution of manufactured products and for balance-of-payments reasons.

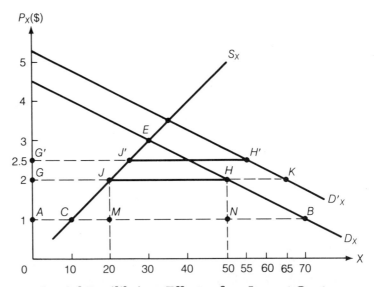

FIGURE 9-1. Partial Equilibrium Effects of an Import Quota

D_x and S_x represent the nation's demand and supply curves of commodity X. Starting from the free trade $P_x = \$1$, an import quota of 30X (*JH*) would result in $P_x = \$2$ and consumption of 50X (*GH*), of which 20X (*GJ*) is produced domestically. If the government auctioned off import licenses to the highest bidder in a competitive market, the revenue effect would also be $30 (*JHNM*), as with a 100 percent import tariff. With a shift in D_x to D_x' and an import quota of 30X (*J'H'*), consumption would fall from 65X to 55X (*G'H'*), of which 25X (*G'J'*) is produced domestically.

The partial equilibrium effects of an import quota can be illustrated with Figure 9–1, which is almost identical to Figure 8–4. In Figure 9–1, D_X is the demand curve and S_X is the supply curve of commodity X for the nation. With free trade at the world price of $P_X = \$1$, the nation consumes 70X *(AB)*, of which 10X *(AC)* is produced domestically and the remainder of 60X *(CB)* is imported. An import quota of 30X *(JH)* would raise the domestic price of X to $P_X = \$2$, exactly as with a 100 percent ad valorem import tariff on commodity X (see Figure 8–4). The reason is that only at $P_X = \$2$ does the quantity demanded of 50X *(GH)* equal the 20X *(GJ)* produced domestically plus the 30X *(JH)* allowed by the import quota. Thus, consumption is reduced by 20X *(BN)* and domestic production is increased by 10X *(CM)* with an import quota of 30X *(JH)*, exactly as with the 100 percent import tariff. If the government also auctioned off import licenses to the highest bidder in a competitive market, the revenue effect would be $30 ($1 on each of the 30X of the import quota), given by area *JHNM*. Then the import quota of 30X would be equivalent in every respect to an "implicit" 100 percent import tariff.

With an upward shift of D_X to D_X', the *given import quota* of 30X *(J'H')* would result in the domestic price of X rising to $P_X = \$2.50$, domestic production rising to 25X *(G'J')*, and domestic consumption falling from 65X to 55X *(G'H')*. On the other hand, with the given 100 percent import tariff (in the face of the shift from D_X to D_X'), the price of X would remain unchanged at $P_X = \$2$ and so would domestic production at 20X *(GJ)*, but domestic consumption would rise to 65X *(GK)* and imports to 45X *(JK)*.

9.2b   Comparison of an Import Quota to an Import Tariff

The shift of D_X to D_X' in Figure 9–1 points to one of several important differences between an import quota and an equivalent (implicit) import tariff. That is, with a given import quota, an increase in demand will result in a higher domestic price and greater domestic production and lower consumption. On the other hand, with a given import tariff, an increase in demand will leave the domestic price and domestic production unchanged but will increase consumption and imports. A downward shift in D_X as well as shifts in S_X can be analyzed in an analogous manner but are left as end-of-chapter problems. Since adjustment to any shift in D_X or S_X occurs in the domestic *price* with an (effective) import quota but in the *quantity of imports* with a tariff, an import quota completely replaces the market mechanism rather than simply altering it (as an import tariff does).

A second important difference between an import quota and an import tariff is that the quota involves the distribution of import licenses. If the government does not auction off these licenses in a competitive market, firms that receive them will reap monopoly profits. In that case, the government must decide the basis for distributing licenses among potential importers of the commodity. Such choices may be based on arbitrary official judgments rather than on efficiency considerations, and they tend to remain frozen even in the face of changes in the relative efficiency of various actual and potential importers of the commodity. Furthermore, since import licenses result in monopoly profits, potential importers are likely to devote a great deal of effort in lobbying and even bribing government officials to obtain them (i.e., in so-called rent-seeking activities). Thus, import quotas not only replace the market mechanism, but also result in waste from the point of view of the economy as a whole and contain the seeds of corruption.

Finally, an import quota limits imports to the specified level with *certainty*, while the trade effect of an import tariff may be uncertain. The reason for this is that the shape or elasticity of D_X and S_X are often not known, making it difficult to estimate the import tariff required to restrict imports to a desired level. Furthermore, foreign *exporters* may absorb all or part of the tariff by increasing their efficiency of operation or by accepting lower profits. As a result, the actual reduction in imports may be less than anticipated. Exporters cannot do this with an import quota since the *quantity* of imports allowed into the nation is clearly specified by the quota. It is for this reason, and also because an import quota is less "visible," that domestic producers strongly prefer import quotas to import tariffs. However, since import quotas are more restrictive than equivalent import tariffs, society should generally resist these efforts.

9.3 Other Nontariff Barriers

In this section, we examine trade barriers other than import tariffs and quotas. These include voluntary export restraints and technical, administrative, and other regulations. Trade restrictions also result from the existence of international cartels and from dumping. In recent years, these **nontariff trade barriers** (**NTBs**) have become more important than tariffs as obstructions to the flow of international trade and now represent a major threat to the world trading system that has evolved since the end of World War II. In this section, we examine NTBs, starting with voluntary export restraints.

9.3a Voluntary Export Restraints

One of the most important of the nontariff trade barriers or NTBs is **voluntary exports restraints** (**VER**). These refer to the case where an importing country induces another nation to reduce its exports of a commodity "voluntarily," under the threat of higher all-around trade restrictions, when these exports threaten an entire domestic industry. Voluntary export restraints have been negotiated since the 1950s by the United States government to curtail textile exports from Japan and more recently also to curb exports of automobiles, steel, shoes, and other commodities from Japan and other nations. These are the mature industries facing sharp declines in employment especially in a period (such as the present one) of sluggish economic growth all over the world. Sometimes called "orderly marketing arrangements," these voluntary export restraints have allowed the United States and other industrial nations making use of them to save at least the appearance of continued support for the principle of free trade.

When voluntary export restraints are successful, they have all the economic effects of (and, therefore, can by analyzed in exactly the same way as) an equivalent import quota, except for the revenue effect, which foreign suppliers of the commodity are now likely to capture by charging higher prices. A clear example of this is provided by the rise in the sticker price of Japanese automobile exports to the United States after Japan "voluntarily" agreed to restrict them to 1.85 million units or less per year from 1981 to 1985. Voluntary export restraints are also likely to be less effective in limiting imports than import quotas because voluntary export restraints are usually administered by the exporting nations, which only reluctantly agree to curb their exports. Furthermore, as a rule only major supplier countries are involved, leaving the door open for other nations to replace part of the exports of the major suppliers and also from transshipments through third countries.

9.3b   Technical, Administrative, and Other Regulations

International trade is also hampered by numerous **technical, administrative, and other regulations.** These include *safety regulations* for automobile and electrical equipment, *health regulations* for the hygienic production and packaging of imported food products, and *labeling requirements* showing origin and contents. While many of these regulations serve legitimate purposes, some (such as the French ban on scotch advertisements and the British restriction on the showing of foreign films on British television) are only thinly veiled disguises for restricting imports.

Other trade restrictions have resulted from laws requiring governments to buy from domestic suppliers (the so-called government procurement policies). For example, under the "Buy American Act" passed in 1933, United States government agencies gave a price advantage of up to 12 percent (50 percent for defense contracts) to domestic suppliers. As part of the Tokyo Round of trade liberalization (see section 9.5d), the United States and other nations agreed on a code on government procurements to bring these practices and regulations into the open and give foreign suppliers a fair chance.

Much attention has been given in recent years to *border taxes*. These are rebates for internal *indirect* taxes given to exporters of a commodity and imposed (in addition to the tariff) on importers of a commodity. Examples of indirect taxes are excise and sales taxes in the United States and the value-added tax in Europe. Since most government revenues are raised through direct taxes (such as income taxes) in the United States and through indirect taxes (such as the value-added tax) in Europe, United States exporters receive much lower rebates than European exporters (or no rebate at all) and are thus at a competitive disadvantage.

International commodity agreements and *multiple exchange rates* also restrict trade. However, as the former are of primary concern to developing nations and the latter relate to international finance, they are discussed in Chapter 11 and Chapter 17, respectively.

9.3c   International Cartels

An **international cartel** is an organization of suppliers of a commodity located in different nations (or a group of governments) that agrees to restrict output and exports of the commodity with the aim of maximizing or increasing the total profits of the organization. Though *domestic* cartels are illegal in the United States and restricted in Europe, the power of *international* cartels cannot easily be countered because they do not fall under the jurisdiction of any one nation.

The most notorious of present-day international cartels is OPEC (Organization of Petroleum Exporting Countries), which, by restricting production and exports, succeeded in quadrupling the price of crude oil between 1973 and 1974. Another example is the International Air Transport Association, a cartel of major international airlines, which meets annually to set international air fares and policies.

An international cartel is more likely to be successful if there are only a few international suppliers of an essential commodity for which there are no close substitutes. OPEC fulfilled these requirements very well during the 1970s. When there are many international suppliers, it is more difficult to organize them into an effective cartel. Similarly, when good substitutes for the commodity are available, the attempt by an international cartel to restrict output and exports to increase prices and profits would only lead buyers to shift to substitute commodities. This explains the failure of, or inability to set up, international cartels in minerals other than petroleum and tin, and in a handful of agricultural products (sugar, coffee, cocoa, and rubber).

Since the power of a cartel lies in its ability to restrict output and exports, there is an incentive for any one supplier to remain outside the cartel or to "cheat" on it by unrestricted sales at slightly below the cartel price. This became painfully evident to OPEC during the 1980s when high petroleum prices greatly stimulated petroleum exploration and production by nonmembers (such as the U.K., Norway, and Mexico). The resulting increase in supply, together with conservation measures which reduced the demand for petroleum products, led to sharply lower petroleum prices in the 1980s as compared to the 1970s. It also showed that, as predicted by economic theory, cartels are inherently unstable and often collapse or fail. If successful, however, a cartel could behave exactly as a monopolist (a **centralized cartel**) in maximizing its total profits (see section A9.1).

9.3d Dumping

Trade barriers may also result from dumping. **Dumping** is the export of a commodity at below cost or at least the sale of a commodity at a lower price abroad than domestically. Dumping is classified into persistent, predatory, and sporadic. **Persistent dumping,** or international price discrimination, is the *continuous* tendency of a domestic monopolist to maximize total profits by selling the commodity at a higher price in the domestic market (which is insulated by transportation costs and trade barriers) than internationally (where it must meet the competition of foreign producers). Section A9.2 shows how a domestic monopolist can determine the exact prices to charge domestically and internationally to maximize total profits in cases of persistent dumping, or international price discrimination.

Predatory dumping is the *temporary* sale of a commodity at below cost or at a lower price abroad in order to drive foreign producers out of business, after which prices are raised to take advantage of the newly acquired monopoly power abroad. **Sporadic dumping** is the *occasional* sale of a commodity at below cost or at a lower price abroad than domestically in order to unload an unforeseen and temporary surplus of the commodity without having to reduce domestic prices.

Trade restrictions to counteract predatory dumping are justified and allowed to protect domestic industries. These restrictions usually take the form of antidumping or countervailing duties to offset price differentials, or the threat to impose such duties. However, it is often difficult to determine the type of dumping, and domestic producers invariably demand protection against any form of dumping. In some cases of persistent and sporadic dumping, the benefit to consumers from low prices may actually exceed the possible production losses of domestic producers.

Over the past decade, Japan was accused of dumping steel and television sets in the United States, and European nations of dumping cars, steel, and other products. Many industrial nations have a tendency of persistently dumping surplus agricultural commodities arising from their farm support programs. When dumping is proved, the violating nation or firm usually chooses to raise its prices (as Volkswagen did in 1976 and Japanese TV exporters in 1977) rather than face antidumping or countervailing duties.

In 1978 the United States government introduced a **trigger-price mechanism** under which a charge that steel is being imported into the United States at prices below those of the lowest-cost foreign producer (presumably Japan) will be subject to a speedy antidumping investigation. If dumping is proved, the United States government will provide quick relief to the domestic steel industry in the form of a duty that will bring the price of the imported steel equal to that of the lowest-cost country.

Export subsidies are also a form of dumping. Though illegal by international agreement, many nations provide them in disguised and not-so disguised forms (such as the granting of tax relief and subsidized loans to potential exporters, and low-interest loans to foreign buyers of the nation's exports). All major industrial nations give foreign buyers of the nation's exports low-interest loans to finance the purchase through agencies such as the U.S. **Export-Import Bank.** These low-interest credits finance about 10 percent of U.S. exports but as much as 40 percent of the exports of Japan and France. Indeed, this is one of the most serious trade complaints that the United States has against other industrial countries today. The amount of the subsidy can be measured by the difference between the interest that would have had to be paid on a commercial loan and what is in fact paid at the subsidized rate. In 1980, the total value of these subsidies given by the United States, Japan, France, the United Kingdom, Germany, Italy, and Canada amounted to between $1.5 and $3.0 billion dollars. The U.S. **Domestic International Sales Corporation (DISC)** also stimulates exports by reducing the effective rate of taxation on export income.

Since the mid-1970s, the number and importance of these nontariff trade barriers (NTBs) have grown so rapidly that they have now become more important than tariffs as obstructions to international trade. They also represent the greatest threat to the fairly liberal world trading system that was so painstakingly put together after World War II and which served the world so well since then. It has been estimated that the number of NTBs have more than quadrupled over the past 15 years or so and that over half of world trade is now subject to some form of nontariff trade barriers. It was primarily to deal with the serious threat posed by these NTBs and to deal with the rapidly growing trade in services (banking, insurance, telecommunications, and so on) that the leading nations agreed to begin a new round of multilateral trade negotiations in 1986 (see section 9.6a).

9.4   Arguments for Protection

In this section, we analyze the various arguments for protection. These range from clearly fallacious propositions to arguments that can stand up, with some qualification, to close economic scrutiny.

9.4a   Fallacious and Questionable Arguments for Protection

One *fallacious* argument is that trade restrictions are needed to *protect domestic labor against cheap foreign labor.* The reason this argument is fallacious is that even if domestic wages are higher than wages abroad, domestic labor *costs* can still be lower if the productivity of labor is sufficiently higher domestically than abroad. Even if this were not the case, mutually beneficial trade could still be based on comparative advantage, with the cheap-labor nation specializing in the production of and exporting labor-intensive commodities, and the expensive-labor nation specializing in the production of and exporting capital-intensive commodities (refer back to section 2.4).

Another *fallacious* argument for protection is the **scientific tariff.** This is the tariff rate that would make the price of imports equal to domestic prices and (so the argument goes) allow domestic producers to meet foreign competition. However, this would eliminate international price differences and trade in all commodities subject to such "scientific" tariffs.

Two *questionable* arguments are that protection is needed (1) to reduce domestic unemployment and (2) to cure a deficit in the nation's balance of payments (i.e., the excess of the nation's expenditures abroad over its foreign earnings). Protection would reduce domestic unemployment and a balance-of-payments deficit by leading to the replacement of imports with domestic production. However, these are *beggar-thy-neighbor* arguments for protection because they come at the expense of other nations. Specifically, when protection is used to reduce domestic unemployment and the nation's balance-of-payments deficit, it causes greater unemployment and worsened balance of payments abroad. As a result, other nations are likely to retaliate and all nations lose in the end. Domestic unemployment and deficits in the nation's balance of payments should be corrected with appropriate monetary, fiscal, and trade policies (discussed in Chapter 17) rather than with trade restrictions.

9.4b   The Infant-Industry Argument for Protection

One argument for protection that stands up to close economic scrutiny (but must nevertheless be qualified) is the **infant-industry argument.** It holds that a nation may have a potential comparative advantage in a commodity, but because of lack of know-how and the initial small level of output, the industry will not be set up or, if already started, cannot compete successfully with more established foreign firms. *Temporary* trade protection is then justified to establish and protect the domestic industry during its "infancy" until it can meet foreign competition, achieve economies of scale, and reflect the nation's long-run comparative advantage. At that time, protection is to be removed. However, for this argument to be valid, the return in the grown-up industry must be sufficiently high also to offset the higher prices paid by domestic consumers of the commodity during the infancy period.

The infant-industry argument for protection is correct but requires several important qualifications which, together, take away most of its significance. First of all, it is clear that such an argument is more justified for developing nations (where capital markets may not function properly) than for industrial nations. Second, it may be difficult to identify which industry or potential industry qualifies for this treatment, and experience has shown that protection, once given, is difficult to remove. Third, and most important, what trade protection (say in the form of an import tariff) can do, an equivalent production *subsidy* to the infant industry can do better. The reason is that a *purely domestic distortion* such as this should be overcome with a *purely domestic policy* (such as a direct production subsidy to the infant industry) rather than with a trade policy that also distorts relative prices and domestic consumption. A production subsidy is also a more direct form of aid and is easier to remove than an import tariff. One practical difficulty is that a subsidy requires revenues, rather than generating them as, for example, an import tariff does. But the principle remains.

9.4c   Other Qualified Arguments for Protection

The same general principle also holds for every other type of domestic distortion. For example, if the private cost of car travel is smaller than the social costs (because of pollution), it is better to overcome this domestic distortion with a domestic tax on car travel or ownership than by a tariff on car imports. Similarly, to induce workers to move from one industry to another (if this is deemed socially desirable), it is better to provide direct subsidies to workers to move and to retrain than to give tariff protection to the growing industry so that it can increase its prices and be able to pay higher wages to attract more workers. The same is true if the nation wants to change the distribution of income among the various domestic factors of production. Attempts to correct these purely domestic distortions with trade policies would also distort relative prices and domestic consumption, and so they would not represent the optimal policies. Tariffs in these cases are second best rather than the optimal policy. The general principle that the best way to correct a *domestic* distortion is with *domestic* policies is shown graphically in section A9.3.

Trade restrictions may be advocated to protect domestic industries important for national defense. But even in this case, direct production subsidies are generally better than tariff protection. Some tariffs can be regarded as "bargaining tariffs" to be used to induce other nations to agree to a mutual reduction in tariffs. Here, political scientists may be more qualified to judge how effective they are in achieving their intended purpose.

The closest we come to a truly valid economic argument for protection is the *optimum tariff* discussed in section 8.4. That is, if a nation is large enough to affect its terms of trade, the nation can exploit its market power and improve its terms of trade and welfare with an optimum tariff. However, other nations may retaliate so that in the end all nations may lose.

9.5   History of United States Commercial Policy

This section surveys the history of United States commercial policy. We start by examining the Trade Agreements Act of 1934 and then discuss the importance of the General Agreement on Tariff and Trade (GATT). Subsequently, we consider the 1962 Trade Expansion Act and the results of the Kennedy

Round of trade negotiations. Finally, the Trade Reform Act of 1974 and the outcome of the Tokyo Round of trade negotiations are examined.

9.5a   The Trade Agreements Act of 1934

During the early 1930s, world trade in general and United States exports in particular fell sharply because of (1) greatly reduced economic activity the world over as a result of the Great Depression and (2) passage in 1930 of the **Smoot-Hawley Tariff Act,** under which the average import duty in the United States reached the all-time high of 59 percent in 1932, provoking foreign retaliation.

The Smoot-Hawley Tariff Bill was originally introduced to aid American agriculture. But through log-rolling in Congress, large tariffs were imposed on manufactured imports as well. The aim was clearly beggar-thy-neighbor to restrict imports and stimulate domestic employment. The bill was passed despite the protest of 36 countries that the tariff would seriously hurt them and that they would retaliate. President Hoover signed the bill into law in spite of a petition signed by more than one thousand American economists urging him to veto it. The result was catastrophic. By 1932, sixty countries retaliated with stiff tariff increases of their own, in the face of the deepening world depression. The net result was a collapse of world trade (American imports in 1932 were only 31 percent of their 1929 level and exports fell even more) and this contributed in a significant way to the spreading and to the deepening of the depression around the world.

To reverse the trend toward sharply reduced world trade, the United States Congress under the new Roosevelt Administration passed the **Trade Agreements Act of 1934**. The general principles embodied in this act remained the basis for all subsequent trade legislation in the United States. The act transferred the formulation of trade policy from the more politically minded Congress to the President and authorized the President to negotiate with other nations *mutual* tariff reductions by as much as 50 percent of the rates set under the Smoot-Hawley Tariff Act. The Trade Agreements Act was renewed a total of 11 times before it was replaced in 1962 by the Trade Expansion Act. By 1947 the average United States import duty was 50 percent below its 1934 level.

The Trade Agreements Act of 1934 and all subsequent trade legislation were based on the **most-favored-nation principle**. This nondiscrimination principle extended to all trade partners any *reciprocal* tariff reduction negotiated by the United States with any of its trade partners. The United States would similarly benefit from any bilateral tariff reduction negotiated between any other two nations that were signatories of the most-favored-nation agreement. However, this **bilateral trade** approach faced the serious shortcoming that tariff reductions were negotiated for the most part only in commodities that *dominated* bilateral trade. Otherwise, many "freeloader" nations, not directly involved in the negotiations and not making any tariff concession (reduction) of

their own, would also have benefitted from reciprocal tariff reductions negotiated between any other two nations.

9.5b   The General Agreement on Tariff and Trade (GATT)

The **General Agreement on Tariff and Trade (GATT)** is an international organization, created in 1947 and headquartered in Geneva (Switzerland), devoted to the promotion of freer trade through *multilateral trade negotiations.*
Originally, it was thought that GATT would become part of the **International
Trade Organization (ITO),** whose charter was negotiated in Havana in 1948
to regulate international trade. When ITO was not ratified by the U.S. Senate
and by the government of other nations and was, therefore, stillborn, GATT
(which was less ambitious than ITO) was salvaged and further evolved on its
own.

GATT rests on three basic principles:

1. *Nondiscrimination.* This refers to the unconditional acceptance of the
   most-favored-nation principle discussed earlier. The only exceptions to
   this principle are made in cases of economic integration, such as customs unions (discussed in Chapter 10), and in the trade between a nation and its former colonies and dominions.
2. *Elimination of nontariff trade barriers* (such as quotas), except for agricultural products and for nations in balance-of-payments difficulties.
3. *Consultation among nations in solving trade disputes* within the GATT
   framework.

Ninety nations (including the United States and all major countries, with the
exception of the Soviet Union and China) are now signatories of GATT and
24 other nations belong on a provisional basis. Today, over four-fifths of international trade comes under GATT rules.

Under the auspices of GATT, tariffs were reduced by a total of about 35
percent in five different trade negotiations between 1947 and 1962. In 1965
GATT was extended to allow preferential trade treatment to developing nations and allow them to benefit from tariff reductions negotiated among industrial nations without reciprocity (these are discussed in Chapter 11).

Greater success in tariff reductions was not achieved because tariff negotiations were conducted on a *product-by-product* basis and because in the 1950s
the United States Congress attached serious protectionist devices to the periodic renewals of the Trade Agreements Act. These protectionist devices were:

1. **Peril-point provisions,** which prevented the President from negotiating
   any tariff reduction that would cause serious damage to a domestic industry.
2. The **escape clause,** which allowed any domestic industry that claimed
   injury from imports to petition the International Trade Commission (the

U.S. Tariff Commission until 1975), which could then recommend to the President to revoke any *negotiated* tariff reduction. A rising share of imports in an industry was sufficient to "prove" injury.

3. The **national security clause,** which prevented tariff reductions (even if already negotiated) when they would hurt industries important for national defense.

Since meaningful tariff reductions *necessarily* hurt some industries (those in which the nation has a comparative disadvantage), these trade restrictions, especially the escape clause, represented a serious obstacle to greater tariff reductions.

9.5c   The 1962 Trade Expansion Act and the Kennedy Round

It was primarily to deal with the new situation created by the formation of the European Economic Community, or Common Market, that the **Trade Expansion Act of 1962** was passed by the United States Congress to replace the Trade Agreements Act.

The Trade Expansion Act of 1962 authorized the President to negotiate across-the-board tariff reductions of up to 50 percent of their 1962 level (and to remove completely duties that were 5 percent or less in 1962). This replaced the product-by-product approach of the Trade Agreements Act. In addition, the 1962 act provided **adjustment assistance** to displaced workers and firms injured by tariff reductions. This replaced the no-injury doctrine and took the form of retraining and moving assistance to displaced workers and tax relief, low-cost loans, and technical help to injured firms.

The principle of adjustment assistance was the most significant aspect of the Trade Expansion Act of 1962 since society at large (which was the beneficiary of the trade expansion resulting from tariff reductions) was made to bear, or at least share, the burden of adjustment. However, until the early 1970s, when the criteria for assistance were relaxed, few workers or firms qualified for adjustment assistance. In 1980, the trade assistance program's peak year, more than half a million workers received about $1.6 billion in assistance. Since then, however, the program has shrunk dramatically, so that in 1984 only about 15 thousand workers received a total of $51 million in aid.

Under the authority of the 1962 Trade Expansion Act, the United States initiated, under GATT auspices, wide-ranging multilateral trade negotiations. These were known as the **Kennedy Round**. Negotiations in the Kennedy Round were completed in 1967 and resulted in an agreement to cut average tariff rates on industrial products by a total of 35 percent of their 1962 level, to be phased over a five-year period. When fully implemented by the end of 1972, average tariff rates on industrial products were less than 10 percent in industrial nations. However, there were still many serious nontariff trade barriers, especially in agriculture.

9.5d   The Trade Reform Act of 1974 and the Tokyo Round

The 1962 Trade Expansion Act was replaced in 1974 by the **Trade Reform Act**. This authorized the President (1) to negotiate tariff reductions of up to 60 percent and remove tariffs of 5 percent or less and (2) to negotiate reductions in nontariff trade barriers. The act also liberalized the criteria for adjustment assistance.

Under the authority of Trade Reform Act of 1974, the United States participated in the multilateral tariff negotiations known as the **Tokyo Round** (actually conducted in Geneva, except for the opening meeting held in Tokyo), which were concluded in 1979. Negotiated tariff reductions phased over an eight-year period, starting in 1980, averaged 31 percent for the United States, 27 percent for the European Common Market, and 28 percent for Japan. A code of conduct for nations to adhere to in applying nontariff trade barriers was also prescribed to reduce the restrictive effect of these nontariff barriers. This code included (1) agreement on a government procurement code, (2) uniformity in the application of countervailing duties in antidumping cases (to be applied only after proof of injury), (3) a "generalized system of preferences" to the manufactured, semimanufactured, and selected other exports of developing nations. (However, textiles, shoes, consumer electronics, steel, and many other products of great importance to developing nations were excluded.)

Before completion of the negotiations, it was estimated that the static gains from trade liberalization under the Tokyo Round would amount to about $1.7 billion annually. Including the dynamic gains rising from economies of scale and greater all-around efficiency and innovations, the figure might rise as high as $8 billion per year. These gains would rise as the volume of world trade grows over time. However, these figures are only very rough "guesstimates." Also to be noted is that labor (the relatively scarce factor in the United States) and those industries with a relatively larger share of small businesses (which are more highly protected in the United States) are likely to be somewhat negatively affected by the negotiated tariff reductions, though the United States as a whole will benefit by sharing in the total gains from trade liberalization.

Figure 9–2 summarizes the history of average tariff rates on dutiable imports in the United States from 1900 to 1985. Note that the average tariff rates shown in the figure fall even without a change in tariff schedules when the proportion of low-tariff imports increases. For example, the fall in average tariff rates after 1972 was due mostly to the sharp increase in low-tariff imports of petroleum in the United States.

9.6   Current Trade Problems

Despite the great success in reducing tariffs through multilateral trade negotiations and reducing them in a nondiscriminatory manner since World War

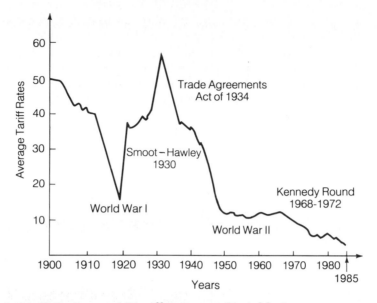

FIGURE 9-2.   U.S. Average Tariff Rates on Dutiable Imports, 1900–1985

Average tariff rates on dutiable imports in the United States ranged from the high of 59 percent reached in 1932 under the Smoot-Hawley Tariff Act of 1930 to less than 5 percent in 1985. The average tariff rates can fall even without a change in tariff schedules when the proportion of low-tariff imports increases (as after 1972 as a result of the sharp rise in low-tariff petroleum imports).
Source: Historical Abstract of the United States (Washington, D.C.: U.S. Government Printing Office, 1972), and *Statistical Abstract of the United States* (Washington, D.C.: U.S. Government Printing Office, 1987) for years since 1971.

II, many problems remain that require future attention. The most important and immediate problem is the rapid proliferation of nontariff trade barriers and the need to reverse this trend by a new round of multilateral trade negotiations. This topic is examined in section 9.6a. In section 9.6b, we discuss other trade problems. These arise from agricultural protection, from the formation of regional trade associations, and from the slowdown in growth and from the huge international debt of developing countries.

9.6a   The New Protectionism and Trade Negotiations

The sharp tariff reductions on industrial goods over the past four decades has resulted from successive rounds of multilateral trade negotiations. This has made possible a very rapid expansion of international trade that significantly contributed to the growth of the world economy. Since the mid-1970s, however, the continued reduction of tariffs was more than offset by the rise of nontariff trade barriers or NTBs, as industrial nations sought to protect industry after industry from the adjustments required by international trade, in a climate of slow domestic growth and rising unemployment.

This fact did not go unnoticed during the Tokyo Round of trade negotiations (1973–79), and indeed codes were negotiated to restrict and regulate the use of NTBs. These codes, however, did not stem the tide of new NTBs, to the point where today these represent the most serious threat to the postwar trading system and world welfare. The great danger is that the continued proliferation of NTBs will lead to sharp retaliation and result in a decline in world trade, as nations revert more and more to bilateral trade deals. This would result in a misallocation of resources internationally, a slowdown in structural adjustments in mature economies and in growth in developing economies, and in an increase in the specter of a trade war in which all nations stand to lose.

Reversing the present drift toward this new and insidious form of trade protectionism will not be easy. The best antiprotectionist measure is the resumption of rapid expansion in the world economy. A resumption of rapid growth not only would slow down the decline of mature industries (such as textile and steel) in developed nations but would also lead to the creation of many additional job opportunities in the rest of the economy, resulting in the absorption of new entrants into the labor force and employment opportunities for displaced workers from declining industries. This, together with increased assistance (in the form of financial assistance, job retraining, and relocation allowances to displaced workers), would greatly reduce demands for trade protection, and arrest or reverse the movement toward the new protectionism.

Perhaps more promising as a way to reverse the trend toward greater protectionism is the agreement to begin a new round of multilateral trade negotiations in 1986. These new trade negotiations will be the eighth that GATT members have conducted since World War II and are expected to last several years. It is widely believed that governments find it easier to resist demands for new trade restrictions when they are engaged in trade-liberalizing negotiations. The crucial problem to be addressed in these new trade negotiations is the current drift toward bilateralism and discriminatory practices in international trade. There is, today, a serious need for the world to return to GATT's most-favored nation principle—that is, to the principle that trade restrictions should not discriminate among sources of supply. Trade disputes should be resolved through GATT, not bilaterally. In particular, "voluntary" export restraints, which are bilateral and discriminatory, should be discontinued and replaced, whenever possible, by more open and transparent devices such as tariffs. As it is, managed trade greatly reduces the volume and the benefits of trade, and generally leads to still more trade restrictions.

The new round of trade negotiations should also address the question as to how far it is legitimate for nations to promote their high-technology industries by restricting market access, by subsidies to exports and to research and development, and by government procurement provisions favoring domestic suppliers. It seems that most industrial and some developing nations (such as

Brazil) are claiming a greater share of high-tech industries than is consistent with world growth of these industries. This not only leads to current trade problems but sows the seeds for even greater trade problems in the future. Japan is a case in point. Having "targeted" the information industry for growth, Japan provides all sorts of trade protection and subsidies to the industry. It is now clear that without some international agreement on the development, expansion, protection, and trade in high-technology products by leading nations, the world will see increasing trade tensions in the future.

One of the major aims of U.S. trade policy today is to include trade in services (banking, insurance, telecommunications, data processing, high technology, and so on) in trade negotiations and to force Japan and other nations to open more widely their markets to American exports. However, liberalizing international trade in services is strongly opposed by some developing nations, under the leadership of Brazil and India, as undermining their own development plans in this crucial field. Negotiations in this area are likely to prove long and difficult, and their success is by no means assured.

Trade policy in the U.S. over the past thirty years has been marked by continuous tensions. While the U.S. generally adhered to the principle of free trade, it has made an increasing number of compromises to protect textiles, automobiles, steel, and other industries in exchange for political support for the general principle of free trade. However, in the process, the U.S. and the world have slipped more and more toward bilateralism and managed trade. There is today a great need for the U.S. to take the lead in checking the further spread of trade restrictions worldwide. Without it, the world is likely to slip more and more into protectionism and managed trade, to the detriment of all.

9.6b   Other Trade Problems

Another problem of trade liberalization of long standing arises from the protection that most industrial nations extend to their agriculture. In all of the multilateral trade negotiations conducted since World War II, agriculture was always granted a special status and was generally exempted from tariff cuts. This is due primarily to the disproportionate power of agricultural interests in the internal affairs of most nations. In the United States and the European Economic Community (EEC), agricultural support programs result in huge surpluses of many products, especially milk and its derivatives, eggs, meat, and wheat. Not only has this prevented greater specialization in these products by nations such as Australia and Canada, but as United States and EEC surpluses are unloaded on the world market or given away as part of foreign aid, they "spoil" the export market of developing nations such as Argentina and Brazil.

Still another problem arises from the formation of regional economic associations, such as the European Economic Community (EEC). These eliminate tariffs among members but retain them against the rest of the world and are, therefore, clearly against the GATT principle of nondiscrimination. They are also against the economic interests of outsiders such as the United States. The United States, nevertheless, has supported efforts to form regional economic associations in Europe, Latin America, and elsewhere because of the greater political stability that they generate. Aside from the possible political benefits, regional economic associations can only be justified on purely economic grounds from the welfare point of view of the world as a whole if they represent a step toward or facilitate lower all-around trade barriers.

The proliferation of nontariff trade restrictions in mature industries (steel, textile, automobiles) in industrial countries has also greatly hampered the development prospects of developing countries and made it very difficult or impossible for them to service their huge international debt. This problem is examined in detail in Chapter 11, which deals with international trade and economic development.

While the static welfare costs of tariff protection have been estimated to range only from 0.5 to 1 percent of GNP for the United States, the static and dynamic welfare costs of nontariff trade barriers are likely to be much greater, especially for nations that rely much more heavily on international trade than does the United States. As pointed out above, the international negotiations that began in 1986 came none too soon as an attempt to reverse the present dangerous trend toward proliferating nontariff trade barriers, widespread protectionist sentiments in the United States, and the inevitable major trade conflicts that they foster.

Finally, it might be argued that if other nations are unwilling to reduce their trade barriers (tariff and nontariff), it is in the best interest of each nation to do so unilaterally. For a nation such as the United States that is large enough to affect its terms of trade, the efficiency benefits resulting from unilaterally eliminating its trade barriers must be weighed against the worsening of its terms of trade. The unilateral elimination of all trade barriers would also be difficult politically because of strong opposition from the very vocal and influential minorities that would be hurt in the process. In fact, at this point, the trend has been toward increasing rather than reducing trade barriers in the United States and in most other nations of the world.

Summary

1. A quota is a direct quantitative restriction on imports or exports. An import quota has the same consumption and production effects as an (equivalent) import tariff. If the government auctions off import licenses to the highest bidder in a competitive market, the revenue effect also is the same. The adjustment to any shift in demand or supply occurs in the domestic price with an import quota and in the quantity of imports with a tariff. If import licenses are not auctioned off, they lead to monopoly profits and possible corruption. An import quota restricts imports with certainty and is in general more restrictive than an equivalent import tariff.

2. Voluntary export restraints refer to the case where an importing nation induces another nation to curb its exports of a commodity "voluntarily," under the threat of higher all-around trade restrictions. When successful, their economic impact is the same as that of an equivalent import quota, except for the revenue effect, which is now likely to be captured by foreign suppliers by charging higher prices. Voluntary export restraints are not likely to be completely successful in limiting imports, however. There are also numerous other nontariff trade restrictions. These have become more important than tariffs as obstructions to the flow of international trade over the past decade and today represent the most serious threat to the world trading system.

3. An international cartel is an organization of suppliers of a commodity located in different nations, or a group of governments, that agrees to restrict output and exports of the commodity with the aim of maximizing or increasing the total profits of the organization. An international cartel is more likely to succeed if there are only a few international suppliers of an essential commodity for which there is no good substitute. There is also an incentive to stay out of or cheat on the cartel. Trade restrictions can also result from dumping. Dumping is the export of a commodity at below cost or at least the sale of a commodity at a lower price abroad than domestically, and it can be persistent, predatory, or sporadic.

4. The argument that tariffs are needed to protect domestic labor against cheap foreign labor and the "scientific tariff" are clearly fallacious. Two questionable beggar-thy-neighbor arguments are that protection is needed to reduce domestic unemployment and a deficit in the nation's balance of payments. A more valid argument for protection is the infant-industry argument. However, what trade protection can do, direct subsidies and taxes can do better in overcoming purely domestic distortions. Similarly, industries important for national defense are better aided with production subsidies than with trade protection. The closest we come to a valid economic argument for protection is the optimum tariff to exploit the market power that the nation has in international markets. However, this may lead to retaliation.

5. The Smoot-Hawley Tariff Act of 1930 resulted in the all-time high average import duty in the United States of 59 percent in 1932, provoking foreign retaliation. The Trade Agreements Act of 1934 authorized the President to negotiate mutual tariff reductions of up to 50 percent under the most-favored-nation princi-

ple. A serious disadvantage was its bilateral approach. The General Agreement on Tariff and Trade (GATT) is devoted to freer trade based on nondiscrimination, consultation, and removal of nontariff trade barriers, except in agriculture and in nations experiencing balance-of-payments difficulties. Until 1962 tariff reduction was seriously limited by product-by-product negotiations and by United States protectionist devices, specifically peril-point provisions, the escape clause, and the national security clause. Under the authority of the 1962 Trade Expansion Act, the United States negotiated tariff reductions averaging 35 percent on industrial products in the Kennedy Round, which was completed in 1967. The 1962 Trade Expansion Act also replaced the no-injury doctrine with adjustment assistance. Under the authority of the Trade Reform Act of 1974, the United States negotiated tariff reductions averaging 31 percent in the Tokyo Round, which was completed in 1979, and accepted a code of conduct for nontariff trade barriers.

6. Despite the great success in reducing tariffs through multilateral trade negotiations, many problems remain. The most important of these are the proliferation of nontariff trade barriers and the problems that arise from the rapid expansion of trade in services. Other problems arise from agricultural protection, from the formation or regional trade associations, and from the slowdown of growth and the huge international debt problem of developing countries. The static gains that would result from the complete elimination of trade barriers seem small, but the dynamic gains from increased efficiency might be much greater. Large countries must balance the efficiency benefits from unilaterally eliminating all trade barriers against the worsening of their terms of trade. Unilateral action would also be very difficult politically.

A Look Ahead

In Chapter 10, we analyze the economic impact of the formation of regional economic associations (such as the European Common Market) on the member nations and on the rest of the world. Regional economic associations eliminate tariff barriers among members but keep them against the outside world. As such, they represent a direct extension of the topics discussed in this chapter. In Chapter 11, we further extend our discussion to analyze the special trade problems of developing nations. Chapter 12 completes Part II of the text with an examination of international resource movements and multinational corporations.

Glossary

Quota   A direct *quantitative* restriction on trade.

Nontariff trade barriers (NTBs)   Trade restrictions other than tariffs, such as voluntary export restraints, and technical, administrative, and other regulations, as well as those arising from international cartels, dumping, and export subsidies.

Voluntary export restraints   Refer to an importing country inducing another country to reduce "voluntarily" its exports of a commodity to the importing nation under the threat of higher all-around trade restrictions.

Technical, administrative, and other regulations   Nontariff trade barriers such as safety, health, and labeling requirements, and border taxes.

International cartel   An organization of suppliers of a commodity located in different nations (or a group of governments) that agrees to restrict output and exports of the commodity with the aim of maximizing or increasing the total profits of the organization. An international cartel that behaves as a monopolist is called a centralized cartel.

Dumping   The export of a commodity at below cost or at least the sale of a commodity at a lower price abroad than domestically.

Persistent dumping   The *continuous* tendency of a domestic monopolist to maximize total profits by selling the commodity at a lower price abroad than domestically; also called international price discrimination.

Predatory dumping   The *temporary* sale of a commodity at a lower price abroad in order to drive foreign producers out of business, after which prices are raised to take advantage of the newly acquired monopoly power abroad.

Sporadic dumping   The *occasional* sale of a commodity at a lower price abroad than domestically in order to sell an unforeseen and temporary surplus of the commodity abroad without having to reduce domestic prices.

Trigger-price mechanism   The antidumping mechanism introduced by the United States in 1978 to protect its steel industry by imposing a duty on under-priced imported steel to make its price equal to that of the lowest-cost foreign producer.

Export subsidies   The granting of tax relief and subsidized loans to potential exporters, and low-interest loans to foreign buyers of the nation's exports.

Export-Import Bank   A U.S. government agency that extends subsidized loans to foreigners to finance U.S. exports.

Domestic International Sales Corporation (DISC)   U.S. tax legislation aimed at stimulating U.S. exports by reducing the effective rate of taxation on export income.

Scientific tariff   The tariff rate that would make the price of imports equal to domestic prices so as to allow domestic producers to meet the foreign competition.

Infant-industry argument   The argument that temporary trade protection is needed to set up an industry and to protect it during its infancy against competition from more established and efficient foreign firms. However, a direct production subsidy is generally a better method of assisting the domestic infant industry.

Smoot-Hawley Tariff Act of 1930   Raised average import duties in the United States to the all-time high of 59 percent in 1932.

Trade Agreements Act of 1934   Authorized the President to negotiate with other nations mutual tariff reductions of up to 50 percent under the most-favored-nation principle.

Most-favored-nation principle   The extension to all trade partners of any reciprocal tariff reduction negotiated by the United States with any other nation.

Bilateral trade Trade between any two nations.

General Agreement on Tariff and Trade (GATT) An international organization devoted to the promotion of freer trade through multilateral trade negotiations.

Multilateral trade negotiations Trade negotiations among many nations.

International Trade Organization (ITO) An international organization that was to regulate international trade after World War II. It was never ratified by the United States Senate and never came into existence. Its place was taken by GATT, which was less ambitious.

Peril-point provisions A protectionist device that prevented the President from negotiating any tariff reduction that would cause serious damage to a domestic industry.

Escape clause A protectionist device that allowed any industry that claimed injury from imports to petition the International Trade Commission, which could then recommend to the President to revoke any negotiated tariff reduction.

National security clause A protectionist device that prevented any tariff reduction (even if already negotiated) that would hurt industries important for national defense.

Trade Expansion Act of 1962 Granted the President authority to negotiate across-the-board tariff reductions of up to 50 percent of their 1962 level and replaced the no-injury principle with adjustment assistance.

Adjustment assistance The provision of the 1962 Trade Expansion Act to assist displaced workers and firms injured by tariff reductions.

Kennedy Round The multilateral trade negotiations that were completed in 1967 (under the authority of the 1962 Trade Expansion Act) under which agreement was reached to reduce average tariff duties on industrial products by 35 percent.

Trade Reform Act of 1974 Granted the President authority to negotiate tariff reductions of up to 60 percent of their post-Kennedy Round level and to negotiate reductions in nontariff trade barriers.

Tokyo Round The multilateral trade negotiations that were completed in 1979 (under the authority of the 1974 Trade Reform Act) in which agreement was reached to cut average tariff rates by about 30 percent and to adopt a uniform international code of conduct for applying nontariff trade barriers.

Questions for Review

1. What is an import quota? How is it mostly used today? What are the partial equilibrum effects of an import quota? How are they similar to and different from the effects of an equivalent import tariff?

2. What is meant by voluntary export restraints? How has the United States used them? What are the technical, administrative, and other nontariff barriers to trade? How do they restrict trade? What is the importance of these nontariff trade barriers relative to tariff barriers today?

3. What are international cartels? How do their operations restrict trade? Which was the most successful international cartel during the 1970s? Why did its power sharply decline in the 1980s? What is meant by dumping? What are the different types of dumping? Why is dumping undertaken? What conditions are required to make dumping possible? Why does dumping usually lead to trade restrictions?

4. What are the fallacious and questionable arguments for protection? Why are they fallacious and questionable? What is the infant-industry argument for protection? How must this argument be qualified? What are the other qualified arguments for protection? In what way must they be qualified?

5. What is the importance of the Trade Agreements Act of 1934? What are the ruling principles of GATT? The major accomplishments of the Kennedy Round? Of the Tokyo Round?

6. Which is the most important trade problem today? What attempt is being made to overcome it? What other trade problems face the world today?

Problems

*1. Starting with D_X and S_X and $P_X = \$1$ with free trade in Figure 9–1, analyze the partial equilibrum effects of an import quota of 30X if:

   (a) D_X shifts down to D_X'' in such a way that D_X'' is parallel to D_X and crosses S_X at $P_X = \$2.50$;

   (b) S_X shifts up to S_X' (parallel to S_X) and crosses D_X at $P_X = \$3.50$;

   (c) S_X shifts down to S_X'' (parallel to S_X) and crosses D_X at $P_X = \$2.50$;

   (d) S_X shifts down to S_X^* (parallel to S_X) and crosses D_X at $P_X = \$2.00$.

2. (a) Starting with D_X and S_X and $P_X = \$4.50$ with free trade in Figure 9–1, analyze the partial equilibrium effects of a negotiated export quota of 30X.

   (b) How are these effects similar to and different from those of an equivalent import tariff or quota?

3. Draw a straight-line demand curve for a commodity crossing both axes and its corresponding marginal revenue curve (lying everywhere halfway between the vertical axis and the demand curve). On the same graph, draw a hypothetical supply curve for the commodity crossing the demand and marginal revenue curves.

   (a) If the demand and supply curves refer to the perfectly competitive market for exports of the commodity, determine the equilibrium price and quantity of exports of the commodity.

   (b) If the supply curve referred instead to a cartel of exporters acting as a monopolist, determine the equilibrium price and quantity of exports of the commodity.

   (c) Compare your results in parts a and b. (Hint: review the perfectly competitive and monopoly models in your principles text or notes.)

*4. Draw three sets of price-quantity axes side-by-side. On the first set of axes (graph), draw a straight-line demand curve (D_1) that is steep and starts at a high price and refers to the domestic market. On the same set of axes, draw the corresponding marginal revenue curve (MR_1). On the second graph, draw a straight-line demand curve (D_2) that is low and flat and refers to the international market. On the same (second) set of axes, draw the corresponding MR_2 curve. On the third graph, sum horizontally the MR_1 and MR_2 curves (ΣMR) and draw a marginal cost curve (MC) that intersects the ΣMR curve from below in the third graph, draw a horizontal dashed line and extend it to the second and first graphs. The point where the horizontal dashed line crosses the MR_1 curve indicates how much the domestic monopolist should sell in the domestic market, and where the horizontal line crosses the MR_2 curve indicates how much he should sell on the international market.

   (a) What price should the monopolist charge in the domestic market (P_1) and in the foreign market (P_2)?

   (b) Why does this represent the best, or optimal, distribution of sales between the two markets?

5. On a set of axes measuring average costs of production on the vertical axis and the level of output on the horizontal axis, illustrate the infant-industry argument for protection by drawing the long-run average cost curve of an efficient foreign firm facing constant returns to scale and the long-run average cost curve of an infant industry in a developing nation that becomes more efficient than established foreign firms as it grows.

6. Suppose that in Figure 8–1, Nation 2 produced at point F at the free trade price of $P_W = 1$.

   (a) Why is this an inefficient production point for Nation 2?

   (b) How could this situation arise?

   (c) What tariff could shift production to point B?

   (d) Why would this not represent the best policy?

   (e) What would be the best policy? Why?

APPENDIX

This appendix analyzes graphically the operation of centralized cartels, international price discrimination, and the use of taxes and subsidies instead of tariffs to correct domestic distortions. It also analyzes state trading.

A9.1   Centralized Cartels

In Figure 9–3, D_X is the world demand curve for exports of commodity X, and MR_X is the corresponding marginal revenue curve. Note that the MR_X curve lies everywhere halfway between the vertical axis and D_X. S_X is the cartel's supply curve of exports of commodity X. S_X is the horizontal summation of the marginal curves of all cartel members (ΣMC_X). Under perfect competition, international equilibrium is at point E, at which 400X are traded at $P_X = \$3$.

An international cartel of exporters of commodity X acting as a monopolist (or *centralized cartel*) would maximize total profits by restricting exports to 300X (given by the intersection of the S_X or ΣMC_X curve with the MR_X curve at point F) and charging $P_X = \$3.50$ (given by point G on D_x). The increase in the total profits of the exporters of commodity X as a group (i.e., of the cartel) is given by the shaded area in the figure. The reason for this is that by restrict-

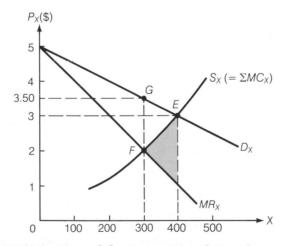

FIGURE 9-3.   Maximization of the International Cartel's Total Profits

D_x is the total demand for exports of commodity X, and S_x is the total supply of exports. Under perfect competition, equilibrium is at point E, at which 400X are traded at $P_x = \$3$. An international cartel of all exporters of commodity X that acts as a monopolist would maximize total profits by restricting exports to 300X (given by the intersection of the MR_x and the S_x or ΣMC_x curves at point F) and charging $P_x = \$3.50$ (given by point G on D_x). The total profits of the cartel are higher by the size of the shaded area in the figure.

ing the total exports of commodity X to 300X, the international cartel eliminated all the exports for which MC_X exceeded MR_X, so that total profits are higher by the sum of those differences.

Problem   Starting with D_X and S_X in Figure 9–3, draw a figure showing the monopoly result if there are only two identical exporters of commodity X and they agree to share the market equally. This is a market-sharing cartel.

A9.2   International Price Discrimination

Persistent dumping, or international price discrimination, is illustrated in Figure 9–4. In the figure, the horizontal summation of the marginal revenue curve in the domestic market (MR_d) and the marginal revenue curve in the foreign market (MR_f) gives ΣMR. Point E, where the MC curve intersects the ΣMR curve from below, indicates that the domestic monopolist should sell a *total* of 300X in order to maximize its total profits. The distribution of the sale of these 300X between the foreign and the domestic market is given by the point where a horizontal line from point E crosses MR_f and MR_d, respectively. Thus, the domestic monopolist should sell 200X in the foreign market at $P_X = \$3$, and 100X in the domestic market at $P_X = \$4$. P_X is higher in the domestic market (which is insulated by transportation costs and trade barriers) than in foreign markets (where the domestic monopolist faces foreign competition).

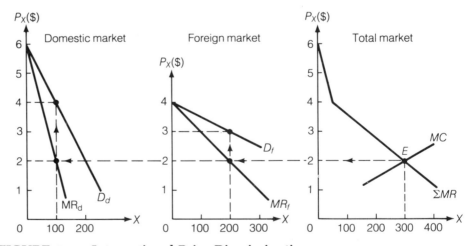

FIGURE 9-4.   International Price Discrimination

The total output that maximizes total profits is 300X and is given by point E, where the ΣMR $(=MR_d + MR_f)$ curve crosses the MC curve. Of these 300X, 200X should be sold in the foreign market (given by the point where a horizontal line from point E crosses MR_f) at $P_x = \$3$, and 100X should be sold in the domestic market (given by the point where a horizontal line from point E crosses MR_d) at $P_x = \$4$. The principle to maximize total profits is that $MR_d = MR_f$.

The general principle to maximize total profits is that $MR_d = MR_f$. If $MR_d \neq MR_f$, total profits could be increased by transferring sales from the market with the lower MR to the market with the higher MR until MR was the same in the two markets. $P_f < P_d$ because D_f is more elastic than D_d in the relevant range. D_f is more elastic than D_d because of the availability of close substitutes on the international market.

Problem If the absolute value of the price elasticity of demand in the domestic market (e_d) is 2 and e_f in the foreign market is 3, and $\Sigma MR = MC = \$10$, calculate at what price the domestic monopolist practicing international price discrimination should sell in the domestic market (P_d) and in the foreign market (P_f) in order to maximize total profits. [Hint: use the formula $MR = P(1 - 1/e)$ from microeconomic theory.]

A9.3   Taxes and Subsidies to Correct Domestic Distortions

In this section, we show graphically that the best, or optimal, policy to correct a domestic distortion is a tax or subsidy in the sector in which the domestic distortion occurs rather than an import tariff.

Figure 9–5 (adapted from Figure 8–1) shows that because of external diseconomies in the production of commodity X, production with free trade takes place at point F (even though the free trade relative commodity price is $P_W = 1$) and consumption is at point H'' on indifference curve III''. The external diseconomies are reflected in the marginal rate of transformation (i.e., the slope of the transformation curve at production point F) being greater than $P_W = 1$.

By imposing a tax of the appropriate size on the production of commodity X and giving it as a subsidy to the production of commodity Y, production can be shifted to point B, where the marginal rate of transformation equals $P_W = 1$. Consumption with free trade would then be at point E on indifference curve III. This is the highest indifference curve that the nation can reach with specialization in production and free trade.

The shift in production from point F to point B could also have been achieved with the appropriate import tariff on commodity X. However, that would make P_X/P_Y to domestic consumers higher than $P_W = 1$ by the amount of the tariff. This would distort domestic consumption away from commodity X and toward commodity Y and lead to a lower level of satisfaction (i.e., an indifference curve lower than III).

Problem By slightly modifying Figure 9–5 show that the best policy to correct external economies in the production of commodity X at the free trade relative price of $P_W = 1$ is to tax the production of Y and subsidize the production of X.

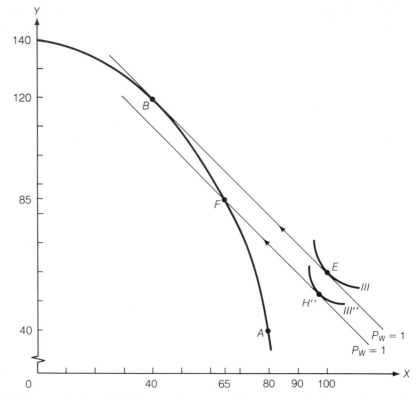

FIGURE 9-5. Optimal Policy to Correct a Distortion in Domestic Production

Because of an external diseconomy in the production of commodity X, production is at point F and consumption is at point H'' with free trade at $P_w = 1$. By taxing the production of X and subsidizing the production of Y, production can be shifted to point B and consumption to point E with free trade at $P_w = 1$. Point E is on the highest indifference curve attainable.

A9.4 State Trading

This book deals with trade among market-oriented economies rather that among centrally planned economies or between the former and the latter. However, we now briefly examine trade among centrally planned economies as well as East-West trade. **Centrally planned economies** are those in which prices are determined not by market forces but by government directives and thus do not reflect opportunity costs or alternatives forgone. Examples of these economies are the Soviet Union, China, North Korea, Vietnam, the communist nations of Eastern Europe, and Cuba. In these nations, a planning board decides how factors of production are used and rewarded, what goods are produced and their prices, and how goods and services are distributed to members of society. (State trading also plays an important role in the export of certain agricultural products in some developing countries with market economies, but this will be discussed in Chapter 11.)

In centrally planned economies, the state decides and controls all international transactions through a number of **state trading companies,** each handling some line of products. Under such a system, the types and amounts of goods imported are determined by the requirements of the national plan over and above domestically available products (i.e., to close the gap in the "materials balance"). The state then decides what goods to export to pay for the required imports. Political considerations play at least as important a role as economic considerations in such a trade, while comparative advantage and relative commodity prices do not play any direct role. Centrally planned economies generally emphasize self-sufficiency and tend to regard international trade as a necessary evil to obtain goods and services (such as high-technology products) that the nation cannot supply for itself.

Trade among centrally planned economies is generally conducted on the basis of bilateral agreements and bulk purchasing. **Bilateral agreements** often involve barter trade in which one good is exchanged for another or at least the attempt is made to balance trade with each nation individually. The reason for this is that the currencies of nonmarket economies are inconvertible into the currencies of Western nations and generally inconvertible even into the currencies of other centrally planned economies. **Bulk purchasing** refers to the agreement of a state trading company to purchase a specified amount of a commodity for a year or over a number of years from a state trading company of another nation.

In 1949, the Soviet Union formed the **Council of Mutual Economic Assistance** (CMCA or COMECON) with the communist bloc nations in Eastern Europe (Bulgaria, Czechoslovakia, East Germany, Hungary, Poland, and Rumania) plus Mongolia (Cuba and Viet Nam joined later). The purpose of this was to divert trade from Western nations and achieve a greater degree of self-sufficiency among communist nations. Under this arrangement, most COMECON members import their oil and natural gas from the Soviet Union in exchange for industrial and farm products. While successful in some respects, trade among the COMECON nations is still mostly bilateral, and their need for Western technology spurs them to seek trade with the West.

Today East-West trade resembles to a large extent the trade between developing and developed nations in that communist nations import the high-technology products that the West allows for export to them in return for raw materials, such as energy products, and simpler labor-intensive products. However, East-West trade represents only about 4 percent of total world trade today. There are several reasons why the volume of trade is so small: (1) the restrictions imposed by Western nations, especially the United States, on the export to communist nations of high-technology products, such as the most advanced computers, which have important military applications; (2) the generally low quality and limited availability of the goods that communist nations can export to pay for their imports; (3) the limited credit availability that the West is willing to extend to communist nations in view of the political risks and the limited means of repayment; (4) lack of most-favored-nation treatment for the U.S.S.R. and some other communist nations.

To overcome their limited export-based capacity to import, the Soviet Union and other communist nations have struck many large bilateral deals with a number of Western nations, particularly West Germany, France, and Italy. These bilateral deals involve the setting up of complete plants (such as the Fiat automobile plant in Russia) financed by long-term borrowing, and the construction of a major gas pipeline from the rich Siberian fields to Western Europe to be paid for in kind (i.e., by future long-term gas flows). The United States was opposed to the gas pipeline deal because it made Western Europe too dependent on the Soviet Union for energy.

West Germany is the largest Western trader, with 6.5 percent of its total exports going to the Soviet Union; France and Italy follow with about 4 percent of their total trade; then comes the United Kingdom with about 2.5 percent. Less than 2 percent of total United States trade is with the Soviet Union; the largest trade deal between them comprised the several huge United States grain sales since 1972. Other communist bloc nations, especially Poland, have reached the limit of their borrowing capacity with the West and can import only limited quantities of Western products.

Since the establishment of full diplomatic relations with China in 1979, trade between the United States and China resumed after three decades. Today, two-way trade (i.e., the sum of exports plus imports) between the United States and China runs between $5 and $6 billion per year. This compares with nearly $20 billion in the two-way trade between the United States and Taiwan. The high hopes of much larger trade with China with the reestablishment of trade relations simply failed to materialize thus far, and may not materialize in the foreseeable future. The reasons are disruptive controversies over trade issues ranging from nuclear reactors to textiles, and the much too low per capita income in China (less than $400 per year) to provide any wide market for American consumer goods, or plants to produce them.

Problem   Explain in what way the Soviet Union's international trade seems to follow the theory of comparative advantage.

Selected Bibliography

For a problem-solving approach to nontariff trade restrictions and United States commercial policy, see:

• D. Salvatore, *Theory and Problems of International Economics*, 2nd ed. (New York: McGraw-Hill, 1984), ch. 6

For a discussion of tariffs, quotas, and other nontariff barriers, see:

• R. M. Stern, "Tariffs and Other Measures of

Trade Control: A survey of Recent Developments," *Journal of Economic Literature*, September 1973.

- R. E. Baldwin, *Nontariff Distortions of International Trade* (Washington, D.C.: Brookings Institution, 1970).
- J. N. Bhagwati, "On the Equivalence of Tariffs and Quotas," in R. E. Baldwin et al., *Trade, Growth and the Balance of Payments: Essays in Honor of Gottfried Haberler* (Chicago: Rand McNally, 1965).
- M. Michaely, *Theory of Commercial Policy* (Chicago: University of Chicago Press, 1977).
- W. E. Takacs, "Pressures for Protectionism: An Empirical Analysis," *Economic Inquiry*, October 1981.
- J. N. Bhagwati, *Lectures on International Trade* (Cambridge, Mass.: M.I.T. Press, 1983).
- J. N. Bhagwati, *The Theory of Commerical Policy* (Cambridge, Mass.: M.I.T. Press, 1983).
- M. Michaely, *Trade, Income Levels, and Dependence.* (New York: North-Holland, 1984).
- W. M. Corden, "The Normative Theory of International Trade," in R. W. Jones and P. B. Kenen, eds. *Handbook of International Economics*, Vol. I (New York: North-Holland, 1984).
- D. Salvatore, "Import Penetration, Exchange Rates, and Protectionism in the United States," *Journal of Policy Modeling*, Spring 1987.
- D. Salvatore, "The Emergence of New Protectionism with Nontariff Instruments," *Vienna Institute for Comparative Economic Studies—Workshop Papers*, Spring 1987.

On international price discrimination and cartels, see:

- D. Salvatore, *Theory and Problems of Microeconomic Theory*, 2nd. ed. (New York: McGraw-Hill, 1984), sects. 11.9 and 12.9
- D. Salvatore, *Microeconomics: Theory and Applications* (New York: Macmillan, 1986), sects. 11.5 and 13.5

The infant-industry argument for protection is clearly presented in:

- H. Myint, "Infant-Industry Arguments for Assistance to Industries in the Setting of Dynamic Trade Theory," in R. F. Harrod and T. D. C. Hague, *International Trade Theory in a Developing World* (London: Macmillan, 1963).

For the theory of domestic distortions, see:

- J. N. Bhagwati and V. K. Ramaswami, "Domestic Distortions, Tariffs, and the Theory of Optimal Subsidy," *Journal of Political Economy*, February 1963. Reprinted in R. E. Caves and H. G. Johnson, *Readings in International Economics*, (Homewood, Ill.: Irwin, 1968).
- H. G. Johnson, "Optimal Trade Intervention in the Presence of Domestic Distortions," in R. E. Baldwin et al., *Trade, Growth and the Balance of Payments: Essays in Honor of Gottfried Haberler* (Chicago: Rand McNally, 1965).
- J. N. Bhagwati, "The Generalized Theory of Distortions and Welfare," in J. N. Bhagwati et al., *Trade, Balance of Payments and Growth* (Amsterdam: Elsevier, North-Holland, 1971).

Trade negotiations are discussed in:

- S. Golt, *The GATT Negotiations 1973–1979: The Closing Stage* (Washington, D.C.: National Planning Association, 1978).
- W. R. Cline et al., *Trade Negotiations in the Tokyo Round: A Quantitative Assessment* (Washington, D.C.: Brookings Institution, 1978).
- M. Kreinin and L. H. Officer, "Tariff Reductions under the Tokyo Round: A Review of Their Effects on Trade Flows, Employment and Welfare," *Weltwirtschaftliches Archiv*, no. 115, 1979.
- Sauvant, K. P. *International Transactions in Services: The Politics of Transborder Data Flows* (Boulder, Co.: Westview Press, 1986).

Estimates of the welfare costs of protection in the United States are found in:

- R. Stern, "The U.S. Tariff and the Efficiency of the U.S. Economy," *American Economic Review*, May 1964.
- G. Basevi, "The Restrictive Effect of the U.S. Tariff on Its Welfare Value," *American Economic Review*, September 1968.
- OECD, *Costs and Benefits of Protection* (Paris: OECD, 1984).

• D. G. Tarr and M. E. Morkre, *Aggregate Costs to the United States of Tariffs and Quotas on Imports* (Washington, D.C.: Federal Trade Commission, 1984).

Two excellent collections of essays on the various aspects of the new protectionism by some of the world's most renowned international economists are:
• D. Salvatore, ed., *The New Protectionism and the Threat to World Welfare,* Special Issue of the *Journal of Policy Modeling,* Spring 1985.
• D. Salvatore, D., ed., *The New Protectionist Threat to World Welfare* (New York: North-Holland, 1987).

For an excellent presentation of recent trade policy in the United States and in other developed countries, see:
• J. N. Bhagwati, ed., *Import Competition and Response.* (Chicago: University of Chicago Press, 1982).

• W. R. Cline, ed. *Trade Policies in the 1980s* (Washington, D.C.: Institute for International Economics, 1983).
• R. E. Baldwin, "Trade Policies in Developed Countries," in R. W. Jones and P. B. Kenen, eds., *Handbook of International Economics,* Vol. I (New York: North-Holland, 1984).
• R. E. Baldwin and A. O. Krueger, *The Structure and Evolution of Recent U.S. Trade Policy* (Chicago: University of Chicago Press, 1984).

For a discussion of state trading, see:
• D. F. Holzman, "Foreign Trade Behavior in Centrally Planned Economies," in H. Rosovsky, *Industrialization in Two Systems* (New York: Wiley, 1966).
• M. Allen, "The Structure and Reform of the Exchange and Payments Systems of Some East European Countries," *IMF Staff Papers,* November 1976.

CHAPTER 10

Economic Integration: Customs Unions

10.1 Introduction

In this chapter, we examine **economic integration** in general and customs unions in particular. The theory of economic integration refers to the commercial policy of discriminatively reducing or eliminating trade barriers only among the nations joining together. The degree of economic integration ranges from preferential trade arrangements to free trade areas, customs unions, common markets, and economic unions.

Preferential trade arrangements provide lower barriers on trade among participating nations than on trade with nonmember nations. This is the loosest form of economic integration. The best example of a preferential trade arrangement is the *British Commonwealth Preference Scheme,* established in 1932 by the United Kingdom with members and some former members of the British Empire.

A **free trade area** is the form of economic integration wherein all barriers are removed on trade among members, but each nation retains its own barriers on trade with nonmembers. The best example of this is the *European Free Trade Association (EFTA),* formed in 1960 by the United Kingdom, Austria, Denmark, Norway, Portugal, Sweden, and Switzerland, with Finland as an associate member.

A **customs union** allows no tariffs or other barriers on trade among members (as in a free trade area), and in addition it harmonizes trade policies

247

(such as the setting of common tariff rates) toward the rest of the world. The most famous example is the *European Economic Community (EEC)*, or *European Common Market*, formed in 1957 by West Germany, France, Italy, Belgium, the Netherlands, and Luxembourg. Another example is the *Zollverein*, or customs union, established in 1834 by a large number of sovereign German states, which proved significant in Bismarck's unification of Germany in 1870.

A **common market** goes beyond a customs union by also allowing the free movement of labor and capital among member nations. The EEC achieved something close to the status of a common market in 1970.

An **economic union** goes still further by harmonizing or even unifying the monetary and fiscal policies of member states. This is the most advanced type of economic integration. An example is *Benelux*, which is the economic union of Belgium, the Netherlands, and Luxembourg formed after World War II (and now part of the EEC). An example of a *complete* economic and monetary union is our own United States.

An interesting recent development that can be analyzed with the same concepts used to analyze customs unions are **duty-free zones** or **free economic zones.** These are areas set up to attract foreign investments by allowing raw materials and intermediate products duty free.

The discussion in this chapter is generally in terms of customs unions, but most of what is said refers also to other forms of regional economic association. In section 10.2, we examine a trade-creating customs union. In section 10.3, we analyze a trade-diverting customs union. Section 10.4 presents the theory of the second best. Section 10.5 examines the dynamic effects of customs unions, and section 10.6 gives a brief history of various attempts at economic integration. The appendix presents the general equilibrium analysis of the static effects of a trade-diverting customs union.

10.2   Trade-Creating Customs Unions

In this section, we first explain the process of trade creation, and then we illustrate the effects of a trade-creating customs union.

10.2a   Trade Creation

The static, *partial equilibrium* effects of forming a customs union are measured in terms of trade creation and trade diversion. **Trade creation** occurs when some domestic production in a nation that is a member of the customs union is replaced by lower cost imports from another *member nation*. Assuming that all economic resources are fully employed before and after formation of the customs union, this increases the welfare of member nations because it leads to greater specialization in production based on comparative advantage.

A **trade-creating customs union** also increases the welfare of nonmembers because some of the increase in its real income (due to its greater specialization in production) spills over into increased imports from the rest of the world.

10.2b Illustration of a Trade-Creating Customs Union

The effects of a trade-creating customs union are illustrated in Figure 10-1, which is adapted from Figure 8-4. D_x and S_x in Figure 10-1 are Nation 2's domestic demand and supply curves of commodity X. Suppose that the free trade price of commodity X is $P_x = \$1$ in Nation 1 and $P_x = \$1.50$ in Nation 3 (or the rest of the world), and Nation 2 is assumed to be too small to affect these prices. If Nation 2 initially imposes a nondiscriminatory ad valorem tariff of 100 percent on all imports of commodity X, then Nation 2 will import commodity X from Nation 1 at $P_x = \$2$. At $P_x = \$2$, Nation 2 consumes 50X (GH), with 20X (GJ) produced domestically and 30X (JH) imported from Nation 1. Nation 2 also collects \$30 (MJHN) in tariff revenues. In the figure, S_1 is Nation 1's perfectly elastic supply curve of commodity X to Nation 2 under

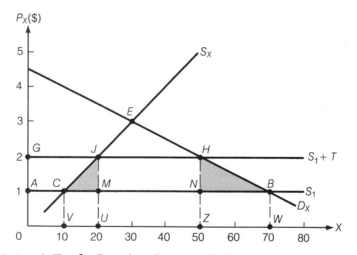

FIGURE 10-1. A Trade-Creating Customs Union

D_x and S_x represent Nation 2's domestic demand and supply curves of commodity X. At the tariff-inclusive $P_x = \$2$ before the formation of the customs union, Nation 2 consumes 50X (GH), with 20X (GJ) produced in Nation 2 and 30X (JH) imported from Nation 1. Nation 2 also collects a tariff revenue of \$30 (MJHN). Nation 2 does not import commodity X from Nation 3 because of the tariff-inclusive $P_x > \$2$. After Nation 2 forms a customs union with Nation 1 only, Nation 2 consumes 70X (AB), with 10X (AC) produced domestically and 60X (CB) imported from Nation 1 at $P_x = \$1$. The tariff revenue disappears, and area AGJC represents a transfer from domestic producers to domestic consumers. This leaves net static gains to Nation 2 as a whole equal to \$15, given by the sum of the areas of shaded triangles CJM and BHN.

free trade, and $S_1 + T$ is the tariff-inclusive supply curve. Nation 2 does not import commodity X from Nation 3 because the tariff-inclusive price of commodity X imported from Nation 3 would be $P_x = \$3$.

If Nation 2 now forms a customs union with Nation 1 (i.e., removes tariffs on its imports from Nation 1 only), $P_x = \$1$ in Nation 2. At this price, Nation 2 consumes 70X (*AB*) of commodity X, with 10X (*AC*) produced domestically and 60X (*CB*) imported from Nation 1. In this case, Nation 2 collects no tariff revenue. The benefit to consumers in Nation 2 resulting from the formation of the customs union is equal to *AGHB* (the increase in the consumers' surplus defined in section 8.5b). However, only part of this represents a *net* gain for Nation 2 as a whole. That is, *AGJC* represents a reduction in rent, or producers' surplus, while *MJHN* represents the loss of tariff revenues. This leaves the sum of the areas of shaded triangles *CJM* and *BHN*, or $15, as the net static welfare gain for Nation 2.

Triangle *CJM* is the production component of the welfare gain from trade creation and results from shifting the production of 10X (*CM*) from less efficient domestic producers in Nation 2 (at a cost of *VUJC*) to more efficient producers in Nation 1 (at a cost of *VUMC*). Triangle *BHN* is the consumption component of the welfare gain from trade creation and results from the increase in consumption of 20X (*NB*) in Nation 2, giving a benefit of *ZWBH* with an expenditure of only *ZWBN*.

Viner, who pioneered the development of the theory of customs unions in 1950, concentrated on the production effect of trade creation and ignored the consumption effect. *Meade* extended the theory of customs unions in 1955 and was the first to consider the consumption effect. *Johnson* then added the two triangles to obtain the total welfare gain of a customs union. (See the selected bibliography for the complete references.)

10.3   Trade-Diverting Customs Unions

In this section, we first explain the meaning of trade diversion, and then we illustrate the effects of a trade-diverting customs union.

10.3a   Trade Diversion

Trade diversion occurs when lower cost imports from outside the customs union are replaced by higher cost imports from a union member. This results because of the preferential trade treatment given to member nations. Trade diversion, by itself, reduces welfare because it shifts production from more efficient producers outside the customs union to less efficient producers inside the union. Thus, trade diversion worsens the international allocation of resources and shifts production away from comparative advantage.

A **trade-diverting customs union** results in *both* trade creation and trade diversion and, therefore, can increase or reduce the welfare of union members, depending on the relative strength of these two opposing forces. The welfare of nonmembers can be expected to decline because their economic resources can only be utilized less efficiently than before trade was diverted away from them. Thus, while a trade-creating customs union leads only to nonmembers, a trade-diverting customs union leads to both trade creation and trade diversion, and can increase or reduce the welfare of members (and will reduce the welfare of the rest of the world).

10.3b Illustration of a Trade-Diverting Customs Union

The effects of a trade-diverting customs union are illustrated in Figure 10-2. In this figure, D_x and S_x are Nation 2's domestic demand and supply curves of commodity X, while S_1 and S_3 are the free trade perfectly elastic supply curves of Nation 1 and Nation 3, respectively. With a nondiscriminatory 100 percent tariff on imports of commodity X, Nation 2 imports commodity X from Nation 1 at $P_x = \$2$, along $S_1 + T$ (exactly as in Figure 10-1). As seen earlier, at $P_x = \$2$, Nation 2 consumes 50X (GH), with 20X (GJ) produced do-

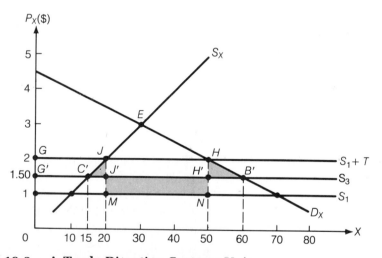

FIGURE 10-2. A Trade-Diverting Customs Union

D_x and S_x represent Nation 2's domestic demand and supply curves of commodity X, while S_1 and S_3 are the free trade perfectly elastic supply curves of commodity X of Nation 1 and Nation 3, respectively. With a nondiscriminatory 100 percent tariff, Nation 2 imports 30X (JH) at $P_x = \$2$ from Nation 1. After forming a customs union with Nation 3 only, Nation 2 imports 45X ($C'B'$) at $P_x = \$1.50$ from Nation 3. The welfare gain in Nation 2 from pure trade creation is $3.75 (given by the sum of the areas of the two shaded triangles). The welfare loss from trade diversion proper is $15 (the area of the shaded rectangle). Thus, this trade-diverting customs union leads to a net welfare loss of $11.25 for Nation 2.

mestically and 30X (*JH*) imported from Nation 1. Nation 2 also collects $30 (*JMNH*) in tariff revenues.

If Nation 2 now forms a customs union with Nation 3 only (i.e., removes tariffs on imports from Nation 3 only), Nation 2 finds it cheaper to import commodity X from Nation 3 at $P_x = \$1.50$. At $P_x = \$1.50$, Nation 2 consumes 60X (*G′B′*), with 15X (*G′C′*) produced domestically and 45X (*C′B′*) imported from Nation 3. In this case, Nation 2 collects no tariff revenue. The imports of commodity X into Nation 2 have now been *diverted* from the more efficient producers in Nation 1 to the less efficient producers in Nation 3, because the tariff discriminates against imports from Nation 1 (which is outside the union). Note that Nation 2's imports of commodity X were 30X before formation of the customs union and 45X afterward. Thus, the trade-diverting customs union also leads to·some trade creation.

The static welfare effects on Nation 2 resulting from the formation of a customs union with Nation 3 can be measured from the shaded areas shown in Figure 10-2. The sum of the areas of shaded triangles *C′JJ′* and *B′HH′* ($3.75) is the welfare gain resulting from pure trade creation, while the area of shaded rectangle *MNH′J′* ($15) is the welfare loss from diverting the *initial* 30X (*JH*) of imports from lower cost Nation 1 to higher cost Nation 3. Specifically, of the gain in consumers' surplus of *G′GHB′* resulting from the formation of the customs union, *G′GJC′* represents a transfer from producers' to consumers' surplus in Nation 2 and, therefore, washes out (i.e., leaves no net gain or loss for Nation 2 as a whole). Of the *JMNH* ($30) tariff revenue collected by Nation 2 before the formation of the customs union with Nation 3, *JJ′HH′* is transferred to consumers in Nation 2 in the form of the lower price of commodity X after the formation of the customs union. This leaves only shaded triangles *C′JJ′* and *B′HH′* as the net gain to Nation 2, and shaded rectangle *MNH′J′* as the still-unaccounted loss of tariff revenue.

Since the area of the shaded rectangle ($15) measuring the welfare loss from trade diversion proper exceeds the sum of the areas of the shaded triangles ($3.75) measuring the welfare gain from pure trade creation, this trade-diverting customs union leads to a net welfare loss of $11.25 for Nation 2. This need not always be the case, however. Looking at Figure 10-2, we can see that the flatter (i.e., the more elastic in the relevant range) D_x and S_x are and the closer S_3 is to S_1, the greater is the sum of the areas of the shaded triangles and the smaller the area of the shaded rectangle. This makes it more likely that even a trade-diverting customs union will lead to a net welfare gain for the nation joining the union (the figure showing this is left as an end-of-chapter problem). The static welfare effects of a trade-diverting customs union are examined within the more advanced general equilibrium framework in the appendix to this chapter.

The several attempts to measure (along the lines discussed above) the static welfare effects resulting from the formation of the European Economic Community all came up with surprisingly small *net static* welfare gains (in the range of 1 percent of GNP or less).

10.4 The Theory of the Second Best and Other Static Welfare Effects of Customs Unions

We now examine the general principle known as the theory of the second best, of which the theory of customs unions is a special case. We then go on to examine the conditions under which a customs union is more likely to lead to trade creation and increased welfare, and finally we examine some other static welfare effects of customs unions.

10.4a The Theory of the Second Best

We saw in Part I that free trade leads to the most efficient utilization of world resources and thus maximizes world output and welfare. Therefore, prior to Viner's work on customs unions in 1950, it was widely believed that any movement toward freer trade would also increase welfare. To the extent that a customs union does not increase trade barriers against the rest of the world, the elimination of trade barriers among union members represents a movement toward freer trade. As such, it was believed to increase the welfare of member and nonmember nations alike.

However, Viner showed that the formation of a customs union could increase or reduce the welfare of member nations and of the rest of the world, depending on the circumstances under which it takes place. This is an example of the **theory of the second best,** which states that if all the conditions required to maximize welfare or reach Pareto optimum cannot be satisfied, trying to satisfy as many of these conditions as possible docs not necessarily or usually lead to the second-best position. Thus, forming a customs union and removing trade barriers only among the members will not necessarily produce the second-best welfare position (as evidenced by the fact that welfare can rise or fall). This somewhat startling conclusion has great significance not only for the field of international economics (from which it originated) but for the study of economics in general. The theory of customs unions is just one example from international trade of this general principle. From its somewhat vague beginning in the work of Viner, the theory of the second best was then fully developed by Meade in 1955 and generalized by *Lipsey* and *Lancaster* in 1957.

10.4b Conditions More Likely to Lead to Increased Welfare

A customs union is more likely to lead to trade creation and increased welfare under the following conditions:

1. The higher are the preunion trade barriers of member countries. There is then a greater probability that formation of the customs union will create trade among union members rather than divert trade from nonmembers to members.

2. The lower are the customs union's barriers on trade with the rest of the world. This makes it less likely that formation of the customs union will lead to costly trade diversion.

3. The greater is the number of countries forming the customs union and the larger their size. Under these circumstances there is a greater probability that low cost producers fall within the union.

4. The more competitive rather than complementary are the economies of member nations. There are then greater opportunities for specialization in production and trade creation with the formation of the customs union. Thus, a customs union is more likely to increase welfare if formed by two competitive industrial nations rather than by an industrial nation and an agricultural (complementary) nation.

5. The closer geographically are the members of the customs union. Then transportation costs represent less of an obstacle to trade creation among members.

6. The greater is the preunion trade and economic relationship among potential members of the customs union. This leads to greater opportunities for significant welfare gains as a result of the formation of the customs union.

The reasons for the greater success of the European Economic Community than the European Free Trade Association are that the nations forming the EEC were much more competitive than complementary, were closer geographically, and had greater preunion trade than the EFTA nations (reasons 4, 5, and 6 above).

10.4c   Other Static Welfare Effects of Customs Unions

There are other *static* welfare effects resulting from the formation of a customs union. One is the administration savings from the elimination of customs officers, border patrols, and so on, for trade among members nations. This benefit arises whether the customs union is trade creating or trade diverting.

Second, a trade-diverting customs union, by reducing its demand for imports from and its supply of exports to the rest of the world, is likely to lead to an improvement in the *collective* terms of trade of the customs union. This can be shown graphically by an inward shift in the customs union's offer curve. However, for a trade-creating customs union, the opposite is likely to be true, since part of the increase in real income resulting from formation of the customs union spills over into a greater demand for imports from the rest of the world. Whether an *individual* member's terms of trade improve, deteriorate, or remain unchanged depends on the circumstances.

Finally, any customs union, by acting as a single unit in international trade negotiations, is likely to have much more bargaining power than all of its members separately. There is no doubt, for example, that this is the case for the EEC.

10.5 Dynamic Benefits from Customs Unions

Besides the static welfare effects discussed earlier, the nations forming a customs union are likely to receive several important *dynamic* benefits. These are due to increased competition, economies of scale, stimulus to investment, and better utilization of economic resources. These will be examined in turn.

The greatest dynamic benefit from the formation of a customs union is the *increased competition* that is likely to result. That is, in the absence of a customs union, producers (especially those in monopolistic and oligopolistic markets) are likely to grow sluggish and complacent behind trade barriers. But when a customs union is formed and trade barriers among member nations are eliminated, producers in each nation must become more efficient to meet the competition of other producers within the union, merge, or go out of business. The increased level of competition is also likely to stimulate the development and utilization of new technology. All of these efforts will cut costs of production to the benefit of consumers. A customs union must, of course, be careful (by passing and enforcing antitrust legislation) that such oligopolistic practices as collusion and market-sharing agreements, which earlier might have restricted competition nationally, are not replaced by similar union-wide practices after the formation of the customs union. The EEC has attempted to do just that.

A second possible benefit from the formation of a customs union is that *economies of scale* are likely to result from the enlarged market. However, it must be pointed out that even a small nation that is not a member of any customs union can overcome the smallness of its domestic market and achieve substantial economies of scale in production by exporting to the rest of the world. For example, it was found that plants in many major industries in such relatively small nations as Belgium and the Netherlands were already of comparable size to United States plants before they joined the EEC and thus already enjoyed substantial economies of scale by producing for the domestic market and for export. Nevertheless, significant economies were achieved after formation of the EEC by reducing the range of differentiated products manufactured in each plant and increasing "production runs" (see section 6.4b).

Another possible benefit is the *stimulus to investment* to take advantage of the enlarged market and to meet the increased competition. Furthermore, the formation of a customs union is likely to spur outsiders to set up production facilities within the customs union to avoid the (discriminatory) trade barriers imposed on nonunion products. These are the so-called **tariff factories.** The massive investments that United States firms made in Europe after 1955 can be explained by their desire not to be excluded from this rapidly growing market.

Finally, in a customs union that is also a common market (as to some extent the EEC after 1970), the free community-wide movement of labor and capital is likely to result in better utilization of the economic resources of the entire community.

These dynamic gains resulting from the formation of a customs union are presumed to be much greater than the static gains discussed earlier and to be very significant. Indeed, the United Kingdom joined the EEC in 1973 primarily because of them. Recent empirical studies seem to indicate that these dynamic gains are about 5 to 6 times larger than the static gains. The monetary aspects of the formation of a customs union are discussed under the heading of "optimum currency areas" in section 19.4.

10.6   History of Attempts at Economic Integration

In this section, we briefly survey the history of attempts at economic integration, starting with the formation of the European Economic Community and the European Free Trade Association and then discussing attempts at economic integration among developing nations.

10.6a   The European Economic Community

The **European Economic Community (EEC),** or European Common Market, was founded by the Treaty of Rome signed in March 1957 by West Germany, France, Italy, Belgium, the Netherlands, and Luxembourg and came into being on January 1, 1958. The common external tariff was set at the average of the 1957 tariffs of the six nations. Free trade in industrial goods within the EEC and a common price for agricultural products were achieved in 1968, and the almost free movement of labor and capital by 1970. Membership increased to twelve as the United Kingdom, Denmark, and Ireland joined in 1973, Greece in 1981, and Spain and Portugal in 1986. With a population of 320 million (one-third more than the population of the United States) and a total output nearly as large as that of the United States, the expanded Community represents the largest trading bloc in the world. By 1969 intra-EEC trade was estimated to be about 50 percent higher than it would have been in the absence of integration.

The formation of the EEC significantly expanded trade in industrial goods with nonmembers. This was due to (1) the very rapid growth of the EEC, which increased its demand for imports of industrial products from outside the union, and (2) the reduction to very low levels of the average tariff on imports of industrial products as a result of the Kennedy and Tokyo Rounds (initiated by the United States, which feared trade diversion).

On the other hand, formation of the EEC resulted in trade diversion in agricultural commodities, particularly in temperate products such as grain from the United States. The development of a *common agricultural policy (CAP)* was particularly troublesome for the EEC. The final outcome sacrificed consumers' interests to those of Community farmers in general, and French farmers in particular, by setting relatively high farm prices. The procedure is as follows. First the Community determines common farm prices, and then it imposes tariffs so as always to make the price of imported agricultural products equal to the high established EEC prices. These are the so-called **variable import levies.** The high farm support price level has also led to huge agricultural surpluses within the EEC, high storage costs, and subsidized exports. This farm policy was a major obstacle to British entry into the EEC because Britain kept agricultural prices low and instead aided its farmers by "deficiency payments" to raise their incomes to desired levels.

At the Lomé Conference in 1975, the EEC eliminated most trade barriers on imports from 46 developing nations in Africa, the Caribbean, and the Pacific region that were former colonies of EEC countries. Earlier, in 1971, the EEC had granted *generalized tariff preferences* to imports of manufactured and semimanufactured products from developing nations. But, as pointed out in section 9.5d, textiles, steel, consumer electronics, shoes, and many other products of great importance to developing nations were excluded. Preferences were extended to trade in tropical products in the Tokyo Round in 1979. However, since these preferences fell short of the complete elimination of trade barriers granted to former colonies, a bitter controversy arose because of alleged trade diversion.

As pointed out earlier, the static welfare benefits resulting from the formation of the EEC are estimated to be 1 percent of GNP or less, and while the dynamic benefits are presumed to be much larger, no serious measurement has been possible. Perhaps the greatest benefit has been political, resulting from unifying into a single economic community nations, such as Germany and France, that were once bitter enemies. However, the road to full economic union for the EEC is paved with almost insurmountable difficulties, as decisions must be reached unanimously by a large group of very disparate countries.

Other highlights in the operation of the EEC are: (1) member nations have adopted a common *value-added tax system*, under which a tax is levied on the value added of the product at each stage of its production and passed on to the consumer. (2) The *Commission* (the executive body of the EEC) has the power to prevent the formation of, or break up, community-wide cartels and monopolies that restrain competition. (3) The *Council of Ministers* (whose members represent their own national governments) makes final decisions but only on the recommendation of the Commission. There is also a *European Parliament* (with membership from the national legislatures but without much power at present) and a *Court of Justice* (with power to rule on the constitutionality of the decisions of the Commission and the Council).

10.6b The European Free Trade Association

In 1960 the free trade area known as the **European Free Trade Association (EFTA)** was formed by the "outer seven" nations: the United Kingdom, Austria, Denmark, Norway, Portugal, Sweden, and Switzerland, with Finland an associate member. The EFTA achieved free trade in industrial goods in 1967, but only a few special provisions were made to reduce barriers on trade in agricultural products.

The maintenance by each nation of its own trade barriers against non-members can lead to the problem of **trade deflection.** This refers to the entry of imports from the rest of the world into the low-tariff member of the association to avoid the higher tariffs of other members. To combat trade deflection requires checking the original source and the final country of destination of all imports. The problem, of course, does not arise in a customs union because of its common external tariff, and it is much less serious in preferential trade arrangements where only small tariff preferences are granted to members.

In 1973 the United Kingdom and Denmark left the EFTA and, together with Ireland, joined the EEC. This lowered the EFTA membership to five, with Finland remaining an associate member. In the early 1980s the EFTA negotiated free trade arrangements in industrial good with the EEC. The EFTA is headquartered in Geneva and does not participate as a single unit in international trade negotiations.

10.6c   Attempts at Economic Integration Among Developing Nations

The success of the EEC encouraged several attempts at economic integration among groups of developing nations as a means to aid their development effort. However, all of these attempts met with only limited success or failed. Examples are: (1) the Central American Common Market (CACM) established by Costa Rica, El Salvador, Guatemala, Honduras, and Nicaragua in 1960 and dissolved in 1969; (2) The Latin American Free Trade Association (LAFTA) established in 1960 by Mexico and most of South America, and its subgroup (The Andean Pact), which hoped to accelerate the process of integration and establish a common market; (3) The Caribbean Free Trade Association (CARIFTA) set up in 1968 and transformed into a common market (CARICOM) in 1973; (4) the East African Economic Community, which was established in 1967 and collapsed in the late 1970s; (5) the Economic Community of West Africa formed in 1974; and (6) the Association of Southeast Asian Nations (ASEAN), which includes Indonesia, Malaysia, the Philippines, Singapore, and Thailand, which in 1976 moved toward a common market. These customs unions are (or were) to a large extent explicitly trade diverting to encourage industrial development.

Perhaps the greatest stumbling block to successful economic integration among groups of developing nations is that the benefits are not evenly distributed among members. Instead, benefits are likely to accrue mainly to the most advanced nations in the group. This leads lagging nations to withdraw, causing the attempt at economic integration to fail. One way to avoid this difficulty is to provide investment assistance through industrial planning (i.e., the assignment of some industries to each member nation). Though this was tried in the Central American Common Market, the effort failed and the union dissolved.

Another difficulty is that many developing nations are not willing to relinquish part of their newly acquired sovereignty to a supranational community body, as required for successful economic integration. Other difficulties arise from lack of good transportation and communications among member nations, the great distance that often separates members, and the basically complementary nature of their economies and competition for the same world markets for their agricultural exports.

Summary

1. Economic integration refers to the commercial policy of discriminatively reducing or eliminating trade barriers only among the nations joining together. In a preferential trade arrangement (such as the British Commonwealth Preference Scheme), trade barriers are reduced on trade among participating nations only. A free trade area (e.g., the EFTA) removes all barriers on trade among members, but each nation retains its own barriers on trade with nonmembers. A customs union (e.g., the EEC) goes further by also adopting a common commercial policy toward the outside world. A common market (as to some extent the EEC after 1970) goes still further by allowing the free movement of labor and capital among member nations as well. An economic union harmonizes (e.g., Benelux) or even unifies (e.g., the United States) the monetary and fiscal policies of its members.

2. The static, partial equilibrium effects of customs unions are measured in terms of trade creation and trade diversion. Trade creation occurs when some domestic production in a union member is replaced by lower cost imports from another member nation. This increases specialization in production and welfare in the customs union. A trade-creating customs union also increases the welfare of nonmembers since some of the increase in its real income spills over into increased imports from the rest of the world.

3. Trade diversion occurs when lower cost imports from outside the customs union are replaced by higher cost imports from another union member. By itself, this reduces welfare because it shifts production away from comparative advantage. A trade-diverting customs union leads to both trade creation and trade diversion and may increase or reduce welfare, depending on the relative strength of these two opposing forces.

4. The theory of customs unions is a special case of the theory of the second best. This states that when all conditions required to reach maximum social welfare or Pareto optimum cannot be satisfied, trying to satisfy as many of these conditions as possible does not necessarily or usually lead to the second-best welfare position. The conditions under which the formation of a customs union is more likely to lead to trade creation and increased welfare are well known theoretically. Other static effects of customs unions are administrative savings and greater bargaining strength. However, a customs union's effect on individual members' terms of trade is unclear.

5. Besides the static welfare gains, the nations forming a customs union are likely to receive significant dynamic benefits from increased competition, economies of scale, stimulus to investment, and better utilization of economic resources.

6. The EEC was formed in 1958 by West Germany, France, Italy, Belgium, the Netherlands, and Luxembourg and were joined by the United Kingdom, Denmark, and Ireland in 1973, Greece in 1981, and Spain and Portugal in 1986. Free trade in industrial goods among the original members and common agricultural prices were achieved in 1968. The EEC led to trade expansion in industrial goods but trade diversion in agricultural products. Development of a common agricultural policy was particularly difficult. The static gains resulting from the formation of the EEC have been estimated to be 1 percent of GNP or less. The dynamic gains are likely to be much greater but have yet to be measured. The best example of a free trade area is the EFTA, established in 1960. Free trade areas face the problem of trade deflection. The several attempts at economic integration among developing nations have had only limited success or have failed.

A Look Ahead

In the next chapter, we examine the special trade problems faced by developing countries. We will find that international trade can contribute significantly to the development of poor nations, but it also gives rise to some special problems requiring joint action by both developed and developing nations. The great poverty in many developing countries and their belief that the present international monetary system operates in a way that hampers their development have led developing nations to demand the establishment of a new international economic order.

Glossary

Economic integration   The commercial policy of discriminatively reducing or eliminating trade barriers only among the nations joining together.

Preferential trade arrangements   The loosest form of economic integration; provide lower barriers to trade among participating nations than on trade with nonparticipating nations. An example is the British Commonwealth Preference Scheme.

Free trade area   Removes all barriers on trade among members, but each nation retains its own barriers on trade with nonmembers. The best example is the European Free Trade Association (EFTA).

Customs union   Removes all barriers on trade among members and harmonizes trade policies toward the rest of the world. The best example is the European Economic Community (EEC).

Common market   Removes all barriers on trade among members, harmonizes trade policies toward the rest of the world, and also allows the free movement of labor and capital among members nations. An example that nearly satisfies these conditions is the EEC after 1970.

Economic union   Removes all barriers on trade among members, harmonizes trade policies toward the rest of the world, allows the free movement of labor and capital among member nations, and also harmonizes or unifies the monetary, fiscal, and tax policies of its members.

Duty-free zones or **free economic zones**   Areas set up to attract foreign investments by allowing raw materials and intermediate products duty free.

Trade creation   Occurs when some domestic production in a member of the customs union is replaced by lower cost imports from another member nation. This increases welfare.

Trade-creating customs union   A customs union that leads to trade creation only and increases the welfare of both member nations and nonmembers.

Trade diversion   Occurs when lower cost imports from outside the union are replaced by higher cost imports from another union member. By itself, this reduces welfare.

Trade-diverting customs union   A customs union that leads to both trade creation and trade diversion and may increase or reduce the welfare of member nations, depending on the relative strength of these two opposing forces.

Theory of the second best   States that when all of the conditions required to reach maximum social welfare or Pareto optimum cannot be satisfied, trying to satisfy as many of these conditions as possible does not necessarily or usually lead to the second-best welfare position.

Tariff factories   Direct investments made in a nation or other economic unit (such as a customs union) to avoid import tariffs.

European Economic Community (EEC)   The customs union formed by West Germany,

France, Italy, Belgium, the Netherlands, and Luxembourg that came into existence in 1958, and expanded to 12 nations with the joining of the United Kingdom, Denmark, and Ireland in 1973, Greece in 1981, and Spain and Portugal in 1986. Also known as the European Common Market.

Variable import levies　The import duties levied by the EEC on imports of agricultural commodities and equal to the difference between the high farm prices established by the EEC and the lower world prices.

European Free Trade Association (EFTA)　The free trade area that was formed in 1960 by the United Kingdom, Austria, Denmark, Norway, Portugal, Sweden, and Switzerland, with Finland an associate member. In 1977 the United Kingdom and Denmark left the EFTA to join the EEC.

Trade deflection　The entry of imports from the rest of the world into the low-tariff member of a free trade area to avoid the higher tariffs of other members.

Questions for Review

1. What is meant by economic integration? A preferential trade arrangement? A free trade area? A customs union? A common market? An economic union? Give an example of each.
2. What is meant by trade creation? What static welfare effects will a trade-creating customs union have on member nations and on the rest of the world? How do these static welfare effects arise? How are they measured?
3. What is meant by trade diversion? What static welfare effects will a trade-diverting customs union have on member nations and on the rest of the world? How do these static welfare effects arise? How are they measured?
4. What is the theory of the second best? In what way is the theory of customs unions an example of the theory of the second best? Under what conditions is the formation of a customs union more likely to lead to trade creation and increased welfare? What are some of the other static welfare effects resulting from the formation of a customs union?

5. What dynamic benefits are the nations forming a customs union likely to receive? How do they arise? How large are they?
6. What was the effect of the formation of the EEC on trade in industrial and agricultural products with the rest of the world? What is the magnitude of the static and dynamic benefits to members resulting from the formation of the EEC? How does the EFTA compare with the EEC? Why have attempts at economic integration among developing nations generally met with limited success or failure?

Problems

*1. Suppose that the autarky price of commodity X is $10 in Nation A, $8 in Nation B, and $6 in Nation C, and Nation A is too small to affect prices in Nations B or C by trading.
　(a) If Nation A initially imposes a nondiscriminatory ad valorem tariff of 100 percent on its imports of commodity X from Nations B and C, will Nation A produce commodity X domestically or import it from Nation B or Nation C?
　(b) If Nation A subsequently forms a customs union with Nation B, will Nation A produce commodity X domestically or import it from Nation B or Nation C?
　(c) Is the customs union that Nation A forms with Nation B trade creating, trade diverting, or neither?

*2. Suppose that the autarky prices of commodity X in Nations A, B, and C are the same as in problem 1, and Nation A is too small to affect prices in Nations B and C by trading.
　(a) If Nation A initially imposes a nondiscriminatory ad valorem tariff of 50 percent (rather than 100 percent) on imports of commodity X from Nations B and C, will Nation A produce commodity X domestically or import it from Nation B or Nation C?
　(b) If Nation A subsequently forms a customs union with Nation B, will Nation A produce commodity X domestically or import it from Nation B or Nation C?

(c) Is the customs union that Nation A forms with Nation B trade creating, trade diverting, or neither?

3. (a) Draw a figure illustrating the effects of a trade-creating customs union.
   (b) Measure the welfare gain of a nation joining this customs union.

4. (a) Draw a figure illustrating the effects of a trade-diverting customs union that *reduces* the welfare of a nation joining it.
   (b) Measure the net welfare loss suffered by a nation joining this customs union.

5. (a) Draw a figure illustrating the effects of a trade-diverting customs union that *increases* the welfare of a nation joining it.
   (b) Measure the net welfare gain of a nation joining this customs union.
   (c) What are the factors that determine whether a trade-diverting customs union leads to a net increase or decrease in the welfare of a member nation?

6. Draw a figure showing what happens if country A forms a customs union with country B only, but the tariff-inclusive prices in country C are less than the free trade prices in country B.

APPENDIX

General Equilibrium Analysis of the Static Effects of a Trade-Diverting Customs Union

In section 10.3, we analyzed the static, partial equilibrium welfare effects of the formation of a trade-diverting customs union. In this appendix, we examine these static welfare effects within the more advanced general equilibrium framework. This brings out some aspects of the trade-diverting customs union not evident from the partial equilibrium analysis. Together they give a fairly complete picture of the static welfare effects resulting from the formation of a customs union.

The general equilibrium analysis of a trade-diverting customs union is illustrated in Figure 10-3. The figure repeats the production frontier of Nation 2 in Figure 8-1. We assume for simplicity that Nation 2 is too small to affect the relative price of commodity X in (large) Nations 1 and 3.

With a nondiscriminatory ad valorem tariff of 100 percent on imports of commodity X, Nation 2 produces at point F, where the marginal rate of transformation, or slope of its transformation curve, equals the tariff-inclusive relative price of commodity X from Nation 1 of $P'_1 = 2$ (not shown in the figure). However, since Nation 2 collects the tariff, it consumes at point H' on indifference curve II′ by exchanging 30Y for 30X with Nation 1 along $P_1 = 1$ (exactly as in Figure 8-1).

If Nation 2 now forms a customs union with Nation 3, it will import commodity X from Nation 3 instead, at the free trade relative commodity price of $P_3 = 1.5$ in Nation 3. Nation 2 might then consume at point B' along the $P_3 = 1.5$ line. Since point B' involves less of both commodities than point H', point B' must be on a lower indifference curve (not shown in the figure). This confirms

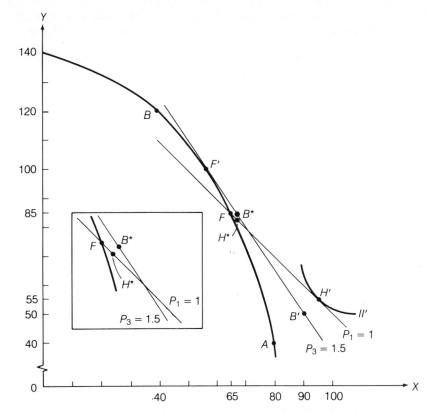

FIGURE 10-3. **General Equilibrium Analysis of a Trade-Diverting Customs Union**

With a 100 percent nondiscriminatory import tariff on commodity X, Nation 2 produces at point F and consumes at point H' on indifference curve II' at the relative commodity price of $P_1 = 1$ (exactly as in Figure 8-1). By forming a customs union with Nation 3 only, Nation 2 produces at point F' at $P_3 = 1.5$ and consumes at $B' < H'$. This trade-diverting customs union leads to a net welfare loss for Nation 2. However, with different tastes, Nation 2 could conceivably consume at point H^* before and at point B^* after the formation of the customs union with Nation 3 and receive a net welfare gain (since $B^* > H^*$).

the partial equilibrium results shown in Figure 10-2, where Nation 2 suffered a net loss of welfare by forming a customs union with Nation 3.

However, with different tastes, Nation 2 might have consumed at point H^* before the formation of the customs union and at point B^* afterward. Since point B^* involves the consumption of both more X and more Y than point H^*, the trade-diverting customs union would lead to a net welfare *gain* for Nation 2. (For greater clarity, the area of the graph showing the relationship between points F, B^*, and H^* is enlarged in the inset inside the transformation curve.) Thus, a trade-diverting customs union may lead to a net welfare gain or loss, depending on the circumstances under which it is formed.

Problem   Starting from Figure 10-3, where Nation 2 produces at point F and consumes at point H', prove graphically that the smaller the relative inefficiency of Nation 3 with respect to Nation 1, the more likely it is that the formation of a customs union between Nation 2 and Nation 3 will lead to a net welfare gain for Nation 2 (even though the customs union would be trade diverting).

Selected Bibliography

For a problem-solving approach to economic integration, see:
• D. Salvatore, Theory and Problems of International Economics, 2nd ed. (New York: McGraw-Hill, 1984), ch. 6 (sect. 6.6).

The classic works on the theory of customs unions are:
• J. Viner, The Customs Union Issue (New York: The Carnegie Endowment for International Peace, 1953).
• J. Meade, The Theory of Customs Unions (Amsterdam: North-Holland, 1955).
• R. G. Lipsey, "The Theory of Customs Unions: A General Survey," Economic Journal, September 1961. Reprinted in R. E. Caves and H. G. Johnson, Readings in International Economics (Homewood, Ill.: Irwin, 1968).

Other interesting contributions on customs unions theory are:
• B. Balassa, The Theory of Economic Integration (Homewood, Ill.: Irwin, 1961).
• C. A. Cooper and B. F. Massell, "A New Look at Customs Union Theory," Economic Journal, December 1965.
• T. Scitovsky, Economic Theory and Western European Economic Integration (Stanford, Cal.: Stanford University Press, 1958).
• J. Vanek, General Equilibrium of International Discrimination: The Case of Customs Unions (Cambridge, Mass.: Harvard University Press, 1965).
• D. Swann, The Economics of the Common Market (London: Penguin, 1978).

• P. J. Lloyd, "3 x 3 Theory of Customs Unions," Journal of International Economics, February 1982.

For the theory of the second best, see:
• J. Meade, The Theory of Customs Unions (Amsterdam: North-Holland, 1955).
• R. G. Lipsey and K. Lancaster, "The General Theory of the Second Best," Review of Economic Studies, October 1956.

Estimates of the welfare effects of customs unions are found in:
• H. G. Johnson, "The Gains from Freer Trade with Europe: An Estimate," Manchester School of Economics and Social Studies, September 1958.
• B. Balassa, "Trade Creation and Trade Diversion in the European Common Market: An Appraisal of the Evidence," The Manchester School, 1974.
• M. Kreinin, Trade Relations of the EEC: An Empirical Investigation (New York: Praeger, 1974).
• M. H. Miller and J. E. Spencer, "The Static Effects of the U.K. Joining the Common Market: A General Equilibrium Approach," The Review of Economic Studies, 1977.
• H. C. Petith, "European Integration and the Terms of Trade," Economic Journal, June 1977.
• N. Owen, Economies of Scale, Competitiveness, and Trade Patterns within the European Economic Community (Oxford: Oxford University Press, 1983).
• R. Harris, "Applied General Equilibrium Analysis of Small Open Economies and Imperfect Competition," American Economic Review, December 1984.

For customs unions among developing countries, see:

- H. G. Johnson, "An Economic Theory of Protectionism, Tariff Bargaining, and the Formation of Customs Unions," *Journal of Political Economy*, 1965.
- C. A. Cooper and B. F. Massell, "Towards a General Equilibrium Theory of Developing Countries," *Journal of Political Economy*, September 1965.
- W. D. Ingram, "Economies of Scale, Domestic Divergencies, and Potential Gains from Economic Integration of Ghana and the Ivory Coast," *Journal of Political Economy*, October 1980.

Two studies analyzing the economic effects of duty-free zones or free economic zones are:

- C. Hamilton and L. E. O. Svensson, "On the Welfare Effects of 'Duty-Free Zone,'" *Journal of International Economics*, 1982.

H. G. Grubel, "Towards a Theory of Free Economic Zones," *Weltwirtschafliches Archiv*, 1982.

CHAPTER 11

International Trade and Economic Development

11.1   Introduction

With the exception of a handful of nations in North America, Western Europe, and Japan, most nations of the world are classified as less developed or, to put it more positively, as developing countries. In relation to developed (or more developed) countries, developing nations are characterized by low (and sometimes extremely low) average real per capita income, a high proportion of the labor force in agriculture and other primary activities such as mineral extraction, a low life expectancy, high rates of illiteracy, high rates of population growth, and low rates of growth in average real per capita income. In international trade, the economic relationship between developed and developing nations has been characterized by developing nations exporting primarily food and raw materials in exchange for manufactured goods from developed nations.

Though the level and the rate of economic development depend primarily on internal conditions in developing nations, international trade can contribute significantly to the development process. There are, however, some economists who strongly believe that international trade and the functioning of the present international monetary system have hindered rather than facilitated development through secularly declining terms of trade and wildly fluctuating export earnings for developing nations. Indeed, these economists contend that standard international trade theory based on comparative advantage is completely irrelevant for developing nations and the development process. Therefore, they advocate industrialization through import substitution (i.e., the domestic production of manufactured goods previously imported) and generally placing less reliance on international trade by developing nations. They also advocate reform of the present international monetary system to make it more responsive to the special needs of developing nations.

In this chapter, we will be examining all of these topics. The presentation will necessarily be brief, since these issues are discussed in detail in courses and textbooks in development economics. In section 11.2, we examine the relationship between international trade and economic development in general. In section 11.3, we discuss the terms of trade and their effect on economic development, and we do the same for export instability in section 11.4. Section 11.5 then examines the policy of development through import substitution or through exports. Finally, in section 11.6, we examine and evaluate the demands of developing nations for a "new international economic order."

11.2   The Importance of Trade to Development

In this section, we first analyze the claim that international trade theory is completely irrelevant for developing nations and to the development process. Then we examine the ways in which international trade operated as an "engine of growth" for the so-called regions of recent settlement in the nineteenth century and the reasons it can no longer be relied upon to the same extent by today's developing nations. We will complete this section on a positive note by examining all of the important ways in which international trade can still contribute to the process of economic development today.

11.2a   Trade Theory and Economic Development

According to traditional trade theory, if each nation specializes in the production of the commodity of its comparative advantage, world output will be greater and, through trade, each nation will share in the gain. With the present distribution of factor endowments and technology between developed and developing nations, the theory of comparative advantage thus prescribes that developing nations should continue to specialize in the production of and export raw materials, fuels, minerals, and food to developed nations in exchange for manufactured products.

While this may maximize welfare in the short run, developing nations believe that this pattern of specialization and trade relegates them to a subordinate position vis-à-vis developed nations, and keeps them from reaping the *dynamic* benefits of industry and from maximizing their welfare in the long run. The dynamic benefits resulting from industrial production are a more trained labor force, more innovations, higher and more stable prices for the nation's exports, and higher income for its people. With developing nations specializing in primary commodities and developed nations specializing in manufactured products, all or most of these dynamic benefits of industry and trade accrue to developed nations, leaving developing nations poor, undeveloped, and dependent. This belief is reinforced by the observation that all developed nations are primarily industrial while all developing nations are primarily agricultural or engaged in mineral extraction.

Thus, developing nations attack traditional trade theory as completely static and irrelevant to the development process. They view traditional trade theory as involving *adjustment* to existing conditions, while development necessarily requires *changing* existing conditions. In short, traditional trade theory may maximize welfare at one point in time but not over time. As a result, developing nations demand changes in the pattern of trade and reform of the present international economic system to take into consideration their special development needs.

These are serious charges which, if entirely true, would indeed make traditional trade theory irrelevant to the process of economic development. However, as shown in Chapter 7 (dealing with economic growth and international trade), traditional trade theory can readily be extended to incorporate changes in factor supplies, technology, and tastes by the technique of comparative statics. What this means is that a nation's pattern of development is not determined once and for all, but must be recomputed as underlying conditions change or are expected to change over time. Therefore, developing nations are not necessarily or always relegated by traditional trade theory to export mostly primary commodities and import mostly manufactured products. For example, as a developing nation accumulates capital and improves its technology, its comparative advantage shifts away from primary products to simple manufactured goods first and then to more sophisticated ones. To some extent, this is already occurring in Brazil, Korea, Taiwan, Mexico, and some other developing nations.

Furthermore, the dynamic benefits from industry can theoretically be incorporated into the original calculations of comparative advantage and in subsequent changes in comparative advantage over time. This may indicate that the expansion of industrial production does not always represent the best use of the developing nation's scarce resources—as some of these nations have now come to realize. Thus, while the need for a truly dynamic theory cannot be negated, comparative statics can carry us a long way toward incorporating dynamic changes in the economy into traditional trade theory. As a result, traditional trade theory, with the qualifications noted above, is of relevance even for developing nations and the development process. At least, this is the feeling of most "middle-of-the-road" economists who have studied the problem.

11.2b Trade as an Engine of Growth

During the nineteenth century, most of the world's modern industrial production was concentrated in Great Britain. Large increases in industrial production and population in resource-poor Britain led to a rapidly rising demand for the food and raw material exports of the **regions of recent settlement** (the United States, Canada, Australia, New Zealand, Argentina, Uruguay, and South Africa). For example, during the century from 1815 to 1913, Britain's population tripled, its real GNP increased 10 times, and the volume of its imports increased 20 times. This growth spread to the rest of the economy of these newly settled lands through the familiar accelerator-multiplier process. Thus, according to *Nurkse*, the export sector was the leading sector that propelled these economies into rapid growth and development. That is, international trade functioned as an **engine of growth** for these nations during the nineteenth century.

The regions of recent settlement were able to satisfy Britain's burgeoning demand for food and raw materials (and in the process grow very rapidly) because of several favorable circumstances. First, these countries were richly endowed with natural resources such as fertile arable land, forests, and mineral deposits. Second, workers with various skills moved in great waves from overpopulated Europe to these mostly empty lands, and so did huge amounts of capital. Though data are far from precise, it seems that from 30 to 50 percent of total capital formation (i.e., investments) in such nations as Canada, Argentina, and Australia was financed through capital inflows. The huge inflows of capital and workers made possible the construction of railroads, canals, and other facilities that allowed the opening up of new supply sources of food and raw materials. Finally, the great improvement in sea transportation enabled these new lands to satisfy the rising demand for wheat, corn, cotton, wool, leather, and a variety of other foods and raw materials more cheaply than traditional sources of supply in Europe and elsewhere.

Thus, all "ingredients" were present for rapid growth in these new lands: the demand for their products was rising rapidly; they had great and unexploited natural resources; and they received huge amounts of capital and millions of workers from Europe. To be sure, there are some economists, notably *Kravis*, who believe (and have presented data that seem to show) that the rapid growth of the regions of recent settlement during the nineteenth century was due primarily to very favorable internal conditions (such as abundant natural resources), with trade playing only an important *supportive* role. Be that as it may, it is generally agreed that today's developing nations can rely much less on trade for their growth and development. This is due both to less favorable demand and supply conditions.

On the demand side, it is pointed out that the demand for food and raw materials is growing much less rapidly today than it was the case for the regions of recent settlement during the nineteenth century. There are several reasons for this. (1) The income elasticity of demand in developed nations for many of the food and agricultural raw material exports of developing nations is less (and sometimes much less) than 1, so that as income rises in developed nations, their demand for the agricultural exports of developing nations increases proportionally less than the increase in income. For example, the income elasticity of demand for coffee is about 0.8, for cocoa 0.5, for sugar 0.4, and for tea 0.1. (2) The development of synthetic substitutes has reduced the demand for natural raw materials; for example, synthetic rubber has reduced the demand for natural rubber, nylon the demand for cotton, and plastics the demand for hides and skins. (3) Technological advances have reduced the raw-material content of many products, such as tin-plated cans and microcircuits. (4) The output of services (with lower raw material requirements than commodities) has grown faster than the output of commodities in developed nations. (5) Developed nations have imposed trade restriction on many temperate exports (such as wheat, vegetables, sugar, oils, and other products) of developing nations.

On the supply side, *Cairncross* has pointed out that most of today's developing nations are much less well endowed with natural resources (except for petroleum-exporting nations) than were the regions of recent settlement during the nineteenth century. In addition, most of today's developing nations are overpopulated, so that most of any increase in their output of food and raw materials is absorbed domestically rather than exported. Furthermore, the international flow of capital to developing nations today is relatively much less than it was in the nineteenth century, and today's developing nations seem also to face an outflow of skilled labor rather than an inflow (these topics are discussed in Chapter 12). Finally, it is also true that until recently developing nations have somewhat neglected their agriculture in favor of more rapid industrialization, thereby hampering their export (and development) prospects.

11.2c   The Contributions of Trade to Development

Even though international trade cannot be expected to be an "engine of growth" today, there are still many ways (besides the static gains from comparative advantage) by which it can contribute to the economic development of today's developing nations. *Haberler*, among others, has pointed out the following important beneficial effects that international trade can have on economic development. (1) Trade can lead to the full utilization of otherwise underemployed domestic resources. That is, through trade, a developing nation can move from an inefficient production point inside its production frontier, with unutilized resources because of insufficient internal demand, to a point on its production frontier with trade. For such a nation, trade would represent a **vent for surplus,** or an outlet for its potential surplus of agricultural commodities and raw materials. This has indeed occurred in many developing nations, particularly those in Southeast Asia and West Africa.

In addition, (2) by expanding the size of the market, trade makes possible division of labor and economies of scale. This is especially important and has actually taken place in the production of light manufactures in such small economic units as Taiwan, Hong Kong, and Singapore. (3) International trade is the vehicle for the transmission of new ideas, new technology, and new managerial and other skills. (4) Trade also stimulates and facilitates the international flow of capital from developed to developing nations. In the case of direct foreign investments, where the foreign firm retains managerial control over its investment, the foreign capital is likely to be accompanied by foreign skilled personnel to operate it. (There is, however, a great deal of controversy surrounding the costs and benefits of foreign capital to the developing host nation. These are examined in detail in the next chapter.) (5) In several large developing nations, such as Brazil and India, the importation of new manufactured products has stimulated domestic demand until efficient domestic production of these goods became feasible. Finally, (6) international trade is an excellent antimonopoly weapon (when allowed to operate) because it stimulates greater efficiency by domestic producers to meet foreign competition. This is particularly important to keep low the cost and price of intermediate or semifinished products used as inputs in the domestic production of other commodities.

Critics of international trade can match this impressive list of benefits with an equally impressive list of the allegedly harmful effects of trade. However, since a developing nation can refuse to trade if it gains nothing or loses, the presumption is that it must also gain from trade. It is true that when most of the gains from trade accrue to developed nations, there is a great deal of dissatisfaction and justification for demands to rectify the situation, but this should not be construed to mean that trade is actually harmful. One can, of course, always find cases where, on balance, international trade may actually have hampered economic development. However, in most cases it can be expected to provide invaluable assistance to the development process. This has been confirmed empirically by *Michaely, Balassa*, and this author. Even the Soviet Union and China, which for security and ideological reasons strive for self-sufficiency, have recently come to appreciate the benefits that international trade can make to their growth and development.

11.3   The Terms of Trade and Economic Development

In this section, we first define the various terms of trade. We then analyze the alleged reasons for expecting the commodity terms of trade of developing nations to deteriorate. Finally, we present the results of some empirical studies that have attempted to measure the change in developing nations' commodity and income terms of trade over time.

11.3a   The Various Terms of Trade

In section 4.5, we defined the commodity, or net barter, terms of trade. However, there are several other types of terms of trade. These are the income terms of trade, the single factoral terms of trade, and the double factoral terms of trade. We will define each of these terms of trade, give an example of each, and explain their significance.

In section 4.5, we defined the **commodity,** or **net barter, terms of trade** (N) as the ratio of the price index of the nation's exports (P_x) to the price index of its imports (P_M) multiplied by 100 (to express the terms of trade in percentages). That is,

$$N = (P_x/P_M)100 \qquad\qquad (11\text{-}1)$$

For example, if we take 1950 as the base year (N = 100), and we find that by the end of 1986 the nation's P_x fell by 5 percent (to 95) while its P_M rose by 10 percent (to 110), then this nation's commodity terms of trade declined to:

$$N = (95/110)100 = 86.36$$

This means that between 1950 and 1986 the nation's export prices fell by about 14 percent in relation to its import prices.

A nation's **income terms of trade** (I) are given by:

$$I = (P_x/P_M)Q_x \qquad\qquad (11\text{-}2)$$

where Q_x is an index of the *volume* of exports. Thus, I measures the nation's export-based capacity to import. Returning to our example, if Q_x rose from 100 in 1950 to 120 in 1986, then the nation's income terms of trade rose to:

$$I = (95/110)120 = (0.8636)(120) = 103.63$$

This means that from 1950 to 1986 the nation's capacity to import (based on its export earnings) increased by 3.63 percent (even though P_x/P_M declined). The change in the income terms of trade is very important for developing nations since they rely to a large extent on imported capital goods for their development.

A nation's **single factoral terms of trade** (S) are given by:

$$S = (P_x/P_M)Z_x \qquad\qquad (11\text{-}3)$$

where Z_x is a *productivity* index in the nation's export sector. Thus, S measures the amount of imports the nation gets per unit of domestic factors of production embodied in its exports. For example, if productivity in the nation's export sector rose from 100 to 1950 to 130 in 1986, then the nation's single factoral terms of trade increased to:

$$S = (95/110)130 = (0.8636)(130) = 112.27$$

This means that in 1986 the nation received 12.27 percent more imports per unit of domestic factors embodied in its exports than it did in 1950. Even though the nation shares part of its productivity increase in its export sector with other nations, the nation is better off in 1986 than it was in 1950 (by more than indicated by the increase in *I* and even though *N* declined).

The concept of the single factoral terms of trade can be extended to measure the nation's **double factoral terms of trade** (*D*), given by:

$$D = (P_x/P_M)(Z_x/Z_M)100 \qquad (11\text{-}4)$$

where Z_m is an *import* productivity index. Thus, *D* measures how many units of domestic factors embodied in the nation's exports are exchanged per unit of *foreign* factors embodied in its imports. For example, if Z_M rises from 100 to 105 between 1950 and 1986, then *D* rises to:

$$D = (95/110)(130/105) = (0.8636)(1.2381)(100) = 106.92$$

Of the four terms of trade defined, *N, I,* and *S* are the most important. *D* does not have much significance for developing nations and is very seldom if ever measured (it was included here only for the sake of completeness). The most significant terms of trade for developing nations are *I* and *S*. However, since *N* is the easiest to measure, most of the discussion in the economic literature has been in terms of *N*. Indeed, *N* is often referred to simply as "the terms of trade." As we have seen in the above examples, *I* and *S* can rise even when *N* declines. This is generally regarded as favorable to a developing nation. Of course, the most favorable situation is when *N, I,* and *S* all increase. On the other hand, the worst possible situation from the point of view of a developing nation occurs when all three terms of trade deteriorate. This may lead to *immiserizing growth,* discussed in section 7.5b.

11.3b Alleged Reasons for Deterioration in the Commodity Terms of Trade

According to such economists as *Prebisch, Singer,* and *Myrdal,* the *commodity terms of trade* of developing nations tend to deteriorate over time. The reason is that most or all of the productivity increases that take place in developed nations are passed on to their workers in the form of higher wages and income, while most or all of the productivity increases that take place in developing nations are reflected in lower prices. Thus, developed nations, so the argument goes, have the best of both worlds. They retain the benefits of their own productivity increases in the form of higher wages and income for their workers, and at the same time they also reap most of the benefits from the productivity increases taking place in developing nations through the lower prices that they are able to pay for the agricultural exports of developing nations.

The very different response to productivity increases in developed and developing nations is due to the widely differing conditions in their internal labor markets. Specifically, because labor is relatively scarce in developed nations and labor unions are strong, most of the productivity increases in developed nations are extracted by labor in the form of higher wages, leaving costs of production and prices more or less unchanged. Indeed, labor in these nations is often able to extract wage increases that are even higher than their productivity increases. This raises costs of production and the prices of the manufactured goods that developed nations export. On the other hand, because of surplus labor, large unemployment, and weak or nonexistent labor unions in most developing nations, all or most of the increases in productivity taking place in these nations are reflected in lower production costs and in lower prices for their agricultural exports.

If all productivity increases were reflected in lower commodity prices in both developed and developing nations, the terms of trade of developing nations should improve over time. The reason is that productivity increases in agriculture are generally smaller than in industry. Therefore, the cost and prices of manufactured goods should fall in relation to the prices of agricultural commodities. Since developed nations export mostly manufactured goods and import mostly agricultural commodities and raw materials, their terms of trade should deteriorate, so that the terms of trade of developing nations (the inverse, or reciprocal) should improve over time. It is because productivity increases are reflected in higher wages in developed countries but in lower prices in developing countries that, according to Prebisch, Singer and Myrdal, we can expect a secular deterioration in the collective terms of trade of developing nations.

Another reason for expecting the terms of trade of developing nations to deteriorate is that their demand for the manufactured exports of developed nations tends to grow much faster than the latter's demand for the agricultural exports of developing nations. This is due to the much higher income elasticity of demand for manufactured goods than for agricultural commodities. For these reasons, the deterioration in the terms of trade of developing nations could be so great as to make them worse off with trade than without it.

While these arguments seem to make some sense, it is difficult to evaluate them on theoretical grounds alone. In the meantime, they have generated a great deal of controversy and have led to many attempts to measure the movement in the terms of trade of developing nations over time.

11.3c Historical Movement in the Commodity and Income Terms of Trade

Prebisch and Singer based their belief that the (commodity) terms of trade of developing nations tend to deteriorate on a 1949 United Nations study that showed that the terms of trade of the United Kingdom rose from 100 in 1870 to 170 in 1938. Since the United Kingdom exported manufactured goods and imported food and raw materials, while developing nations exported food and raw materials and imported manufactured goods, Prebisch and Singer inferred from this that the terms of trade of developing nations (the inverse of the terms of trade of the United Kingdom) fell from 100 to $100/170 = 59$.

This conclusion was seriously challenged on several grounds. First of all, since the prices of exports and imports were measured at dockside in the United Kingdom, a great deal of the observed relative decline in the price of food and raw material imports of the United Kingdom reflected the sharp decline in the cost of ocean transportation that occurred over this period and not lower relative prices received by exporting nations. Second, the higher relative prices received by the United Kingdom for its manufactured exports reflected the greater quality improvements in manufactured goods than in primary commodities. For example, a typewriter today does many more things automatically than a typewriter of twenty or thirty years ago, whereas a pound of coffee today is not much different from a pound of coffee of previous years. Therefore, it is only natural that the price of some manufactured goods should rise in relation to the price of primary commodities. Third, developed nations also export some primary commodities (witness the large agricultural exports of the United States) and developing nations also export some manufactured goods. Consequently, measuring the terms of trade of developing nations as the price of traded primary commodities divided by the price of traded manufactured goods is not entirely valid. Fourth, the study ended in a depression year when prices of primary commodities were abnormally low, so that the increase in the terms of trade of the United Kingdom (and thereafter the decline in the terms of trade of developing nations) was greatly overestimated.

Such criticisms stimulated other empirical studies that attempted to overcome the shortcomings of the United Nations study. One of these is the study published in 1956 by *Kindleberger*, in which he concluded that the terms of trade of developing nations vis-à-vis Western Europe declined only slightly from 1870 to 1952. However, he also could not take quality changes into account. A 1963 study by *Lipsey* found that the terms of trade of developing nations in relation to those of the United States did not suffer any continuous downward trend from 1880 to 1960. They rose before World War I and from World War II to 1952 and declined since then. These conclusions seem confirmed for the post-World War II period by a 1975 United Nations study that found that between 1952 and 1972 the terms of trade of developing nations declined by about 1.6 percent per year when petroleum products were excluded. More recently (1980), *Spraos* dismissed most of the criticisms raised against the original conclusions of Prebisch and Singer and confirmed that the commodity terms of trade of developing nations deteriorated from 1870 to 1938, but much less than they had indicated. By including the postwar period until 1970 into the analysis, however, Spraos found no evidence of deterioration. Finally, by greatly refining the method of measurement, *Michaely* found that the terms of trade of developing countries actually improved somewhat from 1952 to 1970.

Several important conclusions emerge from these studies. First, whatever overall secular trends there may have been in the commodity terms of trade of developing countries, they were relatively small in magnitude. Second, estimating the change in the secular terms of trade inevitably faces serious statistical difficulties. For example, results are very sensitive to which years are taken as the beginning and the end of the data series and the way the price indices of exports and imports are calculated. Third, the movement in the overall terms of trade of all developing nations does not have much relevance for individual developing nations. For example, a developing nation exporting mostly minerals may find its terms of trade rising, while a developing nation exporting primarily tropical products such as rubber, tea, and coffee is likely to experience deteriorating terms of trade. Fourth, most studies found that, regardless of the secular movement in the *commodity terms of trade*, the overall *income terms of trade* of developing nations as a group have increased substantially over time because of sharply rising volumes of exports. For example, *Wilson* found that between 1950 and 1965 the commodity terms of trade of developing nations declined 9 percent, but their income terms of trade increased by 56 percent (and as pointed out earlier, the income terms of trade are more important than the commodity terms of trade for developing nations). Finally, attempts to measure the factoral terms of trade have been seriously hampered by the difficulty of obtaining measures of productivity changes.

11.4   Export Instability and Economic Development

Independently of deteriorating long-run or secular terms of trade, developing nations may also face large *short-run fluctuations* in their export prices and earnings that could seriously hamper their development. In this section, we concentrate on this short-run instability. We first analyze from a theoretical point of view the causes and effects of short-run fluctuations in the export prices and earnings of developing nations. Then we present the results of some empirical studies that have attempted to measure the magnitude of these short-run fluctuations and their actual effect on development. Finally, we discuss briefly international commodity agreements directed at stabilizing and increasing the export prices and earnings of developing nations.

11.4a   Cause and Effects of Export Instability

Developing nations often experience wild fluctuations in the prices of their primary exports. This is due to both inelastic and unstable demand and supply. In Figure 11-1, D and S represent, respectively, the steeply inclined (inelastic) hypothetical demand and supply curves of developing nations' primary exports. With D and S, the equilibrium price is P. If for whatever reason D decreases (shifts to the left) to D' or S increases (shifts to the right) to S', the equilibrium price falls sharply to P'. If both D and S shift at the same time to D' and S', the equilibrium price falls even more, to P''. If then D' and S' shift back to D and S, the equilibrium price rises very sharply and returns to P. Thus, inelastic (i.e., steeply inclined) and unstable (i.e., shifting) demand and supply curves for the primary exports of developing countries can lead to wild fluctuations in the prices that these nations receive for their exports.

But why should the demand and supply curves of the primary exports of developing nations be inelastic and shifting? The demand for many primary exports of developing nations is price inelastic because individual households in developed nations spend only a small proportion of their income on such commodities as coffee, tea, cocoa, and sugar. Consequently, when the prices of these commodities change, households do not significantly change their purchases of these commodities, resulting in a price-inelastic demand. On the other hand, the demand for many minerals is price inelastic because few substitutes are available. At the same time, the demand for the primary exports of developing nations is unstable because of business cycle fluctuations in developing nations.

Turning to the supply side, we find that the supply of the primary exports of developing nations is price inelastic (i.e., the quantities supplied do not respond very much to changes in their prices) because of internal rigidities and inflexibilities in resource uses in most developing nations, especially in the case of tree crops that involve long gestation periods. Supplies are unstable or shifting because of weather conditions, pests, and so on.

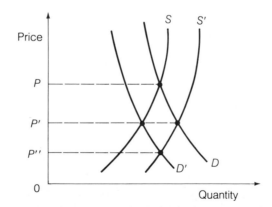

FIGURE 11-1. Price Instability and the Primary Exports of Developing Nations

D and *S* refer, respectively, to the demand and supply curves of the primary exports of developing nations. With *D* and *S,* the equilibrium price is *P*. If *D* shifts to *D'* or *S* to *S'*, the equilibrium price falls sharply to *P'*. If both *D* and *S* shift to *D'* and *S'*, the equilibrium price falls even more, to *P''*. If, subsequently, *D'* and *S'* shift back up to *D* and *S*, the equilibrium price moves back up to *P*. Thus, price-inelastic and unstable *D* and *S* curves may lead to wild price fluctuations.

Because of wildly fluctuating export prices, the export *earnings* of developing nations are also expected to vary significantly from year to year. When export earnings rise, exporters increase their consumption expenditures, investments, and bank deposits. The effects of these are magnified and transmitted to the rest of the economy by the familiar multiplier-accelerator process. The subsequent fall in export earnings results in a multiple contraction of national income, savings, and investment. This alternation of boom and bust periods renders development planning (which depends on imported machinery, fuels, and raw materials) much more difficult.

11.4b   Measurements of Export Instability and Its Effect on Development

In a well-known study published in 1966, *MacBean* found that over the 1946–1958 period the index of instability of export earnings (defined as the average percentage deviation of the dollar value of export proceeds from a five-year moving average and measured on a scale of 0 to 100) was 23 for a group of 45 developing nations and 18 for a group of 18 developed nations for which data were available.

These empirical results seem to indicate that, while **export instability** is somewhat larger for developing nations than for developed nations, the degree of instability itself is not very large *in an absolute sense* when measured on a scale of 0 to 100. MacBean also showed that the greater instability of export earnings of developing nations is not due, as previously believed, to the fact that these nations export only a few commodities or export these commodities to only a few nations (i.e., to commodity and geographic *concentration* of trade) but depends primarily on the type of commodities exported. For example, those nations exporting such commodities as rubber, jute, and cocoa face much more unstable export earnings than developing nations exporting petroleum, bananas, sugar, and tobacco.

MacBean further showed that the greater fluctuation in the export earnings of developing nations did not lead to significant fluctuations in their national incomes, savings, and investments and did not seem to interfere much with their development efforts. This was probably due to the relatively low absolute level of instability and to the fact that very low foreign trade multipliers insulated the economies of developing nations from fluctuations in their export earnings. These results led MacBean to conclude that the very costly international commodity agreements demanded by developing nations to stabilize their export earnings were not justified. The same resources could be used more profitably for truly development purposes than to stabilize export earnings, which were not very unstable to begin with.

Subsequent studies by *Erb* and *Schiavo-Campo* (1969), *Massell* (1970), *Mathieson* and *McKinnon* (1974), *Lancieri* (1978), *Brudel, Horn,* and *Svedberg*

(1980), and *Savvides* (1984) confirm for later periods MacBean's results that export instability was not very large and that it has not hampered development. Despite these conclusions, developing countries continue to demand international commodity agreements to stabilize and increase their export earnings.

11.4c International Commodity Agreements

The stabilization of export prices *for individual producers* in developing nations could be achieved by purely domestic schemes such as the **marketing boards** set up after World War II. These operated by purchasing the output of domestic producers at the stable prices set by the board, which would then export the commodities at fluctuating world prices. In good years, domestic prices were to be set below world prices so that the board could accumulate funds, which it would then disburse in bad years by paying domestic producers higher than world prices. Examples are the cocoa marketing board of Ghana and the rice marketing board of Burma. However, only a few of these marketing boards met with some degree of success because of the great difficulty in correctly anticipating the domestic prices that would average out world prices over time, and because of corruption.

Developing nations, however, are most interested in **international commodity agreements** because they also offer the possibility of *increasing* their export prices and earnings. There are three basic types of international commodity agreements: buffer stocks, export controls, and purchase contracts.

Buffer stocks involve the purchase of the commodity (to be added to the stock) when the commodity price falls below an agreed minimum price, and the sale of the commodity out of the stock when the commodity price rises above the established maximum price. Buffer stock agreements have certain disadvantages: (1) some commodities can be stored only at a very high cost; (2) if the minimum price is set above the equilibrium level, the stock grows larger and larger over time. An example of a buffer stock arrangement is the *International Tin Agreement*. This was set up in 1956 but, after a number of years of successful operation, is now near collapse. The same is true for the *International Cocoa Agreement* and the *International Natural Rubber Agreement*. At the beginning of 1986, the buffer stock of rubber was bulging with 375,000 metric tons of rubber at a cost of about $300 million per year. Yet, rubber prices remain close to the bottom of the support range.

Export controls seek to regulate the quantity of a commodity exported by each nation in order to stabilize commodity prices. The main advantage of an export control agreement is that it avoids the cost of maintaining stocks. The main disadvantage is that (as with any quota system) it introduces inefficiencies and requires that all major exporters of the commodity participate (in the face of strong incentives for each of them to remain outside or cheat on the agreement). An example is the *International Sugar Agreement*. This was negotiated in 1954 but has generally been unable to stabilize and raise sugar prices because of the ability of developed nations to increase their own production of beet sugar. The only exception to the downward price spiral is coffee, the price of which has been successfully stabilized at a high level by the *International Coffee Agreement* set up in 1962. In general, however, commodity prices have been declining during the 1980s. As pointed out in section 9.3c, even OPEC is now in disarray as over-supply of petroleum products and reduced demand has caused large price declines in the 1980s, after the sharp price increases of the 1970s.

Purchase contracts are long-term multilateral agreements that stipulate a minimum price at which importing nations agree to purchase a specified quantity of the commodity and a maximum price at which exporting nations agree to sell specified amounts of the commodity. Purchase contracts thus avoid the disadvantages of buffer stocks and export controls but result in a two-price system for the commodity. An example is the *International Wheat Agreement,* which was signed in 1949. This agreement, however, affects primarily the United States, Canada, and Australia rather than developing nations, and it became inoperative when, as a result of the huge wheat purchases by the Soviet Union since the early 1970s, wheat prices rose sharply above the established price ceiling.

The international commodity agreements mentioned above are the only ones of any significance to have been operational at one time or another since World War II. However, as noted above, with the exception of the International Coffee Agreement, they either failed or have had very limited success in stabilizing and increasing the export prices and earnings of developing nations. One reason for this is the very high cost of operating them and the general lack of support by developed nations since they would have to shoulder most of the burden of setting up and running these international agreements. Developing nations, however, continue to make international commodity agreements the centerpiece of their demands for a new international economic order. This will be discussed in section 11.6d.

To be noted is that in the evaluation of international commodity agreements, it is important to determine whether prices or earnings are to be stabilized and whether instability results from shifts in the demand curve or in the supply curve (this is left as an end-of-chapter problem).

A modest compensatory financing scheme was set up in the early 1970s by the International Monetary Fund (IMF) for developing nations whose export earnings in any one year fall below the previous five-year moving average (this is discussed in Chapter 20). A similar scheme was set up in 1975 with a $400-million fund by the European Economic Community (EEC) for the 46 Lomé Convention countries in Africa, the Caribbean, and the Pacific. However, these are very modest programs and fall far short of what developing nations are demanding. Nevertheless, compensatory financing schemes could provide many of the benefits and avoid most of the problems associated with international commodity agreements.

11.5   Import Substitution Versus Export Orientation

We now examine the reasons why developing nations want to industrialize and the advantages and disadvantages of industrialization through import substitution versus exports. We will then evaluate the results of the policy of import substitution, which most developing nations chose as their strategy for industrialization and development during the 1950s and 1960s.

11.5a.   Development Through Import Substitution versus Exports

During the 1950s and 1960s most developing nations made a deliberate attempt to industrialize rather than continuing to specialize in the production of primary commodities (food, raw materials, and minerals) for export, as prescribed by traditional trade theory. Industrialization was relied upon to provide (1) faster technological progress, (2) the creation of high-paying jobs to relieve the serious unemployment and underemployment problems faced by most developing nations, (3) higher multipliers and accelerators through greater backward and forward linkages in production process, (4) rising terms of trade and more stable export prices and earnings, and (5) relief from balance-of-payments difficulties resulting because the demand of developing nations for manufactured products rises faster than their export earnings. The desire of developing nations to industrialize is natural in view of the fact that all rich nations are industrial while most poor nations are primarily agricultural.

Having decided to industrialize, developing nations had to choose between industrialization through import substitution and export-oriented industrialization. Both policies have advantages and disadvantages. **Industrialization through import substitution** has three main advantages. (1) The market for the industrial product already exists, as evidenced by imports of the commodity, so that risks are reduced in setting up an industry to replace imports. (2) It is easier for developing nations to protect their domestic market against foreign competition than to force developed nations to lower trade barriers against their manufactured exports. (3) Foreign firms are induced to establish so-called tariff factories to overcome the tariff wall of developing nations.

Against these advantages are the following disadvantages. (1) Domestic industries grow accustomed to protection from foreign competition and have no incentive to become more efficient. (2) Import substitution leads to inefficient industries because the smallness of the domestic market in many developing nations does not allow them to take advantage of economies of scale. (3) After the simpler manufactured imports are replaced by domestic production, import substitution becomes more and more difficult and costly (in terms of the higher protection and inefficiency) as more capital-intensive and technologically advanced imports have to be replaced by domestic production.

Export-oriented industrialization also has advantages and disadvantages.

Advantages include the following. (1) It overcomes the smallness of the domestic market and allows a developing nation to take advantage of economies of scale. This is particularly important for the many developing countries that are both very poor and small. (2) Production of manufactured goods for export requires and stimulates efficiency throughout the economy. This is especially important when the output of an industry is used as an input of another domestic industry. (3) The expansion of manufactured exports is not limited (as in the case of import substitution) by the growth of the domestic market.

On the other hand, there are two serious disadvantages. (1) It may be very difficult for developing nations to set up export industries because of the competition from the more established and efficient industries in developed nations. (2) Developed nations often provide a high level of effective protection for their simple labor-intensive commodities in which developing nations already have or can soon acquire a comparative advantage.

During the 1950s and 1960s, most developing nations, particularly the larger ones, strongly opted for a policy of import substitution to industrialize. They protected their infant industries or stimulated their birth with effective tariff rates that rose sharply with the degree of processing. This was done at first to encourage the relatively simple step of assembling foreign parts, in the hope that subsequently more of these parts and intermediary products could be produced domestically (backward linkage). Heavy protection of domestic industries also stimulated the establishment of tariff factories in developing nations.

11.5b   The Experience with Import Substitution

The policy of industrialization through import substitution generally met with only limited success or with failure. Very high rates of effective protection, in the range of 100 to 200 percent or more, were common in such nations as India, Pakistan, Argentina, and Brazil. These led to very inefficient domestic industries and very high prices for domestic consumers. Sometimes the foreign currency value of imported inputs was greater than the foreign currency value of the output produced (negative value added).

Heavy protection and subsidies to industry led to excessive capital intensity and relatively little labor absorption. For example, the capital intensity in the production of steel is almost as high in such a relatively capital-poor nation as India as it is in the United States. This quickly exhausted the meager investment funds available to developing nations and created only a few jobs. Furthermore, the highest priority was given to the construction of new factories and the purchase of new machinery, with the result of widespread idle plant capacity for lack of funds to purchase needed raw material and fuel imports. One-shift operation of plants also contributed to excessive capital intensity and low labor absorption in developing nations.

The policy of import substitution and excessive capital intensity resulted in the absorption of only a small proportion of the yearly increase in the labor force of developing nations, thus generally aggravating their unemployment and underemployment problems. Indeed, it was entirely unrealistic to expect that import substitution could solve the unemployment and underemployment problems of developing nations. For example, even with 25 percent of the labor force in industry and 20 percent growth of industrial output per year, at most 0.5 percent (0.25 times 0.20) of the 2 to 3 percent annual increase in the labor force of developing nations could be absorbed into modern industry. The other workers must be absorbed into agriculture and in the traditional service sector, or remain unemployed. In addition, the hope of finding high-paying jobs in the modern sector attracted many more people to the cities than could find employment, leading to an explosive situation.

The effort to industrialize through import substitution also led to the neglect of agriculture and other primary sectors, with the result that many developing nations experienced a decline in their earnings from traditional exports, and some (such as Brazil) were even forced to import some food products that they had previously exported. Furthermore, the policy of import substitution often aggravated the balance-of-payments problems of developing nations by requiring more imports of machinery, raw materials, fuels, and even food.

The overall result was that those developing nations (such as India, Pakistan, and Argentina) that stressed industrialization through import substitution fared much worse and grew at a much slower rate than the few (smaller) developing economies (such as Singapore, Taiwan, and Hong Kong) that followed from the early 1950s an export-oriented policy. It has been estimated that the policy of import substitution resulted in waste of up to 10 percent of the national income of developing nations.

Starting in the 1970s, many developing nations began to pay more attention to efficiency considerations and to stress an export-oriented policy. They also started paying more attention to their agriculture. However, developing nations faced the significant trade restrictions imposed by developed nations, which limited the possible benefits from this shift in policies (this is discussed in the next section). Nevertheless, some developing nations—such as Brazil, Argentina, Mexico, and the Philippines—are already showing some benefits from their shift in policies through increased efficiency and rising exports. Others (e.g., India, Pakistan, and Turkey) have been much slower to move in this direction and have fared much worse.

Finally, it must be pointed out that a policy of import substitution may be more beneficial in the early stages of development (especially for larger developing nations), while an export orientation may become an absolute necessity only later in the development process. Thus, rather than being alternatives, policies of import substitution and export orientation could profitably be applied to some extent sequentially, especially in the larger developing nations.

11.6 Current Problems and Demands of Developing Countries

In this section, we examine the current problems facing developing countries and the demands which they make to overcome them. The most serious problems facing developing countries today are (1) the conditions of stark poverty prevailing in many countries, particularly those of sub-Sahara Africa, (2) the huge international debt of most developing countries, especially those of Latin America, and (3) the rising protectionism in developed countries against developing countries' exports. Developing countries seek to overcome these problems by demanding a new international economic order based on the establishment of international commodity agreements, increased access of their exports to developed countries' markets, and increased flow of foreign aid. These topics are discussed in order, starting with the conditions of poverty in many developing countries.

11.6a Poverty in Developing Countries

Table 11-1 gives the average gross national product (GNP) per person in 1983, its growth from 1965 to 1983, and expected growth from 1985 to 1995 in developed noncommunist nations and in developing nations (excluding petroleum-exporting nations). We see that per capita GNP in low-income developing nations is far below that in middle-income developing nations and abysmally low in relation to the per capita GNP in developed nations. Even though growth rates are comparable in all three groups of nations, absolute differences in GNP per person will continue to widen. Although this is far from encouraging for the middle-income group of developing nations, prospects for the low-income group are especially dim because of their present extreme poverty. In fact, because of the drought and famine engulfing most of

TABLE 11-1. *GNP per Person, and Growth and Expected Growth in GNP per Person in Developed and Developing Nations: 1965–1995*

	Population in 1983 (million)	GNP per Person (1983 dollars)	Average Annual Real % Growth		
			1965–83	Low Case 1985–95	High Case 1983–1995
Developed	729	11,060	2.5	2.0	3.7
Developing					
Low income	2,335	260	2.7	2.7	3.4
Middle income	1,165	1,310	3.4	2.6	3.6

Source: World Bank, *Annual Report* (Washington, D.C.: World Bank, 1985).

the African continent, the countries of sub-Sahara are expected to continue to face an *absolute decline* in standard of living for the rest of the decade.

11.6b International Debt Problem of Developing Countries

During the past decade, developing countries have accumulated an **international debt** exceeding $600 billion. They are now finding it very difficult to repay or even service (i.e., pay interest on) this huge debt, and this is seriously hampering their development plans. The debt arose as many developing countries borrowed heavily from private banks in developed nations to finance their growing capital needs and to pay for sharply higher oil bills during the 1970s—all this in the face of slowly expanding exports to developed countries (as the latter entered a period of slow growth). By heavily borrowing abroad, developing countries continued to grow at a relatively rapid pace even during the second half of the 1970s. However, in the early 1980s, their huge and rapidly growing foreign debts caught up with them and large scale defaults were avoided only by repeated large-scale official intervention by the IMF.

Even Mexico rapidly accumulated a huge short-term foreign debt with foreign banks, as it overborrowed against its newly found riches from petroleum. When the price of petroleum started to decline in 1982, Mexico was unable to service its foreign debt (August 1982) and the world was plunged into the so-called debt crisis. At the end of 1985, Mexico had a foreign debt of about $97 billion (more than half of it short term) and faced an annual interest payment on the debt of $13 billion, against a positive trade balance of $8.4 billion. Comparable figures (in billions) were $106, $12.5, and $11 for Brazil, $50, $4, and $3 for Argentina, and $37, $2, and $0.7 for Venezuela. These are the most heavily indebted developing countries. Other heavily indebted nations include Korea, Indonesia, the Philippines, Israel, Chile, Nigeria, and Yugoslavia. By the middle of 1985, Mexico and Venezuela had renegotiated and Brazil and Argentina were in the process of renegotiating their debt repayment schedules and interest payments with their creditor banks in the developed countries, with the help of the IMF and under its general direction. As part of the deal, these nations were required to adopt austerity measures to reduce imports still further and to cut inflation, wage increases, and domestic programs, so as to put domestic growth on a more sustainable basis.

Renegotiation of the foreign debt by the heavily indebted nations, however, only avoided defaults on foreign loans and did not provide a long-term solution to the debt crisis. A long-run solution would necessarily involve increased access for the exports of developing countries to developed-country markets.

Toward the end of summer 1985, the heavily indebted countries of Latin America began to reject the austerity plans advocated by the IMF (as a condition for additional loans) and to demand a renegotiation of existing loans under the threat of default. It was under such circumstances that the United States advanced a new plan to deal with the worsening debt problem at the annual meetings of the International Monetary Fund and World Bank held in Seoul in October 1985. Known as the Baker Plan (for the U.S. Secretary of the Treasury who introduced it), the plan stressed growth over austerity in developing countries, based on a much larger flow of capital from developed nations and international institutions (primarily the World Bank). Specifically, the plan called for additional loans of $20 billion from commercial banks in developed nations and an additional $9 billion from the World Bank to the heavily indebted developing countries over the next three years. Developing countries welcomed the plan and the general direction of the new U.S. thinking on the debt problem, but felt that it did not go far enough. Specifically, they advocate a reduction in the huge outflow of debt interest payments (which for Latin American Countries amounted to $32 billion in 1985). While major American commercial banks (which have the largest concentration of third world loans at risk) strongly supported the plan from the beginning, European and small American commercial banks seemed reluctant to pour fresh loans on top of troublesome ones.

In the final analysis, the continued and increased capital flows from developed to developing countries that are necessary for growth to resume in the latter countries require improvement in the creditworthiness of developing countries and a major shift in the *composition* of the capital flows. Whereas in the early 1970s developing countries were receiving about one dollar of equity (direct investments) for every dollar of debt, in the early 1980s they were receiving less than 20 cents of equity for every dollar of external debt. It is this excess leverage that led to the debt crisis in the early 1980s. Thus, for the debt problem to be overcome and for sustained growth to resume in developing countries, an increase in the flow of equity capital in the form of direct investments and less reliance on short-term borrowing is required. Stripped of all its rhetoric, the Baker plan advanced in Seoul seems primarily aimed at avoiding large scale default on past commercial loans, without leaving much for new development projects.

11.6c   Trade Problems of Developing Countries

Over the past decade, developed countries, beset by slow growth and large unemployment, have increased the trade protection they provide to some of their large industries (such as textile, steel, shipbuilding, consumer electronic products, TV sets, shoes, and many other products) against imports from developing countries. These are the very industries in which developing countries have gained or are gaining a comparative advantage. A great deal of the new protectionism has been directed especially against the manufactured exports of the newly industrializing developing countries (NICs). These nations (Brazil, Hong Kong, Korea, Mexico, Singapore, and Taiwan) are characterized by rapid growth in gross domestic product (GDP), in industrial production, and in manufactured exports. Over the past 20 years, the ratio of the industrial exports of the NICs to the total imports of the developed countries rose from about 1 percent to 4 percent. However, it has been the timing and the type of products exported by the NICs that have led to increased trade restrictions by the developed countries (DCs).

The increased protectionism has occurred in spite of the Generalized System of Preferences (GSP), negotiated by Western European countries and Japan in 1971–1972 and by the U.S. in 1976, which grants preferential access to the exports of developing countries into developed countries' markets. Exception after exception to the GSP have been "voluntarily" negotiated by the U.S. and other developed countries in many products, such as textiles, which are of great importance to developing countries. By 1982, the U.S. had negotiated such bilateral agreements with 29 developing countries and the European Economic Community with 21. In addition, in the trade legislation passed by Congress in October 1984 (which renewed the GSP trade privileges to developing countries), the President was given authority to deny GSP privileges to the NICs that did not curb their own unfair trade practices and restricted U.S. exports. This condition was included in the face of the increase in the NICs' trade surplus with the U.S. from just over $2 billion in 1981 to over $20 billion in 1985.

If the present trend toward protectionism is not soon reversed, we may witness a revival (and justification) of **export pessimism** and a return to inward-looking policies in developing countries. At present, nearly a third of developing countries' exports to industrial countries are restricted by quotas and other NTBs. The opening more widely of developed countries' markets to developing countries exports depends, however, on solving or dealing with the sectoral unemployment problems in developed countries. It is to be hoped that the new multilateral trade negotiations now under way will succeed in reversing the trend toward mounting protectionism.

11.6d Demands for a New International Economic Order

In June 1974 the General Assembly of the United Nations called for the creation of a **New International Economic Order (NIEO).** It did so because of the great poverty in most developing nations and because of the widely held belief that the world economy worked in a way that was unfair to developing countries. To be sure, most of the demands incorporated in an NIEO had been made previously at **United Nations Conferences on Trade and Development (UNCTAD)** in Geneva in 1964, New Delhi in 1968, and Santiago in 1972, and were repeated in Nairobi in 1976, Manila in 1979, and Belgrade in 1983. Besides demands to renegotiate their international debt and reduce interest payments (examined in the previous section), developing countries' demands include (1) establishment of international commodity agreements for many commodities aimed at stabilizing and increasing the export earnings of developing nations and financed primarily by developed nations, (2) preferential access in developed nations' markets to the manufactured exports of developing nations, (3) removing trade barriers on agricultural products in developed nations, (4) increasing the transfer of technology to developing nations and regulating multinational corporations, (5) increasing the yearly flow of foreign aid to developing nations, and (6) allowing developing nations a greater role in international decision making. We will now briefly discuss these demands and what if any progress has been made to date toward fulfilling them.

In previous years, developing nations have made their demand for international commodity agreements (the so-called Integrated Program for Commodities) the centerpiece of their demand for a NIEO. Initially, ten commodities were to be involved: sugar, copper, cotton, coffee, rubber, cocoa, tin, tea, jute, and sisal. However, as pointed out in section 11.4c, past experience with international commodity agreements has been all but encouraging. It was shown that such schemes either end up with unmanageable commodity stocks or must make use of export controls that lead to great inefficiencies. To date little if any progress has been made toward setting up international commodity agreements.

While the establishment of international commodity agreements for many commodities would completely supplant the market mechanism and be very inefficient, the other demands of developing nations could be accommodated within the present international economic system and might even lead to greater all around efficiency. This may be the case for the demands that the manufactured exports of developing nations be given preferential access to the markets of developed nations. Preferential access is demanded rather than simply the elimination of trade barriers because developed nations might reap most of the benefits from the elimination of trade barriers by increasing their own exports (as occurred after the Kennedy and Tokyo Rounds of trade negotiations sponsored by GATT). It is estimated that tariff preferences might increase the manufactured exports of developing nations by $2 to $3 billion annually. Some progress has been made in principle along these lines with the establishment of a Generalized System of Preferences by Western European countries and Japan in 1971–1972 and by the United States and Canada in 1976. However, as pointed out in section 9.5c, many of the most important products for developing nations (such as textiles, shoes, bicycles, and many other simple manufactures) were excluded directly or indirectly (with "voluntary" export quotas).

Another demand of developing nations is for the removal of all trade restrictions that developed nations imposed on agricultural imports from developing nations. It is estimated that this would increase the agricultural exports of developing nations by about $3 billion annually. However, to date (1986), almost nothing has been achieved along these lines because of the strong opposition and disproportionate internal political power of agricultural interests in developed nations. The same has been the fate of demands for the development of an appropriate technology for developing nations, increased transfer of technology from developed nations, and internationally agreed rules of behavior and multinational corporations to eliminate abuses.

On the purely financial side, NIEO demands include increasing foreign aid for developing nations to 0.7 percent of the GNP of developed nations and making such aid multilateral rather than bilateral, distribution of new international monetary reserves (Special Drawing Rights, or SDRs) of the IMF as aid to developing nations (the so-called "link" proposal), and renegotiation of all foreign debts of developing nations. To date, most of these demands have remained unmet. Most developed nations are giving less (and sometimes much less) than the demanded 0.7 percent of their GNP in foreign aid. For example, for the U.S. this figure is 0.23 percent. In addition, most of the aid that the developed nations do give is bilateral. Similarly, there are no current plans to implement the link proposal. It also does not seem wise to tie the creation of new liquidity to development needs. Some developed nations have renegotiated the foreign debts of some developing nations, but these are isolated incidents rather than a general pattern.

Developing nations do have a somewhat greater voice today than in the past in decision making in such international bodies as the United Nations, the World Bank, and the International Monetary Fund, but they are far from controlling these crucial organizations, despite the fact that they greatly outnumber developed nations.

To conclude, we might say that while some of the demands of developing nations have been met in very modest ways and some reforms of the international economic system are likely to take place, it is highly unlikely that a completely new international economic order will be established in the near future.

Summary

1. Though the level and the rate of economic development depend primarily on internal conditions in developing nations, international trade can contribute significantly to the development process. However, there are some economists, notably Prebisch, Singer, and Myrdal, who believe that international trade and the functioning of the present international economic system benefit developed nations at the expense of developing nations.
2. Even though the need for a truly dynamic theory of trade remains, the technique of comparative statics can extend traditional trade theory to incorporate changes in factor endowments, technology, and tastes. Due to less favorable demand and supply conditions, international trade today cannot be expected to be the engine of growth that it was for the regions of recent settlement in the nineteenth century. However, trade can still play a very important supportive role.
3. The commodity, or net barter, terms of trade (N) measure the movement over time in the nation's export prices relative to its import prices. The income terms of trade (I) measure the nation's export-based capacity to import. The single factoral terms of trade (S) measure the amount of imports the nation gets per unit of domestic factors embodied in its exports. I and S are more important than N for developing nations, but most of the discussion and controversy has been in terms of N (since it is the easiest to measure). I and S can rise even if N declines. Prebisch and Singer have argued that N has a tendency to de-

cline for developing nations because most of their productivity increases are reflected in lower prices for their agricultural exports. Empirical studies do not indicate that for developing nations N has declined over the past century or that I has increased substantially because of sharply rising volumes of exports.

4. Independently of deteriorating long-run or secular terms of trade, developing nations also face larger short-run fluctuations in their export prices and earnings than developed nations because of price-inelastic and unstable demand for supply of their exports. However, the absolute level of export instability is not very great and, in most cases, it does not seem to have interfered with development. Nevertheless, developing nations demand international commodity agreements to stabilize and increase their export prices and earnings. These may involve buffer stocks, export controls, or purchasing agreements. Only a very few of these are in operation today and none (except the one for coffee) seems particularly effective. The large expenditures that would be required to set up and run commodity agreements may not represent the best use of resources.

5. During the 1950s and 1960s, most developing nations made a deliberate attempt to industrialize through the policy of import substitution. The results were generally inefficient industries, excessive capital intensity and little labor absorption, neglect of agriculture, and even greater balance-of-payments problems. Since the 1970s, many developing nations have shifted toward export-oriented policies and are paying more attention to their agriculture.

6. The most serious problems facing developing countries today are (1) the conditions of stark poverty prevailing in many countries, particularly those of sub-Sahara Africa, (2) the huge international debt of most developing countries, especially those of Latin America, and (3) the rising protectionism in developed countries against developing countries' exports. Developing countries seek to overcome these problems by demanding a new international economic order (NIEO) at the United Nations and its special agency UNCTAD. This involves the establishment of international commodity agreements for many commodities, preferential access for the simple manufactured exports of developing nations to developed nations' markets, removal of the trade restrictions that developed nations impose on agricultural imports from developing nations, increased transfer of technology to developing nations and controls on multinational corporations, and more foreign aid to developing nations. To date, very little progress has been made toward meeting these demands, and it is highly unlikely that an NIEO will be set up in the near future.

A Look Ahead

So far, we have dealt almost exclusively with commodity trade and assumed no international resource movement. However, capital, labor, and technology do move across national boundaries. In the next chapter (which is the last in Part II), we analyze the costs and benefits of international resource movements on the nations involved. Since multinational corporations are an important vehicle for the international flow of capital, labor, and technology, we also devote a great deal of attention to this relatively new and crucial type of economic enterprise.

Glossary

Regions of recent settlement   The mostly empty and resource-rich lands that Europeans settled during the nineteenth century, such as the United States, Canada, Argentina, Uruguay, Australia, New Zealand, and South Africa.

Engine of growth   The view that exports were the leading sector that propelled the economies of the regions of recent settlement into rapid growth and development during the nineteenth century.

Vent for surplus   The view that exports could be an outlet for the potential surplus of agricultural commodities and raw materials in some developing countries.

Commodity, or net barter, terms of trade   The

ratio of the price index of the nation's exports to the price index of its imports times 100.

Income terms of trade The ratio of the price index of the nation's exports to the price index of its imports times the index of the nation's volume of exports.

Single factoral terms of trade The ratio of the price index of the nation's exports to the price index of its imports times the productivity index in the nation's export sector.

Double factoral terms of trade The measure of how many units of domestic factors embodied in the nation's exports are exchanged per unit of foreign factors embodied in its imports.

Export instability Short-run fluctuations in export prices and earnings.

Marketing Boards National schemes set up by several developing nations after World War II to stabilize export prices for individual producers of an agricultural commodity.

International commodity agreements Organizations of producer and consumer nations attempting to stabilize and increase the prices and earnings of the primary exports of developing nations.

Buffer stocks The type of international commodity agreement that involves the purchase of the commodity (to be added to the stock) when the commodity price falls below an agreed minimum price, and the sale of the commodity out of the stock when the commodity price rises above the established maximum price.

Export controls The type of international commodity agreement that seeks to regulate the quantity of the comodity exported by each nation.

Purchase contracts Long-term multilateral agreements that stipulate the minimum price at which importing nations agree to purchase a specified quantity of the commodity and a maximum price at which exporting nations agree to sell specified amounts of the commodity.

Industrialization through import substitution The policy of industrialization pursued by many developing nations especially during the 1950s and 1960s which in-

volves the replacement of industrial imports with domestically produced products.

Export-oriented industrialization The policy of industrialization pursued by some developing nations which involves increasing the output of manufactured goods for export.

Export pessimism The feeling that developing countries' exports to developed countries cannot grow rapidly because of the latter's increased protectionism.

International debt The hundreds of billions of dollars that developing countries owe to commercial banks in developed countries and which they find difficult to repay or even service (i.e., pay interest on).

New International Economic Order (NIEO) The demands made by developing nations as a group at the United Nations for the removal of the alleged injustices in the operation of the present international economic system and for specific steps to be taken to facilitate their development.

United Nations Conferences on Trade and Development (UNCTAD) Special conferences held under the auspices of the United Nations in 1964, 1968, 1972, 1976, 1979, and 1983 at which developing nations advanced their demands to improve the operation of the present international economic system to facilitate their development.

Questions for Review

1. Why do some economists regard traditional trade theory as irrelevant for developing nations and the development process? How can this charge be answered? In what way was international trade an engine of growth for the regions of recent settlement during the nineteenth century? Why can international trade not be expected to be an engine of growth for today's developing nations? In what ways can international trade still play a very important supportive role for development today?

2. What is meant by the commodity, or net barter, terms of trade? The income terms of trade? The single factoral terms of trade? The dou-

ble factoral terms of trade? Which are the most significant terms of trade for developing nations? Why? What reasons did Prebisch, Singer, and Myrdal give for their belief that the commodity terms of trade of developing nations have a tendency to deteriorate over time?

3. What criticisms have been levied against the United Nations study that Prebisch and Singer quoted in their work to confirm their belief? What conclusions can be reached on the basis of the many empirical studies conducted as to the movement of the commodity and income terms of trade of developing nations over the past century and especially since World War II?

4. What is export instability? What are the alleged causes and effects of export instability on economic development? What are the results of empirical studies on export instability and its effects on economic development? What are international commodity agreements? Why do developing nations want them? What is meant by buffer stocks, export controls, and purchasing agreements? Can you give an example of each?

5. Why do developing nations want to industrialize? What is meant by import substitution? By export-oriented policies? What are the advantages and disadvantages of each as a method of industrialization for developing nations? What has been the experience with import substitution during the past decades? What has this experience led to?

6. What are the major problems facing developing countries today? What are their causes? How do developing countries propose to resolve them? What are the prospects of resolving them in the near future?

Problems

1. Draw a hypothetical production frontier for a developing nation exhibiting increasing costs. Have the horizontal axis measure primary commodities and the vertical axis measure manufactured goods.
   (a) Show the effect on the nation's produc-

tion frontier of an improvement in the technology of primary production only.
   (b) What effect is this type of growth likely to have on the terms of trade of this nation? Why? (Hint: see Chapter 7.)
   (c) Can you show on the same figure how trade could be a vent for surplus for this nation?

*2. Taking the index of export prices, import prices, volume of exports, and productivity in the export sector in a developing nation to be all equal to 100 in 1980, what would be in 1990:
   (a) The commodity terms if trade of this nation if the index of its export prices rises by 10 percent but the index of its import prices rises by 20 percent?
   (b) This nation's income terms of trade if the index of export volume grows to 130 by 1990?
   (c) This nation's single factoral terms of trade if its productivity index in the export sector rises to 140 by 1990?
   (d) Is this nation better or worse off in 1990 compared with 1980? Why?

3. (a) Indicate all the ways in which international trade could retard development.
   (b) Counter each of these criticisms of international trade.

*4. Explain with the use of a graph how deteriorating terms of trade resulting from growth can make a developing nation worse off after growth than before.

5. (a) Draw a figure showing that when the supply of a commodity increases, its equilibrium price will fall by a greater amount, the more price inelastic is the demand curve for the commodity;
   (b) Draw two other figures showing that with a negatively inclined demand curve and a positively inclined supply curve, producers' earnings fluctuate more with a shift in demand than with a shift in supply.

6. (a) With the use of diagrams, show how buffer stocks could either lead to unmanageable stocks of the commodity or run out of the commodity.
   (b) Under what conditions will each occur?

Selected Bibliography

For a problem-solving approach to the topics discussed in this chapter, see:
- D. Salvatore, *Theory and Problems of International Economics*, 2nd ed. (New York: McGraw-Hill, 1984), ch. 5 (sect. 6).
- D. Salvatore and E. Dowling, *Theory and Problems of Development Economics* (New York: McGraw-Hill, 1977), chs. 4 and 8.

For an overall theoretical discussion and empirical tests of the relationship between international trade and economic development, see:
- D. Salvatore, "A Simultaneous Equations Model of Trade and Development with Dynamic Policy Simulations," *Kyklos*, March 1983.
- R. Findlay, "Growth and Development in Trade Models," in R. W. Jones and P. B. Kenen, eds., *Handbook of International Economics*, Vol. I (New York: North-Holland, 1984).
- A. O. Krueger, "Trade Policies in Developing Countries," in R. W. Jones and P. B. Kenen, eds., *Handbook of International Economics*, Vol. I (New York: North-Holland, 1984).
- J. N. Bhagwati, *Dependence and Interdependence* (Cambridge, Mass.: M.I.T. Press, 1985).

Many of the following selections dealing with international trade and development are found in:
- J. Theberge, *Economics of Trade and Development* (New York: Wiley, 1968).
- G. M. Meier, *Leading Issues in Economic Development* (New York: Oxford University Press, 1970).

An evaluation of the relevance of trade theory to development is found in:
- H. Chenery, "Comparative Advantage and Development Policy," *American Economic Review*, March 1961.
- G. Haberler, "Comparative Advantage, Agricultural Production and International Trade," *The International Journal of Agrarian Affairs*, May 1964.

- H. Myint, "The 'Classical Theory' of International Trade and the Underdeveloped Countries," *Economic Journal*, June 1958.

For a discussion and evaluation of international trade as an engine of growth, see:
- R. Nurkse, "Patterns of Trade and Development," in R. Nurkse, *Problems of Capital Formation in Underdeveloped Countries and Patterns of Trade and Development* (New York: Oxford University Press, 1970).
- A. K. Cairncross, "Trade and Development," in A. K. Cairncross, ed., *Factors in Economic Development* (London: Allen & Unwin, 1962).
- I. B. Kravis, "Trade as a Handmaiden of Growth: Similarities between the 19th and 20th Centuries," *Economic Journal*, December 1970.

The contribution that trade can make toward development and empirical confirmation of the importance of trade to development are found in:
- G. Haberler, *International Trade and Economic Development* (Cairo: National Bank of Egypt, 1959).
- R. E. Caves, "Vent for Surplus Models of Trade and Growth," in R. E. Baldwin et al., *Trade Growth and the Balance of Payments* (Chicago: Rand McNally, 1965).
- M. Michaely, "Exports and Growth—An Empirical Investigation," *Journal of Development Economics*, December 1977.
- B. Balassa, "Exports and Economic Growth: Further Evidence," *Journal of Development Economics*, June 1978.

For a discussion of the various terms of trade, see:
- G. Meier, *The International Economics of Development* (New York: Harper & Row, 1968), ch. 3.

The reasons for the belief that the terms of trade of developing nations tend to deteriorate over time are found in:
- R. Prebisch, "The Economic Development of Latin America and Its Principal Problems," *Economic Bulletin for Latin America*, 1962.
- R. Prebisch, *Towards a New Trade Policy for*

Development (New York: United Nations, 1964).

- M. J. Flanders, "Prebisch on Protectionism: An Evaluation," *Economic Journal,* June 1964.
- H. Singer, "The Distribution of Gains between Investing and Borrowing Countries," *American Economic Review,* May 1950.
- G. Myrdal, *Development and Underdevelopment* (Cairo: National Bank of Egypt, 1959).

For measurements of the commodity terms of trade of developing nations, see:
- United Nations, *Relative Prices of Exports and Imports of Underdeveloped Countries* (Lake Success, N.Y.: United Nations, 1949).
- C. P. Kindleberger, *The Terms of Trade: A European Case Study* (New York: Wiley, 1956).
- R. E. Lipsey, *Price and Quantity Trends in the Foreign Trade of the United States* (Princeton, N.J.: Princeton University Press, 1963).
- W. A. Lewis, "World Production, Prices and Trade, 1870–1960," *Manchester School of Economic and Social Studies,* 1952.
- J. Spraos, *Inequalizing Trade?* (Oxford: Claredon Press, 1983).
- M. Michaely, *Trade Income Levels and Dependence* (Amsterdam: North-Holland, 1984).
- T. Wilson et al., "The Income Terms of Trade of Developed and Developing Nations," *Economic Journal,* December 1969.

The most important studies on the export instability of developing nations are:
- A. I. MacBean, *Export Instability and Economic Development* (Cambridge, Mass.: Harvard University Press, 1966).
- G. F. Erb and S. Schiavo-Campo, "Export Instability, Level of Development, and Economic Size of Less Developed Countries," *Bulletin of Oxford University Institute of Economics and Statistics,* 1969.
- B. F. Massell, "Export Instability and Economic Structure," *American Economic Review,* September 1970.
- D. J. Mathieson and R. I. McKinnon, "Instability in Underdeveloped Countries: The Impact of the International Economy," in P. David and M. Reder, eds., *Nations and Households in Economic Growth* (New York: Academic Press, 1974).

- E. Lancieri, "Export Instability and Economic Development: An Appraisal," *Banca Nazional Del Lavoro Quarterly Review,* June 1978.
- P. Brundell, H. Horn, and P. Svedberg, "On the Causes of Instability in Export Earnings," *Oxford Bulletin of Economics and Statistics,* 1980.
- A. Savvidas, "Export Instability and Economic Growth: Some New Evidence," *Economic Development and Cultural Change,* April 1984.

The classics on import substitution are:
- I. Little et al., *Industries and Trade in Some Developing Countries* (London: Oxford University Press, 1970).
- A. O. Krueger, "Alternative Strategies and Employment in LDCs," *American Economic Review,* May 1978.

For conditions in and policies toward developing countries, and a discussion of a new international economic order, see:
- H. G. Johnson, *Economic Policies Toward Developing Countries* (New York: Praeger, 1968).
- J. N. Bhagwati, ed. *The New International Economic Order: The North-South Debate* (Cambridge, Mass.: M.I.T. Press, 1977.
- W. R. Cline, ed., *Policy Alternatives for a New International Economic Order* (New York: Praeger, 1979).
- T. Murray, *Trade Preferences for Developing Countries* (London: Macmillan, 1977).
- L. Turner and N. McMullen, *The Newly Industrializing Countries: Trade and Adjustment* (London: George Allen & Unwin, 1982).
- D. Salvatore, ed., *The New Protectionist Threat to World Welfare* (New York: North-Holland, 1987).
- D. Salvatore, ed., *African Development Prospects: A Policy Modeling Approach* (New York: North-Holland, 1987).

On the international debt problem of developing countries, see:

- D. C. McDonald, "Debt Capacity and Developing Country Borrowing: A Survey of the Literature," *International Monetary Fund Staff Papers*, 1982.
- W. R. Cline, *International Debt: Systematic Risk and Response* (Washington, D.C.: Institute for International Economics, 1984).

The most important data sources on developing nations are:

- United Nations, *World Economic Survey* (New York: United Nations, Yearly).
- United Nations, *Statistical Yearbook* (New York: United Nations, Yearly).
- World Bank, *World Bank Development Report* (Washington, D.C.: World Bank, 1986).
- International Monetary Fund, *International Financial Statistics* (Washington, D.C.: International Monetary Fund, Monthly, with Yearly Summaries).

CHAPTER 12

International Resource Movements and Multinational Corporations

12.1   Introduction

So far, we have dealt almost exclusively with commodity trade and assumed no international resource movement. However, capital, labor, and technology do move across national boundaries. In some ways, international trade and movements of productive resources can be regarded as substitutes for one another. For example, a relatively capital-abundant and labor-scarce country, such as the United States, could either export capital-intensive commodities or export capital itself, and either import labor-intensive products or allow the immigration of workers from countries with plentiful labor supplies. As in the case of international trade, the movement of productive resources from nations with relative abundance and low remuneration to nations with relative scarcity and high remuneration has a tendency to equalize factor returns internationally and generally increases welfare.

International trade and movements of productive factors, however, have very different economic effects on the nations involved. It is on the cost and benefits of international resource movements that we focus in this chapter. Since multinational corporations are an important vehicle for the international flows of capital, labor, and technology, we also devote a great deal of attention to this relatively new and crucial type of economic enterprise.

There are two main types of foreign investments: portfolio investments and direct investments. **Portfolio investments** are purely financial assets, such as bonds and stocks, denominated in a national currency. With bonds, the investor simply lends his capital to get fixed payouts or a return at regular intervals and then receives the face value of the bond at a prespecified date. Most foreign investments prior to World War I were of this type and flowed primarily from the United Kingdom to the "regions of recent settlement" for railroad construction and the opening up of new lands and sources of raw materials. With stocks, however, the investor purchases equity, or a claim on the net worth of the firm. Portfolio or financial investments take place primarily through financial institutions such as banks and investment funds.

Direct investments, on the other hand, are real investments in factories, capital goods, land, and inventories where both capital and management are involved and the investor retains control over use of the invested capital. Direct investment usually takes the form of a firm starting a subsidiary or taking control of another firm (for example, by purchasing a majority of the stock). In the international context, direct investments are usually undertaken by multinational corporations engaged in manufacturing, resource extraction, or services. Direct investments are now the principal channel of international private capital flows. International portfolio investments collapsed after World War I and have only revived since the 1960s.

In section 12.2, we present some data on international capital flows. In section 12.3, we examine the motives for portfolio and direct investments abroad. In section 12.4, we analyze the welfare effects of international capital flows on investing and host countries. Section 12.5 deals with multinational corporations—the reasons for their existence and some of the problems they create. Finally, in section 12.6, we discuss the reasons for and welfare effects of the international migration of labor in general and of skilled labor in particular. The appendix deals with the so-called transfer problem associated with international capital flows.

12.2   Some Data on International Capital Flows

We now present some data on the size and composition of United States capital investments in foreign nations and foreign capital investments in the United States from 1950 to the present.

We can see from Table 12-1 that both United States *direct* investments abroad and foreign *direct* investments in the United States grew very rapidly from 1950 to 1984, with the latter growing much faster than the former, especially since 1980. Nevertheless, United States direct investments abroad still exceeded foreign direct investments in the United States by over $70 billion in 1984. United States private holdings of foreign long-term securities (stocks and bonds) and foreign private holdings of United States long-term securities also grew very rapidly from 1950 to 1984, with the latter also growing much faster than the former, especially since 1981. In 1984, United States private

TABLE 12-1. *U.S. Foreign Long-Term Private International Investment Position in Selected Years, 1950–1984 (billions of U.S. dollars, book value at year-end)*

Year	1950	1960	1970	1980	1981	1982	1983	1984
U.S. assets abroad								
Direct investments	11.8	31.9	75.5	215.4	228.3	221.8	227.0	233.4
Foreign securities	4.3	9.5	20.9	62.7	63.5	75.7	84.3	89.9
Foreign assets in the U.S.								
Direct investments	3.4	6.9	13.3	83.0	108.7	124.7	137.1	159.6
U.S. securities	2.9	9.3	34.8	74.1	75.4	93.6	114.7	128.2

Source: U.S. Department of Commerce, *Survey of Current Business* (Washington, D.C.: U.S. Government Printing Office, various issues).

holdings of foreign long-term securities exceeded foreign private holdings of United States long-term securities by nearly $40 billion.

By the end of 1984, total United States assets abroad were $323 billion ($233 billion in direct investments plus $90 billion in foreign securities), and this exceeded foreign assets in the United States of $288 billion ($160 billion in direct investments plus $128 billion in U.S. securities). Thus, at the end of 1984, the United States was still a net creditor nation vis-à-vis the rest of the world by about $35 billion. During 1985, however, and primarily as a result of much higher foreign portfolio investments in the United States during 1985, the United States became a net debtor nation for the first time since 1914. This gave rise to a lively debate among economists, politicians, and government officials in the United States about the benefits and risks of this devel-

TABLE 12-2. *U.S. Direct Investments Abroad by Area in Selected Years, 1950–1984 (billions of U.S. dollars, book value at year-end)*

Area	Total	Canada	Europe	Latin America	Others
1950	11.8	3.6	1.7	4.6	1.9
1960	31.9	11.2	7.0	8.4	5.3
1970	75.5	21.0	25.3	13.0	16.2
1980	215.4	45.1	96.3	38.8	35.2
1981	228.3	47.1	101.6	38.8	40.8
1982	221.8	46.2	99.5	32.7	43.4
1983	227.0	47.6	102.7	29.7	47.0
1984	233.4	50.5	103.7	28.0	51.2

Source: U.S. Department of Commerce, *Survey of Current Business* (Washington, D.C.: U.S. Government Printing Office, various issues).

opment. The change of the United States from a net creditor to a net debtor nation is examined in detail in section 14.6 after our discussion of the balance of payments.

Table 12-2 shows that from 1950 to 1980, United States direct investments in Europe have grown much more rapidly than United States direct investments in Canada, Latin America, and in other parts of the world. The faster growth of United States direct investments in Europe was due to the rapid growth of the European Economic Community and the desire of United States firms to avoid the common external tariff imposed by the EEC on imports from outside the Community. Since 1980, however, United States direct investments in other parts of the world (especially in Japan) have grown much faster than those in Europe and in Canada, and they have actually declined in Latin America (this is related to the international debt problem of the Latin American countries discussed in section 11.6b). Nevertheless, U.S. direct investments in Europe in 1984 were still more than double those in Canada and in other parts of the world, and over three times those in Latin America.

Table 12-3 separates United States direct investments abroad and foreign direct investments in the United States into petroleum, manufacturing, and others (mostly services). United States direct investments abroad in manufacturing grew much more rapidly until 1980 and were larger in 1984 than the other two classes. Since 1980, however, United States direct investments abroad in the petroleum industry grew much more rapidly than in manufacturing and in other industries. On the other hand, foreign direct investments in the United States in sectors other than petroleum and manufacturing, after growing less rapidly than these other sectors from 1950 to 1970, grew so much faster since 1970 that by 1984 totalled more than the sum of the other two sectors.

TABLE 12-3. **U.S. and Foreign Direct Investments by Industry in Selected Years, 1950–1984 (billions of U.S. dollars, book value at year-end)**

	1950	1960	1970	1980	1981	1982	1983	1984
U.S. investments abroad								
Petroleum	3.4	10.8	19.8	47.6	53.2	56.8	60.3	63.3
Manufacturing	3.8	11.1	31.0	89.3	92.4	90.6	90.2	93.0
Other	4.6	10.0	24.7	78.5	82.7	74.4	76.5	77.1
Total	11.8	31.9	75.5	215.4	228.3	221.8	227.0	233.4
Foreign investments in the U.S.								
Petroleum	0.4	1.2	3.0	12.2	15.2	17.7	18.2	24.9
Manufacturing	1.1	2.6	6.1	33.0	40.3	44.1	47.7	50.7
Other	1.9	3.1	4.2	37.8	53.2	62.9	71.1	84.0
Total	3.4	6.9	13.3	83.0	108.7	124.7	137.1	159.6

Source: U.S. Department of Commerce, *Survey of Current Business* (Washington, D.C.: U.S. Government Printing Office, various issues).

12.3   Motives for International Capital Flows

In this section, we examine the motives for portfolio and direct investments abroad. While the motives for both types of foreign investments are basically the same, direct foreign investments require additional explanations not provided by the basic model that explains international portfolio investments.

12.3a   Motives for International Portfolio Investments

The basic motive for international portfolio investments is to earn higher returns abroad. Thus, residents of one country purchase bonds of another country if the returns on bonds are higher in the other country. This is the simple and straightforward outcome of yield maximization and tends to equalize returns internationally. According to the basic (two-nation) Heckscher-Ohlin model, returns on capital are originally higher in the nation having the lower overall capital-labor ratio. Residents of one country may also purchase stock in a corporation in another country if they expect the future profitability of the foreign corporation to be greater than that of domestic corporations. (For simplicity, we abstract here from the greater transaction and other costs usually involved in holding foreign securities.)

The explanation that international portfolio investments occur to take advantage of higher yields abroad is certainly correct as far as it goes. The problem is that it leaves one important fact unexplained. It cannot account for *observed* two-way capital flows. That is, if returns on securities are lower in one nation than in another nation, this could explain the flow of capital investments from the former nation to the latter but is inconsistent with the simultaneous flow of capital in the opposite direction, which is often observed in the real world (see Tables 12-1 and 12-3).

To explain two-way international capital flows, the element of risk must be introduced. That is, investors are interested not only in the rate of return but also in the risk associated with a particular investment. The risk with bonds consists of bankruptcy and the variability in their market value. With stocks, the risk consists of bankruptcy, even greater variability in market value, and the possibility of lower than anticipated returns. Thus, investors maximize returns for a given level of risk and generally accept a higher risk only if returns are higher.

Let us deal with stocks and measure risk by the variability (variance) of returns about the average rate. For example, suppose stocks A and B both have a rate of return of 30 percent on average, but there is a 50-50 chance that the yield will be either 20 percent or 40 percent on stock A but 10 percent or 50 percent on stock B. Stock B is then clearly riskier than stock A. Since both stocks have the same yield on the average, investors should purchase stock A to minimize risks.

However, if the yield on stock A falls when the yield on stock B rises and vice versa (i.e., if changes in yields are inversely, or negatively, correlated over time), then by holding both stocks, the investor can still receive a yield of 30 percent on average but with a much lower risk. That is, the risk of a lower than average yield on stock A at any point is more or less matched by the tendency for the yield on stock B to be higher than average at the same time. As a result, the risk of a portfolio including *both* stock A and stock B is substantially reduced.

Portfolio theory thus tells us that by investing in securities with yields that are inversely related over time, a given yield can be obtained at a smaller risk or a higher yield can be obtained for the same level of risk for the portfolio as a whole. Since yields on foreign securities (depending primarily on the different economic conditions abroad) are more likely to be inversely related to yields on domestic securities, a portfolio including both domestic and foreign securities can have a higher average yield and/or lower risk than a portfolio containing only domestic securities.

To achieve such a balanced portfolio, a two-way capital flow may be required. For example, if stock A (with the same average yield but lower risk than stock B) is available in one country, while stock B (with yields inversely related to the yields on stock A) is available in another country, investors in the first nation must also purchase stock B (i.e., invest in the second nation), and investors in the second nation must also purchase stock A (i.e., invest in the first nation) to achieve a balanced portfolio. **Risk diversification** can thus explain two-way international portfolio investments.

Throughout the preceding discussion, it was implicitly assumed that investors know precisely the average return on stocks and their variability. In reality, this is seldom known in advance. Thus, investors must determine for themselves (from their market knowledge and intuition) what the average returns and variabilities are likely to be in deciding which stocks to purchase. Since different individuals can have different expectations for the same stocks, it is possible that some investors in each nation think that stocks in the other nation are a better buy. This provides an additional explanation for two-way international portfolio investments.

12.3b Motives for Direct Foreign Investments

The motives for direct investments abroad are generally the same as for portfolio investments; that is, to earn higher returns (possibly resulting from higher growth rates abroad, more favorable tax treatment, or greater availability of infrastructures) and to diversify risks. Indeed, it has been found that firms with a strong international orientation, either through exports or through foreign production and/or sales facilities, are more profitable and have a much smaller variability in profits than purely domestic firms.

However, while these reasons are sufficient to explain international portfolio investments, they leave one basic question unanswered with regard to direct foreign investments. That is, they cannot explain why the residents of a nation do not borrow from other nations and themselves make real investments in their own nation rather than accept *direct* investments from abroad. After all, the residents of a nation can be expected to be more familiar with local conditions and thus to be at a competitive advantage with respect to foreign investors. There are several possible reasons for this. The most important is that many large corporations (usually in monopolistic and oligopolistic markets) often have some unique production knowledge or managerial skill that could easily and profitably be utilized abroad and over which the corporation wants to retain direct control. In such a situation, the firm will make direct investments abroad. This involves **horizontal integration,** or the production abroad of a differentiated product that is also produced at home.

For example, IBM has a particular computer technology over which it wants to retain direct control but which it can easily duplicate abroad so as to serve the foreign market better (by adapting to local conditions) than through exports. IBM does not want to license foreign producers because it wants to retain complete control over its trade secrets and patents and to ensure consistent quality and service. Even if IBM were willing to negotiate licensing agreements with foreign producers, this would not be feasible in view of the very rapid rate of technological innovations in the field. The situation is basically the same for Xerox, Gillette, Volkswagen, and many other multinational corporations, and it is the motive behind most direct foreign investments in manufacturing in developed nations.

Another important reason for direct foreign investments is to obtain control of a needed raw material and thus ensure an uninterrupted supply at the lowest possible cost. This is referred to as **vertical integration** and is the form of most direct foreign investments in developing countries and in some mineral-rich developed countries. Thus, American and foreign corporations own mines in Canada, Jamaica, Venezuela, Australia, and other nations and foreigners own some coal mines in the United States. Vertical integration involving multinational corporations can also go *forward* into the ownership of sales or distribution networks abroad, as is the case with most of the world's major automobile producers.

Still other reasons for direct foreign investments are to avoid tariffs and other restrictions that nations impose on imports or to take advantage of various government subsidies to encourage direct foreign investments. Examples of the former are the large-scale direct investments made by United States firms in the EEC countries and some direct foreign investments in manufacturing in developing nations. Examples of the latter are the direct foreign investments made in developing nations and in depressed regions of some developed nations. Other possible reasons for direct foreign investments are to enter a foreign oligopolistic market to share in the profits, to purchase a promising foreign firm to avoid its future competition and possible loss of export markets, or because only a large foreign multinational corporation can obtain the necessary financing to enter the market.

Two-way direct foreign investments can then be explained by some industries being more advanced in one nation (such as the computer industry in the United States) while other industries being more efficient in other nations (such as the small-car industry in Japan and West Germany). Also to be noted is that direct foreign investments have been greatly facilitated (in a sense made possible) by the very rapid advances in transportation (i.e., jet travel) and communications (i.e., international telephone lines and international data transmission and processing) that have occurred since the end of World War II. These permit the headquarters of multinational corporations to exert immediate and direct control over the operations of their subsidiaries around the world, thus facilitating and encouraging direct investments abroad.

12.4 Welfare Effects of International Capital Flows

In this section, we examine the welfare effects of international capital flows on the investing and host countries. Some of these effects can be shown graphically. These are examined first. Subsequently, we examine the effects not revealed in the graphical analysis.

12.4a Effects on the Investing and Host Countries

In Figure 12-1, we examine a world of only two nations (Nation 1 and Nation 2) with a total combined capital stock of OO'. Of this total capital stock, OA belongs to Nation 1 and $O'A$ belongs to Nation 2. the $VMPK_1$ and $VMPK_2$ curves give the value of the marginal product of capital in Nation 1 and Nation 2, respectively, for various levels of investments. Under competitive conditions, the value of the marginal product of capital represents the return, or yield, on capital.

In isolation, Nation 1 invests its entire capital stock OA domestically at a yield of OC. The total product (which can be measured by the area under the value of the marginal product curve) is thus $OFGA$, of which $OCGA$ goes to owners of capital in Nation 1 and the remainder of CFG goes to other cooperating factors, such as labor and land. Similarly, Nation 2 in isolation invests its entire stock $O'A$ domestically at a yield of $O'H$. Total product is $O'JMA$, of which $O'HMA$ goes to owners of capital in Nation 2 and the remainder of HJM goes to other cooperating factors.

Let us assume that free international capital movements are allowed. Since the return on capital is higher in Nation 2 ($O'H$) than in Nation 1 (OC), AB of capital flows from Nation 1 to Nation 2 so as to equalize at BE ($=ON=O'T$) the rate of return on capital in the two nations. Total *domestic product* in Nation 1 is now $OFEB$, to which must be added $ABER$ as the total return on foreign investments, giving a total *national income* of $OFERA$ (ERG greater than before foreign investments). With free international capital flows, the total return on capital in Nation 1 increases to $ONRA$, while the total return on other cooperating factors decreases to NFE.

The inflow of AB of foreign capital into Nation 2 lowers the rate of return

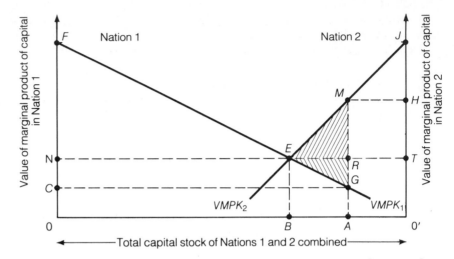

FIGURE 12-1. Output and Welfare Effects of International Capital Transfers

Of the total capital stock of OO', Nation 1 holds OA and its total output is $OFGA$, while Nation 2 holds $O'A$ and its total output is $O'JMA$. The transfer of AB of capital from Nation 1 to Nation 2 equalizes the return on capital in the two nations at BE. This increases world output by EGM (the shaded area), of which EGR accrues to Nation 1 and ERM to Nation 2. Of the increase in total domestic product of $ABEM$ in Nation 2, $ABER$ goes to foreign investors, leaving ERM as the net gain in domestic income in Nation 2.

on capital from $O'H$ to $O'T$. Total domestic product in Nation 2 grows from $O'JMA$ to $O'JEB$. Of the increase in total product of $ABEM$, $ABER$ goes to foreign investors, so that ERM remains as the *net gain* in total product accruing to Nation 2. The total return to domestic owners of capital falls from $O'HMA$ to $O'TRA$, while the total return to other cooperating factors rises from HJM to TJE.

From the point of view of the world as a whole (i.e., the two nations combined), total product increased from $OFGA + O'JMA$ to $OFEB + O'JEB$, or by $ERG + ERM = EGM$ (the shaded area of the figure). Thus, international capital flows increase the efficiency in the allocation of resources internationally and increase world output and welfare. Note that the flatter the $VMPK_1$ and $VMPK_2$ curves are, the greater is the total gain from international capital flows.

12.4b Other Effects on the Investing and Host Countries

Assuming two factors of production, capital and labor, both fully employed before and after the capital transfer, it can be seen from Figure 12-1 that the total and average return on capital increases, whereas the total and average return to labor decreases in the investing country. Thus, while the investing country as a whole gains from investing abroad, there is a redistribution of domestic income from labor to capital. It is for this reason that organized labor in the United States is opposed to United States investments abroad. On the other hand, while the host country also gains from receiving foreign investments, they lead to a redistribution of domestic income from capital to labor. If we allow for less than full employment, foreign investments tend to depress the level of employment in the investing country and increase it in the host country and, once again, can be expected to be opposed by labor in the former and to benefit labor in the latter.

International capital transfers also affect the balance of payments of the investing and host countries. A nation's balance of payments measures its total receipts from and total expenditures in the rest of the world. In the year in which the foreign investment takes place, the foreign expenditures of the investing country increase and cause a balance-of-payments deficit (an excess of expenditures abroad over foreign receipts). This was certainly a major contributor to the huge balance-of-payments deficits of the United States during the 1960s and led to restrictions on United States foreign investments from 1965 to 1974. Of course, the counterpart to the worsening in the investing nation's balance of payments is the improvement in the host nation's balance of payments in the year in which it receives the foreign investment.

However, the initial capital transfer and increased expenditures abroad of the investing country are likely to be mitigated by increased exports of capital goods, spare parts, and other products of the investing country, and by the subsequent flow of profits to the investing country. It has been estimated that the "payback" period for the initial capital transfer is between five and ten years on average. Another effect to consider in the long run is whether foreign investments will lead to the replacement of the investing country's exports and even to imports of commodities previously exported. Thus, while the immediate effect on the balance of payments is negative in the investing country and positive in the host country, the long-run effects are less certain.

Since foreign investments for most developed countries are two-way (see section 12.2), these short-run and long-run balance-of-payments effects are mostly neutralized, except for a nation such as the United States, with investments abroad greatly exceeding foreign investments received (see Table 12-1) and for developing countries that are primarily recipients of foreign investments and chronically face serious balance-of-payments difficulties (see section 11.6c).

Another important welfare effect of foreign investments on both the investing and host countries results from different rates of taxation and foreign earnings in various countries. Thus, if corporate taxes are 48 percent of earnings in the United States but only 40 percent in Switzerland, it is only natural for United States firms to invest in Switzerland or reroute foreign sales through subsidiaries there in order to pay the lower tax rate. Because most nations, including the United States, are signatories of double-taxation agreements (to avoid double taxation—on equity grounds), the United States would collect a tax of only 8 percent on foreign earnings (the difference between the domestic tax rate of 48 percent and the foreign tax rate of 40 percent). As a result, the tax base and the amount of taxes collected declines in the investing and rises in the host country.

Foreign investments, by affecting output and the volume of trade of both investing and host countries, are also likely to affect the terms of trade. However, how these will change depends on conditions in both nations and not much can be said *a priori*. Foreign investments may also affect the investing nation's technological lead and the host country's control over its economy and ability to conduct its own independent economic policy. Since these and other effects of international capital transfers usually result from the operations of multinational corporations, they are examined in the next section.

12.5 Multinational Corporations

One of the most significant international economic developments of the postwar period is the proliferation of **multinational corporations (MNCs).** These are firms that own, control, or manage production facilities in several countries. Today MNCs account for over 20 percent of world output, and *intrafirm* trade (i.e., trade among the parent firm and its foreign affiliates) is more than 25 percent of world trade in manufacturing. Some MNCs, such as Exxon and General Motors, are truly giants with yearly sales in the tens of billions of dollars and exceeding the total national income of all but a handful of nations. Furthermore, most international direct investments today are undertaken by MNCs. In the process, the parent firm usually provides its foreign affiliates with managerial expertise, technology, parts, and a marketing organization in return for some of the affiliates' output and earnings. In this section, we examine the reasons for the existence of MNCs and some of the problems they create for the home and host countries.

12.5a Reasons for the Existence of Multinational Corporations

The basic reason for the existence of MNCs is the competitive advantage of a global network of production and distribution. This competitive advantage arises in part from vertical and horizontal integration with foreign affiliates. By vertical integration, most MNCs can ensure their supply of foreign raw materials and intermediate products and circumvent (with more efficient intrafirm trade) the imperfections often found in foreign markets. They can also provide better distribution and service networks. By horizontal integration through foreign affiliates, MNCs can better protect and exploit their monopoly power, adapt their products to local conditions and tastes, and ensure consistent product quality.

The competitive advantage of MNCs is also based on economies of scale in production, financing, research and development (R&D), and the gathering of market information. The large output of MNCs allows them to carry division of labor and specialization in production much further than smaller national firms. Product components requiring only unskilled labor can be produced in low-wage nations and shipped elsewhere for assembly. Furthermore, MNCs and their affiliates usually have greater access at better terms to international capital markets than do purely national firms, and this puts MNCs in a better position to finance large projects. They can also concentrate R&D in one or a few advanced nations best suited for these purposes because of the greater availability of technical personnel and facilities. Finally, foreign affiliates funnel information from around the world to the parent firm, placing it in a better position than national firms to evaluate, anticipate, and take advantage of changes in comparative costs, consumers' tastes, and market conditions generally.

The large corporation invests abroad when expected profits on additional investments in its industry are higher abroad. Since the corporation usually has a competitive advantage in and knows its industry best, it does not consider the possibility of higher returns in every other domestic industry before it decides to invest abroad. That is, it is differences in expected rates of profits domestically and abroad in the particular industry that is of crucial importance in a large corporation's decision to invest abroad. This explains, for example, Toyota automotive investments in the United States and IBM computer investments in Japan. Indeed, it also explains investments of several Japanese electronics MNCs in the United States as an attempt to invade the latter's computer market. All of the above implies that MNCs are *oligopolists* selling for the most part *differentiated products*, often developed as described by the *technological gap* and *product cycle models*, and produced under strong *economies of scale* (see section 6.4). Examples of the products sold by MNCs are petroleum products, motor vehicles, electronics, metals, office equipment, chemicals, and food.

MNCs are also in a much better position to control or change to their advantage the environment in which they operate than are purely national firms. For example, in determining where to set up a plant to produce a component, an MNC can and usually does "shop around" for the low-wage nation that offers the most incentives in the form of tax holidays, subsidies, and other tax and trade benefits. The sheer size of most MNCs in relation to most host nations also means the MNCs are in a better position than purely national firms to influence the policies of local governments and extract benefits. Furthermore, MNCs can buy up promising local firms to avoid future competition and are in a much better position than purely domestic firms to engage in other practices that restrict local trade and increase their profits. MNCs, through greater diversification, face lower risks and generally earn higher profits than purely national firms.

Finally, by artificially overpricing components shipped *to* an affiliate in a higher-tax nation and underpricing products shipped *from* the affiliate in the high-tax nation, an MNC can minimize its tax bill. This is called **transfer**

pricing and can arise in intrafirm trade as opposed to trade among independent firms or at "arm's length."

In the final analysis, it is a combination of all or most of these factors that gives MNCs their competitive advantage vis-à-vis purely national firms and explains the proliferation and great importance of MNCs today. That is, by vertical and horizontal integration with foreign affiliates, by taking advantage of economies of scale, and by being in a better position than purely national firms to control the environment in which they operate, MNCs have grown to become the most prominent form of private international economic organization in existence today.

Table 12-4 lists the 25 largest MNCs in the world in 1984 in terms of yearly sales, the major industry, and the home nation of the parent firm. Note that

TABLE 12-4.   Largest 25 MNCs in 1984

Rank	Company	Nationality	Industry	Yearly Sales (billion $)
1	Exxon	United States	Petroleum	91
2	Royal Dutch/Shell Group	Netherlands/ United Kingdom	Petroleum	85
3	General Motors	United States	Motor Vehicles	84
4	Mobil	United States	Petroleum	56
5	Ford Motor	United States	Motor Vehicles	52
6	British Petroleum	United Kingdom	Petroleum	51
7	Texaco	United States	Petroleum	47
8	IBM	United States	Office Equipment	46
9	I.E. du Pont de Nemours	United States	Chemicals	36
10	American Tel. & Tel.	United States	Electronics	33
11	General Electric	United States	Electrical	28
12	Standard Oil (Ind.)	United States	Petroleum	27
13	Chevron	United States	Petroleum	27
14	ENI	Italy	Petroleum	26
15	Atlantic Richfield	United States	Petroleum	25
16	Toyota Motors	Japan	Motor Vehicles	24
17	IRI	Italy	Metals	23
18	Unilever	United Kingdom/ Netherlands	Food Products	22
19	Shell Oil	United States	Petroleum	21
20	Elf-Acquitaine	France	Petroleum	21
21	Matsushita Electric	Japan	Electronics	20
22	Chrysler	United States	Motor Vehicles	20
23	Pemex	Mexico	Petroleum	19
24	Hitachi	Japan	Electronics	18
25	U.S. Steel	United States	Steel	18

Source: Fortune Magazine, August 19, 1985, p. 179.

all except one of the largest 25 MNCs are based in developed countries. Twelve out of the 25 are in petroleum, 4 each in motor vehicles and electronics, 2 in metals, and 1 each in office equipment, chemicals, and food.

12.5b Problems Created by Multinational Corporations in the Home Country

While MNCs, by efficiently organizing production and distribution on a worldwide basis, can increase world output and welfare, they also create serious problems in both the home and host countries. The most controversial of the alleged harmful effects of MNCs on the home nation is the loss of domestic jobs resulting from foreign direct investments. That some domestic jobs are so lost is beyond doubt. These are likely to be unskilled and semiskilled production jobs in which the home nation has a comparative disadvantage. It is for this reason that organized labor in the United States and other major home nations is against direct foreign investments by MNCs. However, some clerical, managerial, and technical jobs are also likely to be created in the headquarters of the MNC in the home nation as a result of direct foreign investments. Even if the number of jobs lost exceeds the number created, it may be that the home nation would have lost these jobs anyway to foreign competitors and would have had no jobs created at home without the direct foreign investment. The extent to which this may be true depends, of course, on the type of direct foreign investment and the circumstances under which it takes place.

A related problem is the export of advanced technology to be combined with other cheaper foreign factors to maximize corporate profits. It is claimed that this may undermine the technological superiority and future of the home nation. However, against this possible harmful effect is the tendency of MNCs to concentrate their R&D in the home nation, thus allowing it to maintain its technological lead. Whether or not MNCs, on balance, undermine the technological superiority of the home country is a hotly debated question to which no clear-cut answer is yet possible.

In addition, through transfer pricing and similar practices, and by shifting their operations to lower-tax nations, MNCs reduce tax revenues and erode the tax base of the home country. This results from common international taxing practice. Specifically, the host country taxes the subsidiary's profits first. To avoid double taxation of foreign subsidiaries, the home country then usually taxes only repatriated profits (if its tax rate is higher than in the host country), and only by the difference in the tax rates.

An example will clarify this. Suppose that the corporate profit tax is 50 percent in the home country and 40 percent in the host country, and the before-tax risk-adjusted profit rate is 20 percent abroad but 16 percent at home. The MNC will then invest abroad. When 20 percent is earned abroad, the host country gets 8 percent in taxes and the MNC retains 12 percent. When the MNC repatriates this 12 percent profit, the home country will tax it at the rate of 10 percent (the difference between the domestic and the foreign corporate tax profit rate). Thus, the home country gets only 1.2 percent and only when the profits are repatriated. The reinvestment of profits abroad in the MNC's affiliate thus amounts to an interest-free loan from the home country. If the corporate profit-tax rate of the home and host countries were equal, the home country would collect no tax at all even when the MNC repatriates its profits. Had the MNC invested in the home country to begin with and earned a profit of 16 percent, it would have collected a tax of 8 percent (at the 50 percent tax rate). Thus, MNCs reduce tax revenues and erode the tax base of the home country.

Finally, because of their access to international capital markets, MNCs can circumvent domestic monetary policies and make government control over the economy in the home nation more difficult. These alleged harmful effects of MNCs are of crucial importance to the United States, since it is home for more than half of the largest MNCs. In general, home nations do impose some restrictions on the activities of MNCs, either for balance-of-payments reasons or, more recently, for employment reasons.

12.5c   Problems Created by Multinational Corporations in the Host Country

Host countries have even more serious complaints against MNCs. First and foremost is the allegation that MNCs dominate their economies. This is certainly true for Canada, where almost 60 percent of the total capital in manufacturing is owned or controlled by foreigners (40 percent by Americans). It is also true for some of the smaller developing nations. Foreign domination is felt in many different ways in host countries, including (1) the unwillingness of a local affiliate of an MNC to export to a nation deemed unfriendly to the home nation or the requirement to comply with a *home*-nation law prohibiting such exports; (2) the borrowing of funds abroad to circumvent tight domestic credit conditions and the lending of funds abroad when interest rates are low at home; (3) the effect on national tastes of large-scale advertising for such products as Coca Cola, jeans, and so on.

Another harmful effect of MNCs on the host country is the siphoning off of R&D funds to the home nation. While this may be more efficient for the MNC and the world as a whole, it also keeps the host country technologically dependent. This is especially true and serious for developing nations. MNCs may also absorb local savings and entrepreneurial talent, thus preventing them from being used to establish domestic enterprises that might be more important for national growth and development. However, the extent to which this occurs is not clear. MNCs may also extract from host nations most of the benefits resulting from their investments, either through tax and tariff benefits or through tax avoidance. In developing nations, foreign direct investments by MNCs in mineral and raw material production have often given rise to complaints of foreign exploitation in the form of low prices paid to host nations, the use of highly capital-intensive production techniques inappropriate for labor-abundant developing nations, lack of training of local labor, overexploitation of natural resources, and creating highly dualistic "enclave" economies.

Most of these complaints are to some extent true, particularly in the case of developing host countries, and they have led many host nations to regulate foreign investments in order to mitigate the harmful effects and increase the possible benefits. Thus, Canada imposes higher taxes on foreign affiliates with less than 25 percent Canadian interest. India specifies the sectors in which direct foreign investments are allowed and sets rules to regulate their operation. Some developing nations allow only joint ventures and set rules for the transfer of technology and the training of domestic labor, impose limits on the use of imported inputs and the remission of profits, set environmental regulations, and so on. In the extreme, the host nation can nationalize foreign production facilities. However, this is likely to seriously reduce the future flow of direct foreign investments to the nation.

Even in the United States, the home of about half of the largest MNCs, we are beginning to hear great concern being expressed over foreign control in the light of the recent upsurge of foreign direct investments. Efforts are currently in progress within the EEC, OECD, the UN, and UNCTAD to devise an international code of conduct for MNCs. However, since the interests of home and host countries are generally in conflict, it is virtually impossible for such an international code to be very specific. As a result, it is unlikely to succeed in severely restricting most of the abuses of and problems created by MNCs in home and host countries.

12.6 Motives and Welfare Effects of International Labor Migration

Labor is generally less mobile internationally than capital. However, great waves of immigrants moved from Europe to the New World during the nineteenth century. This relieved population pressures in Europe and contributed significantly to the rapid growth and development of the New World, especially the United States. In this section, we examine the causes of international labor migration and analyze its welfare effects on the countries of emigration and immigration. Those effects that can be illustrated graphically are examined first. Subsequently, we examine the effects which are not apparent from the graphical analysis.

12.6a Motives for International Labor Migration

International labor migration can take place for economic as well as for noneconomic reasons. Some of the international migrations that occurred in the nineteenth century and earlier were certainly motivated by the desire to escape political and religious oppression in Europe. However, most international labor migration, particularly since the end of World War II, has been motivated by the prospect of earning higher real wages and income abroad.

The decision to migrate for economic reasons can be analyzed in the same manner and with the same tools as any other investment decision. Specifically, migration, just like any other type of investment, involves both costs and benefits. The costs include the expenditures for transportation and the loss of wages during time spent relocating and searching for a job in the new nation. In addition, there are many other less quantifiable costs, such as the separation from relatives, friends, and familiar surroundings, the need to learn new customs and often a new language, and the risks involved in finding a job, housing, and so on in a new land. To be sure, many of these noneconomic costs are greatly reduced by the fact that migrations usually occur in waves and in chains, with many migrants moving together and/or to areas with an already substantial number of earlier migrants from the same place of origin.

The economic benefits of international migration can be measured by the higher real wages and income that the migrant worker can earn abroad during his or her remaining working life, over and above what he or she could have earned at home. Other benefits may be greater educational and job opportunities for the migrants' children. From the excess of returns over costs, an internal rate of return for the migration decision can be estimated, just as for any other type of investment. If this rate of return is sufficiently high to also overcome the noneconomic costs associated with migration, then the worker will migrate. Of course, in the real world workers seldom, if ever, do or have the information to carry out this type of cost-benefit analysis explicitly. Nevertheless, they behave as if they did. This is confirmed by the fact that migrants invariably move from low-wage to high-wage nations. Furthermore, younger workers migrate more readily than older workers because, among other things, they have a longer remaining working life over which to benefit from the higher wages abroad. Thus migration, just like education, is an investment in human capital.

12.6b   Welfare Effects of International Labor Migration

The welfare effects of international labor migration on the nations of emigration and immigration can be analyzed with the same diagrammatic technique used to analyze the welfare effects of international capital movements. In Figure 12-2, the supply of labor is OA in Nation 1 and $O'A$ in Nation 2. The $VMPL_1$ and $VMPL_2$ curves give the value of the marginal revenue product of labor in Nation 1 and Nation 2, respectively. Under competitive conditions, $VMPL$ represents the real wages of labor.

Before migration, the wage rate is OC and total product is $OFGA$ in Nation 1. In Nation 2, the wage rate is $O'H$ and total product is $O'JMA$. Now let us assume free international labor migration. Since wages are higher in Nation 2 ($O'H$) than in Nation 1 (OC), AB of labor migrates from Nation 1 to Nation 2

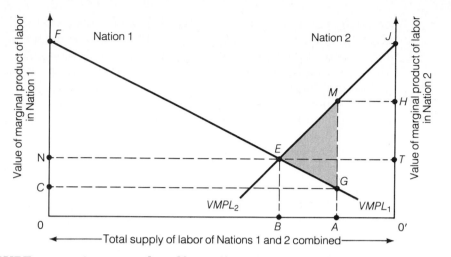

FIGURE 12-2. Output and Welfare Effects of International Labor Migration

With a supply of labor of OA, Nation 1 has a real wage rate of OC and a total output of $OFGA$. With a supply of labor of $O'A$, Nation 2 has a real wage rate of $O'H$ and a total output of $O'JMA$. The migration of AB of labor from Nation 1 to Nation 2 equalizes real wages in the two nations at BE. This reduces total output to $OFEB$ in Nation 1 and increases it in Nation 2 to $O'JEB$, for a net increase in world output of EGM (the shaded area).

so as to equalize wages in the two nations at BE $(=ON=O'T)$. Thus, wages rise in Nation 1 and fall in Nation 2 (and for that reason immigration is generally opposed by organized labor). On the other hand, total product falls from $OFGA$ to $OFEB$ in Nation 1 and rises from $O'JMA$ to $O'JEB$ in Nation 2, for a net gain in world output of EGM (the shaded area in the figure). Note that there is a redistribution of national income toward labor in Nation 1 (the nation of emigration) and toward nonlabor resources in Nation 2. Nation 1 may also receive some remittances from its migrant workers. Note also that if AB of labor had been unemployed in Nation 1 before migration, the wage rate would have been ON and the total product $OFEB$ in Nation 1 with and without migration, and the net increase in world output with migration would have been $ABEM$ (all accruing to Nation 2).

12.6c Other Welfare Effects of International Labor Migration

So far, we have implicitly assumed that all labor is unskilled. However, even casual observation of the real world reveals a great variety in the quality and amount of human capital (in the form of education, training, and health) embodied in different workers and labor groups. The question then arises as to the welfare effects of the migration of a highly skilled worker on the nations of emigration and immigration. These welfare effects are likely to be significantly different from those arising from the migration of unskilled labor. Concern with this question has greatly increased since the 1950s and 1960s as relatively large numbers of scientists and technicians, doctors and nurses, and other highly skilled personnel have moved from developing to developed nations and from Europe to the United States. The problem is vividly conveyed by the term **"brain drain."**

The nations of origin of these skilled migrants charge that they incur a great cost in educating and training these workers only to see them leave and benefit the receiving nations. To be sure, many of these highly skilled workers often cannot be used effectively at home—as, for example, when a doctor only performs nursing services and engineers are used as technicians, as frequently happens in some developing countries. Nevertheless, the fact remains that the nation of origin incurs the great expense of training these workers but receives little, if any, benefit in the form of emigrant remittances. It may also be that the more dynamic, alert, and young workers emigrate, thus reducing the stock of these qualities in the remaining labor force.

The brain drain is often encouraged by national immigration laws (as in the United States, the United Kingdom, and other industrial nations) that facilitate the immigration of skilled persons but generally impose serious obstacles to the immigration of unskilled workers. This has led to demands to tax skilled emigrants at the time of exit or tax their subsequent higher earnings in the nation of immigration, so that the nation of origin could recoup part of the cost incurred in training them. While these proposals seem reasonable, it must be remembered that an important element of personal freedom is involved in the ability to migrate. Thus, it might be more acceptable from the individual's point of view and more efficient from an economic point of view for the government of the receiving nation to somehow compensate, through increased aid or other financial transfer to the nation of origin, for the training costs of skilled immigrants, particularly if the nation of origin is a developing nation.

In the above discussion of the migration of skilled and unskilled workers, we implicitly assumed that the migration decision is more or less permanent. However, a great deal of labor migration, particularly into the European Economic Community, has been of a temporary type. That is, a nation such as West Germany admits foreign workers on a temporary basis when needed (the so-called "guest workers") but refuses to renew work permits during domestic economic downturns when the foreign workers are no longer needed. By doing so, West Germany more or less insulates its economy and its labor force from economic downturns and imposes the adjustment problem on sending nations such as Spain, Portugal, Turkey, and Yugoslavia, which are poorer and less capable of dealing effectively with the resulting unemployment.

In the 1970s, it was estimated that immigrants represented about 10 percent of the labor force of France, Germany, and the United Kingdom, and almost 20 percent of the labor force of Switzerland. In recent years and in the face of high rates of unemployment in many industrial nations, particularly in Europe, temporary migrants have been made to feel increasingly unwelcome and have encountered rising discrimination, even in nations such as France and

England that usually welcomed them. Their work permits have not been renewed and they have been encouraged to return home. As a result, their numbers and proportion of the total labor force in most receiving nations has been decreasing.

There is then the problem of illegal migration. This has become a burning issue in the United States, where millions of illegal immigrants work in the so-called underground economy at below minimum wages and with few if any social benefits. Illegal immigration significantly affects income distribution in the United States by depressing the income of low-skill American workers. This has given rise to vigorous debates in the United States on how to deal with the problem and how to stop or slow down the flood of illegal immigrants.

It has been estimated that there are over 12 million illegal workers, representing about 7 percent of the labor force in the United States. The problem is also worsening by the continuous arrival of hundreds of thousands of additional immigrants illegally each year. Immigrant officials in the United States seem completely overwhelmed by the problem and unable to prevent the thousands who cross the border from Mexico and arrive daily on planes and ships from the Caribbean, Central and South America, and from other parts of the world.

Summary

1. In this chapter we examined the effects of international flows of capital, labor, and technology. In some ways, these are substitutes for international commodity trade. Portfolio investments, such as the purchase of stocks and bonds, are purely financial assets and take place primarily through banks and investment funds. Direct investments are real investments in factories, capital goods, land, and inventories where both capital and management are involved and the investor retains control over the use of the invested capital. International direct investments are usually undertaken by multinational corporations.

2. The total of United States direct investments abroad and United States private holdings of long-term foreign securities rose from $16.1 billion in 1950 to $323.3 billion in 1984 (almost 3/4 being direct investments). Over the same period, the total of foreign direct investments in the United States and foreign private holdings of long-term United States securities rose from $6.3 billion to $287.8 billion (of which $159.6 billion are direct investments). Of the total United States direct foreign investments in 1984, 45 percent was in Europe, 23 percent in Canada, 12 percent in Latin America, and 20 percent in other areas. About 40 percent of United States direct investments abroad in 1984 was in manufacturing, 27 percent in petroleum, and 33 percent in other activities. On the other hand, 15 percent of foreign direct investments in the United States was in manufacturing, 32 percent in petroleum, and 53 percent in other activities (mostly services).

3. The basic motives for international portfolio investments are yield maximization and risk diversification. The latter is also required to explain two-way capital movements. Direct foreign investments require additional explanations. These are: (1) to exploit abroad some unique production knowledge or managerial skill (horizontal integration), (2) to gain control over a foreign source of a needed raw material or a foreign marketing outlet (vertical integration), (3) to avoid import tariffs and other trade restrictions and/or to take advantage of production subsidies, (4) to enter a foreign oligopolistic market, (5) to acquire a foreign firm in order to avoid future competition, or (6) because of unique ability to obtain financing.

4. International capital transfers increase the national income of both the investing and host countries, but in the investing nation the relative share going to capital rises and the share going to labor falls, while the opposite occurs in the host or receiving nation. Thus the level of employment tends to fall in the investing nation and rise in the host nation. In the short run, the balance of payments tends to worsen in the investing nation and improve in the host nation. In the long run, the balance-of-payments effects of foreign investments on the investing and host nations are less clear-cut. Nations with high corporate tax rates encourage investments abroad and thereby lose tax revenues. The terms of trade are also likely to be affected by foreign investments.

5. Multinational corporations have grown to be the most prominent form of private international economic organization today. The basic reason for their existence is the competitive advantage of a global network of production and distribution. Some of the alleged problems created by multinational corporations in the home country are the export of domestic jobs, the erosion of the home nation's technological advantage, avoidance of domestic taxes through transfer pricing, and reduced government control over the domestic economy. On the other hand, host countries complain of loss of sovereignty and domestic research activity, tax avoidance, inappropriate technology, and most benefits flowing to the home nation. As a result, most host nations have adopted policies to reduce these alleged harmful effects and increase the possible benefits.

6. International labor migration can occur for economic and noneconomic reasons. When the decision to migrate is economic, it can be evaluated in terms of costs and benefits just as any other investment in human and physical capital. International migration reduces total output and increases real wages in the nation of emigration while it increases total output and reduces real wages in the nation of immigration. These changes are accompanied by a net increase in world output. The migration of highly skilled and

trained people confers special benefits on the nation of immigration and imposes serious burdens, in the form of sunk and replacement costs, on the nation of emigration. This problem is referred to as the brain drain.

A Look Ahead

This chapter completes Part II, dealing with commercial policies and international resource movements. We next move on to Parts III and IV, in which we will be discussing the monetary sector, or international finance. In Part III, Chapter 13 examines the operation of foreign exchange markets, and Chapter 14 deals with the balance of payments.

Glossary

Portfolio investments   The purchase of purely financial assets, such as stocks and bonds, usually arranged through banks and investment funds.

Direct investments   Real investments in factories, capital goods, land, and inventories where both capital and management are involved and the investor retains control over the use of the invested capital. International direct investments are usually undertaken by multinational corporations.

Portfolio theory   Maintains that by investing in securities with yields that are inversely related over time, a given yield can be obtained at a smaller risk or a higher yield can be obtained for the same level of risk for the portfolio as a whole.

Risk diversification   Investments in securities with yields that are inversely, or negatively, correlated or investments in different lines or products in order to spread and thus reduce the overall risks of the total investments.

Horizontal integration   The production abroad of a differentiated product that is also produced at home.

Vertical integration   The expansion of a firm backward to supply its own raw materials and intermediate products and/or forward to provide its own sales or distribution networks.

Multinational corporations (MNCs)   Firms that own, control, or manage production and distribution facilities in several countries.

Transfer pricing   The over- and underpricing of products in the intrafirm trade of multinational corporations in an attempt to shift income and profits from high- to low-tax nations.

Brain drain   The migration of highly skilled and trained people from developing to developed nations and from other industrial nations to the United States.

Questions for Review

1. In what sense are international flows of productive resources a substitute for international commodity trade? What is meant by portfolio investments? Through what institutions do they usually take place? What is meant by direct investments? By what organizations are they usually undertaken internationally?

2. What was the dollar value of United States direct investments abroad and United States private holdings of long-term foreign securities in 1950 and 1984? How were United States foreign direct investments in 1984 distributed among Europe, Canada, Latin America, and elsewhere? How much of United States foreign direct investments in 1984 went into manufacturing, petroleum, and other activities? Answer the same questions for foreign investments in the United States.

3. What are the basic motives for international portfolio investments? What additional reasons are required to explain direct foreign investments? How can two-way international capital investments be explained? What is meant by risk diversification? Horizontal integration? Vertical integration?

4. What is the effect of foreign investments on the national income of the investing and host nations? What is the effect on the relative share of national income going to capital and labor in each nation? What is the effect of foreign

investments on the balance of payments of the investing and host nations in the short run and in the long run? What problems do nations with high corporate tax rates face?

5. What is the importance of multinational corporations today? What are the reasons for their existence? What are some of the problems created by multinational corporations in the home country? In the host country? How have host countries attempted to limit the alleged harmful effects and increase the beneficial effects of multinational corporations?

6. What are the motives for the international migration of workers? What is the effect of labor migration on real wages, total output, and the relative share of national income going to labor in the nation of emigration and the nation of immigration? What is meant by the brain drain? Why is it a problem? How can it be overcome?

Problems

1. On two sets of price-quantity axes referring to the capital market in the investing country and in the host country, respectively, show the effect of a capital flow on the price of capital in the:
   (a) investing nation;
   (b) receiving nation.

2. From the latest August issue of the *Survey of Current Business*, find the amount of foreign direct investment into the United States by major area or country of origin.

*3. Determine whether the following statement is true or false and explain why. "The profitability of a portfolio of many securities can never exceed the yield of the highest-yield security in the portfolio but it can have a risk lower than the lowest-risk security."

4. Draw a graph similar to Figure 12-1 showing:
   (a) equal gains in the two nations as a result of capital transfers from Nation 1 to Nation 2;
   (b) greater gains in Nation 1 resulting from capital transfers to Nation 2.
   (c) What general principle can you deduce

from your answers to parts a and b and from Figure 12-1 as to the distribution of the total gains from international capital transfers between the investing and host nations?

*5. Using Figure 12-1, explain why:
  (a) organized labor in the United States opposes United States investments abroad;

  (b) labor in developing nations benefits from an inflow of foreign investments.
6. Indicate for each of the 25 largest manufacturing MNCs in the world in terms of yearly sales: the home nation of the parent firm, the major industry, and the amount of yearly sales. (Hint: for the 1984 data, see the August 19, 1985 issue of *Fortune Magazine*, p. 179).

APPENDIX

The Transfer Problem

To be successful, any international long-term capital movement must be accompanied by a transfer of real resources from the investing or lending country to the host or borrowing country. For example, if a nation invests $100 million in another country, the investing nation must free real domestic resources and increase its exports to the host or receiving nation by $100 million in order for the international capital transfer actually to take place. Precisely how this transfer of real resources occurs is discussed in detail in section A16.2 in connection with the income adjustment mechanism to correct balance-of-payments disequilibria. At this point, all that needs to be remembered is that a transfer of real resources must accompany any international transfer of financial resources in order for the latter actually to occur. This is known as the **transfer problem.**

A transfer problem arises not only in the case of international capital movements but also in connection with reparations payments for war damages. Examples of these are the indemnities that France was made to pay to Prussia after the 1870–1871 war and Germany had to pay to France after World War I. A more recent example is the transfer problem that arose from the sharp increase in petroleum prices during the 1970s. Most petroleum-exporting nations, notably Saudi Arabia, Libya, and Kuwait, did not spend all of their petroleum earnings on increased imports from petroleum-importing countries. Most unspent earnings were used for portfolio purchases in developed nations, especially in the United States. To the extent that not all excess earnings were so used, a deflationary tendency arose in the world economy as petroleum-importing nations tried to reduce their collective import surplus. Thus, a transfer problem was at the heart of the petroleum crisis during the 1970s.

Of more immediate interest is the transfer problem arising from the huge net foreign investments in the United States during the 1980s, which resulted in the United States joining the ranks of the debtor nations in 1985, for the first time since 1914. The counterpart to these huge net capital flows to the

United States are the record trade deficits of the United States by which the transfer of real resources was accomplished (see sections 14.6b and A16.2).

Problem   For the period from 1973 to 1980, construct a table showing: (a) the dollar price per barrel of Saudi Arabian petroleum exports, (b) the dollar value of the total exports of the nations belonging to the Organization of Petroleum Exporting Countries (OPEC), (c) the dollar value of the total imports of OPEC, (d) the dollar value of United States petroleum imports. (Hint: consult the 1981 issue of *International Financial Statistics*, published by the International Monetary Fund, in your library).

Selected Bibliography

For a problem-solving approach to the topics covered in this chapter, see:
- D. Salvatore, *Theory and Problems of International Economics*, 2nd ed. (McGraw-Hill, 1984), ch. 5 (probs. 5.27 and 5.28) and ch. 7.

For data on foreign investments from and into the United States, see:
- Department of Commerce, *U.S. Survey of Current Business* (Washington: D.C.: United States Government Printing Office, August issue of any year for data on the previous year).

A clear and simple presentation of portfolio theory is found in:
- R. I. Robinson and D. Wrightman, *Financial Markets: The Accumulation and Allocation of Wealth* (New York: McGraw-Hill, 1974), ch. 5.

The motives for direct foreign investments are presented in:
- C. P. Kindleberger, *American Business Abroad* (New Haven, Conn.: Yale University Press, 1969).
- R. E. Caves, *Multinational Enterprise and Economic Analysis* (Cambridge: Cambridge University Press, 1982).
- N. Hood and S. Young, *The Economics of Multinational Enterprise* (London: Longman, 1979).

For risks and returns on foreign portfolio and direct investments, see:
- H. G. Grubel, "Internationally Diversified Portfolios: Welfare Gains and Capital Flows,"
American Economic Review, December 1968.
- A. Rugman, "Risk Reduction by International Diversification," *Journal of International Business Studies*, September 1976.

The classic article on the welfare effects of foreign investments is:
- G. D. A. MacDougall, "The Benefits and Costs of Private Investment from Abroad: A Theoretical Approach," *Economic Record*, March 1960.

A negative view on foreign investments in less developed nations is found in:
- H. W. Singer, "The Distribution of Gains between Investing and Borrowing Countries," *American Economic Review*, May 1950. Reprinted in R. E. Caves and H. G. Johnson, *Readings in International Economics* (Homewood, Ill.: Irwin, 1968).

For an overall theoretical discussion and empirical test of the relationship between international trade, foreign investments, and economic development, see:
- D. Salvatore, "A Simultaneous Equations Model of Trade and Development with Dynamic Policy Simulations," *Kyklos*, March (No. 1) 1983.

The leading collections of essays on multinational corporations are:
- C. P. Kindleberger, *The International Corporation* (Cambridge, Mass.: Harvard University Press, 1970).
- J. M. Berham, *National Interests and the Multinational Enterprise* (Englewood Cliffs, N.J.: Prentice-Hall, 1970).

• J. H. Dunning, *Studies in International Investment* (London: Allen & Unwin, 1970).

For evaluations of multinationals from a national or regional point of view, see:
  • C. F. Bergsten, et al., *American Multinationals and American Interests* (Washington, D.C.: Brookings Institution, 1978).
  • R. Vernon, *Storm over Multinationals* (Cambridge, Mass.: Harvard University Press, 1977).
  • J. J. Servan-Schreiber, *The American Challenge* (New York: Avon, 1969).
  • K. Levitt, *Silent Surrender* (Toronto: Macmillan, 1970).

For the motives and welfare effects of international labor migrations, see:

• H. G. Grubel and A. D. Scott, "The International Flow of Human Capital," *American Economic Review*, May 1966.
• W. A. Adams, ed., *The Brain Drain* (New York: Macmillan, 1968).
• T. Brinley, *Migration and Economic Growth* (Cambridge: Cambridge University Press, 1972).
• J. N. Bhagwati and M. Parkington, *Taxing the Brain Drain: A Proposal* (Amsterdam: North-Holland, 1976).
• M. J. Piore, *Birds of Passage* (Cambridge: Cambridge University Press, 1979).
• J. N. Bhagwati, *Dependence and Interdependence* (Cambridge, Mass.: M.I.T. Press, 1985), Part IV. Edited by G. M. Grossman.

PART III

Foreign Exchange Markets and the Balance of Payments

Part III (Chapters 13 and 14) deals with foreign exchange markets and the measurement of a nation's balance of payments. A clear grasp of the material in these two chapters is crucial for understanding Part IV, on adjustment to balance of payments disequilibria and Part V on the functioning of the present international monetary system. Besides presenting the theory, Chapter 13 also examines the actual operation of foreign exchange markets and therefore is of great practical relevance for all students of international economics, particularly business majors. Chapter 14 examines the meaning, function, and measurement of the balance of payments and defines the concepts of deficit and surplus in a nation's balance of payments.

CHAPTER 13

The Foreign Exchange Markets

13.1   Introduction

In Parts I and II, we dealt with the "real," as opposed to the monetary, side of the economy. Money was not explicitly considered, and the discussion was in terms of relative commodity prices. We now begin our examination of the monetary aspects of international economics, or international finance. Here, money is explicitly brought into the picture, and commodity prices are expressed in terms of domestic and foreign currency units. We begin our discussion of international finance by examining the functioning of foreign exchange markets.

The **foreign exchange market** is the market in which individuals, firms, and banks buy and sell foreign currencies or foreign exchange. The foreign exchange market for any currency, say, the U.S. dollar, is composed of all the locations (such as London, Zurich, Paris, Hong Kong, Singapore, Tokyo, and New York) where dollars are bought and sold for other currencies. These different monetary centers are connected by a telephone network and via telex and are in constant contact with one another.

In section 13.2, we examine the functions of foreign exchange markets. In section 13.3 we define foreign exchange rates and examine how they are determined under a flexible exchange rate system. We also discuss arbitrage, spot and forward rates, and foreign exchange futures and options. Section 13.4 then deals with foreign exchange risks, hedging, speculation, and the

323

efficiency of foreign exchange markets. Section 13.5 examines covered and uncovered interest arbitrage. Finally, section 13.6 deals with the Eurocurrency, Eurobond, and Euronote markets. In the appendix, we derive the demand and supply curves for a foreign currency, illustrate covered interest arbitrage and interest parity graphically, and derive the formula for the precise calculations of the covered interest arbitrage margin.

13.2   Functions of the Foreign Exchange Markets

By far the principal function of foreign exchange markets is the transfer of funds or purchasing power from one nation and currency to another. This is usually accomplished by a telegraphic transfer, which is a check that is wired rather than mailed. With it, a domestic bank instructs its correspondent bank in a foreign monetary center to pay a specified amount of the local currency to a person, firm, or account. With the recent introduction of direct dialing telephone service anywhere in the world, the telex has become relatively less important.

But why do individuals, firms, and banks want to exchange one national currency for another? The demand for foreign currencies arises when tourists visit another country and need to exchange their national currency for the currency of the country they are visiting, when a domestic firm wants to import from other nations, when an individual wants to invest abroad, and so on. On the other hand, a nation's supply of foreign currencies arises from foreign tourist expenditures in the nation, from export earnings, from receiving foreign investments, and so on. For example, suppose a United States firm exporting to the United Kingdom is paid in pounds sterling (the United Kingdom currency). The United States exporter will exchange the pounds for dollars at a commercial bank. The commercial bank will then sell these pounds for dollars to a United States resident who is going to visit the United Kingdom, to a United States firm that wants to import from the United Kingdom and pay in pounds, or to a United States investor who wants to invest in the United Kingdom and needs the pounds to make the investment.

Thus, a nation's commercial banks operate as *clearing houses* for the foreign exchange demanded and supplied in the course of foreign transactions by the nation's residents. In the absence of this function, a United States importer needing United Kingdom pounds, for instance, would have to locate a United States exporter with pounds to sell. This would be very time consuming and inefficient and would essentially revert to barter trade. Those United States commercial banks that find themselves with an over-supply of pounds will sell these excess pounds (through the intermediary of *foreign exchange brokers*) to commercial banks that happen to be short of pounds in satisfying their customers' demand for pounds. In the final analysis, then, a nation pays for its tourist expenditures abroad, its imports, its investments abroad, and so on, with its foreign exchange earnings from tourism, exports, and the receipt of foreign investments.

If the nation's total demand for foreign exchange in the course of its foreign transactions exceeds its total foreign exchange earnings, the rate at which currencies exchange for one another will have to change (as explained in the next section) to equilibrate the total quantities demanded and supplied. If such an adjustment in the exchange rates were not allowed, the nation's commercial banks would have to borrow from the nation's central bank. The nation's central bank would then act as the "lender of last resort" and draw down its foreign exchange reserves. On the other hand, if the nation generated an excess supply of foreign exchange in the course of its business transactions with other nations (and if adjustment in exchange rates were not allowed), this excess supply would be exchanged for the national currency at the nation's central bank, thus increasing the nation's foreign currency reserves.

Thus, four *levels* of transactors or participants can be identified in foreign exchange markets. At the bottom, or at the first level, are tourists, importers, exporters, investors, and so on. These are the immediate users and suppliers of foreign currencies. At the next, or second, level are the commercial banks, which act as clearing houses between users and earners of foreign exchange. At the third level are foreign exchange brokers, through whom the nation's commercial banks even out their foreign exchange inflows and outflows among themselves. Finally, at the fourth and highest level is the nation's central bank, which acts as the seller or buyer of last resort when the nation's total foreign exchange earnings and expenditures are unequal. The central bank then either draws down its foreign exchange reserves or adds to them.

Because of the special position of the United States dollar as an international as well as the national currency, United States importers and United States residents wishing to make investments abroad could pay in dollars. Then it would be the United Kingdom exporter or investment recipient that would have to exchange dollars for pounds in the United Kingdom. Similarly, United States exporters and United States recipients of foreign investments may require payment in dollars. Then it would be the United Kingdom importer or investor who would have to exchange pounds for dollars in London. This makes *foreign* monetary centers relatively larger than otherwise.

For the world as a whole, the total of foreign exchange trading has been estimated to be above $100 billion per day. Most of these foreign exchange transactions, however, take place through debiting and crediting bank accounts rather than through actual currency exchanges. For example, a United States importer will pay for British goods by debiting his account at his United States bank. The latter will then instruct its corresponding bank in the United Kingdom to credit the account of the United Kingdom exporter with the pound value of the goods.

Another function of foreign exchange markets is the credit function. Credit is usually needed when goods are in transit and also to allow the buyer time to resell the goods and make the payment. In general, exporters allow 90 days for the importer to pay. However, the exporter usually discounts the importer's obligation to pay at the foreign department of his commercial bank. As a result, the exporter receives payment right away, and the bank will eventually collect the payment from the importer when due. Still another function of foreign exchange markets is to provide the facilities for hedging and speculation. These are discussed in section 13.4, after we define foreign exchange rates and show how they are determined in free markets.

With direct dialing telephone service anywhere in the world, foreign exchange markets have become truly global in the sense that currency transactions now only require a simple telephone call and take place twenty-four hours per day. As banks end their regular business day in San Francisco and Los Angeles, they open in Singapore, Hong Kong, Sydney, and Tokyo; and by the time the latter wind down their regular business day, banks open in London, Frankfurt, Zurich, Paris, and Milan; before the latter close, New York and Chicago banks open.

13.3   The Foreign Exchange Rates

In this section, we first define exchange rates and show how they are determined under a flexible exchange rate system. Then we explain how exchange rates between currencies are equalized by arbitrage among different monetary centers. Subsequently, we distinguish between spot and forward exchange rates and examine their significance. Finally, we discuss foreign exchange futures and options.

13.3a   The Equilibrium Foreign Exchange Rates

Assume for simplicity that there are only two nations, the United States and the United Kingdom, with the dollar ($) as the domestic currency and the pound sterling (£) as the foreign currency. The **exchange rate** between the dollar and the pound (R) is equal to the number of dollars needed to purchase one pound. That is, $R = \$/£$. For example, if $R = \$/£ = 2$, this means that two dollars are required to purchase one pound.

Under a flexible exchange rate system of the type we have today, the dollar price of the pound (R) is determined, just like the price of any commodity, by the intersection of the market demand and supply curves for pounds. This is shown in Figure 13-1, where the vertical axis measures the dollar price of pounds, or the exchange rate, $R = \$/£$, and the horizontal axis measures the quantity of pounds. The market demand and supply curves for pounds intersect at point E, defining the equilibrium exchange rate of $R = 2$, at which the quantity of pounds demanded and the quantity supplied are equal at £40 million per day. At a higher exchange rate, the quantity of pounds supplied exceeds the quantity demanded, and the exchange rate will fall toward the equi-

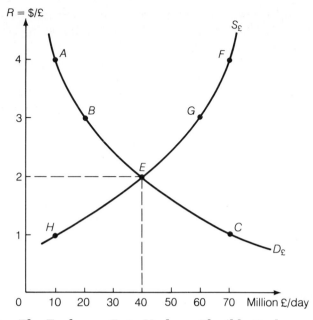

FIGURE 13-1.   The Exchange Rate Under a Flexible Exchange Rate System

The vertical axis measures the dollar price of pounds ($R = \$/£$) and the horizontal axis measures the quantity of pounds. With a flexible exchange rate system, the equilibrium exchange rate is $R = 2$, at which the quantity demanded and the quantity supplied are equal at £40 million per day. This is given by the intersection at point E of the U.S. demand and supply curves for pounds. At a higher exchange rate, a surplus of pounds would result that would tend to lower the exchange rate toward the equilibrium rate. At an exchange rate lower than $R = 2$, a shortage of pounds would result that would drive the exchange rate up toward the equilibrium level.

librium rate of $R = 2$. At an exchange rate lower than $R = 2$, the quantity of pounds demanded exceeds the quantity supplied, and the exchange rate will be bid up toward the equilibrium rate of $R = 2$. If the exchange rate were not allowed to rise to its equilibrium level (as under the fixed exchange rate system that prevailed up to March 1973), then either restrictions would have to be imposed on the demand for pounds of United States residents or the United States central bank (the Federal Reserve System) would have to fill the excess demand for pounds out of its international reserves.

The United States demand for pounds is negatively inclined, indicating that the lower the exchange rate (R), the greater is the quantity of pounds demanded by the United States. The reason is that the lower is the exchange rate (i.e., the fewer the number of dollars required to purchase one pound), the cheaper it is for the United States to import from and to invest in the United Kingdom, and thus the greater is the quantity of pounds demanded by United States residents. On the other hand, the United States supply of pounds is usually positively inclined (as in Figure 13-1), indicating that the higher

the exchange rate (R), the greater is the quantity of pounds earned by or supplied to the United States. The reason is that at higher exchange rates, United
Kingdom residents receive more dollars for each of their pounds. As a result,
they find United States goods and investments cheaper and more attractive
and spend more in the United States, thus supplying more pounds to the
United States. (The actual derivation of the demand and supply curves for
pounds shown in Figure 13-1 is presented in section A13.1 of the appendix.)

If the United States demand curve for pounds shifted up (for example, as a
result of increased United States tastes for British goods) and intersected the
United States supply curve for pounds at point G (see Figure 13-1), the equilibrium exchange rate would be $R = 3$, and the equilibrium quantity of pounds
would be £60 million per day. The dollar is then said to have depreciated
since it now requires three (instead of the previous two) dollars to purchase
one pound. **Depreciation** thus refers to an increase in the domestic price of
the foreign currency. On the other hand, if the United States demand curve
for pounds shifted down so as to intersect the United States supply curve for
pounds at point H (see Figure 13-1), the equilibrium exchange rate would fall
to $R = 1$, and the dollar is said to have appreciated (because fewer dollars are
now required to purchase one pound). **Appreciation** thus refers to a decline
in the domestic price of the foreign currency. An appreciation of the domestic
currency means a depreciation of the foreign currency and vice versa. Shifts
in the United States supply curve for pounds would similarly affect the equilibrium exchange rate and equilibrium quantity of pounds (this is left as an
end-of-chapter problem).

The exchange rate could also be defined as the foreign currency price of a
unit of the domestic currency. This is the inverse, or reciprocal, of our previous definition. That is, if the dollar price of the pound is $R = 2$, then the
pound price of the dollar is $1/R = 1/2$, or it takes half a pound to purchase one
dollar. Though this definition of the exchange rate is sometimes used, we will
use the previous one, or the dollar price of the pound (R). In the real world,
the particular definition of the exchange rate being used is generally spelled
out to avoid confusion.

Finally, while we have dealt with only two currencies for simplicity, in
reality there are numerous exchange rates, one between any pair of currencies.
Thus, besides the exchange rate between the United States dollar and the
British pound, there is an exchange rate between the United States dollar and
the German mark, between the United States dollar and the French franc,
between the British pound and the German mark, between the German mark
and the French franc, between each of these currencies and the Japanese yen,
and so on. Once the exchange rate between each of a pair of currencies with
respect to the dollar is established, the exchange rate between the two currencies themselves can easily be determined. Since over time a currency can
depreciate against some currencies and appreciate against others, an **effective
exchange rate** is calculated. This is a weighted average of the exchange rates
between the domestic currency and the nation's most important trade part-

ners, with weights given by the relative importance of the nation's trade with each of these trade partners.

13.3b Arbitrage

The exchange rate between any two currencies is kept the same in different monetary centers by **arbitrage.** This refers to the purchase of a currency in the monetary center where it is cheaper for immediate resale in the monetary center where it is more expensive in order to make a profit.

For example, if the dollar price of pounds were $1.99 in New York and $2.01 in London, an arbitrageur (usually a foreign exchange dealer of a commercial bank) would purchase pounds at $1.99 in New York and immediately resell them in London for $2.01, thus realizing a profit of $0.02 per pound. While the profit per pound transferred seems small, on £1 million the profit would be $20,000 for only a few minutes work. From this profit must be deducted the cost of the transatlantic telephone call and the other costs associated with arbitrage. Since these costs are very small, we shall ignore them here.

However, as arbitrage takes place, the exchange rate between the two currencies tends to be equalized in the two monetary centers. Continuing our example, we see that arbitrage increases the demand for pounds in New York, thereby exerting an upward pressure on the dollar price of pounds in New York. At the same time, the sale of pounds in London increases the supply of pounds there, thus exerting a downward pressure on the dollar price of pounds in London. This continues until the dollar price of pounds quickly becomes equal in New York and London (say at $2 = £1) thus eliminating the profitability of further arbitrage.

When only two currencies and two monetary centers are involved in arbitrage as in the above example, we have *two-point arbitrage.* When three currencies and three monetary centers are involved, we have *triangular, or three-point, arbitrage.* While triangular arbitrage is not very common, it operates in the same manner to ensure *consistent indirect, or cross, exchange rates* between the three currencies in the three monetary centers. For example, suppose exchange rates are as follows:

$$\$2 = £1 \text{ in New York}$$
$$£0.2 = 1 \text{ mark in London}$$
$$2.5 \text{ marks} = \$1 \text{ in Frankfurt}$$

These cross rates are consistent because:

$$\$2 = £1 = 5 \text{ marks}$$

and there is no possibility of profitable arbitrage. However, if the dollar price of pounds were $1.96 in New York, with the other exchange rates as indicated above, then it would pay to use $1.96 to purchase £1 in New York, use the £1 to buy 5 marks in London, and exchange the 5 marks for $2 in Frankfurt, thus realizing a $0.04 profit on each pound so transferred. On the other hand, if the dollar price of pounds was $2.04 in New York, it would pay to do just the opposite; that is, use $2 to purchase 5 marks in Frankfurt, exchange the 5 marks for £1 in London, and exchange the £1 for $2.04 in New York, thus making a profit of $0.04 on each pound so transferred.

As in the case of two-point arbitrage, triangular arbitrage increases the demand for the currency in the monetary center where the currency is cheaper, increases the supply of the currency in the monetary center where the currency is more expensive, and quickly eliminates inconsistent cross rates and the profitability of further arbitrage. As a result, arbitrage quickly equalizes exchange rates for each pair of currencies and results in consistent cross rates among all pairs of currencies, thus unifying all international monetary centers into a single market.

13.3c Spot and Forward Rates

The most common type of foreign exchange transaction involves the payment and receipt of the foreign exchange within two business days after the day the transaction is agreed upon. The two-day period gives adequate time for the parties to send instructions to debit and credit the appropriate bank accounts at home and abroad. This type of transaction is called *a spot transaction*, and the exchange rate at which the transaction takes place is called the **spot rate.** The exchange rate $R = \$/£ = 2$ in Figure 13-1 is a spot rate.

Besides spot transactions, there are *forward transactions*. These involve an agreement today to buy or sell a specified amount of a foreign currency at a specified future date at a rate agreed upon today (the **forward rate**). For example, I could enter into an agreement today to purchase £100 three months from today at $2.02 = £1. Note that no currencies are paid out at the time the contract is signed (except for the usual 10 percent security margin). After three months, I get the £100 for $202, regardless of what the spot rate is at that time. The typical forward contract is for one month, three months, or six months, with three months the most common. Forward contracts for longer periods are not as common because of the great uncertainties involved. However, forward contracts can be renegotiated for one or more periods when they become due. In what follows we will deal exclusively with three-month forward contracts and rates, but the procedure would be the same for forward contracts of different duration.

The equilibrium forward rate is determined at the intersection of the market demand and supply curves of foreign exchange *for future delivery*. The demand for and supply of forward foreign exchange arise in the course of hedging, from foreign exchange speculation and covered interest arbitrage. These, as well as the close relationship between the spot rate and the forward rate, are discussed next in sections 13.4 and 13.5. All that needs to be said here is that, at any point in time, the forward rate can be equal to, above, or below the corresponding spot rate.

If the forward rate is below the present spot rate, the foreign currency is said to be at a **forward discount** with respect to the domestic currency. On the other hand, if the forward rate is above the present spot rate, the foreign currency is said to be at a **foreign premium.** For example, if the spot rate is $2 = £1 and the three-month forward rate is $1.98 = £1, we say that the pound is at a three-month forward discount of 2 cents or 1 percent (or at a 4 percent forward discount per year) with respect to the dollar. On the other hand, if the spot rate is still $2 = £1 but the three-month forward rate is instead $2.02 = £1, the pound is said to be at a forward premium of 2 cents or 1 percent for three months, or 4 percent per year.

Forward discounts (*FD*) or premiums (*FP*) are usually expressed as percentages per year from the corresponding spot rate and can be calculated formally with the following formula:

$$FD \text{ or } FP = \frac{FR - SR}{SR} \times 4 \times 100 \qquad (13\text{-}1)$$

where *FR* is the forward rate and *SR* is the spot rate (what we simply called *R* in the previous sections). The multiplication by 4 is to express the *FD* (−) or *FP* (+) on a yearly basis, and the multiplication by 100 is to express the *FD* or *FP* in percentages. Thus, when the spot rate of the pound is *SR* = $2.00 and the forward rate is *FR* = $1.98, we get:

$$FD = \frac{\$1.98 - \$2.00}{\$2.00} \times 4 \times 100 = \frac{-\$0.02}{\$2.00} \times 4 \times 100 = -0.01 \times 4 \times 100 = -4\%$$

the same as found earlier without the formula. Similarly, if *SR* = $2 and *FR* = $2.02:

$$FP = \frac{\$2.02 - \$2.00}{\$2.00} \times 4 \times 100 = \frac{\$0.02}{\$2.00} \times 4 \times 100 = 0.01 \times 4 \times 100 = +4\%$$

Table 13-1 gives the spot rate for various currencies with respect to the United States dollar for Wednesday, January 22, 1986, and for Tuesday, January 21, 1986—first defined as the dollar price of the foreign currency and then as the foreign currency price of the dollar. For example, next to Britain, we find that the spot rate was $1.3970/£1 on Wednesday and $1.4110 on Tuesday. On the same line, we find that the pound price of the dollar was £0.7158/$ on Wednesday and £0.7087 on Tuesday. On the next three lines under Britain, we find the 30-day forward rate, the 90-day forward rate, and the 180-day forward rate. The 30-day forward rate of the pound is lower than the spot rate, meaning that the market expects the pound to be weaker in 30 days (and progressively weaker in 90 and 180 days, because the 90-day and

TABLE 13-1. *Foreign Exchange Quotations*

FOREIGN EXCHANGE

Wednesday, January 22, 1986

The New York foreign exchange selling rates below apply to trading among banks in amounts of $1 million and more, as quoted at 3 p.m. Eastern time by Bankers Trust Co. Retail transactions provide fewer units of foreign currency per dollar.

Country	U.S. $ equiv. Wed.	U.S. $ equiv. Tues.	Currency per U.S. $ Wed.	Currency per U.S. $ Tues.
Argentina (Austral) ...	1.2484	1.2484	.801	.801
Australia (Dollar)	.7115	.6995	1.4055	1.4296
Austria (Schilling)	.05841	.05794	17.12	17.26
Belgium (Franc)				
Commercial rate	.02010	.01995	49.75	50.12
Financial rate	.01990	.01980	50.25	50.50
Brazil (Cruzeiro)	.00009615	.00009615	10400.00	10400.00
Britain (Pound)	1.3970	1.4110	.7158	.7087
30-Day Forward	1.3908	1.4047	.7190	.7119
90-Day Forward	1.3790	1.3931	.7252	.7178
180-Day Forward	1.3622	1.3768	.7341	.7263
Canada (Dollar)	.7120	.7118	1.4045	1.4048
30-Day Forward	.7111	.7106	1.4062	1.4073
90-Day Forward	.7082	.7083	1.4121	1.4119
180-Day Forward	.7052	.7053	1.4180	1.4179
Chile (Official rate) ...	.005479	.005479	182.50	182.50
China (Yuan)	.3131	.3131	3.1935	3.1935
Colombia (Peso)	.005837	.005837	171.32	171.32
Denmark (Krone)	.1112	.1110	8.9900	9.0100
Ecuador (Sucre)				
Official rate	.01504	.01504	66.48	66.48
Floating rate	.007952	.007952	125.75	125.75
Finland (Markka)	.1835	.1833	5.4500	5.4550
France (Franc)	.1328	.1326	7.5325	7.5410
30-Day Forward	.1326	.1325	7.5415	7.5500
90-Day Forward	.1315	.1313	7.6050	7.6135
180-Day Forward	.1303	.1301	7.6775	7.6860
Greece (Drachma)	.006680	.006678	149.70	149.75
Hong Kong (Dollar)	.1281	.1280	7.8090	7.8095
India (Rupee)	.08091	.08137	12.36	12.29
Indonesia (Rupiah)	.0008881	.0008881	1126.00	1126.00
Ireland (Punt)	1.2450	1.2390	.8032	.8071
Israel (Shekel)	.0006739	.0006739	1484.00	1484.00
Italy (Lira)	.0006006	.0005988	1665.00	1670.00
Japan (Yen)	.004959	.004942	201.65	202.35
30-Day Forward	.004965	.004948	201.43	202.11
90-Day Forward	.004976	.004959	200.98	201.65
180-Day Forward	.004998	.004981	200.08	200.77
Jordan (Dinar)	2.8265	2.8265	.3538	.2895
Kuwait (Dinar)	3.4542	3.4542	.2895	.2895
Lebanon (Pound)	.05540	.05540	18.05	18.05
Malaysia (Ringgit)	.4058	.4061	2.4645	2.4625
Malta (Lira)	2.3781	2.3781	.4205	.4205
Mexico (Peso)				
Floating rate	z	z	z	z
Netherland(Guilder) .	.3631	.3617	2.7540	2.7645
New Zealand (Dollar)	.5185	.5150	1.9286	1.9417
Norway (Krone)	.1319	.1322	7.5800	7.5650
Pakistan (Rupee)	.06329	.06329	15.80	15.80
Peru (Sol)	.00007173	.00007173	13942.00	13942.00
Philippines (Peso)	.05263	.05263	19.00	19.00
Portugal (Escudo)	.006369	.006390	157.00	156.50
Saudi Arabia (Riyal) ..	.2739	.2739	3.6505	3.6500
Singapore (Dollar)	.4695	.4689	2.1300	2.1325
South Africa (Rand)				
Commercial rate	.4390	.4375	2.2779	2.2857
Financial rate	.3335	.3390	2.9985	2.9498
South Korea (Won)	.001123	.001123	890.66	890.60
Spain (Peseta)	.006523	.006515	153.30	153.50
Sweden (Krona)	.1312	.1312	7.6200	7.6200
Switzerland (Franc) ..	.4810	.4795	2.0790	2.0855
30-Day Forward	.4827	.4813	2.0718	2.0776
90-Day Forward	.4827	.4844	2.0583	2.0645
180-Day Forward	.4904	.4891	2.0390	2.0445
Taiwan (Dollar)	.02523	.02523	39.63	39.63
Thailand (Baht)	.03752	.03752	26.65	26.65
United Arab (Dirham) ..	.2723	.2723	.3673	.3673
Uruguay (New Peso)				
Financial	.008008	.008008	124.875	124.875
Venezuela (Bolivar)				
Official rate	.1333	.1333	7.50	7.50
Floating rate	.06305	.06305	15.86	15.86
W. Germany (Mark) ..	.4075	.4066	2.4540	2.4592
30-Day Forward	.4088	.4079	2.4461	2.4513
90-Day Forward	.4111	.4102	2.4325	2.4380
180-Day Forward	.4145	.4136	2.4124	2.4179
SDR	1.09196	1.09260	0.915789	0.915251
ECU	0.882029	0.885970	.....	.....

Special Drawing Rights are based on exchange rates for the U.S., West German, British, French and Japanese currencies. Source: International Monetary Fund.

ECU is based on a basket of community currencies. Source: European Community Commission.

z-Not quoted.

Source: *The Wall Street Journal,* Thursday January 23, 1986, p. 60.

180-day forward rates are smaller than the spot rate by larger amounts than the 30-day forward rate).

13.3d   Foreign Exchange Futures and Options

An individual, firm, or bank can also purchase or sell foreign exchange futures and options. Trading in foreign exchange futures was initiated in 1972 by the International Monetary Market (IMM) of the Chicago Mercantile Exchange. A **foreign exchange futures** is a forward contract for standardized currency amounts and selected calendar dates traded on an organized market (exchange). The currencies traded on the IMM are the British pound, the German mark, the Swiss franc, the Canadian dollar, the Japanese yen, the Mexican peso, the French franc, and the Dutch guilder.

IMM trading is done in contracts of standard size. For example, the IMM pound contract is for £25,000, the Canadian dollar contract is for C$100,000, and the Japanese yen contract is for Y12,500,000. Only four dates per year are available: the third Wednesday in March, June, September, and December. The IMM imposes a daily limit on exchange rate fluctuations. Buyers and sellers pay a brokerage commission and are required to post a security deposit or margin (of about 4% of the value of the contract). A market similar to the IMM is the London International Financial Futures Exchange (LIFFE), which started operation in September 1982. Currency futures are also exchanged on the COMEX commodities exchange in New York and on the American Board of Trade.

In contrast, a *forward contract* is an agreement between two parties (usually a customer and a bank) to purchase or sell any currency, in any amount, for delivery at any future date, and subject to no daily limit on exchange rate fluctuations. Since it is only by chance that the standard size and particular dates of *futures contracts* will conform exactly to the needs of importers and exporters, they are not as useful as forward contracts. Large firms and financial institutions with a fairly continuous stream of payments and receipts in the traded foreign currencies, however, can find futures contracts useful and cheaper. While the market for currency futures is small compared with the forward market, IMM has grown very rapidly, especially in very recent years. The two markets are also connected by arbitrage when prices differ.

Since 1982, individuals, firms, and banks can also purchase or sell foreign exchange options (in Canadian dollars, pounds, Swiss francs, German marks, and yen) on the Philadelphia Stock Exchange, in German marks on the Chicago Mercantile Exchange since 1984, or from a bank. A **foreign exchange option** is a contract specifying the right, not the obligation, to buy or sell a standard amount of a traded currency within a specified period. Foreign exchange options are in standard sizes that are half those of futures IMM contracts. The buyer of the option has the choice to purchase the currency within the specific period or forego the purchase if it turns out to be unprofitable. The seller of the option, however, must fulfill the contract if the buyer so desires. The buyer pays the seller a premium (the option price) ranging from 1 to 5 percent of the contract's value for this privilege when he enters the contract.

In contrast, neither forward contracts nor futures are options. Though forward contracts can be reversed (e.g., a party can sell a currency forward to neutralize a previous purchase) and futures contracts can be sold back to the futures exchange, both must be exercised (i.e., both contracts must be honored by both parties on the delivery date). Thus, options are less flexible than forward contracts, but in some cases they may be more useful. For example, an American firm making a bid to take over a British firm may be required to *promise* to pay a specified amount in pounds. Since the American firm does not know if its bid will be successful, it will purchase an option to buy the pounds that it would need, and will exercise the option if the bid is successful.

13.4   Foreign Exchange Risks, Hedging, and Speculation

In this section, we examine the meaning of foreign exchange risks and how they can be avoided or covered by individuals and firms whose main business is not speculation. We then discuss how speculators attempt to earn a profit by trying to anticipate future foreign exchange rates.

13.4a   Foreign Exchange Risks

Through time, a nation's demand and supply curves for foreign exchange shift, causing the spot (and the forward) rate to frequently vary. A nation's demand and supply curves for foreign exchange shift over time as a result of changes in tastes for domestic and foreign products in the nation and abroad, different growth and inflation rates in different nations, changes in relative rates of interest, changing expectations, and so on.

For example, if United States tastes for British products increase, the United States demand for pounds increases (the demand curve shifts up), leading to a rise in the exchange rate (i.e., a depreciation of the dollar). On the other hand, a lower rate of inflation in the United States than in the United Kingdom leads to United States products becoming cheaper for United Kingdom residents. This tends to increase the United States supply of pounds (the supply curve shifts to the left) and cause an appreciation of the dollar. Or simply the expectation of a stronger dollar may lead to an appreciation of the dollar. In short, in a dynamic and changing world, exchange rates frequently vary, reflecting the constant change in the numerous economic forces simultaneously at work.

Figure 13-2 shows the great variation in daily exchange rates between the United States dollar and the other major international currencies from 1978 and 1986. Note the sharp appreciation of the United States dollar with respect

(in U.S. cents)

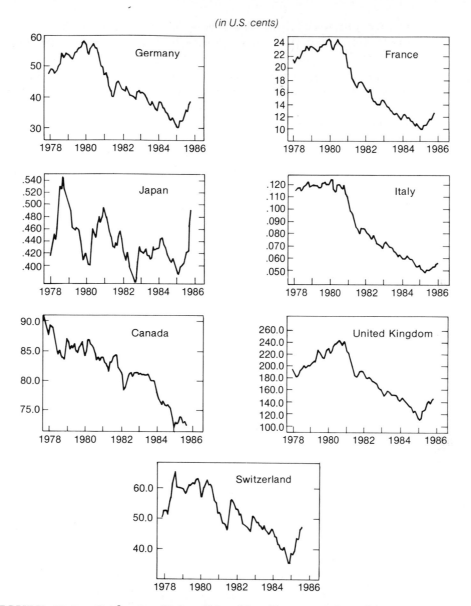

FIGURE 13-2.   Exchange Rates: Monthly Averages of Daily Quotations in the Foreign Exchange Market in the Major Financial Center of the Reporting Country

The exchange rate is defined here as the price of a unit of the foreign currency in U.S. cents. *Source:* International Monetary Fund, *International Financial Statistics* (Washington, D.C.: International Monetary Fund, Various Issues).

to these currencies from the beginning of 1980 until the beginning of 1985, and the large depreciation since then (except for the Canadian dollar).

Since the exchange rate between the United States dollar and the various currencies changed by different amounts and sometimes in different directions over time, the effective exchange rate (defined as the weighted average foreign currency value of the dollar) is shown in Figure 13-3. The sharp appreciation in the effective rate of the dollar from the beginning of 1984 until the beginning of 1985, as well as its depreciation since then, are clearly shown in the figure.

The frequent and relatively large fluctuations in exchange rates shown in Figure 13-2 impose foreign exchange risks on all individuals, firms, and banks that have to make or receive payments in the future denominated in a foreign currency. For example, suppose a United States importer purchases £100,000 worth of goods from the United Kingdom and has to pay in three months in pounds. If the present spot rate of the pound is $SR = \$2/£1$, the current dollar value of the payment that he must make in three months is $200,000. However, in three months the spot rate might change to $SR = \$2.10/£1$. Then he would have to pay $210,000, or $10,000 more, for his imports. Of course, in

FIGURE 13-3.   Effective Exchange Rate of the U.S. Dollar, 1978–1985

The effective exchange rate is here defined as the weighted average foreign currency value of the dollar. *Source:* Federal Reserve Bank of St. Louis, *International Economic Conditions,* January 1986, p. 2.

three months the spot rate might be $SR = \$1.90/\pounds1$, in which case he would have to pay only $190,000 or $10,000 less than he anticipated. However, the importer has enough to worry about in his import business without also having to face this exchange risk. As a result, he will usually want to insure himself against an increase in the dollar price of the pound (i.e., an increase in the spot rate) in three months.

Similarly, a United States exporter who expects to receive a payment of £100,000 in three months will receive only $190,000 (instead of the $200,000 that he anticipates at today's spot rate of $SR = \$2/\pounds1$) if the spot rate in three months is $SR = \$1.90/\pounds1$. Once again, the spot rate could be higher in three months than it is today, so that the exporter would receive more than he anticipates. However, the exporter, like the importer, will usually want to avoid (at a small cost) the exchange risk that he faces. Another example is provided by an investor who buys pounds at today's spot rate in order to invest in three-month British treasury bills paying a higher rate than United States treasury bills. However, in three months, when he wants to convert pounds back into dollars, the spot rate may have fallen sufficiently to wipe out most of the extra interest earned on the British bills or even produce a loss.

What these three examples clearly show is that whenever a future payment must be made or received in a foreign currency, a **foreign exchange risk,** or a so-called "open position," is involved because spot exchange rates vary over time. In general, businessmen will want to avoid or insure themselves against their foreign exchange risk. (Note that arbitrage does not involve any exchange risk since the currency is bought at the cheaper price in one monetary center *to be resold immediately* at the higher price in another monetary center.) A foreign exchange risk arises not only from transactions involving future payments and receipts in a foreign currency (the transaction exposure), but also from the need to value inventories and assets held abroad in terms of the domestic currency for inclusion in the firm's consolidated balance sheet (the translation or accounting exposure), and in estimating the domestic currency value of the future profitability of the firm (the economic exposure). In what follows we concentrate on the transaction exposure or risk.

13.4b Hedging

Hedging refers to the avoidance of a foreign exchange risk, or the *covering* of an open position. For example, the importer of the previous example could borrow £100,000 at the present spot rate of $SR = \$2/\pounds1$ and leave this sum on deposit in a bank (to earn interest) for three months, when his payment is due. By so doing, the importer avoids the risk that the spot rate in three months will be higher than today's spot rate and that he would have to pay more than $200,000 for his imports. The cost of insuring himself against the foreign exchange risk in this way is the positive difference between the interest rate he has to pay on his loan of £100,000 and the lower interest rate he earns on his deposit of £100,000. Similarly, the exporter could borrow £100,000 today, exchange this sum for $200,000 at today's spot rate of $SR = \$2/\pounds1$, and deposit the $200,000 in a bank to earn interest. After three months, the exporter would repay his loan of £100,000 with the payment of £100,000 he receives. The cost of avoiding the foreign exchange risk in this manner is, once again, equal to the positive difference between the borrowing and deposit rates of interest.

Covering the foreign exchange risk in the spot market as indicated above has a very serious disadvantage, however. The businessman or investor must borrow or tie up his own funds for three months. To avoid this, hedging usually takes place in the forward market, where no borrowing or tying up of funds is required. Thus, the importer could buy pounds forward for delivery (and payment) in three months at today's three-month forward rate. If the pound is at a three-month forward premium of 4 percent per year, the importer will have to pay $202,000 in three months for the £100,000 he needs to pay for his imports. Therefore, his hedging cost will be $2,000 (1 percent of $200,000 for the three months).

Similarly, the exporter could *sell* pounds forward for delivery (and payment) in three months at today's three-month forward rate, in anticipation of receiving the payment of £100,000 for his exports. Since no transfer of funds takes place until three months have passed, the exporter need not borrow or tie up his own funds now. If the pound is at a three-month forward discount of 4 percent per year, the exporter will get only $198,000 for the £100,000 he delivers in three months. On the other hand, if the pound is at a 4 percent forward premium, the exporter will receive $202,000 in three months with certainty by hedging.

A foreign exchange risk can also be hedged and an open position avoided in the futures or options markets. For example, suppose that an importer knows that it must pay £100,000 in three months and the three-month forward rate of the pound is $FR = \$2/\pounds1$. The importer could either purchase the £100,000 forward (in which case he will have to pay $200,000 in three months and receive the £100,000) or purchase an option to purchase £100,000 in three months, say at $\$2/\pounds1$, and pay now the premium of, say, 1 percent (or $2,000 on the $200,000 option). If in three months, the spot rate of the pound is $SR = \$1.95/\pounds1$, the importer would have to pay $200,000 with the forward contract, but could let the option expire unexercised and get the £100,000 at the cost of only $195,000 on the spot market. In that case, the $2,000 premium can be regarded as an insurance policy and the importer will save $3,000 over the forward contract.

In a world of foreign exchange uncertainty, the ability of traders and investors to hedge greatly facilitates the international flow of trade and investments. Without hedging there would be smaller international capital flows, less trade and specialization in production, and smaller benefits from trade. Note that a large firm, such as a multinational corporation, that has to make and receive a large number of payments in the same foreign currency at the same time in the future need only hedge its *net* open position. Similarly, a bank has an open position only in the amount of its *net balance* on contracted future payments and receipts in each foreign currency at each future date. The bank closes as much as its open position as possible by dealing with other banks (through foreign exchange brokers), and it may cover the remainder in the spot, futures, or options markets.

13.4c Speculation

Speculation is the opposite of hedging. Whereas a hedger seeks to cover a foreign exchange risk, a speculator accepts and even seeks out a foreign exchange risk, or an open position, in the hope of making a profit. If the speculator correctly anticipates future changes in spot rates, he makes a profit, otherwise he incurs a loss. As in the case of hedging, speculation can take place in the spot, forward, futures, or options markets—most usually in the forward market. We begin by examining speculation in the spot market.

If a speculator believes that the spot rate of a particular foreign currency will rise, he could purchase the currency now and hold it on deposit in a bank for resale. If the speculator is correct and the spot rate does indeed rise, he earns a profit on each unit of the foreign currency he bought equal to the spread between the previous lower spot rate at which he purchases the foreign currency and the higher subsequent spot rate at which he resells it. If the speculator is wrong and the spot rate falls instead, he incurs a loss because he must resell the foreign currency at a price lower than the purchase price.

If, on the other hand, the speculator believes that the spot rate will fall, he borrows the foreign currency for three months, immediately exchanges it for the domestic currency at the prevailing spot rate, and deposits the domestic currency in a bank to earn interest. After three months, if the spot rate on the foreign currency is lower, as he anticipated, he earns a profit by purchasing the currency (to repay his foreign exchange loan) at the lower spot rate. (Of course, for the speculator to earn a profit, the new spot rate must be sufficiently lower than the previous spot rate to also overcome the possibly higher interest rate paid on a foreign currency deposit over the domestic currency deposit.) If the spot rate in three months is higher rather than lower, the speculator incurs a loss.

In both of the above examples, the speculator operated in the spot market and either had to tie up his own funds or had to borrow to speculate. It is to avoid this serious shortcoming that speculation, like hedging, usually takes place in the forward market. For example, if the speculator believes that the spot rate of a certain foreign currency will be higher in three months than its present three-month forward rate, he purchases a specified amount of the foreign currency forward for delivery (and payment) in three months. After three months, if he is correct, he receives delivery of the foreign currency at the lower agreed forward rate and immediately resells it at the higher spot rate, thus realizing a profit. Of course, if the speculator is wrong and the spot rate in three months is lower than the agreed forward rate, he incurs a loss. In any event, no currency changes hands until the three months are over (except for the normal 10 percent security margin that the speculator is required to pay at the time he signs the forward contract).

As another example, suppose that the three-month forward rate on the pound is $FR = \$2.02/\pounds 1$ and the speculator believes that the spot rate of the pound in three months will be $SR = \$1.98/\pounds 1$. He then sells pounds forward for delivery in three months. After three months, if he is correct and the spot rate is indeed as he anticipated, he purchases pounds in the spot market at $SR = \$1.98/\pounds 1$ and immediately resells them to fulfill the forward contract at the agreed forward rate of $\$2.02/\pounds 1$, thereby earning a profit of 4¢ per pound. If the spot rate in three months is instead $SR = \$2.00/\pounds 1$, the speculator earns only 2¢ per pound. If the spot rate in three months is $\$2.02/\pounds 1$, he earns nothing. Finally, if the spot rate in three months is higher than the forward rate, at which he sold the forward pounds, the speculator incurs a loss on each pound equal to the difference between the two rates.

As an alternative, the above speculator (who believes that the pound will depreciate) could have purchased an option to sell a specific amount of pounds in three months at the rate, of say, $\$2.02/\pounds 1$. If in three months, he is correct and the spot rate of the pound is indeed $\$1.98/\pounds 1$ as he anticipated, he will exercise the option, buy pounds in the spot market at $\$1.98/\pounds 1$, and receive $\$2.02/\pounds 1$ by exercising the option. By so doing, the speculator earns 4¢ per pound (from which he deducts the premium or the option price to determine his net gain). In this case, the result will be the same as with the forward contract, except that the option price may exceed the commission on the forward contract, so that his net profit with the option may be a little less. On the other hand, if the speculator is wrong and the spot rate of the pound is much higher than he expected after three months, he will let his option contract expire unexercised and incur only the cost of the premium or option price. With the forward contract, he would have to honor his commitment and incur a much larger loss.

When a speculator buys a foreign currency on the spot, forward, or futures market, or buys an option to purchase a foreign currency in the expectation of reselling it at a higher future spot rate, he is said to take a *long position* in the currency. On the other hand, when he borrows or sells forward a foreign currency in the expectation of buying it at a future lower price to repay his foreign exchange loan or honor his forward sale contract or option, the speculator is said to take a *short position* (i.e., he is now selling what he does not now have).

Speculation can be stabilizing or destabilizing. **Stabilizing speculation** refers to the purchase of a foreign currency when the domestic price of the foreign currency (i.e., the exchange rate) falls or is low, in the expectation that it will soon rise, thus leading to a profit. Or, it refers to the sale of the foreign currency when the exchange rate rises or is high, in the expectation that it will soon fall. Stabilizing speculation moderates fluctuations in exchange rates over time and performs a useful function.

On the other hand, **destabilizing speculation** refers to the sale of a foreign currency when the exchange rate falls or is low, in the expectation that it will fall even lower in the future, or the purchase of a foreign currency when the exchange rate is rising or is high, in the expectation that it will rise even higher in the future. Destabilizing speculation thus magnifies exchange rate fluctuations over time and can prove very disruptive to the international flow of trade and investments. Whether speculation is primarily stabilizing or destabilizing is a very important question, to which we return in Chapter 15 when we analyze in depth the operation of a flexible exchange rate system and in Chapter 19 when we compare the operation of a flexible exchange rate system with that of a fixed exchange rate system. In general, it is believed that under "normal" conditions speculation is stabilizing, and we so assume here.

Speculators are usually wealthy individuals or firms rather than banks. However, anyone who has to make a payment in a foreign currency in the future can speculate by speeding up payment if he expects the exchange rate to rise and delaying it if he expects the exchange rate to fall, while anyone who has to receive a future payment in a foreign currency can speculate by using the reverse tactics. For example, if an importer expects the exchange rate to rise soon, he can anticipate the placing of an order and pay for imports right away. On the other hand, an exporter who expects the exchange rate to rise will want to delay deliveries and extend longer credit terms to delay payment. These are known as *leads* and *lags* and are a form of speculation.

13.5   Interest Arbitrage and the Efficiency of Foreign Exchange Markets

Interest arbitrage refers to the international flow of short-term liquid capital to earn higher returns abroad. Interest arbitrage can be covered or uncovered. These are discussed in turn. We will then examine the efficiency of foreign exchange markets.

13.5a   Uncovered Interest Arbitrage

Since the transfer of funds abroad to take advantage of higher interest rates in foreign monetary centers involves the conversion of the domestic to the foreign currency to make the investment, and the subsequent reconversion of the funds (plus the interest earned) from the foreign currency to the domestic currency at the time of maturity, a foreign exchange risk is involved due to the possible depreciation of the foreign currency during the period of the investment. If such a foreign exchange risk is covered, we have covered interest arbitrage, otherwise we have uncovered interest arbitrage. Even though interest arbitrage is usually covered, we begin by examining the simpler **uncovered interest arbitrage.**

Suppose that the interest rate on three-month treasury bills is 10 percent at an annual basis in New York and 14 percent in London. It may then pay for a United States investor to exchange dollars for pounds at the current spot rate and purchase British treasury bills to earn the extra 1 percent interest for the three months. When the British treasury bills mature, the United States investor may want to exchange the pounds he invested plus the interest he earned back into dollars. However, by that time, the pound may have depreciated so that he would get back fewer dollars per pound than he paid. If the pound depreciates by ½ of 1 percent during the three months of the investment, the United States investor nets only about ½ of 1 percent from his foreign investment (the extra 1 percent interest he earns minus the ½ of 1 percent that he loses from the depreciation of the pound). If the pound depreciates by 1 percent during the three months, the United States investor gains nothing, and if the pound depreciates by more than 1 percent, the United States investor loses. Of course, if the pound *appreciates*, the United States investor gains both from the extra interest he earns and from the appreciation of the pound.

13.5b   Covered Interest Arbitrage

Investors of short-term funds abroad generally want to avoid the foreign exchange risk; therefore, interest arbitrage is usually covered. To do this, the investor exchanges the domestic for the foreign currency at the current spot rate in order to purchase the foreign treasury bills, and at the same time he sells forward the amount of the foreign currency he is investing plus the interest he will earn so as to coincide with the maturity of his foreign investment. Thus, **covered interest arbitrage** refers to the spot purchase of the foreign currency to make the investment and the offsetting simultaneous forward sale *(swap)* of the foreign currency to cover the foreign exchange risk. When the treasury bills mature, the investor can then get the domestic currency equivalent of the foreign investment plus the interest earned without a foreign exchange risk. Since the currency with the higher interest rate is usually at a forward discount, the net return on the investment is *roughly* equal to the positive interest differential earned abroad minus the forward discount on the foreign currency. This reduction in earnings is the cost of insurance against the foreign exchange risk.

As an illustration, let us continue the previous example where the interest rate on three-month treasury bills is 10 percent per year in New York and 14 percent in London, and assume that the pound is at a three-month forward discount of 1 percent per year. To engage in covered interest arbitrage, the United States investor must exchange dollars for pounds at the current exchange rate (to purchase the British treasury bills) and at the same time sell forward a quantity of pounds equal to the amount invested plus the interest he will earn at the prevailing forward rate. Since the pound is at a forward discount of 1 percent per year, the United States investor loses ¼ of 1 percent on the foreign exchange transaction to cover his foreign exchange risk for the three months. His net gain is thus the extra 1 percent interest he earns for the three months minus the ¼ of 1 percent he loses on the foreign exchange transaction, or ¾ of 1 percent.

However, as covered interest arbitrage continues, the possibility of gains diminishes until it is completely wiped out. This occurs for two reasons. First, as funds are transferred from New York to London, the interest rate rises in New York (since the supply of funds in New York diminishes) and falls in London (since the supply of funds in London increases). As a result, the positive interest differential in favor of London diminishes. Second, the purchase of pounds in the spot market increases the spot rate, and the sale of pounds in the forward market reduces the forward rate. Thus, the forward discount on the pound (i.e., the positive difference between the spot rate and the forward rate) rises. With the positive interest differential in favor of London diminishing and the forward discount on the pound rising, the net gain falls for both reasons until it becomes zero. Then the pound is said to be at **interest parity.** Here, the positive interest differential in favor of the foreign monetary center is equal to the forward discount on the foreign currency (both expressed on an annual basis). In the real world, a net gain of at least ¼ percent per year is normally required to induce funds to move internationally under covered interest arbitrage.

If the pound is instead at a forward premium, the net gain to the United States investor will equal the extra interest earned for the three months plus the forward premium on the pound for the three months. However, as covered interest arbitrage continues, the positive interest differential in favor of London diminishes (as indicated earlier) and so does the forward premium on the pound until it becomes a forward discount and all of the gains are once again wiped out. Thus, the spot and the forward rate on a currency are closely related through covered interest arbitrage. This is shown more rigorously with Figure 13-5 in the appendix, where we will also derive the formula to calculate precisely the covered interest arbitrage margin (CIAM).

In the real world, significant covered interest arbitrage margins are often observed for long periods. The reason for this is not that covered interest arbitrage does not necessarily work. Rather, it is likely to be the result of other forces at work not accounted for by the pure theory of covered interest arbitrage. Some of these other forces are the different real growth rates among nations, differential growth in their money supplies, and differences in expectations, in liquidity preferences, in inflation rates, and in fiscal and trade policies. Lack of adequate information and government restrictions on short-term international capital flows can also sometimes account for the persistence of wide covered interest arbitrage margins.

Finally, it must be remembered that behind the demand and supply curves of foreign exchange are not only traders and investors (as explained in section 13.2a), but also hedgers, speculators, and interest arbitrageurs (as explained in this and section 13.4). Governments also operate in foreign exchange markets, both in their normal function of making and receiving foreign payments (such as for economic aid and military expenditures abroad, to maintain embassies abroad, etc.) and in their effort to affect the level and the movement of exchange rates. It is all of these forces together that determine exchange rates at the intersection of the nation's aggregate demand and supply curves for each foreign currency under a flexible exchange rate system (of the type in operation today). We shall return to this topic in much greater detail in the next and subsequent chapters.

13.5c   The Efficiency of Foreign Exchange Markets

A market is said to be *efficient* if prices reflect all available information. The foreign exchange market is said to be efficient if forward rates accurately predict future spot rates. That is, if forward rates reflect all available information and quickly adjust to any new information, so that investors cannot earn consistent and unusual profits by utilizing any available information.

Questions of market efficiency are important because only when markets are efficient do prices correctly reflect the scarcity value of the various resources and result in allocational efficiency. For example, if for whatever reason, the price of a commodity is higher than its value to consumers, then too many resources flow to the production of the commodity at the expense of other commodities that consumers prefer.

By their very nature, tests of the market efficiency are very difficult to formulate and to interpret. Even if foreign exchange markets were efficient, we cannot expect that the forward rate of a currency be identical to the future spot rate of the currency, because the latter also depends on unforseen events. However, if the forward rate exceeds the future spot rate as often as it falls below it, then we could say that the market is efficient, in the sense that there is no available information that investors could systematically use to ensure consistent and unusual profits.

Many empirical tests have been conducted by *Levich* and others on the **efficiency of foreign exchange markets.** Most of these studies seem to indicate that foreign exchange markets are efficient according to this definition of efficiency. For example, several empirical tests show that few opportunities exist for risk-free arbitrage, and deviations from interest rate parity are, for the most part, smaller than transaction costs. Similarly, speculators sometimes earn profits and sometimes incur losses, and seldom face opportunities for certain and large profits.

While most studies seem to indicate that foreign exchange markets are fairly efficient, this conclusion is not unanimous. Exchange rates do seem to respond very quickly to news, are very volatile, and have defied all attempts at being accurately forecasted. Note, however, that though the forward rate may reflect all or nearly all available information and in general seems to exceed the future spot rate as often as it falls below it, the *degree* by which the forward rate exceeds or falls short of the future spot rate (i.e., its variance) may itself be large or small. In recent years this variance has been relatively large. That is, the forward rate seems to be a good but not an efficient predictor of the future spot rate.

In recent years, and as exchange rates have become more volatile, the volume of foreign exchange transactions have grown much faster than the volume of world trade and faster than even the much larger flows of investment capital. The risks associated with all kinds of foreign exchange trading have increased significantly, but so have the awareness of them, the knowledge to deal with them, and the instruments available to cover them.

13.6 Eurocurrency, Eurobond, and Euronote Markets

In this section, we first describe Eurocurrency markets and then examine their operation and effects on the nations involved and on the functioning of the present international monetary system. Finally, we examine the Eurobond and Euronote markets.

13.6a Description of the Eurocurrency Markets

Eurocurrency refers to commercial bank deposits outside the country of issue of the currency. For example, a deposit denominated in United States dollars in a British commercial bank (or even in a British branch of a United States bank) is called a Eurodollar. Similarly, a pound sterling deposit in a French commercial bank or in a French branch of a British bank is a Eurosterling, a mark deposit in an Italian bank is a Euromark, and so on. These balances are usually borrowed or lent by major international banks, international corporations, and governments when they need to acquire or invest additional funds. The market in which this borrowing and lending takes place is called the **Eurocurrency market.**

Initially, only the dollar was used in this fashion and the market was therefore called the Eurodollar market. Subsequently, the other leading currencies (the British pound sterling, the German mark, the Japanese yen, and the French and the Swiss franc) began to be used in this way, and so the market is now more appropriately called the Eurocurrency market. The practice of keeping bank deposits denominated in a currency other than that of the nation in which the deposit is held has also spread to such non-European international monetary centers as Tokyo, Hong Kong, Singapore, and Kuwait. Even though outside Europe and even if denominated in yen, these deposits are often referred to as Eurocurrency (despite the obvious misnomer) because the market has been concentrated in Europe. A more precise name would be *offshore deposits*.

The Eurocurrency market consists mostly of short-term funds with maturity of less than six months. The Eurocurrency market has grown extremely rapidly, from less than $10 billion in the early 1960s to over $1 trillion in 1986.

Slightly more than half of the total value of Eurocurrencies is now in Euro-dollars. There are several reasons for the existence and rapid growth of the Eurocurrency and Eurodollar markets. The following are some of the reasons:

One reason is the higher interest rates often prevailing abroad on short-term deposits. The Federal Reserve System *Regulation Q* put a ceiling on the interest rates that United States member banks could pay on deposits, to levels that were often below the rates paid by European banks. As a result, short-term dollar deposits were attracted to European banks and became Eurodollars. Another important reason is that international corporations often find it very convenient to hold balances abroad for short periods in the currency in which they need to make payments. Since the dollar is the most important "international" (or vehicle) currency in making and receiving international payments (even for communist nations), more than half of the Eurocurrency is in Eurodollars. Still another reason is that international corporations can overcome domestic credit restrictions by borrowing in the Eurocurrency market. A fourth reason for the existence of the Eurocurrency market is that communist nations prefer to keep their dollar deposits outside the United States for fear that they might be frozen in a political crisis. Indeed, this is how the Eurocurrency market originated. The Eurodollar market grew especially rapidly after 1973 with the huge dollar deposits from petroleum-exporting countries, arising from the many-fold increase in the price of petroleum.

European banks are willing to accept deposits denominated in foreign currencies and are able to pay higher interest rates on these deposits than United States banks because they can lend these deposits at still higher rates. In general, the spread between lending and borrowing rates on Eurocurrency deposits is smaller than that of United States banks. Thus, European banks are often able to pay higher deposit rates and lend at lower rates than United States banks. This is the result of (1) the fierce competition for deposits and loans in the Eurocurrency market, (2) the lower operating costs in the Eurocurrency market due to the absence of legal reserve requirements and other restrictions on Eurocurrency deposits (except for United States branches of European banks), (3) economies of scale in dealing with very large deposits and loans, and (4) risk diversification. Arbitrage is so extensive in the Eurocurrency market that interest parity is generally maintained.

13.6b Operation and Effects of Eurocurrency Markets

One important question is whether Eurocurrencies are money. Since Eurocurrencies are, for the most part, time rather than demand deposits, they are money *substitutes* or *near* money rather than money itself, according to the usual narrow definition of money (which includes only currency in circulation and demand deposits). Thus, Eurobanks do not, in general, create money, but are essentially financial intermediaries bringing together lenders and borrowers, and operating more like domestic savings and loan associations (before they established the so-called NOW accounts) than like commercial banks in the United States.

Perhaps more significant than if Eurocurrencies are or are not money and if Eurobanks can or cannot create money is the fact that Eurocurrencies and Euromarkets do increase international liquidity. Of course, a dollar deposit flowing from a bank in Europe to a bank in the United States is no longer a Eurodollar, so that Eurocurrency and Eurodollar deposits can increase or decrease. However, the Eurocurrency market has been growing at a very rapid pace since the 1960s and today net Eurocurrency deposits (mostly very short term) exceed $1 trillion.

In the past, the United States and oil-exporting countries have been the main net lenders of Eurodollar funds, while developing countries, the Soviet Union, and Eastern European countries have been the major net borrowers. Particularly significant has been the crucial intermediation function that the Eurocurrency market performed in *recycling* hundreds of billions of *petrodollars* from oil-exporting nations to oil-importing nations during the 1970s. This, however, also paved the way for the huge international debt problem of developing countries, particularly those of Latin America (see section 11.6b). Eurocurrency markets have also led to a very significant integration of domestic and international financial markets.

The existence, size, and rapid growth of the Eurocurrency market has also created certain problems. One of the most serious is that it reduces the effectiveness of domestic stabilization efforts of national governments. For example, large firms that cannot borrow domestically because of credit restrictions often can and do borrow in the Eurocurrency market, thus frustrating the government effort to restrict credit to fight domestic inflationary pressures. This is particularly true for smaller nations where the volume of domestic financial transactions is small in relation to Eurocurrency transactions. To be sure, this problem is much less serious under a flexible than under a fixed exchange rate system, except when the government intervenes heavily in the foreign exchange market to moderate exchange rate fluctuations (a topic examined in Chapter 19).

A closely related problem is that frequent and large flows of short-term Eurocurrency funds from one international monetary center to another can produce great instability in foreign exchange rates and domestic interest rates. Once again, these "hot money" flows were much more of a problem under the fixed exchange rate system in operation before 1973 than they are today. However, they do still occur, even if in a smaller degree.

Another possible problem is that Eurocurrency markets are largely uncontrolled. As a result, a deep worldwide recession could render some of the system's banks insolvent and possibly lead internationally to the type of bank panics that afflicted capitalist nations during the nineteenth century and the first third of the twentieth century. Domestic bank panics were more or less eliminated by the creation of national central banks to regulate domestic banking through deposit insurance and by setting themselves up as "lenders of last resort" for domestic banks in a liquidity squeeze. However, any attempt on the part of any one nation to impose regulations on the Eurocurrency market would simply result in the market shifting its activity elsewhere. Thus, to be effective, regulation requires a great deal of international cooperation from all major countries, and this has not been forthcoming.

On the positive side, the Eurocurrency market has certainly increased competition and the efficiency of domestic banking, and during the 1970s it has also performed the crucial intermediation between the huge deposits of petroleum-exporting nations and the nations needing to borrow these funds to pay for the sharp increases in petroleum prices. As such, the Eurocurrency market very likely prevented a liquidity crisis in the middle and late 1970s by performing a function that other international institutions were either unable or unwilling to undertake.

Starting on December 3, 1981, international banking facilities (IBFs) were permitted in the United States. That is, United States banks were allowed to accept deposits from abroad and reinvest them overseas and thus to compete directly in the huge Eurodollar market. The new rules exempted foreign deposits in United States banks from federally imposed interest rate ceilings and reserve and insurance requirements. Several states have also passed complementary legislation exempting profits on international banking transactions from state and local taxes. Almost 200 United States banks have entered this market, about half of them in New York, with the rest in Chicago, Miami, New Orleans, and San Francisco. It is expected that within a decade the United States will capture about 20 percent of the huge Eurodollar market and that this will lead to the creation of thousands of new jobs in banking, about half of them in New York City.

13.6c   The Eurobond and Euronote Markets

Eurobonds are long-term debt securities that are sold outside the borrower's country to raise long-term capital in a currency other than the currency of the nation where the bonds are sold. An example is provided by a United States corporation selling bonds in London denominated in German marks, French francs, or United States dollars.

In 1985, corporations, banks, and countries raised a record $135 billion in the Eurobond market ($36 billion by United States corporations and banks), of which 70 percent were denominated in dollars. The total of $135 billion of Eurobonds sold in 1985 represented an increase from $48 billion in 1983 and $80 billion in 1984. The sharp increase was made possible by the opening up of capital markets to Eurobond issues by several countries, including France, Germany, and Japan, and by the elimination of the United States interest-equalization tax. The incentive of Eurobonds is that they generally represent a lower cost of borrowing long-term funds than available alternatives.

In recent years, there has also been a sharp increase in **Euronotes.** These are medium-term financial instruments falling somewhat between short-term Eurocurrency bank loans and long-term Eurobonds that corporations, banks, and countries can use to borrow funds in a currency other than the currency of the nation in which the notes are sold. A large issue of Euronotes is usually negotiated by a group (called a *syndicate*) of banks so as to spread the credit risk among numerous banks in many countries. Euronotes or *Eurocredits* usually have floating rates. That is, the interest rates charged are refixed regularly, usually every three or six months, in line with changes in market conditions.

Interest rates on Eurocredits are expressed as a mark-up or spread over LIBOR (the London interbank offer rate) at which Eurobanks lend funds to one another. The spread varies according to the creditworthiness of the borrower and ranges from ¼ of 1 percent for best or prime borrowers to 2½ percent for borrowers with weak credit ratings. Often, weaker borrowers can negotiate a lower spread by paying various fees up front. These are a management fee for the bank or banks organizing the syndication, a participation fee to all participating banks based on the amount lent by each, as well as a commitment fee on any undrawn portion of the loan.

Because of the size and rapid growth of the Eurocurrency, Eurobond, and Eurocredit (Euronote) markets, and the resulting integration of domestic and international financial markets, we are truly approaching the situation in which all banking functions and markets are viewed globally. That is, we are approaching *global banking*.

Summary

1. Foreign exchange markets are the markets where individuals, firms, and banks buy and sell foreign currencies or foreign exchange. The foreign exchange market for any currency, say the United States dollar, is composed of all the locations, such as London, Zurich, Paris, Hong Kong, Tokyo as well as New York, where dollars are bought and sold for other currencies. These different monetary centers are connected by a telephone network and via telex and are in constant contact with one another.

2. The principal function of foreign exchange markets is the transfer of purchasing power from one nation and currency to another. The demand for foreign exchange arises from the desire to import or purchase goods and services from other nations and to make investments abroad. The supply of foreign exchange comes from exporting or selling goods and services to other nations and from the inflow of foreign investments. A nation's commercial banks operate as clearing houses for the foreign exchange demanded and supplied. Commercial banks then even out their excess supply of or demand for foreign exchange with other commercial banks through the intermediation of foreign exchange brokers. The nation's central bank then acts as the lender or borrower of last resort.

3. The exchange rate (R) is defined as the domestic currency price of the foreign currency. Under a flexible exchange rate system of the type in existence since 1973, the equilibrium exchange rate is determined at the intersection of the nation's aggregate demand and supply curves for the foreign currency. If the domestic currency price of the foreign currency rises, we say that the domestic currency depreciated. In the opposite case, we say that the domestic currency appreciated (and the foreign currency depreciated). Arbitrage refers to the purchase of a currency where it is cheaper for immediate resale where it is more expensive in order to make a profit. This equalizes exchange rates and ensures consistent cross rates in all monetary centers, unifying them into a single market. A spot transaction involves the exchange of currencies within two business days. A forward transaction is an agreement to purchase at a future date (usually one, three, or six months hence) a specified amount of a foreign currency at a rate agreed upon today (the forward rate). When the forward rate is lower than the spot rate, the foreign currency is said to be at a forward discount of a certain percentage per year. In the opposite case, the foreign currency is said to be at a forward premium. A foreign exchange futures is a forward contract for standardized currency amounts and selected calendar dates traded on an organized market (exchange). A foreign exchange option is a contract specifying the right to buy or sell a standard amount of a traded currency within a specified period.

4. Because exchange rates usually change over time, they impose a foreign exchange risk on anyone who expects to make or receive a payment in a foreign currency at a future date. The covering of such an exchange risk is called hedging. Speculation is the opposite of hedging. It refers to the taking of an open position in the expectation of making a profit. Speculation can be stabilizing and destabilizing. Hedging and speculation can take place in the spot, forward, futures, or options markets, usually the forward market.

5. Interest arbitrage refers to the international flow of short-term liquid funds to earn higher returns abroad. Covered interest arbitrage refers to the spot purchase of the foreign currency to make the investment and an offsetting simultaneous forward sale of the foreign currency to cover the foreign exchange risk. The net return from covered interest arbitrage is usually equal to the positive interest differential earned abroad minus the forward discount on the foreign currency. As covered interest arbitrage continues, the net gain is reduced and finally eliminated. When the net gain is zero, the currency is said to be at interest parity. Foreign exchange markets are said to be efficient if forward rates accurately predict future spot rates.

6. Eurocurrency refers to commercial bank deposits outside the country of issue of the currency. Thus, Eurodollars are dollar deposits in banks in Europe or other places outside the United States. The Eurocurrency market has grown very rapidly, from less than $10 billion in the early 1960s to over $1 trillion today. Of this total, slightly more than half is now in Eurodollars. The Eurodollar market grew very rapidly because of higher interest on dollar deposits in Europe, the vehicle function of the dollar as an international currency, and the general lack of regulation. The existence of the Eurocurrency market makes the conduct of national stabilization policies more difficult and can lead to unstable exchange rates. However, it has also increased competition and performed the crucial intermediation of petrodollars. Eurobonds are long-term and Euronotes are medium-term debt securities sold outside the borrower's country and denominated in a currency other than the currency of the country in which the bonds or notes are sold.

A Look Ahead

In the next chapter, we will examine the meaning, function, and measurement of the balance of payments and define the concepts of deficit and surplus in a nation's balance of payments. We will also analyze the United States balance of payments for the year 1984, the latest year for which complete balance-of-payments data were available for the United States as this book went to press.

Glossary

Foreign exchange market The institutional framework in all the monetary centers where foreign currencies are bought and sold. These monetary centers are connected by a telephone network and via telex and are in constant contact with one another.

Exchange rate The domestic currency price of the foreign currency.

Depreciation An increase in the domestic currency price of the foreign currency.

Appreciation A decrease in the domestic currency price of the foreign currency.

Effective exchange rate A weighted average of the exchange rates between the domestic currency and the nation's most important trade partners, with weights given by the relative importance of the nation's trade with each of these trade partners.

Arbitrage The purchase of a currency in the monetary center where it is cheaper for immediate resale in the monetary center where it is more expensive in order to make a profit.

Spot rate The exchange rate in foreign exchange transactions that call for the payment and receipt of the foreign exchange within two business days from the date when the transaction is agreed upon.

Forward rate The exchange rate in foreign exchange transactions involving delivery of the foreign exchange one, three, or six months after the contract is agreed upon.

Forward discount The percentage per year by which the forward rate on the foreign currency is below its spot rate.

Forward premium The percentage per year by which the forward rate on the foreign currency is above its spot rate.

Foreign exchange futures A forward contract for standardized currency amounts and selected calendar dates traded on an organized market (exchange).

Foreign exchange options A contract specifying the right to buy or sell a standard amount of a traded currency within a specified period.

Foreign exchange risk The risk resulting from changes in exchange rates over time and faced by anyone who expects to make or to receive a payment in a foreign currency at a future date; also called an open position.

Hedging The avoidance of a foreign exchange risk (or the covering of an open position).

Speculation The acceptance of a foreign exchange risk, or open position, in the hope of making a profit.

Stabilizing speculation The purchase of a foreign currency when the domestic currency price of the currency (i.e., the exchange rate) falls or is low, in the expectation that the ex-

change rate will soon rise, thus leading to a profit. Or the sale of a foreign currency when the exchange rate rises or is high, in the expectation that it will soon fall.

Destabilizing speculation The sale of a foreign currency when the exchange rate falls or is low, in the expectation that it will fall even lower in the future, or the purchase of a foreign currency when the exchange rate is rising or is high, in the expectation that it will rise even higher in the future.

Interest arbitrage The transfer of short-term liquid funds abroad to earn a higher return.

Uncovered interest arbitrage The transfer of short-term liquid funds to the international monetary center with higher interest rates without covering the foreign exchange risk.

Covered interest arbitrage The transfer of short-term liquid funds abroad to earn higher returns, with the foreign exchange risk covered by the spot purchase of the foreign currency and a simultaneous offsetting forward sale.

Interest parity The situation where the positive interest differential in favor of the foreign monetary center is equal to the forward discount on the foreign currency.

Efficiency of foreign exchange markets The situation in which forward rates accurately predict future spot rates.

Eurocurrency market The market for commercial bank deposits outside the country of issue of the currency. Thus, Eurodollars are dollar deposits in banks in Europe.

Eurobonds Long-term debt securities that are sold outside the borrower's country and denominated in a currency other than the currency of the country in which the notes are sold.

Euronotes Medium-term debt securities sold outside the borrower's country and denominated in a currency other than the currency of the country in which the notes are sold.

Questions for Review

1. What are foreign exchange markets? What is their most important function? How is this function performed? What are the four differ-

ent levels of participants in foreign exchange markets? What are the other functions of foreign exchange markets?

2. What is meant by the exchange rate? How is the equilibrium exchange rate determined under a flexible exchange rate system? What is meant by a depreciation of the domestic currency? An appreciation? What is the effective exchange rate?

3. What is arbitrage? What is its result? What is triangular arbitrage? What are cross rates? What is meant by a spot transaction and the spot rate? A forward transaction and the forward rate? What is meant by forward discount? Forward premium? What is a foreign exchange futures? A foreign exchange option?

4. What is meant by foreign exchange risk? How can foreign exchange risks be covered in the spot, forward, futures, or options market? Why does not hedging usually take place in the spot market? What is meant by speculation? How can speculation take place in the spot, forward, futures, or options markets? Why does not speculation usually take place in the spot market? What is stabilizing speculation? Destabilizing speculation?

5. What is interest arbitrage? Uncovered interest arbitrage? Covered interest arbitrage? How is interest arbitrage covered in the forward market? Why does the net gain from covered interest arbitrage tend to diminish as covered interest arbitrage continues? What is meant by the foreign currency being at interest parity? Why is this often not the case in the real world? How do hedgers, speculators, and interest arbitrageurs, as well as government actions, affect exchange rates? What is meant by market efficiency? Are foreign exchange markets efficient?

6. What is meant by Eurocurrency markets? Eurodollars? Eurosterling? Euromarks? What are the reasons for the existence of the Eurodollar market? What problems do the existence of the Eurocurrency market create? What are some of the important benefits that result from this market? What are Eurobonds? Euronotes?

Problems

1. Redraw Figure 13-1 and show on it *two supply curves* for pounds, one intersecting the demand curve for pounds at point *B* and the other intersecting the demand curve for pounds at point *C*. Assuming a flexible exchange rate system, determine the equilibrium exchange rate and equilibrium quantity of pounds with the supply curve for pounds that intersects the demand curve:
   (a) at point *B*;
   (b) at point *C*.
   (c) If the nation wanted to maintain a fixed exchange rate of $R = 1$ in Figure 13-1 in the text, what amount of pound reserves would the nation's central bank gain or lose per day?

2. Assume the following exchange rates:

$$\$2 = £1 \text{ in New York}$$
$$410 \text{ yen} = £1 \text{ in London}$$
$$200 \text{ yen} = \$1 \text{ in Tokyo}$$

   (a) Indicate how profitable triangular, or three-point arbitrage can take place.
   (b) What are the forces at work that will make the cross rates consistent?
   (c) Which are the consistent cross rates in this case?

*3. Calculate the forward discount or premium for the following spot and three-month forward rates:
   (a) $SR = \$2.00/£1$ and $FR = \$2.01/£1$
   (b) $SR = \$2.00/£1$ and $FR = \$1.96/£1$
   (c) $SR = 2$ French francs/1 mark and $FR = 2.02$ French francs/1 mark
   (d) $SR = 200$ yen/$1 and $FR = 190$ yen/$1

4. Assume that $SR = \$2/£1$ and the three-month $FR = \$1.96/£1$.
   (a) How can an importer who will have to pay £10,000 in three months hedge his foreign exchange risk?
   (b) How can an exporter who expects to receive a payment of £1 million in three months hedge his foreign exchange risk?

5. Assume that the three-month $FR = \$2.00/£1$

and a speculator believes that the spot rate in three months will be $SR = \$2.05/£1$.

(a) How can he speculate in the forward market? How much will he earn if he is correct?

(b) If the speculator believes instead that the spot rate in three months will be $SR = \$1.95/£1$, how can he speculate in the forward market? How much will he earn if he is correct? What will the result be if in three months $SR = \$2.05/£1$ instead?

*6. If the positive interest rate differential in favor of a foreign monetary center is 4 percent

per year and the foreign currency is at a forward discount of 2 percent per year,

(a) roughly how much would an interest arbitrageur earn from the purchase of foreign three-month treasury bills if he covers the foreign exchange risk?

(b) how much would he earn if the foreign currency was instead at a forward premium of 1 percent per year?

(c) what would happen if the foreign currency was at a forward discount of 6 percent per year?

APPENDIX——————————

In this appendix, we derive the demand and supply curves for foreign exchange, illustrate covered interest arbitrage and interest parity graphically, and derive the formula for calculating the covered interest arbitrage margin.

A13.1 Derivation of the Demand and Supply Curves for Foreign Exchange

In this section, we derive the United States demand curve for pounds $(D_£)$ and the United States supply curve for pounds $(S_£)$ shown in Figure 13-1. For simplicity we assume here that the United States demand for pounds arises only from its desire to import commodity Y from the United Kingdom and that the United States supply of pounds comes only from the export of commodity X to the United Kingdom.

We start by deriving the United States demand curve for pounds $(D_£)$. This involves first deriving the United States demand curve for *imports* of commodity Y from the United States domestic demand and supply curves for commodity Y and then expressing United States total expenditures on imports of commodity Y in terms of pounds at various exchange rates.

In the left panel of Figure 13-4, D_Y and S_Y are the domestic demand and supply curves for commodity Y in terms of dollars in the United States. At $P_Y = \$5$, the United States satisfies all of its demands for 40Y by domestic production. Therefore, it demands 0Y of imports (see the right panel of Figure 13-4). At $P_Y = \$4$, the left panel shows that the United States demands 45Y but produces only 35Y domestically. Thus, it demands 10Y of imports, given by point A' in the right panel. At $P_Y = \$3$, the United States demands 50Y but

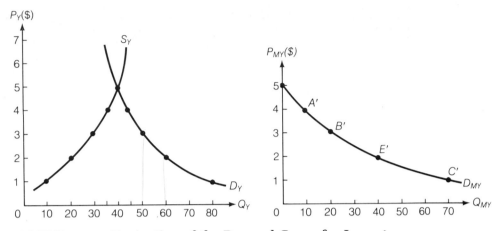

FIGURE 13-4.   Derivation of the Demand Curve for Imports

In the left panel, D_Y and S_Y are the domestic demand and supply curves for commodity Y in terms of dollars in the United States. At $P_Y=\$5$, the United States satisfies all of its demand for 40Y by domestic production. Therefore, it imports 0Y (in the right panel). At $P_Y=\$4$, the left panel shows that the United States demands 45Y but produces only 35Y domestically. Thus, it demands 10Y of imports, given by point A' in the right panel. Other points on the U.S. demand curve for imports of commodity Y are similarly derived by subtracting from the quantity of Y demanded the amount of Y produced domestically.

produces only 30Y domestically (see the left panel), and so it demands 20Y of imports (point B' in the right panel). At $P_Y=\$2$, the United States demands 60Y, produces 20Y domestically, and demands 40Y of imports (point E' in the right panel). Finally, at $P_Y=\$1$, the United States demands 80Y, produces 10Y domestically, and demands 70Y of imports (point C' in the right panel). Note that the United States demand for imports of commodity Y (D_{MY} in the right panel) is more elastic than the United States demand for commodity Y (D_Y) as long as the United States produces some Y. Otherwise, D_{MY} and D_Y would be identical. This latter possibility is more likely to occur in developing than in developed countries.

From the United States demand for imports of commodity Y (D_{MY}) from the United Kingdom, we can derive the United States demand curve for pounds at various exchange rates for the dollar. This is shown in Table 13-2, where we assume that $P_Y=\pounds1$ (column 1) in the United Kingdom and remains the same regardless of how much of commodity Y the United States imports from the United Kingdom. Then if the exchange rate is $R=4$ (column 2), $P_Y=\$4$ in the United States (column 3), and the United States demands 10Y of imports (column 4) from the United Kingdom. If $R=3$, $P_Y=\$3$ and the United States demands 20Y of imports; if $R=2$, $P_Y=\$2$ and the United States demands 40Y of imports; and if $R=1$, $P_Y=\$1$ and the United States demands 70Y of imports. Thus, columns 3 and 4 in Table 13-2 give the United States demand

TABLE 13-2.   Derivation of the U.S. Demand Schedule for Pounds

(1) P_Y in £	(2) $R=\$/£$	(3) P_Y in \$	(4) QD_{MY}	(5) $QD_£$	(6) Point
1	4	4	10	10	A
1	3	3	20	20	B
1	2	2	40	40	E
1	1	1	70	70	C

schedule for imports of commodity Y plotted in the right panel of Figure 13-4. By multiplying the United States QD_{MY} in column 4 by the P_Y in £ given in column 1, we obtain the United States $QD_£$ in column 5. Column 2 and column 5 then give the United States demand schedule for pounds ($D_£$) plotted in Figure 13-1, with the various points given in column 6.

The United States supply of pounds comes from the United States exporting commodity X to the United Kingdom. We assume that $P_X=\$1$ in the United States regardless of how much of commodity X the United Kingdom imports from the United States. By translating this $P_X=\$1$ into the price of commodity X in pounds (by using the exchange rate), we can find the quantity of imports of commodity X the United Kingdom will demand at various exchange rates and the quantity of pounds it will supply to the United States ($S_£$). This is shown in Table 13-3.

In the table, column 1 gives the constant $P_X=\$1$ in the United States, and column 2 gives the exchange rates. By dividing the values in column 2 into the values in column 1, we get P_X in £ given in column 3. If at various P_X in £ in column 3, the United Kingdom demands the imports of commodity X indicated in column 4, it will supply the quantities of pounds shown in column 5. That is, the values in column 5 are obtained by multiplying the values in column 3 by those in column 4. Column 2 and column 5 then give the United States supply schedule for pounds ($S_£$) plotted in Figure 13-1, with the various points given in column 6.

The United Kingdom demand for imports for commodity X from the United States can be derived from the positive difference between the quantity of

TABLE 13-3.   Derivation of the U.S. Supply Schedule for Pounds

(1) P_X in \$	(2) $R=\$/£$	(3) P_X in £	(4) QD_{MX}	(5) $QS_£$	(6) Point
1	4	0.25	280	70	F
1	3	0.33	180	60	G
1	2	0.50	80	40	E
1	1	1.00	10	10	H

commodity X demanded by the United Kingdom at various prices of X in terms of pounds and the quantity it produces domestically at these prices. The higher is P_X in £, the smaller is the quantity of X demanded in the United Kingdom and the greater is the quantity of X produced there, so that the smaller is the United Kingdom demand for imports of commodity X. Note that as P_X in £ rises (column 3), the United Kingdom QD_{MX} falls very rapidly (column 4). This means that the United Kingdom demand for imports of commodity X is very price elastic. That is, each increase in P_X in £ causes a greater than proportionate reduction in QD_{MX} so that the $QS_£$ also fall. If QD_{MX} had been unitary elastic, $QS_£$ would remain the same, and the United States $S_£$ would have been vertical. Finally, if QD_{MX} had been price inelastic, the United States $S_£$ would have been negatively inclined. Thus, while the United States $D_£$ can be assumed to be always negatively inclined, the United States $S_£$ is *usually* positively inclined, but it could also be vertical or even negatively inclined.

Problem (a) Show graphically that the more elastic the United States demand and supply curves for commodity Y are, the more elastic is the United States demand curve for imports of commodity Y. (b) Substitute different hypothetical values in column 4 of Table 13-3 so as to make the United States $S_£$ vertical and then negatively inclined.

A13.2   Covered Interest Arbitrage and Interest Parity Theory

Figure 13-5 illustrates rigorously the relationship, through covered interest arbitrage, between the interest rate differentials between two nations and the forward discount or premium on the foreign currency. The vertical axis measures interest differentials in favor of the foreign country and foreign monetary center expressed in percentages per year. Positive values indicate that interest rates are higher abroad. Negative values indicate that interest rates are higher domestically. The horizontal axis measures the forward discount ($-$) or forward premium ($+$) on the foreign currency expressed in percentages per year.

The solid diagonal line indicates interest parity. Thus, when the positive interest differential is 1 percent per year in favor of the foreign nation, the foreign currency is at a forward discount of 1 percent per year. A negative interest differential of 1.5 percent is associated with a forward *premium* of 1.5 percent. When the interest differential is zero, the foreign currency is neither at a forward discount nor at a forward premium (i.e., the forward rate on the foreign currency is equal to its spot rate).

Above the interest parity line, either the positive interest differential exceeds the forward discount or the forward premium exceeds the negative interest differential. In either case, there will be a net gain from an arbitrage outflow equal to their difference. For example, at point A, the positive interest

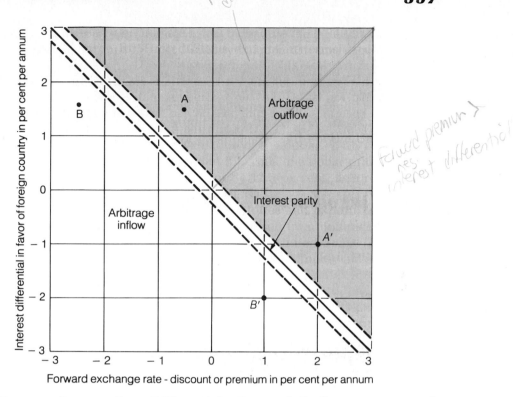

pos. interest diff. > forward discount

forward premium > neg. interest differential

FIGURE 13-5. Interest Rate Differentials, Forward Exchange Rates, and Covered Interest Arbitrage

The vertical axis measures interest differentials in favor of the foreign country in percentages per annum. The horizontal axis measures the forward exchange rate with the minus sign indicating that the foreign currency is at a forward discount and positive values indicating that it is at a forward premium in percent per annum. The solid diagonal line refers to interest parity. Above the interest parity line, either the positive interest differential exceeds the forward discount or the forward premium exceeds the negative interest differential. In either case, there will be a capital outflow under covered interest arbitrage. Below the interest parity line, the opposite is true and there will be an arbitrage inflow. *Source:* Adapted from A. Holmes and F. Scott, *The New York Foreign Exchange Market* (New York: The Federal Reserve Bank of New York, 1965), p. 54.

differential is 1.5 percentage points per year in favor of the foreign nation, while the foreign currency is at a forward discount of 0.5 percent per year. Thus, there is a covered interest arbitrage margin of 1 percent per year in favor of the foreign nation, leading to a capital outflow. On the other hand, point A' involves a forward premium of 2 percent on the foreign currency and a negative interest differential of only 1 percent. Thus, investors have an incentive to invest abroad because they would gain 2 percent on the exchange transaction and lose only 1 percent in interest.

As the arbitrage outflow continues, the net gain diminishes and tends to disappear. Starting from point *A*, the transfer of funds abroad reduces the positive interest differential (say, from +1.5 to +1) and increases the forward discount (say, from −0.5 to −1), as explained in section 13.5b, so as to reach the interest parity line (see the figure). Starting from point *A'*, the transfer of funds abroad will increase the negative interest differential (say, from −1 to −1.5) and reduce the forward premium (say, from +2 to +1.5) so as to once again reach the interest parity line. Specifically, as funds move abroad, interest rates tend to rise at home and decline abroad. Since interest rates were already higher at home, the negative interest differential increases. On the other hand, as investors purchase the foreign currency to invest abroad, the spot rate rises. As they see the foreign currency forward to cover their foreign exchange risk, the forward rate declines. Thus, the forward premium (i.e., the excess of the forward rate over the spot rate) diminishes. With the negative interest differential increasing and the forward premium decreasing, the net gain from arbitrage outflow diminishes until it becomes zero on the interest parity line and the arbitrage outflow comes to an end.

Below the interest parity line, either the forward discount exceeds the positive interest differential (point *B* in the figure) or the negative interest differential exceeds the forward premium (point *B'*). In either case, it pays for foreigners to invest in our country, and there will be an arbitrage *inflow*. However, as the arbitrage inflow continues, the net gain diminishes and then disappears when the interest parity line is reached. In reality, interest arbitrage (inflow and outflow) will come to an end when the net gain reaches about ¼ of 1 percent per year (¹⁄₁₆ of 1 percent for three months). This range is shown by the white area between the diagonal *dashed* lines in the figure.

Problem   With reference in Figure 13-5, explain (a) why there will be an arbitrage inflow at points *B* and *B'* and (b) the forces that tend to eliminate the net gain as arbitrage inflows continue.

A13.3   Derivation of the Formula for the Covered Interest Arbitrage Margin

We now derive the formula for the precise calculation of the covered interest arbitrage margin (CIAM), starting with formula 13A-1:

$$K(1 + i/4) \gtreqless K/SR(1 + i^*/4)FR \tag{13A-1}$$

where
$$
\begin{aligned}
K &= \text{amount of capital invested} \\
i &= \text{domestic interest rate per year} \\
i^* &= \text{foreign interest rate per year} \\
SR &= \text{spot rate} \\
FR &= \text{forward rate}
\end{aligned}
$$

The left-hand side of formula 13A-1 gives the value of the investment (the original capital invested plus the interest earned) when K amount of capital is invested domestically for three months. The right-hand side gives the domestic currency value of the investment (the original capital invested plus the interest earned) when the same amount of capital is invested abroad for three months with the foreign exchange risk covered. Specifically, the right-hand side of the formula gives the foreign currency value of the investment, times one plus the interest earned abroad for three months, times the forward rate (to reconvert the invested capital plus the interest earned back into the domestic currency). Investors will invest domestically if the left-hand side of the formula is larger than the right-hand side; they will invest abroad if the right-hand side is greater than the left-hand side; and they are indifferent if the two sides are equal.

According to the theory of covered interest arbitrage, an arbitrage outflow or inflow will proceed until no net gain remains (i.e., until interest parity). Thus, at interest parity the two sides of formula 13A-1 would be equal. By treating formula 13A-1 as an equation and manipulating it algebraically, we can derive the formula for the covered interest arbitrage margin (CIAM). In doing this, it is convenient to divide both sides by K and omit, for the moment, the division of i and i^* by 4. This will give us the CIAM per dollar per year. By then multiplying the CIAM obtained by the capital invested (K) and dividing by 4, we get the extra dollar earnings in percentage for the three months of the investment with the foreign exchange risk covered.

Treating formula 13A-1 as an equation, and dividing both sides by K and omitting the division of i and i^* by 4 as explained above, we get the equation 13A-2:

$$1 + i = 1/SR(1 + i^*)FR \qquad (13\text{A-}2)$$

Manipulating equation 13A-2 algebraically, we obtain:

$$i = 1/SR(1 + i^*)FR - 1$$
$$i = FR/SR + FRi^*/SR - 1$$
$$i - FRi^*/SR = FR/SR - 1$$
$$(SRi - FRi^*)/SR = FR/SR - 1$$
$$SRi - FRi^* = (FR/SR - 1)SR$$
$$SRi - FRi^* = FR - SR$$
$$(i - i^*)SR + SRi^* - FRi^* = FR - SR$$
$$(i - i^*)SR + SRi^* = FR + FRi^* - SR$$
$$(i - i^*)SR + SRi^* = FR(1 + i^*) - SR$$
$$(i - i^*)SR + SRi^* + SR = FR(1 + i^*)$$
$$(i - i^*)SR + (1 + i^*)SR = FR(1 + i^*)$$

Dividing both sides by $(1 + i^*)$ and transposing, we get formula 13A-3 to calculate the forward rate at interest parity:

$$FR = [(i - i^*)/(1 + i^*)]SR + SR \qquad (13A\text{-}3)$$

Manipulating equation 13A-3 algebraically, we get:

$$(FR - SR)/SR = (i - i^*)/(1 + i^*)$$
$$0 = (i - i^*)/(1 + i^*) - (FR - SR)/SR$$

But when we are not at interest parity, the right-hand side is not equal to zero but gives us equation 13A-4 to calculate the covered interest arbitrage margin (CIAM):

$$\text{CIAM} = (i - i^*)/(1 + i^*) - (FR - SR)/SR \qquad (13A\text{-}4)$$

The first fraction on the right-hand side of equation 13A-4 is the domestic-foreign interest rate differential weighted by 1 plus the foreign interest rate. The second fraction on the right-hand side is the forward discount on the foreign currency weighted by the spot rate. Since equation 13A-4 refers to a whole year, the covered interest arbitrage margin for three months is CIAM/4.

   For example, if $i = 10$ percent per year in New York, $i^* = 14$ percent in London, $SR = \$2.00/£1$, and the three-month annualized $FR = \$1.98/£1$, then CIAM is:

$$\begin{aligned}
\text{CIAM} &= (0.10 - 0.14)/1.14 - (\$1.98 - \$2.00)/\$2.00 \\
&= -0.04/1.14 + 0.02/2.00 \\
&= -0.03509 + 0.01 \\
&= -0.02509
\end{aligned}$$

Dividing this result by 4 (to get the CIAM for the three months of the investment), we obtain -0.00627, or -0.63 percent, for the extra return per dollar invested in three-month British treasury bills with the foreign exchange risk covered. The negative sign results from i^* exceeding i and simply indicates an arbitrage *outflow*. An arbitrage *inflow* would instead have a positive sign. In sections 13.5b and A13.2, the estimate of the CIAM was positive because there we took "the *positive* interest differential in favor of the foreign country," or $(i^* - i)$ instead of $(i - i^*)$. We have used $(i - i^*)$ here because equation 13A-4 is the formula actually used to measure the CIAM, and because the sign for the arbitrage outflow or inflow resulting from the application of equation 13A-4 is consistent with the definition used in the next chapter, dealing with the balance of payments. The CIAM of 0.63 percent found here does not differ much from the rough estimate of 0.75 percent obtained in section 13.5b; the slight difference is due to the weighting factor present in equation 13A-4 but not in the *estimate* used in section 13.5b.

Problem   Using the above data on i, i^*, SR, and FR, determine the dollar amount (principal plus interest) that a United States investor will get back by investing $200,000 for three months in (1) United States treasury bills or (b) British treasury bills with his foreign exchange risk covered. How would your answer to part b differ if you estimated the CIAM as in section 13.5b?

Selected Bibliography

For a problem-solving approach to the topics covered in this chapter, see:
- D. Salvatore, *Theory and Problems of International Economics*, 2nd ed. (New York: McGraw-Hill, 1984), ch. 7.

The operation of foreign exchange markets is explained in detail in:
- R. M. Kurbarych, *Foreign Exchange Markets in the United States* (New York: The Federal Reserve Bank, 1983).
- R. Z. Aliber, *The International Money Game*, (New York: Basic Books, 1979).
- G. Dufey and I. Giddy, *The International Monetary Market* (Englewood Cliffs, N.J.: Prentice-Hall, 1978).
- Federal Reserve Bank of Chicago, *Readings in International Economics* (Chicago: Federal Reserve Bank of Chicago, 1984), Part VI.

An analysis of exchange rate determination is found in:
- A. O. Krueger, *Exchange Rate Determination* (Cambridge: Cambridge University Press, 1983).
- J. F. O. Bilson and R. M. Martson (eds.), *Exchange Rate Theory and Practice* (Chicago: University of Chicago Press, 1984).
- M. Obstfeld and A. Stockman, "Exchange Rate Dynamics," in R. W. Jones and P. B. Kenen (eds.), *Handbook of International Economics*, Vol. II (Amsterdam: North-Holland, 1985).

The classic work on the spot and forward markets for foreign exchange, hedging, and speculation is:
- P. Einzig, *The Dynamic Theory of Forward Exchange* (London: Macmillan, 1967).

The first clear exposition of the theory of covered interest arbitrage is found in:

- J. M. Keynes, *A Tract on Monetary Reform* (London: Macmillan, 1923), pp. 113–139.

For an excellent presentation of the theory of covered interest arbitrage, see:
- A. Holmes and F. Scott, *The New York Foreign Exchange Market* (New York: The Federal Reserve Bank, 1965).

On the efficiency of foreign exchange markets, see:
- J. A. Frenkel and M. L. Mussa, "The Efficiency of the Foreign Exchange Market and Measures of Turbulence," *American Economic Review*, May 1980.
- J. F. O. Bilson, "The 'Speculative Efficiency' Hypothesis," *Journal of Business*, July 1981.
- R. M. Levich, "Empirical Studies of Exchange Rates: Price Behavior, Rate Determination and Market Efficiency," in R. W. Jones and P. B. Kenen (eds.), *Handbook of International Economics*, Vol. II (Amsterdam: North-Holland, 1985).

A discussion of the operation of the Euromarkets is found in:
- G. McKenzie, *Economics of the Eurodollar Market* (London: Macmillan, 1976).
- R. I. McKinnon, *The Eurocurrency Market*, Essays in International Finance, No. 125 (Princeton, N.J.: Princeton University Press, International Finance Section, December 1977).
- Federal Reserve Bank of Chicago, *Readings in International Economics* (Chicago: Federal Reserve Bank of Chicago, 1984), Part V.
- Y. S. Park and J. Zwick, *International Banking in Theory and Practice* (Reading, Mass.: Addison-Wesley, 1985).
- J. O. Grabbe, *International Financial Markets* (New York: Elsevier, 1986).

CHAPTER 14

The Balance of Payments

14.1 Introduction

The **balance of payments** is a summary statement in which, in principle, all the transactions of the residents of a nation with the residents of all other nations are recorded during a particular period of time, usually a calendar year. The United States and some other nations also keep such a record on a quarterly basis. The main purpose of the balance of payments is to inform the government of the international position of the nation and to help it in its formulation of monetary, fiscal, and commercial policies. Governments also regularly consult the balance of payments of important trade partners in making policy decisions. The information contained in a nation's balance of payments is also indispensible to banks, firms, and individuals directly or indirectly involved in international trade and finance.

The definition of the balance of payments given above requires some clarification. First of all, it is obvious that the literally millions of transactions of the residents of a nation with the rest of the world cannot appear *individually* in the balance of payments. As a *summary statement*, the balance of payments aggregates all merchandise trade into a few major categories. Similarly, only the net balance of each type of international capital flow is included. Furthermore, the balance of payments includes some transactions in which the residents of foreign nations are not directly involved, for example, when a nation's central bank sells a portion of its foreign currency holdings to the nation's commercial banks.

An *international transaction* refers to the exchange of a good, service, or asset (for which payment is usually required) between the residents of one nation and the residents of other nations. However, gifts and certain other transfers (for which no payment is required) are also included in a nation's balance of payments. The question of who is a *resident* of a nation also requires some clarification. Diplomats, military personnel, tourists, and workers who temporarily migrate are residents of the nation in which they hold citizenship. Similarly, a corporation is the resident of the nation in which it is incorporated, but its foreign branches and subsidiaries are not. Some of these distinctions are of course arbitrary and may lead to difficulties. For example, a worker may start by emigrating temporarily and then decide to remain abroad permanently. International institutions such as the United Nations, the International Monetary Fund, the World Bank, and GATT are not residents of the nation in which they are located. Also to be remembered is that the balance of payments has a time dimension. Thus, it is the flow of goods, services, gifts, and assets between the residents of a nation and the residents of other nations *during a particular period of time,* usually a calendar year.

In this chapter, we examine the international transactions of the United States and other nations. In section 14.2, we discuss some accounting principles used in the presentation of the balance of payments. In section 14.3, we present and analyze the international transactions of the United States for the year 1984. Section 14.4 then examines some accounting balances and the concept and measurement of disequilibrium under a fixed and a flexible exchange rate system. Section 14.5 presents a brief postwar international monetary history of the United States. Section 14.6 then examines the international investment position of the United States.

In the appendix, we present the complete statement of the international transactions of the United States from 1960 to 1984 and then examine two discontinued but still important measures of the United States balance of payments. Finally, we present the method of measuring the balance of payments that all nations must use in reporting to the International Monetary Fund. This ensures consistency and permits international comparison of the balance of payments of different nations.

14.2 Balance-of-Payments Accounting Principles

In this section, we examine some balance-of-payments accounting principles as a necessary first step in the presentation of the international transactions of the United States. We begin with the distinction between debits and credits, and then we examine double-entry bookkeeping.

14.2a   Debits and Credits

International transactions are classified as debits or credits. **Credit transactions** are those that involve the receipt of payments *from* foreigners. **Debit transactions** are those that involve the making of payments *to* foreigners. Credit transactions are entered with a positive sign and debit transactions are entered with a negative sign in the nation's balance of payments.

Thus, the export of goods and services, unilateral transfers (gifts) received from foreigners, and capital inflows are entered as credits ($+$) because they involve the receipt of payments from foreigners. On the other hand, the import of goods and services, unilateral transfers or gifts made to foreigners, and capital outflows involve payments to foreigners and are entered as debits ($-$) in the nation's balance of payments.

Capital inflows can take either of two forms: an increase in foreign assets in the nation or a reduction in the nation's assets abroad. For example, when a United Kingdom resident purchases a United States stock, foreign assets in the United States increase. This is a capital inflow to the United States and is recorded as a credit in the United States balance of payments because it involves the receipt of a payment from a foreigner. A capital inflow can also take the form of a reduction in the nation's assets abroad. For example, when a United States resident sells a foreign stock, United States assets abroad decrease. This is a capital inflow to the United States (reversing the capital outflow that occurred when the United States resident purchased the foreign stock) and is recorded as a credit in the United States balance of payments because it too involves the receipt of a payment from foreigners.

The definition of capital inflows to the United States as increases in foreign assets in the United States or reductions in United States assets abroad can be confusing and is somewhat unfortunate, but this is the terminology actually used in all United States government publications. Confusion can be avoided by remembering that when a foreigner purchases a United States asset (an increase in foreign assets in the United States), this involves the receipt of a payment from foreigners. Therefore, it is a capital inflow, or credit. Similarly, when a United States resident sells a foreign asset (a reduction in United States assets abroad), this also involves a payment from foreigners, and therefore it too represents a capital inflow to the United States and a credit. Both an increase in foreign assets in the United States and a reduction in United States assets abroad are capital inflows, or credits, because they both involve the receipt of payment from foreigners.

On the other hand, **capital outflows** can take the form of either an increase in the nation's assets abroad or a reduction in foreign assets in the nation because both involve a payment to foreigners. For example, the purchase of a United Kingdom treasury bill by a United States resident increases United States assets abroad and is a debit because it involves a payment to foreigners. Similarly, the sale by a German firm of a United States subsidiary reduces foreign assets in the United States and is also a debit because it involves a payment to foreigners. (The student should study these definitions and examples carefully, since mastery of these important concepts is crucial to understanding what follows.)

To summarize, the export of goods and services, the receipt of unilateral transfers, and capital inflows are credits (+) because they all involve the receipt of payments from foreigners. On the other hand, the import of goods and services, unilateral transfers to foreigners, and capital outflows are debits (−) because they involve payments to foreigners.

14.2b Double-Entry Bookkeeping

In recording a nation's international transactions, the accounting procedure known as **double-entry bookkeeping** is used. This means that each international transaction is recorded twice, once as a credit and once as a debit of an equal amount. The reason for this is that in general every transaction has two sides. We sell something and we receive payment for it. We buy something and we have to pay for it.

For example, suppose that a United States firm exports $500 of merchandise to be paid for in three months. The United States first credits merchandise exports for $500 since this merchandise export will lead to the receipt of a payment from foreigners. *The payment itself* is then entered as a short-term capital debit because it represents a short-term capital outflow from the United States. That is, by agreeing to wait three months for payment, the United States exporter is extending credit to, and has acquired a claim on, the foreign importer. This is an increase in United States assets abroad and a debit. The entire transaction is entered as follows in the United States balance of payments:

	Debit (−)	*Credit (+)*
Merchandise exports		$500
Short-term capital outflow	$500	

As another example of double-entry bookkeeping, suppose that a United States resident visits London and spends $200 on hotels, meals, and so on. The United States resident is purchasing travel services from foreigners requiring a payment. (This is similar to a United States import.) Thus, the United States debits travel services for $200. The payment itself is then entered as a short-term credit because it represents an increase in foreign claims on the United States. Specifically, we can think of the $200 in British hands as "securities" giving the United Kingdom a claim on United States goods and services, equivalent to an increase in foreign assets in the United States. Therefore, it is a capital inflow to the United States and is recorded as a short-term capital credit of $200. The entire transaction is entered as follows in the United States balance of payments:

	Debit (−)	Credit (+)
Travel services purchased from foreigners	$200	
Short-term capital inflow		$200

As a third example, assume that the United States government gives a United States bank balance of $100 to the government of a developing nation as part of the United States aid program. The United States debits **unilateral transfers** for $100 since extending aid involves a United States payment to foreigners. The payment itself is the United States bank balance given to the government of the developing nation. This represents an increase in foreign claims on, or foreign assets in, the United States and is recorded as a short-term capital inflow, or credit, in the United States balance of payments. The entire transaction is thus:

	Debit (−)	Credit (+)
Unilateral transfers made	$100	
Short-term capital inflow		$100

As a fourth example, suppose a United States resident purchases a foreign stock for $400 and pays for it by increasing *foreign* bank balances in the United States. The purchase of the foreign stock increases United States assets abroad. This is a capital outflow from the United States and is recorded as a long-term capital debit of $400 in the United States balance of payments. The increase in foreign bank balances in the United States is an increase in foreign assets in the United States (a short-term capital inflow to the United States) and is entered as a short-term credit in the United States balance of payments. The same would be true if the United States resident paid for the foreign stock by reducing United States bank balances abroad. (This would be a reduction in United States short-term assets abroad, which is also a short-term capital inflow to the United States and a credit.) Note that both sides of this transaction are financial:

	Debit (−)	Credit (+)
Long-term capital outflow	$400	
Short-term capital inflow		$400

Finally, suppose that a foreign investor purchase $300 of United States treasury bills and pays by drawing down his bank balances in the United

States by an equal amount. The purchase of the United States treasury bills increases foreign assets in the United States. This is a capital inflow to the United States and is recorded as a short-term credit in the United States balance of payments. The drawing down of United States bank balances by the foreigner is a reduction in foreign assets in the United States. This is a capital outflow from the United States and is recorded as a short-term capital debit in the United States balance of payments. Note that both entries here are short-term capital flows:

	Debit (−)	Credit (+)
Short-term capital inflow		$300
(the purchase of U.S. treasury bills by a foreigner)		
Short-term capital outflow	$300	
(the reduction in foreign bank balances in the United States)		

If we assume that these five transactions are all the international transactions of the United States during the year, then the United States balance of payments is as follows:

	Debits (−)	Credits (+)
Merchandise		$500
Services	$200	
Unilateral transfers	$100	
Long-term capital	$400	
Short-term capital, net		$200
Total debits and credits	$700	$700

The net short-term capital credit balance of $200 is obtained by adding together the five short-term capital entries (−$500, $200, $100, $400, $300, −$300) examined separately above. Total debits equal total credits because of double-entry bookkeeping.

14.3   The International Transactions of the United States in 1984

Table 14-1 presents a summary of the international transactions of the United States for the year 1984 (the last year for which complete data were available as this book went to press). The complete unabridged statement of United States international transactions for selected years from 1960 to 1984 is presented in Table 14-4 in section A14.1 in the appendix. In Table 14-1, credits

TABLE 14-1. **Summary of U.S. International Transactions for 1984 (billions of dollars)**

Exports of goods and services	**362**
Merchandise	220
Services	142
Imports of goods and services	**−453**
Merchandise	−329
Services	−124
Unilateral transfers, net	**−11**
U.S. government grants	−9
U.S. government pensions and other transfers	−2
Private remittances and other transfers	−1
U.S. assets abroad, net (increase/capital outflow (−))	**−20**
U.S. official reserve assets, net	−3
U.S. government assets, other than official reserve assets, net	−6
U.S. private assets, net	−12
Direct investment abroad	−5
Foreign securities	−5
Nonbank claims	6
Bank claims	−9
Foreign assets in the U.S., net (increase/capital inflow (+))	**97**
Foreign official assets in the U.S., net	3
Other foreign assets in the U.S., net	94
Direct investment in the U.S.	23
U.S. Treasury and other U.S. securities	35
Nonbank liabilities	4
Bank liabilities	32
Allocation of special drawing rights	**0**
Statistical discrepancy	**25**
Memoranda:	
Balance on merchandise trade	−108
Balance on goods and services	−90
Balance on current account	−102
Transactions in official reserve assets:	
Increase (−) in U.S. official reserve assets, net	−3
Increase (+) in foreign official assets in the U.S.	3

Source: U.S. Department of Commerce, *Survey of Current Business* (Washington, D.C.: U.S. Government Printing Office, June 1985).

are entered with positive signs and debits, with negative signs. In few in-stances, the sum of the subtotals differ slightly from the total because of rounding.

Table 14-1 shows that the United States exported $362 billion of goods and services in 1984. Merchandise exports ($220 billion) included high-technol-ogy products such as computers and aircrafts, machinery, chemicals, agricul-tural products, and so on. Service exports ($142 billion) included travel and transportation services provided to foreigners, fees and royalties received from foreigners, and interest and dividends earned on United States foreign invest-ments. Note that while a capital outflow from the United States is recorded as a debit under capital, the earnings received from abroad for the *services* of United States foreign investments are recorded as a credit under services.

On the other hand, the United States imported goods and services for $453 billion in 1984. Merchandise imports included petroleum, automobiles, tele-vision sets, shoes, textiles and many other products. Imports of services in-cluded the travel and transportation services purchased by United States cit-izens from other nations, fees and royalties paid to foreigners, and the interest and dividends paid on foreign investments in the United States. Note that the inflow of foreign capital into the United States is recorded as a credit under capital, while the payments made to foreigners for the services of the foreign capital invested in the United States are recorded as a debit under services in the United States balance of payments.

The United States made *net* unilateral transfers to foreigners of (−) $11 billion during 1984. These included net economic and military grants to for-eign nations (−$9 billion), net United States government pensions and other transfers to foreign nations (−$2 billion), and net private remittances and other transfers (−$1 billion). Private remittances and other transfers refer to the immigrant remittances to relatives "back home" and other private gifts. Since more than these private transfers were made to foreigners than received by United States residents from abroad, the United States had a net debit entry of (−)$1 billion for private remittances and other transfers.

The stock of United States assets abroad increased (a capital outflow of the United States and a debit) by the net amount of (−)$20 billion during 1984. This included a net increase of (−)$3 billion in the stock of United States official reserve assets, a net increase of (−)$6 billion in the stock of United States government assets other than official reserve assets, and a net increase of (−)$12 in the stock of United States private assets abroad. These three subtotals add up to a total of (−)$21 billion instead of (−)$20 billion because of rounding.

The official reserve assets of the United States include the gold holdings of United States monetary authorities, Special Drawing Rights, the United States reserve position in the International Monetary Fund, and the official foreign currencies holdings of United States monetary authorities. Special Drawing Rights (SDRs, or "paper gold") are international reserves created on the books of the International Monetary Fund (IMF) and distributed to member nations according to their importance in international trade. The reserve position in the IMF refers to gold reserves paid in by the nation upon joining the IMF, which the nation can then borrow automatically and without questions asked, in case of need. Membership in the IMF allows nations to borrow further amounts subject to the conditions imposed by the IMF. (SDRs and the nation's reserve position in the IMF are discussed in detail in Chapter 20.)

The increase in United States private assets abroad of (−)$12 billion included the increase in United States foreign direct investments abroad of (−)$5 billion, an increase in United States holdings of foreign securities of (−)$5 billion, a *decrease* in United States long-term and short-term nonbank claims on unaffiliated foreigners of (+)$6 billion, and an increase in United States long-term and short-term bank liabilities of (−)$9 billion. These four subtotals add up to (−)$13 billion instead of (−)$12 because of rounding.

The stock of foreign assets in the United States increased (a capital inflow to the United States and a credit) by the net amount of (+)$97 billion in 1984. This included a net increase in other foreign assets (i.e., other than official) in the United States of (+)$94 billion. The latter included the following net increases: (+)$23 billion in foreign direct investments in the United States, (+)$35 billion in foreign holdings of United States treasury and other United States securities, (+)$4 billion in United States nonbank liabilities to unaffiliated foreigners, (+)$32 billion in United States bank liabilities to foreigners. There was no allocation of SDRs in 1984.

When we sum the total credits of (+)$362 billion credit for United States exports of goods and services and the (+)$97 billion net increase in foreign assets in the United States, we get the overall credit total of (+)$459 billion for the United States international transactions during 1984. On the other hand, adding up the debits of (−)$453 billion for the United States imports of goods and services, (−)$11 billion for the net unilateral transfers, and (−)$20 billion for the net increase in United States assets abroad, we get the overall debit total of (−)$484 billion.

Since the overall debit total of (−)$484 exceeds the overall credit total of (+)$459 billion by $25 billion, there is a credit entry called **statistical discrepancy** of (+)$25 billion in Table 14-1. This entry is required to make the total credits (including the statistical discrepancy) equal to the total debits, as required by double-entry bookkeeping. A statistical discrepancy results because some transactions (or payments) are valued incorrectly or not reported at all. This is especially true for international capital flows. The memoranda items at the bottom of Table 14-1 are discussed next.

14.4 Accounting Balances and Disequilibrium in International Transactions

In this section, we first examine the various accounting balances appearing in the memoranda at the bottom of Table 14-1 and then discuss the concept and the measurement of disequilibrium in international payments under a fixed and under a flexible exchange rate system.

14.4a Accounting Balances

The first accounting balance in the memoranda at the bottom of Table 14-1 is the balance on merchandise trade. In 1984, the United States exported $220 billion and imported $329 billion of merchandise, for a net debit balance on merchandise trade of (−)$108 billion (with −$1 billion rounding error). The United States had a net debit balance on goods and services of (−)$90 billion (from the export of goods and services of $362 billion minus the import of goods and services of $453 billion, and −$1 billion rounding error). Adding the net debit balance of (−)$11 billion on unilateral transfers to the net debit balance of (−)$90 billion on goods and services, we get the current account net debit balance of (−)$102 billion (with $1 billion rounding error). The **current account** thus lumps together all sales and purchases of currently produced goods and services and unilateral transfers and provides the link between the nation's international transactions and its national income.

The last two items in the memoranda deal with transactions in official reserve assets. During 1984 there was a net increase in United States official reserve assets (a capital outflow from the United States) of (−)$3 billion. At the same time, there was a net increase in foreign official assets in the United States (a capital inflow to the United States) of (+)$3 billion. This gives a zero net balance on transactions in official reserve assets (not shown in the memoranda).

The change in United States assets abroad and foreign assets in the United States, *other than official reserve assets*, gives the **capital account** of the United States. This measures the change in the stock of all nonreserve financial assets. The justification for excluding financial reserve assets from the capital account is that changes in reserves reflect government policy rather than market forces. Thus, the capital account of the United States shows a net increase in United States assets abroad (a capital outflow of the United States) of (−)$17 billion (the total of $20 billion minus the $3 billion net increase in United States official reserve assets), and a net increase in foreign assets in the United States (a capital inflow to the United States) of $94 billion (the total of $97 billion minus the $3 billion of the net increase in foreign official assets in the United States). Thus, the United States has a net credit balance (a net capital inflow) in its capital account of (+)$77 billion (−$17 +$94) in 1984.

All transactions in the current and capital accounts are called **autonomous transactions** because they take place for business or profit motives (except for unilateral transfers) and independently of balance-of-payments considerations. Autonomous items are sometimes referred to as "the items above the line." On the other hand, transactions in official reserve assets are called **accommodating transactions** (or "items below the line") because they result from and are needed to balance international transactions. The accommodating or below-the-line items form the **official reserve account,** and the balance on the official reserve account is called the **official settlements balance.**

If total debits exceed total credits in the current and capital accounts, the net *debit* balance measures the deficit in the nation's balance of payments. This deficit must then be settled with an equal net *credit* in the official reserve account. Thus, a **deficit in the balance of payments** can be measured either by the excess of debits over credits in the current and capital accounts or by the excess of credits over debits in the official reserve account. On the other hand, a nation has a **surplus in the balance of payments** if its total credits exceed its total debits in the current and capital accounts. The net credit balance gives the size of the surplus and is settled by an equal debit balance in the official reserve account.

Thus, the zero net balance on transactions in official reserve assets, or items below the line, in Table 14-1 indicates that the United States balance of payments was in equilibrium in 1984 (on the official settlements measure). This is equal to the zero net balance on the items above the line (obtained from the net debit balance of $-\$102$ in the current account, plus the net credit balance of $+\$77$ billion in the capital account, and the $+\$25$ billion credit for the statistical discrepancy—see Table 14-1).

However, this method of measuring the deficit (or surplus) in the balance of payments (as well as the concept itself) is strictly correct only under a fixed exchange rate system, and not under a flexible exchange rate system such as we have today. The reason for this is explained next.

14.4b   Disequilibrium in International Transactions

The difficulty in using the above method to measure the disequilibrium in a nation's balance of payments under a flexible exchange rate system can be examined with Figure 14-1, which is identical to Figure 13-1 except for the addition of the new demand curve for pounds labeled $D_£'$. The United States demand for pounds $(D_£)$ arises from the United States demand for imports of goods and services from the United Kingdom, from United States unilateral transfers to the United Kingdom, and from United States investments in the United Kingdom (a capital outflow from the United States). These are the autonomous debit transactions of the United States that involve payments to the United Kingdom. On the other hand, the supply of pounds $(S_£)$ arises from United States exports of goods and services to the United Kingdom, from unilateral transfers received from the United Kingdom, and the United Kingdom investments in the United States (a capital inflow to the United States). These are the autonomous credit transactions of the United States that involve payments from the United Kingdom. (We are here assuming for simplicity that the United States and the United Kingdom are the only two nations in the world and that all transactions between them take place in pounds.)

With $D_£$ and $S_£$, equilibrium exchange rate is $R = \$/£ = 2$ (point E in Figure 14-1), at which £40 million are demanded and supplied per day (exactly as in Figure 13-1). Now suppose that for whatever reason (such as an increase in United States tastes for United Kingdom products) the United States autonomous demand for pounds shifts up to $D_£'$. If the United States wanted to maintain the exchange rate at $R = 2$, United States monetary authorities would have to satisfy the excess demand for pounds of *TE* (£50 million per day in Figure 14-1) out of their official reserve holdings of pounds. Alternatively, United Kingdom monetary authorities would have to purchase dollars (thus adding to their official dollar reserves) and supply pounds to the foreign exchange market to prevent an appreciation of the pound (a depreciation of the dollar). In either case, the United States official settlements balance would show a deficit of £50 million pounds ($100 million at the official exchange rate of $R = 2$) per day, or £18.25 billion ($36.5 billion) per year.

If, on the other hand, the United States operated under a freely flexible exchange rate system, the exchange rate would rise (i.e., the dollar would depreciate) from $R = 2$ to $R = 3$, at which the quantity of pounds demanded

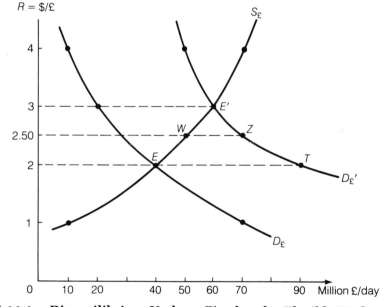

FIGURE 14-1.   Disequilibrium Under a Fixed and a Flexible Exchange Rate System

With $D_£$ and $S_£$, equilibrium is at point *E* at the exchange rate of $R = \$/£ = 2$, at which the quantities of pounds demanded and supplied are equal at £40 million per day. If $D_£$ shifted up to $D_£'$, the United States could maintain the exchange rate at $R = 2$ by satisfying (out of its official pound reserves) the excess demand of £50 million per day (*TE* in the figure). With a freely flexible exchange rate system, the dollar would depreciate until $R = 3$ (point *E'* in the figure). If, on the other hand, the United States wanted to limit the depreciation of the dollar to $R = 2.50$ under a managed float, it would have to satisfy the excess demand of £20 million per day (*WZ* in the figure) out of its official pound reserves.

(£60 million per day) exactly equals the quantity supplied (point E' in Figure 14-1). In this case, the United States would not lose any of its official pound reserves. Indeed, such international reserves would be entirely unnecessary under such a system. The tendency for an excess demand for pounds on autonomous transactions would be completely eliminated by a sufficient depreciation of the dollar with respect to the pound.

However, under a "managed floating exchange rate system" of the type in operation since 1973, United States monetary authorities can intervene in foreign exchange markets to moderate the depreciation (or appreciation) of the dollar. In the above example, the United States might limit the depreciation of the dollar to $R = 2.5$ (instead of letting the dollar depreciate all the way to $R = 3$ as under a *freely* fluctuating exchange rate system). This the United States could do by supplying to the foreign exchange market the excess demand for pounds of WZ, or £20 million per day, out of its official pound reserves (see the figure). Under such a system, part of the *potential* deficit in the United States balance of payments is covered by the loss of official reserve assets of the United States, and part is reflected in the form of a depreciation of the dollar. Thus, we cannot now measure the deficit in the United States balance of payments by simply measuring the loss of United States international reserves or by the amount of the net credit balance in the official reserve account of the United States. Under a managed float, the loss of official reserves only indicates the degree of official intervention in foreign exchange markets to influence the level and movement of exchange rates, and not the exact size of the balance-of-payments deficit (or surplus).

It is for this reason that the United States no longer calculates the balance-of-payments deficit (or surplus) by the official settlements method or by any other method. The statement of international transactions does not even show the net balance on the official reserve account (though it can be easily calculated) in order to be neutral and not to focus undue attention on such a balance, in view of the present system of managed float.

In 1976, besides dropping the official settlements balance, the United States Department of Commerce also (and for the same reason) dropped the two other balances that it had previously calculated. These are the basic balance and the net liquidity balance. The **basic balance** places above the line as autonomous only the current account and *long-term* capital items, while placing *short-term* capital items below the line as accommodating. The **net liquidity balance** includes also the change in short-term private nonliquid assets above the line, while putting the change in short-term private **liquid assets** (i.e., money or assets that could quickly be exchanged for money) below the line. The rationale for the basic balance and the net liquidity balance is presented in section A14.2 in the appendix. These balances are discussed because they are still encountered in writings on international finance, are still used by developing nations and the International Monetary Fund, and the world may even return to some form of fixed exchange rate system in the future.

There is still another method of measuring the deficit or surplus in a nation's balance of payments. This is the method used by the International Monetary Fund and which all member nations must use in reporting yearly to the IMF. Basically, the IMF continues to use the basic balance and the official settlements balance. Section A14.3 presents this method and utilizes it to compare the balance of payments of the United States and a few other important nations in 1984 (the last year for which such data were available when this book went to press).

14.5 Brief Postwar International Monetary History of the United States

In this section we present a brief international monetary history of the United States with the aid of Table 14-2, which is a condensed version of Table 14-4 in the appendix.

From Table 14-2, we see that the United States positive merchandise trade balance (column 4) of the 1960s gave way to a negative merchandise trade balance in the 1970s (for the first time in over 50 years), which became very large after 1982. To a large extent, this reflected the sharp rise in the price of imported petroleum products during the 1970s and the high international value of the dollar in the 1980s. Adding together columns 7 and 8 gives the official settlements balance. Keeping in mind that a positive official settlements balance represents a deficit in United States international transactions, while a negative balance represents a surplus, we see that the United States had its first very large official settlements deficit (of $9 billion) in 1970. The deficit rose sharply in 1971 when it reached $29 billion. The deficit was lower until 1977 and 1978, when it rose above $30 billion. The United States had a surplus of $15 billion in 1979 and then a deficit of $7 billion in 1980. Since 1980, the United States has had either equilibrium in its balance of payments or a very small deficit or surplus.

The huge deficits in the United States balance of payments in 1970 and 1971 were the immediate cause of the collapse of the fixed exchange rate system and establishment of the flexible system in operation today. However, before we turn to that topic, we must clear a few possible pitfalls in the analysis of a nation's statement of international transactions (as summarized in Table 14-2 for the United States). First of all, too much attention is generally placed on the merchandise trade balance and on short-term data. The reason may be that quarterly merchandise trade data are the first to become available. It is also dangerous to extrapolate for the year based on quarterly data. Even the notion of a positive trade balance being favorable is somewhat misleading because a positive trade balance means that the nation has fewer goods to consume domestically.

It is also extremely important to keep in mind that international transactions are closely interrelated rather than independent. For example, cutting

TABLE 14-2. Summary of U.S. International Transactions: 1960–1984 (billions of dollars)

Year (1)	Exports of Goods and Services (2)	Imports of Goods and Services (3)	Balance of Merchandise Trade (4)	Balance on Goods and Services (5)	Balance on Current Account (6)	Increase (−) in U.S. Official Reserve Assets (7)	Increase (+) in Foreign Official Assets in the U.S. (8)
1960	29	−24	5	5	3	2	1
1961	30	−24	6	6	4	1	1
1962	32	−26	5	6	3	2	1
1963	34	−27	5	7	4	0	2
1964	39	−29	7	10	7	0	1
1965	41	−33	5	8	5	1	0
1966	45	−39	4	6	3	1	−1
1967	47	−42	4	6	3	0	3
1968	52	−49	1	4	1	−1	−1
1969	58	−54	1	3	0	−1	−2
1970	66	−60	3	6	2	2	7
1971	69	−67	−2	2	−1	2	27
1972	77	−79	−6	−2	−6	0	10
1973	110	−99	1	11	7	0	5
1974	147	−138	−6	9	2	−1	10
1975	156	−133	9	23	18	−1	6
1976	172	−162	−9	9	4	−3	13
1977	184	−194	−31	−10	−15	0	35
1978	220	−230	−34	−10	−15	1	31
1979	287	−282	−28	5	−1	−1	−14
1980	342	−334	−25	9	2	−8	15
1981	376	−363	−28	13	6	−5	5
1982	350	−350	−36	0	−8	−5	3
1983	334	−366	−62	−32	−41	−1	5
1984	362	−453	−108	−90	−102	−3	3

Source: From Table 14-4 in the appendix to this chapter.

United States foreign aid programs also reduces the ability of recipient nations to import from the United States. Therefore, the possible improvement in the United States balance of payments is likely to be much less than the reduction in the amount of foreign aid given, particularly if the aid is tied to be spent in the United States. Furthermore, an attempt to reduce the United States trade deficit with respect to a nation such as Japan is likely to reduce the United States surplus with respect to Brazil, because Brazil pays for United States goods partly through natural resource exports to Japan. In a world of multilateral trade and highly interdependent transactions, the interpretation of a nation's statement of international transactions must be approached very cautiously, especially when trying to establish causality.

We can now explain the events that led to the collapse of the fixed exchange rate system in 1971 and the establishment of flexible rates in 1973. The discussion is necessarily very brief here. A detailed analysis is presented in Chapter 20. Under the rules of the International Monetary Fund (IMF), established in 1947, member nations were to maintain their exchange rates fixed at declared par values, except in cases of "fundamental disequilibrium." This was broadly defined as a large and persistent, actual or potential deficit. Nations other than the United States intervened with dollars in foreign exchange markets to keep their exchange rates fixed within margins of no more than 1 percent above or below the par value. The United States dollar became an international medium of exchange and together with gold constituted international reserves. The system was thus referred to as the "gold-exchange standard" (the so-called Bretton Woods system). The United States, on its part, was obligated to redeem in gold at the fixed price of $35 per ounce any and all officially foreign-held dollars on demand.

However, as the amount of officially foreign-held dollars began to greatly exceed United States gold reserves, it became evident that the United States could no longer honor its commitment. The problem was aggravated by the large United States balance-of-payments deficit in 1970 and the prospect of an even greater deficit in 1971. These circumstances led the United States to suspend the convertibility of the dollar into gold in August 1971 and to devalue the dollar by about 9 percent in December 1971 (by increasing the price of gold to $38 per ounce). There followed a period of turmoil in international finance that led to another increase in the official price of gold to $42.22 (equivalent to a 10 percent devaluation of the dollar) in February 1973, and finally to the establishment of a flexible exchange rate system in March 1973.

As pointed out in section 14.4b, the present system is a managed float, whereby monetary authorities intervene in foreign exchange markets to influence exchange rate movements. Under such a system, the official settlements balance only measures the degree of government intervention in foreign exchange markets and not the size of the deficit or surplus in a nation's balance of payments. This led the United States to suspend the formal calculation of all three balances (i.e., the basic, the net liquidity, and the official settlements balance). However, most developing nations still peg their exchange rates to a major currency, such as the United States dollar or French franc, or to SDRs. There also seems to be a desire on the part of the United States and other leading nations to reduce exchange rate fluctuations. Thus, an understanding of the concept and measurements of the balance of payments are still relevant.

During the 1980s, the United States began to face much larger merchandise trade deficits. This resulted from the sharp appreciation of the dollar between 1980 and 1984 (see Figure 13-3), which made United States exports much more expensive abroad and imports much cheaper for United States residents.

This led to large job losses in steel, automobile, textile and other United States industries, and to strong pressures in Congress to restrict imports. To avoid trade restrictions (which would lead to foreign retaliation), the United States and other leading nations cooperated during the latter part of 1985 to reinforce the decline in the international value of the dollar that had started in February 1985 (see Figure 13-3). However, it usually takes many months for the trade balance to show significant improvement. Note that the United States avoided large balance-of-payments deficits during the 1980s because of huge capital inflows (see Table 14-2). These topics will be explored in detail in subsequent chapters.

14.6   The International Investment Position of the United States

While a nation's balance of payments measures the international *flow* of goods, services, and capital *during a one-year period*, the **international investment position** measures the total amount and the distribution of a nation's assets abroad and foreign assets in the nation *at the end of the year*. Thus, the balance of payments represents a flow concept and the international investment position (often called the *balance of international indebtedness*) represents a stock concept.

The value of the statement of a nation's international investment position is that it can be used to project the future flow of income or earnings from the nation's foreign investments. Furthermore, adding the nation's capital flows during a year to its international investment position at the end of the *previous* year should theoretically give the international investment position of the nation at the end of the *current* year. In reality, this is seldom, if ever, true because of unrecorded changes in the domestic price (due to inflation) and in the foreign currency price (due to changes in exchange rates) of foreign direct investments and securities over the year.

Table 14-3 gives the international investment position of the United States at the end of 1960, 1970, 1980, 1983, and 1984. We can see that the United States net international investment position increased from $45 billion at the end of 1960 to $106 billion in 1980 and 1983, before declining sharply to $28 billion in 1984. The amount of United States assets abroad increased very rapidly, from $86 billion in 1960 to over $900 billion in 1984. Most of this increase resulted from the rise in United States direct investments abroad and United States bank claims on foreigners (a large part of which represents loans made by American banks to developing countries), with the latter rising even faster than the former. Foreign assets in the United States increased relatively faster than United States assets abroad, from $41 billion in 1960 to $886 billion in 1984. Most of this increase took the form of increases in foreign official assets in the United States (mostly foreign official dollar holdings), foreign holdings of United States securities, and bank claims on the United States.

TABLE 14-3.   International Investment Position of the U.S. in Selected Years: 1960–1984 (billions of dollars, book value at year-end)

	1960	1970	1980	1983	1984
Net U.S. international investment position	**45**	**58**	**106**	**106**	**28**
U.S. assets abroad	**86**	**165**	**607**	**894**	**915**
Official reserve assets	19	14	27	34	35
Gold	18	11	11	11	11
SDRs	0	1	3	5	6
Reserve position in the IMF	2	2	3	11	12
Foreign currencies	0	1	10	6	7
Other government assets	17	32	64	79	85
Private assets	49	119	517	781	795
Direct investments	32	75	215	227	233
Foreign securities	10	21	63	84	90
Bank claims	5	14	204	435	443
Other	3	9	35	35	29
Foreign assets in the U.S.	**41**	**107**	**501**	**788**	**886**
Official assets	12	26	176	195	199
Private assets	29	81	325	593	687
Direct investments	7	13	83	137	160
Other	22	67	242	456	528

Source: U.S. Department of Commerce, *Survey of Current Business* (Washington, D.C.: U.S. Government Printing Office, October 1972 and June 1985).

Three important points can be made with regard to Table 14-3. First, the sharp decline in the United States net international investment position resulted from foreign assets in the United States rising faster than United States assets abroad. This trend continued into 1985, so that during 1985, the net investment position of the United States turned negative (i.e., the United States became a net debtor nation) for the first time since 1914. As the richest nation in the world, one would expect the United States to be a net lender, not a net borrower.

Second, the rapid rise in foreign holdings of United States securities and bank claims on the United States resulted from higher rates of interest in the United States than abroad and financed about half of the huge United States federal budget deficit in the mid-1980s. Thus, while an overvalued dollar led to a huge merchandise trade deficit (which reached nearly $150 billion for the year 1985), the large budget deficit (of nearly $200 billion for 1985) led to high interest rates, which attracted capital from abroad and prevented huge balance of payments deficits, but it also turned the United States into a net debtor nation in 1985.

Third, the figures in Table 14-3 must be interpreted with great caution. For example, direct investments are entered at the lower book value rather than at the much higher replacement value. Since United States direct investments abroad exceed foreign direct investments in the United States, the data in Table 14-3 makes the United States net international investment position seem worse than it is. The same results from the fact that United States' gold holdings are carried at the book value of $42.22 per ounce rather than at the current market price of over $300 per ounce. Working in the opposite direction is the large *cumulative* statistical discrepancies from 1980 to the present, which represent (for the most part) unrecorded capital inflows into the United States.

The turning of the United States from a net creditor to a debtor nation has given rise to a lively debate among economists, politicians, and government officials in the United States regarding the benefits and risks of this recent development. On the benefit side, large foreign investments allowed the United States to finance about half of its budget deficit without the need for still higher interest rates. Foreign investments also went into businesses, farms, real estate, and other property. It has been estimated that this created about 2.5 million jobs in the United States. It also helped rebuild cities, preserve agricultural land, and spread new and more efficient managerial techniques from abroad.

On the negative side, there is the danger that foreigners, for whatever reason, may suddenly withdraw their funds, which would lead to much higher interest rates in this country. Rising income payments to foreigners on their investments also means a worsening of the United States current account balance in the future. On a more general level, some economists and officials fear that foreign companies are used to transfer advanced American technology abroad and lead to some loss of domestic control over political and economic matters, as foreign executives and their lobbyists become ever more familiar figures in the corridors of Congress, state houses, and city halls. There is a bit of irony in all of this—these are the complaints usually heard from Canada, smaller European nations, and developing countries with regard to the large foreign investments (particularly United States investments) in their country. Now the tables are turning.

Summary

1. The balance of payments is a summary statement of all the transactions of the residents of a nation with the rest of the world during a particular period of time, usually a year. Its main purpose is to inform monetary authorities of the international position of the nation and to aid banks, firms, and individuals engaged in international trade and finance in their business decisions.

2. International transactions are classified as debits or credits. Credit transactions are those that involve the receipt of payments from foreigners. Debit transactions are those that involve payments to foreigners. The export of goods and services, unilateral transfers from foreigners, and capital inflows are credits and are entered with a positive sign. The import of goods and services, unilateral transfers to foreigners, and capital outflows are debits and are entered with a negative sign. Each transaction is recorded twice, once as a credit and once as a debit of an equal amount. This is known as double-entry bookkeeping.

3. In 1984, United States exports of goods and

services amounted to $362 billion, while imports of goods and services were $(-)$453 billion. The United States also made net unilateral transfers to foreigners equal to $(-)$11 billion. This gave a net current account deficit of $(-)$108 billion. The United States had a net capital outflow (including official reserve assets) of $(-)$20 billion and a net capital inflow of $(+)$97 billion. A statistical discrepancy credit entry of $(+)$25 billion was necessary to make total credits equal to total debits, as required by double-entry bookkeeping.

4. The change in United States assets abroad and foreign assets in the United States, other than official reserve assets, gives the United States capital account. This showed a net credit balance (a net capital outflow) of $(-)$77 billion in 1984. All transactions in the current and capital accounts are called autonomous, or above-the-line, transactions. If total debits on these autonomous items exceed total credits, the nation has a deficit in its balance of payments equal to the net debit balance. The deficit is then settled by an equal net credit balance on the accommodating, or below-the-line, items. These are the change in United States official reserve assets and the change in foreign official assets in the United States. Together, they form the official reserve account. The United States had a zero net balance in its official reserve account in 1984. However, because of the managed floating exchange rate system, this only means that the United States did not, on balance, intervene in foreign exchange markets during 1984.

5. The United States had its first large official settlements deficit in 1970. This was followed by a much greater deficit in 1971. These were the immediate cause of the collapse of the fixed exchange rate system (the Bretton Woods system) in 1971 and the establishment of the managed floating system in March 1973. Because of this, in 1976 the United States suspended the actual calculation of the official settlements balance, as well as the basic balance and the net liquidity balance. In analyzing a nation's balance of payments, it is important not to give undue attention to the merchandise trade balance and to keep clearly in mind the strong interdependence among most international transactions. During the 1980s, the United States faced huge trade imbalances because of a large dollar overvaluation, and strong pressure in Congress to impose trade restrictions. This led to a coordinated effort on the part of the United States and other leading nations to lower the international value of the dollar during 1985.

6. The international investment position, or balance of indebtedness, measures the total amount and the distribution of a nation's assets abroad and foreign assets in the nation at year-end. Its usefulness is in projecting the future flow of income from foreign investments. In 1985, the United States became a net debtor nation for the first time since 1914. This carries some advantages but also creates problems and risks.

A Look Ahead

This chapter concludes Part III, dealing with foreign exchange markets and the balance of payments. Part IV is concerned with the various mechanisms for adjusting balance-of-payments disequilibria. We begin in Chapter 15 with the discussion of the adjustment mechanism that operates by changing the relationship between domestic and foreign prices. This can be achieved through the operation of the gold standard or with a flexible exchange rate system.

Glossary

Balance of payments A summary statement of all the international transactions of the residents of a nation with the rest of the world during a particular period of time, usually a year.

Credit transactions Transactions that involve the receipt of payments from foreigners. These include the export of goods and services, unilateral transfers from foreigners, and capital inflows.

Debit transactions Transactions that involve payments to foreigners. These include the import of goods and services, unilateral transfers to foreigners, and capital outflows.

Capital inflow   An increase of foreign assets in the nation or a reduction in the nation's assets abroad.

Capital outflow   A decrease of foreign assets in the nation or an increase in the nation's assets abroad.

Double-entry bookkeeping   The accounting procedure whereby each (international) transaction is entered twice, once as a credit and once as a debit of an equal amount.

Unilateral transfers   Gifts or grants extended to or received from abroad.

Statistical discrepancy   The entry made in a nation's balance of payments to make total credits equal to total debits, as required by double-entry bookkeeping.

Current account   All sales and purchases of currently produced goods and services and unilateral transfers. It provides the link between the nation's international transactions and its national income.

Capital account   The change in United States assets abroad and foreign assets in the United States, other than official reserve assets.

Autonomous transactions   International transactions that take place for business or profit motives (except for unilateral transfers) and independently of balance-of-payments considerations; also called above-the-line items.

Accommodating transactions   Transactions in official reserve assets required to balance international transactions; also called below-the-line items.

Official reserve account   The change in United States official reserve assets and the change in foreign official assets in the United States. These are the accommodating, or below-the-line, items.

Official settlements balance   The net credit or debit balance in the official reserve account.

Deficit in the balance of payments   The excess of debits over credits in the current and capital accounts, or autonomous transactions; equal to the net *credit* balance in the official reserve account, or accommodating transactions.

Surplus in the balance of payments   The excess of credits over debits in the current and capital accounts, or autonomous transac-

tions; equal to the net *debit* balance in the official reserve account, or accommodating transactions.

Basic balance   The net balance on all current account and long-term capital transactions.

Net liquidity balance   The net balance on all current account, long-term capital, and short-term nonliquid assets transactions.

Liquid assets   Money or other assets, such as treasury bills, that could easily and quickly be exchanged for money.

International investment position   The total amount and the distribution of a nation's assets abroad and foreign assets in the nation at year-end; also called the balance of international indebtedness.

Questions for Review

1. What is meant by the balance of payments? In what way is the balance of payments a summary statement? What is meant by an international transaction? How is the resident of a nation defined? In what way is the time element involved in measuring a nation's balance of payments?

2. What is a credit transaction? A debit transaction? Which are the broad categories of international transactions classified as credits? As debits? What is double-entry bookkeeping? Why does double-entry bookkeeping usually involve an entry called statistical discrepancy? How does such a statistical discrepancy arise?

3. What is meant by the current account? Did the United States have a deficit or a surplus in the current account in 1984? What was its size? What was the size of the net capital outflow (including United States official reserve assets) in 1984? What was the size of the net capital inflow to the United States in 1984? How was the statistical discrepancy of (+)$25 billion arrived at? By how much did United States official reserve assets increase in 1984? By how much did foreign official reserve assets increase in 1984?

4. Which items does the capital account include? What is meant by the autonomous, or

above-the-line, items? The accommodating, or below-the-line, items? Which items does the official reserve account include? How is an official settlements deficit or surplus measured? Why is the measure of a balance-of-payments deficit or surplus not strictly appropriate under a flexible exchange rate system?

5. What was the immediate cause of the collapse of the fixed exchange rate (Bretton Woods) system in 1971 and the establishment of the flexible exchange rate system in March 1973? What are the most serious pitfalls to avoid in analyzing a nation's balance of payments or statements of international transactions? What was the cause and effect of the large United States trade imbalance during the 1980s?

6. What is meant by the international investment position of a nation, or its balance of international indebtedness? What is its relationship to the nation's balance of payments? What is the most important use of the statement of the international investment position of a nation? What are the benefits and risks of the United States becoming a net debtor nation?

Problems

*1. Indicate how each of the following international transactions is entered into the United States balance of payments with double-entry bookkeeping:
(a) A United States resident imports $500 worth of merchandise from a United Kingdom resident and agrees to pay in three months.
(b) After the three months, the United States resident pays for his imports by drawing down his bank balances in London.
(c) What is the net effect of transactions a and b on the United States balance of payments if they occur during the same year?

2. Indicate how each of the following international transactions is entered into the United States balance of payments with double-entry bookkeeping:

(a) The United States government gives a $100 cash balance in a United States bank to a developing nation as part of the United States foreign aid program.
(b) The developing nation uses the $100 bank balance to import $100 worth of food from the United States.
(c) What is the net effect of transactions a and b on the United States balance of payments if they occur during the same year?
(d) The United States government gives instead $100 worth of food aid to the developing nation.
(e) What is the difference of their effect on the balance of payments between transaction d on the one hand and the next result of transactions a and b on the other?

3. Indicate how each of the following international transactions is entered into the United States balance of payments with double-entry bookkeeping:
(a) A United States resident purchase a $1,000 foreign stock and pays for it by drawing down his bank balances abroad.
(b) During the same year, the United States resident receives a dividend of $100 on his foreign stock and deposits it into his bank account abroad.

*4. Indicate how each of the following international transactions is entered into the United States balance of payments with double-entry bookkeeping:
(a) A foreign investor purchases $400 of United States treasury bills and pays by drawing down his bank balances in the United States.
(b) At maturity (during the same year), the foreign investor receives $440 for the principal and the interest earned and deposits these *dollars* in his bank account in his own nation.

5. Indicate how the following transaction is entered into the United States balance of payments with double-entry bookkeeping:
(a) A United States commercial bank exchanges $800 worth of pounds sterling for dollars at the Federal Reserve Bank of New York.
(b) What effect does this transaction have on

the official settlements balance of the United States?

6. (a) From Table 14-2, calculate the official settlements balance of the United States for each year from 1960 to 1984.

(b) Why is this an appropriate measure for the United States balance of payments position until 1972, but not since 1973?

APPENDIX

In this appendix, section A14.1 presents the complete statement of the international transactions of the United States from 1960 to 1984. Section A14.2 examines the basic balance and the net liquidity balance and compares them with the official settlements balance. Finally, section A14.3 presents the method of measuring the balance of payments that all nations must use in reporting to the International Monetary Fund.

A14.1   The International Transactions of the United States: 1960–1984

Table 14-4 presents the complete statement of United States international transactions from 1960 through 1984 (though the format of the table is strictly appropriate only for the years since 1973, when the flexible exchange rate system came into existence). A summary of the 1984 data in Table 14-4 was presented as Table 14-1 in section 14.3. The line numbers in the first column of Table 14-4 are for ease of reference. The superscript next to some of the entries in the table refers to clarifications given in the footnotes at the end of the table in the source. In Table 14-4, the net exports of goods and services under United States military grant programs (line 16) are reported separately from other United States exports of goods and services, and they are also reported separately (line 30) from other United States government unilateral transfers.

Problem   From the most recent June issue of the *Survey of Current Business* (in your college library), construct a summary table of United States international transactions (similar to Table 14-1) for the previous year.

A14.2   The Basic Balance and the Net Liquidity Balance

Table 14-5 summarizes the United States balance of payments according to the old format and shows and compares the basic balance, the net liquidity balance, and the official settlements balance for 1973, 1974, and 1975 (the last three years for which the United States actually calculated these balances).

The basic balance is the balance on current account and long-term capital. In 1975 the basic balance showed a surplus of (+)$1.4 billion. The net liquidity balance is the balance on current account, long-term capital, non-liquid short-term private capital, the allocation of SDRs, and errors and omissions (the statistical discrepancy). Nonliquid short-term private capital includes such items as short-term international bank loans, which can be converted into cash only when the loan is due. In 1975 the net liquidity balance showed a surplus of (+)$3.1 billion. The official reserve transactions, or settlements, balance adds liquid private capital flows to the net liquidity balance. Liquid private capital flows include such items as changes in foreign bank balances in the United States, which are due on demand, and changes in foreign holdings of United States treasury bills, which can easily and quickly be converted into cash. In 1975 the official settlements balance showed a deficit of (−)$2.5 billion. Thus, the size of the disequilibrium in the balance of payments varies greatly depending on the method of measurement used. This is true for all three years reported in Table 14-5.

The rationale behind the basic balance is the distinction between those items that are more stable and reflect long-run forces and those items (such as short-term international capital flows) that supposedly are more volatile and more responsive to monetary policies in defense of the exchange rate. This distinction is not very convincing, however. For example, long-term international capital flows can sometimes be very volatile, whereas short-term capital flows (especially if related to the financing of trade) may not.

The liquidity balance was introduced in the mid-1950s at a time when the United States government was under obligation to exchange any and all officially foreign-held dollars for gold on demand and at the then fixed price of $35 per ounce. As the stock of United States official gold reserves began to decline while the amount of foreign-held dollars was increasing rapidly, the United States Department of Commerce introduced the liquidity balance to measure the ability of the United States to defend the dollar and maintain its fixed exchange rate. Although the *net* liquidity balance introduced in the early 1970s removed some of the strong criticism levied against the liquidity balance introduced in the mid-1950s, the net liquidity balance too was criticized because of the somewhat artificial distinction that it makes between liquid and nonliquid capital and for its continued attempt to measure the overall liquidity position of the United States.

In 1963 the United States government appointed a committee headed by *Bernstein* to review the method of measuring disequilibrium in the United States balance of payments. In 1965 the Review Committee proposed the official settlements method. As pointed out in section 14-4, the official settlements method considers as accommodating and places below the line only changes in United States official reserve assets and changes in foreign official assets in the United States (i.e., changes in United States liabilities to foreign official agencies). The justification is that it is the United States official or monetary authorities who have the final responsibility for defending the ex-

TABLE 14-4. U.S. International Transactions: 1960–1984 (millions of dollars)

Line	(Credits +; debits −) [1]	1960	1961	1962	1963	1964	1965	1966	1967	1968	1969
1	Exports of goods and services [2]	28,861	29,937	31,803	34,214	38,826	41,087	44,562	47,314	52,363	57,522
2	Merchandise, adjusted, excluding military [3]	19,650	20,108	20,781	22,272	25,501	26,461	29,310	30,666	33,626	36,414
3	Transfers under U.S. military agency sales contracts	335	402	656	657	747	830	829	1,152	1,392	1,528
4	Travel	919	947	957	1,015	1,207	1,380	1,590	1,646	1,775	2,043
5	Passenger fares	175	183	191	205	241	271	317	371	411	450
6	Other transportation	1,607	1,620	1,764	1,898	2,076	2,175	2,333	2,426	2,548	2,652
7	Fees and royalties from affiliated foreigners	590	662	800	890	1,013	1,199	1,162	1,354	1,430	1,533
8	Fees and royalties from unaffiliated foreigners	247	244	256	273	301	335	353	393	437	486
9	Other private services	570	607	585	613	651	714	814	951	1,024	1,160
10	U.S. Government miscellaneous services	153	164	195	236	265	285	326	336	353	343
	Receipts of income on U.S. assets abroad:										
11	Direct investment	3,621	3,823	4,241	4,636	5,106	5,506	5,260	5,603	6,591	7,649
12	Other private receipts	646	793	904	1,022	1,256	1,421	1,669	1,781	2,021	2,338
13	U.S. Government receipts	349	383	473	499	462	510	599	636	756	925
14	Transfers of goods and services under U.S. military grant programs, net	1,695	1,465	1,537	1,562	1,340	1,636	1,892	2,039	2,547	2,610
15	Imports of goods and services	−23,279	−23,591	−25,778	−27,047	−29,222	−32,801	−38,599	−41,606	−48,800	−54,129
16	Merchandise, adjusted, excluding military [3]	−14,758	−14,537	−16,260	−17,048	−18,700	−21,510	−25,493	−26,866	−32,991	−35,807
17	Direct defense expenditures	−3,087	−2,998	−3,105	−2,961	−2,880	−2,952	−3,764	−4,378	−4,535	−4,856
18	Travel	−1,750	−1,785	−1,939	−2,114	−2,211	−2,438	−2,657	−3,207	−3,030	−3,373
19	Passenger fares	−513	−506	−567	−612	−642	−717	−753	−829	−885	−1,080
20	Other transportation	−1,402	−1,437	−1,558	−1,701	−1,817	−1,951	−2,161	−2,157	−2,367	−2,455
21	Fees and royalties to affiliated foreigners	−35	−43	−57	−61	−67	−68	−64	−62	−80	−101
22	Fees and royalties to unaffiliated foreigners	−40	−46	−44	−51	−60	−67	−76	−104	−106	−120
23	Private payments for other services	−593	−588	−528	−493	−527	−461	−506	−565	−668	−751
24	U.S. Government payments for miscellaneous services	−313	−406	−398	−447	−535	−550	−644	−691	−760	−717
	Payments of income on foreign assets in the United States:										
25	Direct investment	−394	−432	−399	−459	−529	−657	−711	−821	−876	−848
26	Other private payments	−511	−535	−586	−701	−802	−942	−1,221	−1,328	−1,800	−3,244
27	U.S. Government payments	−332	−278	−339	−401	−453	−489	−549	−598	−702	−777
28	U.S. military grants of goods and services, net	−1,695	−1,465	−1,537	−1,562	−1,340	−1,636	−1,892	−2,039	−2,547	−2,610
29	Unilateral transfers (excluding military grants of goods and services), net	−2,308	−2,524	−2,638	−2,754	−2,781	−2,854	−2,932	−3,125	−2,952	−2,994
30	U.S. Government grants (excluding military grants of goods and services)	−1,672	−1,855	−1,916	−1,917	−1,888	−1,808	−1,910	−1,805	−1,709	−1,649
31	U.S. Government pensions and other transfers	−214	−235	−245	−262	−279	−369	−367	−441	−407	−406
32	Private remittances and other transfers	−423	−434	−477	−575	−614	−677	−655	−879	−836	−939
33	U.S. assets abroad, net (increase/capital outflow (−))	−4,099	−5,538	−4,174	−7,270	−9,560	−5,716	−7,321	−9,757	−10,977	−11,585
34	U.S. official reserve assets, net [4]	2,145	607	1,535	378	171	1,225	570	53	−870	−1,179
35	Gold	1,703	857	890	461	125	1,665	571	1,170	1,173	−967
36	Special drawing rights										
37	Reserve position in the International Monetary Fund	442	−135	626	29	266	−94	537	−94	−870	−1,034
38	Foreign currencies		−115	19	−112	−220	−346	−538	−1,023	−1,173	822
39	U.S. Government assets, other than official reserve assets, net	−1,100	−910	−1,085	−1,662	−1,680	−1,605	−1,543	−2,423	−2,274	−2,200
40	U.S. credits	−1,214	−1,928	−2,128	−2,204	−2,382	−2,463	−2,513	−3,638	−3,722	−3,489
41	Repayments on U.S. loans [5]	642	1,279	1,288	988	720	874	1,235	1,005	1,386	1,200
42	U.S. foreign currency holdings and U.S. short-term assets, net	−528	−261	−245	−447	−19	−16	−265	209	62	89
43	U.S. private assets, net	−5,144	−5,235	−4,623	−5,986	−8,050	−5,336	−6,347	−7,386	−7,833	−8,206
44	Direct investment	−2,940	−2,653	−2,851	−3,483	−3,760	−5,011	−5,418	−4,805	−5,295	−5,960
45	Foreign securities	−663	−762	−969	−1,105	−677	−759	−720	−1,308	−1,569	−1,549
46	U.S. claims on unaffiliated foreigners reported by U.S. nonbanking concerns	−394	−558	−354	157	−1,108	341	−442	−779	−1,203	−126
47	U.S. claims reported by U.S. banks, not included elsewhere	−1,148	−1,261	−450	−1,556	−2,505	93	233	−495	233	−570
48	Foreign assets in the United States, net (increase/capital inflow (+))	2,294	2,705	1,911	3,217	3,643	742	3,661	7,379	9,928	12,702
49	Foreign official assets in the United States, net	1,473	765	1,270	1,986	1,660	134	−672	3,451	−774	−1,301
50	U.S. Government securities	655	233	1,409	816	432	−141	−1,527	2,261	−769	−2,343
51	U.S. Treasury securities [6]	655	233	1,410	803	434	−134	−1,548	2,222	−798	−2,269
52	Other [7]			−1	12	−2	−7	21	39	29	−74
53	Other U.S. Government liabilities [8]	215	25	152	429	298	65	113	83	−15	251
54	U.S. liabilities reported by U.S. banks, not included elsewhere	603	508	−291	742	930	210	742	1,106	10	792
55	Other foreign official assets [9]										
56	Other foreign assets in the United States, net	821	1,939	641	1,231	1,983	607	4,333	3,928	10,703	14,002
57	Direct investment	315	311	346	231	322	415	425	698	807	1,263
58	U.S. Treasury securities	−364	151	−66	−149	−146	−131	−356	−135	136	−68
59	U.S. securities other than U.S. Treasury securities	282	324	134	287	−85	−358	906	1,016	4,414	3,130
60	U.S. liabilities to unaffiliated foreigners reported by U.S. nonbanking concerns	−90	226	−110	−37	75	178	476	584	1,475	792
61	U.S. liabilities reported by U.S. banks, not included elsewhere	678	928	336	898	1,818	503	2,882	1,765	3,871	8,886
62	Allocations of special drawing rights										
63	Statistical discrepancy (sum of above items with sign reversed)	−1,019	−989	−1,124	−360	−907	−458	629	−205	438	−1,516
	Memoranda:										
64	Balance of merchandise trade (lines 2 and 16)	4,892	5,571	4,521	5,224	6,801	4,951	3,817	3,800	635	607
65	Balance on goods and services (lines 1 and 15) [10]	5,132	6,346	6,025	7,167	9,604	8,285	5,963	5,708	3,563	3,393
66	Balance on goods, services, and remittances (lines 65, 31, and 32)	4,496	5,677	5,303	6,331	8,711	7,239	4,941	4,338	2,320	2,048
67	Balance on current account (lines 65 and 29) [10]	2,824	3,822	3,387	4,414	6,823	5,432	3,031	2,583	611	399
	Transactions in U.S. official reserve assets and in foreign official assets in the United States:										
68	Increase (−) in U.S. official reserve assets, net (line 34)	2,145	607	1,535	378	171	1,225	570	53	−870	−1,179
69	Increase (+) in foreign official assets in the United States (line 49 less line 53)	1,258	741	1,118	1,558	1,362	69	−785	3,368	−759	−1,552

Source: United States Department of Commerce, Bureau of Economic Analysis, Survey of Current Business (Washington, D.C.: U.S. Government Printing Office, June 1985), pp. 40–41 and 69.

1970	1971	1972	1973	1974	1975	1976	1977	1978	1979	1980	1981	1982	1983	1984	Line
65,674	68,838	77,495	110,241	146,666	155,729	171,630	184,276	219,994	286,796	342,485	375,759	350,058	333,586	362,421	1
42,469	43,319	49,381	71,410	98,306	107,088	114,745	120,816	142,054	184,473	224,269	237,085	211,198	200,745	220,316	2
1,501	1,926	1,364	2,559	3,379	4,049	5,454	7,351	7,973	6,516	8,274	10,041	11,907	12,394	10,086	3
2,331	2,534	2,817	3,412	4,032	4,697	5,742	6,150	7,183	8,441	10,588	12,913	12,393	11,408	11,386	4
544	615	699	975	1,104	1,039	1,229	1,366	1,603	2,156	2,591	3,111	3,174	3,037	3,023	5
3,125	3,299	3,579	4,465	5,697	5,840	6,747	7,090	8,136	9,971	11,618	12,560	12,317	12,639	13,799	6
1,758	1,927	2,115	2,513	3,070	3,543	3,531	3,883	4,705	4,980	5,780	5,794	5,561	6,275	6,530	7
573	618	655	712	751	757	822	1,037	1,180	1,204	1,305	1,490	1,572	1,580	1,585	8
1,294	1,546	1,764	1,985	2,321	2,920	3,584	3,848	4,296	4,403	5,158	5,856	6,635	6,857	7,463	9
332	347	357	401	419	446	489	557	620	520	398	499	533	630	624	10
8,169	9,160	10,949	16,542	19,157	16,595	18,999	19,673	25,458	38,183	37,146	32,549	22,600	21,271	23,078	11
2,671	2,641	2,949	4,330	7,356	7,644	8,955	10,881	14,944	23,654	32,798	50,182	58,050	51,920	59,301	12
907	906	866	936	1,074	1,112	1,332	1,625	1,843	2,295	2,562	3,680	4,118	4,832	5,230	13
2,713	3,546	4,492	2,810	1,818	2,207	373	203	236	465	756	679	585	194	190	14
−60,050	−66,569	−79,435	−99,219	−137,519	−133,000	−162,425	−194,170	−230,316	−282,138	−333,536	−362,573	−349,974	−365,524	−452,539	15
−39,866	−45,579	[11]−55,797	[11]−70,499	−103,811	−98,185	−124,228	−151,907	−176,001	−212,009	−249,749	−265,063	−247,642	−262,757	−328,597	16
−4,855	−4,819	[11]−4,784	[11]−4,629	−5,032	−4,795	−4,895	−5,823	−7,352	−8,294	−10,511	−11,224	−12,225	−12,556	−11,851	17
−3,980	−4,373	−5,042	−5,526	−5,980	−6,417	−6,856	−7,451	−8,475	−9,413	−10,397	−11,479	−12,394	−13,997	−16,008	18
−1,215	−1,290	−1,596	−1,790	−2,095	−2,263	−2,568	−2,748	−2,896	−3,184	−3,607	−4,487	−4,772	−5,484	−6,508	19
−2,843	−3,130	−3,520	−4,694	−5,942	−5,708	−6,852	−7,972	−9,124	−10,906	−11,790	−12,474	−11,710	−12,324	−14,666	20
−111	−118	−155	−209	−160	−287	−293	−243	−393	−523	−428	−362	78	67	−187	21
−114	−123	−139	−176	−186	−186	−189	−262	−277	−309	−297	−289	−267	−295	−329	22
−827	−956	−1,043	−1,180	−1,262	−1,551	−2,006	−2,190	−2,573	−2,822	−2,909	−3,002	−3,529	−3,364	−3,762	23
−725	−746	−788	−862	−967	−1,044	−1,227	−1,358	−1,545	1,718	−1,730	−1,865	−2,238	−2,193	−2,133	24
−875	−1,164	−1,284	−1,610	−1,331	−2,234	−3,110	−2,834	−4,211	−6,357	−8,635	−6,898	−3,155	−5,598	−10,188	25
−3,617	−2,428	−2,604	−4,209	−6,491	−5,788	−5,681	−5,841	−8,795	−15,481	−20,893	−28,553	−33,833	−29,198	−38,543	26
−1,024	−1,844	−2,684	−3,836	−4,262	−4,542	−4,520	−5,542	−8,674	−11,122	−12,592	−16,878	−18,285	−17,825	−19,769	27
−2,713	−3,546	−4,492	−2,810	−1,818	−2,207	−373	−203	−236	−465	−756	−679	−585	−194	−190	28
−3,294	−3,701	−3,854	−3,881	[12]−7,186	−4,613	−4,998	−4,617	−5,106	−5,649	−7,077	−6,847	−8,135	−8,852	−11,413	29
−1,736	−2,043	−2,173	−1,938	[12]−5,475	−2,894	−3,146	−2,787	−3,176	−3,550	−4,731	−4,466	−5,501	−6,287	−8,522	30
−462	−542	−572	−693	−694	−813	−934	−971	−1,086	−1,180	−1,302	−1,464	−1,473	−1,581	−1,591	31
−1,096	−1,117	−1,109	−1,250	−1,017	−906	−917	−859	−844	−920	−1,044	−918	−1,160	−984	−1,300	32
−9,337	−12,475	−14,497	−22,874	−34,745	−39,703	−51,269	−34,785	−61,130	−64,331	−86,118	−111,031	−119,218	−55,045	−20,447	33
2,481	2,349	−4	158	−1,467	−849	−2,558	−375	732	−1,133	8,155	−5,175	−4,965	−1,196	−3,131	34
787	866	547					−118	−65	−65		(*)				35
−851	−249	−703	9	−172	−66	−78	−121	1,249	−1,136	−16	−1,824	−1,371	−66	−979	36
389	1,350	153	−33	−1,265	−466	−2,212	−294	4,231	−189	−1,667	−2,491	−2,552	−4,434	−995	37
2,156	382	−1	182	−30	−317	−268	158	−4,683	257	−6,472	−861	−1,041	3,304	−1,156	38
−1,589	−1,884	−1,568	−2,644	[14]366	−3,474	−4,214	−3,693	−4,660	−3,746	−5,162	−6,131	−5,006	−5,516		39
−3,293	−4,181	−3,819	−4,638	−5,001	−5,941	−6,943	−6,445	−7,470	−7,697	−9,860	−9,674	−10,063	−9,967	−9,619	40
1,721	2,115	2,086	2,596	[13]4,826	2,475	2,596	2,719	2,941	3,926	4,456	4,413	4,293	5,012	4,483	41
−16	182	165	−602	[12]541	−9	133	33	−131	25	242	164	−361	−51	−380	42
−10,229	−12,940	−12,925	−20,388	−33,643	−35,380	−44,498	−30,717	−57,202	−59,453	−72,802	−100,758	−108,122	−48,843	−11,800	43
−7,590	−7,618	−7,747	−11,353	−9,052	−14,244	−11,949	−11,890	−16,056	−25,222	−19,222	−9,624	4,424	−5,394	−4,503	44
−1,076	−1,113	−618	−671	−1,854	−6,247	−8,885	−5,460	−3,626	−4,726	−3,568	−5,778	−8,102	−7,007	−5,059	45
−596	−1,229	−1,054	−2,383	−3,221	−1,357	−2,296	−1,940	−3,853	−3,291	−3,174	−1,181	6,626	−6,513	6,266	46
−967	−2,980	−3,506	−5,980	−19,516	−13,532	−21,368	−11,427	−33,667	−26,213	−46,838	−84,175	−111,070	−29,928	−8,504	47
6,359	22,970	21,461	18,388	34,241	15,670	36,518	51,319	64,036	38,752	58,112	83,322	94,447	84,322	97,319	48
6,908	26,879	10,475	6,026	10,546	7,027	17,693	36,816	33,678	−13,665	15,497	4,960	3,672	5,795	3,424	49
9,439	26,570	8,470	641	4,172	5,563	9,892	32,538	24,221	−21,972	11,895	6,322	5,085	6,496	4,857	50
9,411	26,578	8,213	59	3,270	4,658	9,319	30,230	23,555	−22,435	9,708	5,019	5,779	6,972	4,690	51
28	−8	257	582	902	905	573	2,308	666	463	2,187	1,303	−694	−476	167	52
−456	−510	182	936	301	1,517	4,627	1,400	2,476	−40	615	−338	684	552	453	53
−2,075	819	1,638	4,126	5,818	−2,158	969	773	5,551	7,213	−159	−3,670	−1,747	−1,798	663	54
		185	323	254	2,104	2,205	2,105	1,430	1,135	3,145	2,646	−350		−2,549	55
−550	−3,909	10,986	12,362	23,696	8,643	18,826	14,503	30,358	52,416	42,615	78,362	90,775	78,526	93,895	56
1,464	367	949	2,800	4,760	2,603	4,347	3,728	7,897	11,877	16,918	25,195	13,792	11,946	22,514	57
81	−24	−39	−216	697	2,590	2,783	534	[13]2,178	[13]4,960	[13]2,645	[13]2,946	[13]7,052	[13]8,721	22,440	58
2,189	2,289	4,507	4,041	378	2,503	1,284	2,437	2,254	1,351	5,457	7,176	6,392	8,636	12,983	59
2,014	369	815	1,035	1,844	319	−578	1,086	1,889	1,621	6,852	917	−2,383	−118	4,284	60
−6,298	−6,911	4,754	4,702	16,017	628	10,990	6,719	16,141	32,607	10,743	42,128	65,922	49,341	31,674	61
867	717	710							1,139	1,152	1,093				62
−219	−9,779	−1,879	−2,654	−1,458	5,917	10,544	−2,023	12,521	25,431	24,982	20,276	32,821	11,513	24,660	63
2,603	−2,260	−6,416	911	−5,505	8,903	−9,483	−31,091	−33,947	−27,536	−25,480	−27,978	−36,444	−62,012	−108,281	64
5,625	2,269	−1,941	11,021	9,147	22,729	9,205	−9,894	−10,321	4,659	8,950	13,186	84	−31,937	−90,119	65
4,067	610	−3,622	9,078	7,437	21,011	7,354	−11,724	−12,251	2,559	6,604	10,805	−2,549	−34,503	−93,910	66
2,331	−1,433	−5,795	7,140	1,962	18,116	4,207	−14,511	−15,427	−991	1,873	6,339	−8,051	−40,790	−101,532	67
2,481	2,349	−4	158	−1,467	−849	−2,558	−375	732	−1,133	−8,155	−5,175	−4,965	−1,196	−3,131	68
7,364	27,389	10,293	5,090	10,244	5,509	13,066	35,416	31,202	−13,624	14,881	5,298	2,988	5,243	2,971	69

TABLE 14-5. U.S. Balance of Payments Summary—Old Format
(billions of dollars)

	1973	1974	1975
Merchandise exports	70.2	98.3	107.2
Merchandise imports	−69.6	−103.6	−98.1
Merchandise trade balance	**0.6**	**−5.3**	**9.1**
Military transactions, net	−2.2	−2.2	−0.8
Travel and transportation, net	−2.7	−2.7	−2.0
Investment income, net	5.3	10.1	6.0
Other services, net	3.5	3.8	4.2
Balance on goods and services	**4.5**	**3.8**	**16.5**
Remittances, pensions and other transfers	−1.9	−1.7	−1.8
Balances on goods, services and remittances	**2.6**	**2.1**	**14.7**
U.S. government grants (excluding military goods and services)	−1.9	−5.5	−2.8
Balance on current account	**0.7**	**−3.4**	**11.9**
U.S. government capital flows	−1.4	1.1	−1.7
Long-term capital flows, net	0.1	−8.5	−8.8
Balance on current account and long-term capital (basic balance)	**−0.7**	**−10.7**	**1.4**
Nonliquid short-term private capital flow, net	−4.3	−12.9	−2.8
Allocation of SDRs	0.0	0.0	0.0
Errors and omissions, net	−2.8	4.7	4.6
Net liquidity balance	**−7.8**	**−18.9**	**3.1**
Liquid private capital flows, net	2.5	10.5	−5.6
Official reserve transactions balance	**−5.3**	**−8.4**	**−2.5**
Financed by changes in:			
Liabilities to foreign official agencies	5.1	9.8	3.0
U.S. official reserve assets, net	0.2	−1.4	−0.6

Source: U.S. Department of Commerce, Survey of Current Business (Washington, D.C.: U.S. Government Printing Office, June 1974 and March 1976).

change rate of the dollar. However, with the collapse of the fixed exchange rate system and the establishment of a managed floating exchange rate system in March 1973, this method only measures the degree of government intervention in foreign exchange markets, rather than the deficit or surplus in the balance of payments (see section 14.4b).

As a result, in 1976 the United States changed its method of presenting its international transactions and ceased to calculate all three balances. The basic balance and the official settlements balance can still be calculated from the new reporting method, but the net liquidity balance can no longer be calculated because the distinction between liquid and nonliquid capital flows has been discontinued.

Problem Suppose that a commercial bank in the United Kingdom exchanges $1 million for pounds at the central bank of the United Kingdom. Indicate how this transaction affects each of the three measures of the United States balance of payments.

A14.3 The IMF Method of Reporting International Transactions

Table 14-6 summarizes the balance of payments of the United States, West Germany, Japan, France, the United Kingdom, and Brazil for the year 1984 in the standard form required by the International Monetary Fund. This standardized reporting method is valuable because it allows international comparisons.

A few items in Table 14-6 require explanation. In section E, the so-called counterpart items refer to the monetization and demonetization of gold, the allocation and cancellation of SDRs, and valuation changes in reserves. Exceptional financing in section F refers to such things as monetary authorities' borrowing foreign exchange from foreign governments and issuing securities denominated in foreign currencies in order to raise the foreign exchange to intervene in foreign exchange markets in defense of the national currency. The conversion rates at the bottom of the table indicate the United States dollar price of one SDR. The SDR itself is the weighted average of the five leading national currencies (i.e., the currencies of the nations included in the table with the exception of Brazil).

From section A in Table 14-6, we see that only the United States among the six nations had a net debit balance in the current account in 1984. This was equal to almost 100 billion SDRs ($102.4 billion). From section B, we see that Japan had a net debit balance of 49 billion SDRs ($50.5 billion) on long-term capital. Germany and the United Kingdom had smaller net debit balances on long-term capital. The total of groups A and B gives the basic balance. The United States, Japan, and the United Kingdom had a basic balance deficit, while Germany, France, and Brazil had a surplus. The basic balance deficit was largest for the United States (67.8 billion SDRs equal to $69.2 billion). France had the largest basic balance surplus (5.2 billion SDRs equal to $5.4 billion). The total of groups A through E gives the official settlements balance. This was nearly in balance for all countries except the United Kingdom, which had an official settlements deficit of 12.8 billion SDRs ($13.1 billion). The U.S. official settlements deficit of $(-)0.7$ billion SDRs was settled by an equal net credit balance of $(+)0.7$ billion SDRs for the items below the

TABLE 14-6.   *IMF Balance-of-Payments Summary Presentation: U.S., W. Germany, Japan, France, U.K., Brazil in 1984 (in billions of SDRs)*

	U.S.	W. Germany	Japan	France	U.K.	Brazil
A. Current account	**−99.4**	**6.0**	**34.3**	**0.1**	**0.8**	**0.1**
Merchandise exports f.o.b.	215.0	159.5	164.3	90.0	91.4	26.4
Merchandise imports f.o.b.	−320.7	−137.7	−121.0	−94.0	−96.9	−13.6
Trade balance	−105.7	21.8	43.3	−3.9	−5.5	12.8
Services: credit	138.7	45.7	41.2	54.5	47.2	3.1
Services: debit	−120.5	−50.7	−48.7	−47.7	−37.8	−16.0
Private unrequited transfers	−1.3	−3.7	−0.1	−1.0	−0.4	0.2
Official unrequited transfers	−10.6	−7.1	−1.3	−1.8	−2.8	0.0
B. Direct investment and other long-term capital	**31.8**	**−5.1**	**−49.0**	**5.1**	**−14.3**	**1.7**
Direct investment	17.5	−1.9	−5.8	0.3	−0.4	1.5
Portfolio investment	28.6	0.6	−23.6	6.9	−9.5	−0.3
Other long-term capital	−15.2	−3.8	−19.6	−2.0	−4.4	0.4
Total Groups A plus B (Basic Balance)	**−67.6**	**0.9**	**−14.7**	**5.2**	**−13.6**	**1.7**
C. Short-term capital	**43.2**	**−5.7**	**13.1**	**−3.1**	**−0.4**	**−3.1**
D. Net errors and omissions	**24.2**	**3.6**	**3.7**	**0.6**	**1.8**	**0.4**
E. Counterpart items	**−0.6**	**1.1**	**1.4**	**−1.2**	**−0.6**	**1.0**
Total, Groups A through E (Official Settlements Balance).	**−0.7**	**−0.2**	**3.5**	**1.5**	**−12.8**	**0.0**
F. Exceptional financing	**0.0**	**0.0**	**0.0**	**0.0**	**1.6**	**5.8**
G. Liabilities constituting foreign authorities' reserves	**3.2**	**0.8**	**0.0**	**0.1**	**9.4**	**0.5**
H. Total change in reserves	**−2.5**	**−0.6**	**−3.5**	**−1.7**	**1.8**	**−6.3**
Monetary gold	0.2	−0.5	0.0	0.0	0.6	−0.3
SDRs	−1.0	0.2	−0.1	−0.2	0.0	0.0
Reserve position in the Fund	−1.0	−0.3	−0.1	0.0	0.0	0.0
Foreign exchange assets	−0.8	−0.1	−3.3	−2.2	1.2	−7.6
Other claims	0.0	0.1	0.0	0.7	0.0	−0.1
Use of Fund credit	0.0	0.0	0.0	0.0	0.0	1.7
Conversion rates:						
U.S. dollars per SDR	1.03	2.92	243.46	8.96	0.77	1894.2

Source: International Monetary Fund, *Balance of Payments Yearbook* (Washington, D.C.: IMF, 1985).

line. This was given by the sum of the increase in United States liabilities to foreign authorities of (+)3.2 billion SDRs and the decrease in United States reserves of (−)2.5 billion SDRs.

Problem   Measure from Table 14-4 the official settlements balance for the U.S. for 1984 and try to explain the reason for the difference between that result and the one obtained above.

Selected Bibliography

For a problem-solving approach to the material covered in this chapter, see:
- D. Salvatore, *Theory and Problems of International Economics*, 2nd ed. (New York: McGraw-Hill, 1984), ch. 7.

The current presentation of United States international transactions follows the:
- Report of the Advisory Committee on the Presentation of the Balance of Payments Statistics, *Survey of Current Business* (Washington, D.C.: United States Government Printing Office, June 1976), pp. 18–27.

For an excellent discussion of the current method of presenting United States international transactions, see:
- R. M. Stern et al., *The Presentation of the United States Balance of Payments: A Symposium*, Essays in International Finance, No. 123 (Princeton, N.J.: Princeton University Press, International Finance Section, August 1977).

The classic work on the balance of payments is still:
- J. Meade, *The Balance of Payments* (London: Oxford University Press, 1951).

For a discussion and comparison of the basic balance, the liquidity balance, and the official settlements balance, see:
- U.S. Bureau of the Budget, Review Committee for Balance of Payments Statistics, *The Balance of Payments of the United States* (Washington, D.C.: United States Government Printing Office, 1965).
- D. S. Kemp, "Balance of Payments Concepts—What Do They Really Mean?" in Federal Reserve Bank of Chicago, *Readings in International Finance* (Chicago: Federal Reserve Bank of Chicago, 1984).

Data on United States international transactions are presented in:
- U.S. Department of Commerce, Bureau of Economic Analysis, *Survey of Current Business* (Washington, D.C.: United States Government Printing Office, Monthly).

Data on the international transactions of members of the International Monetary Fund are published in:
- International Monetary Fund, *Balance of Payments Yearbook* (Washington, D.C.: IMF, Yearly).

PART IV

Adjustment in the Balance of Payments and Domestic Stability

Part IV (Chapters 15–20) deals with the various mechanisms for adjusting balance-of-payments disequilibria. Chapter 15 discusses the adjustment mechanism that operates by changing the relationship between domestic and foreign prices. The income adjustment mechanism and a synthesis of the automatic adjustment mechanisms are presented in Chapter 16. Chapter 17 examines various adjustment policies; Chapter 18 considers the monetary and the portfolio approaches to the balance of payments; and Chapter 19 compares fixed and flexible exchanges rates. Chapter 20 (the last chapter in the book) examines the operation of the international monetary system through time, especially its present functioning and current international economic problems.

CHAPTER 15

Price Adjustment Mechanism

15.1   Introduction

In Chapter 14, we examined the meaning and measurement of a deficit or surplus in a nation's balance of payments. A deficit simply refers to an excess of debits over credits in the nation's *autonomous* transactions. A surplus refers to the opposite. Balance-of-payments disequilibria cannot go on indefinitely, but require adjustment. We saw in Chapter 14 that a nation can cover or finance a deficit in its balance of payments either out of its international reserves or by borrowing abroad. However, a nation's international reserves are limited, and surplus nations are generally unwilling to extend credit indefinitely to a deficit nation or continue to accumulate "sterile" international reserves once their reserve holdings are deemed adequate.

In discussing adjustments to balance-of-payments disequilibria, we will usually deal with ways to correct a deficit. The correction of a surplus would generally require the opposite techniques. For simplicity, we also define a deficit as an excess of debits over credits in the *current account*, not balanced by an *autonomous* capital inflow, but requiring some *accommodating* transaction, such as the loss of international reserves, official borrowing, or the depreciation or devaluation of the domestic currency.

The methods of correcting balance-of-payments disequilibria are classified as automatic or policy. An **automatic adjustment mechanism** is one that is activated by the balance-of-payments disequilibrium itself, without any government action, and operates until the disequilibrium is eliminated (unless the government takes specific steps to avoid its operation if there are unwanted side effects). On the other hand, **adjustment policies** are specific measures adopted by the government with the primary aim of correcting a balance-of-payment disequilibrium. Whereas automatic adjustment mechanisms are triggered as soon as a disequilibrium arises and continue to operate (if unhampered) until the disequilibrium is eliminated, adjustment policies involve a time lag. That is, it takes time for the existence of a balance-of-payments disequilibrium to be recognized, for the government to adopt the appropriate policies, and for these policies to take effect. However, automatic adjustment mechanisms can have serious negative side effects, which the government may attempt to avoid by using adjustment policies. What must be remembered is that all adjustment methods are somewhat painful (i.e., require some sacrifices), and the nation will want to choose the method that minimizes the cost (or sacrifice) of the adjustment.

Automatic adjustment mechanisms are subdivided into those that operate on prices and those that operate on incomes. In addition, there are automatic monetary adjustments. The **automatic price adjustment mechanism** relies on price changes in the deficit and surplus nations to bring about adjustment. The mechanism operates differently under a flexible exchange rate system than under the gold standard. This mechanism is discussed in this chapter. The **automatic income adjustment mechanism** relies on induced changes in the national income of the deficit and the surplus nation to bring about adjustment. This mechanism is discussed in Chapter 16. The automatic price and income adjustment mechanisms are first discussed separately for pedagogical reasons. Since in the real world, automatic price, income, and monetary adjustments are to some extent likely to operate side by side, the last two sections of Chapter 16 present a *synthesis* of these three automatic adjustment mechanisms. Chapter 17 then discusses adjustment *policies*.

In this chapter, section 15.2 examines adjustment with flexible exchange rates, section 15.3 deals with the closely related topic of the stability of foreign exchange markets, and section 15.4 with real-world elasticities and their measurement. Section 15.5 presents the purchasing-power parity theory. Finally, section 15.6 describes the adjustment mechanism under the gold standard (the so-called price-specie-flow mechanism). In the appendix, we illustrate graphically the effect of a change in the exchange rate on domestic prices, derive mathematically the Marshall-Lerner condition for stability in foreign exchange markets, and demonstrate that unstable foreign exchange markets will eventually become stable for large exchange rate changes. The last section shows graphically how the gold points and international gold flows are determined under the gold standard.

15.2 Adjustment with Flexible Exchange Rates

In this section, we examine the method of correcting a deficit in a nation's balance of payments by a depreciation or a devaluation of the nation's currency. A depreciation implies a flexible exchange rate system. A **devaluation** refers to a deliberate increase in the exchange rate by the nation's monetary authorities from one fixed or pegged level to another. Since the effects of a depreciation and a devaluation are generally the same, they will be discussed together here. We begin by examining the process of adjustment itself, and then show how the demand and supply schedules of foreign exchange are derived. These topics were examined less formally in section 14.4b and section A13.1, respectively (but those sections are not required to understand the derivations presented here). Finally, we examine the effects of a depreciation or devaluation on domestic currency prices and on the nation's terms of trade.

15.2a Balance-of-Payments Adjustments with Exchange Rate Changes

The process of correcting a deficit in a nation's balance of payments by a depreciation or devaluation of its currency is shown in Figure 15-1. In the figure, it is assumed that the United States and the United Kingdom are the only two nations in the world and that there are no international capital flows, so that the United States demand and supply curves for pounds reflect only trade in goods and services. The figure shows that at the exchange rate of $R = \$2/£1$, the quantity of pounds demanded by the United States is £12 million per year, while the quantity supplied is £8 million. As a result, the United States has a deficit of £4 million *(AB)* in its balance of payments.

If the United States demand and supply curves for pounds are given by $D_£$ and $S_£$, a 20 percent devaluation or depreciation of the dollar, from $R = \$2/£1$ to $R = \$2.40/£1$, would completely eliminate the United States deficit. That is, at $R = \$2.40/£1$, the quantity of pounds demanded and the quantity supplied would be equal at £10 million per year (point E in the figure), and the United States balance of payments would be in equilibrium. If, however, the United States demand and supply curves for pounds were more inelastic (steeper), as indicated by $D_£*$ and $S_£*$, the same 20 percent devaluation would only reduce the United States deficit to £3 million *(CF* in the figure), and a 100 percent devaluation or depreciation of the dollar, from $R = \$2/£1$ to $R = \$4/£1$, would be required to completely eliminate the deficit (point E^* in the figure). Such a huge devaluation or depreciation of the dollar might not be feasible (for reasons examined later).

Thus, it is very important to know how elastic the United States demand and supply curves for pounds are. In some cases, the shape of the deficit nation's demand and supply curves for foreign exchange may be such that a devaluation or depreciation would actually increase, rather than reduce or

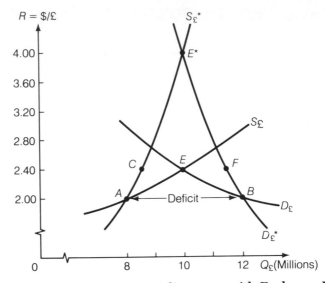

FIGURE 15-1. Balance of Payments Adjustment with Exchange Rate Changes

At $R = \$2/\pounds1$, the quantity of pounds demanded by the United States is £12 million per year, while the quantity supplied is £8 million, so that the United States has a deficit of £4 million *(AB)* in its balance of payments. With $D_\pounds$ and $S_\pounds$, a 20 percent depreciation or devaluation of the dollar would completely eliminate the deficit (point E). With $D_\pounds^*$ and $S_\pounds^*$, a 100 percent depreciation or devaluation would be required to eliminate the deficit (point E^*).

eliminate, the deficit in its balance of payments. These crucial questions are examined next by showing how a nation's demand and supply schedules for foreign exchange are derived.

15.2b   Derivation of the Demand Curve for Foreign Exchange

The United States demand curve for pounds $(D_\pounds)$ shown in Figure 15-1 is derived from the demand and supply curves of United States imports in terms of pounds (shown in the left panel of Figure 15-2). On the other hand, the United States supply curve for pounds $(S_\pounds)$ shown in Figure 15-1 is derived from the demand and supply curves of United States exports in terms of pounds (shown in the right panel of Figure 15-2). Let us start with the derivation of the United States demand curve for pounds $(D_\pounds)$.

In the left panel of Figure 15-2, D_M is the United States demand for imports from the United Kingdom in terms of pounds at $R = \$2/\pounds1$, while S_M is the United Kingdom supply of imports to the United States. With D_M and S_M, the pound price of United States imports is $P_M = \pounds1$, and the quantity of United States imports is $Q_M = 12$ million units per year, so that the quantity of pounds

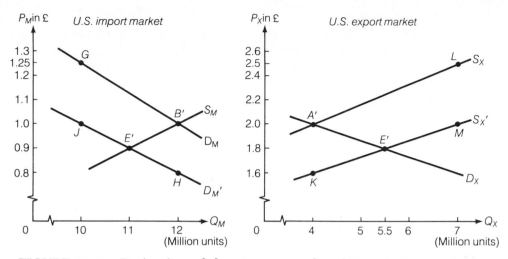

FIGURE 15-2. Derivation of the U.S. Demand and Supply Curves for Foreign Exchange

With D_M (at $R=\$2/\pounds1$) and S_M in the left panel, $P_M=\pounds1$ and $Q_M=12$ million units per year, so that the quantity of pounds demanded by the United States is £12 (point B'). This corresponds to point B in Figure 15-1. With a 20 percent depreciation of the dollar, D_M shifts down to D_M'. Then $P_M=\pounds0.9$ and $Q_M=11$ million units, so that the quantity of pounds demanded by the United States falls to £9.9 million (point E' in the left panel). This corresponds to point E (with £9.9 rounded to £10 million) in Figure 15-1.

With D_X and S_X (at $R=\$2/\pounds1$) in the right panel, $P_X=\pounds2$ and $Q_X=4$ million, so that the quantity of pounds supplied to the United States is £8 million (point A'). This corresponds to point A in Figure 15-1. With a 20 percent depreciation or devaluation of the dollar, S_X shifts down to S_X'. Then $P_X=\pounds1.8$ and $Q_X=5.5$ million units, so that the quantity of pounds supplied to the United States rises to £9.9 million (point E'). This corresponds to point E in Figure 15-1.

demanded by the United States £12 million (point B' in the left panel of Figure 15-2). This corresponds to point B on the United States $D_\pounds$ in Figure 15-1.

When the dollar depreciates by 20 percent to $R=\$2.40/\pounds1$, S_M remains unchanged, but D_M shifts down by 20 percent to D_M' (see the left panel of Figure 15-2). The reason is that for the United States to continue to demand 12 million units of imports (as at point B' on D_M), the pound price of United States imports would have to fall from $P_M=\pounds1$ to $P_M=\pounds0.8$, or by the full 20 percent of the depreciation of the dollar, in order to leave the dollar price of imports unchanged (point H on D_M'). However, at pound prices below $P_M=\pounds1$, the United Kingdom will supply smaller quantities of imports to the United States (i.e., the United Kingdom will move down along S_M), while the United States will demand smaller quantities of imports at pound prices above $P_M=\pounds0.8$

(i.e., the United States will move up along D_M'), until a compromise on price at the new equilibrium point E' is reached (see the left panel of Figure 15-2). The student should reread this paragraph and the previous one, and carefully study the left panel of Figure 15-2 and its relationship to Figure 15-1, because this is a rather important topic and one of the most challenging in international finance.

Note that D_M' is not parallel to D_M because the shift is of a *constant percentage*. Thus, a 20 percent downward shift from point B' (£1.00) is only £0.20, while the same 20 percent downward shift from point G (£1.25) is £0.25. With D_M' and S_M, $P_M = £0.9$ and $Q_M = 11$ million, so that the quantity of pounds demanded by the United States falls to £9.9 million (point E' in the left panel of Figure 15-2). This corresponds to point E (with £9.9 million rounded to £10 million) on $D_£$ in Figure 15-1. Thus, the quantity of pounds demanded by the United States falls from £12 million (given by point B' in the left panel of Figure 15-2) at $R = \$2/£1$ to £10 million (given by point E') at $R = \$2.40/£1$. This corresponds to a movement from point B to point E along $D_£$ in Figure 15-1.

Only in the unusual case when D_M has zero elasticity (is vertical), will the United States quantity demanded of pounds remain exactly the same after the devaluation or depreciation of the dollar as it was before, because in that case the downward shift in D_M leaves D_M unchanged (this is assigned an an end-of-chapter problem). Thus, aside from the unusual case where D_M is vertical, a devaluation or depreciation of the dollar always leads to a reduction in the United States quantity demanded of pounds, so that $D_£$ in (Figure 15-1) is always negatively sloped. The reduction in the United States quantity demanded of pounds when the dollar is devalued or is allowed to depreciate results because both the pound price of United States imports and the quantity of United States imports fall (see the left panel of Figure 15-2).

Furthermore, given S_M, the less elastic (steeper) is D_M, the smaller is the reduction in the United States quantity demanded of pounds and the less elastic (steeper) is the United States demand curve for pounds (this is assigned as another end-of-chapter problem). In that case, a 20 percent devaluation of the dollar might be represented by a movement from point B to point F along $D_£^*$ rather than by a movement from point B to point E along $D_£$ in Figure 15-1.

15.2c   Derivation of the Supply Curve for Foreign Exchange

In the right panel of Figure 15-2, D_X is the United Kingdom demand for United States exports in terms of pounds, and S_X is the United States supply of exports to the United Kingdom at $R = \$2/£1$. With D_X and S_X, the pound price of United States exports is $P_X = £2$, and the quantity of United States exports is $Q_X = 4$ million units, so that the United States quantity of pounds earned or supplied is £8 million (point A' in the right panel of Figure 15-2). This corresponds to point A on $S_£$ in Figure 15-1.

When the dollar is devalued or is allowed to depreciate by 20 percent to $R = \$2.40/\pounds 1$, D_X remains unchanged, but S_X shifts down by 20 percent to S_X' (see the right panel of Figure 15-2). The reason is that the United States would now be willing to export 4 million units (the same as at point A' on S_X) at the pound price of $P_X = \pounds 1.6$, or 20 percent lower than before the depreciation of the dollar, because each pound is now worth 20 percent more in terms of dollars (point K on S_X' in the figure). However, at pound prices below $P_X = \pounds 2$, the United Kingdom will demand greater quantities of United States exports (i.e., the United Kingdom will move down along D_X), while the United States will supply greater quantities of exports at pound prices above $P_X = \pounds 1.6$ (i.e., the United States will move up along S_X'), until the new equilibrium point E' is reached (see the right panel of Figure 15-2).

Note that S_X' is not parallel to S_X because the shift is of a constant percentage. With D_X and S_X', $P_X = \pounds 1.8$ and $Q_X = 5.5$ million units, so that the quantity of pounds supplied to the United States increases to £9.9 million (1.8 times 5.5). This is given by point E' in the right panel of Figure 15-2 and corresponds to point E (with £9.9 million rounded to £10 million) on $S_\pounds$ in Figure 15-1. Thus, the quantity of pounds supplied to the United States rises from £8 million (given by point A' in the right panel of Figure 15-2) at $R = \$2/\pounds 1$ to £10 million (given by point E') at $R = \$2.40/\pounds 1$. This corresponds to a movement from point A to point E along $S_\pounds$ in Figure 15-1.

Note that a devaluation of the dollar reduces the pound price but increases the quantity of United States exports (compare point E' to point A' in the right panel of Figure 15-2). What happens to the quantity of pounds supplied to the United States then depends on the price elasticity of D_X between points A' and E'. Since in this case the percentage increase in Q_X exceeds the percentage reduction in P_X, D_X is price elastic, and the quantity of pounds supplied to the United States increases. If D_X in the right panel of Figure 15-2 had been less elastic (steeper), the same 20 percent devaluation might have resulted in a movement from point A to point C along $S_\pounds^*$ in Figure 15-1 rather than from point A to point E along $S_\pounds$. Thus, the less elastic is D_X, the less elastic is the derived United States supply curve for pounds ($S_\pounds$).

If D_X had been unitary elastic, the devaluation or depreciation of the dollar would have left the United States quantity supplied of pounds completely unchanged, so that the United States supply curve of pounds would have been vertical, or have zero elasticity. (The same would be true if S_X were vertical, so that a depreciation or devaluation of the dollar would leave S_X unchanged.) Finally, if D_X hd been price inelastic, a devaluation or depreciation of the dollar would have actually reduced the United States quantity supplied of pounds, so that the United States supply curve of pounds would have been negatively sloped. (These are assigned as end-of-chapter problems.) Thus, while the United States demand curve for pounds is almost always negatively sloped, the United States supply curve of pounds could be positively sloped, vertical, or even negatively sloped, depending on whether D_X is elastic, unitary elastic, or inelastic, respectively. In section 15.3, we will see that this is crucial in determining the stability of the foreign exchange market.

15.2d   Effect of Exchange Rate Changes on Domestic Prices and the Terms of Trade

Up to now, we have discussed the demand and supply curves of United States imports and exports *in terms of the foreign currency* (the pound) because we were interested in the effect of a devaluation or depreciation of the dollar on the United States balance of payments. However, a devaluation or depreciation of the dollar also has very important effects on United States prices *in terms of dollars.* That is, the reduction of United States imports resulting from the depreciation or devaluation of the dollar stimulates the production of United States import substitutes and exports and will lead to a *rise* in United States dollar prices. Thus, while a devaluation or depreciation of the dollar reduces the pound price of United States imports and exports (see Figure 15-2), it increases the dollar price of United States import substitutes and exports and is inflationary. This is illustrated graphically in section A15.1 in the appendix for the more advanced or eager student.

The greater the devaluation or depreciation of the dollar, the greater is its inflationary impact on the United States economy and the less feasible is the increase of the exchange rate as a method of correcting the deficit in the United States balance of payments. Note that the increase in the dollar price of import substitutes and exports in the United States is a necessary incentive to United States producers to shift resources from the production of nontraded or purely domestic goods to the production of import substitutes and exports. But this also reduces the price advantage conferred on the United States by the devaluation or depreciation of the dollar.

A depreciation or devaluation is also likely to affect the nation's terms of trade. In section 4.5, we defined the terms of trade of a nation as the ratio of the price of its export commodity to the price of its import commodity. Export and import prices must both be measured in terms of either the domestic or the foreign currency. Since the prices of both the nation's exports and imports rise in terms of the domestic currency as a result of its depreciation or devaluation, the terms of trade of the nation can rise, fall, or remain unchanged, depending on whether the price of exports rises by more than, by less than, or by the same percentages as the price of imports.

Since from Figure 15-2 we already know the exact change in the pound prices of United States exports and imports as a result of the 20 percent depreciation or devaluation of the dollar, we can use these prices to measure the change in the United States terms of trade. Before the depreciation or devaluation of the dollar, $P_X = £2$ (see point A' in the right panel of Figure 15-2) and $P_M = £1$ (point B' in the left panel), so that $P_X/P_M = 2/1 = 2$, or 200 percent. After the 20 percent depreciation or devaluation of the dollar, $P_X = £1.8$ (point E' in the right panel) and $P_M = £0.9$ (point E' in the left panel), so that

$P_X/P_M = 1.8/0.9 = 2$, or 200 percent. Therefore, the United States terms of trade in this case remain unchanged. The conclusion would be the same if we used the *dollar* prices of United States exports and imports to measure the change in the United States terms of trade (see Figure 15-5 in the appendix). In general, however, we can expect the terms of trade of a nation to change (as discussed at the end of section A15.2 in the appendix) when its currency is devalued or allowed to depreciate.

15.3 Stability of Foreign Exchange Markets

In this section, we examine the meanings of and the condition for the stability of the foreign exchange market. We have a **stable foreign exchange market** when a disturbance from the equilibrium exchange rate gives rise to automatic forces that push the exchange rate back toward the equilibrium level. We have an **unstable foreign exchange market** when a disturbance from equilibrium pushes the exchange rate further away from equilibrium.

15.3a Stable and Unstable Foreign Exchange Markets

A foreign exchange market is stable when the supply curve of foreign exchange is positively sloped or, if negatively sloped, is less elastic (steeper) than the demand curve of foreign exchange. A foreign exchange market is unstable if the supply curve is negatively sloped *and* more elastic (flatter) than the demand curve of foreign exchange. These conditions are illustrated in Figure 15-3.

The left panel of Figure 15-3 repeats $D_£$ and $S_£$ from Figure 15-1. With $D_£$ and $S_£$, the equilibrium exchange rate is $R = \$2.40/£1$, at which the quantity of pounds demanded and the quantity supplied are equal at £10 million per year (point E). If, for whatever reason, the exchange rate fell to $R = \$2/£1$, there would be an excess demand for pounds (a deficit in the United States balance of payments) of £4 million *(AB)*, which would automatically push the exchange rate back up toward the equilibrium rate of $R = \$2.40/£1$. On the other hand, if the exchange rate rose to $R = \$2.80/£1$, there would be an excess quantity supplied of pounds (a surplus in the United States balance of payments) of £3 million *(NR)*, which would automatically drive the exchange rate back down toward the equilibrium rate of $R = \$2.40/£1$. Thus, the foreign exchange market shown in the left panel of Figure 15-3 is stable.

The center panel of Figure 15-3 shows the same $D_£$ as in the left panel, but $S_£$ is now negatively sloped but steeper (less elastic) than $D_£$. Once again, the equilibrium exchange rate is $R = \$2.40/£1$ (point E). At the lower than equilibrium exchange rate $R = \$2/£1$, there is an excess demand for pounds (a deficit in the United States balance of payments) equal to £1.5 million *(UB)*, which automatically pushes the exchange rate back up toward the equilibrium rate of $R = \$2.40/£1$. At the higher than equilibrium exchange rate of $R = \$2.80/£1$,

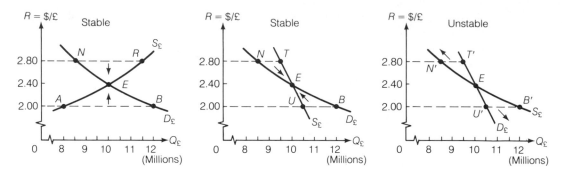

FIGURE 15-3.   Stable and Unstable Foreign Exchange Markets

In all three panels, the equilibrium exchange rate is $R = \$2.40/\pounds1$, at which £10 million are demanded and supplied per year. If, for whatever reason, the equilibrium is disturbed and the exchange rate falls, say to $R = \$2/\pounds1$, the *excess demand* for foreign exchange in the left and center panels will push the exchange rate back up toward the equilibrium rate, but the *excess supply* of foreign exchange in the right panel will cause the exchange rate to fall even lower. Similarly, at $R = \$2.80/\pounds1$, the excess supply in the left and center panels will drive the exchange rate down toward $R = \$2.40/\pounds1$, but the excess demand in the right panel will push the exchange rate even higher. Thus, the left and center panels depict stable markets, while the right panel depicts an unstable market.

there is an excess supply of pounds (a surplus in the United States balance of payments) of £1 million *(NT)*, which automatically pushes the exchange rate back down toward the equilibrium rate of $R = \$2.40/\pounds1$. In this case also, the foreign exchange market is stable.

The right panel of Figure 15-3 looks the same as the center panel, but the labels of the demand and supply curves are reversed, so that now $S_\pounds$ is negatively sloped *and* flatter (more elastic) than $D_\pounds$. The equilibrium exchange rate is still $R = \$2.40/\pounds1$ (point E). Now, however, at any exchange rate, lower than equilibrium, there is an excess quantity *supplied* of pounds, which automatically drives the exchange rate even *lower and farther away* from the equilibrium rate. For example, at $R = \$2/\pounds1$, there is an excess quantity supplied of pounds of £1.5 million *(U'B')*, which pushes the exchange rate even lower and farther away from $R = \$2.40/\pounds1$. On the other hand, at $R = \$2.80/\pounds1$, there is an excess quantity *demanded* for pounds of £1 million *(N'T')*, which automatically pushes the exchange rate even higher and farther away from the equilibrium rate. Thus, the foreign exchange market in the right panel is unstable.

When the foreign exchange market is unstable, a flexible exchange rate system increases rather than reduces a balance-of-payments disequilibrium. Then an appreciation rather than a devaluation of the deficit nation's currency is required to eliminate or reduce a deficit, while a devaluation would be necessary to correct a surplus. These policies are just the opposite from those required under a stable foreign exchange market. Determining whether the foreign exchange market is stable or unstable is, therefore, crucial. Only after the foreign exchange market has been determined to be stable will the elasticity of $D_£$ and $S_£$ (and thus the feasibility of correcting a balance-of-payments disequilibrium with a depreciation or devaluation of the deficit nation's currency) become important.

15.3b   The Marshall-Lerner Condition

If we knew the exact shape of the demand and supply curves of foreign exchange in the real world, it would be rather easy (as indicated above) to determine whether the foreign exchange market in a particular case was stable or unstable and, if stable, the size of the depreciation or devaluation required to correct a deficit in the balance of payments. Unfortunately, this is not the case. As a result, we can only infer whether the foreign exchange market is stable or unstable and the elasticity of the demand for the supply of foreign exchange from the demand for and supply of the nation's imports and exports.

The condition that tells us whether the foreign exchange market is stable or unstable is the Marshall-Lerner condition. The general formulation of the Marshall-Lerner condition is very complex and is presented in section A15.2 in the appendix. Here we present and discuss the simplified version that is generally used. This is valid when the supply curves of imports and exports (i.e., S_M and S_X) are both infinitely elastic, or horizontal. Then the **Marshall-Lerner condition** indicates a stable foreign exchange market if the sum of the price elasticities of the demand for imports (D_M) and the demand for exports (D_X), in absolute terms, is greater than 1. If the sum of the price elasticities of D_M and D_X is less than 1, the foreign exchange market is unstable, and if the sum of these two demand elasticities is equal to 1, a change in the exchange rate will leave the balance of payments unchanged.

For example, from the left panel of Figure 15-2 we can visualize that if D_M were vertical and S_M horizontal, a depreciation or devaluation of the dollar would leave the United States demand for imports and thus the quantity of pounds demanded by the United States completely unchanged. By itself, this would leave the United States balance of payments unchanged. From the right panel of Figure 15-2, we can visualize that given a horizontal S_X which shifts down by the percentage depreciation or devaluation of the dollar, the quantity of pounds supplied to the United States rises, remains unchanged, or falls, depending on whether D_X is price elastic, unitary elastic, or inelastic, respectively. Thus, the sum of the price elasticities of D_M and D_X is equal to the price elasticity of D_X (because we have here assumed D_M to have zero price elasticity), and the United States balance of payments improves if the elasticity of D_X is greater than 1.

If D_M is negatively sloped so that it falls or shifts down by the amount of the depreciation of the dollar, the quantity of pounds demanded by the United States falls, and this, by itself, improves the United States balance of payments. The reduction in the quantity of pounds demanded by the United States is greater the larger is the price elasticity of D_M. Now, even if the price elasticity of D_X is less than 1, so that the quantity of pounds supplied falls as a result of the depreciation of the dollar, the United States balance of payments will still improve as long as the *reduction in the quantity of pounds demanded by the United States is greater than the reduction in the quantity of pounds supplied to the United States.* For this to be the case, the sum of the elasticities of D_M and D_X must be greater than 1. The greater the amount by which the sum of these two elasticities exceeds 1, the greater is the improvement in the United States balance of payments for a given depreciation or devaluation of the dollar.

15.4   Elasticities in the Real World

In this section, we present some real world elasticity estimates and examine the reasons why these elasticity estimates are likely to grossly underestimate true elasticities in international trade.

15.4a   Elasticity Estimates

The Marshall-Lerner condition postulates a stable foreign exchange market if the sum of the price elasticities of the demand for imports and the demand for exports exceeds 1 in absolute value. However, the sum of these two elasticities will have to be substantially greater than 1 for the nation's demand and supply curves of foreign exchange to be sufficiently elastic to make a depreciation or devaluation feasible (i.e., not excessively inflationary) as a method of correcting a deficit in the nation's balance of payments. Thus, it is very important to determine the real world value of the price elasticity of the demand for imports and exports.

Before World War II, it was widely believed not only that the foreign exchange market was stable but that the demand for the supply of foreign exchange was very elastic. *Marshall,* among others, advanced this view in his *Money, Credit and Commerce,* published in 1923, but offered no empirical justification for his belief.

During the 1940s, a number of econometric studies were undertaken to measure price elasticities in international trade. Two representative studies were undertaken by *Chang* (see the selected bibliography), one in 1945 to measure the price elasticity of the demand for imports in 21 nations for which data existed from 1924 to 1938, and the other in 1949 to measure the price elasticity of the demand for exports of 22 nations over the same period. Chang found that the sum of the demand elasticities on the average barely exceeded 1, so that while the foreign exchange market was stable, the demand and supply curves of foreign exchange were probably fairly steep and inelastic (i.e., as $D_£^*$ and $S_£^*$ rather than as $D_£$ and $S_£$ in Figure 15-1). Other studies reached similar conclusions, confirming that the sum of the elasticities of the demand for imports and the demand for exports was either below or very close to 1 in absolute value. Thus, the prewar "elasticity optimism" was replaced by post-war **elasticity pessimism.**

However, writing in 1950, *Orcutt* (see the selected bibliography) provided some convincing reasons for the view that the regression technique used to estimate elasticities led to gross underestimation of the true elasticities in international trade. In short, it was likely that Marshall had been broadly correct, while the new econometric estimates, though seemingly more precise, were in fact likely to be far off the mark.

15.4b Evaluation of Elasticity Measurements

The reasons advanced by Orcutt for the belief that econometric studies grossly underestimated the price elasticity of the demand for imports and exports are the following.

First, there is the so-called **identification problem** in estimation. This is explained with the aid of Figure 15-4. This figure is similar to the right panel of Figure 15-2 in that it shows the effect of a depreciation or devaluation of

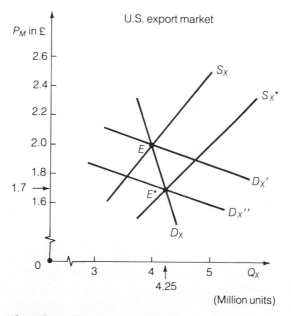

FIGURE 15-4. The Identification Problem

Observed equilibrium points E and E^* are consistent either with non-shifting, inelastic demand curve D_X or with elastic demand curve D_X' shifting down to D_X''. The estimation techniques used in the 1940s ended up measuring the elasticity of (inelastic) demand curve D_X even when the relevant demand curve was elastic D_X'.

the dollar on the United States export market when the foreign demand curve and the United States supply curve of exports are expressed in terms of the foreign currency (pounds). Suppose that points E and E^* are, respectively, the equilibrium points actually observed before and after the United States devalues its currency or allows it to depreciate (none of the curves in Figure 15-4 being observed). The downward shift from S_X to S_X^* in Figure 15-4 is due to the depreciation or devaluation of the dollar (as in the right panel of Figure 15-2). The depreciation or devaluation of the dollar does not affect the foreign demand for United States exports.

If no other change (such as a change in tastes for United States exports) occurs, then the estimated foreign demand curve of United States exports is inelastic, as shown by D_X in Figure 15-4. However, equilibrium points E and E^* are also consistent with elastic demand curve D_X', which shifts down to D_X'' as a result, for example, of reduced foreign tastes for United States exports. Regression analysis will always measure the low elasticity of demand D_X even if the true demand is elastic and given by D_X' and D_X'' (i.e., regression techniques fail to identify demand curves D_X' and D_X''). Since shifts in demand due to changes in tastes or other unaccounted forces frequently occur over time, estimated elasticities are likely to greatly underestimate true elasticities.

The estimated elasticities of the 1940s also measured short-run elasticities in that they were based on quantity responses to price changes over a period of one year or less. *Junz* and *Rhomberg* have identified five possible lags in the quantity response to price changes in international trade. These are the *recognition lag* before the price change becomes evident, the *decision lag* to take advantage of the change in prices, the *delivery lag* of new orders placed as a result of price changes, the *replacement lag* to use up available inventories before new orders are placed, and finally the *production lag* to change the output mix as a result of price changes. Junz and Rhomberg estimated that it takes about three years for 50 percent of the final long-run quantity response to take place and five years for 90 percent to occur. By measuring the quantity response only during the year of the price change, these econometric studies greatly underestimated long-run elasticities.

In fact, it it likely that a nation's trade balance will worsen in the short run in response to a devaluation or depreciation of its currency because of the tendency of the domestic-currency price of imports to rise faster than export prices, with quantities not changing very much. Over time, the quantity of exports rises and the quantity of imports falls and export prices catch up with import prices, so that the initial deterioration in the nation's trade balance is halted and then reversed. For example, the dollar depreciated during 1985 but the trade balance of the United States deteriorated, and it was not expected to improve until 1986 or 1987. Economists call this currency-trade relationship over time the *J-curve*. In practice, however, the curve is often hard to discern from the other influences (such as changes in the level of economic activity and trade policies) on the nation's trade balance.

The regression analysis technique of estimation is also such that errors in the measurement of prices and quantities do not cancel out but systematically lead to the underestimation of elasticities. Furthermore, price changes in international trade were very small during the 1920s and 1940s (the years used in the immediate postwar econometric studies), and some economists believe that some *threshold* price change is required to lead to a quantity response. (The interested reader is referred to the Orcutt article for a more technical and detailed discussion of this.)

Later empirical studies by *Harberger* (1957), *Houthakker* and *Magee* (1969), *Stern, Francis* and *Schumacher* (1976), and *Spitaeller* (1981) (and summarized and reviewed by *Goldstein* and *Khan,* 1985) attempted to overcome some of the estimation problems raised by Orcutt and generally came out with higher elasticities than those found in the empirical studies of the 1940s. The upshot of all of this is that real world elasticities are likely to be high enough to ensure stability of the foreign exchange market and also to result in fairly elastic demand and supply schedules for foreign exchange, especially in the long run. But there is yet no hard and complete evidence to prove this beyond doubt.

15.5   Purchasing-Power Parity

In this section, we present the so-called purchasing-power parity theory in its absolute and relative formulations and evaluate their usefulness.

The **purchasing-power parity (PPP) theory** is a short-cut method of estimating the equilibrium exchange rate when a nation has a balance-of-payments disequilibrium. The need for such a measurement arises because a nation does not usually have knowledge of the exact shape of its demand and supply curves of foreign exchange. Indeed, the theory was introduced by the Swedish economist *Cassel* to estimate the equilibrium exchange rate at which nations could return to the gold standard after the disruption of international trade and the large changes in relative commodity prices in the various nations caused by World War I. Of course, under a freely fluctuating exchange rate system, there is no need for such a measurement since the exchange rate automatically gravitates toward the equilibrium rate. There is an absolute and a relative version of the PPP theory. These will be examined in turn.

15.5a   Absolute Purchasing-Power Parity Theory

The **absolute purchasing-power parity theory** postulates that the equilibrium exchange rate is equal to the ratio of the price levels in the two nations. Specifically:

$$R_{ab} = P_a/P_b \qquad\qquad (15\text{-}1)$$

where R_{ab} equals the exchange rate between the currency of Nation A and the currency of Nation B, and P_a and P_b refer, respectively, to the general price level in Nation A and in Nation B. Thus, if Nation A is the United States and Nation B is the United Kingdom, the exchange rate between the dollar and the pound (defined as the dollar price of the pound) is equal to the ratio of United States to United Kingdom prices. For example, if the general price level in the United States is twice the general price level in the United Kingdom, the absolute PPP theory postulates the equilibrium exchange rate to be $R = \$2/\pounds1$.

For several reasons, this version of the PPP theory is grossly incorrect and cannot be taken seriously. First, it appears to give the exchange rate that equilibrates trade in goods and services so that a nation experiencing capital outflows would have a deficit in its balance of payments, while a nation receiving capital inflows would have a surplus. Second, this version of the PPP theory will not even give the exchange rate that equilibrates trade in goods and services because of the existence of nontraded goods and services.

Nontraded goods include products, such as cement and bricks, for which the cost of transportation is too high for them to enter international trade, except perhaps in border areas. Most services, including those of mechanics, hair stylists, family doctors, and many others also do not enter international trade. International trade tends to equalize the prices of traded goods and services among nations but not the prices of nontraded goods and services. Since the general price level in each nation includes both traded and nontraded commodities and prices of the latter are not equalized by international trade, the absolute PPP theory will definitely not lead to the exchange rate that equilibrates trade. Furthermore, the absolute PPP theory fails to take into account transportation costs or other obstructions to the free flow of international trade. As a result, the absolute PPP theory must be rejected. Whenever the purchasing-power parity theory is used, it is usually in its relative formulation.

15.5b   Relative Purchasing-Power Parity Theory

The more refined **relative purchasing-power parity theory** postulates that the *change* in the exchange rate over a period of time should be proportional to the *relative* change in the price levels in the two nations over the same time period. Specifically, if we let the subscript 0 refer to the base period and 1 to a subsequent period, the relative PPP theory postulates that:

$$R_{ab1} = \frac{(P_{a1}/P_{a0})}{(P_{b1}/P_{b0})} R_{ab0} \qquad (15\text{-}2)$$

where R_{ab1} and R_{ab0} are the exchanges rates in period 1 and in the base period, respectively.

For example, if the general price level does not change in Nation B from the base period to period 1 (i.e., $P_{b1}/P_{b0} = 1$), while the general price level in Nation A increases by 50 percent, the relative PPP theory postulates that the exchange rate between the currency of Nation A and the currency of Nation B (defined as the price of the latter in terms of the former) should be 50 percent higher (i.e., Nation A's currency should depreciate by 50 percent) in period 1 as compared with the base period.

Note that if the absolute PPP held, the relative PPP would also hold, but when the relative PPP holds, the absolute PPP need not hold. For example, while the very existence of capital flows, transportation costs and other obstructions to the free flow of international trade, and government intervention policies lead to the rejection of the absolute PPP, only a *change* in these would lead the relative PPP theory astray.

However, other difficulties remain with the relative PPP theory. One of these results from the fact (pointed out by *Balassa*) that the ratio of the price of nontraded to the price of traded goods and services is systematically higher in developed than in developing nations. One possible reason for this is that techniques in the production of many nontraded goods and services (haircutting, for example) are often quite similar in developed and developing nations. However, for labor to remain in these occupations in developed nations, it must receive wages comparable to the high wages in the production of *traded* goods and services. This makes the price of nontraded goods and services systematically much higher in developed than in developing countries. For example, the price of a haircut may be $5 in the United States but only $1 in Brazil.

Since the general price index includes the prices of both traded and nontraded goods and services, and prices of the latter are not equalized by international trade but are relatively higher in developed nations, the relative PPP theory will tend to undervalue exchange rates for developed nations and overvalue exchange rates for developing nations, with distortions being greater the greater the differences in the levels of development.

Significant structural changes also lead to problems with the relative PPP theory. For example, the PPP theory indicated that the British pound was undervalued (i.e., the exchange rate of the pound was too high) immediately after World War I, when it was obvious that the opposite was the case (and the exchange rate of the pound should have been even higher). The reason was that the United Kingdom had liquidated many of its foreign investments during the war, so that the equilibrium exchange rate predicted by the relative PPP theory (which did not take into consideration the drop in earnings from foreign investments) would have left a large deficit in the United Kingdom balance of payments after the war.

Empirical tests indicate that the relative PPP theory often gives fairly good approximations of the equilibrium exchange rate, particularly in periods of rapid inflation. In Table 15-1, the actual exchange rate between the dollar and

TABLE 15-1.   *Actual Exchange Rates and PPP Indices*

	1977	1978	1979	1980	1981	1982	1983	1984
$/£	1.7455	1.9195	2.1216	2.3263	2.0279	1.7505	1.5170	1.3363
US/UK PPP	1.7455	1.7106	1.9588	2.1216	2.3263	1.9062	1.6946	1.4628
% difference	—	−10.9	−7.7	−8.8	14.7	8.9	11.7	9.5
$/Mark	0.4306	0.4979	0.5456	0.5501	0.4425	0.4121	0.3917	0.3514
US/Germany PPP	0.4306	0.4621	0.5318	0.5804	0.5556	0.4337	0.4079	0.3917
% difference	—	−7.2	−2.5	5.5	25.6	5.2	4.1	11.5
$/Yen	0.00372	0.00475	0.00456	0.00441	0.00453	0.00401	0.00421	0.00421
U.S./Japan PPP	0.00372	0.00410	0.00499	0.00443	0.00476	0.00453	0.00419	0.00432
% difference	—	−13.7	9.4	0.0	5.1	13.0	0.0	2.6
$/Franc	0.2035	0.2216	0.2351	0.2367	0.1840	0.1522	0.1213	0.1144
US/France PPP	0.2035	0.2101	0.2193	0.2475	0.2320	0.1690	0.1387	0.1184
% difference	—	−5.2	−6.7	4.6	26.1	11.0	14.3	3.5

Source: International Monetary Fund, *International Financial Statistics* (Washington, D.C.: IMF, 1985).

the other four most important international currencies is compared with the PPP index (the ratio of the change of United States to foreign wholesale indices) for each year from 1978 through 1984. Wholesale prices exclude services, most of which are not traded. For ease of reference, the PPP indices have been scaled to equal actual exchange rates in 1977.

The table shows that the PPP indices generally move in the same direction as average exchange rates but are close to actual exchange rates only sometimes. *Frenkel* provided empirical evidence that the PPP theory seemed fairly accurate in the long run during the 1920s, and so did *Kravis* and *Lipsey* for the period from 1950 to 1970. On the other hand, Frenkel also found that the PPP theory collapsed during the 1970s, and so did *Hakkio*. But this is disputed by *Davutyan* and *Pippinger* (see the selected bibliography for the sources).

Presumably, the PPP indices would be much closer to and possibly coincide with actual exchange rates if the prices of traded commodities only were used, and adjustments could be made in the PPP indices for structural changes (such as England becoming a petroleum exporting nation during the 1970s), and for changes in international capital flows, tariffs, taxes, and other government intervention policies. However, incorporating all of these changes into the PPP indices would be extremely difficult, if not impossible, and would eliminate much of the usefulness of the PPP theory as a *shortcut* method of estimating equilibrium exchange rates. In the real world, it may be better to let the exchange rate fluctuate for a while (if possible) and allow market forces to define the equilibrium exchange rate. As a method of forecasting short-term exchange rates, the PPP theory is also not very accurate.

15.6 Adjustment Under the Gold Standard

In this last section of Chapter 15, we examine the operation of the international monetary system known as the gold standard. The gold standard also relies on an automatic *price* mechanism for adjustment, but of a different type from the one operating under a flexible exchange rate system.

15.6a The Gold Standard

The **gold standard** operated from about 1880 to the outbreak of World War I in 1914. An attempt was made to reestablish the gold standard after the war, but it failed in 1931 during the Great Depression. Today, there are vague discussions of reestablishing the gold standard, but it is highly unlikely that this will happen. Nevertheless, it is important to understand the advantages and disadvantages inherent in the operation of the gold standard, not only for its own sake, but also because they were to some extent present in the fixed exchange rate system (the Bretton Woods system, or gold-exchange standard) that operated from the end of World War II until it collapsed in 1971.

Under the gold standard, each nation defines the gold content of its currency and passively stands ready to buy or sell any amount of gold at that price. Since the gold content in one unit of each currency is fixed, exchange rates are also fixed. For example, under the gold standard, a £1 gold coin in the United Kingdom contained 113.0016 grains of pure gold, while a $1 gold coin in the United States contained 23.22 grains. This implied that the dollar price of the pound, or the exchange rate, was $R = \$/\pounds = 113.0016/23.22 = 4.87$. This is called the **mint parity.**

Since the cost of shipping £1 worth of gold between New York and London was about 3 cents, the exchange rate between the dollar and the pound could never fluctuate by more than 3 cents above or below the mint parity (i.e., the exchange rate could not rise above 4.90 or fall below 4.84). The reason is that no one would pay more than $4.90 for a £1 since he could always purchase $4.87 worth of gold at the United States Treasury (the Federal Reserve Bank of New York was established only in 1913), ship it to London at a cost of 3 cents, and exchange it for £1 at the Bank of England (the United Kingdom central bank). Thus, the United States supply curve of pounds became infinitely elastic (horizontal) at the exchange rate of $R = \$4.90/\pounds 1$. This was the **gold export point** of the United States.

On the other hand, the exchange rate between the dollar and the pound could not fall below 4.84. The reason for this is that no one would accept less than $4.84 for each pound he wanted to convert into dollars because he could always purchase £1 worth of gold in London, ship it to New York at a cost of 3 cents, and exchange it for $4.87 (thus receiving $4.84 net). As a result, the United States demand curve of pounds became infinitely elastic (horizontal) at the exchange rate of $R = \$4.84/\pounds1$. This was the **gold import point** of the United States.

The exchange rate between the dollar and the pound was determined at the intersection of the United States demand and supply curves of pounds between the gold points and was prevented from moving outside the gold points by United States gold sales or purchases. That is, the tendency of the dollar to depreciate, or the exchange rate to rise above $R = \$4.90/\pounds1$, was countered by gold shipments from the United States. These gold outflows measured the size of the United States balance-of-payments deficit. On the other hand, the tendency of the dollar to appreciate, or the exchange rate to fall below $R = \$4.84/\pounds1$, was countered by gold shipments to the United States. These gold inflows measured the size of the surplus in the United States balance of payments. (For the interested reader, this process is shown graphically in section A15.4 in the appendix.)

Since deficits are settled in gold under this system and nations have limited gold reserves, deficits cannot go on forever but must soon be corrected. We now turn to the adjustment mechanism that automatically corrects deficits and surpluses in the balance of payments under the gold standard.

15.6b   The Price-Specie-Flow Mechanism

The automatic adjustment mechanism under the gold standard is the **price-specie-flow mechanism.** This operates as follows to correct balance-of-payments disequilibria. Since each nation's money supply under the gold standard consisted of either gold itself or paper currency backed by gold, the money supply would fall in the deficit nation and rise in the surplus nation. This caused internal prices to fall in the deficit nation and rise in the surplus nation. As a result, the exports of the deficit nation would be encouraged and its imports would be discouraged until the deficit in its balance of payments was eliminated.

The reduction of internal prices in the deficit nation as a result of the gold loss and reduction of its money supply was based on the so-called **quantity theory of money.** This can be explained by using equation 15-3,

$$MV = PQ \qquad \text{(15-3)}$$

where M is the nation's money supply, V is the velocity of circulation of money (the number of times each unit of the domestic currency turns over on the average during one year), P is the general price index, and Q is physical output. Classical economists believed that V depended on institutional factors and was constant. They also believed that, apart from temporary disturbances, there was built into the economy an automatic tendency toward full employment without inflation (based on their assumption of perfect and instantaneous flexibility of all prices, wages, and interests). For example, any tendency toward unemployment in the economy would be automatically corrected by wages falling sufficiently to ensure full employment. Thus, Q was assumed to be fixed at the full-employment level. With V and Q constant, a change in M led to a direct and proportional change in P (see equation 15-3).

Thus, as the deficit nation lost gold, its money supply would fall and cause internal prices to fall proportionately. For example, a deficit in the nation's balance of payments and gold loss that reduced M by 10 percent would also reduce P by 10 percent in the nation. This would encourage the exports of the deficit nation and discourage its imports. The opposite would take place in the surplus nation. That is, the increase in the surplus nation's money supply (due to the inflow of gold) would cause its internal prices to rise. This would discourage the nation's exports and encourage its imports. The process would continue until the deficit and surplus were eliminated.

Note that the adjustment process is automatic; it is triggered as soon as the balance-of-payments disequilibrium arises and continues to operate until the disequilibrium is entirely eliminated. Note also that the adjustment relies on a change in internal prices in the deficit and surplus nations. Thus, while adjustment under a flexible exchange rate system relies on changing the external value of the national currency, adjustment under the gold standard relies on changing internal prices in each nation. Adjustment under the gold standard also relies on high price elasticities of exports and imports in the deficit and surplus nations, so that the volumes of exports and imports respond readily and significantly to price changes.

The price-specie-flow mechanism was introduced by *Hume* in 1752 and used by him to demonstrate the futility of the mercantilists' belief that a nation could continuously accumulate gold by exporting more than it imported (refer to section 2.2). Hume pointed out that as a nation accumulated gold, domestic prices would rise until the nation's export surplus (which led to the accumulation of gold in the first place) was eliminated. The example used by Hume to make his point is unsurpassed: that is, it is futile to attempt to raise the water level (the amount of gold) above its natural level in some compartment (nation) as long as the compartments are connected with one another (i.e., as long as nations are connected through international trade).

Passively allowing the nation's money supply to change for balance-of-payments considerations meant that nations could not use monetary policy for achieving full employment without inflation. Yet, this created no difficulties for classical economists, since (as pointed out above) they believed that there was an automatic tendency in the economic system toward full employment without inflation.

Note that for the adjustment process to operate, nations were not supposed to *sterilize* (i.e., neutralize) the effect on their money supply of a deficit or surplus in their balance of payments. On the contrary, the **rules of the game of the gold standard** required a deficit nation to reinforce the adjustment process by further restricting credit and a surplus nation to expand credit further. (The actual experience under the gold standard is discussed in Chapter 20.)

Summary

1. Balance-of-payments disequilibria cannot go on indefinitely, but must be corrected. Adjustment is classified as automatic or policy. Automatic mechanisms are triggered by the disequilibria and operate without government intervention, but they may have serious unwanted side effects. Adjustment policies involve explicit government action and face various time lags. The automatic price adjustment mechanism relies on price changes in the deficit and surplus nations to bring about adjustment. This operates differently under a flexible exchange rate system than under the gold standard. The automatic income mechanism operates by changing incomes. To some extent, the price and income adjustment mechanisms operate side-by-side in the real world, but they are discussed separately first (with a synthesis in Chapter 16).

2. A nation can usually correct a deficit in its balance of payments by devaluing its currency or allowing it to depreciate. The more elastic the demand and supply curves of foreign exchange, the smaller is the devaluation or depreciation required to correct a deficit of a given size. The nation's demand for foreign exchange is derived from the demand for and supply of its imports in terms of the foreign currency. The more elastic the latter, the more elastic is the former. A devaluation or depreciation of its currency also increases the domestic currency prices of the nation's exports and import substitutes and is inflationary.

3. The foreign exchange market is stable if the supply curve of foreign exchange is positively sloped or, if negatively sloped, is steeper (less elastic) than the demand curve of foreign exchange. According to the Marshall-Lerner condition, the foreign exchange market is stable if the sum of the price elasticities of the demands for imports and exports exceeds 1. This holds when the supply elasticities of imports and exports are infinite. If the sum of the two demand elasticities equals 1, a change in the exchange rate will leave the nation's balance of payments unchanged. If, on the other hand, the sum of the two demand elasticities is less than 1, the for-

eign exchange market is unstable, and a depreciation will increase, rather than reduce, the nation's deficit.

4. Empirical estimates of elasticities in international trade conducted during the 1940s found that foreign exchange markets were either unstable or barely stable and led to the so-called elasticity pessimism. However, these econometric studies seriously underestimated true elasticities, especially because of the problem of identifying shifts in demand and because they estimated short-run rather than long-run elasticities. Though hard and complete evidence is not yet available, it is now believed that foreign exchange markets are generally stable and that demand and supply curves of foreign exchange may be fairly elastic in the long run.

5. The purchasing-power parity (PPP) theory is a short-cut method of estimating the equilibrium exchange rate in the absence of knowledge of the shape of the demand and supply curves of foreign exchange. The absolute PPP theory is not acceptable. The more refined relative PPP theory postulates that the change in the exchange rate over a period of time should be proportional to the relative change in the price levels in the two nations. However, the existence of nontraded goods and services would lead to undervalued exchange rates for developed countries and overvalued rates for developing countries. Structural and other changes also create difficulties for the relative PPP theory. Nevertheless, empirical tests show that this theory has some value.

6. Under the gold standard, each nation defines the gold content of its currency and passively stands ready to buy or sell any amount of gold at that price. This results in a fixed exchange rate called the mint parity. The exchange rate is determined at the intersection of the nation's demand and supply curves of the foreign currency between the gold points and is prevented from moving outside the gold points by the nation's sales or purchases of gold. The adjustment mechanism under the gold standard is the price-specie-flow mechanism. The loss of gold by the deficit nation reduces its money supply. This causes domestic prices to fall, thus stimulating the nation's exports and discouraging its imports until the deficit is eliminated. The opposite process corrects a surplus.

A Look Ahead

In Chapter 16, we examine in detail the automatic income adjustment mechanism. This relies on induced changes in the national income of the deficit and surplus nations to bring about adjustment. The examination of the income adjustment mechanism requires a review of the concept of the equilibrium level of national income and the multiplier. Since the automatic price and income adjustment mechanisms operate side-by-side in the real world, the last two sections of Chapter 16 present a synthesis of their operation. Chapter 17 will then examine adjustment policies.

Glossary

Automatic adjustment mechanism An adjustment mechanism activated by the balance-of-payments disequilibrium itself, without any government action, and which operates (if unhampered) until the disequilibrium is eliminated.

Adjustment policies Specific measures adopted by a nation's monetary authorities for the primary purpose of correcting a balance-of-payments disequilibrium.

Automatic price adjustment mechanism An adjustment mechanism that relies on price changes in the deficit and surplus nations to correct balance-of-payments disequilibria.

Automatic income adjustment mechanism An adjustment mechanism that relies on induced changes in the national income of the deficit and surplus nations to correct balance-of-payments disequilibria.

Devaluation A deliberate increase in the exchange rate by a nation's monetary authorities from one fixed or pegged level to another.

Stable foreign exchange market The condition in a foreign exchange market where a disturbance from the equilibrium exchange rate gives rise to automatic forces that push the exchange rate back toward the equilibrium rate.

Unstable foreign exchange market The condition in a foreign exchange market where a disturbance from equilibrium pushes the exchange rate farther away from equilibrium.

Marshall-Lerner condition Indicates that the foreign exchange market is stable when the sum of the price elasticities of the *demands* for imports and exports is larger than 1 (when the *supply* elasticities of imports and exports are infinite).

Elasticity pessimism The belief, arising from the empirical studies of the 1940s, that foreign exchange markets were either unstable or barely stable.

Identification problem The inability of the regression technique to identify shifts in demand curves from shifts in supply curves, leading to the underestimation of price elasticities in empirical studies of international trade.

Purchasing-power parity (PPP) Theory A shortcut (but not very accurate) method of estimating the equilibrium exchange rate when a nation has a balance-of-payments disequilibrium.

Absolute purchasing-power parity theory Postulates that the equilibrium exchange rate is equal to the ratio of the price levels in the two nations. This version of the PPP theory is not acceptable.

Relative purchasing-power parity theory Postulates that the change in the exchange rate over a period of time should be proportional to the relative change in the price levels in the two nations. This version of the PPP theory has some value.

Gold standard The international monetary system operating from about 1880 to 1914 under which gold was the only international reserve, exchange rates fluctuated only within the gold points, and balance-of-payments adjustment was described by the price-specie-flow mechanism.

Mint parity The fixed exchange rates resulting under the gold standard from each nation defining the gold content of its currency and passively standing ready to buy or sell any amount of gold at that price.

Gold export point The mint parity plus the cost

of shipping an amount of gold equal to one unit of the foreign currency between the two nations.

Gold import point   The mint parity minus the cost of shipping an amount of gold equal to one unit of the foreign currency between the two nations.

Price-specie-flow mechanism   The automatic adjustment mechanism under the gold standard. It operates by the deficit nation losing gold and experiencing a reduction in its money supply. This in turn reduces domestic prices, which stimulates the nation's exports and discourages its imports until the deficit is eliminated. A surplus is corrected by the opposite process.

Quantity theory of money   Postulates that the nation's money supply times the velocity of circulation of money is equal to the nation's general price index times physical output at full employment. With V and Q assumed constant, the change in P is directly proportional to the change in M.

Rules of the game under the gold standard   The requirement under the gold standard that monetary authorities restrict credit in the deficit nation and expand credit in the surplus nation (thus reinforcing the effect of international gold flows on the nation's money supply).

Questions for Review

1. What are the short-run and long-run forces that can lead to a deficit in a nation's balance of payments? How can a nation cover or finance a deficit in its balance of payments? Why will a nation be unable to run balance-of-payments deficits indefinitely? What is meant by an automatic adjustment mechanism? What are the automatic mechanisms and how do they operate? What is meant by adjustment policies?

2. How does a depreciation or devaluation of a nation's currency eliminate or reduce a deficit in its balance of payments? Why is a depreciation or devaluation of the nation's currency not feasible to eliminate a deficit if the nation's demand and supply curves of foreign exchange are inelastic? How is the nation's demand curve for foreign exchange derived? What determines its elasticity? How is the nation's supply curve of foreign exchange derived? What determines its elasticity? Why is a devaluation or depreciation inflationary?

3. What shape of the demand and supply curves of foreign exchange will make the foreign exchange market stable? Unstable? What is the Marshall-Lerner condition for a stable foreign exchange market? For an unstable market? For a depreciation to leave the nation's balance of payments unchanged? Why will a depreciation of the deficit nation's currency increase rather than reduce the balance-of-payments deficit when the foreign exchange market is unstable?

4. What is meant by elasticity pessimism? How did it arise? What is the J-curve? Why may elasticity pessimism be unjustified? What is the prevailing view today as to the stability of foreign exchange markets and the elasticity of the demand and supply curves of foreign exchange?

5. What is the purchasing-power parity theory? Why is it needed? What is the absolute purchasing-power parity theory? Why is this not acceptable? What is the relative purchasing-power parity theory? What are the difficulties encountered in its use? Do empirical tests confirm or reject the relative purchasing-power parity theory?

6. What is meant by the mint parity? How is it defined? What is meant by the gold export point? The gold import point? How are they defined? How are exchange rates determined under the gold standard? How are balance-of-payments disequilibria adjusted under the gold standard? What is the quantity theory of money? What were the rules of the game under the gold standard?

Problems

*1. From the negatively sloped demand curve and the positively sloped supply curve of a nation's tradeable commodity (i.e., a commodity that is produced at home but is also imported or exported), derive the nation's:

(a) demand curve of imports of the tradeable commodity for below equilibrium prices;

(b) supply curve of exports of the tradeable commodity for above equilibrium prices.

(Hint for part a: see Figure 13-4. Of course, the nation can be either an importer or an exporter of the commodity, but not both.)

2. Draw a figure similar to Figure 15-2, but with D_M vertical in the left panel and with S_X vertical in the right panel, and explain:

(a) from the left panel, why $D_£$ would also be vertical;

(b) from the right panel, why $S_£$ would also be vertical.

3. Draw a figure similar to Figure 15-2, but with D_M and S_X steeper (less elastic) than in Figure 15-2, and explain:

(a) from the left panel, why $D_£$ would be steeper (less elastic) than in Figure 15-1;

(b) from the right panel, why $S_£$ would be steeper (less elastic) than in Figure 15-1 if D_X is price elastic in the relevant range.

*4. Explain why for a small nation:

(a) S_M and D_X are horizontal, or infinitely elastic;

(b) the balance of payments always improves with a depreciation or devaluation of its currency.

5. Draw a figure similar to Figure 15-2, but referring to an unstable foreign exchange market.

6. The average exchange rate between the dollar and the pound was 1.5170 in 1983; the United States wholesale price index was 112.7 in 1983 and 115.4 in 1984, while the United Kingdom wholesale price index was 124.4 in 1983 and 132.1 in 1984. Use the data to calculate the PPP index, or the equilibrium exchange rate predicted by the relative PPP theory, for 1984. (Hint: your result should be the one indicated in Table 15-1.)

APPENDIX

In this appendix, section A15.1 shows graphically the effect of a change in the exchange rate on the domestic currency price of traded commodities. Section A15.2 presents the formal mathematical derivation of the Marshall-Lerner condition for stability in foreign exchange markets. Section A15.3 demonstrates that unstable foreign exchange markets will eventually become stable for large enough exchange rate changes. Finally, section A15.4 shows graphically how the gold points and international gold flows are determined under the gold standard.

A15.1 The Effect of Exchange Rate Changes On Domestic Prices

We said in section 15.2d that the reduction in United States imports resulting from a depreciation or devaluation of the dollar stimulates the production of import substitutes and exports in the United States and leads to a rise in United States dollar prices. This can be shown with Figure 15-5.

In the left panel of Figure 15-5, S_M' is the United Kingdom supply curve of imports to the United States expressed in dollars when the exchange rate is

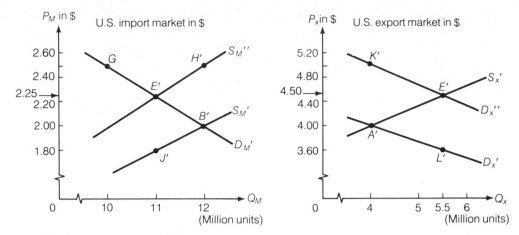

FIGURE 15-5.   Effect of a Depreciation or Devaluation on Domestic Prices

In the left panel, D_M' is the U.S. demand curve of imports in terms of dollars, and S_M' is the U.K. supply curve of imports to the United States at $R=\$2/\pounds1$. With D_M' and S_M', $P_M=\$2$ and $Q_M=12$ million units. When the dollar depreciates or is devalued by 20 percent, S_M' shifts up to S_M'', but D_M' remains unchanged. With D_M' and S_M'', $P_M=\$2.25$ and $Q_M=11$ million units. In the right panel, D_X' is the U.K. demand curve of U.S. exports at $R=\$2/\pounds1$, and S_X' is the U.S. supply curve of exports to the United Kingdom, both in terms of dollars. With D_X' and S_X', $P_X=\$4$ and $Q_X=4$ million units per year. When the dollar depreciates or is devalued by 20 percent to $R=\$2.40/\pounds1$, D_X' shifts up to D_X'', but S_X' remains unchanged. With D_X'' and S_X', $P_X=\$4.50$ and $Q_X=5.5$ million units. Thus, a depreciation or devaluation increases dollar prices in the United States.

$R=\$2/\pounds1$, and D_M' is the United States demand curve for imports in dollars. With D_M' and S_M', equilibrium is at point B', with $P_M=\$2$ and $Q_M=12$ million units per year. When the dollar is devalued or allowed to depreciate by 20 percent to $R=\$2.40/\pounds1$, the United Kingdom supply curve of imports to the United States in terms of dollars falls (i.e., shifts up) by 20 percent to S_M'' because each dollar that United Kingdom exporters earn in the United States is now worth 20 percent less in terms of pounds. This is like a 20 percent per unit tax on United Kingdom exporters. Note that S_M'' is not parallel to S_M' because the shift is of a constant percentage, and that S_M'' is used as the base to calculate the 20 percent upward shift from S_M'. Also, D_M' does not change as a result of the depreciation or devaluation of the dollar. With D_M' and S_M'', $P_M=\$2.25$ and $Q_M=11$ million (point E'). Thus, the dollar price of United States imports rises from $2.00 to $2.25, or by 12.5 percent, as a result of the 20 percent depreciation or devaluation of the dollar.

In the right panel of Figure 15-5, D_X' is the United Kingdom demand curve for United States exports expressed in dollars at $R=\$2/\pounds1$, and S_X' is the United States supply curve of exports in terms of dollars. With D_X' and S_X', equilibrium is at point A', with $P_X=\$4.00$ and $Q_X=4$ million units. When the dollar is devalued or allowed to depreciate by 20 percent to $R=\$2.40/\pounds1$, the United Kingdom demand curve for United States exports in terms of dollars rises (shifts up) by 20 percent to D_X'' because each *pound* is now worth 20 percent more in terms of dollars. This is like a 20 percent per unit subsidy to United Kingdom buyers of United States exports. Note that D_X'' is not parallel to D_X' because the shift is of a constant percentage, and that D_X'' is used as the base to calculate the 20 percent upward shift from D_X'. Also, S_X' does not change as a result of the depreciation or devaluation of the dollar. With D_X'' and S_X', $P_X=\$4.50$ and $Q_X=5.5$ million units (point E'). Thus, the dollar price of United States exports rises from $\$4.00$ to $\$4.50$, or by 12.5 percent, as a result of the 20 percent depreciation or devaluation of the dollar.

The rise in the dollar price of import substitutes and exports is necessary to induce United States producers to shift production from nontraded to traded goods, but it also reduces the price advantage the United States gained from the depreciation or devaluation. Since the prices of import substitutes and exportable commodities are part of the United States general price index, and they both rise, the depreciation or devaluation of the dollar is inflationary for the United States. As a result, the greater the devaluation or depreciation required to correct a deficit of a given size, the less feasible is depreciation or devaluation as a method of correcting the deficit. The elasticity of the demand for and supply of the nation's imports and exports is simply a short-cut indication of the ease or difficulty of shifting domestic resources from nontraded to traded commodities as a result of a devaluation or depreciation of the nation's currency, and of how inflationary the shift will be.

Problem   From Figure 15-5, calculate the United States terms of trade before and after the 20 percent depreciation or devaluation of the dollar. How do your results compare with those obtained in section 15.2d?

A15.2 Derivation of the Marshall-Lerner Condition

We now derive mathematically the Marshall-Lerner condition that the sum of the elasticities of the demand for imports and the demand for exports must exceed 1 for the foreign exchange market to be stable. This condition holds when the *supply* curves of imports and exports are infinitely elastic, or horizontal.

To derive the Marshall-Lerner condition mathematically, let:

P_X and P_M = the foreign currency price of exports and imports, respectively

Q_X and Q_M = the quantity of exports and imports, respectively

V_X and V_M = the foreign currency value of exports and imports, respectively

Then the trade balance (B) is:

$$B = V_X - V_M = Q_X \cdot P_X - P_M \cdot Q_M \qquad (15A\text{-}1)$$

For a small devaluation, the change in the trade balance (dB) is:

$$dB = P_X \cdot dQ_X + Q_X \cdot dP_X - (P_M \cdot dQ_M + Q_M \cdot dP_M) \tag{15A-2}$$

This was obtained by the product rule of differentials $(duv = v \cdot du + u \cdot dv)$. Since S_M is horizontal, P_M does not change (i.e., $dP_M = 0$) with a depreciation or devaluation of the dollar, so that the last term in equation 15A-2 drops out. By then rearranging the first and third terms, we get:

$$dB = dQ_X \cdot P_X + Q_X \cdot dP_X - dQ_M \cdot P_M \tag{15A-3}$$

We now define equation 15A-3 in terms of price elasticities. The price elasticity of the demand for exports (n_X) measures the percentage change in Q_X for a given percentage change in P_X. That is:

$$n_X = -\frac{dQ_X}{Q_X} \div \frac{dP_X}{P_X} = \frac{dQ_X}{Q_X} \div k\left(\frac{P_X}{P_X}\right) = \frac{dQ_X \cdot P_X}{Q_X \cdot k \cdot P_X} \tag{15A-4}$$

where $k = -dP_X/P_X$ (the percentage of depreciation or devaluation of the dollar).

Similarly, the coefficient of price elasticity of the demand for imports (n_M) is:

$$n_M = -\frac{dQ_M}{Q_M} \div \frac{dP_M}{P_M} = -\frac{dQ_M \cdot P_M}{Q_M \cdot dP_M} \tag{15A-5}$$

From equation 15A-4, we get:

$$dQ_X \cdot P_X = n_X \cdot Q_X \cdot P_X \cdot k \tag{15A-6}$$

This is the first term in equation 15A-3. We can also rewrite the second term in equation 15A-3 as:

$$Q_X \cdot dP_X = Q_X (dP_X/P_X) P_X = Q_X(-k) P_X = -Q_X \cdot k \cdot P_X \tag{15A-7}$$

Finally, from equation 15A-5, we get:

$$dQ_M \cdot P_M = -n_M \cdot Q_M \cdot dP_M = -n_M \cdot Q_M \cdot P_M \cdot k \tag{15A-8}$$

where $k = dP_M/P_M$. To be noted is that while $dP_M = 0$ in terms of the foreign currency, it is positive in terms of the domestic currency. Equation 15A-8 is the third term in equation 15A-3.

Substituting equations 15A-6, 15A-7, and 15A-8 into equation 15A-3, we get:

$$dB = n_X \cdot Q_X \cdot P_X \cdot k - Q_X \cdot P_X \cdot k - (-n_M \cdot Q_M \cdot P_M \cdot k) \qquad (15A\text{-}9)$$

Simplifying algebraically, we get:

$$dB = k[Q_X \cdot P_X(n_X - 1) + n_M \cdot Q_M \cdot P_M] \qquad (15A\text{-}10)$$

If to begin with:

$$B = Q_X \cdot P_X - Q_M \cdot P_M = 0 \qquad (15A\text{-}11)$$

then,

$$dB = k[Q_X \cdot P_X(n_X + n_M - 1)] \qquad (15A\text{-}12)$$

and $dB > 0$ if:

$$n_X + n_M - 1 > 0 \text{ or } n_X + n_M > 1 \qquad (15A\text{-}13)$$

where both n_X and n_M are positive.

If the devaluation or depreciation takes place from the condition of $V_M > V_X$, n_M should be given a proportionately greater weight than n_X, and the Marshall-Lerner condition for a stable foreign exchange market becomes more easily satisfied and is given by:

$$n_X + (V_M/V_X)n_M > 1 \qquad (15A\text{-}14)$$

If the price elasticities of the foreign supply of the United States imports (e_M) and the United States supply of exports (e_X) are not infinite, then the smaller are e_M and e_X, the more likely it is that the foreign exchange market is stable even if:

$$n_X + n_M < 1 \qquad (15A\text{-}15)$$

The Marshall-Lerner condition for stability of the foreign exchange market when e_M and e_X are not infinite is given by:

$$\frac{e_X(n_X - 1)}{e_X + n_X} + \frac{n_M(e_M + 1)}{e_M + n_M} \qquad (15A\text{-}16)$$

or combining the two components of the expression over a common denominator:

$$\frac{e_M \cdot e_X(n_M + n_X - 1) + n_M \cdot n_X(e_M + e_X + 1)}{(e_X + n_X)(e_M + n_M)} \qquad (15A\text{-}17)$$

The foreign exchange market is stable, unstable, or remains unchanged as a result of a depreciation or devaluation to the extent that equation 15A-16 or 15A-17 is larger than, smaller than, or equal to 0, respectively. The mathematical derivation of equation 15A-16 is given in Stern (see the selected bibliography).

The condition for a deterioration in the terms of trade of the devaluing nation is also derived in Stern and is given by:

$$e_X \cdot e_M > n_X \cdot n_M \qquad \text{(15A-18)}$$

If the direction of the inequality sign in equation 15A-18 is the reverse, the devaluing country's terms of trade improve, and if the two sides are equal, the terms of trade will remain unchanged.

Problem   Explain why a depreciation or devaluation of a small country's national currency is not likely to affect its terms of trade. (Hint: refer to the statement of problem 5.)

A15.3   Stability of Foreign Exchange Markets Once Again

In this section, we show that an unstable foreign exchange market will eventually become stable for large enough exchange rate changes. Figure 15-6 shows that the foreign exchange market is unstable in the vicinity of equilibrium point E_2 because $S_£$ is negatively sloped and flatter, or more elastic, than $D_£$. However, the foreign exchange market becomes stable at equilibrium points E_3 and E_1 (i.e., for a large enough exchange rate change, such as from R_2 to either R_3 or R_1).

The reason for this is that at very high exchange rates, the dollar price of the United States imports becomes so high that the United States imports nothing, and so $D_£$ cross the vertical axis. For this to occur, $D_£$ has to become more elastic and cross $S_£$, resulting in stable equilibrium point E_3 at R_3. On the other hand, at a very low exchange rate, the pound price of United States exports is so high for United Kingdom residents that the United States is not able to export anything, and so $S_£$ crosses the vertical axis. For this to occur, $S_£$ has to become less elastic and cross $D_£$, resulting in stable equilibrium point E_1 at R_1. However, stable equilibrium points E_3 and E_1 involve such huge exchange rate changes that the fact that the unstable foreign exchange market in the vicinity of R_2 becomes stable at R_3 or R_1 is devoid of any practical significance.

Problem   Explain why the fact that an unstable foreign exchange market eventually becomes stable for large enough exchange rate changes is not of practical importance.

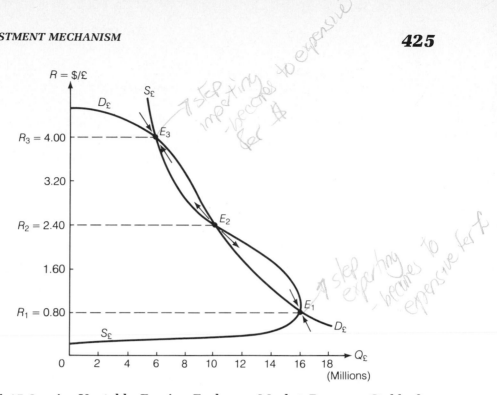

FIGURE 15-6.   An Unstable Foreign Exchange Market Becomes Stable for Large Exchange Rate Changes

At equilibrium point E_2, the foreign exchange market is unstable because $S_£$ is negatively sloped and flatter, or more elastic, than $D_£$. However, for a large depreciation of the dollar from R_2 to R_3, the foreign exchange market becomes stable at point E_3 because $D_£$ becomes flatter, or more elastic, than $S_£$. Similarly, for a large appreciation of the dollar from R_2 to R_1, the foreign exchange market becomes stable at point E_1 because $S_£$ becomes steeper, or less elastic, than $D_£$.

A15.4   Derivation of the Gold Points and Gold Flows Under the Gold Standard

Figure 15-7 shows graphically how the gold points and international gold flows are determined under the gold standard. In the figure, the mint parity is $4.87 = £1 (as defined in section 15.6a). The United States supply curve of pounds ($S_£$) is given by *REABCF* and becomes infinitely elastic, or horizontal, at the United States gold export point of $4.90 = £1 (the mint parity plus the 3 cents cost to ship £1 worth of gold from New York to London). The United States demand curve of pounds ($D_£$) is given by *TEGHJK* and becomes infinitely elastic, or horizontal, at the United States gold import point of $4.84 = £1 (the mint parity minus 3 cents cost to ship £1 worth of gold from London to New York). Since $S_£$ and $D_£$ intersect at point E within the gold points, the

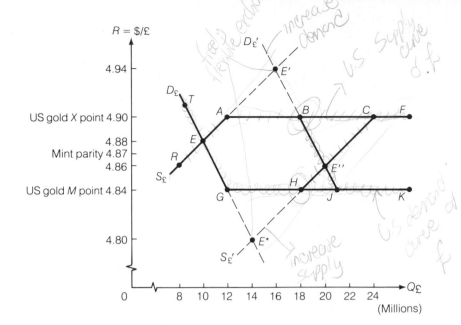

FIGURE 15-7.   Gold Points and Gold Flows

With $D_£$ and $S_£$, the equilibrium exchange rate is $R = \$4.88/£1$ (point E) without any international gold flow, and the U.S. balance of payments is in equilibrium. With $D_£'$ and $S_£$, the exchange rate would be $R = \$4.94$ under a freely flexible exchange rate system, but would be prevented under the gold standard from rising above $R = \$4.90$ (the U.S. gold export point) by U.S. exports of £6 million *(AB)* of its gold. This represents the U.S. balance-of-payments deficit under the gold standard. With $D_£$ and $S_£'$, the exchange rate would be $R = \$4.80$ under a freely flexible exchange rate system, but would be prevented under the gold standard from falling below $R = \$4.84/£1$ (the U.S. gold import point) by U.S. gold imports of £6 million *(HG)*. This represents the U.S. balance-of-payments surplus under the gold standard.

equilibrium exchange rate is $R = \$4.88/£1$ without any international gold flow (i.e., the United States balance of payments is in equilibrium).

If subsequently the United States demand for pounds increases (shifts up) to $D_£'$, there is a tendency for the exchange rate to rise to $R = \$4.94/£1$ (point E' in the figure). However, because no one would pay more than $\$4.90$ for each pound under the gold standard (i.e., the United States supply curve of pounds becomes horizontal at $R = \$4.90/£1$), the exchange rate only rises to $R = \$4.90/£1$, and the United States will be at point B. At point B, the United States quantity demanded of pounds is £18 million, of which £12 million (point A) is supplied from United States exports of goods and services to the United Kingdom and the remaining £6 million *(AB)* is supplied by United States gold exports to the United Kingdom (and represents the United States balance-of-payments deficit).

If, on the other hand, the United States demand curve of pounds does not shift but continues to be given by $D_£$, while the United States supply of pounds increases (shifts to the right) to $S_{£}'$, equilibrium would be at point E^* (at the exchange rate of $R = \$4.80/£1$) under a flexible exchange rate system. However, since no one would accept less than \$4.84 under the gold standard (i.e., the United States demand curve of pounds becomes horizontal at $R = \$4.84/£1$), the exchange rate falls only to $R = \$4.84/£1$, and the United States will be at point H. At point H, the United States quantity supplied of pounds is £18 million, but the United States quantity demanded of pounds is only £12 million (point G). The excess of £6 million *(HG)* supplied to the United States takes the form of gold imports from the United Kingdom and represents the United States balance-of-payments surplus.

The operation of the price-specie-flow mechanism under the gold standard would then cause $D_{£}$ and $S_{£}$ to shift so as to intersect once again within the gold points, thus automatically correcting the balance-of-payments disequilibrium of both nations.

Problem Determine from Figure 15-7 the exchange rate and the size of the deficit or surplus in the United States balance of payments under the gold standard and under a flexible exchange rate system if $D_{£}$ shifts to $D_{£}'$, and $S_{£}$ shifts to $S_{£}'$ at the same time.

Selected Bibliography

For a problem-solving approach to the topics covered in this chapter, see:
- D. Salvatore, *Theory and Problems of International Economics*, 2nd ed. (New York: McGraw-Hill, 1984), ch. 9 (sects. 9.1 to 9.3).

Adjustment under flexible exchange rates is presented by:
- J. Robinson, "The Foreign Exchanges," in J. Robinson, *Essays in the Theory of Employment* (Oxford: Basil Blackwell, 1947). Reprinted in H. S. Ellis and L. A. Metzler, *Readings in the Theory of International Trade* (Homewood, Ill.: Irwin, 1950), pp. 83–103.
- G. Haberler, "The Market for Foreign Exchange and the Stability of the Balance of Payments: A Theoretical Analysis," *Kyklos*, September 1949. Reprinted in R. N. Cooper, *International Finance* (Baltimore: Penguin, 1969).
- F. Machlup, "The Theory of Foreign Exchanges," *Economica*, November 1939. Reprinted in H. S. Ellis and L. A. Metzler, *Readings in the Theory of International Trade* (Homewood, Ill.: Irwin, 1950).

For the Marshall-Lerner condition, see:
- A. Marshall, *Money, Credit and Commerce* (London: Macmillan, 1923).
- A. Lerner, *The Economics of Control* (London: Macmillan, 1944).

The mathematical derivation of the formula for the Marshall-Lerner condition, as well as the derivation of the condition for an improvement in the devaluing nation's terms of trade, is found in:
- R. M. Stern, *The Balance of Payments* (Chicago: Aldine, 1973), pp. 62–69.

For estimates of elasticities in international trade, see:
- T. C. Chang, "International Comparison of Demand for Imports," *Review of Economic Studies*, 1945–1946.
- T. C. Chang, "A Statistical Note on World Demand for Exports," *Review of Economics and Statistics*, February 1948.
- A. C. Harberger, "Some Evidence on the International Price Mechanism," *Journal of Political Economy*, December 1957. Reprinted in R. N. Cooper, *International Finance* (Baltimore: Penguin, 1969).

- H. Houthakker and S. Magee, "Income and Price Elasticities in World Trade," *Review of Economics and Statistics,* May 1969.
- H. Junz and R. Rhomberg, "Price Competitiveness in Export Trade Among Industrial Countries," *American Economic Review,* May 1973.
- R. M. Stern, J. Francis, and B. Schumacher, *Price Elasticities in International Trade - An Annotated Bibliography* (London: Macmillan, 1976).
- E. Spitaeller, "Short-Run Effects of Exchange Rate Changes on the Terms of Trade and Trade Balance," *IMF Staff Papers,* 1980.
- M. Golstein and M. S. Khan, "Income and Price Effects in International Trade," in R. W. Jones and P. B. Kenen, Eds. *Handbook of International Economics* (Amsterdam: North-Holland, 1985).

The problems of elasticity measurements are discussed in:

- G. Orcutt, "Measurements of Price Elasticities in International Trade," *Review of Economics and Statistics,* May 1950. Reprinted in R. E. Caves and H. G. Johnson, *Readings in International Economics* (Homewood, Ill.: Irwin, 1968).
- E. E. Leamer and R. Stern, *Quantitative International Economics* (Boston: Allyn & Bacon, 1970).
- D. Salvatore, *Theory and Problems of Microeconomic Theory,* 2nd ed. (New York: McGraw-Hill, 1983), ch. 6 (sect. 6.6).
- D. Salvatore, *Theory and Problems of Statistics and Econometrics* (New York: McGraw-Hill, 1982), chs. 7 and 8.

The purchasing-power parity theory is presented and tested empirically in:

- G. Cassel, *Money and Foreign Exchange after 1914* (New York: Macmillan, 1923).
- B. Balassa, "The Purchasing Power Parity Doctrine: A Reappraisal," *Journal of Political Economy,* December 1964. Reprinted in R. N. Cooper, *International Finance* (Baltimore: Penguin, 1969).
- I. B. Kravis and R. E. Lipsey, "Price Behavior in the Light of Balance of Payments Theories," *Journal of International Economics,* May 1978.
- L. H. Officer, "The Relation Between Absolute and Relative Purchasing Power Parity," *Review of Economic and Statistics,* November 1978.
- J. A. Frenkel, "Purchasing Power Parity: Doctrinal Perspective and Evidence from the 1920s," *Journal of International Economics,* May 1978.
- I. B. Kravis and R. E. Lipsey, "Price Behavior in the Light of Balance of Payments Theories," *Journal of International Economics,* May 1978.
- J. A. Frenkel, "The Collapse of Purchasing Power Parity in the 1970s," *European Economic Review,* May 1981.
- N. Davutyan and J. Pippenger, "Purchasing Power Parity Did Not Collapse During the 1970s," *American Economic Review,* December 1985.

The operation of the gold standard is discussed in:

- D. Hume, "Of the Balance of Trade," in *Essays, Moral, Political and Literary,* Vol. 1 (London: Longmans Green, 1898). Excerpts reprinted in R. N. Cooper, *International Finance* (Baltimore: Penguin, 1969).
- W. Bagehot, *Lombard Street* (London: Smith, Elder & Co., 1915). Reprinted by Arno Press, New York, 1978.
- R. Nurkse, *International Currency Experience* (Princeton, N.J.: League of Nations, 1944).
- A. I. Bloomfield, *Monetary Policy under the International Gold Standard: 1880–1914* (New York: Federal Reserve Bank, 1959).
- M. Michaely, *Balance-of-Payments Adjustment Policies* (New York: National Bureau of Economic Research, 1968).

CHAPTER 16

The Income Adjustment Mechanism and Synthesis of Automatic Adjustments

16.1 Introduction

In this chapter, we begin by examining the operation of the *automatic income adjustment mechanism*. This relies on induced changes in the national income of the deficit and the surplus nation to bring about adjustment in the balance of payments. The automatic income adjustment mechanism represents the application of Keynesian economics to open economies (i.e., to nations engaging in international transactions). This is distinguished from the "classical" adjustment mechanism (presented in Chapter 15), which relied on automatic price changes to bring about adjustment in the balance of payments.

As in Chapter 15, we assume here that the deficit or surplus arises in the current account of the nation. However, while we implicitly assumed in Chapter 15 that national income remained constant and adjustment was brought about by automatic price changes, we now assume that all prices remain constant and examine how automatic income changes lead to balance-of-payments adjustment. Specifically, in order to isolate the automatic income adjustment mechanism, we begin by assuming that the nation operates under a fixed exchange rate system and that all prices, wages, and interest rates are constant. We also assume initially that nations operate at less than full employment. In the real world, balance-of-payments disequilibria not only affect national incomes but also exert pressure on exchange rates, prices, wages, and interest

429

rates. Thus, to some extent, all automatic adjustments are likely to operate simultaneously. Such a synthesis is presented in the last two sections of this chapter.

In section 16.2, we review (from principles of economics) the concept and the determination of the equilibrium national income and the multiplier in a closed economy. In section 16.3, we extend the concept and examine the determination of the equilibrium level of national income and multiplier in a small open economy. Section 16.4 further extends the presentation to include foreign repercussions arising when the nations are not small. Foreign repercussions arise because any change in a large nation's level of national income and trade affects the national income and trade of the trade partner, and these in turn have secondary effects (repercussions) on the first nation. Indeed, this is how business cycles are transmitted internationally. Section 16.5 examines the price and income adjustment mechanisms together. Finally, section 16.6 discusses monetary adjustments and presents a synthesis of all automatic adjustments, pointing out the disadvantages of each automatic mechanism and the need for adjustment policies. In the appendix, we present the mathematical derivation of the foreign trade multipliers with foreign repercussions, and then we examine the transfer problem (building on the discussion in the appendix to Chapter 12).

16.2 Income Determination in a Closed Economy

In this section, we review the concept and determination of the equilibrium national income and the multiplier in a **closed economy** (i.e., an economy in autarky or without international trade). These concepts were covered in your principles of economics course and represent our point of departure for examining the equilibrium level of national income and the multiplier in a small open economy (in section 16.3).

16.2a Determination of the Equilibrium National Income in a Closed Economy

In a closed economy without a government sector, the **equilibrium level of national income** and production (Y) is equal to the desired or planned flow of consumption (C) plus desired or planned investment expenditures (I), as indicated in equation 16-1:

$$Y = C(Y) + I \qquad\qquad (16\text{-}1)$$

Desired or planned investment (I) is exogenous, or independent of (i.e., it does not change with) the level of national income. On the other hand, desired consumption expenditures, $C(Y)$, are a function of, or depend on, the level of national income. That is, as income (Y) rises, desired consumption

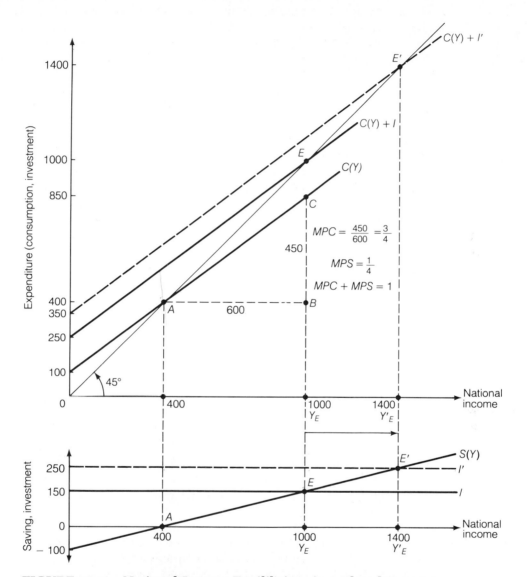

FIGURE 16-1. National Income Equilibrium in a Closed Economy

In the top panel, $C(Y)$ is the consumption function and $C(Y)+I$ is the total expenditure function obtained by adding desired investment to the consumption function. The equilibrium level of national income is at point E, where the $C(Y)+I$ function crosses the 45° line. In the bottom panel, equilibrium is given by point E, where the saving function $S(Y)$ intersects the horizontal investment function. In both panels, the equilibrium level of income is 1000. If investment rises to $I'=250$, the new equilibrium level of national income is 1400, given by point E', where broken-line $C(Y)+I'$ crosses the 45° line or where broken-line I' crosses $S(Y)$.

(C) also rises. The change in consumption (ΔC) associated with a change in income (ΔY) is called the **marginal propensity to consume (MPC).** Since consumers save part of their income, the increase in consumption is less than the increase in income so that MPC < 1. This is illustrated in Figure 16-1.

The top panel of Figure 16-1 measures consumption and investment expenditures along the vertical axis and national income along the horizontal axis. The **consumption function** is shown by line C(Y). Desired consumption equals 100 when income is zero and rises as income rises. The positive level of consumption when income is zero indicates that the nation lives off its past savings, or dissaves. Then as income rises, desired consumption rises, but by less than the rise in income. For example, an increase in income of 600 (from 400 to 1000, given by AB in the top panel) is associated with an increase in consumption of 450 (BC). Thus, marginal propensity to consume, or MPC, equals ΔC/ΔY = 450/600 = ¾, or 0.75.

Adding to the consumption function a hypothetical desired investment expenditure of 150 at every level of income, we get the total expenditure function C(Y) + I in the figure. The C(Y) + I function crosses the 45° line at point E. Every point on the 45° line measures equal distances along the vertical and horizontal axes. Thus, at point E, the total of consumption and investment expenditures of 1000 (measured along the vertical axis) equals the level of production of income of 1000 (measured along the horizontal axis). $Y_E = 1000$ is then the equilibrium level of national income.

At Y > 1000, desired expenditures fall short of output, firms have an *unplanned* accumulation of inventories of unsold goods, and they cut production. On the other hand, at Y < 1000, desired expenditures exceed production, there is an unplanned reduction of inventories, and production is increased. Thus, the equilibrium level of national income $Y_E = 1000$ is stable in the sense that at any other level of national income, desired expenditures either exceed or fall short of the value of output, and the level of national income moves toward $Y_E = 1000$. The equilibrium level of income need not be, and we assume that it is not, the full-employment level of income (Y_F).

In the bottom panel of Figure 16-1, the vertical axis measures the level of saving and investment, and the horizontal axis measures the level of national income (as in the top panel). The level of desired investment is exogenous at I = 150 regardless of the level of income. On the other hand, desired saving is a function of income, so that the **saving function** is,

$$S(Y) = Y - C(Y) \qquad (16-2)$$

Thus, when Y = 0, C = 100 (see the top panel) and S = −100 (in the bottom panel). At Y = 400, C = 400 and S = 0 (point A in both panels). At Y = 1000, C = 850 and S = 150. Note that as income rises, desired saving rises. The change in desired saving (ΔS) associated with a change in income (ΔY) is defined as the **marginal propensity to save (MPS).** For example, an increase in income of 600 (from 400 to 1000) is associated with an increase in saving of 150 in the bottom panel. Thus, the marginal propensity to save, or *MPS*, equals $\Delta S/\Delta Y = 150/600 = \frac{1}{4}$. Since any change in income (ΔY) always equals the change in consumption (ΔC) plus the change in saving (ΔS), $MPC + MPS = 1$, so that $MPS = 1 - MPC$. In the above example, $MPC + MPS = \frac{3}{4} + \frac{1}{4} = 1$, and $MPS = 1 - \frac{3}{4} = \frac{1}{4}$.

In the bottom panel, the desired investment of 150 (an injection into the system) equals desired saving (a leakage out of the system) at $Y = 1000$. Investment is an injection into the system because it adds to total expenditures and stimulates production. Saving is a leakage out of the system because it represents income generated but not spent. The equilibrium level of income is the one at which:

$$S = I \tag{16-3}$$

Graphically, the equilibrium level of income is given at the intersection of the saving function and the **investment function** at point *E*. At $Y > 1000$, the excess of desired saving over desired investment represents an unintended or unplanned inventory investment. Thus, production and income fall toward $Y_E = 1000$. On the other hand, at $Y < 1000$, the excess of desired investment over desired saving represents an unintended or unplanned inventory disinvestment, and income and production rise toward $Y_E = 1000$.

Thus, the equilibrium level of national income is determined either at the intersection of the $C(Y) + I$ function with the 45° line in the top panel or by the intersection of the $S(Y)$ and I functions in the bottom panel. In either case, the equilibrium level of national income is $Y_E = 1000$, and we assume that it is smaller than the full-employment level of income.

16.2b   The Multiplier in a Closed Economy

If, for whatever reason, investment rises by 100 from $I = 150$ to $I' = 250$, the total expenditure function shifts up by 100 from $C(Y) + I$ to $C(Y) + I'$ (the broken line in the top panel of Figure 16-1) and defines equilibrium point E' at $Y_E' = 1400$. Equivalently, an autonomous increase in investment causes the investment function to shift up from $I = 150$ to $I' = 250$ (the broken line in the bottom panel) and intersect the saving function at point E', also defining the equilibrium level of national income at $Y_E' = 1400$.

Starting from the original equilibrium point E in the bottom panel, as investment increases from $I = 150$ to $I' = 250$, $I' > S$ and Y rises. The rise in Y induces S to rise. This continues until Y has risen sufficiently for induced S to equal the new and higher level of I'. For this to occur, Y must rise by 400, from $Y_E = 1000$ to $Y_E' = 1400$, as indicated by the new equilibrium point of E' in the bottom (and top) panel(s).

Thus, an increase in I of 100 results in an increase in Y of 400 in order to induce S to also rise by 100 and reach another equilibrium point. That is:

$$\Delta I = \Delta S = MPS \times \Delta Y$$

So that:

$$\Delta Y = \left(\frac{1}{MPS}\right)\Delta I$$

Therefore, the multiplier *(k)* is:

$$k = \frac{\Delta Y}{\Delta I} = \frac{1}{MPS} = \frac{1}{1 - MPC} \qquad (16\text{-}4)$$

That is, the closed economy **multiplier** *(k)* is equal to the inverse, or reciprocal, of the marginal propensity to save or to the reciprocal of 1 minus the marginal propensity to consume. Since $0 < MPS < 1$, the multiplier is larger than 1. For example, in Figure 16-1, $MPS = \frac{1}{4}$ and $k = 4$, so that the increase in I of 100 leads to an increase in Y of 400 and an induced rise in S also equal to 100.

The reason income rises more than investment is as follows. When investment expenditures rise, producers expand production and hire more workers and use more capital and other factors of production. Since the income generated in the process of production equals the value of the output produced, increasing investment expenditures by 100 has the immediate effect of also increasing income by the same amount. But the recipients of this 100 increase in income will spend ¾ (the MPC) of it. Thus, as incomes rise by 100, consumption expenditures rise by 75. This leads to a further expansion of production and generates an additional income of 75. This new increase in income leads to a further increase in consumption of 56.25 (from 0.75×75).

The process continues, with income rising by smaller and smaller amounts at every step, until the increase in income becomes zero. Thus, income increases by 100 in the first step, by 75 in the second step, by 56.25 in the third step, and so on, until the *sum total* of all the increases in income is 400. When income has risen by 400, from $Y_E = 1000$ to $Y_E' = 1400$, induced saving will have risen by 100, and once again $S = I' = 250$, and the process comes to an end.

16.3   Income Determination in a Small Open Economy

We now extend the discussion of the equilibrium level of national income and the multiplier from a closed economy to a small open economy (i.e., an economy whose international transactions do not perceptibly affect the national income of its trade partner or the rest of the world). We begin by defining the import function of the nation; then we show how the equilibrium level of national income is determined algebraically and graphically; finally, we derive the foreign trade multiplier. In section 16.4, we will relax the assumption that the nation is small and extend the discussion to consider foreign repercussions. For simplicity, we continue to assume that there is no government sector and that the economy operates at less than full employment.

16.3a The Import Function

The **import function** of a nation, $M(Y)$, shows the relationship between the nation's imports and national income. A hypothetical import function is shown in Figure 16-2. Note that $M = 150$ when $Y = 0$ and rises as Y rises. When income is zero, the nation purchases 150 of imports by borrowing abroad or with its international reserves. Then, as income rises, imports also rise.

The change in imports (ΔM) associated with a change in income (ΔY) is called the **marginal propensity to import (MPM).** For example, a movement from point G to point H on the import function in Figure 16-2 involves an increase in imports from $M = 300$ to $M = 450$ for an increase in income from $Y = 1000$ to $Y = 2000$. Thus, $MPM = \Delta M/\Delta Y = 150/1000 = 0.15$. The MPM is equal to the slope of $M(Y)$ and is constant. On the other hand, the ratio of imports to income is called the **average propensity to import (APM)** and falls as income rises (if the import function has a positive vertical intercept, as in Figure 16-2). Thus, at point G, $APM = M/Y = 300/1000 = 0.3$, while at point H, $APM = M/Y = 450/2000 = 0.225$. Then MPM/APM is the **income elasticity of imports** (n_Y). Specifically:

$$n_Y = \frac{\text{percentage change in imports}}{\text{percentage change in income}} = \frac{\Delta M/M}{\Delta Y/Y} = \frac{\Delta M/\Delta Y}{M/Y} = \frac{MPM}{APM} \qquad (16\text{-}5)$$

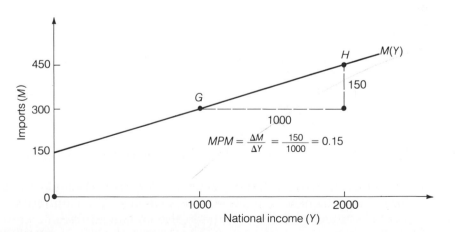

FIGURE 16-2. The Import Function

Import function $M(Y)$ shows that imports are 150 when income is zero and rise as income rises. The slope of the import function (the change in imports resulting from a given change in income) is called the marginal propensity to import (MPM). For the import function shown here, $MPM = \triangle M/\triangle Y = 0.15$ and remains constant.

For the movement from point G to point H in Figure 16-2:

$$n_Y = \frac{150/1000}{300/1000} = \frac{0.15}{0.30} = 0.5$$

A large nation that is well endowed with resources and little dependent on international trade usually has a small APM and MPM. For example, for the United States, $APM = 0.08$ and $MPM = 0.13$, so that $n_Y = 1.63$. Smaller market economies generally have larger APM and MPM. For example, for West Germany, $APM = 0.14$, and $MPM = 0.25$, and $n_Y = 1.79$. For Switzerland, $APM = 0.26$, $MPM = 0.47$, and $n_Y = 1.81$.

16.3b   Determination of the Equilibrium National Income in a Small Open Economy

The analysis of the determination of the equilibrium national income in a closed economy can easily be extended to include foreign trade. In an open economy, exports, just like investment, are an injection into the nation's income stream, while imports, just like saving, represent a leakage out of the income stream. Specifically, exports as well as investment stimulate domestic production, while imports as well as saving constitute income earned but not spent on domestic output.

For a small open economy, exports are also taken to be *exogenous* or independent of the level of income of the nation (just like investment). Thus, the **export function** is also horizontal when plotted against income. That is, the exports of the nation are the imports of the trade partner or the rest of the world and, as such, depend not on the exporting nation's level of income but on the level of income of the trade partner or the rest of the world. On the other hand, imports (like saving) are a function of the nation's income. With this in mind, we can now proceed to specify the condition for the equilibrium level of national income for a small open economy.

In a small open economy, the equilibrium condition relating injections and leakages in the income stream is,

$$I + X = S + M \tag{16-6}$$

Note that this condition for the equilibrium level of national income does not imply that the balance of trade (and payments) is in equilibrium. Only if $S = I$, will $X = M$ and the balance of trade also be in equilibrium.

By rearranging the terms of equation 16-6, we can restate the condition for the equilibrium level of national income as:

$$X - M = S - I \tag{16-7}$$

This points out that at the equilibrium level of national income, the nation could have a surplus in its trade balance (a net injection from abroad) equal to the excess of saving over domestic investment (a net domestic leakage). On the other hand, a deficit in the nation's trade balance must be accompanied by an equal excess of domestic investment over saving at the equilibrium level of national income.

By transposing I from the right to the left side of equation 16-7, we get still another useful and equivalent form of the equilibrium condition:

$$I + (X - M) = S \tag{16-8}$$

The expression $(X - M)$ in equation 16-8 refers to net foreign investment, since an export surplus represents an accumulation of foreign assets to cover the export surplus. Thus, equation 16-8 indicates that at the equilibrium level of national income, domestic investment plus net foreign investment equals domestic saving. If imports exceed exports, the term $(X - M)$ is negative, so that domestic investment exceeds domestic saving by the amount of net foreign disinvestment (i.e., the amount by which foreigners are investing in the nation).

16.3c Graphical Determination of the Equilibrium National Income

The above algebraic statement of the equilibrium level of national income in a small open economy is shown graphically and clarified in Figure 16-3. The top panel of Figure 16-3 represents the determination of the equilibrium level of national income in terms of equation 16-6, while the bottom panel determines the equilibrium level of national income in terms of equation 16-7. Exports are exogenous and are assumed to be equal to 300, and $Y_E = 1000$ in both panels. Specifically, the top panel measures saving plus imports and investment plus exports on the vertical axis, and national income along the horizontal axis. With investment of $I = 150$ (as in Figure 16-1) and exports of $X = 300$, the investment plus exports function is $I + X = 150 + 300 = 450$. The saving plus imports function, $S(Y) + M(Y)$, is obtained by the vertical addition of the import function of Figure 16-2 to the saving function of Figure 16-1. For example, at $Y = 0$, $S = -100$ and $M = 150$, so that $S + M = -100 + 150 = +50$. At $Y = 1000$, $S + M = 150 + 300 = 450$. Note that the slope of the saving plus imports function is equal to the MPS (the slope of the saving function) plus the MPM (the slope of the import function). That is, the slope of $S(Y) + M(Y) = MPS + MPM = 0.25 + 0.15 = 0.40$.

The equilibrium level of national income is $Y_E = 1000$ and is determined where the $I + X$ function crosses the $S(Y) + M(Y)$ function (point E in the top panel). That is, equilibrium is determined where:

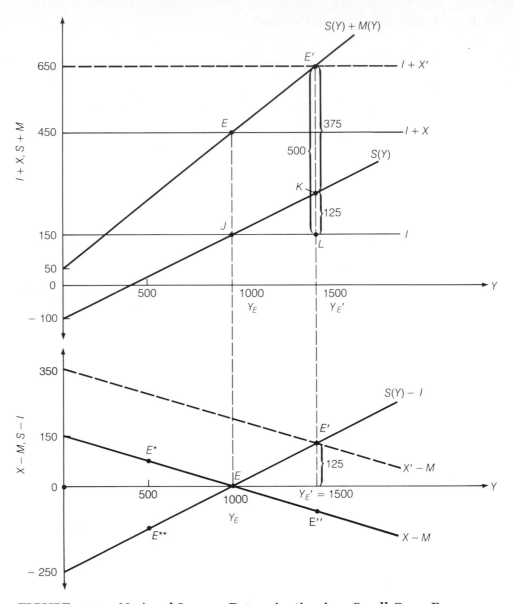

FIGURE 16-3.   National Income Determination in a Small Open Economy

The top panel measures saving plus imports and investment plus exports on the vertical axis and national income along the horizontal axis. The equilibrium level of national income is $Y_E = 1000$ and is determined at point E, where the $I+X$ function crosses the $S(Y)+M(Y)$ function. At $Y_E = 1000$, $S=I=150$ so that $X=M=300$. The bottom panel measures $X-M$ and $S-I$ on the vertical axis and Y on the horizontal axis. The $X-M(Y)$ function falls because we subtract rising M from a constant X as Y rises. The $S(Y)-I$ function rises because we subtract a constant I from rising S as Y rises. $Y_E = 1000$ and is determined at point E, where the $X-M(Y)$ function crosses the $S(Y)-I$ function and $X-M=S-I=0$. An autonomous increase in X of 200 (broken-line $I+X'$ in the top panel and $X'-M(Y)$ in the bottom panel) results in $Y_{E'} = 1500$ and $X'-M = 125$ and $S-I = 125$.

438

$$\text{INJECTIONS} = \text{LEAKAGES}$$
$$I + X = S + M$$
$$150 + 300 = 150 + 300$$
$$450 = 450$$

Note that in this case, $I = S = 150$ so that $X = M = 300$ (*EJ* in the figure). Thus, the trade balance is also in equilibrium at the equilibrium level of national income of $Y_E = 1000$. Y_E is also stable in the sense that if injections did not equal leakages, the economy would automatically gravitate toward Y_E.

The bottom panel of Figure 16-3 measures $X - M$ and $S - I$ on the vertical axis, and Y along the horizontal axis. Since $X = 300$ and $M = 150$ at $Y = 0$, $X - M = 300 - 150 = 150$ at $Y = 0$. The $X - M(Y)$ function declines because we subtract rising M from a constant X as Y rises. That is, the balance of trade deteriorates as Y rises. On the other hand, since $S = -100$ at $Y = 0$ and $I = 150$, $S - I = -100 - 150 = -250$ at $Y = 0$. The $S(Y) - I$ function rises because we subtract a constant I from rising S as Y rises. The equilibrium level of national income is $Y_E = 1000$ (as in the top panel) and is determined where the $X - M(Y)$ function crosses the $S(Y) - I$ function (point E in the bottom panel).

The advantage of using the bottom panel (and equation 16-7) is that the trade balance can be read directly from the figure. Since the $X - M(Y)$ function crosses the $S(Y) - I$ function on the horizontal axis, $X - M = S - I = 0$ at $Y_E = 1000$. That is, the trade balance happens to be in equilibrium at the equilibrium level of national income. This is a convenient point of departure to analyze how a disturbance (such as an autonomous change in exports or investment) affects the nation's equilibrium level of income and the operation of the automatic income adjustment mechanism.

16.3d   The Foreign Trade Multiplier

Starting from the equilibrium point E in the top and bottom panels of Figure 16-3, an autonomous change in exports or investment (the left side of equation 16-6) disturbs the nation's equilibrium level of income. The change in the equilibrium level of national income then induces changes in the amount of saving and imports (the right side of equation 16-6) until the sum of the induced changes in saving and imports equals the sum of the autonomous changes in investment and exports. That is, another equilibrium level of national income is determined where:

$$\Delta I + \Delta X = \Delta S + \Delta M \qquad (16\text{-}9)$$

The *induced* changes in saving and imports when income changes are given by:

$$\Delta S = (MPS)(\Delta Y)$$
$$\Delta M = (MPM)(\Delta Y)$$

Substituting these for ΔS and ΔM in equation 16-9, we get:

$$\Delta I + \Delta X = (MPS)(\Delta Y) = (MPM)(\Delta Y)$$
$$\Delta I + \Delta X = (MPS + MPM)(\Delta Y)$$
$$\Delta Y = \frac{1}{MPS + MPM}(\Delta I + \Delta X)$$

where the **foreign trade multiplier (k')** is:

$$k' = \frac{1}{MPS + MPM} \tag{16-10}$$

For example, starting from equilibrium point E in Figure 16-3, if exports rise exogenously by 200 from $X = 300$ to $X' = 500$:

$$k' = \frac{1}{MPS + MPM} = \frac{1}{0.25 + 0.15} = \frac{1}{0.40} = 2.5$$

$$\Delta Y = (\Delta X)(k') = (200)(2.5) = 500$$
$$Y_{E'} = Y_E + \Delta Y = 1000 + 500 = 1500$$
$$\Delta S = (MPS)(\Delta Y) = (0.25)(500) = 125$$
$$\Delta M = (MPM)(\Delta Y) = (0.15)(500) = 75$$

Therefore, at $Y_{E'}$:

$$\text{CHANGE IN INJECTIONS} = \text{CHANGE IN LEAKAGES}$$
$$\Delta I + \Delta X = \Delta S + \Delta M$$
$$0 + 200 = 125 + 75$$
$$200 = 200$$

At the new equilibrium level of national income of $Y_{E'} = 1500$, exports exceed imports by 125 per period. That is, the automatic change in income induces imports to rise by less than the autonomous increase in exports, so that the adjustment in the balance of payments is incomplete. The foreign trade multiplier $k' = 2.5$ found above is smaller than the corresponding closed economy multiplier $k = 4$ found in section 16.2b because in an open economy, domestic income leaks into both saving and imports.

In the top panel of Figure 16-3, the new higher (broken line) $I + X'$ function crosses the unchanged $S(Y) + M(Y)$ function at point E'. At $Y_{E'} = 1500$, $X' = 500$ $(E'L)$ and $M = 375$ $(E'K)$, so that $X' - M = 125$ (KL). The same outcome is shown in the bottom panel of Figure 16-3 by point E', where the new and higher (broken line) $X' - M(Y)$ function crosses the unchanged $S(Y) - I$ function at $Y_{E'} = 1500$ and defines the trade surplus of $X' - M = 125$.

Note that the smaller $MPS + MPM$ is, the flatter is the $S(Y) + M(Y)$ function in the top panel of Figure 16-3, and the larger would be the foreign trade multiplier and the increase in income for a given autonomous increase in investment and exports. Also to be noted is that Y rises as a result of the exogenous increase in X, and I remains unchanged (i.e., $\Delta I = 0$).

If I instead of X rises by 200:

$$\Delta I + \Delta X = \Delta S + \Delta M$$
$$200 + \quad 0 = 125 + 75$$

and the nation faces a continuous trade deficit of 75, equal to the increase in imports. This could be shown graphically by a downward shift in the $S(Y) - I$ function by 200 so as to cross the unchanged $X - M(Y)$ function at point E'' (see the bottom panel of Figure 16-3) and define $Y_{E}'' = 1500$ and $X - M = -75$.

On the other hand, starting from equilibrium point E in the bottom panel of Figure 16-3, an *autonomous* increase of 200 in saving would shift the $S(Y) - I$ function upward by 200 and define (at point E^*) $Y_{E}^* = 500$ and a trade surplus of $X - M(Y)$ function downward by 200 and define equilibrium point E^{**} (see the bottom panel of Figure 16-3), at which $Y_{E}^{**} = 500$ and the nation would have a trade deficit of $X - M = -125$. The reduction in the equilibrium level of national income results because imports replace domestic production.

16.4   Foreign Repercussions

In this section, we relax the assumption that the nation is small and extend the analysis to consider **foreign repercussions.** In a two-nation world (Nation 1 and Nation 2), an autonomous increase in the exports of Nation 1 arises from and is equal to the *autonomous increase in the imports of Nation 2.* If the autonomous increase in the imports of Nation 2 replaces domestic production, Nation 2's income will fall. This will induce *Nation 2's imports to fall,* thus neutralizing part of the original autonomous increase in its imports. This represents a foreign repercussion on Nation 1 that neutralizes part of the original autonomous increase in its exports. As a result, the foreign trade multiplier for Nation 1 with foreign repercussions is smaller than the corresponding foreign trade multiplier without foreign repercussions.

Assuming that all of the autonomous increase in the exports of Nation 1 replaces domestic production in Nation 2, *the foreign trade multiplier of Nation 1 with foreign repercussions for an autonomous increase in exports (k″)* is:

$$k'' = \frac{\Delta Y_1}{\Delta X_1} = \frac{1}{MPS_1 + MPM_1 + MPM_2(MPS_1/MPS_2)} \qquad (16\text{-}11)$$

where the subscripts 1 and 2 refer, respectively, to Nation 1 and Nation 2. (This and the following formulas are derived in the appendix.) For example, if $MPS_1 = 0.25$ and $MPM_1 = 0.15$ for Nation 1 (as in section 16.3), and $MPS_2 = 0.2$ and $MPM_2 = 0.1$ for Nation 2:

$$k'' = \frac{\Delta Y_1}{\Delta X_1} = \frac{1}{0.25 + 0.15 + 0.10(0.25/0.20)} = \frac{1}{0.525} = 1.90$$

Thus, the original autonomous increase of 200 in the exports of Nation 1 leads to an increase in the equilibrium national income of Nation 1 of $(200)(1.90) = 380$ with foreign repercussions, as compared with $(200)(2.5) = 500$ without foreign repercussions. As a result, $\Delta M_1 = (\Delta Y_1)(MPM_1) = (380)(0.15) = 57$ with foreign repercussions, as opposed to $(500)(0.15) = 75$ without, so that the final trade surplus is 143 instead of 125.

Starting from the equilibrium level of national income and equilibrium in the trade balance (point E in the bottom panel of Figure 16-3), an autonomous increase in investment in Nation 1 (I_1) causes its income (Y_1) to rise and induces its imports (M_1) to rise also, thus opening a deficit in Nation 1's balance of trade (for example, see equilibrium point E‴ in the bottom panel of Figure 16-3). In the absence of foreign repercussions, this is the end of the story. With foreign repercussions, the increase in M_1 is equal to an increase in the exports of Nation 2 (X_2) and induces an increase in Y_2 and M_2. This increase in M_2 is an increase in X_1 (a foreign repercussion on Nation 1) and moderates the original trade deficit of Nation 1.

The foreign trade multiplier in Nation 1 with foreign repercussions for an autonomous increase in investment (k^*) *is:*

$$k^* = \frac{\Delta Y_1}{\Delta I_1} = \frac{1 + MPM_2/MPS_2}{MPS_1 + MPM_1 + MPM_2(MPS_1/MPS_2)} \tag{16-12}$$

Since the denominator of formula 16-12 is identical to the denominator of formula 16-11, using the same information as above, we get:

$$k^* = \frac{\Delta Y_1}{\Delta I_1} = \frac{1 + 0.10/0.20}{0.525} = \frac{1.50}{0.525} = 2.86$$

Thus, $k^* > k' > k''$ and the autonomous increase in I_1 of 200 causes Y_1 to rise by $(200)(2.86) = 572$, instead of 500 in the absence of foreign repercussions. As a result, M_1 rises by $(\Delta Y_1)(MPM_1) = (572)(0.15) = 85.8$ with foreign repercussions, as opposed to $(500)(0.15) = 75$ without. Thus, the deficit in Nation 1's balance of trade is larger (85.8) with than without foreign repercussions (75).

Finally, if there is an autonomous increase in investment *in Nation 2, the foreign trade multiplier in Nation 1 with foreign repercussions for the autonomous increase in* I_2 (k^{**}) *is:*

$$k^{**} = \frac{\Delta Y_1}{\Delta I_2} = \frac{MPM_2/MPS_2}{MPS_1 + MPM_1 + MPM_2(MPS_1/MPS_2)} \tag{16-13}$$

Note that $k^* = k^{**} + k''$. The effect of an autonomous increase in I_2 on Y_1 and the trade balance of Nation 1 is left as an end-of-chapter problem. The mathemetical derivations of the foreign trade multipliers with foreign repercussions given by formulas 16-11, 16-12, and 16-13 are presented in section A16.1 in the appendix.

Note that this is how business cycles are propagated internationally. For example, an expansion in economic activity in the United States spills into imports. Since these are the exports of other nations, the United States expansion is transmitted to other nations. The rise in the exports of these other nations expands their economic activity and feeds back to the United States through an increase in their imports from the United States. Another example is provided by the Great Depression of the 1930s. The sharp contraction in United States economic activity that started in the early 1930s greatly reduced the United States demand for imports. This tendency was reinforced by passage of the Smoot-Hawley tariff, which was the highest tariff in United States history and led to retaliation by other nations (see section 9.5a). The sharp reduction in United States imports had a serious deflationary effect (through the multiplier) on foreign nations, which then reduced their imports from the United States, causing a further reduction in the national income of the United States. Foreign repercussions were an important contributor to the spread of the depression to the entire world. Only a very small nation can safely ignore foreign repercussions.

16.5 The Absorption Approach

In this section, we integrate the automatic price and income adjustment mechanisms and examine the so-called absorption approach. Specifically, we examine the effect of induced (automatic) income changes in the process of correcting a deficit in the nation's balance of payments through a depreciation or devaluation of the nation's currency. These automatic income changes were omitted from Chapter 15 in order to isolate the automatic price adjustment mechanism.

We saw in Chapter 15 that a nation can correct a deficit in its balance of payments by allowing its currency to depreciate or by a devaluation (if the foreign exchange market is stable). Because the improvement in the nation's trade balance depends on the price elasticity of demand for its exports and imports, this method of correcting a deficit is referred to as the **elasticity approach.** The improvement in the deficit nation's trade balance arises because a depreciation or devaluation stimulates the nation's exports and discourages its imports (thus encouraging the domestic production of import substitutes). The resulting increase in production and in the real income of the deficit nation induces imports to rise, which neutralizes part of the original improvement in the nation's trade balance resulting from the depreciation or devaluation of its currency.

However, if the deficit nation is already at full employment, production cannot rise, and only if *real domestic absorption* (i.e., expenditures) is reduced, will the depreciation or devaluation eliminate or reduce the deficit in the nation's balance of payments. If real domestic absorption is not reduced, either automatically or through contractionary fiscal and monetary policies, the depreciation or devaluation will lead to an increase in domestic prices that will completely neutralize the competitive advantage conferred by the depreciation or devaluation, without any reduction of the deficit.

In terms of the bottom panel in Figure 16-3, a depreciation or devaluation of the deficit nation's currency shifts the $X-M(Y)$ function up (because X rises and M falls) and improves the nation's trade balance if the nation operated at less than full employment to begin with (and the Marshall-Lerner condition is satisfied). Note that the net final improvement in the nation's trade balance is less than the upward shift in the $X-M(Y)$ function because domestic production rises and induces imports to rise, thus neutralizing part of the original improvement in the trade balance. However, if the nation started from a position of full employment, the depreciation or devaluation leads to domestic inflation, which then shifts the $X-M(Y)$ function back to its original position without any improvement in the trade balance. Only if domestic absorption is somehow reduced, will some improvement in the trade balance of the deficit nation remain (i.e., the $X-M(Y)$ function will not shift all the way back to its original position).

The above analysis was first introduced by *Alexander*, who named it the **absorption approach.** Alexander began with the identity that production or income (Y) is equal to consumption (C) plus domestic investment (I) plus foreign investment or the trade balance $(X-M)$, all in real terms. That is:

$$Y = C + I + (X - M) \qquad (16\text{-}14)$$

By then letting A equal domestic absorption $(C+I)$ and B equal the trade balance $(X-M)$, we have:

$$Y = A + B \qquad (16\text{-}15)$$

By subtracting A from both sides, we get:

$$Y - A = B \qquad (16\text{-}16)$$

That is, domestic production or income minus domestic absorption equals the trade balance. For the trade balance (B) to improve as a result of a depreciation or devaluation, Y must rise and/or A must fall. If the nation was at full employment to begin with, production or real income (Y) cannot rise, and the depreciation or devaluation can be effective only if domestic absorption (A) falls, either automatically or as a result of contractionary fiscal and monetary policies.

A depreciation or a devaluation of the deficit nation's currency automatically reduces domestic absorption if it redistributes income from wages to profits (since profit earners usually have a higher marginal propensity to save than wage earners). In addition, the increase in domestic prices resulting from the depreciation reduces the value of the real cash balances that the public wants to hold. To restore the value of real cash balances, the public must reduce consumption expenditures. Finally, rising domestic prices push people into higher tax brackets and also reduce consumption. Since we cannot be certain as to the speed and size of these automatic effects, contractionary fiscal and monetary policies may have to be used to cut domestic absorption adequately. These are discussed in the next chapter.

Thus, while the elasticity approach stresses the demand side and implicitly assumes that slack exists in the economy that will allow it to satisfy the additional demand for exports and import substitutes, the absorption approach stresses the supply side and implicitly assumes an adequate demand for the nation's exports and import substitutes. It is clear, however, that both the elasticity approach and the absorption approach are important and both must be considered simultaneously.

Related to the automatic income adjustment mechanism and the absorption approach is the so-called **transfer problem.** This is discussed in section A16.2 in the appendix.

16.6 Monetary Adjustments and Synthesis of the Automatic Adjustments

In this section, we first examine monetary adjustments to balance-of-payments disequilibria. We then present a synthesis of the automatic price, income, and monetary adjustments and how they seem to work in the real world. Finally, we conclude with a discussion of the disadvantages of automatic adjustment mechanisms.

16.6a Monetary Adjustments

Up to now, monetary adjustments have been omitted. However, when the exchange rate is not freely flexible, a deficit in the balance of payments tends to reduce the nation's money supply because the excess foreign currency demanded is obtained by exchanging domestic money balances for foreign exchange at the nation's central bank. Under a fractional-reserve banking system, this loss of reserves causes the nation's money supply to fall by a multiple of the trade deficit. Unless sterilized, or neutralized, by the nation's monetary authorities, the reduction in the money supply induces interest rates to rise in the deficit nation.

The rise in interest rates in the deficit nation discourages domestic investment and reduces national income (via the multiplier process), and this induces a decline in the nation's imports, which reduces the deficit. Furthermore, the rise in interest rates attracts foreign capital, thus helping the nation to finance the deficit. The opposite occurs in the surplus nation. Indeed, it is through these international capital flows and automatic income changes that adjustment seems actually to have occurred under the gold standard (rather than through the price-specie-flow mechanism described in section 15.6b).

The reduction in its money supply and income also tends to reduce prices in the deficit nation relative to the surplus nation, further improving the trade balance of the deficit nation. This adjustment through changes in internal prices is *theoretically* most pronounced and direct under the gold standard, but it also occurs under other international monetary systems. In Chapter 18 we resume and expand this discussion and examine whether the change in the money supply affects the balance of payments primarily through a change in relative prices (as monetarists assert) or through a change in interest rates (as suggested by Keynesian analysis). In what follows, we assume that a change in the money supply affects the balance of payments, to some extent, through both interest rate changes and changes in internal prices.

16.6b   Synthesis of Automatic Adjustments

Let us now integrate the automatic price, income, and monetary adjustments for a nation that faces unemployment and a deficit in its balance of payments at the equilibrium level of income.

Under a freely flexible exchange rate system and a stable foreign exchange market, the nation's currency will depreciate until the deficit is entirely eliminated. Under a managed float, the nation's monetary authorities usually do not allow the full depreciation required to eliminate the deficit completely. Under a fixed exchange rate system (such as the one that operated during most of the postwar period), the exchange rate can depreciate only within the narrow limits allowed, so that most of the balance-of-payments adjustment must come from elsewhere.

A depreciation (to the extent that it is allowed) stimulates production and income in the deficit nation and induces imports to rise, thus reducing part of the original improvement in the trade balance resulting from the depreciation. Under a freely flexible exchange rate system, this simply means that the depreciation required to eliminate a balance-of-payments deficit is larger than if these automatic income changes were not present.

Except under a freely flexible exchange rate system, a balance-of-payments deficit tends to reduce the nation's money supply, thus increasing its interest rates. This, in turn, reduces domestic investment and income in the deficit nation, which induces its imports to fall and thereby reduces the deficit. The increase in interest rates also attracts foreign capital, which helps the nation finance the deficit. The reduction in income and in the money supply also causes prices in the deficit nation to fall relative to prices in the surplus nation, thus further improving the balance of trade of the deficit nation.

Under a fixed exchange rate system, most of the automatic adjustment would have to come from the monetary adjustments discussed above, unless the nation devalues its currency. On the other hand, under a freely flexible exchange rate system, the national economy is to a large extent insulated from balance-of-payments disequilibria, and most of the adjustment in the balance of payments takes place through exchange rate variations. (The fixed and flexible exchange rate systems are evaluated and compared in Chapter 19.)

When all of these automatic price, income, and monetary adjustments are allowed to operate, the adjustment to balance-of-payments disequilibria is likely to be more or less complete even under a fixed exchange rate system. The problem is that automatic adjustments often have serious disadvantages, which nations often try to avoid by the use of adjustment policies (discussed in the next chapter).

16.6c   Automatic Adjustments in the Real World

In the real world, income, prices, interest rates, exports, imports, and other variables change as a result of an autonomous disturbance (such as an increase in expenditures) in one nation, and a disturbance in one nation affects other nations, with repercussions back to the first nation. It is very difficult to trace all of these effects in the real world because of the very intricate relationships that exist among these variables and also because, over time, other changes and disturbances occur, and nations also adopt various policies to achieve domestic and international objectives.

With the advent of large computers, large-scale models of the economy have been constructed, and they have been used to estimate foreign trade multipliers and the net effect on prices, interest rates, exports, imports, and other variables that would result from an autonomous change in expenditures in one nation, or in the rest of the world. While these models are very complex, they do operate according to the general principles examined in this chapter.

Table 16-1 presents the net final result (simulation) of an autonomous and sustained increase of 1 percent in the gross national product (GNP) of the United States on short-term interest rates, imports, and exports of the United States, and the repercussions that these have on the same variables in Germany, Japan, France, Italy, the United Kingdom, and Canada one-and-a-half years after the change occurs.

The 1 percent increase in the GNP of the United States induces (through the multiplier process) its GNP to increase by 1.39 percent one-and-a-half years after the change. A longer period of time would show larger effects, but the results would be blurred even more by the other changes that are likely to occur as the observation period is lengthened. The GDP deflator (a price index) of the United States rises by 0.55 percent. Short-term interest rates increase by 0.89, imports by 2.94 percent, and exports by 0.65 percent. The increase in United States exports results from the increase in the GNP of other nations that are induced by the United States increase in imports. The much

TABLE 16-1. *Estimated Effect of a 1 Percent Increase in Autonomous Expenditures in the United States (in percentages)*

Country	Real GNP	GDP Deflator	Short-Term Interest Rate	Imports	Exports
United States	1.39	0.55	0.89	2.94	0.65
Canada	0.55	0.56	0.60	1.14	2.66
Germany	0.14	0.10	0.41	−0.06	0.35
Japan	0.12	−0.10	−0.12	1.04	0.92
France	−0.07	−0.14	0.29	0.25	0.20
Italy	0.21	−0.27	−0.42	0.43	0.39
United Kingdom	0.10	−0.11	0.02	0.23	0.20

Source: R. C. Fair, "Estimated Output, Price, Interest Rate, and Exchange Rate Linkages among Countries," *Journal of Political Economy*, June 1982.

larger increase in imports than in exports, however, worsens the trade balance of the United States.

The increase in prices and short-term interest rates in the United States affects consumption, investments, capital flows, and other variables in the United States. But these effects are already incorporated in the results shown in the table. That is, the data in the table show the final results in the United States at the end of 18 months from all of the direct (domestic) and indirect (from abroad) effects of the 1 percent increase in the GNP of the United States.

The table also shows that the 1 percent increase in the GNP of the United States results in an increase of 0.56 percent in the GNP of Canada, 0.14 percent in the GNP of Germany, 0.12 percent in the GNP of Japan, −0.7 percent in the GNP of France, 0.21 percent in Italy, and 0.10 percent in the United Kingdom, as part of the increase in the GNP of the United States spills into increased imports. The larger repercussions on Canada than on the other nations result from the smaller size of and the much greater interdependence of the Canadian economy with the United States economy. The increase in the GNP of the United States also results in an increase in short-term interest rates, imports, and exports of most other nations. The negative responses in the table (especially for the GDP deflator) may be due to other changes occurring at the same time in these nations that reversed the expected relationship.

16.6d Disadvantages of Automatic Adjustments

The disadvantage facing a freely flexible exchange rate system may be erratic fluctuations in exchange rates. These interfere with the flow of international trade (even though foreign exchange risks can often be hedged at a cost) and impose costly adjustment burdens (in the form of shifts in the use of domestic resources) that might be entirely unnecessary in the long run.

Under a managed floating exchange rate system, erratic exchange rate fluctuations can be avoided, but monetary authorities may manage the exchange rate so as to keep the domestic currency undervalued to stimulate the domestic economy at the expense of other nations (thus inviting retaliation). Such competitive depreciations or devaluations (beggar-thy-neighbor policies) proved very disruptive and damaging to international trade in the period between the two world wars (see section 20.2b).

On the other hand, the possibility of a devaluation under a fixed exchange rate system can lead to destabilizing international capital flows, which can also prove very disruptive. A fixed exchange rate system also forces the nation to rely primarily on monetary adjustments.

Automatic income changes can also have serious disadvantages. For example, a nation facing an autonomous increase in its imports at the expense of domestic production would have to allow its national income to fall in order to reduce its trade deficit. On the other hand, a nation facing an autonomous increase in its exports from a position of full employment would have to accept domestic inflation to eliminate the trade surplus.

Similarly, for the automatic monetary adjustments to operate, the nation must passively allow its money supply to change as a result of balance-of-payments disequilibria and thus give up its use of monetary policy to achieve the more important objective of domestic full employment without inflation. For all of these reasons, nations often will use adjustment policies to correct balance-of-payments disequilibria instead of relying on automatic mechanisms.

Summary

1. The income adjustment mechanism relies on induced changes in the national income of the deficit and surplus nations to bring about adjustment in the balance of payments. To isolate the income adjustment mechanism, we initially assume that the nation operates under a fixed exchange rate system and that all prices, wages, and interest rates are constant. We also begin by assuming that the nation operates at less than full employment.

2. In a closed economy without a government sector, the equilibrium level of national income (Y_E) is equal to the desired flow of consumption expenditures (C) plus desired investment expenditures (I). That is, $Y = C(Y) + I$. Equivalently, Y_E occurs where $S = I$. If $Y \neq Y_E$, desired expenditures do not equal the value of output and $S \neq I$. The result is unplanned inventory investment or disinvestment, which pushes the economy toward Y_E. An increase in I causes Y_E to rise by a multiple of the increase in I. The ratio of the increase in Y_E to the increase in I is called the multiplier (k), which is given by the reciprocal of the marginal propensity to save (MPS). The increase in Y_E induces S to rise by an amount equal to the autonomous increase in I.

3. In a small open economy, exports (X) are exogenous, or independent of the nation's income, just as I is. On the other hand, imports (M) depend on income, just as S does. The ratio of the change in M for a given change in Y is the marginal propensity to import (MPM). Y_E is determined where the sum of the injections $(I + X)$ equals the sum of the leakages $(S + M)$. The condition for Y_E can also be rewritten as $X - M = S - I$ and as $I + (X - M) = S$. The foreign trade multiplier $k' = 1/(MPS + MPM)$ and is smaller than the corresponding closed economy multiplier (k). An autonomous increase in I and/or X causes Y_E to change by k' times ΔI and/or ΔX. The change in

Y_E induces S to change by *(MPS) (ΔY)*, and M to change by *(MPM) (ΔY)*, but adjustment in the trade balance is incomplete.

4. If the nations are not small, foreign repercussions cannot be safely ignored. In a two-nation world, an autonomous increase in the exports of Nation 1 arises from and is equal to the autonomous increase in the imports of Nation 2. If occurring at the expense of domestic production, this reduces the income and imports of Nation 2 and represents a foreign repercussion of Nation 1 that neutralizes part of the original autonomous increase in the exports of Nation 1. Thus, the foreign trade multiplier of Nation 1 with foreign repercussions is smaller than that without foreign repercussions (see formula 16-11). We can also calculate the foreign trade multiplier for Nation 1 with foreign repercussions for an autonomous increase in investment in Nation 1 (see formula 16-12) and in Nation 2 (see formula 16-13). Foreign repercussions explain how business cycles are transmitted internationally.

5. The absorption approach integrates the automatic price and income adjustment mechanisms. For example, a depreciation or devaluation stimulates the domestic production of exports and import substitutes and increases the level of real national income. This induces an increase in the nation's imports, which neutralizes part of the original improvement in its trade balance. But if the nation is at full employment to begin with, production cannot rise, and the depreciation or devaluation will instead increase domestic prices so as to leave the trade balance completely unchanged, unless real domestic absorption is somehow reduced.

6. When the exchange rate is not freely flexible, a depreciation of the deficit nation's currency will correct part, but not all, of the deficit. The deficit then leads to a reduction in the nation's money supply and an increase in its interest rate. This induces a fall in investment, income, and imports, which reduces the deficit. It also induces a capital inflow. In addition, the reduction in the money supply and income reduces prices in the deficit nation relative to prices in the surplus nation, and this further improves the former's trade balance. All of these automatic adjustment mechanisms together are likely to bring about complete balance-of-payments adjustment, but they sacrifice internal to external balance.

A Look Ahead

Chapter 17 deals with adjustment policies. Specifically, we will examine how a change in the exchange rate, together with the monetary and fiscal policies, can be used to achieve balance-of-payments equilibrium as well as full employment without inflation. If the nation is unwilling to change its exchange rate or allow it to vary, the government could use monetary policy to achieve balance-of-payments equilibrium and fiscal policy to achieve noninflationary full employment. However, achieving internal and external balance simultaneously is much more difficult or even impossible without exchange rate changes (if automatic adjustments are also neutralized and not allowed to operate). The chapter will conclude with a discussion of direct controls over international transactions to correct a balance-of-payments disequilibrium.

Glossary

Closed economy   An economy in autarky or not engaging in international transactions.

Equilibrium level of national income (Y_E)   The level of income at which desired or planned expenditures equal the value of output, and desired saving equals desired investment.

Desired or planned investment   The level of investment expenditures that business would like to undertake.

Marginal propensity to consume (MPC)   The ratio of the change in consumption expenditures to the change in income, or $\Delta C/\Delta Y$.

Consumption function   The relationship between consumption expenditures and income. In general, consumption is positive when income is zero (i.e., the nation dissaves) and rises as income rises, but by less than the rise in income.

Saving function   The relationship between saving and income. In general, saving is negative when income is zero and rises as income rises, in such a way that the increase in consumption plus the increase in saving equals the increase in income.

Marginal propensity to save (MPS) The ratio of the change in saving to the change in income, or $\Delta S/\Delta Y$.

Investment function The relationship between investment expenditures and income. With investment exogenous, the investment function is horizontal when plotted against income. That is, investment expenditures are independent of (or do not change with) the level of national income.

Multiplier (k) The ratio of the change in income to the change in investment; in a closed economy without government, $k = 1/MPS$.

Import function The positive relationship between the nation's imports and national income.

Marginal propensity to import (MPM) The ratio of the change in imports to the change in national income, or $\Delta M/\Delta Y$.

Average propensity to import (APM) The ratio of imports to national income, or M/Y.

Income elasticity of demand for imports (n_Y) The ratio of the percentage change in imports to the percentage change in national income; it is equal to MPM/APM.

Export function The relationship between exports and income. With exports exogenous, the export function is horizontal. That is, exports are independent of (or do not change with) the level of national income.

Foreign trade multiplier (k′) The ratio of the change in income to the change in exports and/or investment. It equals $k' = 1/(MPS + MPM)$.

Foreign repercussions The effect that a change in a large nation's income and trade has on the rest of the world and which the rest of the world in turn has on the nation under consideration. This is how business cycles are transmitted internationally.

Elasticity approach The change in the trade balance resulting from a depreciation or devaluation and depending on the price elasticity of demand for the nation's exports and imports.

Absorption approach Examines and integrates the effect of induced income changes in the process of correcting a balance-of-payments disequilibrium by a change in the exchange rate.

Transfer problem Deals with the conditions under which a large and unusual capital transfer is actually accomplished by an export surplus of the paying nation and an equal import surplus of the receiving nation.

Synthesis of automatic adjustments The attempt to integrate the automatic price, income, and monetary adjustments to correct balance-of-payments disequilibria.

Questions for Review

1. How does the automatic income adjustment mechanism operate to bring about adjustment in a nation's balance of payments? What are the variables that we hold constant to isolate the income adjustment mechanism?

2. What is meant by a closed economy? By desired or planned investment, consumption, and saving? What is meant by investment being exogenous? What is a consumption function, a saving function, and an investment function? What do the MPC and the MPS measure? How is the equilibrium level of national income determined in a closed economy? How is the size of the closed economy multiplier (k) determined?

3. What is meant by exports being exogenous? What is meant by MPM, APM, and n_Y? How is the equilibrium level of national income determined in a small open economy? What is the value of the foreign trade multiplier (k′)? What is meant when we say that the automatic income adjustment mechanism brings about incomplete adjustment in the balance of trade or payments?

4. What is meant by foreign repercussions? When is it not safe to ignore them? What is the multiplier formula for Nation 1 with foreign repercussions for an autonomous increase in its exports that replaces domestic production in Nation 2? What is the multiplier formula for an autonomous increase in investment in Nation 1? In Nation 2? How are foreign repercussions related to international business cycles?

5. What is meant by the elasticity approach? The absorption approach? In what way does the absorption approach integrate the automatic price and income adjustment mechanisms? What happens to the trade balance of a deficit nation if it allows its currency to depreciate or devalues from a position of full employment? How can real domestic absorption be reduced?

6. What is meant by automatic monetary adjustments? How do they help to adjust balance-of-payments disequilibria? How do all the automatic adjustment mechanisms operate together to correct a deficit in a nation's balance of payments under a fixed or managed exchange rate system when the nation operates at less than full employment? What is the disadvantage of each automatic adjustment mechanism?

Problems

1. Given $C = 100 + 0.8Y$ and autonomous investment $I = 100$:
   (a) Draw a figure showing the equilibrium level of national income.
   (b) Write the equation of the saving function.
   (c) Draw a figure showing the equilibrium level of national income in terms of desired saving and investment.

2. Starting from the given values and figures in problem 1, and assuming that autonomous investment expenditures increase by 100 from $I = 100$ to $I' = 200$:
   (a) Draw a figure in terms of total expenditures showing the new equilibrium level of national income.
   (b) Draw a figure in terms of desired saving and investment showing the new equilibrium level of national income.

   (c) Determine the value of the multiplier.

*3. Given $C = 100 + 0.8Y$, $M = 150 + 0.20Y$, $I = 100$, and $X = 350$:
   (a) Determine Y_E algebraically.
   (b) Show the determination of Y_E graphically as in the top panel of Figure 16-3.
   (c) Show the determination of Y_E graphically as in the bottom panel of Figure 16-3.

4. Starting from the algebraic and graphical results of problem 3, determine algebraically and show graphically the effect on Y_E and on $X - M$ of an *autonomous*:
   (a) increase in X of 200;
   (b) increase in I of 200;
   (c) increase in X and I of 200;
   (d) decrease in S of 100;
   (e) decrease in M of 100;
   (f) decrease in S and M of 100.

*5. Assuming that Nation 1 and Nation 2 are both large, and starting from the equilibrium level of national income and equilibrium in the trade balance in Nation 1, and given that $MPS_1 = 0.20$, $MPS_2 = 0.15$, $MPM_1 = 0.20$, and $MPM_2 = 0.10$, find the change in the equilibrium level of national income and the trade balance in Nation 1 for:
   (a) an autonomous increase in the exports of Nation 1 of 200 that replaces domestic production in Nation 2;
   (b) an autonomous increase in investment of 200 in Nation 1;
   (c) an autonomous increase in investment of 200 in Nation 2.
   (d) Do the same as in part c for the numerical example in section 16.4.

6. Starting from your graphical results of problem 4b, show graphically the effect on Y_E and on $X - M$ of a depreciation of the nation's currency from a position of full employment and a trade deficit.

APPENDIX————————————————————————

In this appendix, section A16.1 presents the mathematical derivation of the foreign trade multipliers with foreign repercussions, while section A16.2 examines the transfer problem.

A16.1   Derivation of Foreign Trade Multipliers with Foreign Repercussions

For the purpose of deriving foreign trade multipliers with foreign repercussions, we will simplify the notations by letting non-asterisked symbols refer to Nation 1 and asterisked symbols refer to Nation 2. Furthermore, we will let $s = MPS$ and $m = MPM$.

The changes in the equilibrium level of national income for Nation 1 and Nation 2 (from equation 16-9) are:

$$\Delta I + \Delta X = \triangle S + \Delta M$$
$$\Delta I^* + \Delta X^* = \Delta S^* + \Delta M^* \qquad (16A\text{-}1)$$

But we know that $\triangle S = s\Delta Y$, $\Delta M = m\Delta Y$, and $\triangle S^* = s^*\Delta Y^*$, $\Delta M^* = m^*\Delta Y^*$. We also know that the change in Nations 1's exports (ΔX) equals the change in Nation 2's imports ($\Delta M^* = m^*\Delta Y^*$), and the change in Nation 2's exports (ΔX^*) equals the change in Nation 1's imports ($\Delta M = m\Delta Y$). Substituting these values into equation 16A-1, we get:

$$\Delta I + m^*\Delta Y^* = s\Delta Y + m\Delta Y$$
$$\Delta I^* + m\Delta Y = s^*\Delta Y^* + m^*\Delta Y^* \qquad (16A\text{-}2)$$

From equation 16A-2, we can derive the foreign trade multipliers with foreign repercussions. We begin by deriving the foreign trade multiplier with foreign repercussions for Nation 1 for an autonomous increase in investment in Nation 1 (k^* given by equation 16-12). Since there is no autonomous change in investment in Nation 2, $\Delta I^* = 0$. Solving the second equation of 16A-2 for ΔY^* and substituting into the first equation, we get:

$$m\Delta Y = s^*\Delta Y^* + m^*\Delta Y^*$$
$$m\Delta Y = (s^* + m^*)\Delta Y^*$$
$$\frac{m\Delta Y}{s^* + m^*} = \Delta Y^*$$
$$\Delta I + m^* \frac{(m\Delta Y)}{s^* + m^*} = s\Delta Y + m\Delta Y$$
$$\Delta I = (s + m)\Delta Y - \frac{(m^*m)}{s^* + m^*}\Delta Y$$
$$\Delta I = \left[(s + m) - \frac{m^*m}{s^* + m^*} \right]\Delta Y$$
$$\Delta I = \left[\frac{(s + m)(s^* + m^*) - m^*m}{s^* + m^*} \right]\Delta Y$$
$$\Delta I = \left[\frac{ss^* + m^*m + ms^* + m^*s - m^*m}{s^* + m^*} \right]\Delta Y$$

$$\frac{\Delta I}{\Delta Y} = \frac{ss^* + ms^* + m^*s}{s^* + m^*}$$

$$\frac{\Delta Y}{\Delta I} = \frac{s^* + m^*}{ss^* + ms^* + m^*s}$$

Dividing numerator and denominator by s^*, we get:

$$k^* = \frac{\Delta Y}{\Delta I} = \frac{1 + m^*/s^*}{s + m + m^*s/s^*}$$

This is equation 16-12 given in section 16.4.

Starting once again with equation 16A-2, we can similarly derive the foreign trade multiplier for Nation 1 for an autonomous increase in investment in Nation 2 (k^{**} given by equation 16-13). Since there is no autonomous change in investment in Nation 1, $\Delta I = 0$. Solving the first equation of 16A-2 for $\triangle Y^*$ and substituting into the second equation, we get:

$$\Delta Y^* = \frac{(s+m)}{m^*}\Delta Y$$

$$\Delta I^* + m\Delta Y = s^*\frac{(s+m)}{m^*}\Delta Y + m^*\frac{(s+m)}{m^*}\Delta Y$$

$$\Delta I^* = \left[s^*\frac{(s+m)}{m^*} + m^*\frac{(s+m)}{m^*} - m\right]\Delta Y$$

$$\Delta I^* = \left[\frac{s^*s + s^*m}{m^*} + \frac{m^*s + m^*m}{m^*} - \frac{mm^*}{m^*}\right]\Delta Y$$

$$\Delta I^* = \left[\frac{s^*s + s^*m + m^*s}{m^*}\right]\Delta Y$$

$$\frac{\Delta Y}{\Delta I^*} = \frac{m^*}{s^*s + s^*m + m^*s}$$

$$k^{**} = \frac{\Delta Y}{\Delta I^*} = \frac{m^*/s^*}{s + m + m^*s/s^*}$$

This is equation 16-13 in section 16.4.

We can now derive the foreign trade multiplier with foreign repercussions for Nation 1 for an autonomous increase in the exports of Nation 1 that replaces production in Nation 2 (so that the total combined expenditures in both nations remains unchanged). The autonomous increase in the exports of Nation 1 has the same effect on the equilibrium level of income of Nation 1 as an equal autonomous increase in investment in Nation 1 ($\Delta Y/\Delta I$ given by equation 16-12). The equal decrease in expenditures in Nation 2 has the same effect on the equilibrium level of income of Nation 1 as a decrease in investment in Nation 2 by the same amount ($-\Delta Y/\Delta I^*$ given by equation 16-13). Thus,

$$k'' = \frac{\Delta Y}{\Delta X} = \frac{\Delta Y}{\Delta I} - \frac{\Delta Y}{\Delta I^*}$$

That is, k'' is given by equation 16-12 minus equation 16-13. This gives equation 16-11.

Problem   (a) Starting from equation 16A-2, derive k'' for Nation 1 in the same way that k^* and k^{**} were derived. (b) What is the value of the foreign trade multiplier with foreign repercussions for Nation 1 if the autonomous increase in the exports of Nation 1 represents entirely an increase in expenditures in Nation 2?

A16.2   The Transfer Problem Once Again

This presentation builds on the discussion of the transfer problem in the appendix to Chapter 12. The transfer problem is discussed here because it is related to the automatic income and price adjustment mechanisms. It deals with the conditions under which a large and unusual capital transfer is actually accomplished by an export surplus of the paying nation and an equal import surplus of the receiving nation.

Attention was first focused on this problem in connection with the reparations that Germany had to pay to France after World War I, which gave rise to the now famous debate on the subject between Keynes and Ohlin (see the selected bibliography for the references). Of more immediate interest is the transfer problem that arose between petroleum-importing and petroleum-exporting nations because of the sharp increase in petroleum prices during the 1970s.

We examine the transfer problem by assuming that both the paying and the receiving nation are operating under a fixed exchange rate system and full employment. The transfer of real resources occurs only if expenditures in the paying and/or the receiving country are affected. If the financial transfer is effected out of idle balances (say, idle bank balances) in the paying nation and goes into idle balances (saving) in the receiving nation, expenditures are not affected in either nation and there is no transfer of real resources. For the transfer of real resources to take place, either taxes must be increased in the paying nation, so as to reduce expenditures, and/or expenditures must rise in the receiving nation through a reduction in taxes or an increase in services.

The reduction in expenditures in the paying nation will induce its imports to fall, while the increase in expenditures in the receiving nation will induce its imports to rise. In a two-nation world (the paying and the receiving nation), this leads to a trade surplus in the paying nation and an equal trade deficit in the receiving nation (if both nations had a zero trade balance before the transfer). It is only through the trade surplus of the paying nation and the corresponding trade deficit of the receiving nation that the transfer of real resources can be accomplished.

If the *sum* of the *MPM* in the paying nation and the *MPM* in the receiving nation equals 1, the entire financial transfer is accomplished with an equal transfer of real resources (through the change in trade balances). In this case, we say that the adjustment is *complete*. If, on the other hand, the sum of the *MPM*s in the two nations is less than 1, the transfer of real resources falls short of the transfer of financial resources. In this case, we say that the adjustment is *incomplete*. If the sum of the *MPM*s in the two nations is greater than 1, the transfer of real resources (i.e., the net change in the trade balance in each nation) is greater than the financial transfer, and the adjustment is said to be *overcomplete*. Finally, if the trade balance of the paying nation deteriorates instead of improving (so that the trade balance of the receiving nation improves), the adjustment is said to be *perverse*. In this case, there is a transfer of real resources from the receiving to the paying country instead of the opposite, as is required.

If adjustment via income changes alone is incomplete, the terms of trade of the paying (deficit) nation will have to deteriorate (and those of the surplus nation improve) to complete the adjustment. A deterioration in the paying nation's terms of trade will further reduce its real national income and imports. The reduction in its export prices in relation to its import prices will discourage the nation's imports and encourage its exports still further, thus contributing to completion of the transfer. On the other hand, if adjustment via income changes is overcomplete, the terms of trade of the paying nation must *improve* to make the adjustment merely complete.

For example, suppose that Nation A has to transfer (or lend) $100 million to Nation B, and in the process the income of Nation A falls by $100 million while the income of Nation B increases by the same amount. If $MPM = m = 0.4$ for Nation A and $MPM = m^* = 0.6$ for Nation B, Nation A's imports will fall by $40 million while Nation B's imports (equal to Nation A's exports) rise by $60 million, for a net improvement of $100 million in Nation A's trade balance. As a result, the transfer is complete without any need for the terms of trade to change. If instead $m = 0.2$ and $m^* = 0.5$, Nation A's imports will fall by $20 million while Nation B's imports (A's exports) rise by $50 million, for a net improvement of only $70 million in Nation A's balance of trade. A deficit of $30 million remains in Nation A's balance of payments, and we say that the transfer is incomplete. The terms of trade of Nation A must then deteriorate, and Nation B's terms of trade improve, to complete the transfer. Finally, if $m = 0.5$ and $m^* = 0.7$, Nation A's trade balance will improve by $120 million, and the adjustment will be overcomplete. Then Nation A's terms of trade will have to improve sufficiently to make the adjustment merely complete.

In the real world, we can expect $m + m^* < 1$ and adjustment through income changes alone to be incomplete. A "secondary burden" of adjustment then falls on the terms of trade; that is, the terms of trade of the paying nation must deteriorate (and those of the receiving nation improve) for the transfer to be complete.

Problem Discuss how the transfer problem arising from the sharp increase in petroleum prices during the 1970s was accomplished.

Selected Bibliography

For a problem-solving approach to the income adjustment mechanism, see:
- D. Salvatore, *Theory and Problems of International Economics,* 2nd ed. (New York: McGraw-Hill, 1984), ch. 9 (sect. 9.4).

For a review of income determination in a closed economy, consult your principles of economics text or:
- D. Salvatore and E. Diulio, *Principles of Economics* (New York: McGraw-Hill, 1980), ch. 5.

The pioneering work on the income adjustment mechanism is:
- J. M. Keynes, *The General Theory of Employment, Interest and Money* (London: Macmillan, 1936).

For the application of Keynesian economics of income determination to an open economy with foreign repercussions, see:
- F. Machlup, *International Trade and the National Income Multiplier* (Philadelphia: Blackston, 1943). Reprinted in the Economic Classics Series (New York: A. Kelly, 1965).
- J. E. Meade, *The Theory of International Economic Policy,* Vol. 1, *The Balance of Payments* (New York: Oxford University Press, 1951), parts 2 and 3.

Estimates of the income elasticity of demand for imports are presented in:
- H. Houthakker and S. Magee, "Income and Price Elasticities in World Trade," *Review of Economics and Statistics,* May 1969.
- M. Golstein and M. S. Khan, "Income and Price Effects in International Trade," in R. W. Jones and P. B. Kenen, Eds., *Handbook of International Economics* (Amsterdam: North-Holland, 1985).

The original presentation of the absorption approach is found in:
- S. S. Alexander, "Devaluation versus Import Restriction as an Instrument for Improving Foreign Trade Balance," *International Monetary Fund Staff Papers,* April 1951.

- S. S. Alexander, "Effects of a Devaluation on a Trade Balance," *International Monetary Fund Staff Papers,* April 1952. Reprinted in R. E. Caves and H. G. Johnson, *Readings in International Economics* (Homewood, Ill.: Irwin, 1968).

For an evaluation of the absorption approach and attempts to integrate the elasticity and absorption approaches, see:
- F. Machlup, "Relative Prices and Aggregate Spending in the Analysis of Devaluation," *American Economic Review,* June 1955.
- S. S. Alexander, "Effects of a Devaluation: A Simplified Synthesis of Elasticities and Absorption Approaches," *American Economic Review,* March 1959.
- S. C. Tsiang, "The Role of Money in Trade Balance Stability: Synthesis of the Elasticity and Absorption Approaches," *American Economic Review,* December 1961. Reprinted in R. E. Caves and H. G. Johnson, *Readings in International Economics* (Homewood, Ill.: Irwin, 1968).

The debate on the transfer problem between Keynes and Ohlin appears in:
- J. M. Keynes, "The German Transfer Problem," *Economic Journal,* March 1929. Reprinted in H. S. Ellis and L. M. Metzler, *Readings in the Theory of International Trade* (Homewood, Ill.: Irwin, 1950).
- B. Ohlin, "The Reparation Problem: A Discussion," *Economic Journal,* June 1929. Reprinted in H. S. Ellis and L. M. Metzler, *Readings in the Theory of International Trade* (Homewood, Ill.: Irwin, 1950).
- *L. M. Metzler, "The Transfer Problem Reconsidered," *Journal of Political Economy,* June 1942. Reprinted in H. S. Ellis and L. M. Metzer, *Readings in the Theory of International Trade* (Homewood, Ill.: Irwin, 1950).

Estimates of real world adjustments to disturbances in open economies are presented in:
- R. C. Fair, "Estimated Output, Price, Interest Rate, and Exchange Rate Linkages among Countries," *Journal of Political Economy,* June 1982.
- J. F. Helliwell and T. Padmore, "Empirical

Studies of Macroeconomic Interdependence,''
in R. W. Jones and P. B. Kenen, Eds., *Handbook of International Economics* (Amsterdam: North-Holland, 1985).
• J. D. Sachs, "The Current Account and Macroeconomic Adjustment in the 1970s,"
Brookings Papers on Economic Activity, 1981.
• L. O. Laney, "The Strong Dollar, the Current
Account, and Federal Deficits: Cause and Effect," *Economic Review*, Federal Reserve Bank
of Dallas, January 1984.

CHAPTER 17

Adjustment Policies

17.1 Introduction

In this chapter, we examine the adjustment policies to achieve full employment with price stability and equilibrium in the balance of payments. The need for adjustment policies arises because the automatic adjustment mechanisms discussed in the previous two chapters have serious unwanted side effects (see section 16.6d). The economist most responsible for shifting the emphasis from automatic adjustment mechanisms to adjustment policies is *Meade.*

The most important economic goals or objectives of nations are: (1) internal balance, (2) external balance, (3) a *reasonable* rate of growth, and (4) an *equitable* distribution of income. **Internal balance** refers to full employment or rate of unemployment of no more than 2 or 3 percent per year (the so-called *frictional unemployment* arising in the process of changing jobs) and a rate of inflation of no more than 2 or 3 percent per year. **External balance** refers to equilibrium in the balance of payments (or a desired temporary disequilibrium such as a surplus that a nation may want in order to replenish its depleted international reserves). In general, nations place priority on internal over external balance, but they are sometimes forced to switch their priority when faced with large and persistent external imbalances.

To achieve these objectives, nations have the following policy instruments at their disposal: (1) expenditure-changing, or demand, policies, (2) expenditure-switching policies, and (3) direct controls. **Expenditure-changing policies** include both fiscal and monetary policies. *Fiscal policy* refers to changes in government expenditures, taxes, or both. Fiscal policy is *expansionary* if government expenditures are increased and/or taxes reduced. These actions lead to an expansion of domestic production and income through a multiplier process (just as in the case of an increase in domestic investment or exports) and induce a rise in imports (depending on the marginal propensity to import of the nation). *Contractionary* fiscal policy refers to a reduction in government expenditures and/or an increase in taxes, both of which reduce domestic production and income, and induce a fall in imports.

Monetary policy involves a change in the nation's money supply and affects domestic interest rates. Monetary policy is *easy* if the money supply is increased and interest rates fall. This induces an increase in the level of investment and income in the nation (through the multiplier process) and induces imports to rise. At the same time, the reduction in the interest rate induces a short-term capital outflow or reduced inflow. On the other hand, *tight* monetary policy refers to a reduction in the nation's money supply and rise in the interest rate. This discourages investment, income, and imports, and also leads to a short-term capital inflow or reduced outflow.

Expenditure-switching policies refer to changes in the exchange rate (i.e., a devaluation or revaluation). A devaluation switches expenditures from foreign to domestic commodities and can be used to correct a deficit in the nation's balance of payments. But it also increases domestic production, and this induces a rise in imports, which neutralizes a part of the original improvement in the trade balance. A revaluation switches expenditures from domestic to foreign products and can be used to correct a surplus in the nation's balance of payments. This also reduces domestic production and, consequently, induces a decline in imports, which neutralizes part of the effect of the revaluation.

Direct controls consist of tariffs, quotas, and other restrictions on the flow of international trade and capital. These are also expenditure-switching policies, but they can be aimed at specific balance-of-payments items (as opposed to a devaluation or revaluation, which is a general policy and applies to all items at the same time). Direct controls in the form of price and wage controls can also be used to stem domestic inflation when other policies fail.

Faced with multiple objectives and with several policy instruments at its disposal, the nation must decide which policy to utilize to achieve each of its objectives. According to *Tinbergen* (Nobel Prize in economics in 1969), the nation usually needs as many effective policy instruments as the number of independent objectives it has. If the nation has two objectives, it usually needs two policy instruments to achieve the two objectives *completely*; if it has three objectives, it requires three instruments, and so on. Sometimes a policy instrument directed at a particular objective also helps the nation move closer to another objective. At other times, it pushes the nation even farther away from the second objective. For example, expansionary fiscal policy to eliminate domestic unemployment will also reduce a balance-of-payments surplus, but it would increase a deficit.

Since each policy affects both the internal and external balance of the nation, it is crucial that each policy be paired and used for the objective toward which it is most effective, according to the **principle of effective market classification** developed by *Mundell*. We will see in section 17-5a that if the nation does not follow this principle, it will move even farther from both balances.

In section 17-2, we analyze the use of expenditure-changing and expenditure-switching policies to achieve both internal and external balance. Section 17-3 introduces new tools of analysis to define equilibrium in the goods market, in the money market, and in the balance of payments. In section 17.4, these new analytical tools are used to examine ways to reach internal and external balance under a fixed exchange rate system. Section 17.5 presents and evaluates the so-called assignment problem, or how fiscal and monetary policies must be used to achieve both internal and external balance. Up to section 17.5b, the important assumption is made that domestic prices remain constant until full employment is reached. Section 17.6 then examines direct controls.

In the appendix, we derive the condition for equilibrium in the goods market, in the money market, and in the balance of payments. We then use these tools of analysis to examine how equilibrium can be reached in all three markets at the same time with exchange rate changes. Finally, we give a mathematical summary of these new tools of analysis.

17.2 Internal and External Balance with Expenditure-Changing and Expenditure-Switching Policies

In this section, we examine how a nation can simultaneously attain internal and external balance with expenditure-changing and expenditure-switching policies. For simplicity we assume a zero international capital flow (so that the balance of payments is equal to the nation's trade balance). We also assume that prices remain constant until aggregate demand begins to exceed the full-employment level of output. The assumption of no international capital flow is relaxed in the next section, and the assumption of no inflation until full employment is reached is relaxed in section 17.5d.

In Figure 17-1, the vertical axis measures the exchange rate (R). An increase in R refers to a devaluation and a decrease in R to a revaluation. The horizontal axis measures real domestic expenditures, or absorption (D). Besides domestic consumption and investments, D also includes government expenditures (which can be manipulated in the pursuit of fiscal policy).

The EE curve shows the various combinations of exchange rates and real domestic expenditures, or absorption, that result in external balance. The EE curve is positively inclined because a higher R (due to a devaluation) improves the nation's trade balance (if the Marshall-Lerner condition is satisfied) and must be matched by an increase in real domestic absorption (D) to induce imports to rise sufficiently to keep the trade balance in equilibrium and maintain external balance. For example, starting from point F on EE, an increase in R from R_2 to R_3 must be accompanied by an increase in D from D_2 to D_3 for the nation to maintain external balance (point J' on EE). A smaller increase in D will lead to a balance-of-trade surplus, while a larger increase in D will lead to a balance-of-trade deficit.

On the other hand, the YY curve shows the various combinations of exchange rates (R) and domestic absorption (D) that result in internal balance (i.e., full employment with price stability). The YY curve is negatively inclined because a lower R (due to a revaluation) worsens the trade balance and must be matched with larger domestic absorption (D) for the nation to remain in internal balance. For example, starting from point F on YY, a reduction in R from R_2 to R_1 must be accompanied by an increase in D from D_2 to D_3 to maintain internal balance (point J on YY). A smaller increase in D will lead to unemployment, while a larger increase in D will lead to excess aggregate demand and (demand-pull) inflation.

In Figure 17-1, we see that only at point F (i.e., at R_2 and D_2), defined where the EE and YY curves intersect, will the nation be simultaneously in external and internal balance. With points above the EE curve referring to external surpluses and points below referring to deficits, and with points below the YY curve referring to unemployment and points above referring to inflation, we can define the following four zones of external and internal imbalance (see the figure):

Zone I   External surplus and internal unemployment
Zone II   External surplus and internal inflation
Zone III   External deficit and internal inflation
Zone IV   External deficit and internal unemployment

From the figure we can now determine the combination of expenditure-changing and expenditure-switching policies required to reach point F. For example, starting from point C (deficit and unemployment), both the exchange rate (R) and domestic absorption (D) must be increased to reach point F. By increasing R only, the nation can reach either external balance (point C' on the EE curve) or, with a larger increase in R, internal balance (point C'' on the YY curve), but it cannot reach both simultaneously. Similarly, by increasing domestic absorption only, the nation can reach internal balance (point J on the YY curve), but this leaves an external deficit because the nation will be below the EE curve. Note that although both point C and point H are in zone IV, point C requires an increase in domestic absorption while point H requires a decrease in domestic absorption to reach point F (see the figure).

Even if the nation was already in internal balance, say, at point J on YY, a devaluation alone could get the nation to point J' on EE, but then the nation

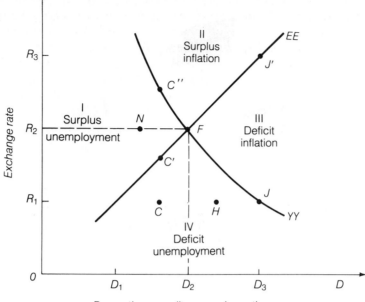

FIGURE 17-1. Swan Diagram

The vertical axis measures the exchange rate and the horizontal axis real domestic expenditures, or absorption. Points on the EE curve refer to external balance, with points to the left indicating external surplus and points to the right indicating external deficit. Points on the *YY* curve refer to internal balance, with points to the left indicating internal unemployment and points to the right indicating internal inflation. The crossing of the *EE* and *YY* curves defines the four zones of external and internal imbalance and helps us determine the appropriate policy mix to reach external and internal balance simultaneously at point *F*.

would face inflation. Thus, two policies are usually required to achieve two goals simultaneously. Only if the nation happens to be directly across from or directly above or below point F will the nation be able to reach point F with a single policy instrument. For example, from point N the nation will be able to reach point F simply by increasing domestic absorption from D_1 to D_2. The reason is that this increase in domestic absorption induces imports to rise by the precise amount required to eliminate the original surplus without any change in the exchange rate. But this is unusual. The precise combination of expenditure-changing and expenditure-switching policies for each of the four zones of Figure 17-1 is left as an end-of-chapter problem. Figure 17-1 is called a "Swan diagram" in honor of *Swan*, the Australian economist who introduced it.

Under the fixed exchange rate system that prevailed from the end of World War II until 1971, industrial nations were generally unwilling to devalue or revalue their currency even when in conditions of *fundamental* disequilibrium. Surplus nations enjoyed the prestige of the surplus and the accumulation of reserves. Deficit nations regarded devaluation as a sign of weakness and feared it might lead to *destabilizing* international capital movements (see Chapter 20). As a result, nations were left with only expenditure-changing policies to achieve internal and external balance. This presented a serious theoretical problem until Mundell showed how to use fiscal policy to achieve internal balance and monetary policy to achieve external balance. Thus, even without an expenditure-switching policy, nations could theoretically achieve both internal and external balance simultaneously.

17.3   Equilibrium in the Goods Market, in the Money Market, and in the Balance of Payments

In order to show how fiscal and monetary policies can be used to achieve both internal and external balance without changing the exchange rate, we use some tools of analysis that are sometimes presented in elementary macroeconomics. Even if this were not the case, these tools of analysis can easily be introduced here and rigorously derived in the appendix. The intuitive presentation here is adequate for our purposes, and there is no need to go to the appendix to understand what follows in the remainder of the chapter. The tools presented in this section will then be utilized in the next section to proceed with our analysis.

The new tools of analysis take the form of three curves: the *IS* curve, showing all points at which the goods market is in equilibrium; the *LM* curve, showing equilibrium in the money market; and the *FE* curve, showing equilibrium in the balance of payments. Short-term capital is now assumed to be responsive to international interest rate differentials. Indeed, it is this response that allows us to direct fiscal policy to achieve internal balance and monetary policy to achieve external balance.

The *IS*, *LM*, and *FE* curves are shown in Figure 17-2. The **IS curve** shows the various combinations of interest rates (r) and national income (Y) that result in equilibrium in the goods market. The goods market is in equilibrium whenever the quantity of goods and services demanded equals the quantity supplied. As pointed out in section 16.3b, this equilibrium condition in an open economy without a government sector occurs when the sum of the injections equals the sum of the leakages (equation 16.6):

$$I + X = S + M$$

The level of investment (*I*) is now taken to be inversely related to the rate of interest (r). That is, the lower the rate of interest (to borrow funds for investment purposes), the higher is the level of investment (and national income,

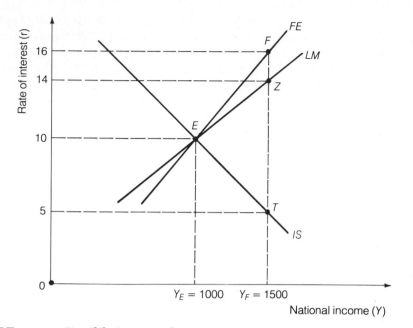

FIGURE 17-2.   Equilibrium in the Goods and Money Markets and in the Balance of Payments

The *IS, LM,* and *FE* curves show the various combinations of interest rates and national income at which the goods market, the money market, and the nation's balance of payments, respectively, are in equilibrium. The *IS* curve is negatively inclined because lower rates of interest (and higher investments) are associated with higher incomes (and higher savings and imports) for the quantities of goods and services demanded and supplied to remain equal. The *LM* curve is positively inclined because higher incomes (and a larger transaction demand for money) must be associated with higher interest rates (and a lower demand for speculative money balances) for the total quantity of money demanded to remain equal to the given supply of money. The *FE* curve is also positively inclined because higher incomes (and imports) require higher rates of interest (and capital inflows) for the nation to remain in balance-of-payments equilibrium. All markets are in equilibrium at point *E*, where the *IS, LM,* and *FE* curves cross at $r = 10\%$ and $Y_E = 1000$. However, $Y_E < Y_F$.

through the multiplier process). As in Chapter 16, the nation's exports (X) are taken to be exogenous, or independent of r and Y in the nation, but depend on national income levels abroad. Also as in Chapter 16, saving (S) and imports (M) are a positive function of, or increase with, the level of income of the nation (Y).

The interest rate of $r = 10\%$ and national income of $Y_E = 1000$ define one equilibrium point in the goods market (point E on the IS curve). The IS curve is negatively inclined because at lower interest rates, the level of investment is higher, so that the level of national income will also have to be higher to induce a higher level of saving and imports to once again be equal to the higher level of investment (and constant exports). For example, at $r = 5\%$, the level of investment will be higher than at $r = 10\%$, and the level of national income will have to be $Y_F = 1500$ (the full-employment level of income) to maintain equilibrium in the goods market (point T on the *IS* curve). At $Y < 1500$ (with $r = 5$ percent), there is unemployment, and at $Y > 1500$ there is inflation.

The ***LM* curve** shows the various combinations of interest rates (r) and national income (Y) at which the demand for money is equal to the given and fixed supply of money, so that the money market is in equilibrium. Money is demanded for transactions and speculative purposes. The **transaction demand for money** are the active working balances held for the purpose of making business payments as they become due. The transaction demand for money is positively related to the level of national income. That is, as the level of national income rises, the quantity demanded of active money balances increases (usually in the same proportion) because the volume of transactions is greater. The **speculative demand for money** arises from the desire to hold money balances instead of interest-bearing securities. The reason for the preference for money balances is to avoid the risk of falling security prices. Furthermore, money balances will allow the holder to take advantage of possible future (financial) investment opportunities. However, the higher the rate of interest, the smaller is the quantity of money demanded for speculative or liquidity purposes because the cost (interest foregone) of holding inactive money balances is greater.

At $r = 10\%$ and $Y_E = 1000$, the quantity of money demanded for transaction purposes plus the quantity demanded for speculative purposes equals the given supply of money, so that the money market is in equilibrium (point E on the *LM* curve). The *LM* curve is positively inclined because the higher the rate of interest (r), the smaller will be the quantity of money demanded for speculative purposes. The remaining larger supply of money available for transaction purposes will be held only at higher levels of national income. For example, at $r = 14\%$, the level of national income will have to be $Y_F = 1500$ (point Z on the *LM* curve) for the money market to remain in equilibrium. At $Y < 1500$ (and $r = 14\%$), the demand for money falls short of the supply of money; while at $Y > 1500$, there is an excess demand for money. To be noted is that the *LM* curve is derived on the assumption that the monetary authorities keep the nation's money supply fixed.

The ***FE* curve** shows the various combinations of interest rates (r) and national income (Y) at which the nation's balance of payments is in equilibrium *at a given exchange rate*. The balance of payments is in equilibrium when a trade deficit is matched by an equal net capital inflow, a trade surplus is matched by an equal net capital outflow, or a zero trade balance is associated with a zero *net* international capital flow. One point of external balance is given by point E on the *FE* curve at $r = 10\%$ *and* $Y_E = 1000$. The *FE* curve is positively inclined because higher rates of interest lead to greater capital inflows (or smaller outflows) and must be balanced with higher levels of national income and imports for the balance of payments to remain in equilibrium.

For example, at $r = 16\%$, the level of national income will have to be $Y_F = 1500$ for the nation's balance of payments to remain in equilibrium (point F on the *FE* curve). To the left of the *FE* curve, the nation has a balance-of-payments surplus and to the right a balance-of-payments deficit. The more responsive international short-term capital flows are to changes in interest rates, the flatter is the *FE* curve. The *FE* curve is drawn on the assumption of a constant exchange rate. A devaluation or depreciation of the nation's currency shifts the *FE* curve down, since the nation's trade balance improves, and so a lower interest rate and smaller capital inflows (or greater capital outflows) are required to keep the balance of payments in equilibrium. On the other hand, a revaluation or appreciation of the nation's currency shifts the *FE* curve upward. Since we are here assuming that the exchange rate is fixed, the *FE* curve does not shift.

In Figure 17-2, the only point at which the nation is simultaneously in equilibrium in the goods market, in the money market, and in the balance of payments is at point E, where the *IS*, *LM*, and *FE* curves cross. Note that this equilibrium point is associated with an income level of $Y_E = 1000$, which is below the full-employment level of national income of $Y_F = 1500$. Also to be noted is that the *FE* curve need not cross at the *IS-LM* intersection. In that case, the goods and money markets would be in equilibrium but not the balance of payments. However, a point such as E, where the nation is simultaneously in equilibrium in all three markets, is a convenient starting point to examine how the nation, by the appropriate combination of fiscal and monetary policies, can reach the full-employment level of national income (and remain in external balance) while keeping the exchange rate fixed.

17.4 Fiscal and Monetary Policies for Internal and External Balance with Fixed Exchange Rates

In this section, we first examine the effect of fiscal policy on the *IS* curve and the effect of monetary policy on the *LM* curve and then show how fiscal and monetary policies can be used to reach internal and external balance, starting from a position of external balance and unemployment (point E in Figure 17-2), alternatively starting from a condition of unemployment and deficit in the balance of payments, and finally assuming that capital flows are perfectly elastic.

17.4a Fiscal and Monetary Policies from External Balance and Unemployment

An expansionary fiscal policy in the form of an increase in government expenditures and/or a reduction in taxes (which increases private consumption) shifts the *IS* curve to the right, so that at each rate of interest the goods market is in equilibrium at a higher level of national income. On the other hand, a contractionary fiscal policy shifts the *IS* curve to the left. An easy monetary policy in the form of an increase in the nation's money supply shifts the *LM* curve to the right, indicating that at each rate of interest the level of national income must be higher to absorb the increase in the money supply. On the other hand, a tight monetary policy reduces the nation's money supply and shifts the *LM* curve to the left. Monetary and fiscal policies will not directly affect the *FE* curve, and since we are here assuming that the exchange rate is fixed, the *FE* curve remains unchanged (i.e., it does not shift).

Figure 17-3 shows that the nation of Figure 17-2 can reach the full-employment level of national income or internal balance and remains in external balance by combining the *expansionary fiscal policy* that shifts the *IS* curve to the right to *IS'* and the *tight monetary policy* that shifts the *LM* curve to the left to *LM'* in such a way that broken curves *IS'* and *LM'* intersect the unchanged *FE* curve at the full-employment level of income of $Y_F = 1500$ and

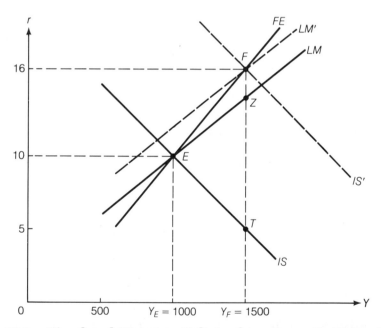

FIGURE 17-3. Fiscal and Monetary Policies from Domestic Unemployment and External Balance

Starting from point *E* with domestic unemployment and external balance, the nation can reach the full-employment level of national income of $Y_F = 1500$ with external balance by pursuing the expansionary fiscal policy that shifts the *IS* curve to the right to *IS'* and the tight monetary policy that shifts the *LM* curve to the left to *LM'*, while holding the exchange rate fixed. All three markets are then in equilibrium at point *F*, where curves *IS'* and *LM'* cross on the unchanged *FE* curve at $r = 16\%$ and $Y_F = 1500$.

$r = 16\%$ (point F). That is, the worsened trade balance resulting from the increase in national income (an induced rise in imports) is matched by an equal increase in capital inflows (or reduction in capital outflows) as the interest rate rises to $r = 16\%$ so as to keep the nation's balance of payments in equilibrium.

The nation could reach the full-employment level of national income by the *easy* monetary policy that shifts the *LM* curve to the right so as to cross the unchanged *IS* curve at point T. However, at point T, the interest rate would be $r = 5\%$ (which is lower than $r = 10\%$ at point E), and so the worsening trade balance as income rises would be accompanied by a smaller capital inflow (or larger capital outflow) as the interest rate falls, leaving a large balance-of-payments deficit. As an alternative, the nation could reach the full-employment level of national income by the expansionary fiscal policy that shifts the *IS* curve to the right so as to cross the *LM* curve at point Z. At point Z, the interest rate is higher than at point E, so that the worsened trade balance would be accompanied by an increased capital inflow (or reduced capital outflow). However, this increased capital inflow or reduced outflow is not sufficient to avoid a deficit in the nation's balance of payments (since point Z is to the right of the *FE* curve).

To reach the full-employment level of national income of $Y_F = 1500$ and also have equilibrium in its balance of payments, the nation should pursue the stronger expansionary policy that shifts the *IS* curve not to point Z on the *LM* curve but to point F on the *FE* curve (as in the figure). The tight monetary policy shown in the figure to shift the *LM* curve to *LM'*, while neutralizing part of the expansionary fiscal policy indicated by *IS'*, also causes the nation's interest rate to rise to $r = 16\%$, as required for external balance. Thus, two *conflicting* policies (an expansionary fiscal policy and a tight monetary policy) are required for this nation to reach internal and external balance simultaneously.

17.4b Fiscal and Monetary Policies from External Deficit and Unemployment

Figure 17-4 shows an initial situation where the *IS* and *LM* curves intersect at point E (as in Figures 17-2 and 17-3) but the *FE* curve does not. That is, the domestic economy is in equilibrium (with unemployment) at $r = 10\%$ and $Y_E = 1000$, but the nation faces a deficit in its balance of payments because point E is to the right of point B on the *FE* curve. That is, external balance requires the level of national income to be $Y = 700$ at $r = 10\%$ (point B on the *FE* curve). Since $Y_E = 1000$ instead, the nation has a deficit in its balance of payments equal to the excess level of national income of 300 $(1000 - 700)$ times the marginal propensity to import (*MPM*). If $MPM = 0.15$ (as in Chapter 16), the deficit in the nation's balance of payments is $(300)(0.15) = 45$. At $Y_E = 1000$, the interest rate would have to be $r = 13\%$ (point B' on the *FE* curve)

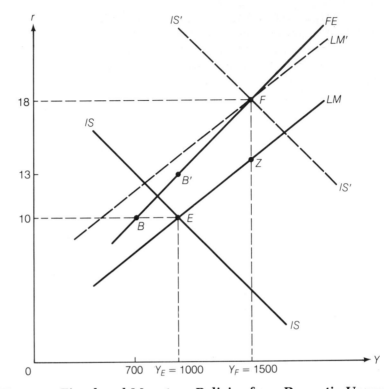

FIGURE 17-4. Fiscal and Monetary Policies from Domestic Unemployment and External Deficit

Starting from point E with domestic unemployment and external deficit, the nation can reach the full-employment level of national income of $Y_F = 1500$ with external balance by pursuing the expansionary fiscal policy that shifts the IS curve to the right to IS' and the tight monetary policy that shifts the LM curve to the left to LM', while keeping the exchange rate fixed. All three markets are then in equilibrium at point F, where curves IS' and LM' cross on the unchanged FE curve at $r = 18\%$ and $Y_F = 1500$. Because of the original external deficit, the nation now requires a higher interest rate than in Figure 17-3 to reach external and internal balance.

for capital inflows to be larger by 45 (or capital outflows smaller by 45) for the nation's balance of payments to be in equilibrium.

Starting from point E, where the domestic economy is in equilibrium with unemployment and a balance-of-payments deficit (of 45 if MPM = 0.15), the nation can reach the full-employment level of output of $Y_F = 1500$ with external balance by using the expansionary fiscal policy that shifts the IS curve to the right to IS' and the tight monetary policy that shifts the LM curve to the left to LM', so that the broken IS' and LM' curves cross the unchanged FE curve at $r = 18\%$ and $Y_F = 1500$ (point F in the figure). Note that in this case the interest rate must rise from $r = 10\%$ to $r = 18\%$ rather than to $r = 16\%$ (as in Figure 17-3) for the nation to also achieve external balance.

A diagram similar to Figure 17-4 could be drawn to show any other combination of internal and external disequilibrium to begin with, together with the appropriate mix of fiscal and monetary policies required to reach the full-employment level of national income with external balance and a fixed exchange rate. This type of analysis is essential not only to examine the workings of the fixed exchange rate system that prevailed from the end of World War II until 1971, but even today because most developing nations and some of the smaller developed nations peg or maintain their exchange rates fixed in terms of the currency of a large developed nation or SDRs. The analysis is also relevant for large developed nations to the extent that they manage their exchange rates by inducing international capital flows.

17.4c   Fiscal and Monetary Policies with Elastic Capital Flows

In Figure 17-5, we return to the initial equilibrium condition where all three markets are simultaneously in equilibrium at point E (as in Figures 17-2 and 17-3), but with perfectly elastic international capital flows (so that the FE curve is now horizontal at $r = 10\%$ prevailing on the world market). This means that a small nation can borrow or lend any desired amount at $r = 10\%$. The condition is particularly relevant for the small nations of Western Europe,

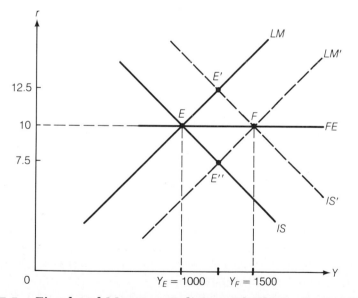

FIGURE 17-5.   Fiscal and Monetary Policies with Elastic Capital Flows

Starting from point E with domestic unemployment and external balance, and perfectly elastic capital flows and a fixed exchange rate, the nation can reach the full-employment level of national income of $Y_F = 1500$ with the expansionary fiscal policy that shifts the IS curve to the right to IS' and with the LM curve shifting to the right to LM' because of capital inflows which the nation is unable to neutralize.

where, as a result of quick and efficient communications and travel, capital markets are highly integrated through the Eurocurrency market. In this extreme case, a small nation can reach the full-employment level of national income with equilibrium in its balance of payments by the appropriate fiscal policy and without any monetary policy. Indeed, in this world of perfectly elastic international capital flows and fixed exchange rates, monetary policy would be entirely ineffective. This can be shown as follows.

Starting from point E, the small nation should pursue the expansionary fiscal policy that shifts the IS curve to the right to IS', so that it crosses the horizontal FE curve at point F, at $Y_F = 1500$. The intersection of the broken IS' curve with the unchanged LM curve at point E' indicates a tendency for the nation's interest rate to rise to $r = 12.5\%$. However, because international capital flows are infinitely elastic at $r = 10\%$ for this small nation, there is a capital *inflow* from abroad that increases the nation's money supply (as the foreign currency is exchanged for domestic currency) and shifts the LM curve to LM'. As a result, broken curves IS' and LM' intersect at point F on the horizontal FE curve, with $r = 10\%$ and $Y_F = 1500$, and the nation is simultaneously in internal and external balance. In this case, it will be impossible for the small nation to prevent its money supply from increasing until the LM curve has shifted all the way to LM'. Only then will capital inflows come to an end and the nation's money supply stabilize (at the level given by LM').

If this small nation attempted to reach point F by the easy monetary policy that shifts the LM curve to the right to LM', the interest rate would tend to fall to $r = 7.5\%$ (point E'' in the figure). This would lead to capital *outflows* which would reduce the nation's money supply to the original level and shift the LM' curve back to the original LM position. If the nation attempted to sterilize, or neutralize, the effect of these capital outflows on its money supply, it would soon exhaust all of its foreign exchange reserves, and the capital outflows would continue until the nation's money supply had been reduced to the original position given by the LM curve. Thus, monetary policy is completely ineffective in the case of elastic capital flows likely to be faced by many small nations in today's world of highly integrated capital markets.

Under a freely flexible exchange rate system, the opposite is the case. That is, fiscal policy is completely ineffective, while a small nation can reach internal and external balance simultaneously with the appropriate monetary policy only. This is assigned as a problem in section 17A.4 in the appendix, after the *IS-LM-FE* analysis is used to examine how any nation can reach the full-employment level of national income and external balance with monetary policy and flexible exchange rates.

17.5 The Policy Mix and Price Changes

In this section, we first examine the reasons for directing fiscal policy to achieve internal balance and monetary policy to achieve external balance. Then we evaluate the effectiveness of this policy mix and the problem created by allowing for cost-push inflation. Finally, we summarize the policy-mix experience of the United States and the other leading industrial nations during the postwar period.

17.5a   The Policy Mix and Internal and External Balance

In Figure 17-6, movements along the horizontal axis away from the origin refer to *expansionary* fiscal policy (i.e., higher government expenditures and/or lower taxes), while movements along the vertical axis away from the origin

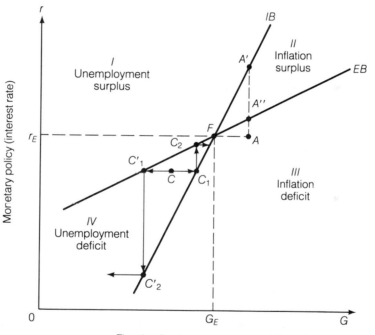

Fiscal policy (government expenditures)

FIGURE 17-6.   Effective Market Classification and the Policy Mix

Moving to the right on the horizontal axis refers to expansionary fiscal policy, while moving upward along the vertical axis refers to tight monetary policy and higher interest rates. The various combinations of fiscal and monetary policies that result in internal balance are given by the *IB* line, and those that result in external balance are given by the *EB* line. The *EB* line is flatter than the *IB* line because monetary policy also induces short-term international capital flows. Starting from point *C* in zone IV, the nation should use expansionary fiscal policy to reach point C_1 on the *IB* line and then tight monetary policy to reach point C_2 on the *EB* line, on its way to point *F*, where the nation is simultaneously in internal and external balance. If the nation did the opposite, it would move to point C_1' on the *EB* line and then to point C_2' on the *IB* line, thus moving farther and farther away from point *F*.

refer to *tight* monetary policy (i.e., reductions in the nation's **money supply** and increases in its interest rate).

The *IB* line in the figure shows the various combinations of fiscal and monetary policies that result in internal balance (i.e., full employment with price stability) in the nation. The *IB* line is positively inclined because an *expansionary* fiscal policy must be balanced by a *tight* monetary policy of a sufficient intensity to maintain internal balance. For example, starting at point *F* in Figure 17-6, an increase in government expenditures that moves the nation to point *A* leads to excess aggregate demand, or demand-pull inflation. This can be corrected or avoided by the tight monetary policy and higher interest rate that moves the nation to point *A'* on the *IB* line. A tight monetary policy that leaves the nation's interest rate below that indicated by point *A'* does not eliminate the excess aggregate demand entirely and leaves some inflationary pressure in the nation. On the other hand, a tighter monetary policy and higher interest rate that moves the nation above point *A'* not only eliminates the inflation created by the increase in government expenditures but leads to unemployment. Thus, to the right of and below the *IB* line there is inflation, and to the left and above there is unemployment.

On the other hand, the *EB* line shows the various combinations of fiscal and monetary policies that result in external balance (i.e., equilibrium in the nation's balance of payments). Starting from a point of external balance on the *EB* line, an expansionary fiscal policy stimulates national income and causes the nation's trade balance to worsen. This must be balanced with a tight monetary policy that increases the nation's interest rate sufficiently to increase capital inflows (or reduce capital outflows) for the nation to remain in external balance. For example, starting from point *F* on the *EB* line, an expansionary fiscal policy that moves the nation to point *A* leads to an external deficit, which can be corrected or avoided by the tight monetary policy and higher interest rate that moves the nation to point *A''* on the *EB* line. As a result, the *EB* line is also positively inclined. A monetary policy that moves the nation to a point below point *A''* leaves an external deficit, while a tighter monetary policy that moves the nation above point *A''* leads to an external surplus. Thus, to the right of and below the *EB* line there is an external deficit, and to the left and above there is an external surplus.

Only at point *F*, where the *IB* and *EB* lines cross, will the nation be at the same time in internal and external balance. The crossing of the *IB* and *EB* curves in Figure 17-6 defines the four zones of internal and external imbalance. Note that the *EB* line is flatter than the *IB* line. This is always the case whenever short-term international capital flows are responsive to international interest differentials. This can be explained as follows. Expansionary fiscal policy raises national income and increases the transaction demand for money in the nation. If monetary authorities increase the money supply sufficiently to satisfy this increased demand, the interest rate will remain unchanged. Under these circumstances, fiscal policy affects the level of national income but not the nation's interest rate. On the other hand, monetary policy operates by changing the money supply and the nation's interest rate. The change in the nation's interest rate affects the level of investment and national income (through the multiplier process) but also affects international capital flows. As a result, monetary policy is more effective than fiscal policy in achieving external balance, and so the *EB* line is flatter than the *IS* line.

Following the *principle of effective market classification*, monetary policy should be assigned to achieve external balance and fiscal policy to achieve internal balance. If the nation did the opposite, it would move farther and farther away from internal and external balance. For example, if from point *C* in Figure 17-6, indicating unemployment and a deficit (zone IV), the nation used a contractionary fiscal policy to eliminate the external deficit and moved to point C_1' on the *EB* line, and then used an easy monetary policy to eliminate unemployment and moved to point C_2' on the *IB* line, the nation would move farther and farther away from point *F*. On the other hand, if the nation appropriately used an expansionary fiscal policy to reach point C_1 on the *IB* line, and then used a tight monetary policy to reach point C_2 on the *EB* line, the nation would move closer and closer to point *F*. In fact, the nation could move from point *C* to point *F* in a single step by the appropriate mix of expansionary fiscal and contractionary monetary policies (as in the *IS-LM-FE* models in Figures 17-3 and 17-4). The nation could similarly reach point *F* from any other point of internal and external imbalance by the appropriate combination of fiscal and monetary policies. This is left as an end-of-chapter problem.

The more responsive international short-term capital flows are to interest rate differentials across nations, the flatter is the *EB* line in relation to the *IB* line. On the other hand, if short-term capital flows did not respond at all to interest differentials, the *EB* line would have the same slope (and coincide with) the *IB* line, so that no useful purpose could be served by separating fiscal and monetary policies as was done above. In that case, the nation could not achieve internal and external balance at the same time without also changing its exchange rate. This would bring us back to the case examined in section 17.2.

17.5b   Evaluation of the Policy Mix with Price Changes

The combination of fiscal policy to achieve internal balance and monetary policy to achieve external balance with a fixed exchange rate faces several criticisms. One of these is that short-term international capital flows may not respond as expected to international interest rate differentials, and their response may be inadequate or even erratic and of a once-and-for-all nature, rather than continuous (as assumed by Mundell). According to some economists, the use of monetary policy merely allows the nation to *finance* its deficit in the *short run*, unless the deficit nation continues to tighten its monetary policy over time. Long-run adjustment may very well require exchange rate changes, as pointed out in section 17.2.

Another criticism is that the government and monetary authorities do not know precisely what the effects of fiscal and monetary policies will be and that there are various lags—in recognition, policy selection, and implementation—before these policies begin to show results. Thus, the process of achieving internal and external balance described in section 17.5a using Figure 17-6 is grossly oversimplified. Furthermore, in a nation such as the United States, it is difficult to coordinate fiscal and monetary policies because fiscal policy is conducted by one branch of the government while monetary policy is determined by the semi-autonomous Federal Reserve Board. However, the nation may still be able to move closer and closer to internal and external balance on a step-by-step basis (as indicated by the arrows from point C in Figure 17-6) if fiscal authorities pursue only the objective of internal balance and disregard the external imbalance, and monetary authorities can be persuaded to pursue only the goal of external balance without regard to the effect that monetary policies have on the internal imbalance.

Another difficulty arises when we relax the assumption that prices remain constant until the full-employment level of national income is reached. In today's world, prices usually begin to rise well before full employment is attained and rise faster as the economy nears full employment. (The controversial inverse relationship, or trade-off, between the rate of unemployment and the rate of inflation is summarized by the **Phillips curve.**) Price increases resulting from upward shifts in aggregate demand at or before full employment are referred to as **demand-pull inflation.** On the other hand, price increases resulting from upward shifts in aggregate supply (arising from wages rising faster than productivity) are usually referred to as **cost-push inflation.** With price increases or inflation occurring even at less than full employment, the nation has at least three objectives: full employment, price stability, and equilibrium in the balance of payments, thus requiring three policies to achieve all three objectives completely. The nation might then have to use fiscal policy to achieve full employment, monetary policy to achieve price stability, and exchange rate changes to achieve external balance. In unusual circumstances, the government may also impose direct controls to achieve one or more of its objectives when other policies fail. These are examined in the next section.

Modern nations also have as a fourth objective an "adequate" rate of growth, which usually requires a low long-term interest rate to achieve. The nation may then attempt to "twist" the interest rate structure (i.e., change the relationship that would otherwise prevail between short-term and long-term interest rates), keeping long-term interest rates low (as required by the growth objective) and allowing higher short-term interest rates (as may be required for price stability or external balance). Monetary authorities may try to accomplish this by open market sales of treasury bills (to depress their price and raise short-term interest rates) and purchases of long-term bonds (to increase their price and lower long-term interest rates). There is some indication that the United States actually tried to do this during the early 1960s but without much success.

17.5c   Policy Mix in the Real World

If we look at the actual policy mix that the United States and the other leading nations actually followed during the fixed exchange rate period of the 1950s and 1960s, we find that most of these nations generally used fiscal and monetary policies to achieve internal balance and switched their aims only when the external imbalance was so serious that it could no longer be ignored. Even then, these nations seemed reluctant to use monetary policy to correct the external imbalance and instead preferred using direct controls over capital flows (discussed in the next section).

During the period of flexible but managed exchange rates since 1971, the leading nations seemed content to leave to the exchange rate the function of adjusting to external imbalances and generally directed fiscal and monetary policies to achieve internal balance. Indeed, during the oil crisis of the 1970s, nations even attempted to manage the exchange rate to support their efforts to contain domestic inflationary pressures. However, since financial markets were subject to rapidly changing expectations and adjusted much more quickly than real markets (e.g., exports and imports), there was a great deal of volatility and overshooting of exchange rates about equilibrium rates. As inflationary pressures subsided during the first half of the 1980s, the leading nations generally continued to direct fiscal and monetary policies to achieve internal balance but (except for the United States) sometimes switched monetary policy toward the external imbalance, as they attempted to manage their exchange rates.

By 1985, it became evident that the dollar was grossly overvalued and showed no tendency to drop in value as a result of purely market forces. The huge *budget* deficit of the United States kept real interest rates higher in the United States than abroad, and this attracted very large capital inflows to the United States, which resulted in a large overvaluation of the dollar, huge trade deficits, and calls for protectionism (see section 14.5). The United States then organized a coordinated international effort with the other four leading industrial nations (Germany, Japan, France, and England) to intervene in foreign exchange markets to correct the overvaluation of the dollar. The United States also advocated (in 1986) a simultaneous, equal, and coordinated reduction in interest rates in the leading nations so as to stimulate growth and reduce unemployment, without directly affecting trade and capital flows, (A more complete discussion of the functioning of the international monetary system during the postwar period is presented in chapter 20.)

17.6   Direct Controls

Direct controls to affect the nation's balance of payments can be subdivided into trade or **commercial controls** (such as tariffs, quotas, and other quantitative restrictions on the flow of international trade) and financial or **exchange controls** (such as restrictions on international capital flows and multiple exchange rates). In general, commercial controls are both less important and less acceptable than exchange controls. Direct control can also take the form of price and wage controls in an attempt to restrain domestic inflation when more general policies have failed.

17.6a   Commercial Controls

One of the most important commercial controls is the import tariff. This increases the price of imported goods to domestic consumers and stimulates the domestic production of import substitutes. On the other hand, export subsidies make domestic goods cheaper to foreigners and encourage the nation's exports. In general, an import tariff and an export subsidy of a given percentage applied across the board on all commodities are equivalent to a devaluation of the nation's currency by the same percentage. However, import duties and export subsidies are usually applied to specific items rather than across the board. As pointed out in Chapter 9, we can always find an import tariff equivalent to an import quota. Both are expenditure-switching policies, just as a devaluation, and both stimulate domestic production. In general, nations today are not allowed to impose new import tariffs and quotas except temporarily when in serious balance-of-payments difficulties.

Another commercial control, frequently applied today by developing nations but also by some developed nations, is the requirement that the importer make an advance deposit at a commercial bank of a sum equal to the value or a fraction of the value of the goods he wishes to import, for a period of time of varying duration, and at no interest. This has the effect of increasing the price of imports by the interest foregone on the sum deposited with the commercial bank, and also discourages imports. The nation can impose an advance deposit of a different amount and length of time on each type of commodity. Advance deposits are thus flexible devices, but they can be difficult and costly to administer. A deficit nation may also impose restrictions on foreign travel and tourist expenditures abroad. A more detailed discussion of commercial controls and their welfare effects is presented in Chapter 9.

17.6b   Exchange Controls

Turning to financial, or exchange, controls, we find that developed nations sometimes impose restrictions on capital exports when in balance-of-payments deficit and on capital imports when in surplus. For example, in 1963 the United Stated imposed the Interest Equalization Tax on portfolio capital exports and voluntary (later mandatory) restraints on direct investments abroad to reduce its balance-of-payments deficit. However, while this improved the U.S. capital account, it certainly reduced U.S. exports and the subsequent return flow of interest and profit on U.S. foreign investments, with an uncertain net effect on the overall balance of payments.

On the other hand, West Germany and Switzerland have sought to discourage capital imports by allowing lower or no interest on foreign deposits, in the face of large balance-of-payments surpluses and in order to insulate their economies from worldwide inflationary pressures. In the late 1960s and early 1970s, France and Belgium established a two-tier foreign exchange market and allowed the exchange rate on capital transactions to fall (i.e., the "financial franc" to appreciate) as a result of large capital inflows, while keeping the exchange rate higher on current account transactions (i.e., on the "commercial franc") in order not to discourage their exports and to encourage their imports. Italy has had a two-tier foreign exchange market since the collapse of the Bretton Woods system in 1971, even though it is administratively difficult and costly to keep the two markets apart.

In addition, developed nations facing balance-of-payments surpluses and huge capital inflows often engage in forward sales of their currency to increase the forward discount and discourage capital inflows. On the other hand, deficit nations often engage in forward purchases of their currency to increase the forward premium on their currency and discourage capital outflows. The funds for such forward purchases are often borrowed from surplus nations. For example, under the General Arrangements to Borrow, negotiated within the framework of the International Monetary Fund in 1962 (and renewed in 1979), the Group of Ten most important industrial nations (the United States, the United Kingdom, West Germany, Japan, France, Italy, Canada, the Netherlands, Belgium, and Sweden) agreed to lend up to $6 billion to any member of the group facing large short-term capital outflows (see section 20.4b).

Many developing nations today have **multiple exchange rates,** with higher exchange rates on luxury and nonessential imports and lower rates on essential imports. The higher exchange rate on luxuries and nonessentials makes these foreign products more expensive to domestic buyers and discourages their importation, while the lower exchange rate on essential imports (such as capital equipment deemed necessary for development) makes these products cheaper to domestic users and encourages their importation. An extreme form of exchange control requires exporters and other earners of foreign exchange to turn in all their exchange earnings to monetary authorities, who then proceed to allocate the available supply of foreign exchange to importers through import licenses and at various rates depending on how important the monetary authorities consider the particular import commodity. This, however, encourages black markets, transfer pricing (i.e., under- or overinvoicing—see section 12.5a), and corruption.

17.6c   Other Direct Controls and International Cooperation

Government authorities sometimes impose direct controls to achieve a purely domestic objective, such as inflation control, when more general policies have failed. For example, in 1971 the United States imposed price and wage controls, or an income policy, to control inflation. However, these price and wage controls were not very successful and were later repealed. From an efficiency point of view, monetary and fiscal policies and exchange rate changes are to be preferred to direct controls on the domestic economy and on international trade and finance. The reason being that direct controls often *interfere with* the operation of the market mechanism, while the more general expenditure-changing and expenditure-switching policies *work through* the market. Nevertheless, when these general policies take too long to operate, when their effect is uncertain, and when the problem affects only one sector of the economy, nations may turn to direct controls as temporary measures to achieve specific objectives. An example is the "voluntary" export quotas on Japanese cars negotiated by the United States in 1981.

In general, for direct controls and other policies to be effective, a great deal of international cooperation is required. For example, the imposition of an import quota by a nation may result in retaliation by the other nations affected (thus nullifying the effect of the quota) unless these nations were consulted and understand and agree to the need for such a temporary measure. The same is true for the exchange rate that a nation seeks to maintain. Similarly, an increase in the interest rate by a nation to attract more foreign capital may be completely neutralized if other nations increase their interest rates by the same amount so as to leave international interest rate differentials unchanged. A more detailed discussion of the process by which most direct controls were dismantled by developed nations after World War II under the leadership of the IMF and GATT is presented in Chapter 20.

Summary

1. Adjustment policies are needed because the automatic adjustment mechanisms discussed in the previous two chapters have unwanted side effects. The most important economic goals or objectives of nations are internal and external balance. Internal balance refers to full employment with price stability. External balance refers to equilibrium in the balance of payments. To reach these goals, nations have at their disposal expenditure-changing policies (i.e., fiscal and monetary policies) and expenditure-switching policies (devaluation or revaluation). According to the principle of effective market classifica-

tion, each policy should be paired or used for the objective toward which it is most effective.

2. In the Swan diagram, the positively inclined *EE* curve shows the various combinations of exchange rates and domestic absorption that result in external balance. To the left of *EE* we have external surpluses, and to the right external deficits. The negatively inclined *YY* curve shows the various combinations of exchange rates and domestic absorption that result in internal balance. To the left of *YY* there is unemployment, and to the right inflation. The intersection of the *EE* and *YY* curves defines the four possible combinations of external and internal imbalance and helps us determine the policy mix required to reach internal and external balance simultaneously (given by the point of intersection on the two curves).

3. The goods market is in equilibrium whenever the quantities of goods and services demanded and supplied are equal. The money market is in equilibrium whenever the quantity of money demanded for transactions and speculative purposes is equal to the given supply of money. The balance of payments is in equilibrium whenever a trade deficit is matched by an equal net capital inflow or a trade surplus is matched by an equal net capital outflow. The *IS*, *LM*, and *FE* curves show the various combinations of interest rates and national income at which the goods market, the money market, and the balance of payments, respectively, are in equilibrium. The *IS* curve is negatively inclined, while the *LM* and *FE* curves are usually positively inclined. The more responsive capital flows are to interest rate changes, the flatter is the *FE* curve. If the three curves intersect at the same point, the three markets are simultaneously in equilibrium at that point.

4. Expansionary fiscal policy shifts the *IS* curve to the right, and tight monetary policy shifts the *LM* curve to the left, but they leave the *FE* curve unchanged as long as the exchange rate is kept fixed. Starting from a condition of domestic unemployment and external balance, the nation can achieve internal and external balance simultaneously by the appropriate expansionary fiscal policy and tight monetary policy without changing the exchange rate. The same general policy mix is required for the nation to achieve internal and external balance starting from a condition of internal unemployment and external deficit. With perfectly elastic capital flows and a horizontal *FE* curve, monetary policy is completely ineffective, and the nation can reach internal and external balance with the appropriate fiscal policy alone, under a fixed exchange rate system.

5. The *IB* and *EB* lines show the various combinations of fiscal and monetary policies required for the nation to achieve internal and external balance, respectively. They are both positively inclined, but the *EB* curve is flatter, or more effective for achieving external balance, because monetary policy also induces short-term international capital flows. The nation should use fiscal policy to achieve internal balance and monetary policy to achieve external balance. (If the nation does the opposite, it will move farther and farther away from internal and external balance.) This policy mix, however, is relevant only in the short run. In the long run, external balance may require a change in the exchange rate. The existence of inflation at less than full employment adds price stability as a third objective. Growth may be a fourth objective. Then, four policy instruments are usually required. In the mid-1980s, the United States advocated a coordinated effort among the leading industrial nations to achieve these objectives.

6. Direct controls can be subdivided into commercial controls and exchange controls. Commercial controls refer to tariffs, quotas, advance deposits on imports, and other selective restrictions on the flow of international trade. Exchange controls include restrictions on international capital movements, forward market intervention, and multiple exchange rates. Other direct controls sometimes applied to reduce inflation when more general policies have failed are price and wage controls. In general, direct controls lead to inefficiencies because they frequently interfere with the operation of the market mechanism. For direct controls and other policies to be effective, international cooperation is often essential.

A Look Ahead

Chapter 18 presents some recent developments in the theory of balance-of-payments adjustments and exchange rate determination. These are the monetary and the portfolio balance approaches. The monetary approach argues that changes in the balance of payments and exchange rates are purely monetary phenomena that result directly from changes in the nation's money supply. The portfolio approach extends the analysis to include also the effect of changes in investors' holdings of domestic and foreign bonds. These are to be contrasted to the Keynesian view, which postulates that the money supply affects the nation's balance of payments and exchange rates only indirectly, through the effects of the money supply on the rate of interest. Chapter 19 evaluates and compares a fixed with a flexible exchange rate system. Chapter 20 examines the operation of the international monetary system over time.

Glossary

Internal balance   The objective of full employment with price stability; usually a nation's most important economic objective.

External balance   The objective of equilibrium in a nation's balance of payments.

Expenditure-changing policies   Fiscal and monetary policies directed at changing the level of aggregate demand of the nation.

Expenditure-switching policies   Devaluation or revaluation of a nation's currency directed at switching the nation's expenditures for foreign to domestic or from domestic to foreign goods.

Principle of effective market classification   Maintains that policy instruments should be paired or used for the objective toward which they are most effective.

IS curve   The negatively inclined curve showing the various combinations of interest rates and national income levels at which the goods market is in equilibrium.

LM curve   The usually positively inclined curve showing the various combinations of interest rates and national income levels at which the money market is in equilibrium.

Transaction demand for money   The demand for active money balances to carry on business transactions; varies directly with the level of national income and the volume of business transactions.

Speculative demand for money   The demand for inactive money balances in preference to interest-bearing securities (which can fall in price) so that one may take advantage of future investment opportunities. The speculative, or liquidity, demand for money varies inversely with the rate of interest.

FE curve   The usually positively inclined curve showing the various combinations of interest

rates and national income levels at which the nation's balance of payments is in equilibrium.

Phillips curve   The controversial inverse relationship, or trade-off, between unemployment and inflation.

Demand-pull inflation   Increases in the general price level resulting from upward shifts in the aggregate demand curve.

Cost-push inflation   Increases in the general price level resulting from upward shifts in the aggregate supply curve, due to wages rising faster than productivity.

Commercial controls   Tariffs, quotas, advance deposits on imports, and other restrictions imposed by a nation on international trade.

Exchange controls   Restrictions on international capital flows, official intervention in forward markets, multiple exchange rates, and other financial and monetary restrictions imposed by a nation.

Multiple exchange rates   The different exchange rates often enforced by developing nations for each class of imports depending on the usefulness of the various imports as determined by the government.

Questions for Review

1. Why do nations need policies to adjust balance-of-payments disequilibria? Which are the most important objectives of nations? What policies can nations utilize to achieve these objectives? How do these policies operate to achieve the intended objectives? What is meant by the principle of effective market classification? Why is it crucial that nations follow this principle?

2. What does the *EE* curve in the Swan diagram show? What does the *YY* curve show? What are the four zones of external and internal imbalance defined by these two curves? What does the point of intersection of the *EE* and *YY* curves show? How does the Swan diagram help us determine the policy mix to reach external and internal equilibrium simultaneously? Under what conditions does a

single policy instrument help a nation reach both external and internal balance simultaneously?

3. What does the *IS* curve show? Why is it negatively inclined? What does the *LM* curve show? What is meant by the transaction and speculative demands for money? Why is the *LM* curve usually positively inclined? What does the *FE* curve show? Why is it usually positively inclined? What determines the slope of the *FE* curve? Under what condition are the goods market, the money market, and the nation's balance of payments simultaneously in equilibrium? Is this necessarily the full-employment level of income?

4. What effects do expansionary and contractionary fiscal policies have on the *IS* curve? What effects do easy and tight monetary policies have on the *LM* curve? Do fiscal and monetary policies directly affect the *FE* curve? What would cause the *FE* curve to shift down? To shift up? How can fiscal and monetary policies be used to achieve full employment and external balance, starting from a condition of domestic unemployment and external balance? Why is monetary policy completely ineffective when international capital flows are perfectly elastic?

5. What does the *IB* curve show? Why is it positively inclined? What does the *EB* curve show? Why is it positively inclined? Why is the *EB* curve usually flatter than the *IB* curve? Why should the nation use fiscal policy to achieve internal balance and monetary policy to achieve external balance? What happens if the nation does the opposite? What are the criticisms faced by the above policy mix? What happens when the additional objectives of price stability and growth are recognized as separate goals?

6. What is meant by direct controls? Commercial controls? Exchange controls? Explain how the most important forms of commercial and exchange controls operate to affect the nation's balance of payments. What is the advantage and the disadvantage of direct controls? Why do direct controls to affect the nation's balance of payments require international cooperation to be effective?

Problems

1. Indicate for each of the twelve points in the following figure (similar to Figure 17-1) the expenditure-changing and expenditure-switching policies required to achieve external and internal balance simultaneously.

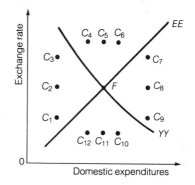

*2. From the following figure (similar to Figure 17-2):
   (a) Indicate whether the nation faces a deficit or surplus in its balance of payments at $Y_E = 1000$.
   (b) Determine the size of the deficit or surplus that the nation faces at $Y_E = 1000$ if its marginal propensity to import is $MPM = 0.15$.

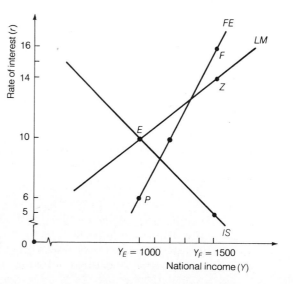

(c) Show how the nation can reach full employment with external balance by using the appropriate mix of fiscal and monetary policies.

*3. Draw on graph paper a figure similar to Figure 17-4, but without the broken curves IS' and LM' and assuming that the full-employment level of national income is $Y_F = 1200$. Indicate on your figure the appropriate mix of fiscal and monetary policies required for the nation to achieve simultaneously internal and external balance under a fixed exchange rate system.

4. Repeat problem 3 for the assumption that the full-employment level of national income is $Y_E = Y_F = 1000$.

5. Draw on graph paper a figure similar to Figure 17-2, but interchanging the labels of the LM and FE curves so that the FE curve is now flatter than the LM curve. (This is unusual but it will serve to bring out an important point.)

(a) Show on your graph the appropriate mix of fiscal and monetary policies required by the nation to reach full employment with external balance.

(b) How does the required policy mix in this case differ from that required for the case shown in Figure 17-2 discussed in section 17.4?

(c) What would happen if international capital flows were perfectly elastic?

6. Indicate for each of the twelve points in the following figure (similar to Figure 17-6) the appropriate direction of the fiscal and monetary policies required to reach point F in a single step.

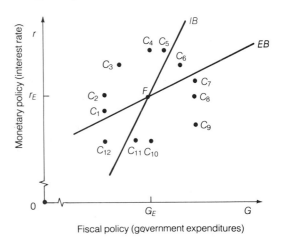

APPENDIX

In this appendix, we show how the IS, LM, and FE curves of Figure 17-2 are derived and the effects on these curves of fiscal policy, monetary policy, and a depreciation or devaluation of the nation's currency. We then examine how a nation can reach internal and external balance with monetary and fiscal policies under a flexible exchange rate system or with expenditure-switching policies. Finally, we summarize the analysis mathematically.

A17.1 Derivation of the *IS* Curve

Figure 17-7 consists of four panels labeled I to IV as we move clockwise, which are used to derive the IS curve in panel I. The IS curve shows the various combinations of interest rates (r) and levels of national income (Y) at which the goods market is in equilibrium in the sense that the leakage from the income stream in the form of domestic saving (S) plus imports (M) are equal to the injections into the income stream in the form of investment (I)

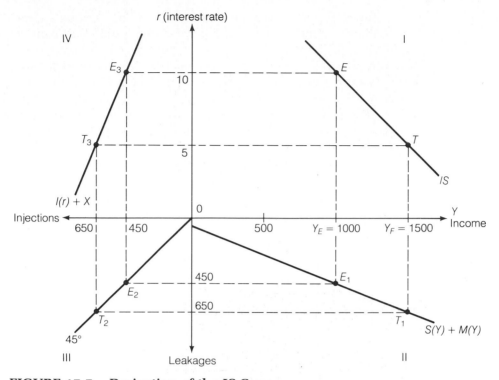

FIGURE 17-7.   Derivation of the *IS* Curve

Panel II shows the positive relationship between the leakages of saving plus imports and national income. The 45° line in panel III shows the equilibrium condition that leakages $(S+M)$ equal injections $(I+X)$. Panel IV shows the total injections function of investment (which is inversely related to the interest rate) and exogenous exports. The *IS* curve in panel I shows the various combinations of r and Y at which the goods market is in equilibrium (given by leakages equal injections). Expansionary fiscal policy shifts the total injections function to the left by the increase in government expenditures (G) and shifts the *IS* curve to the right by the increase in G times the open economy multiplier (k'). A depreciation or devaluation shifts the total leakages function up by the reduction in M at each Y, shifts the total injections function to the left by the increase in X, and shifts the *IS* function to the right by the increase in $X-M$ times k'.

plus exports (X), and assuming for the moment the absence of a government sector.

In panel II, the saving plus import function $[S(Y)+M(Y)]$ from the top panel of Figure 16-3 is plotted showing the positive relationship between total leakages and the level of national income. The 45° line in panel III shows the equilibrium condition that leakages $(S+M)$ equal injections $(I+X)$. Panel IV shows total injections in the form of the investment function (where investment is inversely related to the rate of interest) plus the exogenous export function $[I(r)+X]$. The investment function is usually referred to as the marginal efficiency of investment schedule. For example, at $Y_E = 1000$, $S + M = 450 = I + X$ at $r = 10\%$, so that we derive point E in panel I. Similarly, at $Y_F = 1500$, $S + M = 650 = I + X$ at $r = 5\%$, so that we derive point T in panel I. Assuming that the IS curve is a straight line, we can derive the IS curve by joining point E and point T in panel I. This is the IS curve in Figure 17-2.

The inclusion of government expenditures (G) will lead to a total injections function of $I(r) + X + G$ which is to the left of the total injections function shown in panel IV by the amount of G, and an IS function which is to the right of the one shown in panel I by the amount of G times the open economy multiplier. The equilibrium condition that total injections equal total leakages is then:

$$I + X + G = S + M \qquad (17A\text{-}1)$$

The inclusion of government expenditures (G) will allow us to use the diagram to analyze the effect of fiscal policy on the IS curve. Taxes were not introduced as a leakage by assuming that G is for fiscal policies purposes only.

The diagram can also be used to examine the effect of a depreciation or devaluation on the IS curve. Specifically, a depreciation or devaluation of the nation's currency will reduce its imports at each level of income, so that the total leakages function in panel II shifts up by the reduction of imports at each level of income. At the same time, the nation's exports will increase, shifting the total injections function in Panel IV to the left by the increase in exports. The IS function in panel I will then shift to the right by the improvement in the nation's trade balance ($X - M$) times the nation's open economy multiplier.

Problem   Trace (i.e., pencil in) in each of the four panels of figure 17-7 the effect of an expansionary fiscal policy that increases government expenditures (G) from 0 to 50. Assume that the government changes the money supply as it pursues this expansionary fiscal policy in such a way as to keep the interest rate unchanged. Assume also that the open economy multiplier for the nation is $k' = 2.5$ (as in section 16.3d under the assumption that the nation is small enough that there are no foreign repercussions).

A17.2   Derivation of the *LM* Curve

The four panels of Figure 17-8 are used to derive the LM curve in panel I. The LM curve shows the various combinations of interest rates (r) and levels of national income (Y) at which the money market is in equilibrium in the sense that the quantity of money demanded for transaction and speculative purposes is equal to the given and fixed supply of money.

Panel II shows the positive relationship between the transaction demand for money (MT) and national income (with MT a constant fraction of Y). Panel

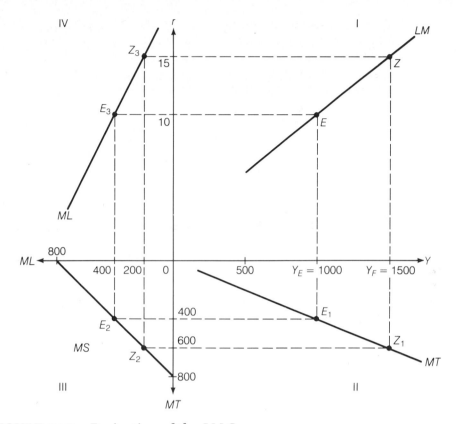

FIGURE 17-8. Derivation of the *LM* Curve

Panel II shows the positive relationship between the transaction demand for money (*MT*) and national income (*Y*). Panel III shows how much of the assumed total supply of money of *MS* = 800 is held for transaction purposes and how much is left for speculative purposes. Panel IV shows the speculative, or liquidity, demand for money (*ML*) as a decreasing function of the rate of interest. The *LM* curve in panel I shows the various combinations of r and Y at which the money market is in equilibrium (given by the equality of the total demand for money to the fixed supply of money). Easy monetary policy shifts the *MS* curve down in panel III and the *LM* curve to the right in panel I in order to reestablish equilibrium in the money market. A depreciation or devaluation shifts the *MT* curve down in panel II and the *LM* curve to the left in panel I.

III shows how much of the assumed total supply of money of *MS* = 800 is held for transaction purposes and how much is left for speculative purposes. Panel IV shows the speculative, or liquidity, demand for money (*ML*) as a decreasing function of the rate of interest. That is, the higher the rate of interest or the opportunity cost of holding money balances, the smaller is the quantity demanded for speculative, or liquidity, purposes.

For example, at $Y_E = 1000$, *MT* = 400, leaving another 400 (out of *MS* = 800) to be held for liquidity purposes at $r = 10\%$. This defines point E in panel I. Similarly, at $Y_F = 1500$, $MT = 600$, leaving 200 of the fixed money supply of $MS = 800$ to be held for liquidity purposes at $r = 15\%$. This defines point Z in panel I. Joining points E and Z in panel I, we derive the LM curve (on the assumption that the LM curve is a straight line). This is the LM curve in Figure 17-2.

An increase in the supply of money as a result of easy monetary policy will shift the MS curve down in panel III and shift the LM curve to the right in panel I until equilibrium in the money market is reestablished. On the other hand, a depreciation or devaluation of the nation's currency will increase domestic prices and the transaction demand for money (i.e., MT shifts down in panel II) and shift the LM curve to the left in panel I until equilibrium in the money market is reestablished.

Problem   Starting from point E on the LM curve in panel I, trace (i.e., pencil in) in each of the four panels of Figure 17-8 the effect of (a) an easy monetary policy that increases the nation's money supply by 100, on the assumption that the entire increase in the money supply will be held for transaction purposes, and (b) a depreciation that shifts the MT function down by 200 in panel II on the assumption that monetary authorities keep MS at 800. (c) What happens if instead monetary authorities increase MS by 200 to $MS = 1000$ in part (b)?

A17.3   Derivation of the *FE* Curve

The four panels of Figure 17-9 are used to derive the FE curve in panel I. The FE curve shows the various combinations of interest rate and national income at which the nation's balance of payments is in equilibrium.

In panel II, the trade balance $(X - M)$ from the bottom panel of Figure 16-3 is plotted as a *decreasing* function of national income. The 45° line in panel III shows the external equilibrium condition that a balance-of-trade deficit be matched by an equal net short-term *capital inflow* or a balance-of-trade surplus be equal to a net short-term *capital outflow*. Panel IV shows net short-term capital inflows (SC) as an increasing function of the interest rate in the nation (and interest differential in favor of the nation on the assumption of constant interest rates abroad). For example, at $Y_E = 1000$, $X - M = 0 = SC$ at $r = 10\%$. This defines point E in panel I. Similarly, at $Y_F = 1500$, $X - M = -75$ and $SC = +75$ (so that $X - M + SC = 0$) at $r = 16\%$. This defines point F in panel I. By joining points E and F, we derive the FE curve in panel I and in Figure 17-2. Note that at $Y < Y_E$, $X - M > 0$ and $SC < 0$ (i.e., there is a net capital outflow from the nation), so that $X - M + SC = 0$ and we get another point on the FE curve to the left of point E.

The FE curve is drawn on the assumption that the exchange rate is fixed.

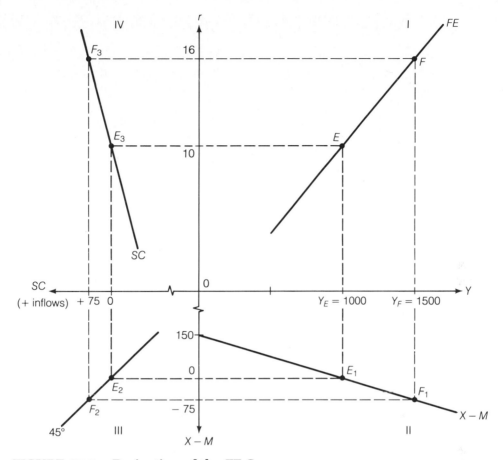

FIGURE 17-9.   Derivation of the *FE* Curve

Panel II shows the negative relationship between the trade balance $(X - M)$ and national income (from the bottom panel of Figure 16-3). The 45° line in panel III shows the external equilibrium condition that a balance-of-trade deficit be matched by an equal net short-term capital inflow (*SC*). Panel IV shows *SC* as an increasing function of r. The *FE* curve shows the various combinations of r and Y for external balance. A depreciation or devaluation shifts the $X - M$ function up at each Y so that a smaller *SC* at a lower r is needed to maintain external balance (i.e., the *FE* curve shifts down).

A depreciation or devaluation from a condition of less than full employment in the nation shifts the $X - M$ function up and improves the nation's trade balance at each level of income, so that a smaller net short-term capital inflow (or even an outflow) is needed at a lower r to keep the balance of payments in equilibrium (i.e., the *FE* curve shifts down in panel I).

Problem   Starting from point E on the *FE* curve in panel I, trace (i.e., pencil in) in each of the four panels of Figure 17-9 the effect of a depreciation or devaluation that shifts the $X - M$ function up by 50 in panel II.

A17.4   The *IS-LM-FE* Model with Exchange Rate Changes

In this section, we utilize the *IS-LM-FE* model to examine how equilibrium in all three markets can be reached simultaneously with monetary policy under a freely flexible exchange rate system or with exchange rate changes.

We start from point E in Figure 17-10, where all three markets are in equilibrium with external balance and unemployment (exactly as in Figure 17-2). The government could use the easy monetary policy that shifts the *LM* curve to the right to *LM'* so as to intersect the *IS* curve at point T, at $Y_F = 1500$ and $r = 5\%$. Since point T is to the right of the *FE* curve, the nation has an external deficit (because Y is higher and r is lower than at point E).

Under a flexible exchange rate system, the nation's currency depreciates and the *FE* curve shifts to the right. At the same time, the depreciation improves the nation's trade balance (if the Marshall-Lerner condition is satisfied), and the *IS* curve also shifts to the right. The depreciation will also increase domestic prices and the transaction demand for money and shift the *LM'* curve to the left (as the *real* money supply declines). Equilibrium will be

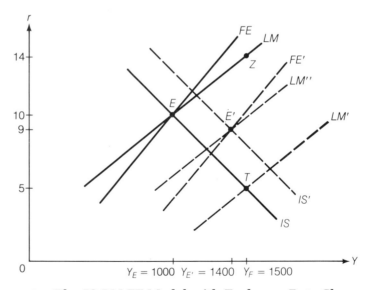

FIGURE 17-10.   The *IS-LM-FE* Model with Exchange Rate Changes

Starting from point E, where all three markets are in equilibrium with an external deficit and domestic unemployment, the nation could use easy monetary policy to shift the *LM* curve to the right to *LM'* so as to cross the *IS* curve at point T and reach the full-employment level of income of $Y_F = 1500$. However, since point T is to the right of the *FE* curve, the nation has an external deficit. Under a flexible exchange rate system, the nation's currency depreciates and shifts the *FE* and *IS* curves to the right and the *LM'* curve to the left until curves *FE'*, *IS'*, and *LM''* cross at point E', with $Y_{E'} = 1400$. The process can be repeated with additional doses of easy monetary policy until all three markets are in equilibrium at $Y_F = 1500$.

reestablished in all three markets where curves IS' and LM'' intersect on the FE' curve at a point such as E', with $Y_{E'} = 1400$ and $r = 9\%$. The process can be repeated with additional doses of easy monetary policy until all three markets are in equilibrium at the full-employment level of national income of $Y_F = 1500$. Note that with flexible exchange rates, equilibrium in all three markets will always be on the FE curve.

The analysis is analogous if, in order to reach the full-employment level of income from point E, the nation uses the expansionary fiscal policy that shifts the IS curve to the right so as to cross the LM curve at point Z. Since point Z is to the right of the FE curve, the nation will have a deficit in its balance of payments. Therefore, the currency depreciates, and this induces a shift in all the curves until the IS and the LM curves intersect on the FE curve and all three markets are simultaneously in equilibrium. Note, however, that when the nation starts with an easy monetary policy rather than expansionary fiscal policy, it ends up with a lower interest rate, which is a stimulus to its long-run growth.

What is important is that when the nation uses expenditure-changing (i.e., monetary and/or fiscal) policies to achieve internal balance, it will have to allow the exchange rate to vary or engage in expenditure-switching policies to achieve external balance simultaneously. We are then back to the analysis in section 17.2 and the Swan diagram of Figure 17-1. Note that there is an inconsistency between the LM and FE curves, since the former is based on the *stock* of money and the latter on the *flow* of capital.

Problem Starting from point E in Figure 17-5, explain why, under perfectly elastic capital flows, fiscal policy is completely ineffective in reaching full employment with external balance under a freely flexible exchange rate system.

A17.5 Mathematical Summary

The above discussion can be summarized mathematically in terms of the following three equations, respectively, the equilibrium condition in the goods market, in the money market, and in the balance of payments, in terms of the three unknowns of the system, which are the level of national income (Y), the rate of interest (r), and the exchange rate (R).

As pointed out in section A17.1, equilibrium in the goods market for an open economy with a government sector occurs where the sum of the injections of investment (I) plus government expenditures (G^*, used as a fiscal policy variable) plus exports (X) equals the sum of the leakages of saving (S) plus imports (M):

$$I(\overset{-}{r}) + G^* + X(\overset{+}{R}) = S(\overset{+}{Y}) + M(\overset{+}{Y},\overset{-}{R}) \tag{17A-1}$$

where the variables in parentheses denote functional independence and the positive or negative sign above the variables refers to a direct or inverse functional relationship. For example, $I(\bar{r})$ means that investment is inversely related to or is a decreasing function of the rate of interest.

For the money market to be in equilibrium, the transaction demand for money (MT) plus the speculative, or liquidity, demand for money (ML) must be equal to the money supply, which is determined by the monetary authorities and is used as a monetary policy variable (MS*):

$$MT(\overset{+}{Y},\overset{+}{R}) + ML(\overset{-}{r}) = MS^* \tag{17A-2}$$

Finally, for the balance of payments to be in equilibrium, the balance on net short-term international capital flows (SC) must be equal in absolute amount and opposite in sign to the trade balance (TB):

$$SC(\overset{+}{r}) = TB(\overset{-}{Y},\overset{+}{R}) \tag{17A-3}$$

Given the value of policy variables G^* and MS^*, we can determine the equilibrium value of Y, r, and R. Graphically, this corresponds to a point such as point E in Figure 17-10, where the IS, LM, and FE curves intersect and the three markets are simultaneously in equilibrium.

Since G^* appears only in equation 17A-1, fiscal policy affects only the goods market and shifts only the IS curve. Since MS^* appears only in equation 17A-2, monetary policy affects only the money market and shifts the LM curve only. Since R appears in all three equations, a change in the exchange rate affects all three markets and shifts all three curves (as indicated in section 17A.4).

Problem Use the above three equations to trace the effects of (a) a contractionary fiscal policy, (b) a tight monetary policy, and (c) an appreciation or revaluation of the nation's currency.

Selected Bibliography

For a problem-solving approach to the topics covered in this chapter, see:

- D. Salvatore, *Theory and Problems of International Economics*, 2nd ed. (New York: McGraw-Hill, 1984), ch. 10.

The classics on the theory of economic policy in general and balance-of-payments adjustment policies in particular are:

- Jan Tinbergen, *On the Theory of Economic Policy* (Amsterdam: North-Holland, 1952).
- J. E. Meade, *The Theory of International Eco-* *nomic Policy. Vol. I, The Balance of Payments* (London: Oxford University Press, 1951), parts 3 and 4.
- T. Swan, "Longer-Run Problems of the Balance of Payments," in H. W. Arndt and W. M. Corden, *The Australian Economy: A Volume of Readings* (Melbourne: Cheshire Press, 1955). Reprinted in R. E. Caves and H. G. Johnson, *Readings in International Economics* (Homewood, Ill.: Irwin, 1968).

The classics on internal and external balance in a world with money are:

- R. A. Mundell, "The Appropriate Use of

Monetary and Fiscal Policy for Internal and External Stability," *International Monetary Fund Staff Papers,* March 1962. Reprinted in R. A. Mundell, *International Economics* (New York: Macmillan, 1968).
• M. J. Fleming, "Domestic Financial Policies under Fixed and under Floating Exchange Rates," *International Monetary Fund Staff Papers,* November 1962. Reprinted in R. N. Cooper, *International Finance* (Baltimore: Penguin, 1969).

For an evaluation and extension of the *IS-LM-FE* model, see:
• R. Mundell, *International Economics* (New York: Macmillan, 1968).
• R. Stern, *The Balance of Payments: Theory and Economic Policy* (Chicago: Aldine, 1973).
• M. Mussa, "Macroeconomic Interdependence and the Exchange Rate Regime," in R. Dornbusch and J. A. Frenkel, Eds., *International Economic Policy* (Baltimore: John Hopkins, 1979).
• R. C. Bryant, *Money and Monetary Policy in Interdependent Nations* (Washington, D.C.: Brookings Institution, 1980).
• P. B. Kenen, "Macroeconomic Theory and Policy: How the Closed Economy Was Opened," in R. W. Jones and P. B. Kenen, Eds., *Handbook of International Economics,* Vol. II (Amsterdam: North-Holland, 1985).
• R. C. Marston, "Stabilization Policies in Open Economies," in R. W. Jones and P. B. Kenen, Eds., *Handbook of International Economics,* Vol. II (Amsterdam: North-Holland, 1985).

The experience with fiscal, monetary, and exchange rate policies to achieve internal and external balance is examined in:
• M. Michaely, *The Responsiveness of Demand Policies to Balance of Payments: The Postwar Patterns* (New York: NBER, 1971).
• S. W. Black, "The Relationship Between Exchange Rate Policy and Monetary Policy in Ten Industrial Countries," in J. F. O. Bilson and R. C. Marston, Eds., *Exchange Rate Theory and Practice* (Chicago: University of Chicago Press, 1984).
• L. O. Laney, "The Strong Dollar, the Current Account, and Federal Deficits: Cause and Effect," *Economic Review,* Federal Reserve Bank of Dallas, January 1984.

For an evaluation of and information on direct controls, see:
• R. Stern, "Tariffs and Other Measures of Trade Control: A Survey of Recent Developments," *Journal of Economic Literature,* March 1973.
• A. Gutowski, "Flexible Exchange Rates vs. Controls," in F. Machlup, A. Gutowski, and F. A. Lutz, *International Monetary Problems* (Washington, D.C.: American Enterprise Institute, 1972).
• International Monetary Fund, *Annual Report on Exchange Arrangements and Exchange Restrictions* (Washington, D.C.: IMF, Annual).
• J. N. Bhagwati, *Anatomy and Consequences of Exchange Control Regimes* (Cambridge, Mass.: Ballinger, 1978).

CHAPTER 18

The Monetary and Portfolio Balance Approaches

18.1 Introduction

In Chapter 15, we examined the *elasticity approach* to balance-of-payments adjustment. In Chapter 16, we examined the *income-multiplier approach* and the *absorption approach*. In Chapter 17, we analyzed the *policy approach*. While each of these approaches stressed a particular aspect of the adjustment process, they were not mutually exclusive and could be and were to some extent reconciled. Starting toward the end of the 1960s and becoming fully developed in the 1970s, a completely different approach was developed, primarily by *Mundell* and *Johnson*, called the *monetary approach* to the balance of payments. During the 1970s, still another approach called the *portfolio balance approach* was developed, along the same general lines as the monetary approach. In this chapter we will first examine the monetary approach in detail and then discuss the portfolio approach.

The new monetary approach is an extension of domestic monetarism (stemming from the Chicago school) to the international economy in that it views the balance of payments as an *essentially monetary phenomenon*. That is, money plays the crucial role in the long run both as a disturbance and adjustment in the nation's balance of payments. The new monetary approach is often presented as a superior alternative to the traditional approaches and frequently leads to diametrically opposing predictions and policy implications from those of the traditional approaches.

According to the **monetary approach to the balance of payments,** a deficit in a nation's balance of payments *results* from an excess in the nation's money supply over its demand for money. The excess supply of money flows abroad and represents the deficit in the nation's balance of payments under a fixed exchange rate system. On the other hand, a balance of payments surplus arises from an excess demand for money which is satisfied by an inflow of money from abroad. After the excess supply of money has flowed out of the nation or the nation's excess demand for money has been satisfied by an inflow of money from abroad, the deficit or surplus in the nation's balance of payments is eliminated. (The monetary approach under a flexible exchange rate system is discussed in section 18.4.) Thus, according to the monetary approach, there is a long-run automatic tendency toward equilibrium in the balance of payments.

The monetary approach views the balance of payments from "the bottom up" rather than from "top to bottom" as in the more traditional approaches. That is, the monetary approach concentrates attention on the *official settlements balance,* discussed in Chapter 14, and on the effect that a change in such a balance has on the nation's monetary base and money supply. In doing so, the monetary approach lumps together all the "above-the-line items" in the current and capital accounts of the balance-of-payments statement without analyzing or explaining them. To some economists, this represents a dangerous oversimplification. However, the ranks of those who subscribe to the monetary approach are growing, and this new approach does seem to offer at times a better explanation of some important economic events, such as the worldwide inflation of the 1970s, than the traditional approaches.

In section 18.2, the monetary approach is analyzed under a system of fixed exchange rates. Section 18.3 presents some of the policy implications of this new approach, and examines the causes of inflation and the mechanism by which inflation is transmitted internationally. In section 18.4, we analyze the monetary approach under a flexible exchange rate system. Section 18.5 presents the portfolio balance approach and examines exchange rate dynamics. Finally, section 18.6 presents an evaluation of the monetary and portfolio approaches and draws upon some empirical tests on their predictive accuracy and usefulness. The appendix presents a formal mathematical model of the monetary and the portfolio approaches which summarize the more descriptive analysis of the chapter. This is suggested only for the more advanced student.

18.2 The Monetary Approach Under Fixed Exchange Rates

In this section, we examine the causes of external imbalances according to the monetary approach and the process of adjustment under a fixed exchange rate system. We then examine the reason why, according to the monetary approach, non-reserve-currency countries have no control over their money supply in the long run under a fixed exchange rate system, while a reserve-currency country, such as the United States, does retain dominant control over its money supply.

18.2a Causes and Adjustment of External Imbalances

The monetary approach begins by postulating that the demand for *nominal* money balances is positively related to the level of *nominal* national income and is stable in the long run. This can be seen by starting with equation *MV* = *PQ*, representing the quantity theory of money discussed in Chapter 15. In this equation (sometimes called the equation of exchange), *V* is the velocity of circulation of money, *P* is the general price index, and *Q* is real output. Defining $1/V = k$ and $Q = Y$, we obtain the equation representing the **demand for money** as:

$$M_d = kPY \qquad (18\text{-}1)$$

where M_d = quantity demanded of nominal money balances
      k = desired ratio of nominal money balances to nominal national income
      P = domestic price level
      Y = real output

In equation 18-1, *PY* is the nominal national income or output (GNP). This is assumed to be at or to tend toward full employment in the long run. With *k* constant, M_d is a stable and positive function of the domestic price level and real national income. For example, if GNP = *PY* = \$1 billion and *V* = 5 (so that *k* = 1/*V* = 1/5), then M_d = (1/5) *PY* = (1/5)(\$1 billion) = \$200 million. Though not included in equation 18-1, the demand for money is also related, but inversely, to the interest rate (*r*) or opportunity cost of holding inactive money balances rather than interest-bearing securities. Thus, M_d is directly related to *PY* and inversely related to *r*. (This more complete money demand function is formally presented in the appendix to this chapter.) To simplify the analysis, however, we assume for now that M_d is related only to *PY*, or the nation's nominal GNP.

On the other hand, the nation's **supply of money** is given by:

$$M_s = m(D + F) \qquad (18\text{-}2)$$

where M_s = the nation's total money supply
      D = domestic component of the nation's monetary base
      F = international or foreign component of the nation's monetary base
      m = money multiplier

The domestic component of the nation's monetary base (D) is the domestic credit created by the nation's monetary authorities or the domestic assets backing the nation's money supply. The international or foreign component of the nation's money supply (F) refers to the international reserves of the nation, which can be increased or decreased through balance-of-payments surpluses or deficits, respectively. $D+F$ is called the **monetary base** of the nation, or "high-powered money." Under a fractional-reserve banking system, (such as we have today), each new dollar of D or F deposited in any commercial bank results in an increase in the nation's money supply by a multiple of $1. This is the money multiplier, m, in equation 18-2.

For example, a new deposit of $1 in a commercial bank allows the bank to lend (i.e., to create demand deposits for borrowers of) $0.80 if the legal reserve requirement (LRR) is 20 percent. The $0.80 lent by the first bank is usually used by the borrower to make a payment and ends up as a deposit in another bank of the system, which proceeds to lend 80 percent of it ($0.64), while retaining 20 percent ($0.16) as reserve. The process continues until the original $1 deposit has become the reserve base of a total of $1.00 + $0.80 + $0.64 + \ . \ . \ . \ = \$5$ in demand deposits (which are part of the nation's total money supply). The figure of $5 is obtained by dividing the original deposit of $1 by the legal reserve requirement of 20 percent, or 0.2. That is, $\$1/0.2 = 5 = m$. However, due to excess reserves and leakages, the real world multiplier is likely to be smaller. In what follows we assume for simplicity that the money multiplier (m) is constant over time.

Starting from a condition of equilibrium where $M_d = M_s$, an increase in the demand for money (resulting, say, from a once-and-for-all increase in the nation's GNP) can be satisfied either by an increase in the nation's domestic monetary base (D) or by an inflow of international reserves, or balance of payments surplus (F). If the nation's monetary authorities do not increase D, the excess demand for money will be satisfied by an increase in F. On the other hand, an increase in the domestic component of the nation's monetary base (D) and money supply (M_s), in the face of unchanged money demand (M_d), flows out of the nation and leads to a fall in F (a deficit in the nation's balance of payments). Thus, a surplus in the nation's balance of payments results from an excess in the stock of money demanded that is not satisfied by an increase in the domestic component of the nation's monetary base, while a deficit in the nation's balance of payments results from an excess in the stock of the money supply of the nation that is not eliminated by the nation's monetary authorities but is corrected by an outflow of reserves.

For example, an increase in the nation's GNP from $1 billion to $1.1 billion increases M_d from $200 million (1/5 of $1 billion) to $220 million (1/5 of $1.1 billion). If the nation's monetary authorities keep D constant, F will ultimately have to increase (a surplus in the nation's balance of payments) by $4 million, so that the nation's money supply also increases by $20 million (the $4 million increase in F times the money multiplier of $m = 5$). Such a balance-of-payments surplus could be generated from a surplus in the current account or the capital account of the nation, as explained in section 18.2b. At this point, all that is important is that the excess demand for money will lead to a balance-of-payments surplus that increases M_s by the same amount. On the other hand, an excess in the stock of money supplied will lead to an outflow of reserves (a balance-of-payments deficit) sufficient to eliminate the excess supply of money in the nation.

To summarize, a *surplus* in the nation's balance of payments *results* from an *excess in the stock of money demanded* that is not satisfied by domestic monetary authorities. A *deficit* in the nation's balance of payments *results* from an *excess in the stock of money supplied* that is not eliminated or corrected by the nation's monetary authorities. The nation's balance-of-payments surplus or deficit is temporary and self-correcting in the long run; that is, after the excess demand for or supply of money is eliminated through an inflow or outflow of funds, the balance-of-payments surplus or deficit is corrected and the international flow of money dries up and comes to an end.

18.2b   Further Aspects of the Adjustment Process

The adjustment process operates as described above unless the nation sterilizes, or neutralizes, the effect that a change in its international reserves (F) has on its monetary base $(D+F)$, or unless the cause of the disturbance persists. For example, if the nation's monetary authorities engage in open market purchases of securities (which puts money into the hands of the public and increases D) by an amount equal to the balance-of-payments deficit and reduction in the nation's international reserves (F), then the nation's monetary base remains unchanged, and the deficit will persist until the nation runs out of international reserves or stops the sterilization. In other words, the deficit will persist as long as the excess supply of money remains.

For example, a persistent balance-of-payments disequilibrium may result from continuous growth of the economy, if the resulting continuous increase in the nation's demand for money is not satisfied with a sufficient and continuous expansion of the domestic component of its monetary base (D). Then, the nation will face a balance-of-payments surplus and inflow of reserves, year after year. This is how the monetary approach explains the persistent balance-of-payments surpluses of a nation such as West Germany during the 1960s and early 1970s; that is, by the growth of West Germany's GNP and demand for money exceeding the growth of the domestic component of its money supply. Note that while the growth of the nation's GNP induces imports to rise, causing a *deterioration* in its trade balance and balance of payments under the Keynesian income-multiplier approach, it leads to an inflow of reserves and an *improvement* in the nation's balance of payments under the monetary approach.

Aside from asserting that a balance-of-payments surplus arises from an excess demand for money in the nation not met by the monetary authorities, and that a balance-of-payments deficit results from an excess supply of money in the nation not eliminated by the monetary authorities, the monetary approach does not explain in detail the dynamic process of adjustment to a balance-of-payments disequilibrium. Presumably, an excess demand for money will lead to a reduction of expenditures on goods, services, and investments in the nation (in an attempt to increase money balances), leaving more goods and services to be exported (thus improving the nation's trade balance) and leaving more domestic investment opportunities to foreigners (resulting in an inflow of capital that improves the nation's capital account). On the other hand, starting from a condition of full employment, the public will get rid of an excess supply of money by importing more goods and services and making more portfolio and direct investments abroad. This outflow of money represents the deficit in the nation's balance of payments.

The adjustment process outlined by the monetary approach is similar to the price-specie-flow mechanism advanced by Hume, and discussed in Chapter 15, in that they both rely on a movement of money or international reserves among nations to automatically correct balance-of-payments disequilibria. However, under the price-specie-flow mechanism, the flow of gold or international reserves leads to a change in relative commodity prices in the deficit and surplus nations that changes the flow of trade and corrects the balance-of-payments disequilibrium, whereas no difference in relative commodity prices between the two nations is required or even possible under the monetary approach in the long run. According to the monetary approach, relative commodity prices will be identical in the deficit and surplus nations in the long run under a fixed exchange rate system when expressed in the same currency (if we abstract from transportation costs, tariffs, and so on). The excess demand for or supply of money simply results in an inflow or outflow of international reserves, respectively, as described above and without causing any long-run *difference* in prices between the deficit and surplus nations.

Specifically, the short-run tendency for the domestic price of traded goods and investment assets to rise as the public increases its expenditures to get rid of an excess supply of money is prevented in the long run by an inflow of substitute commodities from abroad and an outflow of investment funds abroad. As a result, there is an outflow of money from the nation and a deterioration in its trade and capital account balances without resulting in any difference in prices (when expressed in terms of the same currency) or interest rates between the two nations in the long run. For extreme or **global monetarists,** there is a single integrated market for traded goods and capital in the world, so that the purchasing-power parity theory and the **law of one price** hold in the long run. The tendency for the price of nontraded commodities and purely domestic investment assets to rise in the nation in the short run is also checked in the long run by the substitution of traded commodities and other investment assets.

On the other hand, the tendency for the domestic price of traded commodities and investment assets to fall in the short run as the public reduces expenditures to eliminate an excess demand for money is prevented in the long run by an increased foreign demand for the nation's goods and services and investment assets. Therefore, there is an inflow of money from abroad and an improvement in the nation's trade and capital balances without resulting in any difference in prices (when expressed in terms of the same currency) or interest rates between the two nations in the long run. At least, this is what global monetarists believe. Finally, the tendency for the price of nontraded goods and purely domestic investment assets to fall in the nation in the short run is checked in the long run by the substitution of traded commodities and other investment assets.

18.2c   Control Over the Nation's Money Supply

According to the monetary approach, the nation has no control over its total money supply under a fixed exchange rate system in the long run. The attempt by monetary authorities to increase the nation's total money supply (M_s) in the face of an unchanged demand for money (M_d) will simply lead to the outflow of the excess money supply and a reduction in the nation's international reserves (F). Thus, the long-run effect of attempting to increase the total money supply (easy monetary policy) will simply be to change the composition of the nation's monetary base (i.e., it will increase D but this will lead to an equal reduction in F) without any change in the nation's total monetary base ($D+F$). Similarly, the attempt to reduce the nation's total money supply by reducing D (tight monetary policy) in the face of unchanged M_d will result in an equal increase in F, leaving the total monetary base and total money supply of the nation completely unchanged.

The case is different, however, for a **reserve-currency country (RCC)** such as the United States. Since the dollar is used as an international currency or reserve, an outflow of dollars from the United States will leave the U.S. money supply unchanged if foreign nations hold these dollars as international reserves on deposit in the United States. (The outflow of dollars from the United States will be matched by the inflow of dollar deposits to the United States, leaving the United States monetary base completely unchanged.) However, the increase in foreign-owned dollar balances represents an increase in the international reserves (F) and in the monetary base of other nations, as described earlier. Thus, there is an *asymmetry* in the effect of an international flow of a reserve currency on the monetary base of the reserve-currency country as opposed to non-reserve-currency countries. The international component of the monetary base of non-reserve-currency countries is affected while the monetary base of the reserve-currency country is not affected by an inflow or outflow of the reserve currency.

As a result, the reserve-currency country retains a large degree of control over its money supply, which allows it to use monetary policy effectively. The control that the United States retains over its money supply because of its reserve-currency status is further reinforced by the fact that the United

States has a relatively small foreign sector, so that any inflow or outflow of its currency is small in relation to its total money supply. On the other hand, non-reserve-currency countries are powerless in the long run to change their money supply under fixed exchange rates or even to sterilize an inflow or outflow of international reserves originating in or resulting from the actions of a reserve-currency country. This is particularly true for such small open non-reserve-currency countries as Belgium and Holland, and to some extent even for such relatively large and open reserve-currency countries as West Germany and France when dealing with the much larger United States economy.

18.3 Policy Implications of the Monetary Approach Under Fixed Exchange Rates and Inflation in the World Economy

In this section, we examine the policy implications of the monetary approach under a fixed exchange rate system. We also examine the causes and effects of inflation in the world economy and how inflation is transmitted internationally from the point of view of the monetary approach.

18.3a Policy Implications of the Monetary Approach under Fixed Exchange Rates

According to the monetary approach, the only way that a policy can affect a nation's balance of payments is through its effect on the demand for and supply of money in the nation. Any policy that increases the nation's demand for money relative to its supply will lead to an inflow of money (reserves) from abroad, which represents the surplus in the nation's balance of payments under fixed exchange rates. On the other hand, any increase in the nation's money supply relative to its demand will be met by an outflow of money (reserves) abroad, which represents the deficit in the nation's balance of payments.

Thus, a devaluation of the nation's currency, the imposition of an import tariff or quota, and multiple exchange rates increase the domestic price of internationally traded commodities. The price of nontraded commodities also increases, though usually by less, because of the substitution in consumption and production between traded and nontraded commodities. The increase in domestic prices resulting from these policies leads to an increase in the demand for nominal money balances in the nation.

If this increase in the demand for money is not met by an equal increase in the supply of money by the nation's monetary authorities, it will be satisfied from an inflow of money or reserves from abroad (a balance-of-payments surplus) until the excess demand for money is entirely eliminated and equilibrium between the stock of money demanded and the stock supplied is reestablished. If, however, the nation's monetary authorities increase the money supply to match exactly the increase in the demand for money resulting from a devaluation, the imposition of a tariff or quota, or multiple exchange rates, then these policies will not lead to any inflow of money or reserves from abroad and the devaluation will be completely ineffective in improving the nation's balance of payments. The exact opposite would occur as a result of a revaluation or the removal of an import tariff, quota, or multiple exchange rates.

However, changes in exchange rates, tariffs, quotas, or multiple exchange rates have only transitory effects on the nation's balance of payments. Their effects will last only until the balance-of-payments disequilibrium is corrected. Since, according to the monetary approach, a balance-of-payments disequilibrium will automatically be corrected anyway in the long run by an international flow of money or reserves under a fixed exchange rate system, these policies are completely unnecessary except, perhaps, to speed up the process of adjustment by helping to eliminate the excess demand for or supply of money. For example, a devaluation aimed at correcting a deficit in the balance of payments will increase domestic prices and thus help absorb the excess supply of money, but it will have no effect on the nation's real economic variables in the long run.

Turning to growth, we can conclude that if monetary authorities do not increase the domestic component of the nation's money supply sufficiently to meet the increased demand for money resulting from the growth of the nation's GNP over time, then an inflow of money or reserves will take place to make up the difference (a surplus in the nation's balance of payments). This surplus will continue, year in and year out, as long as the growth of the nation's money supply falls short of the growth in its demand for money.

This is the opposite of what the traditional income-multiplier approach predicts. That is, according to the income-multiplier approach, a growing real GNP induces imports to rise (via the marginal propensity to import), causing a *deterioration* in the nation's balance of trade and balance of payments (other things being equal). The monetary approach predicts instead an *improvement* in the nation's balance of payments. These opposing conclusions could possibly be reconciled in this case by a sufficiently large improvement in the nation's capital account to more than overcome the deterioration in the trade account (predicted by the income-multiplier approach) so as to improve the nation's balance of payments as a whole, as predicted by the monetary approach.

Similarly, if monetary authorities do not increase the domestic component of the nation's money supply sufficiently to satisfy entirely the increased demand for money resulting from an exogenous increase in energy prices (with the nation's real income unchanged), there will be an inflow of money or reserves from abroad (a surplus in the nation's balance of payments) to make up the difference. The traditional elasticity approach would instead predict a balance-of-payments deficit for the nation. However, the different predictions of the two approaches could be reconciled through the capital account, as in the growth case discussed above.

The same is true if monetary authorities do not increase the money supply sufficiently to completely satisfy the increased demand for money resulting from an exogenous fall in the nation's interest rate. The increased demand for money arises because the fall in the interest rate reduces the opportunity cost of holding inactive money balances. A smaller increase in the supply of money will lead to an inflow of money or reserves from abroad and a surplus in the nation's balance of payments. The traditional approach postulates instead an outflow of capital from the nation and a deficit in its balance of payments as a result of the fall in the interest rate.

One important conclusion emerges from the monetary approach with regard to the short-run effectiveness of policies, such as a devaluation, to correct a deficit in a nation's balance of payments, namely, that an improvement will occur in the short run only if monetary authorities do not increase the nation's money supply to match exactly the increase in the demand for money resulting from the devaluation or other adjustment policies. Since a balance-of-payments deficit would in any event be corrected automatically in the long run by an inflow of money or reserves from abroad under fixed exchange rates, the persistence of a deficit in a nation's balance of payments implies excessive money expansion by the nation's monetary authorities, according to the monetary approach.

18.3b The Monetary Approach and Inflation in the World Economy under Fixed Exchange Rates

According to the monetary approach, if each nation maintained a balanced budget (i.e., did not pursue expansionary or contractionary fiscal policies) and increased its money supply at the same rate as its real growth, the price level would be stable in each nation (other things equal). Price stability would result on the average even if the growth in the supply of money in some nations exceeded their real growth, as long as this was balanced by real growth exceeding money growth in other nations. That is, if the rate of growth in the total world money supply were equal to the growth of real world GNP, the average price level would tend to be constant for the world as a whole in the long run.

Other things being equal, those nations growing more rapidly than the world average tend to face an excess demand for money (and a balance-of-payments surplus). This excess demand for money will be eliminated by an inflow of money or reserves from the rest of the world *under fixed exchange rates*. On the other hand, those nations growing more slowly than the world average tend to face an excess supply of money (and a balance-of-payments deficit), which will be eliminated by an outflow of money or reserves to the rest of the world. Nevertheless, adherents to the monetary approach believe that if money growth matches real growth for the world as a whole, the average price level for the entire world tends to be stable in the long run.

Thus, the monetary approach postulates that worldwide inflation can only result from excessive world money growth and is more or less directly related to the rate by which money growth exceeds real growth for the world as a whole. For example, other things being equal, a world money growth exceeding the world's real growth by 10 percent will lead to an inflation rate of 10 percent on the average to absorb completely the excess supply of money created. Those nations in which the excess money growth is greater than the average will face a money or reserve outflow under fixed exchange rates, thus exporting some of their inflationary tendency abroad. This is particularly true for a very large nation such as the United States, whose excessive money expansion during the latter part of the 1960s and early 1970s was facilitated by its reserve-currency status.

Deficit and surplus nations could not continuously sterilize the international flows of money or reserves and prevent them from affecting their money supply under fixed exchange rates. In the long run, a surplus nation would either have to give up its goal of domestic price stability or allow its currency to appreciate. This is to a large extent what happened to West Germany during the 1960s, when the large inflow of reserves from abroad led to some domestic inflation and a revaluation of the mark in 1961 and 1969. Expectations of a lower inflationary rate in West Germany than abroad also played an important part in making the revaluations of the mark necessary. World inflationary tendencies are also reinforced because industrial prices today are flexible upward but tend to be sticky downward.

18.4   The Monetary Approach Under Flexible Exchange Rates

Under a flexible exchange rate system, balance-of-payments disequilibria are immediately corrected by automatic changes in the exchange rate without any international flow of money or reserves. Thus, under a flexible exchange rate system, the nation retains dominant control over its money supply and monetary policy. Adjustment takes place as a result of the change in domestic prices that accompanies the change in the exchange rate. For example, a deficit in the balance of payments (resulting from an excess money supply) leads to an automatic depreciation of the nation's currency, which causes prices and therefore the demand for money to rise, thus absorbing the excess supply of money and automatically eliminating the balance-of-payments deficit.

On the other hand, a surplus in the balance of payments (resulting from an excess demand for money) automatically leads to an appreciation of the nation's currency, which tends to reduce domestic prices, thus eliminating the excess demand for money and the balance-of-payments surplus. While under fixed exchange rates, a balance-of-payments disequilibrium is defined as and results from an international flow of money or reserves (so that the nation has no control in the long run over its money supply and domestic monetary policy), under a flexible exchange rate system, a balance-of-payments disequilibrium is immediately corrected by an automatic change in exchange rates and without any international flow of money or reserves (so that the nation retains dominant control over its money supply and domestic monetary policy).

The actual exchange value of a nation's currency in terms of the currencies of other nations is determined by the rate of growth of the money supply and real income in the nation relative to the growth of the money supply and real income in the other nations. For example, assuming zero growth in real income and the demand for money, as well as in the supply of money, in the rest of the world, growth in the nation's money supply in excess of the growth in its real income and demand for money leads to an increase in prices and in the exchange rate (a depreciation of the currency) of the nation. On the other hand, an increase in the nation's money supply that falls short of the increase in its real income and demand for money tends to reduce prices and the exchange rate (an appreciation of the currency) of the nation. The process by which exchange rates are determined under the monetary approach is shown mathematically in section A18.2 of the appendix.

Thus, a currency depreciation results from excessive money growth in the nation over time, while a currency appreciation results from inadequate money growth in the nation, according to the monetary approach. Put differently, a nation facing greater inflationary pressure than other nations (resulting from its more rapid monetary growth in relation to the growth in its real income and demand for money) will find its exchange rate rising (its currency depreciating). On the other hand, a nation facing lower inflationary pressure than the rest of the world will find its exchange rate falling (its currency appreciating). According to monetarists, the depreciation of the United States dollar and appreciation of the German mark during the 1970s were due to excessive monetary growth and inflationary pressure in the United States, and to the much smaller rate of monetary growth and inflationary pressure in West Germany than in the rest of the world.

With flexible exchange rates, the rest of the world is to some extent shielded from the monetary excesses of some nations. The nations with excessive money growth and depreciating currencies will now transmit inflationary pressures to the rest of the world primarily through their increased imports (i.e., through the usual Keynesian foreign trade multiplier) rather than directly through the export of money or reserves. This will take some time to occur and will depend on how much slack exists in the world economy and on structural conditions abroad.

Under a managed floating exchange rate system of the type in operation today, the nation's monetary authorities intervene in foreign exchange markets and either lose or accumulate international reserves to prevent an "excessive'' depreciation or appreciation of the nation's currency, respectively. Under such a system, part of a balance-of-payments deficit is automatically corrected by a depreciation of the nation's currency and part is corrected by a loss of international reserves. As a result, the nation's money supply is affected by the balance-of-payments deficit, and domestic monetary policy loses some of its effectiveness. Under a managed float, the nation's money supply is similarly affected by the inflationary or deflationary monetary policies undertaken by other nations, though to a smaller extent than under a fixed exchange rate system. The operation of the present floating exchange rate system is discussed in detail in Chapters 19 and 20.

18.5   The Portfolio Balance Approach and Exchange Rate Dynamics

In this section, we extend the monetary approach to include financial assets other than domestic money, and we utilize the model to examine exchange rate dynamics (such as the tendency of exchange rates in the short run to "overshoot" their long-run equilibrium level).

18.5a   The Portfolio Balance Approach

Until this point, we have presented the monetary approach. It concentrates attention on the domestic demand for and supply of money. When the quantity supplied of domestic money exceeds the quantity demanded by the nation's residents, there will be an outflow of domestic money (a deficit in the nation's balance of payments) under a fixed exchange rate system or a depreciation of the nation's currency under flexible exchange rates. On the other hand, when the quantity demanded of domestic money by the nation's residents exceeds the quantity supplied, there will be a capital inflow (a balance of payments surplus) under fixed exchange rates, or an appreciation of the domestic currency under flexible rates. The demand for financial assets other than domestic money is not considered by the monetary approach. This shortcoming is overcome by the portfolio balance approach.

The **portfolio balance approach** postulates that domestic money is only one among a spectrum of financial assets that the residents of a nation may want to hold. In the simplest portfolio balance model, individuals and firms hold their financial wealth in some combination of domestic money, a domestic bond, and a foreign bond denominated in the foreign currency. The incentive to hold bonds (domestic and foreign) results from the yield or interest that they provide. They also carry, however, the risk of default and the risk arising from the variability of their market value over time. Holding domestic money, on the other hand, is riskless but provides no yield or interest. Thus, the opportunity cost of holding domestic money is the yield foregone on holding bonds. The higher the yield or interest on bonds, the smaller is the quantity of money that individuals and firms will want to hold. At any particular point in time, an individual will want to hold part of his financial wealth in money and part in bonds, depending on his particular set of preferences and degree of risk aversion. Individuals and firms *do* want to hold a portion of their wealth in the form of money (rather than only in bonds) in order to make business payments (the transaction demand for money). But the higher the interest on bonds, the smaller is the amount of money that they will want to hold (i.e., they will economize on the use of money).

The choice, however, is not only between holding domestic money, on the one hand, and bonds in general, on the other, but among holding domestic money, the domestic bond, and the foreign bond. The foreign bond denominated in the foreign currency carries the additional risk that the foreign currency may depreciate, thereby imposing a capital loss in terms of the holder's domestic currency. But holding foreign bonds also allows the individual to spread his risks because disturbances that lower returns in one country are not likely to occur at the same time in other countries (see section 12.3a). Thus, a financial portfolio is likely to hold domestic money (to carry out business transactions), the domestic bond (for the return it yields), and the foreign bond (for the return and for the spreading of risks it provides). Given the holder's tastes and preferences, his wealth, the level of domestic and foreign interest rates, his expectations as to the future value of the foreign currency, rates of inflation at home and abroad, and so on, he will choose the portfolio that maximizes his satisfaction (i.e., that best fits his tastes).

A change in any of the underlying factors (i.e., the holder's preferences, his wealth, domestic and foreign interest rates, expectations, and so on) will prompt the holder to reshuffle his portfolio until he achieves the new desired (equilibrium) portfolio. For example, an increase in the domestic interest rate raises the demand for the domestic bond but reduces the demand for money and the foreign bond. An increase in the foreign interest rate raises the demand for the foreign bond but reduces the demand for money and the domestic bond. An increase in wealth increases the demand for money, for the domestic bond, and for the foreign bond. According to the portfolio balance approach, equilibrium in each financial market occurs only when the quantity demanded of each financial asset equals its supply. It is because investors hold diversified and balanced (from their individual point of view) portfolios of financial assets that this model is called the portfolio balance approach. This simple portfolio balance model is presented mathematically in section A18.3 of the appendix.

18.5b Exchange Rate Dynamics

We have seen above that a change in interest rates, wealth, expectations, and so on, disturb equilibrium and lead each investor to reallocate financial assets to achieve a new equilibrium or balanced portfolio. The adjustment involves a change in the *stock* of the various financial assets in the portfolio. Having been accumulated over a long period of time, the total *stock* of financial assets in investors' portfolios in the economy is very large in relation to the yearly *flows* (additions to the stock) through usual savings and investments. Not only is the total stock of financial assets in investors' portfolios very large at any point in time, but any change in interest rates, expectations, or other forces that affect the benefits and costs of holding the various financial assets are likely to lead to an immediate or very rapid change in their stock, as investors attempt to quickly reestablish equilibrium in their portfolios.

For example, an increase in the interest rate abroad will lead the investor to reduce his holdings of domestic money and the domestic bond, and increase his holdings of the foreign bond. This stock adjustment can be very large and usually occurs immediately or over a very short time. This is to be contrasted to a change in the *flow* of merchandise trade that results from, say, a depreciation of the nation's currency, and which takes place only gradually and over a longer period of time (previous contracts have to be honored and new orders may take many months to fulfill). Thus, *stock* adjustments in financial assets are usually much larger and quicker to occur than adjustments in trade *flows*.

The difference in the size and quickness of stock adjustments in financial assets as opposed to adjustments in trade flows have very important implications for the process by which exchange rates are determined and change (their dynamics) over time. For example, an increase in the interest rate abroad is likely to lead to a large and quick increase in the demand for the foreign currency in order to increase investors' stocks of the foreign bond. This would lead to an immediate and large depreciation of the domestic currency, which is likely to swamp the smaller and more gradual changes that take place through real markets, such as changes in trade flows. Of course, the opposite occurs if the nation's interest rate rises relative to the interest rate abroad. To be sure, in the long run, the effect on exchange rates of changes in real markets will prevail, but in the short or very short run (i.e., during the period of a day, week, or month), changes in exchange rates are likely to reflect mostly the effect of stock adjustments in financial assets and expectations.

The above can also help explain why, in the short-run, exchange rates tend to overshoot or bypass their long-run equilibrium level as they move toward their long-run equilibrium level. Since adjustments in trade flows occur only gradually over time, most of the burden of adjustment in exchange rates must come from financial markets in the very short and short runs. Thus, the exchange rate must overshoot or bypass its long-run equilibrium level for equilibrium to be quickly reestablished in financial markets. Over time, as the cumulative contribution to adjustment coming from the real (e.g., trade) sector is felt, the exchange rate reverses its movement and the overshooting is eliminated.

For example, suppose that a disturbance requires a 10 percent depreciation of the nation's currency for the exchange rate to be in equilibrium in the long run. In the short run, the nation's currency may have to depreciate by more than 10 percent, say 14 percent, for financial markets to quickly return to equilibrium (as required). Most of the short-run adjustment in the exchange rate must come from financial markets because the real or trade sector only contributes to the adjustment in exchange rates gradually over a longer period of time. In the long run, as the nation's exports expand and imports fall as a result of the depreciation of the nation's currency, the exchange rate will *appreciate* from its excessive short-run depreciation of 14 percent, until only a 10 percent depreciation remains, as required for long-run equilibrium.

Thus, an excessive depreciation in the nation's currency in the short run is likely to be eliminated by a subsequent partial appreciation of the currency as the exchange rate moves toward its long-run equilibrium level. Similarly, an excessive short-run appreciation is likely to be corrected by a subsequent partial depreciation. Of course, if other disturbances occur before the exchange rate reaches its long-run equilibrium level, the exchange rate will be continually fluctuating, always moving toward its long-run equilibrium level, but never quite reaching it. This seems to conform well with the recent real world experience with exchange rates. Specifically, since 1971, exchange rates have been characterized by a great deal of volatility, overshooting, and subsequent correction, but always fluctuating in value.

18.6 Evaluation and Empirical Tests of the Monetary and Portfolio Balance Approaches

The most significant contribution of the monetary approach to the balance of payments is to highlight the role of money in the adjustment process and counteract the tendency of the traditional approaches to concentrate attention on real variables to the almost complete neglect of the monetary factors. The portfolio balance approach extended the analysis to include stock adjustments in other financial assets in addition to money. In doing so, the portfolio approach removed the major shortcoming of the Mundell-Fleming model (section 17.4), which treated international capital flows resulting from interest rate differentials across nations as continuous flows rather than as stock adjustments.

However, the monetary approach itself may have gone too far in emphasizing the role of money and long-run equilibrium over real variables and short-run effects. For example, monetary authorities have a great deal of flexibility and retain a large degree of control over the nation's money supply and monetary policy in the short run, even under fixed exchange rates. Furthermore, by lumping together all the above-the-line items of the balance of payments, the monetary approach overlooks important relationships. For example, a trade deficit may be balanced by a private capital inflow which, while leaving the nation's monetary base unchanged, will increase the foreign debt of the nation and the burden of servicing it. Some of these defects are overcome by the portfolio balance approach, but more general models that fully incorporate the financial and real sectors and deal with the medium run (which is the most relevant period for policies) in addition to the short run and long run are needed, and these are only now being developed.

In the final analysis, it is the ability to predict more accurately and to better explain real world economic events that determines the superiority of an economic theory over others. Empirical testing is rendered somewhat easier in the case of the monetary approach by the fact that it often leads to diametrically opposing predictions and implications from those of the traditional approaches. For example, the monetary approach predicts that more rapid real growth in the nation than abroad, a slower money expansion at home than abroad, and a smaller rise in the interest rate at home than abroad will all lead to a balance-of-payments surplus for the nation, while traditional models predict balance-of-payments deficits for the nation (other things equal). Similarly, the global monetarists' prediction that the law of one price holds in the long run can be empirically tested.

Though Keynesian explanations along the traditional approaches are not lacking, the monetary approach does seem to provide a more convincing explanation for the German hyperinflation of the 1920s, and a somewhat better explanation for the persistent balance-of-payments surpluses and tendency for the German mark to appreciate during the 1970s, and for balance-of-payments deficits and tendency for the U.S. dollar and the British pound to depreciate over the same period of time (see the bibliography for references). Similarly, the explanation put forth by the monetary approach and running in terms of excessive world money expansion seems to better fit the steep inflationary spiral that engulfed the world during the 1970s. However, there are many other studies that found no empirical support for the monetary approach, especially for the experience of the 1970s. For example, many empirical studies reached only mixed and somewhat inconclusive results with regard to the global monetarists' belief in the law of one price.

Similarly, we have mixed or inconclusive results for empirical tests of the portfolio balance approach. Empirical tests of the portfolio approach are further hampered by the limited availability of data on the various financial assets that would be relevant for inclusion in the model. While empirical studies of exchange rate dynamics and overshooting tend to be supported by the empirical evidence, results from the application of the portfolio model to out-of-sample data are very poor. In short, we do not have, at present, an accepted general portfolio balance model and we have yet to develop a complete and acceptable theory of exchange rate variation.

Clearly more theoretical works needs to be done to reconcile the monetary and the portfolio balance approaches with the older traditional approaches, and more empirical tests need to be conducted for the models now being developed along these lines. It is likely, however, that the best we can hope for in the foreseeable future, after the smoke has settled, is that many aspects of the monetary and portfolio models (perhaps in somewhat watered-down fashions) will be incorporated into and will enrich the more traditional approaches without replacing them. At least this has often been the experience in the past.

Summary

1. The monetary approach views the balance of payments as an essentially monetary phenomenon, with money playing the key role in the long run as both the cause and the cure of a nation's balance-of-payments disequilibrium. That is, a surplus in a nation's balance of payments results from an excess in the nation's money demand relative to supply. This excess demand for money is satisfied by an inflow of money (reserves) from abroad and represents the surplus in the nation's balance of payments under a fixed exchange rate system. A balance-of-payments deficit arises from an excess supply of money in the nation, which leads to and is corrected by an outflow of money (reserves) abroad. The monetary approach concentrates attention on the official settlements balance, while lumping together all current and capital account, or above-the-line, items without analyzing them. Because of these criticisms, the more general portfolio balance approach was developed.
2. According to the monetary approach, the nominal demand for money is stable in the long run and positively related to the level of nominal national income but inversely related to the interest rate. The nation's money supply is equal to its monetary base times the money multiplier. The nation's monetary base is equal to the domestic credit created by its monetary authorities plus its international reserves. Unless satisfied domestically, an excess demand for money in the nation results in an inflow of reserves, or a balance-of-payments deficit results from an excess supply of money that is not eliminated by domestic monetary authorities. According to global monetarists, commodity prices and interest rates are the same throughout the world in the long run (the law of one price), and nations have no control over their money supply in the long run under fixed exchange rates.

3. A currency devaluation, the imposition of a tariff or quota, and multiple exchange rates increase prices and the demand for money in the nation. If monetary authorities do not increase the nation's money supply sufficiently to match the increased demand for money, an inflow of money or reserves from abroad will take place (a surplus in the nation's balance of payments). This speeds up the long-run automatic adjustment tendency postulated by monetarists. The same is true if the increase in the supply of money provided by monetary authorities falls short of the increased demand for money resulting from real growth in the nation. According to the monetary approach, worldwide inflation can be explained primarily by excessive monetary growth in the world economy.
4. Under a flexible exchange rate system, balance-of-payments disequilibria are immediately corrected by automatic changes in the exchange rate without any international flow of money or reserves. Thus, the nation retains dominant control over its money supply and monetary policy. A deficit nation will find its currency depreciating. This increases prices and the demand for money in the nation, thus absorbing the excess supply of money and eliminating the balance-of-payments deficit. The opposite takes place in a surplus nation. A nation's currency depreciates as a result of excessive monetary growth, but now the world is shielded from these inflationary pressures, except through an increased demand for its exports. A managed float combines to some extent the characteristics of a flexible and a fixed exchange rate system.
5. While the monetary approach considers only the demand and supply of money, the portfolio balance approach extends the analysis to the demand and supply of other domestic and foreign financial assets as well. In the long run, exchange rates are likely to reflect mostly flow adjustments in the real or trade sector. In the short

run, however, the portfolio balance approach postulates that exchange rates reflect primarily stock adjustments in financial assets. This also means that, in the short run, exchange rates are likely to overshoot or bypass their long-run equilibrium level in the process of moving toward that level.

6. The monetary and portfolio balance approaches emphasize the role of money and other financial assets, and concentrate on the long run and the short run, respectively. Traditional approaches stress real variables and the medium run (the period of one to a few years, which is most relevant for policies) to the almost complete neglect of monetary factors and the short and long runs. The results of empirical tests for the monetary and portfolio approaches are mixed and controversial. Thus, more empirical tests are needed, as well as more theoretical work to reconcile the monetary and portfolio approaches with the traditional approaches.

A Look Ahead

The next chapter examines and compares the advantages and disadvantages of flexible versus fixed exchange rate systems with a view to determining which type of system is "better." The evaluation will be conducted in terms of the degree of uncertainty arising under each system, the type of speculation that each system is likely to give rise to, the likely effect of each system on the rate of inflation, and the policy implications of each system. The conclusion will be reached that each system has some advantages and disadvantages and each may be more appropriate under different sets of circumstances.

Glossary

Monetary approach to the balance of payments   The approach that views the balance of payments as an essentially monetary phenomenon, with money playing the key role in

the long run as both the cause and the cure of balance-of-payments disequilibria.

Demand for money   According to the monetary approach, the nation's demand for nominal money balances is stable in the long run and is directly related to nominal national income but inversely related to the rate of interest in the nation.

Supply of money   The nation's total money supply is equal to the nation's monetary base times the money multiplier.

Monetary base   The domestic credit created by the nation's monetary authorities plus the nation's international reserves.

Global monetarists   Extreme monetarists who believe that national income will be at or will automatically tend toward full employment (or the natural rate of unemployment) in the long run and that the law of one price prevails throughout the world.

Law of one price   The global monetarists' view that the world consists of a fully integrated market for all internationally traded goods and capital so that commodity prices (when expressed in terms of the same currency) and interest rates will be the same throughout the world in the long run.

Reserve-currency country (RCC)   A country, such as the United States, whose currency is held by other nations as international reserves.

Portfolio balance approach   The model that postulates that domestic money is only one among a spectrum of financial assets that the residents of a nation may want to hold, and which stresses the stock adjustment process in achieving diversified and balanced portfolios of financial assets.

Questions for Review

1. What are the traditional approaches to balance-of-payments adjustments? What is meant by the monetary approach to the balance of payments? In what crucial way does it differ from the traditional approaches?
2. According to the monetary approach, what is

the demand for money equal to? What is the supply of money of the nation? What is meant by the monetary base of the nation? The money multiplier? How does a surplus in the nation's balance of payments arise, according to the monetary approach? How does a deficit arise? How does this differ from the traditional approaches? What is meant by global monetarists? The law of one price? Why do nations lose control over their money supply in the long run under fixed exchange rates?

3. What effect on the balance of payments does the monetary approach predict for a devaluation, an import tariff or quota, multiple exchange rates, a decrease in the nation's interest rate, or growth in the nation's GNP? How do these effects differ from those postulated by the traditional approaches?

4. How does the monetary approach explain the process by which a balance-of-payments disequilibrium is corrected under a flexible exchange rate system? How does this differ from the case of fixed exchange rates? What determines the value of the exchange rate and its change under a flexible exchange rate system according to the monetary approach? How does a managed floating exchange rate system compare with a flexible and fixed exchange rate system from the point of view of the monetary approach?

5. What is meant by the portfolio balance approach? In what ways does it differ from the monetary approach? What is the relative importance of stock adjustments in financial assets as compared with adjustments in trade flows for exchange rate changes in the short run and in the long run according to the portfolio approach? How does the portfolio approach explain the overshooting in exchange rates often observed in foreign exchange markets today?

6. What are the results of empirical tests on the monetary and portfolio approaches as compared with the traditional approaches? What additional theoretical and empirical work needs to be done? What is likely to be the outcome of this additional work in the foreseeable future?

Problems

1. Suppose that the velocity of circulation of money is $V = 4$ and the nominal GNP of the nation is $200 billion.
   (a) What is the quantity of money demanded by the nation?
   (b) By how much will the quantity of money demanded rise if the nation's nominal GNP rises to $220 billion?
   (c) What happens to the nation's demand for money if its nominal GNP increases by 10 percent each year?

2. Suppose that the domestic credit created by the nation's monetary authorities is $8 billion and the nation's international reserves are $2 billion, and that the legal reserve requirement for the nation's commercial banking system is 25 percent.
   (a) How much is the monetary base of the nation?
   (b) What is the value of the money multiplier?
   (c) What is the value of the total supply of money of the nation?

3. Assuming fixed exchange rates, find the size of the deficit or surplus in the balance of payments of the nation described in:
   (a) problems 1a and 2 above;
   (b) problems 1b and 2 above;
   (c) problems 1c and 2 above.

4. How is the balance-of-payments disequilibrium corrected if monetary authorities do not change the domestic component of the nation's monetary base:
   (a) in problem 3b above;
   (b) in problem 3c above;
   (c) What happens if monetary authorities completely sterilize, or neutralize, the balance-of-payments disequilibrium with a change in the domestic component of the nation's monetary base? How long can this go on?

*5. Suppose that a nation's nominal GNP $= 100$, $V = 4$, and $M_s = 30$.
   (a) Explain why this nation has a deficit in its balance of payments.
   (b) What is the size of the remaining deficit

in this nation's balance of payments if domestic prices rise by 10 percent as a result of a devaluation of the nation's currency?

(c) What if domestic prices in the nation rise by 20 percent as a result of a larger devaluation of the nation's currency?

*6. Under the law of one price, the price of an internationally traded commodity in one nation in a two-nation world is equal to the exchange rate times the price of the same commodity in the other nation. Assuming that such a law holds, explain why, if the first nation would otherwise face no inflation at home, it will not be able to maintain in the long run both constant prices and a constant exchange rate in the face of inflation in the other nation.

7. (a) Suppose that individuals and firms in a nation are holding the desired proportion of their wealth in foreign bonds to begin with. Suppose that there is then a once-and-for-all decrease in the exchange rate (i.e., the domestic currency appreciates and the foreign currency depreciates). What is the adjustment that the portfolio balance theory postulates?

(b) What happens, according to the portfolio approach, when the rate of inflation is expected to rise abroad?

APPENDIX

A18.1 A Mathematical Model of the Monetary Approach

This appendix presents a formal mathematical model of the monetary approach to the balance of payments, which summarizes the more descriptive analysis presented in the chapter.

We begin by assuming that the complete demand function for money takes the following form:

$$M_d = (P^a Y^b u)/(r^c) \tag{18A-1}$$

where M_d = quantity demanded of nominal money balances
P = domestic price level
Y = real income or output
r = interest rate
a = price elasticity of demand for money
b = income elasticity of demand for money
c = interest elasticity of demand for money
u = error term

Equation 18A-1 shows M_d to be directly related to PY, or GNP, and inversely related to r, as explained in section 18.2a.

On the other hand, the nation's supply of money is assumed to be:

$$M_s = m(D + F) \tag{18A-2}$$

where M_s = the nation's total money supply

m = money multiplier

D = domestic component of the nation's monetary base

F = international or foreign component of the nation's monetary base

The amount of D is determined by the nation's monetary authorities, and the sum $D + F$ represents the nation's total monetary base, or high-powered money.

In equilibrium, the quantity of money demanded is equal to the quantity of money supplied:

$$M_d = M_s \tag{18A-3}$$

Substituting equation 18A-1 for M_d and equation 18A-2 for M_s into equation 18A-3, we get:

$$(P^a Y^b u)/(r^c) = m(D + F) \tag{18A-4}$$

Taking the natural logarithm (ln) of both sides of equation 18A-4, we have:

$$a\ln P + b\ln Y + \ln u - c\ln r = \ln m + \ln(D + F) \tag{18A-5}$$

Differentiating equation 18A-5 with respect to time (t), we get:

$$a(1/P)(dP/dt) + b(1/Y)(dY/dT) + (1/u)(du/dt) - c(1/r)(dr/dt) =$$
$$(1/m)(dm/dt) + [D/(D+F)](1/D)(dD/dt) + [F/(D+F)](1/F)(dF/dt) \tag{18A-6}$$

Simplifying the notation by letting $D + F = H$, $(1/P)(dP/dt) = gP$, $(1/Y)(dY/dt) = gY$, and so on, we have:

$$agP + bgY + gu - cgr = gm + (D/H)gD + (F/H)gF \tag{18A-7}$$

Rearranging equation 18A-7 to make the last term on the right-hand side the dependent variable on the left-hand side, we get the general form of the equation usually used in empirical tests of the monetary approach to the balance of payments:

$$(F/H)gF = agP + bgY + gu - cgr - gm - (D/H)gD \tag{18A-8}$$

According to equation 18A-8, the weighted growth rate of the nation's international reserves $[(F/H)gF]$ is equal to the *negative* weighted growth rate of the domestic component of the nation's monetary base $[(D/H)gD]$ if the rate of growth of prices, real income, interest rate, and money multiplier is zero.

What this means is that, other things being equal, when the nation's monetary authorities change D, an equal and opposite change automatically occurs in F. Thus, the nation's monetary authorities can only determine the *composition* of the nation's monetary base (i.e., $H=D+F$) but not the size of the monetary base itself. That is, under fixed exchange rates, the nation has no control over its money supply and monetary policy.

On the other hand, a growth in Y, with constant P, r, and m, must be met either by an increase in D or F or by a combination of both. If the nation's monetary authorities do not increase D, there will be an excess demand for money in the nation that will be satisfied by an inflow of money or reserves from abroad (a surplus in the nation's balance of payments) under fixed exchange rates. Equation 18A-8 can similarly be used to determine the effect of a change in any other variable included in the equation on the nation's balance of payments.

Empirical tests along the lines of equation 18A-8 seem to lend support to the monetary approach to the balance of payments. However, more empirical tests are needed and more theoretical work is required to try to reconcile the monetary approach with the traditional approaches.

Problem Suppose that the values obtained by estimating equation 18A-8 for a particular nation over a specified period of time are $a=b=c=1$ and $gu=gr=gm=0$. Suppose also that at the beginning of the period of the analysis, $D=100$ and $F=20$ in this nation and during the period of the analysis $gP=10\%$ and $gY=4\%$ and the nation's monetary authorities increase D from 100 to 110. Estimate the value of this nation's international reserves (F) at the end of the period under fixed exchange rates.

A18.2 The Exchange Rate Under the Monetary Approach

In section 13.3a, we defined the exchange rate as the domestic currency price of a unit of the foreign currency. With the dollar ($) as the domestic currency and the pound sterling (£) as the foreign currency, the exchange rate (R) was defined as the number of dollars per pound, or $R=\$/£$. For example, if $R=\$2/£1$, this means that two dollars are required to purchase one pound.

If markets are competitive and if there are no tariffs, transportation costs, or other obstructions to international trade, then according to the law of one price postulated by the purchasing power parity theory, the price of a commodity must be the same in the United States as the United Kingdom. That is, $P_X(\$)=RP_X(£)$. For example, if the price of a unit of commodity X is $P_X=£1$ in the United Kingdom, then $P_X=\$2$ in the United States. The same is true for every other traded commodity and for all commodities together (price indices). That is,

$$P=RP^* \tag{18A-9}$$

where P is the index of dollar prices in the United States, R is the exchange rate of the dollar, and P^* is the index of pound prices in the United Kingdom.

We can show how the exchange rate between the dollar and the pound is determined according to the monetary approach by starting with the nominal demand for money function of the United States (M_d, from 18-1) and for the United Kingdom (M^*_d):

$$M_d = kPY \text{ and } M^*_d = k^*P^*Y^* \tag{18A-10}$$

where k is the desired ratio of nominal money balances to nominal national income in the United States, P is the price level in the United States, and Y is real output in the United States, while the asterisked symbols have the same meaning for the United Kingdom.

In equilibrium, the quantity of money demanded is equal to the quantity of money supplied. That is, $M_d = M_s$ and $M^*_d = M^*_s$. Substituting M_s for M_d and M^*_s for M^*_d in equation 18A-10, and dividing the resulting United Kingdom function by the United States function, we get:

$$\frac{M^*_s}{M_s} = \frac{k^*P^*Y^*}{kPY} \tag{18A-11}$$

By then dividing both sides of 18A-11 by P^*/P and M^*_s/M_s, we get:

$$\frac{P}{P^*} = \frac{M_s}{M^*_s} \frac{k^*Y^*}{kY} \tag{18A-12}$$

But since $P = RP^*$ (from 18A-9), we have:

$$R = \frac{M_s}{M^*_s} \frac{k^*Y^*}{kY} \tag{18A-13}$$

Since k^* and Y^* in the United Kingdom and k and Y in the United States are constant, R is constant as long as M_s and M^*_s remain unchanged. For example, if $k^*Y^*/kY = \frac{1}{2}$ and $M_s/M^*_s = 4$, then $R = \$2/\pounds1$. In addition, changes in R are proportional to changes in M_s and inversely proportional to changes in M^*_s. For example, if M_s increases by 10 percent in relation to M^*_s, R will increase (i.e., the dollar will depreciate) by 10 percent, and so on.

Several important things need to be noted with respect to equation 18A-13. First, it depends on the purchasing power parity (PPP) theory (equation 18A-9). Secondly, equation 18A-13 was derived from the demand for nominal money balances in the form of equation 18-1 (which does not include the interest rate) as opposed to equation 18A-1 (which does include the interest rate). However, since according to the monetary approach, capital markets are internationally integrated, interest rates are identical in the two nations (because of interest arbitrage). Since the interest rate term of the United States would appear in the numerator of equation 18A-13 and the interest rate of the United Kingdom in the denominator, and they are equal, they would cancel out. Third, the exchange rate adjusts to clear money markets in each country without any flow or change in reserves. Thus, for a small country, the PPP theory determines the price level under fixed exchange rates and the exchange rate under flexible rates. Finally, the exchange rate is also affected by the *expected* rate of inflation in each nation. If suddenly the rate of inflation is expected to be 10 percent higher in the United States than in the United Kingdom, then the dollar will immediately depreciate by 10 percent.

Problem   Starting with equation 13A-3 for the forward rate at interest parity, and assuming that the forward rate reflects market expectations precisely, show that the expected percentage change in the exchange rate is equal to the difference in the expected percentage rate of inflation in the two nations.

A18.3   A Mathematical Model of the Portfolio Balance Approach

In this section we present mathematically a simple one-country portfolio balance model in which individuals and firms hold their financial wealth in some combination of domestic money, a domestic bond, and a foreign bond denominated in the foreign currency.

The basic equations of the model can be written as follows:

$$M = a(i, i^*)W \qquad \text{(18A-14)}$$
$$D = b(i, i^*)W \qquad \text{(18A-15)}$$
$$RF = c(i, i^*)W \qquad \text{(18A-16)}$$
$$W = M + D + RF \qquad \text{(18A-17)}$$

where M is the quantity demanded of nominal money balances by domestic residents, D is the demand for the domestic bond, R is the exchange rate (defined as the domestic currency price of a unit of the foreign currency), RF is the demand for the foreign bond in terms of the domestic currency, W is wealth, i is the interest rate at home, and i^* is the interest rate abroad.

The first three equations postulate that the quantity demanded of domestic money balances, the domestic bond, and the foreign bond by the nation's residents are functions of the domestic interest rate, the foreign interest rate, and are equal to a particular proportion of wealth. The sum $a + b + c = 1$. That is, the total wealth of the nation (W) equals $M + D + RF$.

Specifically, the above model postulates that M, D, and RF are fixed proportions of W. In addition, M is inversely related to i and i^*. D is directly related to i and inversely related to i^*. RF is inversely related to i and directly related to i^*. An increase in i raises D but reduces M and RF. An increase in i^* raises RF but reduces M and D. Through savings, W increases over time, and an increase in W increases M, D, and F.

According to the portfolio balance approach, equilibrium in each financial market occurs only when the quantity demanded of each financial asset equals its supply. Assuming that each financial market is in equilibrium to begin with and solving for *RF* in equation 18A-17, we get:

$$RF = W - M - D = W - a(i,i^*)W - b(i,i^*)W = (1 - a - b)W \qquad \text{(18A-18)}$$

Equation 18A-18 can be rewritten as:

$$RF = (1 - a - b)W = f(i,i^*)W \qquad \text{(18A-19)}$$

Thus,

$$R = f(i,i^*)W/F \qquad \text{(18A-20)}$$

From equation 18A-20 we can postulate that the exchange rate is directly related to *i* and *W* and inversely related to *i** and *F*. That is, an increase in wealth resulting from an increase in savings increases the demand for all three financial assets, but as the nation exchanges the domestic for the foreign currency to purchase more of the foreign bond, the exchange rate will rise (i.e., the domestic currency depreciates). Similarly, when the interest rate rises abroad, domestic residents purchase more of the foreign bond and *R* rises. On the other hand, an increase in the supply of *F* will lower its price and reduce the wealth of domestic residents. When this occurs, they will reduce their holdings of all financial assets, including the foreign bond. But as foreign bonds (which are denominated in the foreign currency) are sold and the foreign currency exchanged for the domestic currency on the exchange market, the exchange rate falls (i.e., the domestic currency appreciates). The same is true if the domestic interest rate rises.

The portfolio balance model presented above faces several shortcomings. First, it abstracts from the determinants of real income. Second, it does not deal with trade flows. Third, it provides no role for expectations. The model, however, can be extended (much more readily than the monetary approach) to overcome these shortcomings.

Problem   Using the portfolio balance model presented above, examine the effect (a) on the exchange rate of an increase in the domestic money supply and (b) of a once-and-for-all depreciation of the domestic currency.

Selected Bibliography

For a problem-solving approach to the monetary approach to the balance of payments, see:
- D. Salvatore, *Theory and Problems of International Economics*, 2nd ed. (New York: McGraw-Hill 1984), ch. 11, sects. 11.1 to 11.3.

The domestic monetarist principles from which the monetary approach to the balance of payments stemmed are found in:
- M. Friedman, "The Role of Monetary Policy," *American Economic Review*, March 1968.
- M. Friedman and A. Schwartz, *A Monetary History of the United States: 1867–1960*

(Princeton, N.J.: Princeton University Press, 1971).

The monetary approach to the balance of payments originated with:
- R. Mundell, *International Economics* (New York: Macmillan, 1968), chs. 9, 11, and 15.
- R. Mundell, *Monetary Theory: Inflation, Interest and Growth in the World Economy* (Pacific Palisades, Cal.: Goodyear, 1971).
- H. Johnson, "The Monetary Approach to the Balance of Payments Theory," *Journal of Financial and Quantitative Analysis,* March 1972. Reprinted in M. Connoly and A. Swoboda, *International Trade and Money* (Toronto: University of Toronto Press, 1973).

Other works on the monetary approach to the balance of payments are:
- R. Dornbusch, "Currency Depreciation, Hoarding and Relative Prices," *Journal of Political Economy,* July-August 1973.
- R. Dornbush, "Devaluation, Money and Nontraded Goods," *American Economic Review,* December 1973.
- M. Mussa, "A Monetary Approach to the Balance of Payments Analysis," *Journal of Money, Credit and Banking,* August 1974. Reprinted in J. Frenkel and H. Johnson, *The Monetary Approach to the Balance of Payments* (London: Allen & Unwin, 1975, and Toronto: University of Toronto Press, 1976).
- D. Kemp, "A Monetary View of the Balance of Payments," *Federal Reserve of St. Louis Review,* April 1975.
- J. Frenkel and H. Johnson, *The Monetary Approach to the Balance of Payments* (London: Allen & Unwin, 1975).
- F.A. Frenkel and M. Mussa, "Asset Markets, Exchange Rates, and the Balance of Payments," in W.R. Jones and P.B. Kenen, Eds., *Handbook of International Economics,* Vol. II (Amsterdam: North-Holland, 1985).

Studies in the international transmission of inflation in the world economy are:
- L. Krause and W. Salant, *Worldwide Inflation: Theory and Recent Experience* (Washington, D.C.: Brookings Institution, 1977).
- N. Fieleke, "The International Transmission of Inflation," in *Managed Exchange-Rate Flexibility: The Recent Experience* (Boston: Federal Reserve Bank of Boston, 1978).
- M.R. Darby et al., *The International Transmission of Inflation* (Chicago: University of Chicago Press, 1983).

The most important references for the portfolio balance approach are:
- R.I. McKinnon and W.E. Oates, *The Implications of International Economic Integration for Monetary, Fiscal, and Exchange Rate Policies* (Princeton, N.J.: International Finance Section, Princeton University, 1969).
- W.H. Branson, "Stocks and Flows in International Monetary Analysis," in A. Ando, R. Herring, and R. Martson, Eds., *International Aspects of Stabilization Policies* (Boston, Federal Reserve Bank of Boston, 1975).
- W.H. Branson, "Portfolio Equilibrium and Monetary Policy with Foreign and Nontrade Assets," in E. Claassen and P. Salin, Eds., *Recent Issues in International Monetary Economics* (Amsterdam: North-Holland, 1976).
- P.R. Allen and P.B. Kenen, *Asset Markets, Exchange Rates, and Economic Integration* (London, Cambridge University Press, 1980).
- W.H. Branson and D.W. Henderson, "The Specification and Influence of Asset Markets," in W.R. Jones and P.B. Kenen, Eds., *Handbook of International Economics,* Vol. II (Amsterdam: North-Holland, 1985).

For exchange rate dynamics and overshooting, see:
- R. Dornbusch, "Expectations and Exchange Rate Dynamics," *Journal of Political Economy,* December 1976.
- J.A. Frenkel, "Flexible Exchange Rates, Prices, and the Role of 'News': Lessons from the 1970s," *Journal of Political Economy,* August 1981.
- J.F.O. Bilson, "Exchange Rate Dynamics," in J.F.O. Bilson and R.C. Marston, Eds., *Exchange Rate Theory and Practice* (Chicago: University of Chicago Press, 1984).
- M. Mussa, "The Theory of Exchange Rate Determination," in J.F.O. Bilson and R.C. Marston, Eds., *Exchange Rate Theory and Prac-*

tice (Chicago: University of Chicago Press, 1984).

- M. Obstfeld and A.C. Stockman, "Exchange Rate Dynamics," in W.R. Jones and P.B. Kenen, Eds., *Handbook of International Economics*, Vol. II (Amsterdam: North-Holland, 1985).

Evaluations and empirical testing of the monetary and portfolio balance approaches are found in:

- B.B. Aghevli and M.S. Khan, "The Monetary Approach to the Balance of Payments: An Empirical Test," in *The Monetary Approach to the Balance of Payments* (Washington, D.C.: International Monetary Fund, 1977).
- M. Kreinin and L. Officer, *The Monetary Approach to the Balance of Payments: A Survey*. Princeton Studies in International Finance (Princeton, N.J.: Princeton University Press, 1978).
- J.F.O. Bilson, "The Monetary Approach to Exchange Rate: Some Empirical Evidence," *IMF Staff Papers*, 1978.
- R. Dornbusch, "Exchange Rate Economics: Where Do We Stand?" *Brookings Papers on Economic Activity*, No. 1, 1980.
- F.A. Frenkel, "Exchange Rates, Prices, and Money: Lessons from the 1920s," *American Economic Review*, 1980.
- A.O. Krueger, *Exchange Rate Determination* (Cambridge: Cambridge University Press, 1983).
- J.A. Frenkel, "Tests of Monetary and Portfolio Balance Models of Exchange Rate Determination," in J.F.O. Bilson and R.C. Marston, Eds., *Exchange Rate Theory and Practice* (Chicago: University of Chicago Press, 1984).

CHAPTER 19

Flexible Versus Fixed Exchange Rates

19.1 Introduction

In Chapters 15 through 17, we examined separately the process of adjustment to balance-of-payments disequilibria under a flexible and under a fixed exchange rate system. In this chapter, we evaluate and compare the advantages and disadvantages of a flexible as opposed to a fixed exchange rate system, as well as the merits and drawbacks of hybrid systems that combine various characteristics of flexible and fixed exchange rates.

In general, advocates of flexible exchange rates argue that such a system is more efficient than a system of fixed exchange rates to correct balance-of-payments disequilibria. Furthermore, they stress that by allowing a nation to achieve external balance easily and automatically, flexible rates facilitate the achievement of internal balance and other economic objectives of the nation. On the other hand, advocates of fixed exchange rates argue that by introducing a degree of uncertainty not present under fixed rates, flexible exchange rates reduce the volume of international trade and investment, are more likely to lead to destabilizing speculation, and are inflationary.

A careful review of the theoretical arguments raised by each side does not lead to any clear-cut conclusion that one system is overwhelmingly superior to the other. To be sure, at the time of the collapse of the fixed exchange rate system in the early 1970s, the majority of economists seemed to lean toward flexible exchange rates. However, as a result of the great volatility in exchange rates experienced over the past decade, the balance today seems to be a little toward fixed or more managed rates. It seems that economists often compare the painfully obvious weaknesses of whatever the prevailing exchange rate system is to an idealized alternative system. This is contrasted to the more or less consistent preference for fixed rates, or at least greatly restrained fluctuations, of businessmen, bankers, and government officials.

No one can deny the important benefits of having a single currency throughout a nation and thus *permanently* fixed exchange rates between the various areas of the nation (for example, one dollar in New York can be exchanged for a dollar in San Francisco or in any other part of the United States). But then the debate over fixed versus flexible exchange rates becomes essentially a debate over what is an "optimum currency area," or how large can be the area covered by permanently fixed exchange rates before the benefits of fixed rates are overcome by their drawbacks. In the final analysis, whether flexible or fixed exchange rates are better may very well depend on the nation involved and the conditions under which it operates.

In section 19.2, we analyze the case for flexible exchange rates. In section 19.3, we examine the case for fixed exchange rates. Section 19.4 presents the closely related theory of optimum currency areas. Finally, sections 19.5 and 19.6 examine the advantages and disadvantages of hybrid systems that combine some of the characteristics of flexible and fixed exchange rates in various degrees. These include systems with different exchange rate bands of fluctuation about a par value or fixed exchange rate and systems characterized by adjustable pegs, crawling pegs, and managed floating.

19.2   The Case for Flexible Exchange Rates

We saw in Chapter 15 that under a truly flexible exchange rate system, a deficit or surplus in the nation's balance of payments is automatically corrected by a depreciation or an appreciation of the nation's currency, respectively, without any government intervention and loss or accumulation of international reserves by the nation. On the other hand, pegging or fixing the exchange rate at one level, just as fixing by law the price of any commodity, usually results in excess demand for or excess supply of foreign exchange (i.e., a deficit or a surplus in the nation's balance of payments), which can only be corrected by a change in economic variables other than the exchange rate. This is inefficient, may lead to policy mistakes, and requires the use of policies (such as monetary policy) which, therefore, are not available to achieve purely internal economic objectives.

19.2a   Market Efficiency

Under a flexible exchange rate system, only the exchange rate needs to change to correct a disequilibrium in a nation's balance of payments. Balance-of-payments equilibrium would also be achieved under a fixed exchange rate system (such as the price-specie-flow mechanism under the gold standard) if all internal prices were perfectly flexible in the nation. However, it is argued that it is more efficient or less costly to change only one price (i.e., the exchange rate) than to rely on all internal prices changing in order to bring about adjustment in the balance of payments. The reasoning is the same as that for changing to daylight saving time during the summer months rather than rescheduling all events for one hour earlier. Furthermore, internal prices are sticky and far from perfectly flexible in today's world, especially downward.

According to its advocates, a flexible exchange rate system corrects balance-of-payments disequilibria smoothly and continuously as they occur. This results in stabilizing speculation, which dampens fluctuations in exchange rates. Whatever fluctuations remain in exchange rates can then be hedged at a small cost. On the other hand, the inability or unwillingness of a nation to adjust the exchange rate when out of equilibrium under a fixed exchange rate system is likely to give rise to destabilizing speculation and eventually force the nation to make a large discrete change in its exchange rate. This jolts the economy, imposes serious adjustment costs on the nation, and interferes with the smooth flow of international trade and investments.

Flexible exchange rates clearly identify the degree of comparative advantage and disadvantage of the nation in various commodities when these equilibrium exchange rates are translated into domestic prices. On the other hand, fixed exchange rates are often out of equilibrium in the real world, and when this is the case, they distort the pattern of trade and prevent the most efficient allocation of resources throughout the world.

For example, an exchange rate that is too high may lead the nation to export more of a commodity than would be justified at the equilibrium exchange rate. In extreme cases, it may even lead the nation to export a commodity in which, in reality, the nation has comparative *disadvantage*. That is, the commodity may be cheaper in relation to competitive foreign commodities (when expressed in terms of the same currency) at the nation's undervalued exchange rate, even though it would be more expensive at the equilibrium exchange rate. This interferes with the most efficient utilization of world resources and reduces the benefits from international specialization in production and trade.

19.2b Policy Advantages

A flexible exchange rate system also means that the nation need not concern itself with its external balance and is free to utilize all policies at its disposal to achieve purely domestic goals of full employment with price stability, growth, and equitable distribution of income, and so on. For example, we saw in Chapter 17 that under a fixed exchange rate system, the nation could use fiscal policy to achieve internal balance and monetary policy to achieve external balance. Other things being equal, the achievement of internal balance would certainly be facilitated if monetary policy were also free to be used alongside fiscal policy to attain this goal. Or monetary policy could be utilized to achieve other purely internal objectives, such as growth. In view of the limited number of effective policy instruments usually available to nations, this is no small benefit. In addition, the possibility of policy mistakes and delays in achieving external balance would also be minimized under a flexible exchange rate system.

An additional standard argument for flexible exchange rates is that they enhance the effectiveness of monetary policy (in addition to freeing it to be used for domestic objectives). For example, an anti-inflationary policy that improves the trade balance will result in an appreciation of the domestic currency. This further reduces domestic inflationary pressures by encouraging imports and discouraging exports.

Different nations also have different trade-offs between inflation and unemployment. For example, the United Kingdom and Italy seemed to tolerate double-digit inflation more readily than the United States to keep their unemployment rates low. Japan also seems more willing than West Germany to tolerate inflation to keep its unemployment rate very low. Flexible exchange rates allow each nation to pursue domestic policies aimed at reaching its own desired inflation-unemployment trade-off. Under fixed exchange rates, different inflationary rates in different nations result in balance-of-payments pressures (deficit in the more inflationary and surplus in the less inflationary nations), which restrain or prevent each nation from achieving its optimum inflation-unemployment trade-off. However, the benefit from flexible exchange rates along these lines may be only temporary.

Flexible exchange rates would also prevent the government from setting the exchange rate at a level other than equilibrium in order to benefit one sector of the economy at the expense of another or to achieve some economic objective that could be reached by less costly means. For example, developing nations usually maintain an exchange rate that is too low in order to encourage the importation of capital equipment needed for development. However, this discourages exports of agricultural and traditional commodities. The government then uses a maze of exchange and trade controls to eliminate the excess demand for foreign exchange resulting at its lower-than-equilibrium exchange rate. Other things being equal, it would be more efficient to allow the exchange rate to find its own equilibrium level and give a subsidy to the nation's industrial producers. This is generally better because a subsidy is more evident and comes under legislative scrutiny and because trade and exchange controls introduce many distortions and inefficiencies into an economy.

Finally, a flexible exchange rate system does not impose the cost of government interventions in the foreign exchange market required to maintain exchange rates fixed. Flexible exchange rates are generally preferred by those, such as Nobel Laureate Milton Friedman, who advocate a minimum of government intervention in the economy and a maximum of personal freedom.

The above represents the strongest possible case that could be made for flexible exchange rates, and while generally correct in its broad outlines, it needs to be greatly qualified. This is undertaken in the next two sections in the context of making a case for fixed exchange rates and in examining the theory of optimum currency areas. Also to be pointed out is that we are here examining the case for a **freely floating exchange rate system** in which there is no government intervention at all in foreign exchange markets. A system that permits even a minimum of government intervention in foreign exchange markets simply to smooth out excessive short-run fluctuations without affecting long-run trends or trying to support any specific set of exchange rates does not qualify as a truly flexible exchange rate system. This is referred to as a managed floating exchange rate system and will be examined in section 19.6.

19.3   The Case for Fixed Exchange Rates

In this section, we consider the case for fixed exchange rates. This rests on the alleged smaller degree of uncertainty that fixed exchange rates introduce into international trade and finance, on fixed exchange rates being more likely to lead to stabilizing rather than destabilizing speculation, and on the greater price discipline (i.e., less inflation) under fixed than under flexible rates. Each of these arguments in favor of fixed exchange rates is presented, together with the reply by advocates of flexible exchange rates as well as whatever empirical evidence is available on the issue.

19.3a   Less Uncertainty

According to its advocates, a fixed exchange rate system avoids the wild day-to-day fluctuations that are likely to occur under flexible rates and which discourage specialization in production and the flow of international trade and investments. That is, with flexible exchange rates, the day-to-day shifts in a nation's demand for and supply of foreign exchange would lead to very frequent changes in exchange rates. Furthermore, because the demand and supply curves of foreign exchange are supposedly inelastic (i.e., steeply inclined), not only would exchange rates fluctuate frequently, but these fluctuations would be very large. These wild fluctuations in exchange rates would interfere with and reduce the degree of specialization in production and the flow of international trade and investments. In this form, the case in favor of fixed rates is as much a case *against* flexible exchange rates as it is a case in favor of fixed rates.

For example, in Figure 19-1, the shift over time in the United States demand curve for pounds from the average of $D_£$ to $D_£'$ and then to $D_£*$ causes the exchange rate to fluctuate from R' to $R*$ when the United States supply curve of pounds is $S_£$, or more elastic, and from R'' to $R**$ when the United States supply curve of pounds is $S_£'$, or less elastic.

Turning to the real world and back to Figure 13-2, on page 335, we see that

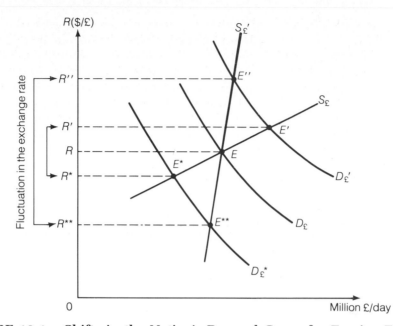

FIGURE 19-1. Shifts in the Nation's Demand Curve for Foreign Exchange and Uncertainty

The shift over time in the U.S. demand curve for pounds from the average $D_£$ to $D_£'$ and then to $D_£^*$ causes the exchange rate to fluctuate from R' to R^* when the U.S. supply curve of pounds is $S_£$, or elastic, and from R'' to R^{**} when the U.S. supply curve is $S_£'$, or inelastic.

the exchange rate between the United States dollar and the currencies of the largest industrial nations and Switzerland did fluctuate widely on a daily basis from 1973 to 1979. To be noted is that since 1973 most nations have had managed rather than freely floating exchange rates. However, to the extent that the intervention of national monetary authorities in foreign exchange markets had some success in their alleged aim of smoothing out short-run fluctuations in exchange rates, fluctuations in exchange rates would have been even greater under a freely floating exchange rate system.

The question of time is also crucial. That is, elasticities are likely to be higher and thus exchange rate fluctuations lower in the long run than in the short run. But it is with the short-run instability in exchange rates that we are now primarily concerned. Excessive short-run fluctuations in exchange rates under a flexible exchange rate system may be costly in terms of higher frictional unemployment, if they lead to overfrequent attempts at reallocating domestic resources among the various sectors of the economy. The short-run tendency of exchange rates to overshoot their long-run equilibrium level has also been noted in section 18.5b.

According to advocates of flexible exchange rates, the uncertainty and instability surrounding the large discrete changes in par values that periodically become necessary under a fixed exchange rate system are even more damaging and disruptive to the smooth flow of international trade and investments than the uncertainty inherent in fluctuating exchange rates. Furthermore, while the latter uncertainty can generally be hedged, the former cannot. However, it must be pointed out that under a *truly* fixed exchange rate system, such as the gold standard, the exchange rate is always kept fixed, and so this source of uncertainty would be absent.

19.3b   Stabilizing Speculation

According to advocates of fixed exchange rates, speculation is more likely to be *destabilizing* under a flexible than under a fixed exchange rate system. With destabilizing speculation, speculators purchase a foreign currency when the exchange rate is rising, in the expectation that the exchange rate will rise even more, and sell the foreign currency when the exchange rate is falling, in the expectation that the exchange rate will fall even more. In the process, the fluctuations in exchange rates resulting from business cycles are amplified and so are the uncertainty and risks involved in international transactions. The opposite occurs under stabilizing speculation.

This is illustrated in Figure 19-2. Curve *A* shows the hypothetical fluctuation in the exchange rate that accompanies the business cycle in the absence of speculation (along an implicit depreciating trend of the dollar over the entire cycle). Curve *B* shows the smaller fluctuation in the exchange rate with stabilizing speculation, and curve *C* shows the larger fluctuation in the exchange rate with destabilizing fluctuation. The amplified fluctuations in exchange rates with destabilizing speculation increase the uncertainty and risks of international transactions and reduce the international flow of trade and investments. According to advocates of a fixed exchange rate system, this is more likely to occur when exchange rates are free to vary than when they are kept fixed.

Once again, advocates of flexible exchange rates disagree. They point out that destabilizing speculation is less likely to occur when exchange rates adjust continuously than when they are prevented from doing so until a large discrete adjustment can no longer be avoided. Anticipating a large change in exchange rates, speculators will then sell a currency that they believe is going to be devalued and buy a currency that they believe is going to be revalued (destabilizing speculation), and their expectations often become self-fulfilling. However, this is generally true only under a fixed exchange rate system of the Bretton Woods type, which did allow exchange rate changes in cases of "fundamental disequilibrium." Under a *truly* fixed exchange rate system, such as the gold standard, exchange rates are always kept fixed, and a balance-of-payments adjustment is achieved by other means, no matter how painful. In that case, speculation is almost certain to be stabilizing. But, then, so is likely to be the case under a *truly* flexible exchange rate system.

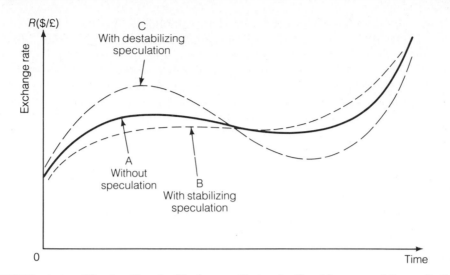

FIGURE 19-2. Fluctuation in Exchange Rates in the Absence of Speculation and with Stabilizing and Destabilizing Speculation

Curve A shows the fluctuation in the exchange rate over the business cycle in the absence of speculation. Curve B shows the smaller fluctuation in the exchange rate with stabilizing speculation, while curve C shows the large fluctuation in the exchange rate with destabilizing speculation.

According to Milton Friedman, speculation is stabilizing on the average because destabilizing speculation would lead to continuous losses by speculators, which would drive them out of business. That is, with destabilizing speculation, speculators buy a foreign currency when its price is rising in the expectation that its price will rise even more, but if it does not, they are forced to resell the currency at a lower price, thus incurring losses. If the process continues, it will bankrupt many of them. For speculators to make profits and remain in business, they must be able to purchase a foreign currency when it is cheap and resell it when it is expensive. This implies that speculation is stabilizing on the average. Some economists reject this argument and point out that the ranks of speculators who behave in a destabilizing manner are always replenished, so that speculation can be destabilizing over a long period of time. Furthermore, the fact that destabilizing speculation would bankrupt them did not prevent speculators from behaving in a destabilizing fashion during the stock market crash in 1929 at the start of the Great Depression.

This is one of those arguments that could possibly be resolved only by examining real world experiences. But when we turn to these, we find conflicting evidence. The interwar experience (i.e., between World War I and World War II) with flexible exchange rates clearly indicated the prevalence of destabilizing speculation, according to *Nurkse* (but this has more recently been subject to revision). This interwar experience strongly influenced the Allies of the close of World War II to establish a fixed exchange rate system (the Bretton Woods system). The Canadian experience with flexible exchange rates during the 1950s showed that stabilizing speculation was prevalent.

The last days of the Bretton Woods system in the early 1970s were marred by chaotic conditions in foreign exchange markets, several exchange rate realignments, and clearly destabilzing speculation. On the other hand, the gold standard period (1880–1914) was definitely a time of stabilizing speculation. Under the managed floating system in operation since 1973, exchange rates have fluctuated widely on a daily basis, but there is no general agreement on whether speculation has been stabilizing or destabilizing on average. Perhaps there has been some of both.

Thus, destabilizing speculation can occur under a managed floating system of the type in operation today as well as under a fixed exchange rate system of the Bretton Woods type. However, a majority of economists seem to believe that, under "normal" conditions, speculation was for the most part stabilizing under both systems. Under a *truly* flexible and a *truly* fixed exchange rate system, speculation is almost certain to be stabilizing.

19.3c   Price Discipline

Fixed exchange rates impose a price discipline on the nation not present under flexible exchange rates (the so-called "anchor" argument). That is, a nation with a higher rate of inflation than the rest of the world is likely to face persistent deficits in its balance of payments and loss of reserves under a fixed exchange rate system. Since deficits and reserve losses cannot go on forever, the nation needs to restrain its excessive rate of inflation and thus faces some price discipline. There is no such price discipline under a flexible exchange rate system, where balance-of-payments disequilibria are, at least in theory, automatically and immediately corrected by changes in the exchange rate. Knowing this, elected officials are more likely to overstimulate the economy in order to increase their chances of reelection.

On theoretical grounds, flexible exchange rates do seem more inflationary than fixed exchange rates. We saw in Chapter 15 that a depreciation in a nation's currency increases its domestic prices. On the other hand, an appreciation does not result in a reduction in prices because of the downward inflexibility of prices in today's world. To be sure, a devaluation under a fixed exchange rate system is also inflationary, while a revaluation fails to reduce domestic prices. However, since fluctuating exchange rates lead to overshooting of the equilibrium exchange rate in both directions and cause prices to rise when depreciating but fail to reduce prices when appreciating (the so-called "ratchet" effect), inflation is likely to be higher under a flexible than under a fixed exchange rate system.

As pointed out earlier, we have had no real world experience with *truly* flexible exchange rates, and so we must rely on the experience under the managed floating system. Managed floating since 1973 has coincided with sharp inflationary pressures throughout most of the world until the early 1980s, but not afterwards. Furthermore, the inflationary pressures during the 1970s were as much, or even primarily, the result of the sharp increase in petroleum prices and excessive money creation in most nations (and the resulting inflationary psychology) as due to flexible exchange rates as such.

Advocates of a flexible exchange rate system acknowledge that flexible rates can be more inflationary than fixed exchange rates. However, this results because nations desire different inflation–unemployment trade-offs, and flexible exchange rates allow each nation to pursue its own stabilization policies, that is, to trade more inflation for less unemployment (or vice versa) as the nation sees fit. Advocates of flexible exchange rates view this as an important advantage of a flexible exchange rate system.

Flexible exchange rates to a large extent insulate the domestic economy from *external* shocks (such as an exogenous change in the nation's exports) much more than do fixed exchange rates. As a result, flexible rates are particularly attractive to nations subject to large external shocks. On the other hand, a fixed exchange rate system provides more stability to an open economy subject to large *internal* shocks.

For example, an autonomous increase in investment in the nation increases the level of national income according to the familiar multiplier process. The increase in income induces imports to rise and possibly causes a deficit in the nation's balance of payments under a fixed exchange rate system. At least for a time, the nation can finance the deficit out of its international reserves. Under a flexible exchange rate system, however, the nation's currency will automatically depreciate and stimulate its exports, which reinforces the tendency for the nation's income to rise. But the outcome can vary greatly when international capital flows are also considered. Furthermore, since 1973, business cycles seem to have become more, rather than less, synchronized even though exchange rates were floating.

By the way of a summary, we might say that a flexible exchange rate system does not seem to compare unfavorably to a fixed exchange rate system as far as the type of speculation to which it gives rise and the degree of uncertainty that it introduces into international transactions when all factors are considered. On the other hand, flexible exchange rates are generally more efficient and do give nations more flexibility in pursuing their own stabilization policies. At the same time, flexible exchange rates are generally more inflationary than fixed exchange rates and less stabilizing and suited for nations facing large internal shocks. The greatest attraction of flexible exchange rates as far as monetary authorities are concerned is that they allow the nation to retain greater control over its money supply and possibly achieve a lower rate of unemployment than would be possible under a fixed or adjustable-peg exchange rate system. However, this benefit is greatly reduced when, as in today's world, international capital flows are very large. The greatest disadvantage of flexible exchange rates is the lack of price discipline and the large day-to-day volatility and overshooting of exchange rates.

In general, a fixed exchange rate system is preferable for a small open economy that trades mostly with one or a few larger nations and in which disturbances are primarily of a monetary nature. On the other hand, a flexible exchange rate system seems superior for a large, relatively closed economy with diversified trade and a different inflation–unemployment trade-off than its main trading partners, and facing primarily disturbances originating in the real sector abroad.

19.4   Optimum Currency Areas

In this section, we examine the theory of optimum currency areas developed by *Mundell* and *McKinnon* during the 1960s. We are particularly interested in this theory for the light that it can shed on the conflict over fixed versus flexible exchange rates. An **optimum currency area** or **bloc** refers to a group of nations whose national currencies are linked through *permanently* fixed exchange rates and the conditions that would make such an area optimum. The currencies of member nations could then float jointly with respect to the currencies of nonmember nations. Obviously, regions of the same nation, sharing as they do the same currency, are optimum currency areas.

The formation of an optimum currency area eliminates the uncertainty that arises when exchange rates are not permanently fixed, thus stimulating specialization in production and the flow of trade and investments among member regions or nations. The formation of an optimum currency area also encourages producers to view the entire area as a single market and to benefit from greater economies of scale in production.

With permanently fixed exchange rates, an optimum currency area is likely to experience greater price stability than if exchange rates could change between the various member nations. The greater price stability arises because random shocks in different regions or nations within the area tend to cancel each other out, and whatever disturbance may remain is relatively smaller when the area is increased. This greater price stability encourages the use of money as a store of value and to effect economic transactions, and discourages inefficient barter deals arising under more inflationary circumstances. An optimum currency area also saves the cost of official interventions in foreign exchange markets involving the currencies of member nations, the cost of hedging, and the cost of exchanging one currency for another when citizens travel between member nations (if the optimum currency area also adopts a common currency).

Perhaps the greatest disadvantage of an optimum currency area is that each member nation cannot pursue its own independent stabilization and growth policies attuned to its particular preferences and circumstances. For example, a depressed region or nation within an optimum currency area might require expansionary fiscal and monetary policies to reduce an excessive unemployment rate, while the more prosperous region or nation might require contractionary policies to curb inflationary pressures. To some extent, these costs of an optimum currency area are reduced by the greater flow (arbitrage) of capital and labor from regions and nations of excess supply (where returns and earnings tend to be low) to regions and nations of excess demand (where returns and earnings are higher). However, while helpful, this is not likely to eliminate interregional and international differences within the optimum currency area, as proved by the persistent relative poverty in depressed regions of the same nation (e.g., Appalachia in the United States and Southern Italy).

The formation of an optimum currency area is more likely to be beneficial on balance under the following conditions: (1) the greater is the mobility of resources among the various member nations, (2) the greater are their structural similarities, and (3) the more willing they are to closely coordinate their fiscal, monetary, and other policies. An optimum currency area should aim at maximizing the benefits from permanently fixed exchange rates and minimizing the costs. However, it is extremely difficult to actually measure the net benefits accruing to each member nation from forming an optimum currency area.

Within the national framework, few would suggest that depressed regions would do better by seceding and setting themselves up as separate nations in order to better address their special problems. Instead, what is usually done in these cases is for the central government to provide special aid, such as investment incentives, to depressed regions. However, East Pakistan, charging exploitation, did break away from West Pakistan and proclaimed itself Bangladesh, and Quebec has threatened to secede from Canada for economic as well as cultural reasons.

Since the early 1970s, the European Economic Community (EEC) has expressed a strong commitment to (and made some attempt at) forming an optimum currency area. This involves permanently fixing exchange rates among member nations, coordinating fiscal and monetary policies, establishing a regional policy to aid depressed areas within the EEC, and eventually establishing a common currency. However, attempts to fix exchange rates permanently among member nations and to establish a joint float with respect to currencies of nonmember nations (the so-called European "snake") have not been generally very successful. An adequate degree of coordination of fiscal and monetary policies among member nations is still far from being a reality, and a regional policy to aid depressed areas within the EEC is still in its infancy. Finally, plans for a common currency have also been shelved for the time being until circumstances become more propitious (see Chapter 20). Nevertheless, in 1979, the EEC did form the European Economic System (discussed in Chapter 20), which was conceived to eventually become an optimum currency area.

Some of the benefits provided by the formation of an optimum currency area can also be obtained under the looser form of economic relationship provided by fixed exchange rates. Thus, the case for formation of an optimum currency area is to some extent also a case for fixed as opposed to flexible exchange rates. The theory of optimum currency areas can be regarded as the special branch of the theory of customs unions (discussed in Chapter 10) that deals with monetary factors.

19.5 Exchange Rate Bands, Adjustable Pegs, and Crawling Pegs

In this section, we examine the advantages and disadvantages of hybrid exchange rate systems that combine some of the characteristics of fixed and flexible exchange rates in various degrees. These involve different exchange rate bands of fluctuation about a par value, or fixed exchange rate, adjustable peg systems, and crawling pegs. Managed floating is discussed separately in section 19.6.

19.5a Exchange Rate Bands

All fixed exchange rate systems usually allow the exchange rate to fluctuate within narrowly defined limits. That is, nations decide on the exchange rate, or par value, of their currencies and then allow a narrow band of fluctuation above and below the par value. For example, under the Bretton Woods system, which operated during the postwar period until 1971, the exchange rate was allowed to fluctuate within 1 percent above and below the established par value, or fixed exchange rate. Under the gold standard, the exchange rate, say, between the dollar and the pound, could fluctuate above and below the mint parity (the so-called gold points) by the cost of transporting £1 worth of gold between New York and London (see section 15.6a).

The actual exchange rate under a fixed exchange rate system is then determined by the forces of demand and supply (as explained in Chapter 13) within the band of fluctuation, and it is prevented from moving outside this band by official interventions in foreign exchange markets under a fixed exchange rate not tied to gold, and by gold shipments under the pure gold standard. In what follows, we concentrate on a fixed exchange rate system not tied to gold. The advantage of the small band of fluctuation under a fixed exchange rate system is that monetary authorities will not have to intervene constantly in foreign exchange markets to maintain the established par value, but only to prevent the exchange rate from moving outside the allowed limits of fluctuation.

In the top panel of Figure 19-3, the par value, or fixed exchange rate, between the dollar and the pound is assumed to be $R = \$/\pounds = 2$ and is allowed to fluctuate within 1 percent above and below the par value (as under the Bretton Woods system). As a result, the band of fluctuation (given by the dashed

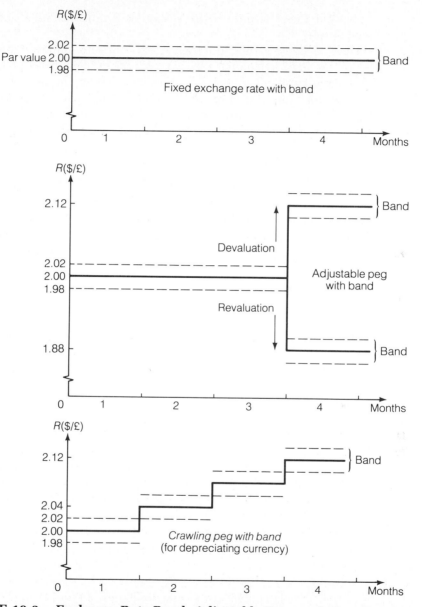

FIGURE 19-3.   Exchange Rate Band, Adjustable Pegs, and Crawling Pegs

In the top panel, the par value is $R=\$2/\pounds1$, and the exchange rate is allowed to fluctuate by 1 percent above and below the par value established. The middle panel shows the nation devaluing its currency from $R=\$2.00$ to $R=\$2.12$ to correct a balance-of-payments deficit, or revaluing from $R=\$2.00$ to $R=\$1.88$ to correct a surplus in its balance of payments. The bottom panel shows the nation devaluing its currency by about 2 percent at the end of each of three months to correct a deficit in its balance of payments.

horizontal lines) is defined by $R = \$1.98$ (the lower limit) and $R = \$2.02$ (the upper limit).

Thus, a fixed exchange rate system exhibits some elements of flexibility about the fixed exchange rate, or par value. Technically, nations could increase the band of allowed fluctuation and let the actual exchange rate be determined more and more by market forces, thus reducing more and more the need for official intervention. Ultimately, the band of allowed fluctuation could be made so wide as to eliminate all official intervention in foreign exchange markets. This would essentially represent a flexible exchange rate system. A preference for fixed exchange rates would allow only a very narrow band of fluctuation, while a preference for flexible exchange rates would make the band very wide.

19.5b Adjustable Peg Systems

An **adjustable peg system** requires defining the par value and the allowed band of fluctuation, with the stipulation that the par value will be changed periodically and the currency devalued to correct a balance-of-payments deficit or revalued to correct a surplus. The Bretton Woods system (see Chapter 20) was originally set up as an adjustable peg system, with nations allowed to change the par value of their currencies when faced with a "fundamental" disequilibrium. Nowhere was fundamental disequilibrium clearly defined, but it broadly referred to a large actual or potential deficit or surplus persisting over several years.

However, under the Bretton Woods system, nations—both for national prestige reasons and for fear that frequent changes in exchange rates would encourage destabilizing speculation (and for the United States also because the dollar was held as international reserves)—were generally unwilling to change par values until practically forced to do so, often under conditions of destabilizing speculation. Thus, while the Bretton Woods system was set up as an adjustable peg system, in fact it operated more nearly as a truly fixed exchange rate system.

A truly adjustable peg system would be one under which nations with balance-of-payments disequilibria would in fact take advantage (or be required to take advantage) of the flexibility provided by the system and change their par values, without waiting for the pressure for such a change to become unbearable. This is shown in the middle panel of Figure 19-3, where the original par value is the same as in the top panel, and then the nation at the beginning of the fourth month *either* devalues its currency (raises the exchange rate) if faced with a balance-of-payments deficit *or* revalues (lowers the exchange rate) if faced with a surplus.

However, for an adjustable peg system to operate as intended, some objective rule would have to be agreed upon and enforced to determine when the nation must change its par value (such as when the international reserves of the nation fell by a certain percentage). Any such rule would to some extent be arbitrary and would also be known to speculators, who could then predict a change in the par value and profitably engage in destabilizing speculation.

19.5c Crawling Pegs

It is to avoid the disdavantage of relatively large changes in par values and possibly destabilizing speculation that the **crawling peg system** or system of "sliding or gliding parties" was devised. Under this system, par values are changed by small preannounced amounts or percentages at frequent and clearly specified intervals, say every month, until the equilibrium exchange rate is reached. This is illustrated in the bottom panel of Figure 19-3 for a nation requiring a devaluation of its currency. Instead of a single devaluation of 6 percent required after three months, the nation devalues by about 2 percent at the end of each of three consecutive months.

The nation could prevent destabilizing speculation by manipulating its short-term interest rate so as to neutralize any profit that would result from the scheduled change in the exchange rate. For example, an announced 2 percent devaluation of the currency would be accompanied by a 2 percent increase in the nation's short-term interest rate. However, this would interfere with the conduct of monetary policy in the nation. Nevertheless, a crawling peg system can eliminate the political stigma attached to a large devaluation and prevent destabilizing speculation. The crawling peg system can achieve even greater flexibility if it is combined with wide bands of fluctuation.

Note that if the upper limit of the band before a mini-devaluation coincides with (as in the figure) or is above the lower limit of the band after the mini-devaluation, then the devaluation may result in no change in the actual spot rate. Nations wanting to use a crawling peg must decide the frequency and amount of the changes in their par values and the width of the allowed band of fluctuation. A crawling peg seems best suited for a developing country that faces real shocks and differential inflation rates. As of December 1984, Brazil, Chile, Colombia, Peru, Portugal, and Somalia had adopted crawling peg systems that seem to function fairly well.

19.6 Managed Floating

Even if speculation were stabilizing, exchange rates would still fluctuate over time (if allowed) because of the fluctuation of real factors in the economy over the business cycle. Destabilizing speculation and overshooting would amplify these intrinsic fluctuations in exchange rates. As we have seen, any exchange rate fluctuation reduces the flow of international trade and investments. Under a **managed floating exchange rate system,** the nation's monetary authorities are entrusted with the responsibility to intervene in foreign exchange markets to smooth out these short-run fluctuations without attempting to affect the long-run trend in exchange rates. To the extent that they are successful, the nation receives most of the benefits that result from fixed exchange rates (see section 19.4) while at the same time retaining flexibility in adjusting balance-of-payments disequilibria.

One possible difficulty is that monetary authorities may be in no better position than professional speculators, investors, and traders to know what the long-run trend in exchange rates is. Fortunately, knowledge of the long-run trend is not needed to stabilize short-run fluctuations in exchange rates if the nation adopts a policy of **leaning against the wind.** This requires the nation's monetary authorities to supply, out of international reserves, a portion (not all) of any short-run excess demand for foreign exchange in the market (thus moderating the tendency of the nation's currency to depreciate) and absorb (and add to its reserves) a portion of any short-run excess supply of foreign exchange in the market (thus moderating the tendency of the nation's currency to appreciate). This reduces short-run fluctuations without affecting the long-run trend in exchange rates.

Note that under a managed float there is still a need for international reserves, whereas under a freely floating exchange rate system, balance-of-payments disequilibria are immediately and automatically corrected by exchange rate changes (with stable foreign exchange markets) without any official intervention and need for reserves. However, the freely floating exchange rate system will experience exchange rate fluctuations that the managed float attempts to moderate.

What proportion of the short-run fluctuation in exchange rates monetary authorities succeed in moderating under a managed floating system depends on what proportion of the short-run excess demand for or supply of foreign exchange they absorb. This, in turn, depends on their willingness to intervene in foreign exchange markets for stabilization purposes and on the size of the nation's international reserves. The larger the nation's stock of international reserves, the greater is the exchange rate stabilization that it can achieve.

There is, however, the danger that if the rules of leaning against the wind discussed earlier are not spelled out precisely (as it has been the case since 1973), a nation might be tempted to keep the exchange rate high (i.e., its currency at a depreciated level) to stimulate its exports. This is a disguised beggar-thy-neighbor policy and invites retaliation by other nations when they face an increase in their imports and a reduction of their exports. This type of floating is sometimes referred to as **dirty floating.** Thus, in the absence of clearly defined and adhered-to rules of behavior, there exists the danger of distortions and conflicts that can be detrimental to the smooth flow of international trade and investments.

The world has had a managed floating system of sorts since 1973. To be sure, this system was not deliberately chosen but was imposed by the collapse of the Bretton Woods system under chaotic conditions in foreign exchange markets and unbearable destabilizing speculation. In the early days of the managed floating system, serious attempts were made to devise specific rules for managing the float to prevent dirty floating and the inevitable conflicts that would follow. However, all of these attempts to date have failed. What is true is that neither the best expectations of those who favored flexible rates in the early 1970s, nor the worst fears of those opposed flexible rates have in fact materialized over the past 15 years or so of the managed float. What is also probably true is that no fixed exchange rate system would have survived the great turmoil of the 1970s arising from the sharp increase in petroleum prices and consequent worldwide inflation and recession.

Nevertheless, the large depreciation of the dollar from 1978 to 1980 and during 1985, as well as its large appreciation from 1981 until the beginning of 1985 clearly indicate that large exchange rate disequilibria can arise and persist over several years under the present managed floating exchange rate system. This has renewed calls for reform of the present international monetary system along the lines of establishing target zones of allowed fluctuations for the leading currencies and for more international cooperation and coordination of policies among the leading nations. It now remains to be seen how successful these new attempts at reform will be.

It must be pointed out, however, that less than one-third of the 149 nations that were members of the International Monetary Fund (IMF) in 1982 have opted for a managed float. But these include all the large industrial nations (the United States, West Germany, Japan, France, Britain, Italy, and Canada) and some of the largest developing and semi-industrialized nations, such as India, Indonesia, the Philippines, Mexico, Argentina, and Spain. In addition, about four-fifths of total world trade today moves between nations operating under a managed floating system.

Most of the remaining two-thirds of the IMF member nations have adopted some kind of a pegged system. About one-third of these nations peg their currencies to the United States dollar (these are primarily the nations of South America, the Caribbean, Africa, and the Middle East). Another third peg their currencies to the French franc (mainly former French colonies in Africa), to Special Drawing Rights (SDRs), or to other currencies. The remaining third peg their currencies to a basket of currencies rather than to a single one. The exchange rate arrangement of each of the 149 members of the International Monetary Fund is presented in the appendix.

The present system thus exhibits a large degree of flexibility and more or less allows each nation to choose the exchange rate regime that best suits its preferences and circumstances. In general, large industrial nations and nations suffering from greater inflationary pressures than the rest of the world have opted for greater exchange rate flexibility than smaller developing nations or highly specialized open economies. Under the 1976 Jamaica Accords (which more or less formally recognized the de facto managed floating system in operation since 1973), a nation may change its exchange rate regime as conditions change, as long as this does not prove disruptive to trade partners and the world economy (more will be said on this in Chapter 20).

Summary

1. While we earlier examined separately the process of adjustment under flexible and fixed exchange rate systems, in this chapter we evaluated and compared the advantages and disadvantages of a flexible as opposed to a fixed exchange rate system, as well as the merits and drawbacks of hybrid systems combining various characteristics of flexible and fixed exchange rates.

2. The case for a flexible exchange rate system rests on its alleged greater market efficiency and its policy advantages. A flexible exchange rate system is said to be more efficient than a fixed exchange rate system because: (1) it relies only on changes in exchange rates, rather than on changing all internal prices, to bring about balance-of-payments adjustment; (2) it makes adjustment smooth and continuous rather than occasional and large; and (3) it clearly identifies the nation's degree of comparative advantage and disadvantage in various commodities. The policy advantages of a flexible exchange rate system are: (1) it frees monetary policy for domestic goals; (2) it enhances the effectiveness of monetary policy; (3) it allows each nation to pursue its own inflation-unemployment trade-off; (4) it removes the danger that the government will use the exchange rate to reach goals that can be better achieved by other policies; and (5) it eliminates the cost of official interventions in foreign exchange markets.

3. The case for a fixed exchange rate system rests on the alleged lower uncertainty, on the belief that speculation is more likely to be stabilizing, and on fixed rates being less inflationary. However, on both theoretical and empirical grounds, it seems that a flexible exchange rate system does not compare unfavorably with a fixed exchange rate system as far as the type of speculation to which it gives rise. On the other hand, flexible exchange rates are generally more efficient and do give nations more flexibility in pursuing their own stabilization policies, but they are generally more inflationary than fixed exchange rates and less stabilizing and suited for nations facing large internal shocks. They also seem to lead to excessive exchange rate volatility.

4. An optimum currency area or bloc refers to a group of nations whose national currencies are linked through permanently fixed exchange rates. The advantages of an optimum currency area are that it (1) eliminates the uncertainty that arises when exchange rates are not permanently fixed, (2) encourages producers to view the entire area as a single market, (3) leads to greater price stability, and (4) saves the cost of official interventions, hedging, and exchanging one currency for another within the area (if a common currency is adopted). Its main disadvantage is that each nation cannot pursue its own independent stabilization and growth policies.

5. All fixed exchange rate systems usually allow the exchange rate to fluctuate within narrowly defined limits. But by increasing the band of allowed fluctuation under a fixed exchange rate system other than the pure gold standard, more and more of the adjustment could be achieved through exchange rate changes. An adjustable peg system would require nations periodically to change their exchange rates when in balance-of-payments disequilibrium. The disadvantage of an adjustable peg system is that it may lead to destabilizing speculation. This can be overcome by a crawling peg system, wherein par values are changed by small amounts at frequent and specified intervals (if the nation also manipulates its short-term interest rates so as to neutralize the profit that speculators could receive from exchange rate changes).

6. Even if speculation were stabilizing, exchange rates would still fluctuate because of the business cycle. Under a managed floating system, monetary authorities intervene in foreign exchange markets to smooth out these short-run fluctuations (with a policy of leaning against the wind) without attempting to affect the long-run trend in exchange rates. However, without clearly defined and adhered-to rules of behavior, a nation might be tempted to keep its exchange rate high (depreciated) to encourage its exports. The world has had a managed floating exchange rate system since 1973. Because of large exchange rate volatility, there are calls today for the establishment of target zones of allowed fluctuation for the leading currencies and for greater international cooperation and coordination of policies.

A Look Ahead

In Chapter 20 (the last chapter in the book), we will examine the operation of the international monetary system from the gold standard period to the present. Fragments of this experience were presented as examples as the various mechanisms of balance-of-payments adjustment were examined. However, in Chapter 20, we will bring it all together and evaluate the process of balance-of-payments adjustment as it actually occurred under the various international monetary systems that existed from 1880 through 1986.

Glossary

Freely floating exchange rate system The flexible exchange rate system under which the exchange rate is always determined by the forces of demand and supply without any government intervention in foreign exchange markets.

Optimum currency area or bloc Refers to a group of nations whose national currencies are linked through permanently fixed exchange rates and the conditions that would make such an area optimum.

Adjustable peg system The system under which exchange rates or par values are periodically changed to current balance-of-payments disequilibria.

Crawling peg system The system under which par values or exchange rates are changed by very small preannounced amounts at frequent and clearly specified intervals until the equilibrium exchange rate is reached.

Managed floating exchange rates system The policy of intervention in foreign exchange markets by monetary authorities to smooth out short-run fluctuations without attempting to affect the long-run trend in exchange rates.

Leaning against the wind The policy of monetary authorities supplying part of the excess demand or absorbing part of the excess supply of foreign exchange in the market to smooth out short-run fluctuations in exchange rates.

Dirty floating Managing the nation's exchange rate to achieve aims other than simply the smoothing out of short-run fluctuations. For example, monetary authorities may intervene in foreign exchange markets to keep the nation's currency undervalued so as to stimulate its exports.

Questions for Review

1. How does a flexible exchange rate system in general adjust balance-of-payments disequilibria? How does a fixed exchange rate system in general adjust balance-of-payments disequilibria? Why is the choice between these two basic types of adjustment system important?

2. What are the two main types of advantage of a flexible as opposed to a fixed exchange rate system? What are the specific advantages subsumed under each main type of advantage of a flexible exchange rate system?

3. What are the alleged advantages of a fixed over a flexible exchange rate system? How would the advocates of flexible exchange rates reply? On the basis of the theoretical and empirical evidence available, what overall conclusion can be reached on which system is to be preferred?

4. What is meant by an optimum currency area or bloc? What are the main advantages and disadvantages of an optimum currency area? What are the conditions required for the establishment of an optimum currency area?

5. What is the effect of increasing the allowed band of exchange rate fluctuation under a fixed exchange rate system? What is meant by an adjustable peg system? What is the advantage and disadvantage of an adjustable peg system with respect to a system of permanently fixed exchange rates? What is meant by a crawling peg system? How can such a system overcome the disadvantage of an adjustable peg system?

6. What is meant by a managed floating exchange rate system? How does the policy of

"leaning against the wind" operate? What is the advantage of a managed floating system with respect to a freely floating exchange rate system and a fixed exchange rate system? What is meant by "dirty" floating? How well is the present managed floating system operating?

Problems

*1. Suppose that the price of a commodity is $7 in the United States and £4 in the United Kingdom, the actual exchange rate between the dollar and the pound is $R = \$2/£1$, but the equilibrium exchange rate $R' = \$1.50/£1$.
   (a) Will the United States export or import this commodity?
   (b) Does the United States have a comparative advantage in this commodity?

*2. Explain why monetary policy would be completely ineffective under a fixed exchange rate system and perfectly elastic international capital flows.

3. Draw a figure similar to Figure 19-1, but showing that for given shifts in the nation's supply curve of foreign exchange, the exchange rate would fluctuate less when the demand for foreign exchange is elastic than when it is inelastic.

4. (a) Draw a figure similar to Figure 19-2 showing the fluctuation in the exchange rate over the business cycle without speculation, with stabilizing speculation, and with destabilizing speculation when there is no long-run trend in the exchange rate over the cycle.
   (b) Draw the same set of curves assuming an implicit appreciating trend of the dollar over the business cycle.

5. Starting with the exchange rate of $R = \$2/£1$, draw a figure showing the exchange rate under a crawling peg system with the nation appreciating its currency by 1 percent at the end of each month for three months, with an allowed band of fluctuation of 1 percent above and below the par value.

6. Starting with the solid line (curve A) showing the fluctuation in the exchange rate over the business cycle in the absence of speculation in Figure 19-2, draw a figure showing the fluctuation in the exchange rate over the cycle (under a managed floating exchange rate system and no speculation) with a policy of leaning against the wind that eliminates about one-half of the fluctuation in the exchange rate.

APPENDIX————————————————————

Exchange Rate Arrangments

In this appendix we present the exchange rate arrangement of each of the 149 members of the International Monetary Fund as of December 31, 1985. This is shown in Table 19-1. The table shows that the present system exibits a large degree of freedom for each nation to choose the exchange regime that best suits it. As a result, some have referred to the present system as a "nonsystem." A nation may also change its exchange regime as long as the change is not disruptive to its trade partners and to the world economy.

Problem   What kind of exchange rate arrangement do the nations of the European Economic Community have?

TABLE 19-1. Exchange Rate Arrangements (As of January 31, 1986)[1]

Currency pegged to					Flexibility Limited in terms of a Single Currency or Group of Currencies		More Flexible		
US Dollar	French Franc	Other currency	SDR	Other composite[2]	Single currency[3]	Cooperative arrangements[4]	Adjusted according to a set of indicators[5]	Other managed floating	Independently floating
Antigua & Barbuda	Benin	Bhutan (Indian Rupee)	Burma	Algeria	Afghanistan	Belgium	Brazil	Argentina	Australia
Bahamas	Burkina Faso	Gambia, The (Pound Sterling)	Burundi	Austria	Bahrain	Denmark	Chile	Costa Rica	Bolivia
Barbados	Cameroon	Lesotho (South African Rand)	Iran, I. R. of	Bangladesh	Qatar	France	Colombia	Ecuador	Canada
Belize	C. African Rep.	Swaziland (South African Rand)	Jordan	Botswana	Saudi Arabia	Germany	Portugal	El Salvador	Dominican Rep.
Djibouti	Chad	Tonga (Australian Dollar)	Kenya	Cape Verde	United Arab Emirates	Ireland	Somalia	Greece	Guinea[3]
Dominica	Comoros		Rwanda	China, P.R.		Italy		Guinea-Bissau	Jamaica
Egypt	Congo		São Tomé & Principe	Cyprus		Luxembourg		Iceland	Japan
Ethiopia	Côte d'Ivoire		Seychelles	Fiji		Netherlands		India	Lebanon
Ghana	Equatorial Guinea		Sierra Leone	Finland				Indonesia	New Zealand
Grenada	Gabon		Vanuatu	Guyana				Israel	Philippines
Guatemala	Mali		Viet Nam	Hungary				Korea	South Africa
Haiti	Niger			Kuwait				Mexico	Uganda
Honduras	Senegal			Madagascar				Morocco	United Kingdom
Iraq	Togo			Malawi				Nigeria	United States
Lao P.D. Rep.				Malaysia				Pakistan	Uruguay
Liberia				Maldives				Spain	Zaire
Libya				Malta				Sri Lanka	Zambia
Nicaragua				Mauritania				Turkey	
Oman				Mauritius				Western Samoa	
Panama				Mozambique				Yugoslavia	
Paraguay				Nepal					
Peru				Norway					
St. Christopher & Nevis				Papua New Guinea					
St. Lucia				Romania					
St. Vincent				Singapore					
Suriname				Solomon Islands					
Syrian Arab Rep.				Sudan					
Trinidad and Tobago				Sweden					
Venezuela				Tanzania					
Yemen Arab Rep.				Thailand					
Yemen, P.D. Rep.				Tunisia					
				Zimbabwe					

[1]Excluding the currency of Democratic Kampuchea, for which no current information is available. For members with dual or multiple exchange markets, the arrangement shown is that in the major market.
[2]Comprises currencies which are pegged to various "baskets" of currencies of the members' own choice, as distinct from the SDR basket.
[3]Exchange rates of all currencies have shown limited flexibility in terms of the U.S. dollar.
[4]Refers to the cooperative arrangement maintained under the European Monetary System.
[5]Includes exchange arrangements under which the exchange rate is adjusted at relatively frequent intervals, on the basis of indicators determined by the respective member countries.
Source: IMF, International Financial Statistics, March 1986, p. 18.

Selected Bibliography

For a problem-solving approach to the topics presented in this chapter, see;

- D. Salvatore, *Theory and Problems of International Economics*, 2nd ed. (New York: McGraw-Hill, 1984), ch. 11, sects. 11.4 to 11.6.

The debate over flexible versus fixed exchange rates is found in:

- M. Friedman, "The Case for Flexible Rates," in M. Friedman, *Essays in Positive Economics* (Chicago: University of Chicago Press, 1953). Reprinted in abbreviated form in R. E. Caves and H. G. Johnson, *Readings in International Economics* (Homewood Ill.: Irwin, 1968).
- E. Sohmen, *Flexible Exchange Rates: Theory and Controversy*, rev. ed. (Chicago: University of Chicago Press, 1969).
- H. G. Johnson, "The Case for Flexible Exchange Rates," in G. N. Halm, *Approaches to Greater Flexibility of Exchange Rates* (Princeton, N.J.: Princeton University Press, 1969).
- R. Stern, *The Balance of Payments: Theory and Economic Policy* (Chicago: Aldine, 1973).
- J. R. Artus and J. H. Young, "Fixed and Flexible Rates: A Renewal of the Debate," *IMF Staff Papers*, December 1979.
- M. Goldstein, *Have Flexible Rates Handicapped Macroeconomic Policy*, Special Papers in International Finance, No. 14 (Princeton, N.J.: Princeton University Press, June 1980).
- R. Dornbusch, *Open Economy Macroeconomics* (New York: Basic Books, 1980).

The classics of the theory of optimum currency areas are:

- R. Mundell, "The Theory of Optimum Currency Areas," *American Economic Review*, September 1961.
- R. McKinnon, "Optimum Currency Areas," *American Economic Review*, September 1963.

For other works on the theory of optimum currency areas, see:

- H. G. Johnson and A. Swoboda, *Madrid Conference on Optimum Currency Areas* (Cambridge, Mass.: Harvard University Press, 1973).
- T. D. Willett and E. Towers, *The Theory of Optimum Currency Areas and Exchange Rate Flexibility*, Special Papers in International Economics, No. 11 (Princeton, N.J.: Princeton University Press, International Finance Section, May 1976).

For the original analysis of the interwar currency experience, see:

- R. Nurkse, *The Interwar Currency Experience: Lessons of the Interwar Period* (Geneva: United Nations, 1944).

The present managed floating system is discussed and evaluated in:

- G. Haberler, "The International Monetary System After Jamaica and Manila," *Contemporary Economic Problems*, No. 2 (Washington, D.C.: American Enterprise Institute, 1977).
- P. A. Tosini, *Leaning Against the Wind: A Standard for Managed Floating*, Essays in International Finance, No. 126, (Princeton, N.J.: Princeton University Press, December 1977).
- J. R. Artus and A. D. Crocket, *Floating Exchange Rates and the Need for Surveillance*, Essays in International Finance, No. 127, (Princeton, N.J.: Princeton University Press, May 1978).
- M. Mussa, *The Role of Official Intervention*, Occasional Paper No. 6 (New York: The Group of Thirty, 1981).
- O. Emminger, *Exchange Rate Policy Reconsidered*, Occasional Paper No. 10 (New York: Group of Thirty, 1982).
- V. Argy, "Exchange Rate Management in Theory and Practice," *Princeton Studies in International Finance*, October 1982.
- R. N. Cooper et al. (Eds.) *The International Monetary System under Flexible Exchange Rates* (Cambridge, Mass.: Ballinger, 1982).
- J. Williamson, *The Exchange Rate System* (Washington, D.C.: Institute for International Economics, 1983).
- W. H. Branson, "Exchange Rate Policy after a

Decade of 'Floating,' " in J. F. O. Bilson and R. C. Marston, Eds., *Exchange Rate Theory and Practice* (Chicago: University of Chicago Press, 1984).

• R. C. Marston, "Exchange Rate Unions as an Alternative to Flexible Rates: The Effects of Real and Monetary Disturbances," in J. F. O. Bilson and R. C. Marston, Eds., *Exchange Rate Theory and Practice* (Chicago: University of Chicago Press, 1984).

• R. C. Marston, "Stabilization Policies in Open Economies," in R. W. Jones and P. B. Kenen, Eds., *Handbook of International Economics,* Vol. 2, (Amsterdam: North-Holland, 1985).

See also the references at the end of Chapter 20.

CHAPTER 20

The International Monetary System: Past and Present

20.1 Introduction

In this chapter, we examine the operation of the international monetary system from the gold standard period to the present. Fragments of this experience were presented as examples as the various mechanisms of balance-of-payments adjustment were examined. We now bring it all together and evaluate the process of balance-of-payments adjustment as it actually occurred under the various international monetary systems that existed from 1880 to the present. Though the approach is historical, the evaluation of the operation of the various international monetary systems will be conducted in terms of the analytical framework developed in Chapters 15 through 19.

An **international monetary system** (sometimes referred to as an international monetary *order* or *regime*) refers to the rules, customs, instruments, facilities, and organizations for effecting international payments. International monetary systems can be classified according to the way in which exchange rates are determined or according to the form that international reserve assets take. Under the exchange rate classification, we can have a fixed exchange rate system with a narrow band of fluctuation about a par value, a fixed exchange rate system with a wide band of fluctuation, an adjustable peg system, a crawling peg system, a managed floating exchange rate system, or a freely floating exchange rate system. Under the international reserve classification, we can have a gold standard (with gold as the only international reserve as- set), a pure fiduciary standard (such as a pure dollar or exchange standard without any connection with gold) or a gold-exchange standard (a combina- tion of the previous two).

The various classifications can be combined in various ways. For example, the gold standard is a fixed exchange rate system. However, we can also have a fixed exchange rate system without any connection with gold, but with in- ternational reserves composed of some national currency, such as the United States dollar, that is no longer backed by gold. Similarly, we can have an adjustable peg system or a managed float with gold and foreign exchange or with only foreign exchange as international reserve. Under a freely floating exchange rate system, there is, of course, no need for reserves since exchange rate changes automatically and immediately correct any balance-of-payments disequilibrium as it develops. Throughout the period of our analysis, most of the international monetary systems possible were in operation at one time or another or for some nations, as described in this chapter.

A good international monetary system is one that maximizes the flow of international trade and investments and leads to an "equitable" distribution of the gains from trade among the nations of the world. An international mon- etary system can be evaluated in terms of adjustment, liquidity, and confi- dence. **Adjustment** refers to the process by which balance-of-payment dise- quilibria are corrected. A good international monetary system is one that minimizes the cost of and the time required for adjustment. **Liquidity** refers to the amount of international reserve assets available to settle temporary bal- ance-of-payments disequilibria. A good international monetary system is one that provides adequate international reserves so that nations can correct bal- ance-of-payments deficits without deflating their own economies or being in- flationary for the world as a whole. **Confidence** refers to the knowledge that the adjustment mechanism is working adequately and that international re- serves will retain their absolute and relative values.

In section 20.2, we examine the gold standard as it operated from about 1880 to 1914 and the experience between World War I and World War II. The gold standard was, of course, a fixed exchange rate system with gold as the only international reserve asset. The interwar period was characterized first by a system of flexible exchange rates and subsequently by the attempt to reestablish the gold standard—an attempt doomed to failure. Sections 20.3, 20.4, and 20.5 examine the establishment, the operation, and the collapse of the Bretton Woods system, the fixed or adjustable-peg gold-exchange standard that operated from the end of World War II until August 1971. From then through March 1973, an adjustable-peg dollar standard prevailed. Section 20.6 examines the present managed floating exchange rate system, which is char- acterized by fiduciary reserves (mostly United States dollars but also other convertible currencies and Special Drawing Rights, as well as the total reserve positions of member nations in the IMF). Finally, the appendix presents the composition and value of international reserves from 1950–1985.

20.2   The Gold Standard and the Interwar Experience

In this section, we examine first the gold standard as it operated from about 1880 to the outbreak of World War I in 1914. Then we examine the interwar experience with flexible exchange rates between 1919 and 1924 and the subsequent attempt to reestablish the gold standard (this attempt failed with the deepening of the Great Depression in 1931).

20.2a   The Gold Standard Period (1880–1914)

The *gold standard* operated from about 1880 to 1914. Under it, as explained in section 15.6a, each nation defined the gold content of its currency and passively stood ready to buy or sell any amount of gold at that price. Since the gold content in one unit of each currency was fixed, exchange rates were also fixed. This was called the *mint parity*. The exchange rate could then fluctuate above and below the mint parity (i.e., within the *gold points*) by the cost of shipping an amount of gold equal to one unit of the foreign currency between the two monetary centers.

The exchange rate was determined within the gold points by the forces of demand and supply and was prevented from moving outside the gold points by gold shipments. That is, the tendency of a currency to depreciate past the *gold export point* was halted by gold outflows from the nation. These gold outflows represented the deficit in the nation's balance of payments. Conversely, the tendency of a nation's currency to appreciate past the *gold import point* was halted by gold inflows. These gold inflows measured the surplus in the nation's balance of payments. Since deficits were supposed to be settled in gold and nations had limited gold reserves, deficits could not go on forever but had to be corrected quickly.

The adjustment mechanism under the gold standard, as explained by *Hume*, was the automatic *price-specie-flow mechanism* (see section 15.6b), which operated as follows. Since each nation's money supply consisted of either gold itself or paper currency backed by gold, the money supply would fall in the deficit nation and rise in the surplus nation. This would cause internal prices to fall in the deficit nation and rise in the surplus nation (the *quantity theory of money*). As a result, the exports of the deficit nation would be encouraged and its imports discouraged until its balance-of-payments deficit was eliminated. The opposite would occur in the surplus nation.

Passively allowing its money supply to change for balance-of-payments considerations meant that a nation could not use monetary policy for achieving full employment without inflation. But this created no difficulties for classical economists, since they believed that there was an automatic tendency in the economic system toward full employment without inflation.

For the adjustment process to operate, nations were not supposed to *sterilize* (i.e., neutralize) the effect of a balance-of-payments deficit or surplus. On the contrary, the *rules of the game* of the gold standard required a deficit nation to reinforce the adjustment process by further restricting credit and a surplus nation to further expand credit. However, *Nurkse* and *Bloomfield* found that monetary authorities often did not follow the rules of the game during the period of the gold standard but sterilized part, though not all, of the effect of a balance-of-payments disequilibrium on the nation's money supply. *Michaely* argued that this was necessary to moderate the adjustment process and prevent an excessive reduction in the deficit nation's money supply and an excessive increase in the surplus nation's money supply.

The above is how the adjustment mechanism was supposed to have worked under the gold standard. In reality, *Taussig* and some of his students at Harvard found in the 1920s that the adjustment process seemed to work much too quickly and smoothly and with little, if any, transfer of gold among nations. Taussig found that balance-of-payments disequilibria were settled mostly by international capital flows rather than through gold shipments (as described above). That is, when the United Kingdom had a balance-of-payments deficit, its money supply fell, interest rates rose, and this attracted a short-term capital inflow to cover the deficit.

The United Kingdom reinforced this incentive for capital inflows by deliberately raising its discount rate (called the *bank rate* there), which increased interest rates and capital inflows even more. Furthermore, the reduction in the United Kingdom money supply as a result of a deficit seems to have reduced domestic economic activity more than prices, and this discouraged imports (as described by the automatic *income* adjustment mechanism discussed in Chapter 16). The opposite process corrected a surplus in the United Kingdom balance of payments.

Not only did most of the adjustment under the gold standard not take place as described by the price-specie-flow mechanism, but if the adjustment process was quick and smooth, this was due to the special conditions that existed during the period of the gold standard. This was a period of great economic expansion and stability throughout most of the world. The pound sterling was the only important international currency and London the only international monetary center. Therefore, there could be no lack of confidence in the pound and shifts into other currencies and to other rival monetary centers. There was greater price flexibility than today, and nations subordinated internal to external balance. Under such circumstances, any international monetary system would probably have worked fairly smoothly.

Reestablishing the gold standard today without at the same time recreating the conditions that ensured its smooth operation during the thirty years or so before World War I would certainly lead to its collapse. Nevertheless, the period of the gold standard is surrounded by an aura of nostalgia about "the good old days" that is difficult to dispel and which to some extent lingers on even today. However, it is very improbable that the gold standard or anything closely resembling it will be reestablished in the foreseeable future.

20.2b The Interwar Experience

With the outbreak of World War I, the classical gold standard came to an end. Between 1919 and 1924, exchange rates fluctuated wildly and led to a desire to return to the stability of the gold standard. In April 1925, the United Kingdom reestablished the convertibility of the pound into gold *at the prewar price* and lifted the embargo on gold exports that it had imposed at the outbreak of World War I. Other nations followed the United Kingdom's lead and went back to gold. (The United States had already returned to gold in 1919.) However, the new system was more in the nature of a gold-exchange standard than a pure gold standard in that both gold and currencies convertible into gold (mostly pounds but also United States dollars and French francs) were used as international reserves. This economized on gold, which (at the prewar price and in the face of a substantial increase in other prices as a result of the war) had become a much smaller percentage of the total value of world trade.

However, since the United Kingdom had lost a great deal of its competitiveness (especially to the United States) and had liquidated a substantial portion of its foreign investments to pay for the war effort, reestablishing the prewar parity left the pound grossly overvalued (see the discussion of Cassell's purchasing power theory in section 15.5). This led to balance-of-payments deficits and to deflation as the United Kingdom attempted to contain its deficits. On the other hand, France faced large balance-of-payments surpluses after the franc was stabilized at a depreciated level in 1926.

Seeking to make Paris an international monetary center in its own right, France passed a law in 1928 requiring settlement of its balance-of-payments surpluses in gold rather than in pounds or other currencies. This was a serious drain in the meager United Kingdom gold reserves and led to a shift of short-term capital from London to Paris and New York. When France also sought to convert all of its previously accumulated pounds into gold, the United Kingdom was forced in September 1931 to suspend the convertibility of the pound into gold, devalued the pound, and the gold-exchange standard came to an end (the United States actually went off gold in 1933).

While France's decision to convert all of its pounds into gold was the immediate cause of the collapse of the gold-exchange standard, the more fundamental causes were (1) the lack of an adequate adjustment mechanism as nations sterilized the effect of balance-of-payments disequilibria on their money supplies in the face of grossly inappropriate parities, (2) the huge destabilizing capital flows between London and the emerging international monetary centers of New York and Paris, and (3) the outbreak of the Great Depression (to which the malfunction of the international monetary system contributed). However, it is likely that any international monetary system would have collapsed under the tremendous strain of worldwide depression.

There followed, from 1931 to 1936, a period of great instability and competitive devaluations as nations tried to "export" their unemployment. The United States even devalued the dollar (by increasing the dollar price of gold from $20.67 to $35 an ounce) in 1933–1934, from a position of balance-of-payments *surplus,* in order to stimulate its exports. Needless to say, this was a serious policy mistake. Expansionary domestic policies would have stimulated the United States economy and at the same time corrected or reduced its balance-of-payments surplus. By 1936 exchange rates among the major currencies were approximately the same as they had been in 1930, before the cycle of competitive devaluations began. The only effect was that the value of gold reserves was increased. However, most foreign exchange reserves had been eliminated by mass conversions into gold as protection against devaluations.

This was also a period when nations imposed very high tariffs and other serious import restrictions, so that the international trade was cut almost in half. For example, in 1930 the United States passed the *Smoot-Hawley Tariff Act,* which raised United States import duties to an all-time high (see section 9.5a). By 1939, of course, depression gave way to full employment—and war.

According to *Nurske,* the interwar experience clearly indicated the prevalence of destabilizing speculation and the instability of flexible exchange rates. This experience strongly influenced the Allies at the close of World War II to establish an international monetary system with some flexibility but with a heavy emphasis on fixity as far as exchange rates were concerned. (This is discussed in the next section.) More recently, the interwar experience has been reinterpreted to indicate that the wild fluctuations in exchange rates during the 1919–1924 period reflected the serious pent-up disequilibria that had developed during World War I and the instability associated with postwar reconstruction, and that in all likelihood no fixed exchange rate system could have survived during this period.

20.3 The Bretton Woods System

In this section, we describe the so-called Bretton Woods system and the International Monetary Fund (the institution created to oversee the operation of the new international monetary system and provide credit to nations facing temporary balance-of-payments difficulties).

20.3a The Gold-Exchange Standard (1947–1971)

In 1944 representatives for the United States, and the United Kingdom, and 42 other nations met at Bretton Woods, New Hampshire, to decide on the international monetary system to establish after the war. The system devised at Bretton Woods called for the establishment of the **International Monetary Fund (IMF)** for the purposes of (1) overseeing that nations followed a set of agreed rules of conduct in international trade and finance and (2) providing *borrowing* facilities for nations in *temporary* balance-of-payments difficulties.

The new international monetary system reflected the plan of the American delegation, headed by *White* of the United States Treasury, rather than the plan submitted by *Keynes,* who headed the British delegation. Keynes had called for the establishment of a *Clearing Union* able to *create* international liquidity based on a new unit of account called the "bancor," just as a national central bank (the Federal Reserve in the United States) can create money domestically. The IMF opened its doors on March 1, 1947, with a membership of 30 nations. By 1986 IMF membership had grown to 149 nations, with practically all of the world's nations belonging, the main exceptions being Switzerland, and some communist nations, including the Soviet Union.

The **Bretton Woods System** was a gold-exchange standard. The United States was to maintain the price of gold fixed at $35 per ounce and be ready to exchange on demand dollars for gold at that price, without restrictions or limitations. Other nations were to fix the price of their currencies in terms of dollars (and thus implicitly in terms of gold) and intervene in foreign exchange markets to keep the exchange rate from moving by more than 1 percent above or below the par value. Within the allowed band of fluctuation, the exchange rate was determined by the forces of demand and supply.

Specifically, a nation would have to draw down its dollar reserves to purchase its own currency in order to prevent it from depreciating by more than 1 percent from the agreed par value, or the nation would have to purchase dollars with its own currency (adding to its international reserves) to prevent an appreciation of its currency by more than 1 percent from the par value. Until the late 1950s and early 1960s, when other currencies became fully convertible into dollars, the United States dollar was the only **intervention currency,** so that the new system was practically a gold-dollar standard.

Nations were to finance temporary balance-of-payments deficits out of their international reserves and by borrowing from the **IMF.** Only in a case of **fundamental disequilibrium** was a nation allowed, after the approval of the Fund, to change the par value of its currency. Fundamental disequilibrium was nowhere clearly defined but broadly referred to large and persistent balance-of-payments deficits or surpluses. Exchange rate changes of less than 10 percent were, however, allowed without Fund approval. Thus, the Bretton Woods system was in the nature of an adjustable peg system, at least as originally conceived, combining general exchange rate stability with some flexibility. The stress on fixity can best be understood as resulting from the strong desire of nations to avoid the chaotic conditions in international trade and finance that prevailed during the interwar period.

After a period of transition following the war, nations were to remove all restrictions on the full convertibility of their currencies into other currencies and into the United States dollar. Nations were forbidden to impose additional trade restrictions (otherwise **currency convertibility** would not have much meaning), and existing trade restrictions were to be removed gradually in multilateral negotiations under the sponsorship of GATT (see section 9.5b). Restrictions on international liquid capital flows were, however, permitted to allow nations to protect their currencies against large destabilizing, or "hot," international money flows.

Borrowing from the Fund (to be described below) was restricted to cover temporary balance-of-payments deficits and to be repaid within three to five years so as not to tie up the Fund's resources in long-term loans. *Long-run* development assistance was to be provided by the **International Bank for Reconstruction and Development (IBRD** or **World Bank)** and its affiliates, the **International Development Association** (established in 1960 to make loans at subsidized rates to the poorer developing nations) and the **International Finance Corporation** (established in 1956 to stimulate *private* investments in developing nations from indigenous and foreign sources).

The Fund was also to collect and propagate balance-of-payments, international trade, and other economic data of member nations. Today the IMF publishes, among other things, *International Financial Statistics* and *Direction of Trade Statistics,* the most authoritative sources of comparable time series data on the balance of payments, trade, and other economic indicators of member nations.

20.3b   Borrowing from the International Monetary Fund

Upon joining the IMF, each nation was assigned a quota based on its economic importance and the volume of its international trade. The size of a nation's quota determined its voting power and its ability to borrow from the Fund. The total subscription to the Fund was set in 1944 at $8.8 billion. As the most powerful nation, the United States was assigned by far the largest quota, 31 percent. Every five years quotas were to be revised to reflect changes in the relative economic importance and international trade of member nations. By 1986 the total subscription of the Fund had grown to 90 billion SDRs (about $98 billion) through increased membership and periodic increases in quotas. The United States quota had declined to 21 percent of the total, the United Kingdom quota was 7 percent, that of West Germany about 6 percent, and that of France and Japan about 5 percent.

Upon joining the IMF, a nation was to pay 25 percent of its quota to the Fund in gold and the remainder in its own currency. In borrowing from the Fund, the nation would get convertible currencies approved by the Fund in exchange for depositing equivalent (and additional) amounts of its own currency into the Fund, until the Fund held no more than 200 percent of the nation's quota in the nation's currency.

Under the original rules of the Fund, a member nation could borrow no more than 25 percent of its quota in any one year, up to a total of 125 percent of its quota over a five-year period. The nation could borrow the first 25 percent of its quota, the so-called **gold tranche,** almost automatically, without any restrictions or conditions. For further borrowings (in subsequent years), the so-called **credit tranches,** the Fund charged higher and higher interest rates and imposed more and more supervision and conditions to ensure that the deficit nation was taking appropriate measures to eliminate the deficit.

Repayments were to be made within three to five years and involved the nation's repurchase of its own currency from the Fund with other convertible currencies approved by the Fund, until the IMF once again held no more than 75 percent of the nation's quota in the nation's currency. The Fund allowed repayments to be made in currencies of which it held less than 75 percent of the issuing nation's quota. If before a nation (Nation A) completed repayment, another nation (Nation B) borrowed Nation A's currency from the Fund, then Nation A would end repayment of its loan as soon as the Fund's holdings of Nation A's currency reached 75 percent of its quota.

If the Fund's holding of a nation's currency fell below 75 percent of its quota, the nation could borrow the difference from the Fund without having to repay its loan. This was called the **super gold tranche.** In the event that the Fund ran out of a currency altogether, it would declare the currency "scarce" and allow member nations to discriminate in trade against the scarce currency nation. The reason for this was that the Fund viewed balance-of-payments adjustment as the joint responsibility of both deficit and surplus nations. However, the Fund has never been called upon to invoke this scarce currency provision during its many years of operation.

A nation's gold tranche plus its super gold tranche (if any) or minus the amount of its borrowing (if any) is called the nation's **net IMF position.** Thus, the nation's net IMF position is given by the size of its quota minus the Fund's holding of its currency. The amount of gold reserves paid in by a nation upon joining the Fund is called the nation's reserve position in the Fund and is added to the nation's other international reserves of gold, Special Drawing Rights (SDRs—see the next section), and other convertible currencies to obtain the total value of the nation's international reserves (see section 14.3).

20.4   Operation and Evolution of the Bretton Woods System

In this section, we examine the operation of the Bretton Woods system from 1947 until it collapsed in 1971. We also examine the way in which the system evolved over the years, in response to changing conditions, from the blueprint agreed upon in 1944.

20.4a   The Operation of the Bretton Woods System

While the Bretton Woods system envisaged and allowed changes in par values in cases of fundamental disequilibrium, in reality industrial nations were very reluctant to change their par values until such action was long overdue and was practically forced on them by the resulting destabilizing speculation. Deficit nations were reluctant to devalue their currencies because they regarded this as a sign of national weakness. Surplus nations resisted needed revaluations, preferring instead to continue accumulating international reserves. Thus, from 1950 until August 1971, the United Kingdom devalued only in 1967; France devalued only in 1957 and 1969; West Germany *revalued* in 1961 and 1969; and the United States, Italy, and Japan never changed their par values. Meanwhile Canada (defying the rules of the IMF) had fluctuating exchange rates from 1950 to 1962 and then reinstituted them in 1970. Developing nations, on the other hand, devalued all too often.

The unwillingness of industrial nations to change their par values as a matter of policy when in fundamental disequilibrium had two important effects. First, it robbed the Bretton Woods system of most of its flexiblity and mechanism for adjusting balance-of-payments disequilibria. We will see in section 20.5 that this played a crucial role in the collapse of the system in August 1971. Second, and related to the first point, the reluctance of industrial nations to change their par value when in fundamental disequilibrium gave rise to huge destabilizing international capital flows by providing an excellent one-way gamble for speculators.

Specifically, a nation such as the United Kingdom, with chronic balance-of-payments deficits over most of the postwar period, was plagued by huge liquid capital outflows in the expectation that the pound would be devalued. Indeed, these expectations became self-fulfilling, and the United Kingdom was forced to devalue the pound in 1967 (after a serious deflationary effort to avoid the devaluation). On the other hand, a nation such as West Germany, with chronic balance-of-payments surpluses, received huge capital inflows in the expectation that it would revalue the mark. This made revaluation of the mark inevitable in 1961 and again in 1969.

The convertibility of the dollar into gold resumed soon after World War II. The major European currencies became convertible for current account purposes de facto in 1958 and de jure, or formally, in 1961. The Japanese yen became formally convertible into United States dollars and other currencies in 1964. As pointed out in section 20.3a, capital account restrictions were permitted to allow nations some protection against destabilizing capital flows. Despite these restrictions, the postwar era experienced periods of huge destabilizing capital flows, which became more frequent and more disruptive, culminating in the collapse of the Bretton Woods in August 1971. These very large destabilizing "hot" money flows were facilitated by the establishment and very rapid growth of *Eurocurrency markets* during the 1960s (see section 13.6).

Under the *Trade Expansion Act of 1962* and GATT auspices (see section 9.5c), the United States initiated and engaged in wide-ranging multilateral trade negotiations (the *Kennedy Round*), which lowered average tariffs on manufactured goods to less than 10 percent. However, many nontariff barriers to international trade remained, especially in agriculture and on simple manufactured goods, such as textiles, which are of special importance to developing nations. This was also the period when several attempts were made at economic integration, the most successful being the European Common Market (see section 10.6).

20.4b   Evolution of the Bretton Woods System

Over the years, the Bretton Woods system evolved in several important directions in response to changing conditions. In 1962 the IMF negotiated the **General Arrangements to Borrow (GAB)** up to $6 billion from the so-called "group of ten" most important industrial nations (the United States, the United Kingdom, West Germany, Japan, France, Italy, Canada, the Netherlands, Belgium, and Sweden) and Switzerland to supplement its resources if needed to help nations with balance-of-payments difficulties. This sum of $6 billion was over and above the periodic increases in the Articles of Agreement that established the IMF. GAB was renewed in 1979.

Starting in the early 1960s, member nations began to negotiate **standby arrangements.** These refer to advance permission for future borrowings by the nation at the IMF. Once a standby arrangement was negotiated, the nation paid a small commitment charge of one-fourth of 1 percent of the amount earmarked and was then able to borrow up to this additional amount *immediately* when the need arose at a 5.5 percent charge per year on the amount actually borrowed. Standby arrangements were usually negotiated by member nations as a first line of defense against anticipated destabilizing hot money flows. After several increases in quotas, the total resources of the Fund reached $28.5 billion by 1971 (of which $6.7 billion, or about 23.5 percent, was the United States quota). By the end of 1971, the Fund had lent about $22 billion (mostly after 1956), of which about $4 billion was outstanding. The Fund also changed the rules and allowed member nations to borrow up to 50 percent of their quotas in any one year (up from 25 percent).

National central banks also began to negotiate so-called **swap arrangements** to exchange each other's currency, to be used to intervene in foreign exchange markets to combat hot money flows. A central bank facing large liquid capital flows could then sell the foreign currency forward in order to increase the forward discount or reduce the forward premium on the foreign currency and discourage destabilizing hot money flows (see sections 13.3 to 13.5). Swap arrangements were negotiated for specific periods of time and with an exchange rate guarantee. When due, they could either be settled by a reverse transaction or be renegotiated for another period. The United States and European nations negotiated many such swap arrangements during the 1960s. In the early 1980s, the total amount of swap arrangements exceeded $30 billion.

The most significant change introduced into the Bretton Woods system was the creation of **Special Drawing Rights (SDRs)** to supplement the international reserves of gold, foreign exchange, and reserve position in the IMF. Sometimes called *paper gold*, SDRs are accounting entries in the books of the

IMF. SDRs are not backed by gold or any other currency but represent genuine international reserves *created* by the IMF. Their value arises because member nations have so agreed. SDRs can only be used in dealings among central banks to settle balance-of-payments deficits and surpluses and not in private commercial dealings. A charge of 1.5 percent (subsequently increased to 5 percent and now based on market rates) was applied on the amount by which a nation's holdings of SDRs fell short of or exceeded the amount of SDRs allocated to it. The reason for this was to put pressure on both deficit and surplus nations to correct balance-of-payments disequilibria.

At the 1967 meeting of the IMF in Rio de Janeiro, it was agreed to create SDRs in the amount of $9.5 billion, to be distributed to member nations according to their quotas in the IMF, in three installments in January 1970, 1971, and 1972. Further allocations of SDRs were made in the 1979–1981 period (see section 20.6a). The value of one SDR was originally set equal to one United States dollar but rose above $1 as a result of the devaluations to the dollar in 1971 and 1973. Starting in 1974, the value of SDRs was tied to a basket of currencies, as explained in section 20.6a.

In 1961 the so-called **gold pool** was started by a group of industrial nations under the leadership of the United States to sell officially held gold on the London market to prevent the price of gold from rising above the official price of $35 an ounce. This was discontinued as a result of the gold crisis of 1968, when a **two-tier gold market** was established. This kept the price of gold at $35 an ounce in official transactions among central banks, while allowing the commercial price of gold to rise above the official price and be determined by the forces of demand and supply in the market. These steps were taken to prevent depletion of United States gold reserves.

Over the years, membership in the IMF increased to include most nations of the world, except Switzerland and some communist nations. Despite the shortcomings of the Bretton Woods system, the postwar period until 1971 was characterized by world output growing quite rapidly and international trade growing even faster. Overall, it can thus be said that the Bretton Woods system served the world community well, particularly until the mid-1960s.

20.5 United States Balance-of-Payments Deficits and Collapse of the Bretton Woods System

In this section, we briefly examine the causes of the United States balance-of-payments deficits over most of the postwar period and their relationship to the collapse of the Bretton Woods system in August 1971. We then consider the more fundamental causes of the collapse of the system and their implications for the present managed floating exchange rate system.

20.5a   The United States Balance-of-Payments Deficits

From 1945 to 1949, the United States ran huge balance-of-payments surpluses with Europe and extended Marshall Plan aid to help pay for them. With European recovery more or less complete by 1950, the United States balance of payments turned into deficit. Up to 1957, United States deficits were rather small, averaging about $1 billion each year. These United States deficits allowed European nations and Japan to build up their international reserves. This was the period of the **dollar shortage.** The United States settled its deficits mostly in dollars. Surplus nations were willing to accept dollars because (1) the United States stood ready to exchange dollars for gold at the fixed price of $35 an ounce, making the dollar "as good as gold"; (2) dollars could be used to settle international transactions with any other nation (i.e., the dollar was truly an international currency); and (3) dollar deposits earned interest while gold did not.

Starting in 1958, United States balance-of-payments deficits increased sharply and averaged over $3 billion per year. Contributing to the much larger United States deficits since 1958 was first the huge increase in capital outflows (mostly direct investments in Europe) and then the high United States inflation rate (connected with the excessive money creation during the Vietnam war period), which led to the virtual disappearance of the traditional United States trade balance surplus, starting in 1968. The United States financed its balance-of-payments deficits mostly with dollars, so that by 1970 foreign official dollar holdings were more than $40 billion, up from $13 billion in 1949. (Foreign private dollar holdings were even larger, and these could also be potential claims on United States gold reserves.) At the same time, United States gold reserves declined from $25 billion in 1949 to $11 billion in 1970.

Because the dollar was an international currency, the United States felt that it could not devalue to correct its balance-of-payments deficits. Instead, it adopted a number of other policies which, however, had only very limited success. One of these was the attempt in the early 1960s to keep short-term interest rates high to discourage short-term capital outflows, while at the same time trying to keep long-term interest rates relatively low to stimulate domestic growth (operation twist). The United States also intervened in foreign exchange markets and sold forward strong currencies, such as the German mark, to increase the forward discount and discourage liquid capital outflows under covered interest arbitrage (see section 13.5b). It also intervened in the spot market in support of the dollar.

The resources for these interventions in the spot and forward markets were usually obtained from swap arrangements with other central banks and from standby arrangements with the IMF. The United States took additional steps to encourage its exports, reduced military and other government expenditures abroad, and tied most of its foreign aid to be spent in the United States. Furthermore, during the 1963–1968 period, the United States introduced a number of direct controls over capital outflows. These were the Interest Equalization Tax, the Foreign Direct Investment Program, and restrictions on bank loans to foreigners.

As the United States deficits persisted and rose over time, United States gold reserves declined while foreign-held dollar reserves grew to the point where they began to exceed the United States gold reserves in the early 1960s. To discourage foreign official holders of dollars from converting their excess dollars into gold at the Federal Reserve and further reducing United States gold reserves, the United States created the so-called **Roosa bonds.** These were medium-term treasury bonds denominated in dollars but with an exchange rate guarantee. Nevertheless, United States gold reserves continued to decline, while foreign-held dollar reserves continued to rise until by 1970 they exceeded total United States gold reserves by a multiple of about 4.

In the face of large and persistent United States balance-of-payments deficits and sharply reduced United States gold reserves, it became evident that a realignment of parities was necessary. The United States sought unsuccessfully in 1970 and early 1971 to persuade surplus nations, particularly West Germany and Japan, to revalue their currencies. The expectation then became prevalent that the United States would sooner or later have to devalue the dollar. By now international capital markets had become highly intergrated through Eurocurrency markets. This led to huge destabilizing capital movements out of dollars and into stronger currencies, particularly the German mark, the Japanese yen, and the Swiss franc. On August 15, 1971, President Nixon was forced to suspend the convertibility of dollars into gold. The "gold window" had been shut. The Bretton Woods system was dead. At the same time, the United States imposed wage and price controls as well as a temporary 10 percent import surcharge, to be lifted after the required currency realignment took place.

The ability of the United States to settle its balance-of-payments deficits with dollars had conferred an important privilege on the United States not available to other nations (which faced the strict limitation imposed by their limited supplies of gold and foreign exchange on the balance-of-payments deficits that they could incur). The benefit accruing to a nation from issuing the currency or when its currency is used as an international currency is referred to as **seigniorage.** However, the United States paid a heavy price for its seigniorage privilege. It was unable to devalue the dollar (as other nations, such as the United Kingdom and France, occasionally did) without bringing down the Bretton Woods system. The use of monetary policy was more constrained in the United States than in other nations. Consequently, the United States had to rely more heavily on fiscal policy to achieve domestic objectives and on *ad hoc* measures (such as controls over capital flows) to correct balance-of-payments deficits.

It is difficult to determine whether on balance the United States benefited or was harmed as a result of the dollar becoming an international currency. In any event, France, West Germany, Japan, and other surplus nations began to view the United States as abusing its position as the world's banker by supplying excessive liquidity with its large and persistent balance-of-payments deficits. The unwillingness of West Germany and Japan to revalue forced the United States to devalue the dollar, thus bringing the Bretton Woods system down. To a large extent, this was a political decision to remove the United States from its unique position as the "world's banker" or to take away from the United States this "exorbitant" privilege (to use Charles de Gaulle's words). The irony of it all is that the dollar remained an international currency without any backing of gold after the Bretton Woods system collapsed in August 1971, and even after the dollar was allowed to fluctuate in value in March 1973. Indeed, the amount of foreign-held dollars has risen dramatically in the years since 1971 (see section 20.6).

20.5b   The Collapse of the Bretton Woods System

As explained above, the *immediate* cause of the collapse of the Bretton Woods system was the expectation in late 1970 and early 1971, in the face of huge balance-of-payments deficits, that the United States would soon be forced to devalue the dollar. This led to a massive flight of liquid capital from the United States, which prompted President Nixon to suspend the convertibility of the dollar into gold on August 15, 1971, and to impose a temporary 10 percent import surcharge.

In December 1971, representatives of the "Group of Ten" nations met at the Smithsonian Institution in Washington and agreed to increase the dollar price of gold from $35 to $38 an ounce. This implied a devaluation of the dollar of about 9 percent. At the same time, the German mark was revalued by about 17 percent and the Japanese yen by about 14 percent with respect to the dollar, and other currencies by smaller amounts. In addition, the band of fluctuation was increased from 1 percent to 2.25 percent on either side of the new central rates, and the United States removed its 10 percent import surcharge. Since the dollar remained inconvertible into gold, the world was now essentially on a **dollar standard.** President Nixon hailed this **Smithsonian Agreement** as the "most significant monetary agreement in the history of the world" and promised that the dollar "would never again be devalued."

However, with another huge United States balance-of-payments deficit in 1972 ($10 billion on the official settlements method—see Table 14-2), it was felt that the Smithsonian Agreement was not working and that another devaluation of the dollar was required. This expectation led to renewed speculation against the dollar and became self-fulfilling in February 1973, when the United States was once again forced to devalue the dollar, this time by about 10 percent (achieved by increasing the official price of gold to $42.22 an ounce). At the same time, the dollar remained inconvertible into gold. In March 1972, the original six member nations of the European Common Market decided to let their currencies float jointly against the dollar with a *total* band of fluctuation of only 2.25 percent, instead of the 4.5 percent agreed in December 1971.

This was named the **European "snake"** or the "snake in the tunnel" and lasted until March 1973.

When speculation against the dollar flared up again in March 1973, monetary authorities in the major industrial nations decided to let their currencies float either independently (the United States dollar, the British pound, the Japanese yen, the Italian lira, the Canadian dollar, and the Swiss franc) or jointly (the German mark, the French franc, and the currencies of six other central and northern European nations—the snake with the maximum total spread of 2.25 percent between the strongest and the weakest currency with respect to the dollar). The present managed floating exchange rate system was born. France abandoned the snake in 1974, Norway in 1977, and Sweden in 1978 (the United Kingdom, Italy, and Ireland had not joined in 1973).

While the immediate cause of the collapse of the Bretton Woods system was the huge balance-of-payments deficits of the United States in 1970 and 1971, the *fundamental* cause is to be found in the interrelated problems of liquidity, adjustment, and confidence. Liquidity refers to the amount of international reserves available in relation to the need for them. International reserves comprise official holdings of gold, foreign exchange (mostly United States dollars), the reserve position of member nations in the IMF, and SDRs. Table 20-1 shows that most of the increase in liquidity under the Bretton Woods system resulted from the increase in official holdings of foreign exchange, mostly dollars to finance United States balance-of-payments deficits.

In Table 20-1, all international reserves are expressed in terms of United States dollars, even though the IMF now expreses all international reserves in terms of SDRs. One SDR was equal to $1 up to 1970, about $1.09 in 1971, and 1972, and about $1.21 in 1973 (see section 20.6a). Gold reserves were valued at the official price of gold of $35 an ounce up to 1970, at $38 an ounce in 1971 and 1972, and at $42.22 an ounce in 1973. Valued at the London free market price of gold of $112.25 an ounce prevailing at the end of 1973, total world gold reserves were $115 billion. For simplicity, all reserves were valued in United States dollars instead of SDRs and gold reserves were valued at official prices.

TABLE 20-1. *International Reserves, 1950–1973 (billions of U.S. dollars, at year-end)*

	1950	1960	1969	1970	1971	1972	1973
Gold (at official price)	33	38	39	37	39	39	43
Foreign exchange	13	19	33	45	82	105	124
SDRs	—	—	—	3	6	9	11
Reserve position in the IMF	2	4	7	8	7	7	7
Total	48	61	79	93	134	160	184

Source: IMF, *International Financial Statistics Yearbook*, 1979 and 1981.

International liquidity is needed so that nations can finance temporary balance-of-payments deficits without trade restrictions while the adjustment mechanisms supposedly operate to eventually correct the deficit. Inadequate liquidity hampers the expansion of world trade. Excessive liquidity leads to worldwide inflationary pressures. But this raised a serious dilemma, according to *Triffin*. Under the Bretton Woods system, most liquidity was provided by an increase in foreign exchange arising from United States balance-of-payments deficits. However, the longer these balance-of-payments deficits persisted and the more unwanted dollars accumulated in foreign hands, the smaller was the confidence in the dollar. The dollar shortage of the 1950s had given way to the **dollar glut** of the 1960s.

It was in response to this problem and in the hope that the United States would soon be able to correct its deficits that the IMF decided to create $9.5 billion of SDRs in 1967. These SDRs were distributed in three installments in January 1970, 1971, and 1972, at the very time when the world was suffering from excessive increases in liquidity resulting from huge United States balance-of-payments deficits. Note that the increase in SDRs from 1970 to 1971 and 1972 shown in Table 20-1 reflects not only the new installments of SDRs distributed to member nations in January of 1971 and 1972 but also the increase in the dollar value of SDRs as a result of the dollar devaluation in December 1971. Similarly, there was no new distribution of SDRs between 1972 and 1973, but the value of one SDR rose from about $1.09 in 1972 to $1.21 in 1973.

As we have seen, the United States was unable to correct its large and persistent balance-of-payments deficits primarily because of its inability to devalue the dollar. Thus, the Bretton Woods system lacked an adequate adjustment mechanism that nations would be willing and able to utilize as a matter of policy. United States balance-of-payments deficits persisted, and this undermined confidence in the dollar. Thus, the fundamental cause of the collapse of the Bretton Woods system is to be found in the interrelated problems of adjustment, liquidity, and confidence.

20.6   The Present International Monetary System

In this section, we examine the operation of the present managed floating exchange rates system, the establishment of the European Monetary System, and the most important current international economic problems and the need for reforms.

20.6a   The Operation of the Present System

Since March 1973, the world has had a managed floating exchange rate system. Under such a system, nations' monetary authorities are entrusted with the responsibility to intervene in foreign exchange markets to smooth out short-run fluctuations in exchange rates without attempting to affect long-run trends. This could be achieved by a policy of "leaning against the wind" (see section 19.6). To be sure, this system was not deliberately chosen but was imposed on the world by the collapse of the Bretton Woods system in the face of chaotic conditions in foreign exchange markets and huge destabilizing speculation.

In the early days of the managed floating system, serious attempts were made to devise specific rules for managing the float to prevent competitive exchange rate depreciations (which nations might use to stimulate their exports), thus possibly returning to the chaotic conditions of the 1930s. However, as the worst fears of abuses did not materialize and the managed floating system seemed to work fairly smoothly, all of the these attempts failed. Indeed, the 1976 **Jamaica Accords** formally recognized the managed floating system and allowed nations the choice of foreign exchange regime as long as their actions did not prove disruptive to trade partners and the world economy. These Jamaica Accords were ratified and took effect in April 1978.

By 1986 less then one-third of the 149 nations that were members of the IMF had opted for a managed float. However, these included all the large industrial nations and many large developing nations, so that about four-fifths of total world trade moved between nations that managed the exchange rate, either independently or jointly (as the EEC). Most of the remaining nations pegged their currencies to the United States dollar, the French franc, SDRs, or a basket of currencies (see section 19.6). During the period from 1974 to 1977 and, again, from 1981 to 1985, the United States generally followed a policy of **benign neglect** by not intervening in foreign exchange markets to stabilize the value of the dollar.

Under the present managed float, nations still need international reserves in order to intervene in foreign exchange markets to smooth out short-run fluctuations in exchange rates. At present such interventions are made mostly with dollars. Between 1979 and 1981 there was another allocation of SDRs, so that by 1986 the total holdings of SDRs by all nations were 16 billion SDRs (the IMF itself was holding another 5 billion SDRs). An interest charge now related to market rates is imposed on the amount of SDRs used by a nation. SDRs can only be used in transactions among central banks and with the IMF. However, the SDR has started to replace the dollar as the unit of account, or *numeraire*. For example, the IMF now keeps all of its accounts in SDRs.

Up to 1971, one SDR was valued at $1. After the devaluation of the dollar in December 1971, one SDR was valued at $1.0857, and after the February 1973 devaluation of the dollar, one SDR was valued at $1.2064. In 1974 the value of one SDR was made equal to weighted average of a "basket" of 16 leading currencies. This was done to stabilize the value of SDRs. In 1981 the number of currencies included in the basket was reduced to the following five (with their relative weights given in parentheses): United States dollar (42%); German mark or Deutschemark (19%); British pound, French franc, and Japanese yen (13% each). At the beginning of 1986, one SDR was valued at about $0.92.

The quotas of the IMF member nations have been increased across-the-board several times, so that by 1986, the Fund resources totaled $98 billion (up from $8.8 billion in 1947). In 1979 the IMF renewed and expanded the General Agreements to Borrow. Borrowing rules at the Fund were also relaxed, and new credit facilities were added that greatly expanded the overall maximum amount of credit available to a member nation. However, this total amount of credit consists of several different credit lines subject to various conditions. IMF loans are now specified in terms of SDRs. There is an initial fee, and the interest charged is based on the length of the loan, the facility used, and prevailing interest rates.

The new credit facilities set up by the IMF include: (1) the Compensatory Financing Facility (CFF), which enables members to draw from the Fund up to 100 percent of their quota when they experience balance-of-payments difficulties produced by temporary shortfalls in export receipts; (2) the Buffer Stock Financing Facility (BSFF), which may be used by members to draw up to 50 percent of their quota to finance international buffer stock arrangements; (3) the Extended Fund Facility (EFF), which allows members to draw up to 140 percent of their quota phased over a period of three years when facing serious structural imbalances; (4) the Supplementary Financing Facility (SFF), which provides supplementary financing when member nations need resources in much larger amounts and for longer periods than are available under regular and standby arrangements; and (5) the Oil Facility (OF), under which the IMF borrowed funds from some surplus nations to lend to deficit nations at competitive rates. This last facility was set up in 1974 and extended in 1975, but by 1976 it had already been fully utilized for a total of 6.9 billion SDRs (about $7.5 billion at the SDR rate of the beginning of 1986) and is now no longer operational. The use of total Fund credit reached an all-time high of $16 billion in 1977, but was about $11 billion at the beginning of 1986, as repayments have exceeded new loans.

In the face of the huge international debt problems of many developing countries since 1982, particularly the large countries of Latin America, the IMF has engaged in a number of debt rescheduling and rescue operations. As a condition for the additional loans and special help, the IMF usually required reduction in government spending, in growth of the money supply, and in wage increases in order to reduce imports, stimulate exports, and make the country more nearly self-sustaining. This, however, is very painful and has led to riots and even the toppling of governments, and to accusations that the IMF does not take into account the social needs of debtor nations and the political consequences of its demands, and that its policies are "all head and no heart." To this, supporters of the IMF reply that desperate situations require harsh choices in the use of the very limited funds from very "stingy" donors. In recent years and in the face of growing resistence from debtor nations, the IMF and its sister institution, the World Bank, are now reevaluating their operation (see the discussion of the international debt in section 20.6c).

In January 1975, United States citizens were allowed for the first time since 1933 to own gold, and the United States sold a small portion of its gold holdings on the free market. The price of gold on the London market temporarily rose above $800 an ounce in January 1980, but it was below $350 an ounce at the beginning of 1986. As part of the Jamaica Accords, the IMF sold one-sixth of its gold holdings on the free market between 1976 and 1980 (and used the proceeds to aid the poorest developing nations) to demonstrate its commitment to eliminate gold (the "barbarous relic"—to use Keynes' words) as an international reserve asset. The official price of gold was abolished, and it was agreed that there would be no future gold transactions between the IMF and member nations. The IMF also continued to value its gold holdings at the pre-1971 official price of $35 or 35 SDRs an ounce. The gold tranche has now become the reserve tranche. However, it may be some time before gold completely "seeps out" of international reserves—if it ever will.

Since 1974 the IMF has measured all reserves and other official transactions in terms of SDRs instead of United States dollars. Table 20-2 shows the composition of international reserves both in United States dollars and in SDRs (valued at $1.0984) at the end of 1985. (For the composition of international reserves from 1950 to 1985 in terms of SDRs as presented by the IMF, see the appendix.)

20.6b The European Monetary System

In March 1979 the European Economic Community (EEC) announced the formation of the **European Monetary System (EMS)** as part of its aim toward greater monetary integration among the nine full members of the EEC, including the ultimate goal of creating a common currency. The main features of the EMS are: (1) the creation of a **European Currency Unit (ECU),** defined as the weighted average of the nine EEC currencies (plus the currency of Greece after

TABLE 20-2. *International Reserves, 1985 (billions of U.S. dollars and SDRs, at year-end)*

	U.S. Dollars	SDRs
Foreign exchange	374	341
SDRs	20	18
Reserve position in the IMF	43	39
Total minus gold	437	398
Gold at market price	310	282
Total with gold	747	680

Source: IMF, *International Financial Statistics,* March 1986.

September 1984) to be used for accounting purposes among member nations. However, ECUs are also being used in private transactions because of their more stable value as compared with national currencies and have already become a major international currency. (2) Defining the central rate or par value of each EEC currency in terms of ECUs and allowing central rates to fluctuate by a maximum of 2.25 percent with respect to other EEC currencies (Italy was allowed a band of fluctuation of 6 percent, the United Kingdom has refused so far to join, and Greece, Spain, and Portugal have postponed joining). Thus, the EMS is a fixed but adjustable exchange rate system among member countries but with the currencies of member countries floating jointly against he dollar and other currencies. (3) The establishment of the **European Monetary Cooperation Fund (EMCF)** to provide short- and medium-term balance-of-payments assistance to EEC members.

The formation of the EMS thus attempted to revive the European snake but also to push monetary integration much further. Even though the United Kingdom chose not to join the EMS at the start, the pound was included in the calculation of the ECU in the expectation that the United Kingdom would later join. When the fluctuation of a member nation's currency reaches 75 percent of its allowed range, a "threshold of divergence" has been reached, and the nation is expected to take a number of corrective steps to prevent its currency from fluctuating outside the allowed range. Member nations were assigned a quota into the EMCF, 20 percent to be paid in gold (valued at the market price) and the remainder in dollars, in exchange for ECUs. The amount of ECUs is rapidly growing as member nations convert more and more of their dollars and gold into ECUs. Indeed, ECUs have already become an important international asset and intervention currency, and may eventually rival the United States dollar. The EMCF is to evolve eventually into an EEC central bank, similar to the United States Federal Reserve, and engage in foreign exchange market intervention and open market operations.

By the beginning of 1986, the total reserve pool of the EMCF was over $50 billion, and the value of one ECU was about $0.88. There have been a total of eleven currency realignments since the start of the system. In general, high inflation countries such as Italy and France need to periodically devalue their currency with respect to the ECU in order to maintain competitiveness in relation to a low inflation country such as Germany. This points to the fundamental weakness of the EMS in attempting to keep exchange rates among member nations within narrowly defined limits without at the same time integrating their monetary, fiscal, and other policies.

The desire on the part of the EEC to stabilize exchange rates is understandable in view of the large exchange rate fluctuations since 1973. Figure 20-1 shows the percentage change in the effective exchange rates of the seven most important industrial nations from the first quarter of 1981 to the first quarter of 1986. From the figure, we see that the United States dollar depreciated by about 30 percent between its peak value reached in the first quarter of 1985 to the first quarter of 1986, while the Japanese yen appreciated by nearly 30

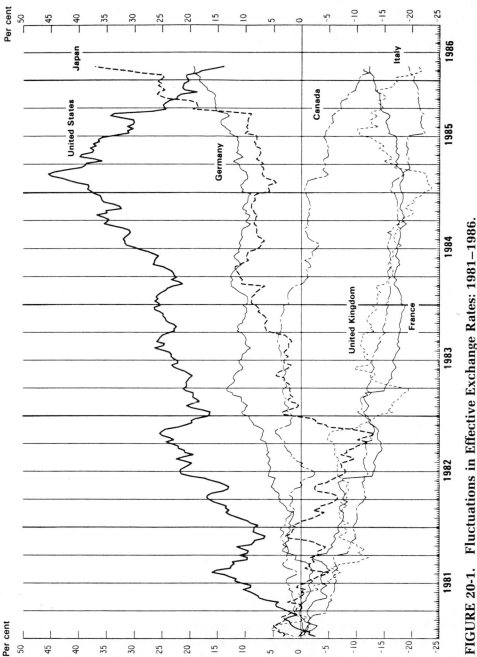

FIGURE 20-1. Fluctuations in Effective Exchange Rates: 1981–1986.

The figure shows the percentage change in the effective exchange rates (weekly averages of daily figures) of the seven most important industrial nations from the first quarter of 1981 to the first quarter of 1986. We see that the U.S. dollar had appreciated by over 45 percent by the first quarter of 1985, but subsequently it depreciated by about 30 percent. On the other hand, the Japanese yen appreciated by nearly 30 percent from the third quarter of 1985 to the first quarter of 1986.
Source: OECD

567

TABLE 20-3. *Important Dates in Modern Monetary History*

1880–1914	Classical gold standard period
April 1925	U.K. returns to the gold standard
October 1929	U.S. stock market crashes
September 1931	U.K. abandons the gold standard
February 1934	U.S. raises official price of gold from $20.67 to $35 an ounce
July 1944	Bretton Woods Conference
March 1947	IMF begins operation
September 1967	Decision to create SDRs
March 1968	Two-tier gold market established
August 1971	U.S. suspends convertibility of the dollar into gold—end of Bretton Woods system
December 1971	Smithsonian Agreement (official price of gold increased to $38 an ounce; band of allowed fluctuation increased to 4.5%)
March 1972	Beginning of European "snake" with band of allowed fluctuation limited to 2.25%
February 1973	U.S. raises official price of gold to $42.22 an ounce
March 1973	Managed floating exchange rate system comes into existence
October 1973	OPEC selective embargo on petroleum exports and start of sharp increase in petroleum prices
January 1976	Jamaica Accords (agreement to recognize the managed float and abolish the official price of gold)
April 1978	Jamaica Accords take effect
Spring 1979	Second oil shock
March 1979	Establishment of the European Monetary System (EMS)
January 1980	Gold price rises temporarily above $800 per ounce
August 1982	International debt problem becomes evident
September 1985	Plaza agreement to intervene to lower value of dollar
December 1985	Gold price falls to $311 per ounce
Fall 1986	New round of GATT multilateral trade negotiations begins

percent from the third quarter of 1985 to the first quarter of 1986. The effective exchange rate of other countries changed by smaller percentages.

By the way of summary, Table 20-3 presents the most important dates in the monetary history of the world over the past century.

20.6c Problems with Present Exchange Rate Arrangements

The world faces a number of serious and closely interrelated international economic problems today. One of the most serious is the excessive volatility of exchange rates and the persistence of large disequilibria in exchange rates under the present floating system.

We have seen in sections 13.4a and 18.5b that since 1971, exchange rates have been characterized by very large volatility and overshooting. This can greatly discourage the flow of international trade. Even more serious is the fact that under the present managed floating exchange rate system large exchange rate disequilibria can arise and persist for several years (see section 19.6). This is clearly evident from the large depreciation of the dollar from 1978 to 1980 and during 1985, as well as the excessive appreciation of the dollar from 1981 until the beginning of 1985. The excessive appreciation of the dollar during the first half of this decade led to huge trade deficits for the United States and almost irresistible calls for increased trade protection.

To be sure (see section 17.5c), the large overvaluation of the dollar from 1981 to 1985 was closely related to the huge federal budget deficits of the United States, which kept real interest rates high and attracted large capital inflows to the United States. Indeed, by the middle of 1985, these large budget deficits and capital inflows turned the United States from a creditor nation (appropriate for its position as the richest nation in the world) into a debtor nation, for the first time since 1914 (see sections 12.2 and 14.6). Nevertheless, the persistence of disequilibrium and great volatility of exchange rates has led to renewed calls for reform of the present international monetary system along the lines of establishing target zones of allowed fluctuations for the major currencies and for more international cooperation and coordination of policies among the leading nations. The earlier debate on the relative merits of fixed versus flexible rates has been superseded by discussions of the optimal degree of exchange rate flexibility and policy cooperation.

Some increased cooperation has already occurred. For example, in September 1985, the United States negotiated with Germany, Japan, France, and the United Kingdom (the so-called Plaza agreement in New York City) a coordinated effort to intervene in foreign exchange markets to lower the value of the dollar. This effort, together with changed market conditions, led to a sharp depreciation of the dollar by early 1986 that removed most of the previous appreciation. Another proposal advanced by the United States is for a simultaneous coordinated reduction in interest rates in the leading nations so as to stimulate growth and reduce unemployment (which has exceeded 10 percent of the labor force in most nations of Europe over most of the past decade) without directly affecting trade and capital flows (see section 17.5c). A more formal and comprehensive type of cooperation, however, is being advocated to be negotiated at an international monetary conference.

One of the best and most articulated of the proposals for greater international coordination of policies has been advanced by *Ronald McKinnon* (1984) of Stanford University. The rationale for this proposal can be understood by recalling (from Chapter 19) that the movement to a system of floating exchange rates by the leading industrial nations did not increase very much their ability to pursue independent targets on inflation and unemployment. This is due to disagreement on the choice of the appropriate inflation–unemployment trade-off in a world grown much more interdependent (see sections 1.2 and 16.6c) and in the face of very large capital flows resulting from closely integrated financial markets (see section 13.6).

McKinnon advocates a return to pegged exchange rates with joint monetary policy for key reserve currency countries. Only by joint monetary policy by the United States, Germany, and Japan (at a minimum) can international price stability be maintained, according to McKinnon. Exchange rate movements would provide important leading indicators for monetary policy. A currency appreciation would signal the need for domestic monetary expansion and a currency depreciation would require domestic monetary contraction. McKinnon proposes a two-stage program. In the first stage, the leading nations would coordinate (limit) the growth of their money supply to achieve price stability and manage exchange rates toward their equilibrium level. Stage two would involve more complete financial unification among reserve currency countries and exchange rates pegged within narrow limits.

Adoption of McKinnon's proposal would go a long way toward avoiding the large and persistent exchange rate disequilibria and volatility that has afflicted the world since 1973. The question is whether the leading nations are prepared to give up most of their monetary independence as required by the plan. As *Richard Cooper* of Harvard points out (1985), in a world of large and growing interdependence, only through international cooperation and policy coordination can sovereignty be wisely and usefully exercised. At this point, it remains to be seen if the leading nations are prepared to give up some of their autonomy in the coming years in order to have greater success in achieving their economic objectives, or if they will waste yet another opportunity at improving the functioning of the present system. Under the current loose form of exchange rate arrangements the danger of competitive currency depreciations is always present.

A closely related problem is the huge **dollar overhang** held by foreigners and ready to move from monetary center to monetary center in response to variations in international interest differentials and expectations of exchange rate changes. These "hot money" flows have been greatly facilitated by the extremely rapid growth of Eurocurrency markets (see section 13.6). One proposal of long standing aimed at eliminating this problem involves converting all foreign-held dollars into SDRs by the introduction of a **substitution account** by the IMF. No action, however, has been taken on this proposal so far, and there are several unresolved problems, such as what interest rate to pay on these SDRs and the procedure whereby the United States can purchase back these dollars from the IMF. At least for the foreseeable future, it seems likely that the dollar will retain most of its importance as the leading international and intervention currency.

20.6d   Other Current International Economic Problems

The problems arising from the present exchange rate arrangements are closely interrelated to the other serious problems faced today by developed and developing countries alike. These are (1) rising protectionism in developed countries, (2) the huge international debt of developing countries, and (3) the poverty and development problems facing the poorest developing countries.

We now examine each of these and the proposals or policies advocated to solve them.

1. *Rising Protectionism in Developed Countries.* We have seen in section 9.6a that since the mid-1970s, there has been rapid proliferation of nontariff trade barriers (NTBs), as industrial nations sought to protect industry after industry from the adjustments required by international trade, in a climate of slow domestic growth and rising unemployment. Today these NTBs represent the most serious threat to the postwar trading system and world welfare. By interfering with the flow of international trade, they lead to a misallocation of resources internationally, a slowdown in structural adjustments in mature economies and in growth in developing economies, and raise the specter of a trade war.

This crucial problem can only be resolved by a new round of multilateral trade negotiations (scheduled to start in fall 1986). The new round of negotiations should also address the question as to how far it is legitimate for nations (especially Japan) to promote their high-technology industries by restricting market access, by subsidies to exports and to research and development, and by government procurement provisions favoring domestic suppliers (see section 9.6a). The proliferation of nontariff trade restrictions in mature industries (steel, textile, automobiles) in industrial countries as well as their heavy protection of domestic agriculture have also greatly hampered the development prospects of developing countries and made it very difficult or impossible for them to service their huge international debt—to which we now turn.

2. *The International Debt Problem of Developing Countries.* We have seen in section 11.6a that during the past decade, developing countries accumulated a huge international debt that they are now finding very difficult to repay or even service. The debt arose as many developing countries borrowed heavily from private banks in developed nations to finance their growing capital needs and to pay for sharply higher oil bills during the 1970s. By heavily borrowing abroad, developing countries continued to grow at a relatively rapid pace even during the second half of the 1970s. In the early 1980s, however, their huge and rapidly growing foreign debts caught up with them and large-scale defaults were avoided only by repeated large-scale interventions by the IMF. Such defaults would make some of the largest commercial banks in the United States insolvent and possibly even lead to a world financial collapse reminiscent of the 1930s.

In 1985, the heavily indebted countries of Latin America began to reject the austerity plans advocated by the IMF (as a condition for additional loans) and to demand a renegotiation of existing loans under the threat of default. It was under these circumstances that the United States advanced a new plan based on a much larger flow of capital from developed nations and international institutions (primarily the World Bank) to the heavily indebted developing nations. This plan, however, seemed designed primarily to avoid defaults. For the debt problem to be overcome and for sustained growth to resume in developing countries, a large increase in the flow of equity capital in the form of direct investments and the opening of developed countries' markets more widely to their exports is required. For a more detailed discussion of the debt problem of developing countries, see section 11.6a.

3. *Poverty and Development Problems of Developing Countries.* In section 11.6a, we have seen that the real per capita GNP in low-income developing nations is far below that in middle-income developing nations and abysmally low in relation to that in developed nations. In addition, absolute differences in GNP per person continue to widen. Prospects for the low-income group are especially dim because of their present extreme poverty. In fact, as a result of the drought and famine engulfing most of the African continent, the countries of the sub-Sahara are expected to continue to face an actual *decline* in standard of living for the rest of the decade.

An international economic system that has spread the benefits from international trade and specialization so unevenly can hardly be said to be functioning properly—not to say equitably. A world where millions of people starve is not only unacceptable from an ethical point of view but can hardly be expected to be a world in which peace and tranquility can prevail. Many proposals have been advanced through the United Nations Conference on Trade and Development (UNCTAD) and in other international forums on how to ameliorate conditions in developing nations and stimulate their development. These proposals seem to have lost some of their immediacy in recent years, not because needs have diminished in developing countries (indeed they are today even greater than a decade ago), but because developed countries have become absorbed mostly with their own domestic problems of inflation, monetary instability, recession, and slow growth (stagflation).

As part of the demands for a New International Economic Order (NIEO— see section 11.6d), developing countries have been demanding both a greater access for their exports to the developed countries' markets as well as a much greater flow of aid. As a way to increase aid, it has been proposed that more SDRs be created to be distributed as development assistance. This is the *LINK Proposal*—a long-standing demand made as early as 1962 in the Stamp Plan (even before SDRs were actually created). In general, however, it would not be wise to combine the creation of more SDRs with development assistance because there is no theoretical connection between the problems of liquidity and poverty, and so they would be better resolved by separate policies and tools. Nevertheless, the LINK proposal may very well represent the only realistic way to raise development assistance from its declining trend.

While we have discussed the international economic problems facing the world today separately, they are in fact closely interrelated. For example, the huge federal budget deficit of the United States, by keeping real interest rates higher in the United States than abroad, induces large capital inflows to the United States, which keeps the dollar overvalued and leads to huge trade deficits and calls for protectionism. High interest rates in the United States also make the debt service problems of developing countries that much more difficult to manage, as do increased trade restrictions in developed countries against the imports of developing countries. These, in turn, hamper development and increases the gap between the rich and the poorest developing countries. The close connection between these problems also shows the strong links between the theory of international trade discussed in the first half of the text (Chapters 2–12) and international finance discussed in the second half (Chapters 13–20).

To be sure, the problems facing the world today are less serious than those of the 1970s and early 1980s. In that earlier period, the above problems were greatly compounded by sharply increasing petroleum prices, steep inflation, and deep recession. Since then, oil prices have been falling and today they are much lower than in the late 1970s. Inflation has also fallen to acceptable levels. This provides a much better framework and opportunity for successfully tackling the other long-standing problems facing the world today. There are reasons for cautious optimism here. After all, the world community has weathered during the past decade the most serious international economic problems since the Great Depression without much strife but in a spirit of cooperation and understanding. In that spirit, today's problems can also be resolved or greatly alleviated.

Summary

1. In this chapter, we examined the operation of the international monetary system from the gold standard period to the present. An international monetary system refers to the rules, customs, instruments, facilities, and organizations for effecting international payments. International monetary systems can be classified according to the way in which exchange rates are determined or according to the form that international reserve assets take. A good international monetary system is one that maximizes the flow of international trade and investments and leads to an equitable distribution of the gains from trade among nations. An international monetary system can be evaluated in terms of adjustment, liquidity, and confidence.

2. The gold standard operated from about 1880 to the outbreak of World War I in 1914. Most of the actual adjustment under the gold standard seems to have taken place through stabilizing short-term capital flows and induced income changes, rather than through induced changes in internal prices, as postulated by the price-specie-flow mechanism. Adjustment was also greatly facilitated by buoyant and stable eco-

nomic conditions. The period from 1919 to 1924 was characterized by wildly fluctuating exchange rates. Starting in 1925 an attempt was made by Britain and other nations to reestablish the gold standard. This attempt failed with the deepening of the Great Depression in 1931. There followed a period of competitive devaluations as each nation tried to "export" its unemployment. This, together with the serious trade restrictions imposed by most nations, cut international trade almost in half.

3. The Bretton Woods system agreed upon in 1944 called for the establishment of the International Monetary Fund (IMF) for the purposes of (1) overseeing that nations followed a set of agreed rules of conduct in international trade and finance and (2) providing borrowing facilities for nations in temporary balance-of-payments difficulties. This was a gold-exchange standard with gold and convertible currencies (only United States dollars at the beginning) as international reserves. Exchange rates were allowed to fluctuate by only 1 percent above and below established par values. Par values were to be changed only in cases of fundamental disequilibrium and after approval by the Fund. Each nation was assigned a quota into the Fund depending on its importance in international trade. A nation had to pay 25 percent of its quota in gold and the remaining 75 percent in its own currency. A nation in balance-of-payments difficulties could borrow 25 percent of its quota from the Fund each year by depositing more of its currency in exchange for convertible currencies, until the Fund held no more than 200 percent of the nation's quota in the nation's currency.

4. Under the Bretton Woods system, industrial nations in fundamental disequilibrium were very reluctant to change par values. The convertibility of the dollar into gold was resumed soon after the war and that of other industrial nations' currencies by the early 1960s. Tariffs on manufactured goods were lowered to an average of less than 10 percent by 1971. Through increased membership and quota increases, the resources of the Fund rose to $28.5 billion by 1971. The Fund also negotiated the General Arrangements to Borrow to further augment its resources. Nations negotiated standby arrangements with the Fund and swap arrangements with other central banks. The IMF also began to allow member nations to borrow up to 50 percent of their quota in any one year. In 1967 the IMF decided to create $9.5 billion of Special Drawing Rights (distributed in 1970–1972) to supplement international reserves. In 1961 the gold pool was set up, but it collapsed in 1968 and the two-tier system was established. During the Bretton Woods period, the EEC and the Eurocurrency markets came into existence; world output grew rapidly, and international trade grew even faster.

5. Use of the dollar as the principal international currency conferred the benefit of seigniorage on the United States, but the United States could not devalue to correct balance-of-payments deficits and its monetary policy was seriously constrained. The immediate cause of the collapse of the Bretton Woods system was the huge balance-of-payments deficit of the United States in 1970 and the expectation of an even larger deficit in 1971. This led to massive destabilizing speculation against the dollar, suspension of the convertibility of the dollar into gold on August 15, 1971, and a realignment of currencies in December 1971. The fundamental cause of the collapse of the Bretton Woods system is to be found in the lack of an adequate adjustment mechanism. The persistence of United States balance-of-payments deficits provided for the system's liquidity but also led to the loss of confidence in the dollar. The dollar was devalued again in February 1973. In March 1973, in the face of continued speculation against the dollar, the major currencies were allowed to fluctuate either independently or jointly.

6. Since March 1973, the world has operated under a managed float.This has been formally, recognized in the Jamaica Accords, which took effect in April 1978. By 1986, $21 billion of SDRs had been created (of which $5 billion were held by the IMF itself). Today the value of one SDR is equal to a weighted average of the five most important international currencies. Borrowing rules at the IMF have been relaxed, and significant new credit facilities have been created. In January 1975, United States citizens were again allowed to own gold. In March 1979, the European Monetary System was established. This was based on the creation of a European Currency Unit of account, revival of the snake, and establishment of the European Monetary Cooperation Fund. The most significant economic problems confronting the world today are (1) excessive volatility and persistent disequilibria in exchange rates, (2) rising protectionism in developed countries, (3) the huge international debt of developing countries, and (4) the poverty and development problems facing the poorest developing countries. Various plans or proposals have been advanced to solve these.

Glossary

International monetary system   The rules, customs, instruments, facilities, and organizations for effecting international payments.

Adjustment   The process by which balance-of-payments disequilibria are corrected.

Liquidity   The amount of international reserve assets available to nations to settle temporary balance-of-payments disequilibria.

Confidence   The knowledge that the balance-of-payments adjustment mechanism is working adequately and that international reserves will retain their absolute and relative values.

International Monetary Fund (IMF) The international institution created under the Bretton Woods system for the purposes of (1) overseeing that nations followed a set of agreed rules of conduct in international trade and finance and (2) providing borrowing facilities for nations in temporary balance-of-payments difficulties.

Bretton Woods system The international monetary system or gold-exchange standard established after World War II, which collapsed in 1971.

Intervention currency A convertible national currency (primarily the United States dollar) used by nations' monetary authorities to intervene in foreign exchange markets in order to keep the exchange rate from moving outside the allowed or desired range of fluctuation.

Fundamental disequilibrium Large and persistent balance-of-payments deficits or surpluses.

Currency convertibility The ability to exchange one national currency for another without any restriction or limitation.

International Bank for Reconstruction and Development (IBRD or World Bank) The international institution established after World War II to provide long-run development assistance to developing nations.

International Development Association (IDA) The affiliate of the International Bank for Reconstruction and Development set up in 1960 to make loans at subsidized rates to the poorer developing nations.

International Finance Corporation (IFC) The affiliate of the International Bank for Reconstruction and Development set up in 1956 to stimulate *private* investments in developing nations from indigenous and foreign sources.

Gold tranche The 25 percent of a nation's quota into the IMF that the nation was originally required to pay in gold and could then borrow from the Fund almost automatically.

Credit tranches The amounts that a member nation could borrow from the IMF over and above the gold tranche.

Super gold tranche The amount by which the IMF's holdings of a nation's currency are below 75 percent of the nation's quota, which the nation could borrow from the Fund without the need to repay.

Net IMF position The size of a nation's quota in the IMF minus the Fund's holdings of the nation's currency.

General Arrangements to Borrow (GAB) The arrangements under which the IMF negotiated to borrow up to $6 billion from the "Group of Ten" (most important industrial nations) and Switzerland to augment its resources if needed to help nations with balance-of-payments difficulties.

Standby arrangements The arrangements under which member nations negotiate with the IMF advance permission for future borrowings from the Fund so they will be immediately available when needed.

Swap arrangements The arrangements under which national central banks negotiate to exchange each other's currency, to be used to intervene in foreign exchange markets to combat international hot money flows.

Special Drawing Rights (SDRs) International reserves created by the IMF to supplement other international reserves and distributed to member nations according to their quotas in the Fund.

Gold pool The agreement reached in 1961 by a group of industrial nations under United States leadership to supply gold to the London market in order to prevent the price of gold from rising above the then official price of $35 an ounce. The gold pool collapsed in 1968, and the two-tier gold market was set up.

Two-tier gold market The gold market set up when the gold pool collapsed in 1968, whereby the official price of gold remained at $35 an ounce, while the private price of gold was determined by the forces of demand and supply and allowed to rise above the official price.

Dollar shortage The inability of war-torn nations during the late 1940s and early 1950s to accumulate substantial dollar reserves.

Roosa bonds   Medium-term treasury bonds denominated in dollars but with an exchange rate guarantee, created by the United States in the early 1960s to induce foreign monetary authorities to continue to hold dollars rather than exchange them for gold at the Federal Reserve.

Seigniorage   The benefit accruing to a nation from issuing the currency or when its currency is used as an international currency and reserve.

Dollar standard   The international monetary system that emerged from the Smithsonian Agreement in December 1971 under which the United States dollar remained an international currency and reserve without any gold backing.

Smithsonian Agreement   The agreement reached in December 1971 in Washington under which the dollar was devalued by about 9 percent (by increasing the dollar price of gold from $35 to $38 an ounce), other strong currencies were revalued by various amounts with respect to the dollar, the dollar convertibility into gold remained suspended, and exchange rates were allowed to fluctuate by 2.25 percent on either side of the new par values.

European "snake"   The decision of the original six members of the European Common Market in March 1972 to allow their currencies to float jointly against the dollar but to limit the total band of fluctuation to only 2.25 percent. The composition of the European snake changed over time.

Dollar glut   The excess supply of dollars in the hands of foreign monetary authorities that developed during the late 1950s and early 1960s.

Jamaica Accords   The agreements reached in January 1976 and ratified in April 1978 that recognized the managed float and abolished the official price of gold.

Benign neglect   The policy of nonintervention in foreign exchange markets followed by the United States from March 1973 until the end of 1977 and from 1981 to 1985.

European Monetary System (EMS)   The orga-nization formed by the members of the European Economic Community (EEC) in 1979 based on the creation of the European Currency Unit (ECU) of account, revival of the snake, and formation of the European Monetary Fund (EMF). The United Kingdom is presently not a member.

European Currency Unit (ECU)   The unit of account defined by the European Monetary System, based on the weighted average of the currencies of the EEC members.

European Monetary Cooperation Fund (EMCF)   The institution of the European Monetary System that provides short-term and medium-term balance-of-payments assistance to member nations.

Dollar overhang   The large amount of foreign-held dollars resulting from past United States balance-of-payments deficits, the movement of which from monetary center to monetary center can lead to large exchange rate fluctuations and complicates the conduct of monetary policies.

Substitution account   The account proposed to be used to exchange all foreign-held dollars for SDRs at the IMF to solve the problem of the dollar overhang.

LINK proposal   The proposal to distribute future additions of SDRs only to developing nations as development assistance.

Questions for Review

1. What is meant by an international monetary system? How can international monetary systems be classified? What are the characteristics of a good international monetary system? How can an international monetary system be evaluated?

2. How was adjustment to balance-of-payments disequilibria under the gold standard explained by Hume? How did adjustment actually take place under the gold standard? What type of international monetary system operated from 1920 to 1924? What happened between 1925 and 1931? What happened after 1931?

3. What are the two basic functions of the Inter-

national Monetary Fund? What is meant by the Bretton Woods system being a gold-exchange standard? How were exchange rates determined under the Bretton Woods system? Under what conditions were nations allowed to change their exchange rates? What was the procedure for nations to borrow from the IMF?

4. In what way did the Bretton Woods system operate as intended? In what way did it not? How did the Bretton Woods system evolve over the years? What is meant by the General Arrangements to Borrow? Standby arrangements? Swap arrangements? Special Drawing Rights? Gold pool? Two-tier gold market?

5. What was meant by the dollar shortage? Dollar glut? What were Roosa Bonds? What was the purpose of the Interest Equalization Tax and the Foreign Direct Investment Program? What is meant by seigniorage? What was the Smithsonian Agreement? What is meant by the European snake? The dollar standard? Adjustment, liquidity, and confidence?

6. What was agreed at the Jamaica Accords? How is the value of the SDR determined today? What additional credit facilities have been set up by the IMF? What are the most significant features of the European Monetary System? What are the major problems facing the world today? What is being proposed to solve them?

Problems

*1. (a) How do economic conditions today differ from those prevailing during the gold standard period?
  (b) How would the different economic conditions today make the reestablishment of a smoothly working gold standard impossible?

2. With respect to a nation with a quota of $100 million in the IMF:
  (a) Indicate how the nation was to pay in its quota to the IMF and the amount that the nation could borrow from the Fund in any one year under the original rules.
  (b) Explain the procedure whereby the nation borrowed from the Fund the maximum amount allowed for the first year.
  (c) Explain the procedure whereby the nation borrowed the maximum amount allowed in each subsequent year.

3. With regard to the nation of problem 2:
  (a) How and when was the nation to repay its loan from the IMF?
  (b) What happens if the nation (say, Nation A) stops borrowing after the first year, but before it repays its loan, another nation borrows $10 million of Nation A's currency from the IMF?

*4. Explain how a nation could attempt to discourage large destabilizing capital *inflows* under the Bretton Woods system by intervening:
  (a) in the forward market;
  (b) in the spot market.

5. With respect to the Bretton Woods system, explain:
  (a) the role of the dollar;
  (b) the immediate cause of its collapse;
  (c) the fundamental causes of its collapse.

6. (a) Explain briefly the operation of the present international monetary system.
  (b) Identify the most significant international economic problems facing the world today.

APPENDIX———————————————————————

International Reserves: 1950–1985

In this appendix, we present historical data on the amount of international reserves in terms of SDRs, as reported by the IMF. The IMF includes gold reserves at the official price of SDR 35 an ounce. Table 20-4 also includes

TABLE 20-4. International Reserves, 1950–1985 (billions of SDRs, at year-end)

	1950	1951	1952	1953	1954	1955
1. Foreign exchange	13.3	13.5	14.0	15.4	16.5	16.7
2. SDRs	—	—	—	—	—	—
3. Reserve position in the IMF	1.7	1.7	1.8	1.9	1.8	1.9
4. Total reserves minus gold	15.0	15.2	15.8	17.3	18.3	18.6
5. Gold at SDR 35/ounce	33.2	33.5	33.5	33.9	34.6	35.0
6. Total with gold at SDR 35/ounce	48.2	48.7	49.3	51.2	52.9	53.6
7. Gold at SDR market price	33.0	33.2	33.3	33.6	34.6	35.0
8. Total with gold at SDR market price	48.0	48.4	49.1	50.9	52.9	53.6
9. U.S. dollars per SDR	1.0000	1.0000	1.0000	1.0000	1.0000	1.0000

	1956	1957	1958	1959	1960	1961	1962	1963	1964	1965
1.	17.8	17.1	17.1	16.1	18.5	19.1	19.9	22.7	24.2	24.0
2.	—	—	—	—	—	—	—	—	—	—
3.	2.3	2.3	2.6	3.3	3.6	4.2	3.8	3.9	4.2	5.4
4.	20.0	19.4	19.7	19.4	22.1	23.3	23.7	26.6	28.4	29.4
5.	35.9	37.1	37.8	37.8	37.9	38.9	39.2	40.2	40.7	41.8
6.	55.9	56.4	57.5	57.1	60.0	62.0	62.9	66.8	69.1	71.2
7.	35.8	37.1	37.9	37.8	38.6	38.9	39.2	40.3	40.9	41.9
8.	55.8	56.5	57.6	57.2	60.7	62.2	62.9	66.9	69.3	71.3
9.	1.0000	1.0000	1.0000	1.0000	1.0000	1.0000	1.0000	1.0000	1.0000	1.0000

	1966	1967	1968	1969	1970	1971	1972	1973	1974	1975
1.	25.7	29.4	32.6	33.1	45.3	75.4	96.6	102.9	127.7	138.8
2.	—	—	—	—	3.1	5.9	8.7	8.8	8.9	8.8
3.	6.3	5.7	6.5	6.7	7.7	6.4	6.3	6.2	8.8	12.6
4.	32.0	35.2	39.1	39.8	56.2	87.6	111.6	117.8	145.4	160.2
5.	40.8	39.4	38.8	39.0	37.1	35.9	35.7	35.7	35.7	35.6
6.	72.8	74.6	77.8	78.7	93.3	123.5	147.3	153.5	181.1	195.8
7.	41.0	39.6	46.4	39.2	39.5	41.3	61.0	95.1	155.4	122.0
8.	73.0	74.7	85.5	79.0	132.8	164.8	208.3	248.6	336.5	317.8
9.	1.0000	1.0000	1.0000	1.0000	1.0000	1.0857	1.0857	1.2064	1.2244	1.1707

	1976	1977	1978	1979	1980	1981	1982	1983	1984	1985
1.	161.7	203.7	224.1	249.7	292.9	292.6	284.3	307.0	345.0	340.7
2.	8.7	8.1	8.1	12.5	11.8	16.4	17.7	14.4	16.5	18.2
3.	17.7	18.1	14.8	11.8	16.8	21.3	25.5	39.1	41.6	38.7
4.	188.1	229.9	247.0	274.0	321.6	330.3	327.5	360.6	403.0	397.6
5.	35.5	36.0	36.3	33.0	33.4	33.4	33.2	33.2	33.1	33.2
6.	223.6	265.9	283.3	307.0	355.0	363.7	360.7	393.8	436.1	430.8
7.	117.6	139.8	179.8	367.1	440.5	325.5	392.9	345.2	297.6	282.2
8.	341.2	405.7	463.1	674.1	795.5	689.2	753.6	739.0	733.7	713.0
9.	1.1618	1.2147	1.3028	1.3173	1.2754	1.1640	1.1031	1.0470	0.9802	1.0984

Source: IMF, *International Financial Statistics*, 1979 and 1985 Yearbook, and March 1986.

gold reserves at market prices in terms of SDRs, as well as the dollar value of one SDR at year-end. Note that the SDR conversion rate for the dollar for 1984 given at the bottom of Table 19-1 is the average for the year and differs from the year-end value given at the bottom of Table 20-4. A few of the totals in the table are subject to very small rounding errors. The SDR market price of gold was practically identical to the official price of SDR 35 per ounce until the two-tier gold market was established in 1968. Note the sharp increase in foreign exchange reserve (mostly dollars) and gold reserves at market prices since the breakdown of the Bretton Woods system in 1971.

Problem (a) Calculate the ratio of the total dollar value of international reserves (with gold measured at market values) to the total dollar value of world imports from 1950 to 1985. (b) What can you say about the change in international liquidity over the years? (c) Why may international liquidity be excessive under the present international monetary system?

Selected Bibliography

For a problem-solving approach to the topics covered in this chapter, see:
- D. Salvatore, *Theory and Problems of International Economics,* 2nd ed. (New York: McGraw-Hill, 1984), ch. 12.

The operation of the gold standard is discussed in:
- D. Hume, "Of the Balance of Trade," in *Essays, Morals, Political and Literary,* Vol. 1 (London: Longmans Green, 1898). Excerpts reprinted in R. N. Cooper, *International Finance* (Baltimore: Penguin, 1969).
- R. Nurkse, *International Currency Experience* (Princeton, N.J.: League of Nations, 1944).
- A. I. Bloomfield, *Monetary Policy under the International Gold Standard: 1880–1914* (New York: Federal Reserve Bank, 1959).
- M. Michaely, *Balance-of-Payment Adjustment Policies* (New York: National Bureau of Economic Research, 1968).
- W. Bagehot, *Lombard Street* (New York: Arno Press, 1978).
- M. D. Bordo, "The Classical Gold Standard: Some Lessons for Today," *Federal Reserve Bank of St. Louis Review,* May 1981.

For the presentation and evaluation of the interwar experience, see:

- R. Nurkse, *The Interwar Currency Experience: Lessons of the Interwar Period* (Geneva: United Nations, 1944).
- R. Z. Aliber, "Speculation in Foreign Exchanges: The European Experience, 1919–1926," *Yale Economic Essays,* vol. 2, 1962.
- S. C. Tsiang, "Fluctuating Exchange Rates in Countries with Relatively Stable Economies: Some European Experiences after World War I," *International Monetary Fund Staff Papers,* October 1959.

The operation, evolution, and problems faced by the Bretton Woods system are examined in:
- R. Solomon, *The International Monetary System* (New York: Harper & Row, 1982).
- R. Triffin, *Gold and the Dollar Crisis* (New Haven, Conn.: Yale University Press, 1960).
- R. Triffin, *Our International Monetary System: Yesterday, Today and Tomorrow* (New York: Random House, 1968).
- G. N. Halm, *Jamaica and the Par Value System,* Essays in International Finance, No. 135 (Princeton, N.J.: Princeton University Press, March 1977).
- R. I. McKinnon, *Money in International Exchange: The Convertible Currency System* (New York: Oxford University Press, 1979).
- R. N. Cooper et al. (Eds.), *The International Monetary System under Flexible Exchange Rates* (Cambridge, Mass.: Ballinger, 1982).

• J. Williamson, *The Lending Policies of the International Monetary Fund* (Washington, D.C.: Institute for International Economics, 1982).
• IMF, *The European Monetary System: The Experience* (Washington, D.C.: IMF, 1983).
• H. Hungerer et al., "The European Monetary System: The Experience 1979–1982," *IMF Occasional Paper*, No. 19, May 1983.
• S. W. Black, "International Money and International Monetary Arrangements," in R. W. Jones and P. B. Kenen, *Handbook of International Economics*, vol. 2 (Amsterdam: North-Holland, 1985).
• J. Williamson, *The Exchange Rate System* (Washington, D.C.: Institute for International Economics, 1985).
• Council of Economic Advisers, *Economic Report of the President* (Washington, D.C.: U.S. Government Printing Office, February 1986).
• International Monetary Fund, *Annual Report* (Washington, DC.: IMF, Annual).
• International Montery Fund, *IMS Survey* (Washington, D.C.: IMF, Bimonthly).
• See also the references at the end of Chapter 19.

For current international economic problems and proposed reforms, see:
• G. Audiz and J. Sachs, "Macroeconomic Policy Coordination among Industrial Economies," *Brookings Papers on Economic Activity*, No.1, 1948.
• R. N. Cooper, "Economic Interdependence and Coordination of Policies," in R. W. Jones and P. B. Kenen, *Handbook of International Economics*, vol. 2 (Amsterdam: North-Holland, 1985).
• J. N. Bhagwati, *Dependence and Interdependence* (Cambridge, Mass.: M.I.T. Press, 1985).
• R. I. McKinnon, *An International Standard for Monetary Stabilization* (Washington, D.C.: Institute for International Economics, 1984).
• P. B. Kenen, "The Use of the SDR to Supplement or Substitute for Other Means of Finance," in G. M. von Furstenberg, Ed., *International Money and Credit: The Policy Roles* (Washington, D.C.: IMF, 1983).

• M. Stamp, "The Stamp Plan—1962 Version," *Moorgate and Wall Street*, Autumn 1962.
• Y. S. Park, *The Link Between Special Drawing Rights and Development Finance*, Essays in International Finance, No. 100 (Princeton, N.J.: Princeton University Press, 1973).
• W. R. Cline, *Trade Policy in the 1980s* (Washington, D.C.: Institute for International Economics, 1982).
• R. E. Baldwin, "Trade Policies in Developed Countries," in R. W. Jones and P. B. Kenen, *Handbook of International Economics*, vol. 1 (Amsterdam: North-Holland, 1984).
• D. Salvatore, "The New Protectionism and World Welfare," *Journal of Policy Modeling*, Spring 1985. Reprinted in *Economic Impact*, March-April 1986.
• D. Salvatore (ed.), *The New Protectionist Threat to World Welfare* (New York: North-Holland, 1987).
• D. Salvatore, "Import Penetration, Exchange Rates and Protectionism in the United States," *Journal of Policy Modeling*, Spring 1987.
• D. Salvatore, "The Emergence of New Protectionism with Nontariff Instruments," *Vienna Institute of Comparative Economic Studies—Workshop Papers*, Spring 1987.
• W. R. Cline, *International Debt: Systematic Risk and Response* (Washington, D.C.: Institute for International Economics, 1984).
• D. Salvatore, "Petroleum Prices, Exchange Rate Changes, and Domestic Inflation in Developing Nations." *Weltwirtsschafliches Archiv*, March 1984.
• S. W. Black, *Learning from Adversity: Policy Responses to Two Oil Shocks*, Essays in International Finance (Princeton, N.J.: Princeton University Press, 1985).
• D. Salvatore, "Oil Import Costs and Domestic Inflation in Industrial Countries." *Weltwirtsschafliches Archiv*, June 1986.
• World Bank, *World Bank Development Report* (Washington, D.C.: World Bank, 1986).
• D. Salvatore, "A Simultaneous Equations Model of Trade and Development with Dynamic Policy Simulations." *Kyklos*, March, 1983.
• D. Salvatore (ed.), *African Development*

Prospects: A Policy Modeling Approach (New York: North-Holland, 1987).
- D. Salvatore (ed.), *World Population Trends and their Impact on Economic Development* (Westport, Conn.: Greenwood Press, 1987).

International financial and trade data of nations that are members of the International Monetary Fund, monthly from 1951 and summarized yearly to the present, are found in:
- International Monetary Fund, *International Financial Statistics* (Washington, D.C.: IMF, Monthly).
- International Monetary Fund, *Balance of Payments Statistics* (Washington, D.C.: IMF, Monthly).
- International Monetary Fund, *Direction of Trade Statistics* (Washington, D.C.: IMF, Monthly).
- International Monetary Fund, *Government Finance Statistics Yearbook* (Washington, D.C.: IMF, vols. I–V).

Answers to Selected Problems

CHAPTER 1

1. a. The economic news of an international character in the daily newspapers are likely to include: demands for protection against imports by U.S. labor; the high value of the dollar in relation to other currencies; the large U.S. trade deficit; the interntional debt of developing nations, and trade negotiations.

   b. Protection against imports by U.S. labor would affect the number of workers employed in some large American industries such as steel, textile, and automobiles; the high international value of the dollar encourages imports to and discourages exports from the U.S.; a large trade deficit may result in the U.S. imposing some import restrictions; the huge international debt of developing nations affects the profitability and solvency of some major U.S. commercial banks; trade negotiations may remove some of the obstructions to the flow of trade in goods and services between the U.S. and other countries.

   c. Protection against imports will make imported goods (such as shoes, stereos, cameras, automobiles, and so on) more expensive to Americans; the high international value of the dollar makes imported goods and foreign travel cheap for Americans; a large trade deficit may result in restrictions on imports and foreign trips and investments; the large international debt of developing nations at risk of not being repaid means that the stocks of the American commercial banks that have lent the money are valued less than otherwise; trade negotiations may lower the price of many imported products to the American consumer.

6. Parts I and II deal with the international trade, while Parts III and IV deal with international finance. Part I deals with the pure theory of international trade, while Part II deals with trade policies. Similarly, Part III deals with foreign exchange markets and the balance of payments, while Part IV deals mostly with adjustment policies. Thus, the text follows very closely the natural breakdown of the subject matter of international economics.

CHAPTER 2

1. a. In case A, the U.S. has an absolute advantage in wheat and the U.K. in cloth; in case B, the U.S. has an absolute advantage (so that the U.K. has an absolute disadvan-

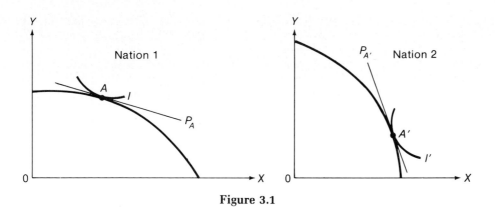

Figure 3.1

tage) in both commodities; in case C, the U.S. has an absolute advantage in wheat but has neither an absolute advantage nor disadvantage in cloth; in case D, the U.S. had an absolute advantage over the U.K. in both commodities.

b. In case A, the U.S. has a comparative advantage in wheat and the U.K. in cloth; in case B, the U.S. has a comparative advantage in wheat and the U.K. in cloth; in case C, the U.S. has a comparative advantage in wheat and the U.K. in cloth, in case D, the U.S. and the U.K. have a comparative advantage in neither commodities.

c. In case A, trade is possible based on absolute advantage; in case B, trade is possible based on comparative advantage; in case C, trade is possible based on compar-

ative advantage; in case D, no trade is possible because the absolute advantage that the U.S. has over the U.K. is the same in both commodities.

2. a. The U.S. gains 1C.
   b. The U.K. gains 4C.
   c. $3C < 4W < 8C$.
   d. The U.S. would gain 3C while the U.K. would gain 2C.

CHAPTER 3

3. a. See Figure 3.1.
   b. Nation 1 has a comparative advantage in X and nation 2 in Y.
   c. If the relative commodity price line has equal slope in both nations.

4. a. See Figure 3.2.

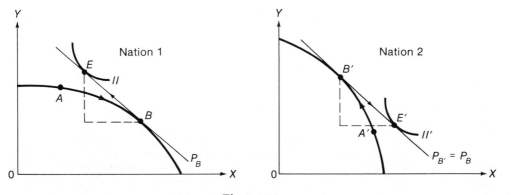

Figure 3.2

b. Nation 1 gains by the amount by which point E is to the right and above point A and nation 2 by the excess of E' over A'. Nation 1 gains more from trade because the relative price with trade differs more from its pretrade price than for nation 2.

CHAPTER 4

3. a. See Figure 4.1.
   b. The quantity demanded of imports by na-

tion 1 at $P_{F'}$ exceeds the quantity of exports of Y supplied by nation 2. As a result, P_x/P_y declines (i.e., P_x/P_y rises) until the quantity demanded of imports of Y by nation 1 equals the quantity of exports of Y supplied by nation 2 at $P_B = P_{B'}$.
   c. That nation 1 is willing to give up less of X for larger amounts of Y.

6. a. See Figure 4.2.
   b. See Figure 4.3.
   c. See Figure 4.4.

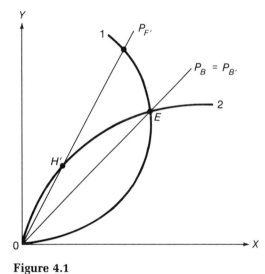

Figure 4.1

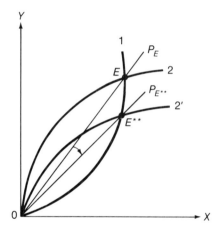

Figure 4.3

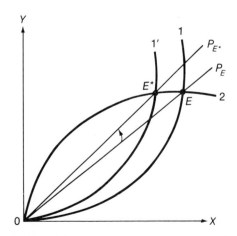

Figure 4.2

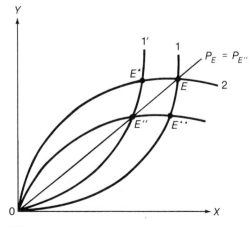

Figure 4.4

CHAPTER 5

5. a. See Figure 5.1. Nation 1 has a comparative advantage in commodity X.

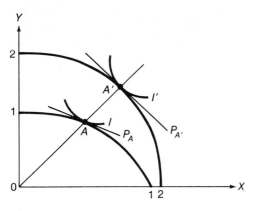

Figure 5.1

b. See Figure 5.2.
6. a. P_x/P_y will be lower in nation 1 because point A will move to the left.
   b. r/w will rise in nation 1.

CHAPTER 6

1. The statement was made by Gottfried Haberler in his *A Survey of International Trade Theory*, Special Papers in International Economics, No. 1 (Princeton, N.J.: Princeton University Press, International Finance Section, July 1961), p. 18. While the statement is true, it does not detract from Samuelson's great contribution in rigorously showing the conditions under which trade would bring about the complete equality in returns to homogeneous factors among nations.

3. a. See Figure 6.1.

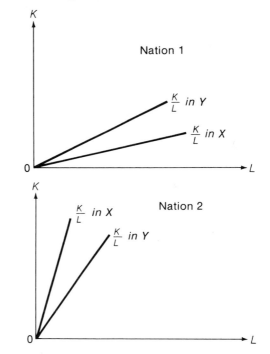

Figure 6.1

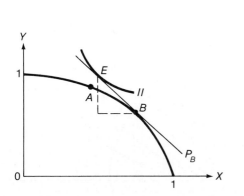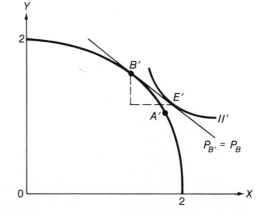

Figure 5.2

b. If the substitutability of K for L in the production of X was much much greater than
for Y and r/w was lower in nation 2 than
nation 1.

c. Minhas found factor reversal to be fairly
frequent. However, by correcting an important source of bias in the Minhas study,
Leontief showed that factor reversal was
much less frequent. Ball tested another
aspect of Minhas' conclusion and con-

firmed Leontief's results that factor reversal was rare.

CHAPTER 7

1. a. See Figure 7.1.
   b. See Figure 7.2.
   c. See Figure 7.3.
   d. See Figure 7.4.
5. See Figure 7.5.

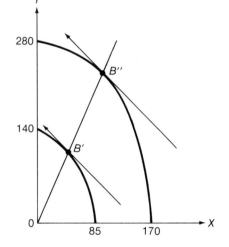

Figure 7.1

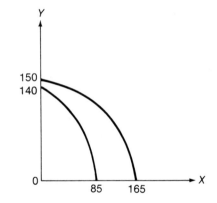

Figure 7.3

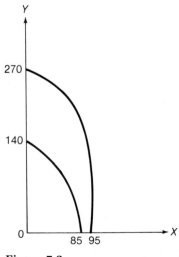

Figure 7.2

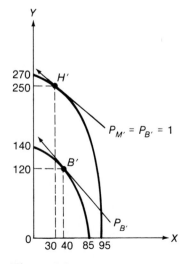

Figure 7.4

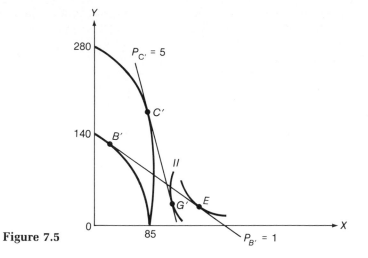

Figure 7.5

CHAPTER 8

1. See Figure 8.1.
2. a. The real income of labor falls and that of capital rises.
   b. P_y/P_x rises for domestic producers and consumers. As production of Y (the K-intensive commodity) rises and of X falls, the demand and income of K rises and that of L falls. Therefore, r rises and w falls.
   c. Nation 1's terms of trade rise and the real income of L may also rise.

tioning off import licenses, the revenue effect would be $15.
   b. $P_x = 2.50$. Consumption is 40X, of which 10X are produced domestically. The revenue effect is $45.
   c. $P_x = \$2$, domestic production and consumption are 50X, and revenue zero.
   d. $P_x = 1$. Consumption is 70X, production is 30X, and revenue is zero.
4. a. P1 = $4 and P2 = $3 in Figure 9-4 in Appendix A9.1.
   b. Any other distribution of sales in the two markets gives less revenue.

CHAPTER 9

1. a. $P_x = \$1.50$. Consumption is 45X, of which 15X are produced domestically. By auc-

CHAPTER 10

1. a. Nation A will produce commodity X domestically.

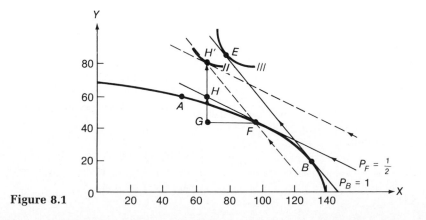

Figure 8.1

b. Nation A will import commodity X from nation B.

c. Trade-creating.

2. a. Nation A will import commodity X from nation C.

b. National A will import commodity X from nation B.

c. Trade-diverting.

CHAPTER 11

2. a. 91.2.

b. 118.6.

c. 128.2.

d. Better off because its income and single factoral terms of trade rose.

4. See Figure 7-6 in the text on immiserizing growth.

CHAPTER 12

3. The statement is true. The profitability of a portfolio is equal to the weighted average of the yield of the securities included in the portfolio. Therefore, the profitability of a portolio of many securities can never exceed the yield of the highest-yield security in the portfolio. The second part of the statement is also true if the portfolio includes securities for which yields are inversely correlated over time.

5. a. U.S. investments abroad reduce the K/L ratio and the productivity and wages of labor in the U.S.

b. An inflow of foreign capital leads to an increase in the K/L ratio and in the productivity and wages of labor or employment in developing nations.

CHAPTER 13

3. a. The pound is at a three-month forward premium of 1¢ or 0.5% (or 2%/year) with respect to the dollar.

b. The pound is at a three-month forward discount of 4¢ or 2% (or 8%/year) with respect to the dollar.

c. The mark is at three-month forward premium of 1% (or 4%/year) with respect to the French franc.

d. The dollar is at three-month forward discount of 0.5% (or 2%/year) with respect to the yen.

6. a. 2% per year.

b. 5% per year.

c. It would pay for investors to transfer funds from the higher- to the lower-interest center and lose 4% interest but gain 6% from the foreign exchange transaction, for a net gain of 2% per year.

CHAPTER 14

1. a. The U.S. debits its current account by $500 (for the merchandise imports) and credits short-term capital by the same amount (for the increase in foreign assets in the U.S.).

b. The U.S. credits its short-term capital by $500 (the drawing down of its bank balances in London, a capital inflow) and debits short-term capital by an equal amount (to balance the short-term capital credit that the U.S. importer received when the U.K. exporter accepted to be paid in three months).

c. The U.S. is left with a $500 debit in its current account and a net credit balance in its short-term capital account of $500.

4. a. The U.S. credits its short-term capital account by $400 (for the purchase of the U.S. treasury bills by the foreign resident) and debits its short-term capital account by the same amount.

b. The U.S. debits its current account by $40 for the interest paid, debits its short-term capital account by $400 (for the capital outflow), and then credits its short-term capital account by $440 (the increase in foreign holdings of U.S. assets, a credit).

CHAPTER 15

1. a. See Figure 15.1.

b. See Figure 15.2.

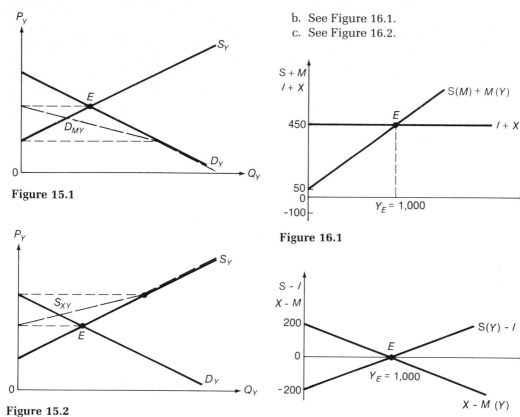

Figure 15.1

Figure 15.2

b. See Figure 16.1.
c. See Figure 16.2.

Figure 16.1

Figure 16.2

4. a. S_M is infinitely elastic because a small nation can demand any quantity of imports without affecting its price; similarly, D_X is infinitely elastic because a small nation can sell any amount of its export good without having to reduce its price.

b. Because the small nation's quantity demanded of pounds always falls (unless D_M is vertical) and its quantity supplied of pounds always rises.

CHAPTER 16

3. a. $S(Y) + M(Y) = -100 + 0.2Y + 150 + 0.2Y = 50 + 0.4Y$
$I + X = 100 + 350 = 450$
$50 + 0.4Y = 450$; therefore,
$YE = 400/0.4 = 1000$.

5. a. $k'' = \dfrac{1}{MPS1 + MPM1 + MPM2(MPS1/MPS2)} = $
$\dfrac{1}{0.20 + 0.20 + 0.10(0.20/0.15)} = $
$\dfrac{1}{0.533} = 1.88$
$\Delta YE = (\Delta X)(k'') = (200)(1.88) = 376$
$\Delta M = (\Delta YE)(MPM1) = (376)(0.20) = 75.2$
therefore, nation's 1 trade balance will improve by 200-75.2 = 124.8.

b. $k^* = \dfrac{1 + MPM2/MPS2}{MPS1 + MPM1 + MPM2(MPS1/MPS2)} = $
$\dfrac{1 + 0.10/0.15}{0.533} = \dfrac{1.667}{0.533} = 3.13$
$\Delta YE = (\Delta I)(k^*) = (200)(3.13) = 626$
$\Delta M = (\Delta YE)(MPM1)(= (626)(0.20) = 125.2 =$ nation 1's trade balance deficit.

c. $k^{**} = \dfrac{MPM2/MPS2}{MPS1 + MPM1 + MPM2(MPS1/MPS2)} =$

$\dfrac{0.10/0.15}{0.533} = \dfrac{0.667}{0.533} = 1.25$

$\Delta YE = (\Delta I^*)(k^{**}) = (200)(1.25) = 250$

$\Delta M = (\Delta YE)(MPM1) = (250)(0.20) = 50 =$ nation 1's trade balance deficit.

d. $k^{**} = \dfrac{0.5}{0.525} = 0.95$

$\Delta YE = (\Delta I^*)(k^{**}) = (200)(0.95) = 190$

$\Delta M = (\Delta YE)(MPM1) = (190)(.15) = 28.5 =$ nations 1's trade balance deficit.

CHAPTER 17

2. a. Surplus because P is below E.
   b. $(200)(0.15) = 30 =$ surplus.
   c. With the expansionary fiscal policy that shifts IS upward until it crosses the FE line at point F and the tight monetary policy that shifts LM upward until it also crosses the FE line at point F.

3. See Figure 17.1.

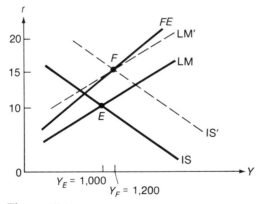

Figure 17.1

CHAPTER 18

5. a. $Md = 100/4 = 25$ falls short of $Ms = 30$ and there will be an outflow of international reserves (a deficit in the nation's balance of payments).
   b. If P increases by 10%, $Md = 110/4 = 27.5$

and the nation will have a $2.5/4 = 0.625$ deficit in its balance of payments.

c. If P increases by 20%, $Md = 120/4 = 30 = Ms$ and the nation's balance of payments will be in equilibrium.

6. According to the monetary approach, inflation in the second nation is caused by excessive money creation there. As result, either the first nation's exchange rate has to appreciate to keep its balance of payments in equilibrium or the first nation's monetary base will rise so that inflation will spread to nation 1.

CHAPTER 19

1. a. The U.S. will export the commodity because at $R = 2$, $P = \$7$ in the U.S. and $P = \$8$ in the U.K.
   b. The U.S. has a comparative disadvantage in this commodity at the equilibrium exchange rate.

2. Under a fixed exchange rate system and perfectly elastic international capital flows, the attempt on the part of the nation to reduce its money supply (tight monetary policy) tends to increase interest rates in the nation and attract capital inflows. This frustrates the attempt on the part of the nation's monetary authorities to reduce the nation's money supply. On the other hand, the attempt of the nation's monetary authorities to increase the money supply of the nation will be frustrated by the tendency of the nation's interest rate to fall, resulting in a capital outflow that would leave the nation's money supply unchanged (see section 17.4c).

CHAPTER 20

1. a. The primary goal of nations today is internal balance, while during the heyday of the gold standard nations gave priority to external balance. The gold standard days were also characterized by much greater price flexibility than today. Furthermore, London was then the undisputed center of international trade and finance and as a result there were no destabilizing international capital flows, as frequently occur

today between the different international monetary centers.

b. The reestablishment of the gold standard today would require the reestablishment of all the conditions that made for its smooth operation from 1880 until 1914. Nations would have to place priority on external over internal balance and give up their use of monetary policy. They would have to eliminate domestic restrictions on price flexibility (i.e., abolish price ceilings, minimum wages, interest restrictions etc.), and reestablish the supremacy of one international monetary center (New York or London) so as to avoid destabilizing capital flows among the international monetary centers in existence today. Needless to say, this is impossible.

4. a. By purchasing the foreign currency forward to reduce the forward discount or increase the forward premium on the foreign currency.

b. By purchasing the foreign currency in the spot market. This tends to appreciate the foreign currency and discourage capital inflows.

Glossary Index

Absolute advantage, 33
Absolute purchasing-power parity theory, 417
Absorption approach, 451
Accommodating transactions, 382
Ad valorem tariff, 201
Adjustable peg system, 541
Adjustment, 574
Adjustment assistance, 237
Adjustment in the balance of payments, 8
Adjustment policies, 417
Antitrade production and consumption, 171
Appreciation, 351
Arbitrage, 351
Autarky, 55
Automatic adjustment mechanism, 417
Automatic income adjustment mechanism, 417
Automatic price adjustment mechanism, 417
Autonomous transactions, 382
Average propensity to import (APM), 451

Balance of payments, 8, 381
Balanced growth, 171
Basic balance, 382
Basis for trade, 33
Benign neglect, 576
Bilateral trade, 237
Brain drain, 317
Bretton Woods system, 575
Buffer stocks, 291

Capital account, 382
Capital inflow, 382
Capital outflow, 382
Capital-intensive commodity, 111
Capital-labor ratio (K/L), 111
Capital-saving technical progress, 171
Closed economy, 450
Comparative statics, 171
Commercial controls, 482
Commercial policies, 201
Commodity or net barter terms of trade, 79, 290-291
Common market, 260

Community indifference curve, 55
Complete specialization, 34
Compound tariff, 201
Confidence, 574
Constant opportunity costs, 33
Constant returns to scale, 111
Consumers' surplus, 201
Consumption effect of a tariff, 201
Consumption function, 450
Cost-push inflation, 482
Covered interest arbitrage, 351
Crawling peg system, 541
Credit tranche, 575
Credit transactions, 381
Currency convertibility, 575
Current account, 382
Customs union, 260

Debit transactions, 381
Debt-servicing problem, 291
Deficit in the balance of payments, 382
Demand for money, 512
Demand-pull inflation, 482
Depreciation, 350
Derived demand, 112
Desired or planned investment, 450
Destabilizing speculation, 351
Devaluation, 417
Differentiated products, 142
Direct investments, 316
Dirty floating, 541
Dollar glut, 576
Dollar shortage, 575
Dollar standard, 576
Dollar overhang, 576
Domestic International Sales Corporation (DISC), 236
Domestic value added, 201
Double factoral terms of trade, 291
Double-entry bookkeeping, 382
Dumping, 236
Duty-free zones or free economic zones, 260
Dynamic analysis, 171

Economic integration, 260
Economic union, 260
Effective exchange rate, 351
Efficiency of foreign exchange markets, 351
Elasticity approach, 451
Elasticity of substitution, 142
Elasticity pessimism, 417
Engine of growth, 290
Equilibrium commodity terms of trade, 34
Equilibrium level of national income (Y_E), 450
Equilibrium relative commodity price in isolation, 55
Equilibrium relative commodity price with trade, 55
Escape clause, 237
Eurobonds, 351
Eurocurrency market, 351
Euronotes, 351
European Currency Unit (ECU), 576
European Economic Community (EEC), 260-261
European Free Trade Association (EFTA), 261
European Monetary Cooperation Fund (EMCF), 576
European Monetary System (EMS), 576
European "snake", 576
Exception to the law of comparative advantage, 33
Exchange controls, 482
Exchange rate, 350
Expenditure-changing policies, 482
Expenditure-switching policies, 482
Export-Import Bank, 236
Export subsidies, 236
Export controls, 291
Export function, 451
Export instability, 291
Export pessimism, 291
Export tariff, 201
Export-oriented industrialization, 291
External balance, 482

Factor abundance, 112
Factor endowments, 112
Factor-intensity reversal, 142
Factor-price equalization (H-O-S) theorem, 112
Factor-proportions of factor-endowments theory, 112
FE curve, 482
Free trade area, 260
Freely floating exchange rate system, 541
Foreign exchange futures, 351
Foreign exchange markets, 8, 350
Foreign exchange options, 351

Foreign exchange risk, 351
Foreign repercussions, 451
Foreign trade multiplier (k'), 451
Forward discount, 351
Forward premium, 351
Forward rate, 351
Fundamental disequilibrium, 575

Gains from specialization, 55
Gains from trade, 33, 55
General Agreement on Tariff and Trade (GATT), 237
General Arrangements to Borrow (GAB), 575
General equilibrium model, 79
Global monetarists, 512
Gold export point, 417
Gold import point, 418
Gold pool, 575
Gold standard, 417
Gold tranche, 575

Heckscher-Ohlin (H-O) theorem, 112
Heckscher-Ohlin (O-H) theory, 112
Hedging, 351
Horizontal integration, 316
Human capital, 142

Immiserizing growth, 172
International debt, 291
International cartel, 236
Identification problem, 417
Import function, 451
Import substitutes, 142
Import tariff, 201
Income elasticity of imports (n_Y), 451
Income terms of trade, 291
Incomplete specialization, 55
Increasing opportunity costs, 55
Increasing returns to scale, 142
Industrialization through import substitution, 291
Inferior goods, 171
Input-output table, 142
Infant-industry argument, 236
Interdependence, 8
Interest arbitrage, 351
Interest parity, 351
Internal balance, 482
Internal factor mobility, 112
International Bank for Reconstruction and Development (IBRD or World Bank), 575
International commodity agreements, 291
International Development Association (IDA), 575

International factor mobility, 112
International Finance, 8
International Finance Corporation (IFC), 575
International investment position, 382
International Monetary Fund (IMF), 575
International monetary system, 574
International Trade Organization, 237
Intervention currency, 575
Intra-industry trade, 142
Investment function, 451
IS curve, 482

Jamaica Accords, 576

Kennedy Round, 237

Labor theory of value, 33
Labor-capital ratio (L/K), 111
Labor-intensive commodity, 111
Labor-saving technical progress, 171
Laissez-faire, 33
Law of comparative advantage, 33
Law of one price, 512
Leaning against the wind, 541
Leontief paradox, 142
LINK proposal, 576
Liquid assets, 530
Liquidity, 574
LM curve, 482

Macroeconomic, 8
Managed floating exchange rate system, 541
Marginal propensity to consume (MPC), 450
Marginal propensity to import (MPM), 451
Marginal propensity to save (MPS), 451
Marginal rate of substitution (MRS), 55
Marginal rate of transformation (MRT), 55
Marketing boards, 291
Marshall-Lerner condition, 417
Mercantilism, 33
Metzler case, 201
Microeconomic, 8
Mint parity, 417
Monetary approach to the balance of payments, 512
Monetary base, 512
Monopoly, 142
Most-favored-nation principle, 236
Multilateral trade negotiations, 237
Multinational corporations (MNCs), 317
Multiple exchange rates, 482
Multiplier (k), 451

National security clause, 237
Net IMF position, 575

Net liquidity balance, 382
Neutral production and consumption, 171
Neutral technical progress, 171
New International Economic Order (NIEO), 291
Nominal tariff, 201
Nontariff trade barriers, 236
Nontraded goods and services, 143
Normal goods, 171

Offer curve, 79
Official reserve account, 382
Official settlements balance, 382
Oligopoly, 142
Opportunity cost theory, 33
Optimum currency area or bloc, 541
Optimum tariff, 201

Partial equilibrium analysis, 143
Pattern of trade, 33
Perfect competition, 111
Peril-point provisions, 237
Persistent dumping, 236
Phillips curve, 482
Portfolio balance approach, 512
Predatory dumping, 236
Preferential trade arrangements, 260
Price-specie-flow mechanism, 418
Principle of effective market classification, 482
Portfolio investments, 316
Portfolio theory, 316
Product cycle model, 143
Production effect of a tariff, 201
Production possibility frontier, 33
Prohibitive tariff, 201
Protection cost or deadweight loss of a tariff, 201
Protrade production and consumption, 171
Purchase contracts, 291
Purchasing-power parity (PPP) theory, 417
Pure theory of trade, 8

Quantity theory of money, 418
Quota, 236

Rate of effective protection, 201
Reciprocal demand curve, 79
Regions of recent settlement, 290
Relative commodity prices, 34
Relative factor prices, 112
Relative purchasing-power parity theory, 417
Rent or producers' surplus, 201
Reserve-currency country (RCC), 512
Revenue effect of a tariff, 201
Risk diversification, 316

Roosa bonds, 576
Rules of the game under the gold standard, 418
Rybczynski theorem, 171

Same technology, 111
Saving function, 450
Scientific tariff, 236
Seignorage, 576
Single factoral terms of trade, 291
Small country case, 34
Smithsonian Agreement, 576
Smoot-Hawley Tariff Act of 1930, 236
Special Drawing Rights (SDRs), 575
Specific-factors model, 112
Specific tariff, 201
Speculation, 351
Speculative demand for money, 482
Sporadic dumping, 236
Spot rate, 351
Stabilizing speculation, 351
Stable foreign exchange market, 417
Standby arrangements, 575
Statistical discrepancy, 382
Stolper-Samuelson theorem, 201
Substitution account, 576
Super gold tranche, 575
Supply of money, 512
Surplus in the balance of payments, 382
Synthesis of automatic adjustments, 451
Swap arrangements, 575

Tariff factories, 260
Technical, administrative and other regulations, 236

Technological gap model, 143
Terms of trade, 79
Terms-of-trade effect, 171
Theory of commercial policy, 8
Theory of the second best, 260
Tokyo Round, 237
Trade Agreements Act of 1934, 236
Trade creation, 260
Trade deflection, 261
Trade diversion, 260
Trade effect of a tariff, 201
Trade Expansion Act of 1962, 237
Trade Reform Act of 1974, 237
Trade-creating customs union, 260
Trade-diverting customs union, 260
Transaction demand for money, 482
Transfer pricing, 317
Transfer problem, 451
Transportation costs, 143
Trigger-price mechanism, 236
Two-tier gold market, 575

Uncovered interest arbitrage, 351
Unilateral transfers, 382
United Nations Conference on Trade and Development (UNCTAD), 291
Unstable foreign exchange market, 417

Variable import levies, 261
Vent for surplus, 290
Vertical integration, 316
Voluntary export restraints, 236

Wealth effect, 171

Name Index

Adams, J., 10
Adams, W. A., 320
Aghevli, B. B. 521
Alexander, S. S. 444, 457
Aliber, R. Z., 361, 579
Allen, P. R., 520
Allen, M., 246
Ando, 520
Arrow, K., 148, 150
Artus, J. R., 544
Audiz, G., 580

Bagehot, W., 428, 579
Balassa, B., 125, 134, 149, 215, 216, 264, 271,
    293, 411, 428
Baldwin, R. E., 10, 129, 149, 245, 246, 580
Ball, D. P. S., 131, 148, 149
Basevi, G., 245
Bergesten, C. F., 320
Berham, J. M., 319
Berstein, E. M., 385
Bhagwati, J., 10, 38, 65, 122, 163, 179, 215,
    245, 246, 293, 294, 320, 493, 580
Bilson, J. F. O., 361, 520, 521
Black, W. S., 493, 580
Bloomfield, A. I., 428, 549, 579
Bordo, M. D., 579
Bowen, H. P., 150
Branson, W. H., 129, 149, 520, 544
Brundell, P., 278, 294
Bryant, R. C., 493

Cairncross, A. K., 270, 293
Cassell, G., 409, 428
Caves, R. E., 10, 293, 319
Chamberlin, E. H., 150
Chang, T. C., 406, 427
Chenery, H. B., 148, 150, 293
Chipman, J., 10, 38, 122
Cline, W. R., 245, 246, 294, 295, 580
Cooper, C. A., 215, 264, 265
Cooper, R. N., 544, 570, 579, 580

Corden, W. M., 179, 215, 245
Crockett, A. D., 544

Darby, M. R., 520
Davutyan, N., 412, 428
de Gaulle, C., 560
de Graff, V. J., 215
Dornbusch, R., 520, 521, 544
Dowling, E., 293
Dufey, G., 361
Dunning, J. H., 320

Edgeworth, F. Y., 67
Einzig, P., 361
Ellis, H. S., 10, 65
Erb, G. F., 278, 294

Fair, R. C., 457
Fieleke, N., 520
Findlay, R., 179, 293
Flanders, M. J., 294
Fleming, M. J., 493
Francis, J., 409, 428
Frenkel, J. A., 361, 412, 428, 520, 521
Friedman, M., 519, 525, 544

Gayer, A. D., 38
Giddy, I., 361
Goldstein, H. N., 409, 428
Goldstein, M., 457, 544
Golt, S., 245
Grabbe, J. O., 361
Grubel, H. G., 134, 150, 215, 265, 319, 320
Gruber, W., 137, 150
Grubert, H., 179
Gutowski, A., 493

Haberler, G., 24, 38, 65, 90, 123, 270, 293, 427,
    544
Halm, G. N., 579
Hamilton, C., 265
Harberger, A. C., 409, 427
Harris, R., 264

Heckscher, E. F., 99, 122, 123
Helliwell, J. F., 457
Helpman, E., 134, 150
Henderson, D. W., 520
Herring, R., 520
Hicks, J. R., 156, 180
Holmes, A., 361
Holzman, D. F., 246
Hood, N., 319
Horn, H., 248, 294
Houthakker, H. S., 127, 149, 409, 428, 457
Hume, D., 415, 428, 548, 579
Hungerer, H., 580

Ingram, W. D., 265

Johnson, H. G., 10, 122, 179, 215, 245, 250,
    264, 265, 294, 494, 520, 544
Jones, R. W., 10, 122, 148
Junz, H., 408, 428

Keesing, D. B., 129, 149
Kemp, D. S., 180, 391, 520
Kenen, P. B., 10, 65, 129, 148, 149, 215, 493,
    520, 580
Keynes, J. M., 5, 361, 457, 552
Khan, M. S., 409, 428, 457, 521
Kindleberger, C. P., 275, 294, 319
Krause, L., 520
Kravis, I. B., 129, 149, 269, 293, 412, 428
Kreinin, I. B., 245, 264, 521
Krueger, A. O., 293, 294, 361, 521
Krugman, P. R., 134, 150
Kubarych, R. M., 361

Laney, L. O., 457, 493
Lancaster, K., 122, 134, 150, 253
Lancieri, E., 278, 294
Leamer, E. E., 129, 149, 428
Leontief, W. W., 65, 126, 148, 149
Lerner, A. P., 65, 90, 215, 427
Levich, R. M., 344
Levitt, K., 320
Lewis, W. A., 294
Linder, S. B., 149
Lipsey, R. E, 253, 264, 275, 294, 412, 428
Lipsey, R. G., 253, 264
Little, I., 294
Lloyd, P. J., 134, 150, 264
Lombardi, J., 216
Long, N. V., 180

MacBean, A. I., 278
MacDougal, G. D. A., 124, 149, 319

Machlup, F., 427, 457
Magee, S., 409, 428, 457
Marshall, A., 5, 67, 406, 427
Marston, R. M., 361, 493, 545
Maskus, K. E., 129, 149
Massell, B. F., 264, 265, 278, 294
Mathieson, D. J., 278, 294
McDonald, D. C., 295
McKenzie, G., 361
McKinnon, R. I., 278, 294, 361, 520, 532, 544,
    569, 579, 580
McMullen, N., 294
Meade, J. E., 10, 67, 90, 250, 264, 391, 457,
    459, 492
Metha, D., 137, 150
Meier, G. M., 293
Metzler, L. A., 10, 65, 215, 457
Michaely, M., 149, 215, 245, 271, 293, 294,
    428, 493, 549, 579
Miller, M. H., 264
Mill, J. S., 5
Minhas, B. S., 131, 148, 149, 150
Monoyios, N., 129, 149
Mussa, M. L., 122, 361, 493, 520, 544
Mundell, R. A., 461, 492, 493, 494, 520, 532,
    544
Murray, T., 294
Myint, H., 245, 293
Myrdal, G., 273, 294

Newman, P. C., 38
Nixon, R. M., 559, 560
Nurkse, R., 293, 428, 529, 544, 549, 551, 579

Oates, W. E., 520
Obstefeld, M., 361, 521
Officer, L. H., 428, 521
Ohlin, B., 99, 122, 123, 457
Orcutt, G. H., 407, 428
Owen, N., 264

Padmore, T., 457
Pareto, V., 253
Park, Y. S., 361, 580
Petith, H. C., 264
Pippenger, J., 412, 428
Posner, M. V., 150
Prebish, R., 273, 293

Ramaswani, V. K., 245
Rhomberg, R., 408, 428
Ricardo, D., 5, 17, 38, 123
Richardson, J. D., 10
Robinson, J., 427

Robinson, R. I., 319
Rugman, A., 319
Rybczynski, T. M., 179

Sachs, J. D., 457, 580
Salant, W., 520
Salvatore, D., 10, 38, 65, 90, 121, 148, 150, 179, 215, 244, 245, 246, 264, 293, 294, 319, 361, 391, 427, 428, 457, 492, 519, 544, 579, 580
Samuelson, P. A., 5, 65, 104, 122, 215
Sauvant, K., 245
Savvidas, A., 279, 294
Schiavo-Campo, S., 278, 294
Schumacher, B., 409, 428
Scitovsky, T., 215, 264
Scott, A. D., 320
Scott, F., 361
Servan-Screiber, J. J., 320
Singer, H., 273, 294, 319
Smith, A., 5, 14, 38, 180
Sodersten, B., 215
Sohmen, E., 544
Solomon, R., 579
Solow, R. M., 148, 150
Spenser, M. H., 38
Spitaeller, E., 409, 428
Spraos, J., 275, 294
Srinivisan, T. N., 10
Stamp, M., 580
Stern, R., 10, 125, 129, 149, 244, 245, 391, 409, 427, 428, 493, 544
Stockman, A. C., 361, 521

Stolper, W. F., 122, 215
Svedberg, P., 278, 294
Svensson, L. E. O., 565
Swan, T., 463, 492
Swann, D., 264
Swoboda, A., 544
Szenberg, M., 216

Takacs, W. E., 245
Taussig, F., 549
Theberge, J., 293
Tinbergen, J., 460, 492
Tosini, P. A., 544
Towers, E., 544
Triffin, R., 562, 579
Tsiang, S. C., 457, 579
Turner, L., 294

Vanek, J., 264
Vernon, R., 137, 150, 320
Vind, K., 215
Viner J., 38, 90, 250, 264

White, H. D., 552
Willett, T. D., 544
Williamson, J., 544, 580
Wilson, T., 294
Wrightman, D., 319

Yeats, A. J., 216
Young, J. H., 544
Young, S., 319

Subject Index

Absolute advantage, 15-17, 33
Absolute factor-price equalization, 105-107, 118-119
Absolute purchasing-power parity theory, 409-410
Absorption, 443-444, 461-463
Absorption approach, 443-445
Absorptive capacity, 444
Accelerator, 278, 281
Accommodating transactions, 371-372, 395
Accounting, balance of payments, 363-367, 371
Ad valorem tariff, 183-184, 201
Adjustment in balance of payments (*See* Balance of payments adjustment)
Adjustable peg system, 536-537, 551-562
Adjustment assistance, 229, 237
Adjustment policy, 396, 449, 459-477
Advance deposits on imports, 478
Agriculture, protection, 233-234, 256-257
Anchor argument against flexible exchange rates, 530
Antitrade production and consumption, 158-159, 171
Antitrust laws, 255
Appreciation, 328
Arbitrage:
  currency, 329-330
  triangular, 329
  (*See also* Interest, arbitrage)
Argentiana, 107, 108, 233, 269, 282, 283, 285, 539
Autarky, 45, 52, 55, 67, 68, 430
Automatic adjustment mechanism:
  in real world, 447-448
  theory, 395
Automatic income adjustment mechanism, 396, 429-443
Automatic price adjustment mechanism, 396-415
Autonomous transactions, 371, 395
Average propensity to import, 435

Balanced growth, 152-153, 171
Balance of indebtedness, 378

Balance of payments:
  accounting, 363-367
  deficit, 372, 374, 377, 395, 498
  defined, 4, 362-363
  disequilibrium, 370, 372-375, 395-396
  effect of foreign direct investment on, 305
  effect of foreign aid on, 376
  fundamental disequilibrium, 377
  purposes, 362
  statistics, 367-370, 384-391
  surplus, 372, 377, 395, 498
Balance of payments adjustment:
  automatic, 395
  income, 396, 429-443
  policy, 396, 449, 459-477
  price, 396-415
  role of money, 494
  under a flexible exchange rate system, 397-403, 446-447
  under a managed floating exchange rate system, 446
  under the gold-exchange standard, 413
  under the gold standard, 413-415, 548-549
  with exchange controls, 478-479
Balance of payments problems of the U.S., 375-380, 477, 558-560
Balance of trade, 371, 375, 378, 444, 488
Bancor, 552
Barter trade, 243
Basic balance, 374, 384-389
Basis for trade, 13, 15-18, 21-32, 33, 47-51, 52-54, 66, 91, 100, 131-137
Beggar-thy-neighbor policies, 225, 227, 449, 538
Belgium, 248, 256, 479, 501, 556
Benign neglect, 563
Bilateral trade, 227, 232-233, 236, 243-244
Bilateral trade agreement, 243-244, 287
Border taxes, 221
Box diagram (*See* Edgeworth box diagram)
Brain drain, 314
Brazil, 107, 183, 233, 268, 271, 282, 283, 285, 376, 537
Bretton Woods system:

description, 534, 551-552
fundamental cause of collapse, 561-562
immediate cause of collapse, 375, 560-561
operation, 554-556
evolution, 556-557
Buffer stocks, 279, 564
Bulk purchasing, 243
Business cycle, international transmission, 443
Buy American Act (1933), 221

Canada, 129, 224, 233, 269, 280, 288, 299, 310-311, 380, 479, 533, 539, 555, 556
Capital-abundant country, 97-98
Capital account, 371
Capital flows:
  controls on, 478-480
  destabilizing, 464, 555, 559
  direct, 297-299
  elastic, 471-472
  inflow, 269, 364-365, 378, 395
  liquid, 385, 389, 558
  long-term, 374, 385
  nonliquid, 385, 389
  official, 371
  outflow, 364-365
  portfolio, 296-297, 300-301
  short-term, 374, 385, 464, 475
  speculative, 347, 560, (See also Speculation, currency)
  stabilizing, 549
Capital-intensive commodity, 59, 93, 94-96, 98, 100, 111, 127
Capital-labor ratio, 59, 64-65, 93, 94-96, 111, 127, 178-179
Capital-saving technical progress, 156, 171
Capital transfer (See Capital flows)
Cartel (See International Cartel)
Central American Common Market (CACM), 258
Central bank swap, 556
Central rates, 566
China, trade with, 244
Closed economy, 430
Cobb-Douglas production function, 147-148
COMEA or COMECON (Council of Mutual Economic Assistance), 243
Commercial controls, 478
Commercial franc, 479
Commercial policy, 183, 201, 247 (See also Tariff; Quotas)
Commodity price stabilization, 279-280
Common Agricultural Policy, 256-257
Common Market (See European Economic Community)

Commonwealth preferences, 247
Communist countries, 242-244, 552, 557
Community indifference curves, 42-45, 55
Comparative advantage, 17-27, 36-38, 46-47, 77-78, 91, 100
Comparative disadvantage, 18
Comparative statics, 121, 152, 171, 222
Compensation principle, 44-45
Complete Specialization, 31, 33, 50, 72, 133
Compound tariff, 184, 201
Confidence problem, 547, 561
Constant elasticity of substitution production function (CES), 148
Constant opportunity costs, 24-26, 33, 72
Constant returns to scale, 58, 93, 111
Consumers' surplus, 195, 201
Consumption effect of a tariff, 184-191, 193-196, 201
Consumption function, 432
Consumption possibility frontier, 27, 49, 161
Contract curve, production, 63-65, 114-115
Convertibility, 243, 377, 550, 552
Convertible currencies, 550, 552, 555
Cost-push inflation, 476
Council of Mutual Economic Assistance, 243
Countervailing duty, 223, 230
Covered interest arbitrage margin (CIAM), 343, 358-360
Covered interest arbitrage, 342-344, 356-358
Crawling peg system, 536
Credit tranches, 553-554
Credit transaction, 364
Currency:
  appreciation, 328, 505, 530
  convertibility, 243, 377, 550, 552
  depreciation, 328, 397, 402, 421, 443, 505, 530
  devaluation, 397, 402, 421, 443, 461, 463, 478, 530, 555
  revaluation, 460, 461, 463, 528, 530, 555, 559-560
Current account:
  defined, 371
  deficit, 372, 395
  surplus, 372
Customs union:
  dynamic effects, 255-256
  history of, 256-259
  monetary integration, 248, sect 19.4
  second best argument for, 253-254
  static effects, 249-250, 252, 253-254, 262-264
  theory of, 247-252, 534
  trade creation and trade diversion, 248-252, 262-264

Debit transaction, 364
Debt problem, international, 285-286
Debt service, 285, 571
Debt-servicing problem, 234, 285-286, 571-572
Decreasing costs, 50
Deficit in balance of payments, 372, 374, 377, 395, 498
Deflation, 547, 550
Demand for:
    exports, 103, 239
    factors of production, 97, 100, 106-107
    foreign exchange, 324-329, 353-356, 398-400
    imports, 67, 70, 75-77, 85, 398-400
    money, 496-498
Demand-pull inflation, 462, 476
Depreciation, currency, 328, 397, 421, 443
Derived demand, 97, 112
Desired or planned investment, 430
Destabilizing speculation, 341, 522, 524, 526, 528-530, 551
Devaluation, currency:
    competitive, 449, 550-551
    defined, 397, 461
    domestic absorption, 443-445
    of dollar, 402, 421
    effect on domestic prices, 402-403, 419-421
    effectiveness of policy of, 397, 406
Developing countries:
    barriers to export from, 183, 270, 283
    commodity terms of trade, 273-276
    debt problem, 234, 285-286, 571-572
    demands for a NIEO, 287-289, 572
    expropriation of foreign investments in, 311
    foreign aid received, 288-289, 572
    foreign direct investments in, 286, 299
    growth of exports, 276
    import-substitution, 218, 267, 281-283
    income terms of trade, 276
    industrialization, 225, 233, 267, 281-283
    instability of export earnings, 278-279
    per capita income, 165, 267, 284
    population growth, 165, 267
    poverty in, 284-285, 572
    regional integration among, 258-259
    trade policies, 225, 286
    UNCTAD, 572
Differentiated products, 134-135, 142, 255, 307
Diminishing returns, law of, 119
Direct controls, 460-461, 478-480
Direct foreign investments:
    balance of payments effects of, 305
    defined, 297
    effects on home country, 303-306
    effects on host country, 303-306

    foreign control of, 311
    joint ventures, 311
    of foreign nations in the U.S., 297-299, 370, 378-380
    of multinational corporations, 302
    of U.S. abroad, 297-299, 370, 378-380
    policies toward, 248
    restrictions on, 311, 479
    theory of, 297, 301-303
    welfare effects of, 303-306
Direct taxes, 183, 198, 201, 241
Dirty float, 538-539
Dollar:
    devaluation, 374, 377, 397, 402, 408, 421, 539, 550, 560-561, 569
    foreign holdings of, 385, 558-560
    glut, 562
    overhang, 570
    reserve currency, 377
    shortage, 558
    standard, 560
    surplus, 562
    suspension of gold convertibility, 377, 555, 559-560
Domestic distortions, 226, 241-242
Domestic International Sales Corporation (DISC), 224, 236
Domestic value added, 196, 201, 213-214
Double-entry bookkeeping, 365
Double-factoral terms of trade, 273
Double-taxation agreements, 305
Dumping:
    defined, 223
    persistent, 223, 240
    predatory, 223
    sporadic, 223
    measures against, 223, 230
Dynamic analysis, 152, 171

East-West trade, 242-244
Economic development, 267-280
Economic integration:
    among developing countries, 258-259
    among developed countries, 256-258
Economic growth:
    with factor immobility, 176-177
    and specific-factors model, 176-177
Economic union, 247-248
Economies of scale, 131-134, 230, 255, 270, 282, 307, 346
ECU (European Currency Unit), 565-566
Edgeworth box diagram:
    definition of, 60
    derivation of, 60-64, 114-115

factor-price equalization, 115-117
EEC (*See* European Economic Community)
Effective exchange rate, 328-329, 336
Effective tariff protection, 196-200, 201, 213-
214
Elasticity (*See* Price elasticity)
Elasticity approach, 403-409, 443
Elasticity of substitution, 130, 142, 146-147
Elasticity optimism, 407
Elasticity pessimism, 407
Emigrant remittances,314
Engine of growth, 268-270
England (*See* United Kingdom)
Equation of exchange, 496
Equilibrium:
    commodity terms of trade, 30, 33
    exchange rate, 326-327, 330, 409-410
    level of national income, 430-441
    relative commodity price in isolation, 45-47,
        55
    relative commodity price with trade, 49, 55,
        70-72, 87-88
    volume of trade, 48-49, 70-72, 87-88
Errors and omissions (*See* Statistical discrep-
    ancy)
Escape clause, 228-229, 236
Euler's theorem, 118
Eurobond, 348
Eurocurrency, 345-347
Eurocurrency market, 345-348, 555
Eurodollar, 345-397
Eurodollar market, 345-346
Euronote, 348-349
European Currency Unit (ECU), 565-566
European Economic Community (EEC), 198-
        199, 229-230, 233, 248, 254, 255, 256-257,
        533
European Free Trade Association (EFTA), 247,
        254, 257
European Monetary Cooperation Fund (EMCF),
        566
European Monetary System (EMS), 565-568
European "snake," 533, 561
Exception to the law of comparative advan-
        tage, 20-21
Exchange controls, 478-479
Exchange rate (*See* Foreign exchange rate)
Exchange rate system (*See* International mone-
        tary systems)
Excise taxes, 221
Expansion path, 58-59
Expenditure-changing policies, 459-464
Expenditure-switching policies, 460-464
Export:

controls, 279-280
function, 436
instability, 276-280
pessimism, 387
quota, 218
subsidy, 223-224, 232, 236, 257, 478
tariff, 183, 193, 201
Export-Import Bank, 224, 236
Export oriented industrialization, 281-282
External balance, 459, 461-464
External economies, 241
Externalities (*See* Domestic distortions)

Factor:
    abundance, 96, 112
    endowments, 42, 99-104, 112
    growth, 152-155, 159-161
    intensity, 94-96
    intensity reversal, 129-131, 144-148
    mobility, 5, 23, 94, 107, 112, 296 (*See also*
        Capital flows; Labor migration)
    price, 100, 106-107
    price equalization, 109, 115-119
    price equalization theorem, 104-109, 112,
        130
    proportions, 100, 112
    substitution, 130, 142, 146-147
Factoral terms of trade:
    double, 273
    single, 272
FE curve, 464, 465-467, 488-489
Federal Reserve System, 327, 552
Financial franc, 479
Fiscal policy:
    defined, 460
    and internal balance, 467-469, 473
Fixed exchange rate systems:
    advantages, 522, 526-532
    disadvantages, 449, 524
    dollar standard, 560
    gold-exchange standard, 547, 551-562
    gold standard, 413-415, 528, 530
Fixed factor proportions, 23, 25, 42, 199, 214
Flexible exchange rates:
    advantages, 522, 523-526, 531-532
    and balance of payments adjustment, 397-
        403, 446-447
    disadvantages, 448-449, 528, 530-531
Floating, dirty, 538-539 (*See also* Managed
        floating exchange rate system)
Floating exchange rates system (*See* Flexible
        exchange rates; Managed floating exchange
        rate system)

Foreign aid:
    amount of, 288-289, 376, 572
    bilateral, 289
    multilateral, 289
    tied, 376, 558
    untied, 289
Foreign borrowing (*See* Capital inflow)
Foreign direct investments (*See* Direct foreign
    investments)
Foreign exchange:
    futures, 333, 338
    options, 333-334, 338, 340
Foreign exchange demand, 324-329, 353-356
Foreign exchange market:
    forward, 338, 339-340
    functions, 324-326
    efficiency, 344-345
    intervention, 377, 477, 526-527, 569
    spot, 337-338, 339
    stable, 403-406, 424-425
    unstable, 403-406, 424-425
Foreign exchange rate:
    defined, 326
    dynamics, 507-509
    equilibrium, 326-327, 330, 409-410
    forward, 330, 344
    multiple, 222, 479
    overshooting, 477, 508-509, 527, 531, 568
    volatility, 336, 477, 509, 522-523, 531, 568
    spot, 330, 344
Foreign exchange rate band, 534-536
Foreign exchange reserves (*See* International
    reserves)
Foreign exchange risk, 334-337
Foreign exchange supply, 324-329, 353-356
Foreign investment, net, 379, 437 (*See also*
    Capital flows; Direct Foreign investments;
    Portfolio investments)
Foreign lending, returns on, 341, 346 (*See also*
    Capital flows)
Foreign repercussions, 441-443
Foreign trade multiplier, 439, 453-455
Forward discount, 331, 479
Forward exchange:
    contract, 330, 333
    exchange market, 338, 339-340
    exchange rate, 330
Forward premium, 331, 479
Fractional reserve system, 445, 497
France, 2, 14, 107, 135, 224, 244, 248, 256,
    314, 348, 477, 479, 539, 550, 553, 555,
    556, 559, 566
Free trade, classical arguments for, 16
Free trade area, 247

Freely floating exchange rate system, 374, 448,
    446, 526, 527
Full employment income, 415, 461-464
Fundamantal disequilibrium, 377, 464, 528,
    536, 552
Futures market, 333-334

Gains from specialization, 51-52, 55
Gains from trade, 13, 19-20, 27-32, 33, 47-52,
    230, 250
GATT (*See* General Agreement on Tariffs and
    Trade)
General Agreement on Tariffs and Trade
    (GATT), 228-229, 232, 236, 363
General Arrangments to Borrow (GAB), 479
General equilibrium model, 77-78, 79, 87-88,
    100-101, 109-110
Generalized System of Preferences (GSP), 230,
    287, 288
Germany (*See* West Germany)
Global banking, 349
Global monetarists, 499
Gold:
    convertibility, 413, 550, 552
    export point, 413, 548
    import point, 414, 548
    points, 413-414, 425-427, 534, 548
    pool, 557
    price, 413, 548, 552, 565
    reserves, 414, 550-551, 554
    two-tier system, 557
Gold exchange standard, 457, 551-562, (*See
    also* Bretton Woods system)
Gold standard:
    adjustment process under, 413-415, 548-549
    and capital flows, 446, 549
    historical experience with, 548-549
    monetary policy under, 549
    price-specie-flow mechanism, 414-415, 548
    reestablishment of, 413, 548-549
    rules of the game of the, 415, 549
Gold tranche, 553, 565
Government procurements, 221, 230, 232
Great Britain (*See* United Kingdom)
Great Depression, 227, 413, 443, 529, 548, 550
Group of Ten, 479, 556, 560
Growth, economic (*See* Economic growth)
Guest workers, 314

Hechscher-Ohlin (H-O) Theorem, 99-104, 112,
    130, 146
Heckscher-Ohlin (H-O) Theory:
    and complementary trade theories, 131-137,
    139-141

empirical testing of, 126-131
extensions of, 131-137, 139-141
factor movements, 94
factor-price equalization, 104-109, 115-119, 130, 146
Leontief paradox, 126-131, 142, 144-148
natural resources, 128-129, 131
Hedging:
  forward market, 338
  high-powered money, 497
  spot market, 337-338
Homogeneous of degree one, 58
Horizontal integration, 302, 306
Hot money flow, 347, 553, 555-556
Human capital, 128-129, 142, 312

Identification problem, 407
IMF (*See* International Monetary Fund)
IMF position, net, 554
Immiserizing growth, 163-165, 171, 273
Import:
  duty (*See* Import, tariff)
  function, 435
  licensing, 219-220
  quota, 218
  substitutes, 127, 142
  substitution, 281-283
  tariff, 183, 193, 201
Income:
  adjustment mechanism, 396, 429-443
  elasticity of imports, 127, 165, 269-270, 274, 435
  policy (*See* Price and wage controls)
  redistribution effect of tariff, 188, 193, 203-208
  terms of trade, 272
Incomplete specialization, 31, 50, 55, 72, 93
Increasing costs, 40-42, 47-52, 55
Increasing returns to scale, 131-132, 142
India, 2, 107, 109, 233, 271, 282, 283, 311
Indifference curves (*See* Community indifference curves)
Indirect taxes, 221
Industrialization through import substitution, 281-283
Infant industry argument, 225-226
Inferior goods, 161, 171
Inflation:
  cost-push, 476
  demand-pull, 462, 476
  devaluation and, 402-403, 419-421
  flexible exchange rates and, 402-403, 419-421
  relative to abroad, 530

Input-output table, 126, 142
Interdependence, 2-4
Interest:
  arbitrage, 341-344, 356-360
  Equalization Tax, 348, 479, 559
  parity, 343, 346, 356-360
  rate, 97, 104-105, 107-109, 117, 119
Internal balance, 459, 461-464
Internal factor mobility, 94
International Bank for Reconstruction and Development (IBRD), 363, 553
International cartel, 222, 236, 239-240
International Coffee Agreement, 280
International commodity agreements, 222, 279-280, 288
International debt problem, 285-286
International Development Association (IDA), 553
International factor mobility, 92, 94, 311-315
International finance, 4
International Finance Corporation (IFC), 553
International investment position, of the United States, 297, 299, 378-380
International liquidity, 347, 547, 561-562
International Monetary Fund (IMF):
  credit facilities, 564
  establishment of, 551-552
  evolution of, 564-565
  functions, 551-555
  General Agreement to Borrow (GAB), 556
  operation, 389-391, 552
  reserve position in, 369-370, 554
  Special Drawing Rights (SDRs), 369, 389, 553, 563
International monetary systems:
  adjustable peg, 536-537, 546, 551-562
  Bretton Woods, 551-562
  crawling peg, 536, 546
  dollar standard, 547
  fixed exchange rate, 546, 548-549, 551-562
  flexible exchange rate, 546, 550-551
  gold standard, 547, 548-549
  gold exchange standard, 547, 551-562
  managed floating exchange rate, 537-539, 546
International reserves, 369, 377, 395, 550, 556-557, 577-579
International reserve assets, 371
International Sugar Agreement, 279
International Tin Agreement, 279
International trade:
  basis of, 13, 15-18, 21-32, 33
  development, 13-14, 267-271
  gains from, 13, 19-20, 27-32, 33

International trade (*cont.*)
  volume of, 75-77, 107, 134, 158-166, 189-193, 232, 243
  growth of, 230-233
International Trade Organization (ITO), 228, 236
Interregional economics, 4-5
Interregional factor movement, 4-5
Intervention currency, 552
Interwar period, 550-551
Intra-industry trade, 134-135, 142
Investment:
  domestic, 430, 437, 446
  foreign, 296-303
  function, 433
  multiplier, 442
  (*See also* Capital flows; Direct foreign investments; Portfolio investments)
IS curve, 464-466, 484-486
IS-LM-FE model:
  derivation of curves, 484-489
  with fixed exchange rates, 467-472
  with freely flexible exchange rates, 490-491
Isocost curve, 58-59
Isoquant, 57-59
Italy, 2, 3, 107, 224, 244, 248, 256, 479, 525, 539, 556, 566

Jamaica Accords, 539, 563
Japan, 2, 3, 107, 109, 136, 137, 198-199, 220-221, 223-224, 230, 233, 288, 307, 348, 376, 477, 525, 539, 553, 555, 556, 559, 571
J-curve effect, 408

Kennedy Round, 229, 237, 555
Key currencies, 570
Keynesian model of income determination, 429-439

Labor-abundant country, 97-98, 127
Labor-capital ratio, 93, 111
Labor-intensive commodity, 59, 93, 94-96, 98, 100, 111, 127
Labor migration:
  brain drain, 314
  effect of on country of emigration, 312-315
  effect of on country of immigration, 312-315
  motives, 311-312
Labor-saving technical progress, 156, 171
Labor surplus economy, 274
Labor theory of value, 23, 33
Laissez-faire, 16, 33
Latin American Free Trade Association (LAFTA), 258

Law of comparative advantage, 17-18, 20-21, 33
Law of one price, 499
Leads and lags, 341
Leaning against the wind, 538, 563
Leontief paradox:
  definition, 126-127
  empirical testing, 128-129
  factor-intensity reversal, 129-131, 142, 144-148
  human capital, 128-129
  natural resources, 128-129, 131
Less developed countries (*See* Developing countries)
LINK proposal, 289, 572
Liquid assets, 374
Liquidity (*See* International liquidity)
Liquidity balance, 384-389
Liquidity preference, 562
LM curve, 464, 486-488
Long-term capital:
  account, 385
  definition, 385
  movements, 385
(*See also* Capital flows; Direct foreign investments; Portfolio investments)
Low income countries (*See* Developing countries)

Macroeconomic, 4, 5, 464
Managed floating exchange rate system, 446, 505-506, 527, 531, 537-539, 562-565 (*See also* Dirty float)
Marginal cost, 239-241
Marginal propensity to:
  consume, 432
  import, 435
  save, 432
Marginal rate of:
  substitution, 44, 55
  technical substitution (MRTS), 58
  transformation, 26, 41, 55, 241
Marginal revenue, 239-241
Marketing boards, 279
Marshall-Lerner condition, 405-406, 421-424
Marshall Plan, 558
Mercantilism, 14-15, 415
Merchandise balance, 371, 375
Metzler case, 191, 201, 205-207
Mexico, 108, 222, 258, 268, 283, 285, 314, 539
Microeconomic, 4, 5
Migration (*See* Labor migration)
Mint parity, 413, 534, 548
MNC (*See* Multinational corporations)

Monetarism (*See* Monetary approach to the balance of payments)
Monetary approach to the balance of payments:
  adjustment to balance of payments disequilibrium, 445-446, 501-503
  control over the nation's money supply, 500-501
  empirical evidence on, 509-511
  exchange rate determination and, 516
  global monetarism, 499
  mathematical model of, 514-518
  origin, 494
  relation to traditional approaches, 494-495, 499
  under fixed exchange rates, 495-504, 501-504
  under flexible exchange rates, 504-506
Monetary base, 497
Monetary policy:
  defined, 460
  and external balance, 467-472, 474
  under fixed exchange rates, 467-472
  under flexible exchange rates, 472
  under the gold standard, 549
  with perfect capital mobility, 471-472
Money demand, 496-498
Money multiplier, 496-497, 515
Money supply, 414-415, 445, 496-498, 500-501, 515
Monopoly, 133, 136, 142, 219-220, 222-223, 239-241, 255, 257
Monopsony, 210
Most-favored-nation principle, 227-228, 232
Multilateral trade, 233, 376
Multilateral trade negotiations, 224, 228-234, 236, 287, 555, 571
Multinational corporation (MNC):
  advantages of, 306-309
  control of, 310-311
  developing nations, 302
  effect on the home country, 309-310
  effect on the host country, 310-311
Multiple exchange rates, 222, 479
Multiplier:
  closed economy, 433-434
  money, 496-497, 515
  open economy, 436-441
  with foreign repercussions, 441-443, 453-455
  without foreign repercussions, 440

National defense, 16, 229
National security clause, 229, 237
Natural resources, 14, 110, 128-129, 131, 148, 152 (*See also* Factor, endowments)

Negative effective protection, 198
Net foreign investment, 379, 437
Net IMF position, 554
Net liquidity balance, 374, 384-389
Netherlands, 248, 255, 256, 479, 556
Neutral production and consumption, 158-159, 171
Neutral technical progress, 156-158, 161-162
New International Economic Order (NIEO), 287-289, 572
New protectionism (*See* Nontariff trade barriers)
Nominal tariff, 196, 201
Noneconomic arguments for tariffs, 183, 224-225
Nontariff trade barriers (NTBs), 217, 220-224, 228, 230, 232, 234, 236, 571
Nontraded commodities, 137, 143
Normal goods, 85, 161, 171

Offer curve:
  defined, 67, 79
  derivation, 67-70, 77, 83-87
  elasticity, 74-75, 85, 88, 189
  shifts in, 73, 75-77, 169-170, 189
Official reserve account, 372
Official reserve transactions, 371-372
Official settlements balance, 372, 384-389, 495
Oil facility, 564
Oligopoly, 133, 142, 255, 307
OPEC (Organization of Petroleum Exporting Countries), 222, 280
Open market operations:
  purchases, 477, 498
  sales, 477
Operation twist, 476, 558
Opportunity cost theory, 24, 33
Opportunity costs:
  constant, 24-26, 33, 72
  decreasing, 50
  increasing, 40-42, 47-52, 55
Optimum currency area or block, 523, 532-534
Optimum tariff, 191-193, 201, 208-210
Organization of Petroleum Exporting Countries (OPEC), 222, 280
Overinvoicing, 479

Paper gold (*See* Special drawing rights)
Par value, 377, 523, 534, 536, 546, 552
Pareto optimum, 253
Partial equilibrium analysis, 137, 143, 193-196, 210-213, 218-219, 248
Pattern of trade, 13, 33, 99-100, 130, 135
Perfect competition, 93-94, 100, 111, 239

Pegged exchange rate system, 536-537 (*See also* Gold-exchange standard)
Peril-point provisions, 228, 236
Persistent dumping, 223, 240
Petrodollars, 347
Phillips curve, 476
Policy instruments, 459-461
Policy mix:
　in real world, 477
　theory, 472-477
Portfolio balance approach:
　adjustment to balance of payments disequilibrium, 506-507
　and exchange rate dynamics, 507
　empirical evidence on, 509-511
　mathematical model of, 518-519
　relation to monetary approach, 494
Portfolio investments, 296-297, 300-301
Portfolio theory, 301
Predatory dumping, 223
Preferential trade arrangements, 247
Price adjustment mechanism, 396-415
Price discipline, 530-532
Price discrimination, third degree, 240-241
Price elasticity:
　of demand, 75, 195, 241, 276-277, 356, 400-401, 403-409, 421
　of supply, 75, 195, 249, 251, 276-277, 356, 400-401, 403-406, 421
Price taker, 71
Price-specie-flow mechanism, 414-415, 548
Price and wage controls, 460, 478, 480
Primary products, 267-268, 275, 281
Principle of effective market classification, 461, 475
Private capital movements, 385
Producer's equilibrium, 58-59
Producer's' surplus, 195, 201, 213
Product contract cruve, 63-65, 114-115
Product cycle model, 135-137, 143, 307
Product differentiation (*See* Differentiated products)
Production effect of a tariff, 184-191, 193-196, 201, 212
Production function, 57-59
Production possibility frontier:
　constant costs, 24-26
　defined, 24, 33, 63
　increasing costs, 40-42, 98-99
Prohibitive tariff, 187, 201
Protection cost of tariff, 194-196, 201, 234
Protrade production and consumption, 158-159, 171
Purchase contracts, 280

Purchasing-power parity (PPP) theory:
　absolute, 409-410
　relative, 410-411
　usefulness, 409
Pure theory of trade, 4

Quantitative restructions (*See* Quotas)
Quantity theory of money, 414, 496, 548
Quotas:
　agricultural products, 218
　comparison to tariff, 219-220
　developed countries, use by, 218
　developing countries, use by, 218
　effects of, 218-219
　GATT rules on, 228
　import quotas, 218
　IMF rules on, 553, 564

R & D (*See* Research and Development)
Rate of effective protection, 196-200, 201, 213-214
Rate of exchange (*See* Foreign exchange rate)
Real cash balance effect, 445
Recession, 572
Reciprocal demand curve (*See* Offer curve)
Recognition lag, 408, 476
Regional integration (*See* Economic integration)
Regions of recent settlement, 269
Regulation Q, 346
Relative factor-price equalization, 105-107, 115-118
Relative prices:
　commodity, 26-27, 29-30, 33
　factor, 59, 65, 96-97, 100-101, 107-109, 112
Relative purchasing-power parity theory, 410-411
Rent (*See* Consumers' surplus; Producers' surplus)
Replacement lag, 408
Research and Development, 128, 137, 232, 306, 309-310
Reserve assets, international, 371
Reserve currency, 500
Reserve currency country, 496, 500
Retaliation, and optimum tariff, 191-193
Revaluation (*See* Currency, revaluation)
Revenue effect of tariff, 195-196, 201, 212
Ricardian trade model, 17-23, 124-126
Risk:
　aversion, 507
　diversification, 301, 346, 507
　foreign exchange, 334-337, 507
　minimization, 300-301

premium, 337
Rome Treaty (1957), 256
Roosa bonds, 559
Rules of the gold standard, 415
Rybezynski theorem, 154-155, 171, 173-175
    and magnification effect, 155

Same technology, 93
Saving function, 432
Scientific tariff, 225, 236
SDRs (*See* Special Drawing Rights)
Second best, theory of, 253-254
Seignorage, 559
Services, 137, 143, 224, 233, 270, 363, 369,
    411
Short-term capital flows, 374, 385, 465, 475
Single factoral terms of trade, 272
Skilled labor, 109, 129, 136-137, 270
Small country case, 30-32, 33, 50-51, 71-72,
    184-188, 314
Smithsonian Agreement, 560
Smoot-Hawley Tariff, 227, 236, 551
Snake in the tunnel (*See* European "snake")
Soviet bloc countries, 242-243
Soviet Union, 3, 228, 242-243, 271, 280, 552
Specific-factors model, 107, 112, 119-121, 207-
    208
Specific tariff, 184, 201
Special Drawing Rights (SDRs), 369, 556, 563
Specialization in production with trade:
    complete, 31, 33, 50, 72, 133
    incomplete, 31, 50, 55, 72, 93
Speculative demand for money, 466
Speculation, currency:
    defined, 339-340
    destabilizing, 341, 522, 524, 526, 528-530,
        551
    stabilizing, 340, 524, 526, 528-530
Sporadic dumping, 223
Spot exchange rate, 330, 344 (*See also* Foreign
    exchange rate)
Stabilizing speculation, 340, 522, 524, 526,
    528-530
Stable foreign exchange market, 403-406, 424-
    425
Stagflation, 572
Stamp plan, 572
Standby arrangements, 556
State trading, 242-244
Statistical discrepancy, 370, 380
Sterilization of changes in international re-
    serves, 415, 445, 498, 548-549
Stolper-Samuelson theorem, 188, 201, 203-205
Structural inflation (cost-push inflation), 476

Subsidy of exports, 223-224, 232, 236, 257
Substitution account, 570
Super gold tranche, 554
Supply of:
    factors of production, 97, 100-101, 106-107,
        176-177
    foreign exchange, 324-329, 353-356, 400
    exports, 67, 70, 211-212, 239, 400
    imports, 67, 70, 398-400
    money, 414-415, 445, 496-498, 500-501, 515
Surplus in balance of payments:
    definition, 372, 498
    measures, 372, 498
Swan diagram, 463
Swap arrangements, 342, 556, 558
Sweden, 247, 258, 479
Switzerland, 2, 3, 228, 247, 258, 314, 479, 527,
    552, 556, 557
Synthesis of automatic adjustments, 446-449

Tariff:
    ad valorem (nominal), 196, 201
    arguments for, 181, 224-226
    balance of payments effect of, 225
    consumption effect of, 184-191, 193-196, 212
    cost of protection, 194-196, 201, 212-213,
        234
    effective, 196-200, 201, 212-214
    factories, 255, 281
    GATT, 228-229
    general equilibrium analysis of, 185-191
    history of, 227-230
    income redistribution effect of, 188, 193,
        207-208
    infant industry argument for, 225-226
    most-favored-nation priciple of, 227-228, 232
    negotiations, 227-230
    nominal, 196, 201
    noneconomic arguments for, 183, 224-225
    optimum, 191-193, 208-210
    partial equilibrium in small nation of, 193-
        196
    partial equilibrium effect in large nation,
        210-213
    preferences for developing countries, 257,
        288
    prohibitive, 187
    protective effect of, 197
    retaliation, 191-193
    revenue effect of, 195-196, 201, 212
    revenue source, as a, 183, 187, 193
    scientific, 225, 236
    specific-factors model and, 207-208
    structure, theory of, 196-200

Tariff (*cont.*)
    terms of trade effect of, 184-193
Tastes:
    effects of changes in, 75-77, 109-110, 121,
       169-170
    trade based on a difference in, 52-54
Taxes:
    direct, 183, 198, 201, 241
    indirect, 221
    excise, 221
    on corporations income, 305-306, 307, 309-
       311
Technical, administrative and other regula-
       tions, 221-222, 236
Technical progress:
    labor-saving, 156, 177-179
    capital-saving, 156, 177-179
    neutral, 156-158, 161-162, 177-179
    and the terms of trade, 158-170
    and the volume of trade, 158-170
    and welfare, 159-170
Technological gap model, 135-137, 143, 307
Terms of trade:
    commodity or net barter, 73, 79, 272
    developing nations, 273-274
    double factoral, 273
    effect, 73, 163, 171, 271–276
    income, 272
    single factoral, 272
Theory of commercial policy, 4
Theory of the second best, 253-254
Tied aid, 376
Tokyo Round, 221, 230, 232, 237, 257
Trade:
    bias, 127-128
    creation, 248-250
    deficit, 4, 372, 374, 377, 395
    deflection, 258
    diversion, 243, 250-252, 256, 258, 262-264
    effect of a tariff, 195-196, 201, 212
    effect on distribution of income, 44, 107-109,
       119-121
    engine of growth, 268-270
    free, 16, 23, 192
    liberalization, 227-234
    negotiations, 4, 224, 228-234, 236, 287, 555,
       571
    policy (*See* Commercial policy)
    restrictions, 183-200, 217-224, 232, 460, 551
    surplus, 233
Trade Agreements Act of 1934, 227-228, 236
Trade-creating customs union, 248-250
Trade-diverting customs union, 250-252

Trade Expansion Act of 1962, 229, 237, 555
Trade indifference curves:
    definition, 81-82
    derivation, 80-83
    usefulness, 83-87
Trade liberalization, 227-234
Trade Reform Act of 1974, 230, 237
Tranche, IMF:
    credit, 553-554
    gold, 553, 565
Transaction demand for money, 466
Transfer payments (unilateral transfers), 366
Transfer pricing, 307-308, 309
Transfer problem, 318-319, 445, 455-456
Transformation curve (*See* Production possi-
      bility frontier)
Transportation costs, 23, 94, 108, 137-139, 143,
      240
Travel expenditures, 324-325, 478
Triangular arbitrage, 329
Trigger-price mechanism, 223, 236
Two-tier gold price, 557

Unbalanced growth, 153
Uncovered interest arbitrage, 341-342
Uncovered position, 339
Underdeveloped countries (*See* Developing
    countries)
Underinvoicing, 479
Unemployment, 274, 281, 415 (*See also* Inter-
    nal balance)
Unilateral transfers, 366
United Kingdom, 2, 3, 14, 107, 124, 135, 222,
    224, 244, 247, 256, 257, 275, 297, 314,
    477, 479, 539, 549, 550, 555, 556, 566
United Nations Conference on Trade and De-
    velopment (UNCTAD), 287, 572
United States:
    as a debtor nation, 298, 379-380, 569
    balance of payments statistics of, 367-370,
      375-378, 384-389
    collapse of the Bretton Woods system, 560-
      562
    control on capital outflows from, 558-559
    developing countries, 299
    economic policies of, 477-480, 550-551
    EEC, 299
    Eurocurrency market, 345-346
    gold reserves of, 377, 559
    import composition of, 2-3
    import propensities of, 2, 443
    international investment position of, 297-
      299, 378-380

international-currency status of, 325, 377, 500, 558
policy of benign neglect, 563
trade policy of, 183-184, 198-199, 226-230, 233-234
Unstable foreign exchange market, 403-406, 424-425
U.S. Tariff Commission, 229

Value added, 196, 201
Value added tax, 221, 257
Value of marginal product:
of capital, 119, 177, 208, 303
of labor, 119, 176-177, 208, 312-313
Variable factor proportions, 23, 42
Variable import levies, 257
Vehicle currency, 346
Vent for surplus, 270

Vertical integration, 302, 306
Voluntary export restraints, 217, 220-221, 232, 236, 480

Wage and price controls, 460, 478, 480, 559
Wages, 21, 23, 97, 104-105, 107-109, 117, 119-121, 124, 129, 146, 188, 203-205, 207-208, 273-274, 312-313
Welfare gain with trade, 163, 166, 250
Wealth effect, 163, 166, 171
West Germany, 2, 3, 107, 108, 135, 224, 244, 248, 256, 314, 348, 477, 479, 498, 504, 525, 539, 553, 555, 556, 559, 566
World Bank (See International Bank for Reconstruction and Development)

Yield (See Interest, rate)

Zollverein, 248